An Introduction to
GOVERNMENT and POLITICS

A CONCEPTUAL APPROACH

FIFTH EDITION

An Introduction to
GOVERNMENT and POLITICS

A CONCEPTUAL APPROACH

MARK O. DICKERSON
UNIVERSITY OF CALGARY

TOM FLANAGAN
UNIVERSITY OF CALGARY

I(T)P Nelson

an International Thomson Publishing company

Toronto • Albany • Bonn • Boston • Cincinnati • Detroit • London • Madrid • Melbourne
Mexico City • New York • Pacific Grove • Paris • San Francisco • Singapore • Tokyo • Washington

I(T)P® **International Thomson Publishing**
The ITP logo is a trademark under licence
www.thomson.com

Published in 1998 by
I(T)P® **Nelson**

A division of Thomson Canada Limited
1120 Birchmount Road
Scarborough, Ontario M1K 5G4
www.nelson.com

Canadian Cataloguing in Publication Data

Dickerson, M.O., 1934–
    An introduction to government and politics : a conceptual approach

5th ed.
Includes bibliographical references and index.
ISBN 0-17-607364-7

1. Political science. I. Flanagan, Thomas, 1944– . II. Title.
JC131.D52   1998   320   C98-930281-4

Publisher and Team Leader	Michael Young
Acquisitions Editor	Nicole Gnutzman
Project Editor	Jenny Anttila
Senior Production Editor	Tracy Bordian
Production Coordinator	Brad Horning
Art Direction	Sylvia Vander Schee
Cover Design	ArtPlus
Cover Image	Damir Frkovic/Masterfile
Senior Composition Analyst	Alicja Jamorski

Printed and bound in Canada
  3 4 (WC) 01 00 99

CONTENTS

PREFACE

The revisions to the fifth edition of *An Introduction to Government and Politics* are not as sweeping as those made to the fourth edition. The new Chapter 1 on the discipline of political science is an expansion of material previously discussed in more condensed form in the Introduction. Otherwise, no new chapters have been added, although parts of several have been revised to incorporate improvements suggested by various readers.

The text continues with the pedagogical method E.D. Hirsch calls "selective exemplification." That is, we try to provide readers with "a carefully chosen but generous sampling of factual data that are set forth in a meaningful web of inferences and generalizations about the larger domain."[1] According to Hirsch, educational research shows this method yields better results than either an abstract discussion of general principles or an encyclopedic recitation of isolated facts. Of course, selective exemplification will only work if the examples make sense to students; so, as with each previous edition, we have taken care to update our examples to make them as current as possible.

This is a text for a first-year course in political science. Although designed for use in Canadian universities and colleges, it does not focus solely on Canadian government. We use Canadian illustrations of general principles together with examples from the British and American political systems—both historically of great importance to Canada.

In thirty years of teaching introductory courses in political science, we have encountered thousands of students. This experience has taught us something about the virtues and vices of the present approach to social studies in Canadian schools. On the positive side, many students come to university with an active curiosity about politics and a healthy scepticism about orthodox opinions. They are eager to learn more about a field that they recognize as important.

At the same time, many students are handicapped by certain deficiencies in the social-studies curriculum:

- They have been offered little historical information and historical perspective on events. History has suffered perhaps more than any other discipline on being integrated into social studies. Students without a historical perspective are adrift intellectually. They lack the important bearings that make sense of Canada's unique history, as well as of the development of Western civilization and the rise and fall of other civilizations.

- They have little specific information about the institutions of Canadian government. Most students entering university are unable to say how a judge is appointed or what an order-in-council is. Their knowledge of government is focused more on current affairs, with heavy emphasis on issues as portrayed in the mass media.

- They are accustomed to discussing politics but not to using rigorously defined concepts. They are used to applying looser reasoning than is required for an academic discipline.

Our textbook addresses each of these problems. We can do relatively little about students' lack of historical background, since the course for which this book is designed cannot replace the systematic study of history. However, we do attempt to put important topics in a historical or developmental perspective, and we supply some information about watershed events such as the French and Russian Revolutions. Also, we refer whenever possible to authors, from Plato to Keynes, whose reputations are established and who are important historical figures in their own right.

We can spend only limited time on the details of Canadian political institutions, for those would require a course in Canadian government; we have chosen rather to emphasize concepts. The material in this book follows a careful sequence. Concepts are introduced one at a time, discussed at length, and then used as the basis for explaining further ideas. Important terms are boldfaced where they first occur or where they are thoroughly explained; these terms are used consistently throughout the text and are listed and defined in the Glossary at the back of the book for easy reference. We believe that this will equip the student with a comprehensive and logically consistent vocabulary for the study of politics. In the last part of the book we offer a method for conceptualizing the process of politics and for organizing or arranging the many ideas and concepts introduced in the earlier parts. Thinking about politics as a coherent process is an essential first step in becoming a student of politics, evaluating politics, and becoming a critic of one's own political system. We hope that this approach will be of value not only to students who intend to major in political science but also to those who are seeking a shorter path toward becoming informed political observers (and, of course, participants).

We are keenly aware that this effort at consistency means simplifying the meaning of some important terms. Political scientists often disagree on the meaning and use of many significant political terms: *politics*, *nation-state*, and *democracy* are a few well-known examples of this problem. Our experience has been that students at the introductory level cannot absorb all these debates about meaning, especially when they are subjecting these terms to serious analysis for the first time. For this reason we have narrowed the meaning of many terms—without, we hope, departing from the mainstream of current usage. Readers will undoubtedly criticize our handling of this or that concept, but we hope the pedagogical benefit of applying a consistent vocabulary will compensate for any resulting problems. It is a considerable advantage to be able to explain, for example, liberalism in terms of previously established concepts such as society, state, and coercion that the student has already assimilated.

The book is divided into four parts that together constitute what we believe is a logical way to begin the study of government and politics. Part One defines those terms, ideas, and concepts that are basic to political science. An understanding of terms such as *state*, *society*, *authority*, *legitimacy*, *law*, and *sovereignty* is essential to a systematic study of politics. Part Two discusses the ideological basis of modern political systems. Liberalism and socialism, the fundamental ideological systems in the modern world, are discussed in the context of the political spectrum that runs from communism to fascism. The emergent ideologies of feminism and environmentalism are also discussed here and placed in context. Part Three looks at forms of government. Here we discuss different types of political systems: liberal–democratic, authoritarian, and totalitarian; parliamentary and presidential; federal and unitary. In Part Four we examine government as a process. A complex interaction of individuals and political institutions produces law and public policies for a society, and we try to view this interaction as a systemic process. The model of politics we offer is hypothetical; however, we draw examples from Canada, the United Kingdom, the United States, and other countries to illustrate how the process works in reality.

This conceptual approach makes it advisable for students to cover the material in the order in which we present it. It is particularly important to read Part One before Part Two, and Parts One and Two (which focus on theory) before Parts Three and Four (which deal more with institutions). However, it would be acceptable to reverse the order of Parts Three and Four.

Our work is meant to be objective and dispassionate, but that does not mean that it is value-free or without commitment. We consistently try to point out the value of the leading ideas of the Western world's political tradition. We pay particular attention to two different and sometimes conflicting groups of ideas, both of which are of great importance. One group centres on constitutionalism and includes notions such as the rule of law and individual freedom; the other centres on democracy and allied concepts such as majority rule and popular sovereignty. For the past two centuries, the Western world has tried to combine these two idea "clusters" into the system of government known as constitutional or liberal democracy, in which majorities rule within a legal framework intended to prevent the oppression of minorities. This form of government has not always been stable and successful, even in the countries in Western Europe and North America where it originated, and it has been adopted only with much difficulty in other parts of the world. In Canada, where liberal democracy seems securely established, we are apt to take this system for granted; but it is far from being an obvious or universal form of government. We hope that better understanding of liberal democracy will help it to flourish.

Special thanks are due to Margaret Ogrodnick for making useful suggestions for the revision of Chapter 15, and to Jim Keeley and Terry Terriff for revising and updating Chapter 9, "International Order." We would also like to thank Judi Powell for help with word processing, Martin West for updating the bibliographies found at the end of each chapter, and Nancy Bleses for compiling the Glossary. As always, our greatest debt is to our students, whose reaction to the book leads us toward further refinements each year we teach.

ITP Nelson would like to thank those reviewers who commented on the text: Marlene Hancock, Douglas College; Robert J. Keaton, Concordia University; Stephen Tomblin, Memorial University; Sharn Tyakoff, Douglas College; and Dr. Edwin Webking, University of Lethbridge.

Basic Concepts

PART 1

POLITICAL SCIENCE

Political science is the systematic study of government and politics, which are defined at greater length in the next chapter. But before getting into the subject matter, students may find it useful to learn a little about the discipline itself.

🝫🝫🝫🝫🝫🝫🝫🝫

HISTORY OF POLITICAL SCIENCE

The origins of political science lie in the classical period of Greek philosophy, whose greatest writers were Plato and Aristotle. The Greek philosophers did not approach political science as a specialized discipline in the modern sense, but they thought and wrote systematically about government. They were concerned above all with how politics can contribute to a life of excellence and virtue. Greek philosophy, and with it the habit of systematic reflection upon government, became part of the cultural tradition of the Western world. Political science continued to exist as a branch of moral philosophy, and important contributions were made by authors who also wrote in other areas of philosophy, such as Thomas Aquinas, Thomas Hobbes, and John Locke. Such writings, extending over more than two millennia, constitute a rich body of wisdom that is still the foundation of political science.

In the eighteenth century, political science started to differentiate itself from moral philosophy—not yet as an independent study, but as part of the new science of political economy. Writers like Adam Smith, who held the chair of moral philosophy at the University of Glasgow, began to study and write about the workings of the market. They did not do this in a vacuum; in the society of the time, market processes were being freed from mercantilist policies predicated on governmental control of the economy. The study of government was a junior partner in the new science of **political economy,** which emphasized market forces. Government was seen as an auxiliary that could perform certain functions that free trade did not perform well. In the late eighteenth and early nineteenth centuries, universities established chairs of political economy. During this period, much work that today we would call political science was also done in faculties of history and law, especially under the guise of comparative and constitutional law.

Economics and political science began to diverge in the second half of the nineteenth century as scholars began to specialize. The discovery of the principle of marginal utility in the 1870s made it possible for economics to become mathematical, and hence more specialized and remote from the everyday concerns of government and politics. Universities in the United States took the lead in establishing autonomous departments of political science, which united the work of professors who might previously have gravitated to political economy, history, and law. Political science in its modern academic form thus stems from developments in the United States in the late nineteenth century. The first American department of political science was founded at Columbia University in 1880; by the outbreak of World War I in 1914, there were forty such departments in U.S. universities.[1]

Why in the United States? Partly because this rapidly expanding country was opening scores of new universities that were not bound by old traditions about academic specialties. But the more important reason is that because the United States—a nation founded on a political act of revolution—has always been fascinated with government. Political science at the university level was a logical extension of the civics education that was so important in the public schools. Also, these early political scientists tended to be moralistic crusaders for governmental reform—a good example being Woodrow Wilson, the only political science professor ever to become an American president.

In the first half of the twentieth century, political science as an academic discipline remained largely an American phenomenon, with only a few chairs established in universities in other countries. Of course, the substance of political science was pursued elsewhere, but it was usually conducted within departments of law, political economy, economics, or history. However, after World War II, political science was adopted as an independent discipline around the world. This was partly in imitation of the American cultural behemoth. A deeper reason, perhaps, was the tremendous expansion of the scope of government in the second half of the twentieth century. The small state of the **laissez-faire** era could be understood fairly easily within the study of political economy; the large, interventionist state of the present era seems to demand its own specialized discipline.

Political science in Canada must be seen in this historical context. In 1950 there were only about thirty political scientists in Canada, most of them employed in university departments of political economy.[2] Their main periodical was the *Canadian Journal of Economics and Political Science (CJEPS)*. In the 1960s, as enrolments increased and more staff were hired to cope with an unprecedented expansion of universities, these departments began to split into separate departments of economics and political science. In 1967 the *CJEPS* was split into the *Canadian Journal of Economics (CJE)* and the *Canadian Journal of Political Science (CJPS)*, while two separate professional associations also emerged: the Canadian Economics Association (CEA) and the Canadian Political Science Association (CPSA).

Some years later, as part of the general movement of Quebec nationalism, political scientists in that province formed their own association, the Société québécoise de science politique, with its own journal, *Politique et Sociétés*. The two associations maintain cooperative relations with one another, and there is a good deal of cross-membership; but in political science, as in so many other areas, the reality of Canada is that Quebec is a "distinct society."

In any case, the academic emancipation of political science in Canada is now complete. Two major universities, Saskatchewan and Toronto, maintained joint departments of economics and political science into the 1980s, but even these two departments have now divided themselves along disciplinary lines. Reflecting the older tradition, about 20 percent of Canadian universities have departments of "political studies" (Queen's, Saskatchewan) or simply "politics" (Brock), but in practice this is a distinction without a difference. Whatever the department is called, those employed in it consider that they are teaching political science.

The term *political economy* no longer embraces the entire territory of economics and politics as it once did. It now has several special uses. In some circles, it refers to the study of certain narrower subjects—such as economic intervention by government—that require information and insights from both disciplines in order to be understood. In other circles, it denotes a historical–materialist approach to the study of politics that draws heavily, though not exclusively, on the thought of Karl Marx and writers in the Marxist tradition. Within the Canadian political-science community, the practitioners of political economy in this latter sense are a recognized subgroup whose members tend to work together with like-minded historians, economists, and sociologists. Together, they maintain their own academic network and help to support an interdisciplinary journal, *Studies in Political Economy*.

APPROACHES TO POLITICAL SCIENCE

When political science achieved academic autonomy, its practitioners brought to it the methods of their forebears in philosophy, political economy, law, and history. These methods were chiefly the narrative, chronological, and descriptive study of political institutions, complemented by philosophical reflection about matters of good and evil as applied to government. Great changes have taken place since that beginning.

In the 1940s, sociology and social psychology began to exert enormous influence, and political scientists became familiar with methods of research common in those disciplines, such as attitude scales, sample surveys, and statistical analysis. The rapidly increasing use of these methods was closely tied to a shift in emphasis away from formal constitutional structures and toward other phenomena, such as political parties, pressure groups, elections, and collective behaviour. This transition—often referred to as the **behavioural revolution**—brought political science closer to the other social sciences.

A second phase of the behavioural revolution began in the 1950s and is still far from ending. It is characterized by the influence of rational-choice models of analysis that were first developed in economics and mathematics. Increasingly, some political scientists are using deductive models derived from branches of mathematics such as game theory and information theory to explain the data gathered in their empirical investigations. This phase is more abstract and theoretical in nature than the first and is drawing political science closer to natural sciences such as biology and cybernetics, which utilize the same mathematical models. We provide a small example of this approach by presenting the game theory model known as the prisoner's dilemma in the appendix to Chapter 2.

There were acrimonious divisions within the discipline in the 1950s and 1960s between supporters and opponents of the new methods, with many extreme claims being made on both sides. That furor, however, has now largely subsided. Political scientists who use quantitative methods now co-exist peacefully with colleagues who rely on the old techniques of description and reflection. It seems to be accepted that political science is inherently pluralistic and is united, not by adherence to a single method, but by concern with a common subject. Because different questions of politics and government lend themselves to different approaches, political scientists may resemble philosophers, sociologists, historians, lawyers, economists, or anthropologists in their research methods; yet all feel that they are united in a joint enterprise to understand the many facets of government and politics.

The methodological battles have subsided but have been followed by equally noisy ideological strife. In the late 1960s, political economists and others rooted in the Marxist tradition enunciated a vigorous challenge of what they saw as the capitalist bias of most political science. Their criticism was soon augmented by distinctive new points of view such as environmentalism, feminism, and multiculturalism; each of these argues that fragile and ill-defended assumptions amounting to bias exist in conventional political science. There is no immediate prospect for consensus on such issues, and political science remains what it has always been—an inherently pluralistic discipline in which different points of view clash and final victory is never achieved.

In this respect, political science is very different from the natural sciences. At any given time, probably 99 percent of physicists, chemists, or biologists agree on about 99 percent of the contents of their respective disciplines. They may disagree heatedly about research on the frontiers, but overall, the areas of such disagreement are small. Those who challenge the fundamentals of such disciplines are often regarded as cranks and banished to the periphery. In contrast, political science is an ongoing debate in which honest differences of opinion over fundamental issues are the norm.

Nonetheless, in spite of such deep-seated divisions, there are large areas of agreement. Although feminist and conservative political scientists may disagree profoundly on the larger implications, they should be able to agree on how many women sit in the House of Commons, on what the statistical trend has been over time, and on at least some of the reasons why the percentage (1) used to be extremely low, (2) has risen in recent years, and (3) is still far below the percentage of men. Such agreement is important in itself, even if it is immersed in vigorous polemics about whether the trends are good or bad, and whether additional measures ought to be enacted to accelerate the changes.

To introduce some technical terminology, political scientists can hope for agreement on **empirical** (i.e., factual) questions, such as what is the shape of the political world, and how does that world function? Although disagreement on such questions always exists, it can in principle be overcome by more research and better evidence. But disagreement on **normative** (i.e., evaluative) questions is harder, perhaps impossible, to resolve, because it may stem from different value commitments. To go back to the preceding example, even after feminist and conservative political scientists reach agreement on a host of empirical issues relating to the representation of women in the House of Commons, they might continue to disagree on the normative question of whether one *ought* to take steps to increase that level of representation.

ORGANIZATION OF THE DISCIPLINE

Political science, like all academic disciplines, has become so large that internal specialization is necessary. Political scientists typically think of themselves as working in one or two particular fields, and university and college departments of political science organize their course offerings accordingly. The following, most common, way of carving up the discipline is based more on convenience than on any profound intellectual rationale:

- political philosophy
- Canadian politics
- comparative politics
- international relations

Political philosophy is treated as a separate field because it has its own long tradition and because its methods are mainly reflective and conceptual rather than empirical. Yet political philosophy often generates empirical hypotheses that can be tested against evidence in all of the other fields.

Canadian politics is treated as a field simply because we live in Canada and the requirements of citizenship make it important to understand the politics of the country where we live. Each country treats its own national politics as a distinct field. Thus, American and British universities have separate fields of American and British politics and teach Canadian politics (if they do) as part of comparative politics.

Comparative politics is the study of politics in different countries. Canadian universities teach American and British politics as part of comparative politics, even though these would be considered separate fields in the United States and Great Britain. This is mainly a matter of convenience. Politics has many similarities and differences all around the world, and everyone understands their own national politics better through comparison with those of other countries. This book, while written for Canadian students, tries to bring in comparative material from many other countries, particularly the United States and Great Britain, to give Canadians a better understanding of their own system.

International relations studies the way in which independent states relate to one another. As explained at greater length in Chapter 9, international politics is characterized by the absence of overall sovereignty, which makes it a unique field of study. In fact, it is so different that some universities have separate programs or even departments of international relations.

Beyond this traditional fourfold division of political science, still found in almost every university catalogue, there is a variety of fields and subfields that crop up more or less widely. The department of political science in which you are studying may group courses under headings such as public administration, public law, public policy, political behaviour, research methods, and many others. These groupings usually cut across the traditional divisions between the four fields described above. For example, public policy—the study of government's role in health care, to take one example—will be both Canadian and comparative. Policy studies also have both philosophical and empirical dimensions to the extent that values are involved and evaluations of effectiveness are made.

When we debated these matters in our department at the University of Calgary, someone proposed the metaphor of "fields and streams," based on the title of a well-known hunting-and-fishing magazine. The four traditional areas can be thought of as expansive territorial divisions—the fields—while the special concerns, such as public policy—can be seen as streams meandering through all the fields. Don't take it too seriously; it's just a metaphor. But we found it helpful in organizing our research and teaching in political science.

WHY STUDY POLITICAL SCIENCE?

There are at least four answers to this question.

1. There is no professional category of political scientist, as there is of economist, chemist, or geologist. Nonetheless, the knowledge imparted by political

science is highly useful in several professions, and many students major in political science as a sort of pre-professional degree. One can take political science as a preparation for studying law, entering the civil service, or working in party politics. Political science is an obvious springboard for anyone interested in these professions, although other disciplines such as history and economics can also serve the same purpose.

2. Political science is a form of education for citizenship. Everyone in the modern world lives under the jurisdiction of a government and is a potential participant in politics. Even those who are not particularly interested in politics—and not everyone is or needs to be—are required to pay taxes and encouraged to vote. Studying political science can help you become a more effective citizen by enhancing your understanding of the environment in which you operate.

3. The study of political science can be part of a broad liberal arts education. Political philosophy is particularly useful in this respect. Systematic reflection on government has natural linkages to other liberal disciplines such as philosophy, history, and literature.

4. For a few who have the time, inclination, and ability to go on to postgraduate studies, political science can lead to a career in research and teaching in universities, colleges, and research institutes. Someone who takes this path becomes part of the same type of scientific community that exists for all disciplines. It is a life dedicated to the advancement of knowledge in your chosen field.

All of the above are valid reasons for studying political science. Whatever your own reasons—you probably have more than one—we hope this book provides an entry into the discipline. It's just a first step, not the last word. Take what you learn and build on it. We, as the authors, will be more than compensated if you remember the words of the philosopher Friedrich Nietzsche: "You badly repay your teacher if you always remain a student."

FURTHER READING

Archer, Keith, et al. *Parameters of Power: Canada's Political Institutions.* Scarborough, Ont.: Nelson Canada, 1995.

Baxter-Moore, Nicolas, Terrance Carroll, and Roderick Church. *Studying Politics: An Introduction to Argument and Analysis.* Toronto: Copp Clark Longman, 1994.

Cairns, Alan C. "Political Science in Canada and the Americanization Issue," *Canadian Journal of Political Science* 8, 1975.

Dahl, Robert Alan. *Modern Political Analysis.* Englewood Cliffs, N.J.: Prentice-Hall, 1991.

Finifter, Ada W. *Political Science: The State of the Discipline II*. Washington, D.C.: American Political Science Association, 1993.

Guy, James John. *People, Politics & Government: Political Science: A Canadian Perspective*, 3rd ed. Scarborough, Ont.: Prentice-Hall, 1995.

Marsh, David and Gerry Stoker, eds. *Theory and Methods in Political Science*. London: Macmillan, 1995.

Ricci, David M. *The Tragedy of Political Science: Politics, Scholarship, and Democracy*. New Haven: Yale University Press, 1984.

Richter, Melvin. *The History of Political and Social Concepts: A Critical Introduction*. New York: Oxford University Press, 1995.

White, Louise G. *Political Analysis: Technique and Practice*, 3rd ed. Belmont, Calif.: Wadsworth Pub. Co., 1994.

SOCIETY, GOVERNMENT, AND POLITICS

We are all social beings who need the support of others not merely to live well but to survive. There is no record of a time when human beings lived as isolated individuals, coming together only to mate. As far as we know, people have always lived in groups at least as large as the family or band. The usual term for such groups, large or small, is *society*.

SOCIETY: LIVING TOGETHER

No one created or designed society. It has arisen from an infinite number of human transactions, from which stable and predictable patterns have emerged. Society is not a person or organization with a will of its own but a setting in which we carry out our lives. We often speak metaphorically of society doing or wanting something, but this must not be taken literally. Only individual men and women have wills, which they can combine through deliberate techniques of organization. Society as a whole, since it is not a conscious formation, cannot act or decide anything.

Sociologists usually define society as a human group whose members live by common rules of conduct and which has a plausible claim to self-sufficiency. Both of these points need clarification. By rules of conduct we mean not just enforceable commands but regular and predictable behaviour. All human activities, such as marriage, work, and recreation, are carried on within a framework of such rules. **Society** exists when people share so many rules of conduct that they are able to understand and predict one another's behaviour.

For example, adults in North America and northern Europe have a clear conception about how close two people should stand or sit next to each other. In impersonal business situations, they generally maintain a distance of between one and two metres. But the people of Arab countries do not use this intermediate spacing; they transact business either closer together or farther apart—the distance depends on factors that would not be immediately apparent to us.[1] Such behavioural differences may cause considerable discomfort and misunderstanding in cross-cultural contact. The physical distance between people is not important in itself, but it is vital that it be understood in the same way by everyone concerned. Understanding and living by the rules that govern interpersonal relations is the essence of social order.

Human beings are not the only social animals. There are social insects (bees, termites, ants) as well as mammals (hyenas, wolves, chimpanzees, baboons). In recent decades the study of animal societies has grown to become one of the most dynamic scientific fields and has yielded many insights that, with appropriate caution, can sometimes be transferred to the study of human society.[2] The common denominator in both animal and human societies is rules of conduct—predictable, regular patterns of behaviour that integrate the individual with the social whole. The major difference between animal and human societies is this: the vastly greater intelligence of human beings allows them not only to understand social rules of conduct but also to change them by conscious decision.

Self-sufficiency is a more problematic concept. Few, if any, societies have ever been self-sufficient in the literal sense of requiring nothing at all from other societies—no husbands or wives, no trade goods, no new ideas or techniques. Perhaps a more reasonable test of self-sufficiency is this: would a society survive if its ties with other societies were broken? But even this test does not give very clear results. Western society could undoubtedly survive if deprived of oil from Third World exporters, but it would have to undergo substantial changes to do so.

When we look at both rules of conduct and self-sufficiency, we see that it is impossible to draw clear lines between societies in the modern world. The international movement of people, commodities, and ideas is so vast that self-sufficiency has almost vanished. Rules of conduct have also become widely diffused. The ascendancy of Western society since the fifteenth century has spread many Western cultural practices around the earth: formal education and literacy, modes of dress, table manners, forms of economic activity, and much more. To a great extent, the world has become one society, with regional differences increasingly blurred. A person can travel to and even work in any major city on any continent without feeling that any profound lines of social demarcation have been crossed.

The term *society* is so vague that we use it in different ways to express different realities. We use the term *Western society* broadly to refer to the peoples of Europe and the new societies they founded overseas as extensions of their mother countries. In this broad sense, Western society is more or less a synonym for Western civilization. At other times, we speak of societies as if their boundaries were the same as the legal and territorial boundaries established by governments. Thus, it is common to refer to Canadian society or American society, and even to Alberta or Toronto society.

Both the Meech Lake Accord and the Charlottetown Accord referred to Quebec as a *distinct society*. Such language was deliberately chosen for political purposes, chiefly to avoid the potential separatist implications of calling Quebec a nation. It is understandable why the phrase "distinct society" emerged, but for analytical purposes it is essential to remember that societies are not sharply distinguished from one another, certainly not by boundaries of governmental jurisdiction.

GOVERNMENT: MAKING PUBLIC DECISIONS

Society is a general matrix of activity formed by similarity of conduct and frequent interaction; **government** is a specialized activity of those individuals and institutions that make and enforce public decisions that are binding upon the whole community. All effective governments carry out at least the following functions: they protect society from external attack, enforce rules of conduct within society, and settle disputes between members of society. The common denominator of these functions is order, both internal and external. Governments selectively use force to maintain a stable and durable social order. Beyond this minimum function, government may also provide services for members of society. This is particularly true of modern governments, which deliver mail, pave highways, operate health insurance schemes, and provide old-age pensions. But these service functions are optional; the essence of government is to maintain peace within the social order.

We may conjecture that the earliest concern of government was to ensure the very survival of the group. To defend against attack and to choose where to hunt or forage were potentially matters of life and death; cooperation could not be left purely to individual whim. Lack of agreement about fighting or hunting might endanger the entire group, so the need for cooperation inevitably led to some degree of coercion. Survival depended not only on self-defence and on finding food, but also on the preservation of peace within the group. That meant that members had to conduct themselves according to accepted rules—for example, rules pertaining to property and marriage. Violation of these rules might have endangered the group's survival, so coercive action had to be possible to punish violators.

But why should rules of conduct need enforcement? Why do human beings not always obey them spontaneously? The problem of obedience is vastly more complicated in our species than in any other because of our greater intelligence. Humans are able not only to follow rules but also to understand and formulate them, reflect upon them, and manipulate them for their own ends. Because of this, there may be differences of opinion about what rules of conduct apply to particular situations.

Even if we could always agree in the abstract about which rule of conduct to follow, there would still be the problem of enforcement. In many situations, cooperation offers benefits, yet the existence of those benefits creates an incentive for self-interested individuals to cheat. For example, almost all of us benefit from paying taxes if the money is used to pave the roads; yet any one person will benefit still more by evading the taxes while continuing to use the roads for which others are paying. However, the benefit disappears if enough people default on their taxes, in which case there will not be enough revenue to pay for the paving of the roads. It is an outcome that no one really wants but that no one can avoid if all are motivated only by narrow self-interest. (If you have a taste for simple mathematics, turn to the appendix of this chapter for a discussion of the so-called prisoner's dilemma as a model of social cooperation.)

There is a profound paradox at the centre of human existence. People need society to survive, and peaceful social life depends on following common rules. Yet the existence of rules inexorably sets up an incentive for some to try to gain special advantages over others by breaking the rules by which others abide. It is in the rule breakers' long-range interest to observe the rules so that society may exist, but it is in their short-range interest to break the rules for as long as others follow them.

The iteration of social transactions is part of the answer to this problem. When people are in close and repeated contact, they learn to get along with each other, and patterns of spontaneous cooperation emerge. In Daniel Defoe's famous novel, Robinson Crusoe and Friday were able to help each other on a desert island even though no one was in charge. But mere repetition is less likely to produce coopera-tion as numbers increase and people have fewer personal connections with each other. There is less incentive to learn to cooperate if one cannot count on dealing tomorrow with the same familiar partners. Government is an attempt to promote cooperation in larger, more impersonal societies. It increases compliance with rules by punishing those who break them. The intelligence that enables people to under-stand and break social rules has also encouraged the evolution of government to punish violations.

There is yet another paradox. If governments were too successful in enforcing rules, progress would be impossible. One aspect of social change is the replacement of one rule of conduct by another, and this is only possible if pioneers are able to experiment with new ways of doing things. If society is to progress, either govern-ment must be less than totally efficient or it must be agreed that some areas of social life fall outside the sphere where rules are enforced. Western limited government opts for the latter solution; it accepts that individuals have the right to establish or vary their own rules of conduct as long as they do not destroy the right of others to do the same.

Up to this point we have described government as a process, a set of activities extending over time. Now we will look at the structure of government—that is, at who performs the activities and how the performers are organized for collective action. The study of government structures is a major part of political science, for although the process of government is universal in all societies, the structure of gov-ernment is infinitely variable.

In the "primitive" governments found in tribal societies, there is little or no specialized structure. Necessary activities are performed by all qualified members of the tribe—usually males who have reached the age of maturity. As required, they hear and settle disputes, decide when to travel or rest, punish lawbreakers, and organize the defence of the tribe. Good examples are the native Indian tribes, such as the Sioux and Blackfoot, that once roamed the Great Plains of North America. There were tribal chiefs, but they did not wield the coercive power we associate with government today. They could persuade others but could not enforce their will. Indeed, during much of the year these tribes were split into small, nomadic bands that were basically extended families.

A specialized structure of government existed only when the families assembled for collective action, such as the buffalo hunt. Then the authority of the chief was enforced by men from the military societies, who became a temporary and voluntary police force. They settled quarrels and enforced the rules necessary for a successful hunt, such as not prematurely attacking the buffalo herd. During this period of close cooperation, men from the military societies could seize and destroy property, flog offenders, and even inflict the death penalty; but when the hunt was over, this temporary apparatus of government disappeared. The Cree and Ojibwa, whose life in the northern forests did not include a buffalo hunt, had even less formal government. The traders of the Hudson's Bay Company, since they could not always identify the leaders within these tribes, sometimes virtually created chiefs by singling men out for special attention.[3]

There is a broad, evolutionary correlation between the increasing complexity and sophistication of social life and the increasing specialization and permanence of governmental institutions. The native peoples of the northern forests did not need any organized authority to coordinate their solitary hunting; the peoples of the plains needed at least an intermittent structure of authority to maintain order during buffalo hunts. Where agriculture exists, the land is subdivided and property rights are created, and this usually leads to a permanent structure of government. (This doesn't apply when the group practises simple slash-and-burn agriculture; such tribes are still very mobile.) The growth of cities and large-scale enterprises such as irrigation brings an increase in the size, complexity, and permanence of governmental institutions, and this requires the creation of monarchs, armies, judges, tax collectors, and so on.

From now on, when we speak of government, we mean this sort of enduring, specialized structure that is found in all complex societies. (The concept of the state is similar but slightly different; but we will not use this word until after Chapter 5, in which certain of its other connotations are introduced.) There is no such thing as a society without at least the process of government, but it is quite proper to speak of a **stateless society**. Indeed, that is a common way of describing societies such as those of the Sioux and Blackfoot, which had little or no specialized structure of government. Again we see why it is so important not to confuse society with government or the state.

POLITICS: GATHERING SUPPORT

A concept always associated with government is **politics.** The word comes from the Greek *polis*, usually translated as "city-state." The polis was the typical Greek form of political community at the time of Socrates, Plato, and Aristotle, the founders of political science. The polis consisted of a city, such as Athens or Sparta, plus some surrounding hinterland, including smaller towns and villages. It has given us a number of related words having to do with the idea of the common good, such as *politics* and *police*.

Curiously, politics is one of the most disputed terms in the vocabulary of political science. Almost everyone uses it as an occasional synonym for government, but beyond that it has taken on a wide variety of meanings, some of which are discussed in this chapter. The various definitions tend to emphasize different aspects of politics. We believe that each contains an element of truth and that a satisfactory understanding of politics must be comprehensive and multifaceted.

One definition comes from a French writer, Bertrand de Jouvenel. According to Jouvenel, "we should regard as 'political' every systematic effort, performed at any place in the social field, to move other men in pursuit of some design cherished by the mover."[4] For him, politics is the activity of gathering and maintaining support for human projects.

Jouvenel's conception of politics emphasizes support. Another common approach is to equate politics with conflict. J.D.B. Miller writes that politics "is about disagreement or conflict."[5] Alan Ball carries this even further; for him, politics "involves disagreements and the reconciliation of those disagreements, and therefore can occur at any level. Two children in a nursery with one toy which they both want at the same time present a political situation."[6]

Ball's definition is not too far from Jouvenel's, for in real life mobilizing supporters for a project almost always involves overcoming conflicts of opinion or desire. Certainly conflicts arise that do not seem political in any usual sense: there is conflict if a mugger tries to take my wallet, but it is a simple crime, not a political action, because no collective project is envisioned. To be political, a crime must be linked to some vision of reordering society. It is thus a political act—as well as a crime—for a revolutionary group to kidnap a politician in the hope of exciting the people to rise against the government.

Yet another conception of politics is expressed in the title of Harold Lasswell's book, *Politics: Who Gets What, When, How.*[7] In Lasswell's view, politics is the distribution of the good things of earthly life: wealth, comfort, safety, prestige, recognition, and so on. David Easton means the same thing when he says that politics is the authoritative allocation of values—values meaning not moral ideals but those things in life that people desire.[8] There is certainly much merit in this approach, in that it draws attention to the fact that the winners in a conflict—that is, those who succeed in mobilizing support for their projects—usually allocate to themselves and their followers a generous share of material and social benefits. At the same time, however, the distributive approach tends to risk merging politics with other activities. Wealth, for example, can be distributed through the impersonal economic transactions of buying and selling, which are not political acts. Such transactions can become political—for example, when governments or corporations exhort consumers to buy products manufactured within the country—but they are not intrinsically political.

Having looked at many definitions, we would promote this one, which is a slight variation on Jouvenel's: politics is a process of conflict resolution in which support is mobilized and maintained for collective projects. Government—which involves making and enforcing rules—is thus laden with politics at every stage. A government cannot carry out its various functions unless it has some popular support. It will probably lose that support if it is unable to maintain internal and external peace and to provide services desired by the population. Government in a democracy must have an especially high level of popular support, and elections are an important way of acquiring it. This is why the term politics has come to be associated with elections and related phenomena, such as political parties. Going into politics usually means running for elective office. This popular usage is valid as far as it goes but is only one aspect of politics in the broader sense.

Politics has been called the art of the possible and the art of compromise because it must resolve disagreements among people with different opinions and desires. Compromise is usually necessary if violence and coercion are to be avoided. Political problems rarely have a satisfying solution; usually the best that can be obtained is a settlement—that is, an arrangement that makes no one perfectly happy but with which everyone can live.[9] When this is achieved, politics approximates the definition put forward by the English political scientist Bernard Crick: "the activity by which different interests within a given unit of rule are conciliated by giving them a share in power in proportion to their importance to the welfare and the survival of the whole community."[10] Citing Aristotle, Crick argues that politics is not unity but harmony—that is, the peaceful and cooperative co-existence of different groups, not their reduction to a single imposed pattern. This is a good description of politics as it can be and sometimes is practised; but in reality there is often a breakdown of harmony and a resorting to coercive measures.

COALITIONS: POLITICS IN ACTION

The fundamental unit of political activity is the **coalition,** defined in a recent book as "the joining of forces by two or more parties during a conflict of interest with other parties."[11] Coalitions involve both conflict and cooperation. They draw a boundary within which cooperation takes place to defeat or gain advantage over an external opponent. Political coalitions are formed precisely to exclude others and thereby exercise power over them.

There are at least three kinds of coalitions. The first kind has parallels among the primates and the social carnivores, whose coalitional behaviour can be observed both in zoos and in natural settings; the other two are distinctively human because they depend on language and the manipulation of symbols.

1. In small-scale settings, coalitions are based on personal relationships among individuals. For example, in any parliamentary system, the prime minister must keep the support of the party caucus—the party's elected members of parliament—in order to remain in office. Prime Minister Brian Mulroney continued to excel at this form of face-to-face politics even after his standing in public opinion polls slumped badly during his second term of office (1988–93). Half a dozen Quebec MPs, led by Mulroney's erstwhile friend Lucien Bouchard, left the Conservative caucus to form the Bloc Québécois, and three anglophone MPs were either expelled or left the Tory caucus to sit as independents, but the Conservatives' majority in the House of Commons was never seriously jeopardized. Considering the stresses that the caucus had to withstand in these years—the collapse of the Meech Lake Accord, the disastrous referendum campaign leading to the defeat of the Charlottetown Accord, and a protracted recession—Mulroney's success at keeping its support showed anyone who might have doubted it that he was a genius at building personal coalitions.

2. Coalitions can also be formal alliances. For example, in the Gulf War of 1991, a number of governments, led by the United States but acting under the auspices of the United Nations, joined together to wage war against Iraq. In domestic politics, cabinets are sometimes formed by coalitions when no single party has a majority of seats in the elected legislature. The party caucuses, acting through their leaders, make an explicit agreement to support each other and to divide up the seats in the cabinet. The cabinets of many European democracies—for example, Germany, Italy, Denmark, and the Netherlands—are routinely put together in this way.

3. Less formally, the building of coalitions is a characteristic of the mass politics of modern democracies. Party leaders form electoral coalitions by proposing policies to attract certain groups of voters. For example, the Progressive Conservative victories of 1984 and 1988 were anchored by a rather fragile coalition of francophone voters in Quebec and anglophone voters in Western Canada and parts of Ontario. Many Québécois were particularly attracted by the Conservatives' promise to pursue constitutional change—specifically, to negotiate a constitutional agreement that Quebec could consent to signing.

(The constitution had been patriated in 1982 without the approval of provincial politicians in Quebec.) The anglophone voters outside Quebec were motivated more by the perception that the Conservatives stood for fiscal responsibility, smaller government, and traditional social values.

Although strikingly successful in the short term, Mulroney's coalition was intrinsically fragile because most of the anglophone voters in Western Canada and Ontario were opposed to the constitutional concessions the Conservatives were offering to Quebec francophones. The resulting strains caused the coalition to fracture. When this happened, two new parties formed—the Reform Party in Western Canada and the Bloc Québécois in Quebec. Both were backed largely by voters who had supported the PCs in 1984 and 1988. The same talent that allowed the prime minister to hold most of his caucus together was not sufficient to overcome the deep rifts in the electoral coalition he had created.

The individuals or groups that make up any type of coalition are not necessarily permanent partners. Political coalitions are often formed to respond to specific issues and circumstances. For example, after World War II a dominant coalition virtually monopolized Canadian federal politics; as a result, Liberal governments were elected for 32 of the 38 years between 1946 and 1984. Significant groups in this coalition included Quebeckers, both francophone and anglophone; immigrants and ethnic minorities in many parts of the country; Roman Catholics; and many individuals in the media and in the academic community. One factor holding these disparate groups together was a belief in the state's ability to guide change, progress, and economic development in Canadian society. When those years produced expensive bureaucracies and programs that did not always work as intended, the stage was set for the breakup of the dominant coalition, and the Conservatives in 1984 seized the opportunity to create a new one, which in turn fell apart in the early 1990s.

To recapitulate: government and politics are universal aspects of human existence. *Government is the process that makes and enforces rules and decisions for society; politics is the activity of reconciling conflicts and gathering support that makes government possible.* Government and politics both arise from the need for people to live in societies; for a society to succeed, people must settle conflicts and abide by common rules in such a way that the community is not endangered. Government and politics involve coercion, but not for its own sake. One reason rulers resort to force is to lessen the use of force by private individuals against each other.

Government and politics become more and more indispensable as civilization advances. The more complicated our way of life becomes, the less we can afford to have our plans upset by random intrusions of others on our person, property, or expectations. Government can be the great guarantor of the stability of expectations and the force that makes it possible for other human endeavours, such as religion, art, science, and business, to flourish. When a government is working well, the political process continually and unobtrusively resolves those conflicts that might otherwise tear society apart. In fact, politics may work so well that the ordinary person may take it for granted and have very little need to be concerned with it.

Even though government is essential, we are not always reconciled to it. There is in Western history a persistent belief that we may someday attain a perfectly harmonious, conflict-free society in which government will be unnecessary. One form of this belief is the Judeo–Christian tradition of the Kingdom of the Saints or the Kingdom of God on earth.[12] According to this idea, human conflict will cease with the advent (Judaism) or return (Christianity) of the Messiah, and there will be no ruler except this divinely authorized figure.

Secular versions of this scenario also exist. The early French socialist Henri Saint-Simon (1760–1825) wrote that eventually "the government of men" would be replaced by the "administration of things"—a formula later echoed by Lenin.[13] They both hoped that in a future world where everyone was comfortable and gross inequalities had vanished, people would become so peaceable that governmental coercion would be unnecessary. The same expectation is embodied in the Marxist doctrine of "the withering away of the state," which teaches that government will eventually become obsolete after a communist revolution.[14] But none of these visions has ever come to pass, and we must still rely on politics and government to mediate the conflicts that arise among self-interested individuals. Politics and government will be inevitable as long as human beings are motivated by individual self-interest.

ꙮꙮꙮꙮꙮꙮꙮ

APPENDIX TO CHAPTER 2
The Prisoner's Dilemma

The prisoner's dilemma is drawn from a branch of mathematics known as game theory. It is presented here as a simple example of the mathematical models that are increasingly being used in the literature of political science. The mathematics is not complicated; all that is required from the reader is a willingness to think logically.

Assume that two men, Mark and Tom, are arrested by the police for possession of illegal drugs and suspected of trafficking. The police interrogate them separately and do not allow them to communicate with each other. The police, furthermore, say the same thing to each prisoner: "We know you are guilty, but we need proof. If you inform on your partner while he remains silent, you can go free, and he will get ten years in jail. But if the situation is reversed—if he informs on you while you remain silent—he will go free and you will get ten years. If you both talk, you will both get eight years. But if neither of you talks, you will each get one year on the lesser charge of possession, which is all that our evidence will sustain without further testimony from one of you."

Mark and Tom will achieve the most favourable outcome if they both keep silent; if they do that, each will escape with a light sentence. But that is not likely to happen in the situation as described; instead, each will probably end up informing on the other and thus both will receive the heavier sentence of eight years. To understand why, consider the following payoff matrix:

Prisoner's Dilemma		Mark	
		Silent	Talk
Tom	Silent	-1,-1	-10,0
	Talk	0,-10	-8,-8

Each cell in the matrix contains a pair of numbers separated by a comma. The first number represents the payoff in a given situation to the row player (Tom), the second number represents the payoff in the same situation to the column player (Mark). The upper right-hand cell, for example, shows that if Mark talks while Tom remains silent, Mark will go free while Tom will get ten years in jail.

Now consider how each player will reason if he has complete information about the game and if he is rational in the sense of caring first about his own self-interest. Tom will say to himself, "I face two possibilities. Mark can either remain silent or talk. If he remains silent, I can either remain silent or talk. If I remain silent, I get one year in jail; if I talk, I go free—so I had better talk. But Mark may talk, in which case I again have two choices. If he talks and I remain silent, I get ten years in jail. If he talks and I also talk, I only get eight—so in this case also, it is better for me to talk. No matter what Mark does, I will be better off if I talk." Mark will reason the same way, for his column payoffs are a mirror image of Tom's row payoffs.

This result is both interesting and paradoxical. By a rigorous analysis of his self-interest, each prisoner is led to talk, which ensures that they both achieve the less desirable outcome of eight years in jail. If each could trust the other to remain silent, both could achieve the more desirable outcome of one year in prison. But in the game as described, if we assume self-interested players, neither has reason to have faith in the other's reliability.

The players might obtain a better joint outcome if the rules of the game were relaxed so they could communicate with each other. They could then agree in advance not to inform on each other. But communication in itself is not sufficient to resolve the prisoner's dilemma, for each player still has an incentive to break the agreement if he believes he can count on the other to keep his side of the bargain. That is, if Tom and Mark agree to keep silent, thus ensuring their best possible joint outcome, Tom (or Mark) can do even better by breaking the agreement and playing the other for a sucker. Thus we may still expect each to betray the other.

The game of prisoner's dilemma is a model of the general problem of obtaining social cooperation. In the terminology of the social sciences, a model is a simplified abstraction, often mathematical in character, used to represent a more complex process. No one pretends that a model can capture all the aspects of a situation. Prisoner's dilemma is an obvious simplification: people are not just individuals but also members of families and communities, and they are not purely self-interested but also care about others and feel obligated to follow general rules of conduct. Nonetheless, a model can illuminate important aspects of a given situation—in this case, the tendency to forego cooperation in the pursuit of self-interest. Of course, in this particular instance, what is good for the two players is bad for the larger society. But it still shows that voluntary cooperation requires a degree of confidence that the behaviour will be reciprocated.

There are two ways to resolve the prisoner's dilemma. One is iteration. If the game is played repeatedly, Mark and Tom can learn from experience how to achieve the best outcome for both. A brilliant study based on computer simulations of iterated prisoner's dilemma has shown that the most effective strategy is tit for tat. Do not be the first to defect; trust the other player as long as he cooperates; but punish him if he defects. At the same time, do not hold a grudge: return to cooperation as soon as he does.[15] Perhaps not surprisingly, this conforms to the working morality of most normal social behaviour: approach others in a cooperative way; cooperate as long as they do; but don't let yourself be played for a sucker. The other way to resolve the prisoner's dilemma is to enforce agreements. If Tom and Mark can find some way to ensure—or at least to increase the probability—that both will keep their promises, each will be able to rely on the other and be willing to cooperate to their mutual benefit.

꧁꧁꧁꧁꧁꧁꧁

FURTHER READING

Ball, Alan R. *Modern Politics and Government*, 5th ed. New Jersey: Chatham, 1993.

Bateman, Thomas M.J., Manuel Mertin, and David M. Thomas, eds. *Braving the New World: Readings in Contemporary Politics*. Scarborough, Ont.: Nelson Canada, 1995.

Crick, Bernard. *In Defence of Politics*, rev. ed. London: Pelican Books, 1964.

Evans, Peter, ed. *State-society Synergy: Government and Social Capital in Development*. Berkeley, Calif.: University of California at Berkeley, International and Area Studies, 1997.

Franks, C.E.S., et al. *Canada's Century: Governance in a Maturing Society: Essays in Honour of John Meisel*. Montreal: McGill-Queen's University Press, 1995.

Klosko, George. *The Principle of Fairness and Political Obligation.* Savage, Md.: Rowman & Littlefield, 1992.

Lasswell, Harold D. *Politics: Who Gets What, When, How.* New York: Meridian Books, 1958.

Leftwich, Adrian, ed. *What Is Politics? The Activity and Its Study.* Oxford: Basil Blackwell, 1984.

Mair, Lucy. *Primitive Government,* 2nd ed. Harmondsworth: Penguin Books, 1977.

Miller, J.D.B. *The Nature of Politics,* rev. ed. Harmondsworth: Penguin Books, 1965.

Roninger, Luis and Ayse Gunes-Ayata, eds. *Democracy, Clientelism, and Civil Society.* Boulder, Colo.: Lynne Rienner, 1994.

Walsh, David F. *Governing Through Turbulence: Leadership and Change in the Late Twentieth Century.* Westport, Conn.: Praeger, 1995.

POWER

Power in the broadest sense is the capacity to achieve what one wants. The word is derived from the French verb *pouvoir*, "to be able." Power can be the physical ability to perform a task such as lifting or running, the intellectual capacity to solve a problem, or the social ability to induce others to do what one wants.

In political science, power has this latter meaning. Power is to politics what money is to economics: the medium of exchange, the universal common denominator. Political power, however, is not a simple thing. There are three main forms of it: influence, coercion, and authority.

INFLUENCE

Influence is the ability to persuade some to do the will of another, to convince others to desire the same objective. The important point is that the targets of persuasion act voluntarily; they are not conscious of restraints on their will because they have freely chosen to agree. Of course, they may agree either because they have come to think that the action is right and justified in itself or because they think they will reap personal benefit from it.

Influence takes many forms, which in the hard light of reality often overlap:

- appeals to the intellect (i.e., convincing people that a given action is intrinsically best)

- appeals to the passions (i.e., persuading people to act by playing directly on the emotions)

- appeals to self-interest (i.e., persuading people to support a cause because of "what is in it for us")

- appeals to group solidarity (i.e., persuading people to work on behalf of a community to which they belong)

Because there are so many ways to influence others, there are also many resources that can be deployed in the task. The following list, while by no means exhaustive, gives some possibilities:

- Intelligence, knowledge, and research can be used to construct convincing arguments.
- Those with money and expertise can produce effective advertising.
- Those who control wealth can offer financial inducements (bribes).
- Those with organizational connections can offer career prospects (jobs, contracts, patronage in all its forms).
- Those who control the apparatus of government can offer what political scientists call "policy outputs" (i.e., promises to legislate in ways that will benefit their supporters).

Influence is always at work in government. Candidates for office in a democratic system win elections by persuading their fellow citizens to vote for them. Once in office, they are in turn besieged by individuals and groups who want government to do something on their behalf—for example, to build a road along one route rather than another, or to lower their taxes (and make up the revenue by increasing taxes on another group). For its part, government seeks to influence the behaviour of the electorate. For example, the government of Canada runs extensive advertising campaigns exhorting Canadians to exercise more, stop smoking, drink less alcohol, conserve energy, and support Canadian unity.

᯾᯾᯾᯾᯾᯾᯾

COERCION

Coercion is the deliberate subjection of one will to another through fear of harm or threats of harm. When it is applied, compliance is not voluntary but results from fear of unpleasant consequences.

Coercion can take many forms. **Violence** involves physical harm, such as beatings, torture, and murder. Imprisonment, while not directly violent, is enforced by violence if the prisoner tries to leave custody. Other forms of coercion include monetary penalties (e.g., fines imposed by government) and strikes, in which workers combine to threaten employers with losses in the marketplace. The number of ways of harming or threatening people is infinite and most methods ultimately rely on violence. We must pay a fine for a traffic violation to avoid imprisonment. Employers must submit to the economic setback of a legal strike. If they repudiated their agreements to bargain collectively with the unions, discharged their workers, and tried to hire a new workforce, they would be breaking the law and could be fined or even imprisoned.

A case that straddles the border between coercion and persuasion involves the manipulating of individuals by means of false or misleading information. Motivating someone to act on false information is probably closer to coercion even though it takes the form of persuasion. The actions of the one who is persuaded would not have been voluntary had the truth been available, so the result is similar to coercion in that it secures involuntary compliance.

Manipulation is a ubiquitous reality in politics. Political leaders quite deliberately rehearse their statements with professional advisers, the "spin doctors," to test them for effect. Words are chosen, and themes are omitted or included, to achieve a desired effect. Statements about future consequences of policies generally emphasize the positive and suppress the negative. Political advertising is even more manipulative than politicians' statements because it is often designed to appeal directly to the emotions.

Modern governments try to control most forms of outright coercion, especially violence. Ordinary people are prohibited from violently assaulting each other or seizing property. They are supposed to refrain from violence except in self-defence or in disciplining their children, and limits are enforced even in these situations. Government uses its near-monopoly on violence to protect society from external attack, and to enforce rules of conduct and punish those who violate them. To these ends, every government has developed a complex apparatus of armed forces, police forces, prisons, and courts.

One partial exception to the governmental control of coercion involves industrial relations. In the twentieth century, governments have accepted that collective bargaining is an arena in which employees and employers may resort to economic coercion to achieve their objectives. Yet the exception is perhaps not as great as it seems: collective bargaining was introduced to civilize labour relations, which were for a long time marked by a great deal of overt violence. Governments now try, more or less successfully, to legalize a degree of economic coercion and thus keep both sides from resorting to violence.

Government forbids all individuals or groups to use violence against it. Whatever their other differences, all governments are identical in their resistance to acts of political violence, because such acts undermine the very existence of the state. The use of force and the threat to use force against government are defined as political crimes.[1] A government that cannot resist such threats will not survive long.

Coercion is a powerful tool, yet no government can depend on it entirely. Society has so many members engaging in so many different activities that everything cannot be coercively directed. Even if it were possible, it would be too expensive because coercion is so labour-intensive. In any case, it is logically impossible for everything to depend on coercion because there must be a coalition of the coercers to get the job done. What holds them together? More coercion? If so, who provides it? At some point, societies must go beyond coercion to a principle that holds its followers together for joint action, that makes it possible for them to coerce others—in a word, authority.

The Chinese communist leader Mao Zedong (1893–1976) expressed this truth when he wrote, "Political power grows out of the barrel of a gun. Our principle is that the Party commands the gun; the gun shall never be allowed to command the Party."[2] (The first clause of this statement is often quoted out of context.) To be sure, the gun is significant, as was demonstrated at Tiananmen Square in 1989, when the Chinese government put down the democracy movement with tanks. But it is noteworthy that the army did nothing until the Communist Party had sorted out its internal disagreements and resolved upon a repressive course of action. Until there was clear direction from the party, the army was unwilling to use its firepower against unarmed civilians. The point is that coercion is not the ultimate form of power but a highly useful adjunct to authority.

AUTHORITY

Authority is a form of power in which people obey commands not because they have been rationally or emotionally persuaded or because they fear the consequences of disobedience, but simply because they respect the source of the command. The one who issues the command is accepted as having a right to do so, and those who receive the command accept that they have an obligation to obey. The relationship between parents and young children is a model of authority. Sometimes the parents will persuade the child to do something, and occasionally they may have to resort to coercion, but most of the time they can command with the expectation of being obeyed.

All governments possess at least some authority and strive to have as much as possible, for obvious reasons. Something more than influence is necessary to guarantee predictable results. Coercion produces compliance, but it is also very expensive and furthermore is possible only if a substantial number of agents of coercion are held together by authority. Clearly, authority is an inescapable necessity of government.

It is safe to say that most people most of the time are acting in deference to authority when they do what their government wishes. They stop at red lights and file tax returns because they realize that such actions have been commanded. (Of course, they may have other motives as well.) Perhaps their consciences bother them if they disobey authority. How else can we explain such obedience even in circumstances where punishment is highly unlikely? Most drivers obey traffic lights even at 3 a.m. on a deserted street, and not solely because they fear a hidden police cruiser—almost certainly, they feel a little uncomfortable about violating an authoritative rule. Nevertheless, not everyone is always deferential to authority; this is why coercion is extremely useful—it motivates by fear those who are not susceptible to feelings of obligation. Coercion is present as a background threat, as with a soldier who may be prompted to obey out of fear of a court-martial. But this coercion, though important, is only a tool of authority. Coercion by itself could not produce the united action necessary to hold a court-martial.

We must distinguish between **natural** and **public authority.** The former exists whenever one person spontaneously defers to the judgment of another. Little children tagging after big children, and students seeking out teachers in the early days of the medieval university, are instances of natural authority. Every individual is always surrounded by numerous natural authorities—friends, relatives, colleagues—and acts as an authority to others on occasion. Natural authority is simply another term for the human tendencies to follow and imitate, as well as lead and initiate. These are some of the bonds that hold society together.

Public authority, in contrast, is deliberately created by human agreement. The English language recognizes the difference between natural and public authority in an interesting way. We say that an expert on baseball statistics is "an authority" in his chosen field, but not that he is "in authority" in that field. But when we describe, for example, a policewoman, we do not say she is "an authority" by virtue of any personal quality, but rather that she is "in authority" by virtue of the power entrusted to her by government. Her uniform is a visible sign of the public or artificial authority that she wields. To be a natural authority, one must have special personal qualities; to hold public authority, one has only to be in a position or office that carries with it rights of command.

What is the relationship between public authority and social order? Power is required to order any society, but it must be more than coercive power if a given society is to be open and free. An advantage of authoritative power over coercive power is that most individuals voluntarily submit to it. But why would people submit to any power that restricts their freedom of action? The answer is not easy to find, and political philosophers have grappled with the question for centuries, searching for the roots of consent to authority. One writer has put the issue this way:

> … the authority of government does not create the order over which it presides and does not sustain that order solely by its own fiat or its accredited power. There is authority beyond the authority of government. There is a greater consensus without which the fundamental order of the community would fall apart.[3]

Consent to authority arises from a consensus about the social order, often called legitimacy. We will discuss that subject further in the next chapter.

Political science, at least with respect to modern government, is largely the study of public authority. However, natural authority still plays a significant role. Particularly in revolutionary or unstable situations, people are drawn to unusual leaders who seem to exude a personal magnetism. As a leader of the Métis, Louis Riel had influence on his followers that transcended any formal office. He was charismatic in the proper sense of that much-abused word, which will also be discussed in the next chapter.

🔲🔲🔲🔲🔲🔲🔲🔲

FURTHER READING

Baldwin, David Allen. *Paradoxes of Power*. Oxford: Blackwell, 1989.

Champlin, John R. *Power*. New York: Atherton Press, 1971.

Jaffe, Erwin. *Healing the Body Politic: Rediscovering Political Power*. Westport, Conn.: Praeger, 1993.

Kittrie, Nicholas N. *The War Against Authority: From the Crisis of Legitimacy to a New Social Contract*. Baltimore: Johns Hopkins University Press, 1995.

Lukes, Steven. *Power: A Radical View*. London: Macmillan, 1974.

Tinder, Glenn. *Political Thinking*, 6th ed. New York: Harper Collins, 1995.

Wrong, Dennis H. *Power: Its Forms, Bases and Uses*. Oxford: Basil Blackwell, 1979.

LEGITIMACY AND AUTHORITY

Although we often speak of having or possessing authority, that usage is misleading because it makes authority sound like a quality some people have, like red hair or a deep voice. In fact, authority is a social relationship; an individual has it only if others respect and obey it. Authority is one pole of a relationship in which the other pole is **legitimacy.** When we emphasize the right to command, we speak of authority; when we emphasize the response to command, we speak of legitimacy. Authority is focused in the one who commands; legitimacy is the feeling of respect for authority that exists in those who obey—it is what makes authority possible. It is the same type of relationship as exists between leadership and "followership." Neither makes sense without the other.

Both authority and legitimacy are moral or ethical concepts; that is, they involve perceptions of right and wrong. We feel that someone in authority has a right to command. Similarly, we feel that it is right to obey, that we have a duty or obligation to do so. Governmental power without legitimacy is only coercion or force; with legitimacy, power becomes authority.

Obligation is the link between authority and legitimacy, as illustrated in the following diagram:

authority ———— **obligation** ———— **legitimacy**
right of command   sense of duty   belief in rightness
of government

We feel obligated to respond to commands when we are convinced that those who exercise authority are justified in doing so.

Public authority survives only as long as it has some degree of legitimacy in society. It is not necessary that literally everyone, or even a numerical majority, accept the legitimacy of a particular government; but there must be at least a loyal minority, strong and united, to withstand potential opposition. If such a minority exists and is willing to use coercion, it can sustain itself in power for a surprising length of time in the face of widespread popular opposition.

It was obvious for decades that the numerical majorities in the Republic of South Africa and in the communist countries of Eastern Europe would have chosen other rulers if they had been effectively consulted. Yet those governments were in little danger of falling as long as they maintained their weapons monopoly and the political support of a determined minority. All these regimes finally changed when reform movements were established within the governments themselves. In each case, substantial elements of the ruling elite, led by the head of government, decided to break with the past. In each case the system had long before lost its legitimacy, but this in itself was not sufficient to topple the structure of authority.

Legitimacy rests upon beliefs and values that are not static; these things change over time, and legitimacy is challenged when government actions no longer correspond with them. According to Carl Friedrich:

> The process of aging leadership in consensual power situations is usually associated with the disintegration of authority. The actions of the "old one" are no longer understood, because they make no sense in terms of the altered values and beliefs; his capacity for reasoned elaboration is declining and finally is gone. This often carries with it a decline of power, though just as often the power continues, but it gradually becomes more coercive, less consensual.[1]

One of the great advantages of democracy is that regular, nonviolent changes of government are possible at periodic intervals. If a government ignores ongoing changes in beliefs and values, it can be voted out of office. Democracy provides a safety valve that enables voters to change governments without having to change the nature of the political system. Legitimacy is maintained for the system as a whole even as authority is transferred within it.

Because authority and legitimacy are so central to political life, they are an important focus of study in political science. One of the most important contributions to understanding them was made by the German sociologist Max Weber (1864–1920), who identified three kinds of authority/legitimacy: traditional, legal, and charismatic.[2] These "ideal types," as Weber called them, are always found mixed together in political systems. They are intellectual models that never exist in pure form in the real world yet help observers to understand what they see.

᠊᠊᠊᠊᠊᠊᠊᠊

TRADITIONAL AUTHORITY

Traditional authority is domination based on inherited position. Hereditary monarchs are a good example of traditional authority. They hold the right of command not because of extraordinary personal qualities or because they have been chosen by others, but because they have inherited a position from a parent or other relative. The arrangement is regarded as legitimate because it has the sanction and prestige of tradition: things have been done that way from time immemorial. The principle of inherited authority also draws support from its similarity to the workings of the family, the most fundamental social institution.

The feudal system of medieval Europe was based mainly on traditional authority. At the apex of authority were the hereditary monarchs. They appointed judges, administrators, and military commanders who owed them personal allegiance; their authority was only an extension of the monarch's. Many governmental functions were performed by members of the caste of nobles, whose social positions were also by right of birth. The system depended on the work of the common people, who were born into a social position out of which it was extremely difficult to rise. Throughout the system, command and obedience were associated with inherited social rank and sanctified by tradition. A similar arrangement characterized much of the rest of the world until very recently; it still prevails in Saudi Arabia and other Gulf sheikhdoms, where authority is vested in the royal family and a number of related clans.

LEGAL AUTHORITY

The central concept of **legal authority** is that general rules exist that are binding on all participants in the system. Authority is exercised only when it is called for by these rules. It is not associated with individuals who inherit their status, but with legally created offices that can be filled by many different incumbents. It is a "rule of law, not of men." (See Chapter 8 for a further discussion of this phrase.)

In Canada and Great Britain, authority is primarily legal, although the external symbolism is still traditional. A hereditary monarch reigns but does not rule, and actual power is wielded by politicians who are elected to office under a strictly defined system of laws. A prime minister is in authority while in office but has no personal status once dismissed. Those who work for government are no longer the personal servants of the monarch; their allegiance to the Crown means loyalty to the government as a whole, not to a particular person within it. There is no longer a hereditary caste of nobles carrying out governmental functions. The House of Lords, which still survives in Great Britain, is merely a symbolic reminder of the vanished age of traditional authority. The system derives its legitimacy not from the acceptance of status or from loyalty to personal authority, but from loyalty to the constitution, which is a legal system stronger than any individual.

However, there are still traditional elements within contemporary legal authority. Law itself is hallowed by tradition. As rule-following animals, we quickly build up habits of compliance to those in power. Over time, it begins to seem right to obey, simply because that is the way things have been done in the past. It is undoubtedly true that habit is a powerful source of governmental legitimacy. We obey because we are accustomed to, because we have always done so. Reflective thought is not necessarily involved.

Such habits of obedience are necessary, for if we continually had to reconsider the legitimacy of government, we would have time for little else. Those habits break down in times of revolutionary transition, when one form of authority is replaced by another. Yet they quickly re-establish themselves as part of the new government's legitimacy.

The great trend of development in modern political history is for traditional authority to be replaced by legal authority. This long, slow, and painful process began in Great Britain and its American colonies in the seventeenth century, continued in Europe in the eighteenth and nineteenth centuries, and has engulfed the entire world in the twentieth century. It is the political aspect of the wider social process known as **modernization.** Social changes gradually and cumulatively changed people's notions of political legitimacy; this process was punctuated at certain times with the dramatic collapse of a traditional regime and its replacement by a new system of legal authority. The great popular revolutions of modern history must be seen in this context:

1688 Glorious Revolution	Stuarts overthrown by English Parliament
1776 American Revolution	American colonies declare independence from British Crown
1789 French Revolution	Bourbon dynasty replaced by a republic
1911 Chinese Revolution	Manchu dynasty replaced by a republic
1917 Russian Revolution	Romanov dynasty overthrown; Russian Empire becomes Soviet Union

These are only a few of the many revolutions that in three centuries have transformed the political face of the globe. Together they make up what is often called the world revolution. The essence of this world revolution was memorably stated by the French writer Alexis de Tocqueville, who made an extended tour in 1831–32 of the United States and Canada, and noted the great social inequality of the traditional order of Europe:

On the one side were wealth, strength, and leisure, accompanied by the refinements of luxury, the elegance of taste, the pleasures of wit, and the cultivation of the arts; on the other were labor, clownishness, and ignorance. But in the midst of this coarse and ignorant multitude it was not uncommon to meet with energetic passions, generous sentiments, profound religious convictions, and wild virtues.

The social state thus organized might boast of its stability, its power, and, above all, its glory.

But the scene is now changed. Gradually the distinctions of rank are done away; the barriers which once severed mankind are falling down; property is divided, power is shared by many, the light of intelligence spreads and the capacities of all classes are equally cultivated.[3]

This social equalization described by de Tocqueville is inseparable from legal authority, in which individuals are governed by universal rules applicable to all. It cannot co-exist for long with the hereditary classes and ranks of traditional authority. The worldwide transition from traditional to legal authority is the single most important political event of our times, and furnishes the context in which everything else takes place.

The collapse of communism in the Soviet Union and Eastern Europe was a further development in this direction. Communism as an ideology promised the benefits of legal authority and social equalization, but the communist regimes never came close to attaining these goals. In practice, they resembled a kind of bureaucratic feudalism, with great emphasis on the personal authority of the party leaders and disregard for impersonal legal norms. The party leaders constituted a privileged elite as oppressive as any traditional aristocracy. In their enthusiastic response to Mikhail Gorbachev's reform policy of *glasnost* (openness), Soviet citizens demonstrated their desire to complete the transition to legal authority that had long been promised under communism.

CHARISMATIC AUTHORITY

Charismatic authority is based on the projection and perception of extraordinary personal qualities. Weber defined charisma as "a certain quality of an individual personality by virtue of which he is set apart from ordinary men and treated as endowed with supernatural, superhuman, or at least specifically exceptional powers or qualities."[4]

Charisma was originally a theological term, derived from the Greek word for "grace" or "spiritual favour." Generally speaking, charismatic leaders are prophets, saints, shamans, or similar figures. Their legitimacy does not depend on tradition or law but on their followers' belief that they speak to them directly from God. Their transcendental claim to authority often places them in conflict with traditional or legal authorities. Some of our most striking and well-known historical figures were charismatic in this sense: the biblical prophets of the Hebrews, as well as Joan of Arc, whose heavenly visions inspired her to help drive the English from France.

Louis Riel is Canada's best example of a charismatic leader. On December 8, 1875, he experienced a mystical illumination that convinced him he was the "Prophet of the New World." He saw himself as endowed by God with a personal mission to create a new religion in North America in which his own people, the Métis, would be a chosen people like the Hebrews. Riel wanted the Métis to adopt certain Old Testament practices, such as polygamy and circumcision; these would eventually be merged with a revised version of Roman Catholicism. Riel preached this novel doctrine to the Métis at Batoche during the North-West Rebellion of 1885. The rebels formed a sort of provisional government, but Riel did not hold office in it—he preferred to be recognized as a prophet. Each morning he assembled the Métis forces to tell them of the divine revelations he had received during the night. He promised his followers that God would work a miracle to defeat the expeditionary force sent by Canada. The miracle did not happen and the uprising was crushed. Riel was later convicted of high treason. He went to the scaffold believing that he, like Christ, would rise from the dead on the third day after his execution.[5]

The term *charisma* is also applied to political leaders who base their claim to rule on an alleged historical mission. Adolf Hitler, for example, believed that he had a special mission to restore Germany's greatness. He came to this conviction as he lay in hospital in 1918, having been blinded by a British gas attack on the Western front. His blindness coincided in time with Germany's surrender, and when he recovered his sight, he became convinced that he might also be the means of Germany's restoration to greatness. The title he always preferred was *Führer*, the German word for leader; it emphasized that his authority radiated from his personality, not from any office that he happened to occupy.

Charisma is sometimes collectively shared, as in the political thought of the Ayatollah Khomeini (1902–89), the symbol and leader of the revolution that swept the Shah of Iran from power in 1979. Khomeini was a jurist who specialized in the study of the *Shari'a*, the Islamic law. "The jurists," according to Khomeini, "have been appointed by God to rule."[6] The state, he said, must also have secular legislative and executive authorities, but the jurists as a group have an overriding and divinely given power and responsibility to ensure that all government is carried on within the principles of the *Shari'a*. Khomeini saw himself less as a special individual than as the most prominent representative of a charismatic class.

In popular culture today, the term charisma has been debased to mean little more than popularity. It has been attributed to democratic politicians who have never made claims like those of Riel or Hitler. John F. Kennedy never claimed to be anything more than an officeholder in a structure of legal authority, nor did Pierre Trudeau. Certainly, neither politician claimed to rule on the basis of divine inspiration or a world-historical mission. Although they were not charismatic in the technical sense of the term as used here, it must be admitted that some politicians—as well as prominent movie stars, rock musicians, and athletic heroes—have a certain aura reminiscent of charisma. Even if they do not claim a literal right to rule, they project themselves as models for admiration and emulation. When during the 1993 election the Progressive Conservatives put up posters bearing the slogan *Kim!*, there was at least a faint hint of charisma, although it did not last very long during the rigours of the campaign.

Charisma, like authority in general, is not a thing that a leader has; it is a social relationship based on the followers' perception of the legitimacy of the leader's claims. The most important question is not how Joan of Arc, Louis Riel, or Adolf Hitler could utter such extraordinary claims about themselves, but how they could find such a receptive audience. The short answer is that charismatic leaders are accorded legitimacy in times of crisis or grave unrest when other forms of authority appear to have failed. Joan of Arc came to the rescue of France during the Hundred Years' War at a time when England had the upper hand and France was in danger of being conquered. The traditional authority of the French monarch seemed incapable of meeting the challenge. Riel preached his radical gospel to the Métis at a time when the disappearance of the buffalo and the replacement of their ox-trains by railways and steamboats threatened to destroy their way of life. It was a challenge that the traditional Métis authorities, the patriarchs of the clans, were helpless to meet. Hitler came to power during a turbulent phase of German history. The traditional authority of the Kaiser had been destroyed by Germany's defeat in World War I. The legal authority of the Weimar Republic, never deeply rooted, was gravely shaken by the runaway inflation of the early 1920s and the international depression of the early 1930s. Driven to desperation, the German people, particularly the middle class, listened to Hitler's promises of salvation.

If charisma is a response to crisis, it is difficult to see how it can be very long-lasting. As stability is restored, we would expect a return to traditional or legal authority. Weber was well aware of this tendency, which he called the "routinization of charisma."[7] The more success prophets or leaders have in creating a following, the more either they or their followers find it necessary to create an enduring structure of authority that can exist over generations. If Riel had been successful in the North-West Rebellion, he would eventually have had to take on some role other than prophet. Once the Shah was overthrown, Khomeini approved a new Iranian constitution that institutionalized and regularized the authority of the Islamic jurists, who have carried on since his death. Political history seems to alternate short, intense upheavals of charismatic authority with longer periods of normalcy.

FURTHER READING

Connolly, William, ed. *Legitimacy and the State*. Oxford: Basil Blackwell, 1984.

Frank, Thomas. *The Power of Legitimacy among Nations*. New York: Oxford University Press, 1990.

Friedrich, Carl J., ed. *Authority*. Cambridge, Mass.: Harvard University Press, 1958.

Nelson, Daniel N. *After Authoritarianism: Democracy or Disorder?* Westport, Conn.: Greenwood Press, 1995.

Nevitte, Neil. *The Decline of Deference: Canadian Value Change in Cross-Cultural Perspective.* Peterborough, Ont.: Broadview Press, 1996.

Raz, Joseph. *Authority*. Oxford: Blackwell, 1990.

Russell, Bertrand. *Authority and the Individual*. Boston: Beacon Press, 1960.

Sennet, Richard. *Authority*. New York: Knopf, 1980.

Shaar, John H. *Legitimacy and the Modern State*. New Brunswick, N.J.: Transaction Publishers, 1989.

Vidrich, Arthur J., and Ronald M. Glassman, eds. *Conflict and Control: Challenge to Legitimacy of Modern Government*. Beverly Hills, Calif.: Sage, 1979.

Zartman, I. William, ed. *Collapsed States: The Disintegration and Restoration of Legitimate Authority*. Boulder, Colo.: Lynne Rienner, 1995.

SOVEREIGNTY AND THE STATE

CHAPTER 5

The term *sovereign*, derived from the Latin *super*, meaning "above," literally denotes one who is superior. It was first used in its modern sense by the French author Jean Bodin toward the end of the sixteenth century. Writing at a time of fierce wars between Catholics and Protestants, Bodin sought to obtain civil peace by establishing the king as the supreme authority whose will could decide such disputes. Bodin's idea was that in any community there ought to be a single highest authority who is not subject to other human authority. He wrote in *Six Livres de la République* (1583) that "sovereignty is the absolute and perpetual power of a commonwealth. The sovereign Prince is only accountable to God ... Sovereignty is not limited with respect to power, scope, or duration ... The Prince is the image of God."[1]

The Romans had a similar concept, which they called *imperium*—the concentrated, undivided power of government. Bodin, who was a student of Roman law, was trying to revive the idea of centralized power in an age in which it did not exist or existed only in an imperfect way. To understand why this was so, we must recall some facts about the feudal society of medieval Europe. Everyone was subject to a feudal overlord, but there was no effective pyramid of authority with the monarch at its peak. For all practical purposes, the nobles were often autonomous, as were many city-states in Italy and along the Rhine. The pope exercised a claim to rule in religious matters through his bishops. The Church maintained its own system of ecclesiastical courts; it even had the power to gather taxes, by which means money flowed to Rome. Nowhere was there a single sovereign—a highest authority—and indeed, except for the authority of God, the concept did not exist. This helps to explain why the religious wars of the Protestant Reformation were so protracted. Various nobles gave their support to one side or the other, and there was no effective central power to keep them all in check.

Bodin's idea of the sovereign took hold at a time of revulsion against this warfare and became well established in the seventeenth and eighteenth centuries. This was the age of absolute monarchs—so called not because they could do whatever they pleased, but because there was no human authority superior to theirs.

However, it is less the person than the power that is of interest here. **Sovereignty** is the authority to override all other authorities. Family, employer, church—all social authorities—must yield to the sovereign's power when it is turned in their direction. More concretely, sovereignty is a bundle of powers associated with the highest authority of government. One is the power to enforce rules of conduct—by establishing tribunals, compensating victims, punishing offenders, and so on—and includes the power of life and death. Another is the power to make law, that is, to create new law, amend existing law, and repeal old law. Sovereignty also includes the control of all the normal executive functions of government such as raising revenue, maintaining armed forces, minting currency, and providing other services to society. In the British tradition sovereignty also implies an underlying ownership of all land. Private ownership of land "in fee simple" is a form of legal delegation from the sovereign, who can reclaim any parcel of land through expropriation. Compensation to the private owner is customary but not required. Finally, sovereignty always means the power to deal with the sovereigns of other communities as well as the right to exercise domestic rule free from interference by other sovereigns.

Sovereignty was exercised by individual sovereigns in the Age of Absolutism (in the seventeenth and eighteenth centuries), but it can also be placed in the hands of a small group or an entire people. In England, the Stuarts' claims to absolute monarchy were decisively defeated by Parliament in the Glorious Revolution of 1688. This victory ultimately led to the theory of **parliamentary sovereignty,** articulated by William Blackstone in his *Commentaries on the Laws of England* (1765–69). Blackstone held that the supreme authority in England was Parliament, defined as the Commons, Lords, and Crown acting together under certain procedures.

Parliamentary sovereignty is still the main principle of the British constitution. It means that Parliament may make or repeal whatever laws it chooses; one Parliament cannot bind its successors in any way. Parliament is still the highest court in the land and cannot be overruled by the judiciary. The executive authority of government symbolized by the Crown can be exercised only by ministers who are responsible to Parliament. One hundred years ago, A.V. Dicey, one of the greatest British constitutional experts, claimed facetiously that "Parliament can do anything except make a man into a woman." The progress of medical science has now removed even that limitation.

While Blackstone was developing the theory of parliamentary sovereignty, Jean-Jacques Rousseau's *Social Contract* (1762) set forth the great alternative of **popular sovereignty**. Rousseau taught that supreme authority resided in the people themselves and could not be delegated. Laws should be made by the people meeting in direct-democratic fashion, not by electing representatives to legislate for them (indirect democracy). "The people of England," wrote Rousseau, "deceive themselves when they fancy they are free; they are so, in fact, only during the election of members of Parliament: for, as soon as a new one is elected, they are again in chains, and are nothing."[2]

Rousseau's ideal of direct democracy is extremely difficult to attain in a commonwealth of any size. Subsequent writers have kept alive the notion of popular sovereignty by softening the definition. For example, the American Declaration of Independence (1776) states that governments derive "their just powers from the consent of the governed." This moderate formulation of popular sovereignty, which stresses consent rather than direct rule, underlies modern representative democracy.

The three alternatives of personal, parliamentary, and popular sovereignty are not mutually exclusive. All three have to be examined to explain the present reality of, for example, British government. The present monarch, Elizabeth II, is still sovereign in the symbolic sense that she represents the power of the state; she "reigns but does not rule," as the saying goes. Parliament is legally sovereign in its control over legislation and all aspects of government, but Parliament does not exist in a political vacuum. The most important part of Parliament is the House of Commons, whose members are elected by the people at large. Interpreters of the British system argue that popular sovereignty exists in the political sense that Parliament depends on public support. If Parliament uses its legal sovereignty in a way that runs counter to public opinion, the people will elect new members to the House of Commons when the opportunity arises. In the long run, popular sovereignty is as much a fact of British politics as is parliamentary sovereignty.

The British situation is complex, the Canadian one even more so. Canada has a heritage of representative democracy on the British model, and Canadians share the same balance of personal, parliamentary, and popular sovereignty. The Queen is the sovereign of Canada, as she is of Great Britain and of some other members of the Commonwealth, and Canada has a legally sovereign Parliament whose political composition is determined by a voting population. But Canada's political system also divides power between levels of government. The national Parliament and the provincial legislatures each have a share of sovereign law-making power. The provinces, for example, have control of education but cannot issue money or raise an army. The government of Canada controls trade and commerce but not property and civil rights, which are provincial matters.

The inevitable disputes between levels of government regarding the precise distribution of powers are settled in the courts, which have a power not needed or possessed by the British courts: judicial review. **Judicial review** is the power of the courts to declare that actions taken by other branches of government violate the Constitution. Canadian courts have the power to nullify legislation passed by one level of government that invades the jurisdiction of the other. The Canadian system is thus a variant of British parliamentary sovereignty, in the sense that sovereignty is shared by a number of parliaments or legislatures and tempered by the courts' power to declare legislation unconstitutional. In other words, Canadian sovereignty is divided, not concentrated. This arrangement is vastly different from Bodin's original conception of sovereignty as a single, undivided centre of power.

The same is true in the United States, where sovereign power is also divided between levels of government. A further complexity of the American constitution is that the president, the chief executive officer, is neither a symbolic figure like the Queen nor an actual ruling sovereign like a seventeenth-century king. Sovereignty is divided between the president and Congress; the two branches must cooperate in order to make law, wage war, and perform other governmental acts.

Sovereignty may also be delegated to administrative agencies or even private bodies. Marketing boards enforcing production quotas, professional associations licensing practitioners, corporations exploiting mineral rights obtained from the Crown, and trade unions requiring all employees to abide by a collective agreement are all exercising a small, delegated share of sovereignty. Much of modern politics consists of a competitive struggle among organized groups to get the government to delegate a share of sovereign power to them, so that they may use it to benefit their members.

Clearly, Bodin's original desire to locate sovereignty entirely in one place has not been fully realized. The bundle of sovereign powers that exists conceptually may be divided among different hands. Some fragmentation of power helps to ensure that sovereignty is exercised within the rules established by the constitution. It is perhaps better for a free society that power be divided in this way, for concentrated, unopposed power is a standing temptation to abuse by those who wield it.

It might even be best to abandon the concept of sovereignty altogether for purposes of domestic politics and to admit that no person or group is sovereign in the original sense of the term. Metaphorically, we might say that the constitution is sovereign, that is, that all political power is constrained by constitutional rules that establish and limit the exercise of public authority. Different authorities exercise sovereign power at different moments in the political process: the people in voting for candidates to office, parliamentarians in voting on legislation, the head of state in giving assent to legislation, the courts in exercising judicial review. Each exercise of power takes place within constitutional limits, so that no one group or person is sovereign in the original sense.

However, even if sovereignty is internally constrained, divided, and delegated within the state, it still makes sense to inquire whether a government is able to control a certain population on a given territory, free from interference by other governments. This is actually the most frequent use of the term today—that is, to denote autonomy from outside control in international affairs. Sovereignty in this sense is claimed by all governments and recognized by international law.

THE STATE

The preceding discussion of sovereignty makes it possible to develop the concept of **state,** which has been mentioned previously but not fully explained. A state is defined by the joint presence of three factors: population, territory, and sovereignty.

A state exists when a sovereign power effectively rules over a population residing within the boundaries of a fixed territory. Canada is a state, as are Great Britain and France. Quebec, on the other hand, is not a state; it has people and territory but not a sovereign government (except to the limited extent in which a province in the Canadian system has a share of sovereignty). It is the program of the Bloc Québécois and the Parti Québécois to turn Quebec into a state by attaining full sovereignty, but that is a project for the future, not a current reality.

The state is the universal form of political organization in the modern world. The earth's entire land mass, with the exception of Antarctica, is divided into territories under the control of approximately 190 ostensibly sovereign states. It is difficult to say precisely how many states there are, because of certain anomalous cases. Some ministates, such as Monaco, Andorra, and San Marino, do not carry on a full range of relationships with other states; their foreign policy is conducted by larger neighbours. Other difficult cases include governments-in-exile, states that lack universal recognition—for example, Taiwan—and puppet or buffer states. Various states claim portions of Antarctica, but the claims conflict and have never been resolved. Despite all this, we tend to take the state for granted as the only conceivable form of political organization, even though the combination of people, territory, and sovereignty that we call the state is, historically speaking, a fairly recent invention. The word itself was not widely used before Machiavelli wrote *The Prince* (1513).

Governmental processes in tribal societies are carried on without the state form of organization. Before the coming of the Europeans, the peoples of the North American plains did not have fixed territories with stable boundaries. They had traditional lands on which they hunted and gathered food, but these lands always overlapped with those of neighbouring tribes. The peoples themselves were in constant movement. The Cree and Ojibwa, for example, only moved off the Canadian Shield and onto the Prairies after the fur traders appeared and gave them firearms. Using their new weapons, they compelled other tribes to make room for them.

If there were no stable borders, there was also no rigid definition of a people. Tribes could split apart (as did the Sioux and Assiniboine), or become close allies in spite of linguistic differences (as did the members of the Blackfoot Confederacy, even though the Sarcee speak a language totally unrelated to Blackfoot). Nor, as described at some length in Chapter 2, was there any specialized structure of government culminating in sovereign authority.

Like hunting societies, the earliest agricultural societies were also stateless. Farming took place in autonomous villages that could handle their collective affairs without a specialized machinery of government. How then did the state arise? The answer almost certainly lies in warfare. Armed clashes between hunting tribes do not lead to the formation of a state as long as the losers can migrate to new hunting grounds; roughly the same is true of primitive agriculturalists, as long as arable land is available. But where new land is not readily accessible, warfare produces a social hierarchy of victors and vanquished enforced by coercion. A specialized state machinery of armies, courts, tax gatherers, and other officials evolves as the conquerors enrich themselves at the expense of the conquered.[3] When a strong monarch consolidates conquered territory, the state form of organization emerges.

Recent research in anthropology and human biology has stressed that reproductive competition was interwoven with competition for land and other resources in the rise of the early states.[4] Tribes victorious in warfare commonly seized women from their conquered opponents. Chiefs and headmen used their power to take and support a larger number of wives. Early states were almost all characterized by polygamy in the upper classes, with kings and powerful noblemen maintaining harems of remarkable size. (Solomon reputedly had 700 wives and 300 concubines.)[5]

Once created, the state was a powerful expansive force. It easily prevailed over neighbouring agricultural communities if these had not formed their own states. It found tougher opposition in warlike nomads, who at times even overran territorial states, as happened often in the history of Europe and Asia. Over thousands of years, tribe after tribe of invaders from the steppes of Eurasia descended upon the empires of China, India, the Middle East, and Europe. Often the conquerors did not destroy the state; rather, they took it over and installed themselves as rulers, and were sometimes able to extend the state's territories. At other times, the conquest was such a shock that the state machinery deteriorated and required a long period to be rebuilt.

The modern European states arose from such an interregnum. Invasions by Germans and other peoples destroyed the highly developed Roman Empire. The invaders installed themselves as rulers in medieval Europe but did not initially create a full-fledged state system. There were rudimentary specialized structures of government, but territorial boundaries between authorities were not clear. For hundreds of years England's kings were nominally vassals of the French kings, because England had important territorial holdings in France. The Roman Catholic Church in all parts of Europe carried on activities, such as raising revenue and conducting court trials, that today would be considered governmental. The political history of modern times is the history of the emergence of separate, sovereign states out of the overlapping, interlocking jurisdictions of medieval Europe.

This development of the state runs like a thread through the familiar epochs into which Western history is customarily divided. Although the subject is far too big for a complete discussion here, we can at least mention some of the main stages.

During the Renaissance (in the fifteenth and sixteenth centuries) there was a great revival of interest in classical antiquity. Knowledge of Latin and Greek became more widespread, and many forgotten works of art, literature, and science were recovered. This revival culminated in what is often referred to as humanism, one of the great contributions of the Renaissance. One consequence of this was a heightened knowledge of Roman law, whose concept of imperium helped clear the way for sovereignty. Legal advisers trained in Roman law guided monarchs toward assertion of centralized control over their territories.

The Reformation (in the sixteenth and seventeenth centuries) broke the political power of the Roman Catholic Church. In England and parts of Germany, new Protestant churches were created that were firmly subordinated to the state. (The Queen is still head of the Church of England, for example.) In countries such as France and Spain, which remained Roman Catholic, church administration was shorn of independent political power and the pope lost the ability to intervene in internal political disputes. Another aspect of the Reformation, the increased use of vernacular languages rather than Latin, strengthened the developing states of Europe by fostering the notion of a different official language for each state. The dialect of Paris became the language of France, the "King's English" became the standard speech of Britain, and so on.

The Enlightenment (in the eighteenth century) saw a relaxation of religious tensions. Exhausted by more than a century of religious warfare, people turned their energies to secular matters. Science and philosophy flourished under the patronage of kings, who founded institutions such as the Royal Society of London to promote the advancement of learning. Scepticism, science, and individual freedom contributed to the development of the name by which the Enlightenment is best known: the Age of Reason. Hope and optimism became the qualities of a civilization that perceived itself as peaceful and reasonable.

Interestingly, the Enlightenment in its political aspect is often known as the Age of Absolutism. The European continent was now more or less clearly divided into territorial states ruled by strong monarchs, who established standing armies, court systems, and police forces and in other ways developed a virtual monopoly on law enforcement and armed coercion. Further, they founded a professional bureaucracy that was capable of raising money through taxes and of offering public services to the population, such as the construction of harbours and highways and the promotion of agriculture. It was in the eighteenth century that the state first took on a shape we would recognize if we could return to that era.

There was an important contradiction between the political thought of the Enlightenment, which was generally individualistic, and the political practices of that age, which were absolutist and monarchical. "L'état c'est moi" (I am the State), said Louis XIV, emphasizing his personal sovereignty. In England this contradiction had been partly resolved through the establishment of parliamentary sovereignty in 1688. On the continent of Europe the revolution was delayed for a century and was correspondingly more violent when it came. The year 1789 saw a popular uprising against the French monarchy that proved to be the beginning of the end of personal sovereignty and traditional authority. Since then, all the great royal dynasties have been overthrown or made merely symbolic, as in Britain. Yet the age of popular revolutions did not abolish the states created by the absolute monarchs; on the contrary, it extended and perfected those states. Modern governments control armies, police, and bureaucracies that Louis XIV could never have imagined.

CITIZENSHIP

In the nineteenth and twentieth centuries, the state became more participatory. The absolute monarchs ruled over **subjects;** the reality of the modern state is **citizenship.** This was dramatically illustrated during the French Revolution, when for a time the legislature forbade the use of the titles *Monsieur* and *Madame* in favour of *Citoyen* and *Citoyenne.*[6] Today every individual is potentially a citizen, a member of an association in which all participate. Citizenship brings a variety of rights: personal rights, such as freedom of speech; political rights, such as the vote; economic rights, such as public education and pensions. The personal sovereign is now chiefly a symbol of the governmental powers exercised by a parliament in response to the wishes of the citizens. In Weber's terms, the modern state is the triumph of legal authority over traditional authority. Ideally, the modern state is not just a power imposed over society by force; it is a specialized instrument of society for the achievement of common goals. In its pursuit of these ends, it can become an association of all citizens, who share popular sovereignty and may be chosen to help wield parliamentary sovereignty.

Today all human beings in the world, with the exception of some refugees who may be stateless, are citizens of at least one state. Even resident aliens usually retain their prior citizenship unless and until they are admitted to citizenship in their new homeland. Sovereignty, state, and citizenship are so much a part of our lives that it is hard to remember that they are not facts of nature but the result of centuries of political evolution.

The participatory aspects of the modern state, however, must not blind us to its origins in warfare and conquest. Any state is fundamentally an enormous engine of coercion, even when that coercive power is restrained by the legal form of authority. States are still predatory in their relations with one another; whatever the pious pronouncements about sovereignty, weak states are often wholly or partly controlled by more powerful ones. Also, the state's internal machinery offers a temptation to the ambition and greed of social groups. Such concentrated coercive power can easily be used by one group within the state to elevate itself at the expense of another. Groups will try to protect themselves from taxation while loading taxes onto others, or campaign for official sponsorship of their language or religion, or argue that public services should flow in their direction rather than toward others. Such efforts by special-interest groups to use the state for their own purposes are as old as the state itself. Their existence should scarcely be surprising, since the original purpose of the state was to protect the spoils of conquest. The modern legal and participatory state is a delicate and sometimes fragile modification of a brutal enterprise.

As a summary, let us link together the four key concepts that have been discussed thus far: society, state, politics, and government. Society is the voluntary, spontaneously emerging order of relationships in which we co-exist with and serve the needs of one another. It is what makes possible human comfort and even survival. The state is the community organized and armed with coercive power to protect the social order from internal disruption and external attack, and to provide certain public services to the community. Government is the decision-making structure and process of the state, while politics is the never-ending struggle for support in the public realm. Social factions put pressure on public authorities, hoping to influence their decisions in certain ways, and provide support if the desired decisions are made.

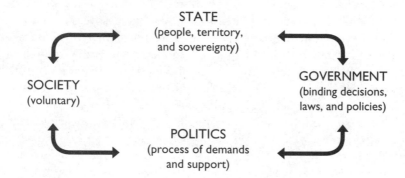

Although the concepts of state and government overlap to a considerable extent, there is a subtle distinction of emphasis between them. Government is the process of decision making and the structure of offices that sustains the process. The state is the entire territorial community, organized for collective action through its government. The state is a more abstract and permanent entity. Governments come and go as politicians and civil servants change in office, but the state remains, unless it is destroyed through civil war, conquest, or annexation by another state. Also, the state is perceived as more universal and impartial than government. For example, political writers would usually refer to medicare as state medical insurance, not government medical insurance. In a program such as medicare, government organizes the resources of the entire community for the enduring welfare of the population. Government is the agent of the state when it acts collectively, but more than government is involved.

FURTHER READING

Albo, Gregory, David Langille, and Leo Panitch. *A Different Kind of State? Popular Power and Democratic Administration.* Toronto: Oxford University Press, 1993.

Camilleri, Joseph. *The End of Sovereignty? The Politics of a Shrinking and Fragmenting World.* Aldershot, England: Elgar, 1992.

Dyson, Kenneth. *The State Tradition in Western Europe.* Oxford: Martin Robertson, 1980.

Elkins, David J. *Beyond Sovereignty: Territory and Political Economy in the Twenty-First Century.* Toronto: University of Toronto Press, 1995.

Esberey, Joy E., and L.W. Johnston. *Democracy and the State: An Introduction to Politics.* Peterborough, Ont.: Broadview Press, 1994.

Guehenno, Jean-Marie, trans. by Victoria Elliott. *The End of the Nation-State.* Minneapolis: University of Minnesota Press, 1995.

Harding, Alan. "The Origins of the Concept of the State," *History of Political Thought* 15, Spring 1994.

Jouvenel, Bertrand de. *Sovereignty.* Chicago: University of Chicago Press, 1963.

Klein, Robert A. *Sovereign Equality among States: The History of an Idea.* Toronto: University of Toronto Press, 1974.

Lubasz, Heinz. *The Development of the Modern State.* New York: Macmillan, 1964.

Magocsi, Paul Robert. *The End of the Nation-State? The Revolution of 1989 and the Future of Europe.* Kingston, Ont.: Kashtan Press, 1994.

McLennan, Gregor. *The Idea of the Modern State/The State and Society.* Milton Keynes, U.K.: Open University Press, 1984.

Oppenheimer, Franz. *The State.* Montreal: Black Rose Books, 1975. First published in 1914.

Poggi, Gianfranco. *The Development of the Modern State.* Stanford, Calif.: Stanford University Press, 1978.

————. *The State: Its Nature, Development, and Prospects.* Stanford, Calif.: Stanford University Press, 1990.

Tivey, Leonard, ed. *The Nation State: The Formation of Modern Politics.* Oxford: Martin Robertson, 1981.

Vincent, Andrew. *Theories of the State.* Oxford: Blackwell, 1987.

THE NATION

CHAPTER 6

What we described in the previous chapter as the modern, legal, participatory state, many authors prefer to call the **nation-state**. The word *nation* is added to state to emphasize that the state is participatory—that it is an association of citizens, not just a power coercively imposed on subjects. For reasons that will become clear later in this chapter, the term *nation-state* raises all sorts of problems in Canada, and we prefer to use it sparingly. However, the term is widely employed in political science, and the student will undoubtedly encounter it many times. Why does the word *nation* have these connotations of voluntary consent and active participation when it is added to state?

First of all, *nation* can be almost a synonym for state. The United Nations is an organization to which only states can belong, which means that bodies like the Palestine Liberation Organization can have only observer status. Could the United Nations just as well have been called the United States if that name had not already been taken by our southern neighbour? Probably not, for United States suggests an association of governments, whereas United Nations suggests an association of the peoples of the world. They may communicate with each other through their governments, but if the term means anything, they are also involved as peoples.

This brings us to the nub of the issue. There are social realities called nations, which are conceptually distinct from states. Typical nations are the Americans, the French, the Germans. Who exactly are the Germans? They are not simply those who speak the German language, for German is also spoken in Austria and parts of Switzerland, Luxembourg, and Belgium. Nor can the Germans be identified with reference to a single state, for after World War II there were two German states—the German Democratic Republic (East Germany) and the Federal Republic of Germany (West Germany)—which did not merge until 1990. Nor is religion the explanation, for the Germans are about equally divided between Protestants and Catholics. The French writer Ernest Renan explored this topic in a well-known essay, *Qu'est-ce qu'une Nation?* (1882). He wrote:

A nation is a soul, a spiritual principle ... A nation is a great solidarity, created by the sentiment of the sacrifices which have been made and of those which one is disposed to make in the future. It presupposes a past; but it resumes itself in the present by a tangible fact: the consent, the clearly expressed desire to continue life in common. The existence of a nation is a plebiscite of every day, as the existence of the individual is a perpetual affirmation of life.[1]

In contemporary language, we would say that a **nation** is an identity shared by a large number of people based upon, but not reducible to, objective factors such as common race, language, religion, customs, and government.

The nation, like the participatory state, is a product of modern European history. It did not exist in medieval Europe. People in that era thought of themselves in both broader and narrower terms: on the one hand as Christians or subjects of the Holy Roman Empire, on the other in terms of limited local identities. The first discernible nations to emerge were the English, French, and Spanish, and in each instance the pattern was approximately the same. A strong monarchy established a stable territorial state within which local identities were merged over centuries into a wider national identity. The language of the court became current throughout the realm, while local dialects were suppressed. The monarch's religion was made a state religion, and nonconforming groups were stripped of power or even expelled (Huguenots from France, Jews and Moors from Spain). Social disparities between the nobility and the common people were gradually reduced as the monarchy, employing many commoners in its official service, stripped away the privileges of the aristocracy. The estates of medieval society—nobility, clergy, freemen, serfs—were levelled into one category: citizens. Out of this often brutal exercise of state power emerged nations conscious of a common identity and destiny. Events in France after the Revolution of 1789 indicate the emergence of the French nation. With the king overthrown and Austria and Prussia—the traditional enemies of France—threatening war, the French rose to defend *la nation*. With the introduction of military conscription, huge armies of citizen-soldiers overran Europe, defeating the professional and mercenary armies of other states.

It was the French Revolution more than anything else that awakened the spirit of nationality in Europe. Other peoples began to think of themselves as nations, even though they were not associated with a single strong state like the French or the English. The Italians and the Germans, for example, had lived for centuries divided among many large and small states. Now movements of unification began, which eventually resulted in the formation of the Kingdom of Italy (1861) and the German Empire (1871). Other peoples, such as the Irish and the Greeks, who had long been ruled by foreign masters, began to assert their nationhood in frequent popular uprisings. One of the great themes of European history since 1789 has been the emergence of nations demanding their own nation-states. The process is now largely complete in Western Europe, though a few small groups (such as the Basques, Scots, and Bretons) remain submerged minorities. A striking political phenomenon of recent years has been the "mininationalism" of such small groups—their attempts to assert themselves as full-fledged nations, even to the point of demanding political independence.[2]

In Eastern Europe, the struggle to define national identities has resumed with a vengeance after half a century of suppression under communist rule. The breakup of Czechoslovakia into Slovakia and the Czech Republic; the three-cornered war between Serbs, Croats, and Muslims in Bosnia; the war between ethnic Russians and ethnic Romanians in Moldova; the numerous wars in the Caucasus mountains, of which the struggle of Chechnya for independence is one example—these and many other conflicts in the area are just the beginning of a long process of sorting out nations and boundaries.

Colonization created new nations elsewhere in the world. European immigrants flocked to the United States and Canada, Australia and New Zealand, Argentina and Chile. In different ways and at different times, each of these nations gained independence from its mother country; political autonomy became the focus of new national identities. These are open, synthetic nations composed of immigrants of varied origins; the traditional European nations are more closed, having evolved over centuries of common history.

A major development of the twentieth century is the spread of European-style nationalism to the rest of the world. The rapid pace of global change has made the nation the chief source of political legitimacy by weakening traditional social institutions such as the family, tribe, and village. It has also meant the destruction of ancient empires and the emergence of new nations from the wreckage. Related to this is the attempt to fuse tribal identities into nationalities. In the nineteenth century most of Africa was divided by the European powers on more or less arbitrary lines that bore little relation to patterns of tribal habitation. The European powers are now gone, but their colonial boundaries remain as the borders between sovereign African states. In most of these states, tribal identities are far more important than national ones. The tragic civil war between Hutu and Tutsi tribes in Rwanda is the most publicized, but far from the only, recent example of such tribal conflict. Still, something similar could have been said of England or France 500 years ago. Over time, at least some of these new states may develop viable national identities. In the meantime, many have been devastated by chronic civil war among tribes, and the continent of Africa is troubled with millions of refugees who have been driven from their homes by political violence.

This brief historical survey confirms that nationality is not tied to any single objective factor. National identity is usually based on some combination of language, race, religion, and government, but none of these is either necessary or sufficient. The Swiss as a nation are divided by religion between Protestant and Catholic, and are linguistically divided among speakers of German, French, Italian, and Romansch; the focus of identity is government. Government is also the focus in the United States, which is a multiracial nation with European, African, Asian, and Native-American elements; also, there are now about 30 million Americans whose first language is not English but Spanish. In contrast to Switzerland and the United States, the small country of Lebanon, where all are of the same race and all speak Arabic, might seem well favoured to develop a coherent nationality; yet that country was torn for much of the 1980s by civil war among Christians and several sects of Muslims. One must look at each case separately to see what factors contribute to or work against the growth of national identity. The only safe generalization is that there is no universal formula.

As a form of identity, the nation is a subjective or psychological reality that transcends objective factors. That is what Renan meant when he called it "a plebiscite of every day"—nations are created by human will. Ultimately, identity is a matter of what you wish to call yourself and what you can get others to accept.

RACE, TRIBE, AND ETHNIC GROUP

The nation as a psychological entity is a particular kind of social group, which in this section will be distinguished from other kinds of groups. Some of the most important groups that overlap with the nation are racially, tribally, or ethnically based.

A **race** is a biologically defined group whose members share a gene pool, giving them common physical characteristics, such as skin, eye, and hair colour. A race is the same as a subspecies; members of a race are physically identifiable and distinctive, but they can interbreed with members of other races and produce fertile offspring (as well as new races). A race differs from a nation in that it is only a biological group. Members of the same race, such as American and African blacks, may have little in common except genetically. In Canada, it was once customary to speak of the French and English as different races, and that usage is still sometimes encountered; but most writers avoid it today, for it implies a biological difference that does not really exist.

A **tribe** has both biological and psychological dimensions. It is a group of people who are tied together by a myth of common ancestry and who think of themselves as blood relations. It is a sort of expanded family, and its identity is reinforced by distinctive language and customs. It differs from a nation in that members of a nation do not usually think of themselves as literally related by ties of common ancestry. Tribes and nations are fairly similar in the way they furnish identity to their members, but they are different social structures that have arisen at different stages of social evolution.

Members of an **ethnic group** usually share a common descent from some region of Europe, Asia, Africa, or Latin America. They now feel American or Canadian but may well wish to preserve distinctive identity while remaining part of the larger nation. The nation is an independent identity that stands on its own; the ethnic group, as we use that term within the modern nation-state, can be understood only as a part of the nation.

Although we may differentiate between a race, a tribe, an ethnic group, and a nation, all are forms of human community that have grown out of the fundamental reality of kinship. Until the rise of agriculture, human beings lived in small bands of usually fewer than 200 members, all of them connected by ties of marriage and descent. Larger communities are tied together by a sense of group solidarity growing out of this primordial community. Not surprisingly, national identity is often expressed through kinship symbols: mother tongue, fatherland, mother country, *fraternité*. Communal identification becomes more complex in modern societies, which tend to be highly mobile both socially and geographically, but it is unlikely to disappear because it expresses an important aspect of being human.[3]

Given that the concept of nationhood is inherently subjective, the distinction between a nation and a race, tribe, or ethnic group is often far from clear. Furthermore, nations have a certain prestige that other types of groups lack. As a result, a group will typically assert itself against other groups by insisting that it is a nation, while others try to cut it down to size by countering that it is really a race, tribe, or ethnic group. Several North American examples readily come to mind.

In the United States the religious movement popularly known as the Black Muslims (their most famous adherent is the boxer Muhammad Ali) maintains that African Americans are a nation—to be precise, the "Lost Found Nation of Islam."[4] This assertion is tied to the demand that, as a nation with a full-fledged identity, African Americans should have their own sovereign state. Critics of the Black Muslims counter that African Americans are a special group within, but still part of, the American nation. In Canada, the Dene of the Northwest Territories elevated themselves from tribe to nation in the Dene Declaration of 1975: "We the Dene of the Northwest Territories insist on the right to be regarded by ourselves and the world as a nation."[5] In this they followed the Métis, who have insisted for a century and a half that they too are a nation, the "New Nation." Aboriginal peoples in general in Canada now refer to themselves as "the First Nations";[6] and that position was roundly endorsed by the 1996 report of the Royal Commission on Aboriginal Peoples, which called for "nation rebuilding and nation recognition" of Aboriginal peoples as "a crucial first component" in restructuring Canada as a multinational confederacy.[7]

French Canadians are often regarded by English Canadians as an ethnic group, although, at least in Quebec, they generally regard themselves as a nation, one of the two "founding nations" of Canada. The difference is vitally important. If Aboriginal Canadians, Métis, and French Canadians are ethnic groups, they are only several among many within the Canadian nation. If they are nations, they are members of a multinational state. Furthermore, nationhood implies at least the possibility of sovereignty. It is implicit that a nation should be able to survive as a nation-state.[8]

Objectively, there is no precise definition of a nation. It is not a scientific issue but a strategic one relating to whether one social group has the power and the right to assert itself against others.

NATION AND STATE

Let us now return to the relationship between nation and state. There are several typical situations. Nation-states exist where the limits of common identity coincide with the boundaries of sovereign authority. The United States is a good example. There is a clearly defined frontier, within which live a multitude of people who recognize the legitimacy of the state and share a common identity of being American. Other contemporary examples are Sweden or Poland; in both, the state contains a relatively homogeneous population. Perhaps more numerous are those nation-states where one nation is clearly preponderant but minorities cannot be ignored. England has its Celtic fringe and its nonwhite immigrants; France has its Basques and Bretons; Finland has its Swedish minority. When these minorities accept the legitimacy of the state, they can be regarded as ethnic groups within the nation. But in many cases the minorities are not content to be ethnic groups and struggle vigorously for national status or even a nation-state of their own, as do some Basques in France and Spain.

A second situation is that of the **binational** or **multinational state.** In such cases, two or more nations co-exist under a single government. From one point of view, Canada is a binational state, a partnership of English Canadians and French Canadians that is enriched by various ethnic groups and by racial and tribal minorities. Belgium is a binational state, a partnership of Flemings and Walloons. India is a vast multinational state, as were the Soviet Union and the Austro-Hungarian, Ottoman, and Russian Empires.

If there are multinational states, there are also multistate nations. Prime examples are the German people, who were divided into East and West Germany from 1945 to 1990; the Koreans, who are still split into North and South Korea; the Poles, whose state was parcelled out among Russia, Austria, and Prussia at the end of the eighteenth century; and the Basques, who straddle the border between France and Spain. Nations can live submerged for hundreds of years with no state of their own and then suddenly reappear, as the Poles did after World War I when their state was reconstituted.

Applying these concepts to Canada is a challenging exercise. There is no single correct view, but a variety of views that reflect differing political positions. The "official view" of the Canadian government is that Canada is a bilingual, multicultural nation-state that holds two great linguistic groups—anglophones and francophones—as well as many cultural groups, which may adopt one or the other of the official languages; at the same time, there is only one overarching Canadian identity. There is only one Canadian nation, even though it is internally pluralistic. This view can be traced back to the Confederation debates, when it was strongly enunciated by Quebec's leading spokesman, George-Étienne Cartier. Cartier called the new state of Canada a "political nationality,"[9] by which he meant that the existence of a common government would create a national identity transcending linguistic and regional differences. These differences would continue to exist and would be reflected in provincial governments, but they would not be great enough to destroy Canada as one nation. Canadians, like the Swiss, would constitute a single nation, even if they spoke more than one language.

Cartier's view appeals today to most English-speaking Canadians, who are a large majority within this political nationality. It is less palatable to minorities. Most Québécois believe, with considerable justification, that they constitute a nation separate from *les Anglais*. They can point not only to language but to a heritage of religion, laws, and customs that makes them unique in North America. This consciousness of national identity does not necessarily imply a political claim for a separate French-Canadian state, although that is the goal of the Parti Québécois and the Bloc Québécois. It does imply a different attitude toward Confederation, in which French Canada is accepted as a partner in a binational state rather than as only one group among many within the Canadian political nationality. Smaller groups, such as Aboriginal peoples, are now practising the same strategy by also identifying themselves as nations. If their claims are accepted, Canada will become a multinational state.

That these are vital political issues, not just conceptual quibbles, was obvious during the Canadian referendum campaign of 1992. Supporters of the Charlottetown Accord often spoke of "two founding nations" (English and French) or even three (English, French, and Aboriginal). They saw the Accord, with its proposals for special guarantees for Quebec and a "third order" of government for Aboriginal Canadians, as a means of reflecting these national differences in Canada's political institutions. Many opponents of the Accord spoke of the "equality" of individuals and provinces within Canada. In their view, Canada was a single nation of equal citizens, and no group required elaborate protections.

The "one Canada" view won the referendum, but that does not mean the debate is over. The view that there are two (now three) "founding nations" will remain alive because it articulates the political aspirations of significant social groups with robust identities. Their leaders, like all political leaders, will continue to use words as weapons in their struggle to attain political power. These different views of Canada are manifested in different views of Canadian federalism, which will be discussed in Part Three of this text.

FURTHER READING

Breuilly, John. *Nationalism and the State*, 2nd ed. Chicago: University of Chicago Press, 1994.

Conlogue, Ray. *Impossible Nation: The Longing for Homeland in Canada and Quebec*. Stratford, Ont.: Mercury Press, 1996.

Gellner, Ernest. *Nations and Nationalism*. Oxford: Basil Blackwell, 1983.

Gottlieb, Gidon. *Nation Against State: A New Approach to Ethnic Conflicts and the Decline of Sovereignty*. New York: Council on Foreign Relations Press, 1993.

Grant, George. *Lament for a Nation: The Defeat of Canadian Nationalism*, new ed. Ottawa: Carleton University Press, 1994.

Ignatieff, Michael. *Blood and Belonging*. Toronto: Penguin Books, 1994.

LAW

CHAPTER 7

Law in the broadest sense means a rule or regularity in behaviour of any element in the universe. The laws of gravitation describe the motion of falling bodies on the earth or of the planets in the heavens; the laws of evolution describe changes over time in living species; the laws of supply and demand describe human behaviour in dealing with scarce resources. Laws or regularities such as these make the universe intelligible. Law is also the foundation of society, which is essentially a group of people living together under the same laws or rules of conduct.

Although law is all-embracing, it is not monolithic. There is a subtle change in the character of law as one ascends the scale of creation from inanimate objects through plant and animal life to human beings. The higher levels have a greater element of self-guidance or freedom in the way they follow laws. Planets stay in their orbits exactly. Crops grow under certain conditions, but only the average yield can be predicted, not the growth of a particular plant. Animals mate at certain times of year, but not with clockwork regularity. People usually try to buy cheap and sell dear in the marketplace, but any individual may depart from this model for personal reasons.

The variability of human behaviour raises the problem of enforcement (a problem that does not exist for inanimate objects and lower life forms but may have parallels among the higher, social animals). From now on, when we use the term **law,** we shall mean a rule of human conduct that is enforced by the community, by means of coercion or violence if necessary.

Law is only one of several kinds of rules that we follow. Our behaviour is guided by instincts of which we may not even be aware. Innate desires to sleep, find nourishment, and reproduce surely contribute to regularities of human behaviour. However, these basic impulses are always mediated by higher forms of rules. A purely personal rule of conduct is usually called a **habit.** We must all drink, but some of us habitually drink coffee, while others take tea at certain times of the day. Habit gradually merges with **custom** as social forces come more into play. Most adults in the Western world drink either coffee or tea because they see others drink the same beverages. In other spheres, the social element is even more influential. Such things as politeness, appropriate clothing, and table manners are elaborate codes of conduct, learned through imitation and parental instruction, which every society has.

Habits and customs create regularities in human behaviour without coercive enforcement in situations where the incentives to violate or ignore them are small or nonexistent. Language, for example, is primarily what theorists call a coordination game; its purpose is to communicate with others. We suffer a disadvantage if we depart from its rules, because we will not be understood. It does not matter what the rules are; once they exist, it is to our advantage to abide by them. The conventions are more or less self-enforcing. Similarly, we lose out when we flout normal customs of politeness, because others avoid the company of those who create unpleasantness. In these instances there is no true enforcement—only a spontaneous reaction that helps keep our conduct within accustomed channels.

Some things, however, cannot be left to spontaneous self-correction. Typically, enforcement is required when the rules are of primary importance to peaceful cooperation and when the rewards of breaking the rules are attractive relative to the costs. Ordered society demands that, at the very least, we know which family we belong to and which material things are within our control. This is why all societies have rules about the family and property that are coercively enforced. Violating table manners makes one incur heavy social penalties for little apparent gain, so that enforcement is unnecessary; stealing someone's property, on the other hand, can be such an attractive proposition that sanctions against such behaviour become necessary.

The enforcement of law performs a number of functions for society, which can be conveniently remembered as the four Rs: retribution, restitution, rehabilitation, and restraint. Retribution is the punishment of those who violate the norms of society. Restitution is the provision of compensation to those who have been harmed by rule breakers. Rehabilitation is a change in conduct that will prevent lawbreaking in the future. And restraint is roughly the same as deterrence—the fear we instill in those who cannot be swayed by influence or authority.

Two general points about rules are worth noting. First, we do not need to know what a rule is in order to follow it—we only need to know how to act. Language, for example, is a complex system of rules. We all learn to speak by imitation before we acquire the ability to read those rules in grammar books. Similarly, children learn what kind of behaviour is fair long before they develop a conscious understanding of the rules of justice. A child of three or four, who does not even know the word justice, can honour a rule not to grab other children's toys. Second, rules are not necessarily designed by conscious intelligence. They may also grow over time in an evolutionary process of trial and error, as is true of habits, customs, and a great many laws.

CUSTOMARY LAW AND COMMON LAW

These observations help to explain the two main kinds of law. The older kind of law, found in all societies, is evolutionary or **customary law;** this kind arises gradually and cannot be traced to an identifiable moment in time. The newer kind of law, **legislation,** is consciously formulated and deliberately constructed. Both kinds of law are equally enforceable and so equally valid. Let us first consider customary law.

All human communities have enforceable rules of conduct. They may not be written down, and no one may be able to articulate them; even so, they exist and are enforced. Such laws are an embodiment of the experience a community has gained in its struggle to survive. With the passage of time, the actors discover methods of cooperation, that is, rules that promote internal order and external strength.

Primitive societies repel or kill external attackers; their most severe method of enforcement against internal rule breakers is usually ostracism. To be permanently cast out of the small hunting band, to lose the support of one's family and kin, is tantamount to a death sentence. To be temporarily shunned is usually enough to make the rule breaker return to accepted norms of conduct.

Laws of this type represent reason—tacit reason—rather than command, because no one has ever issued them. Typically, the community attributes divine origin to them. For example, the Jews regarded the Mosaic law as a product of divine revelation. According to the Old Testament, Moses received the Law on the top of Mount Sinai, enveloped in fire and smoke. God himself wrote the Ten Commandments on two tablets of stone, and the face of Moses shone as he brought the tablets down from the mountain.[1] From the social scientist's point of view, attributing divine origin to law is a way of saying that law does not depend on the will of people alive today and that its importance transcends mere individual preferences.

Society took a step forward in assuming conscious control of law when laws began to be written down instead of merely being honoured in practice and entrusted to collective memory. This deliberate recording of laws, however, should not be confused with true legislation. Early legal systems, such as the laws of Hammurabi in Babylon and the Twelve Tables in Rome, were regarded not as a new creation by the sovereign but as a recording of ancient laws that had existed from time immemorial.[2] These laws had always been valid, but they were now being recorded to avoid misunderstanding and dispute.

A rather similar attitude underlies the **common law** of the English-speaking peoples. Before the Norman Conquest (1066), there were several bodies of law in the different regions of England. The Norman kings set up a unified system of courts throughout the realm that for a time competed with older local courts. The traditional courts gradually fell into disuse as the English found the king's justice to be fairer and more predictable. The king's courts, for their part, continued to interpret the old customary laws; many of these were generally acceptable and became common to all the courts of the realm. Thus there was never a radical break with the past.

Common law is essentially the sum of a vast number of cases decided by English courts since the Middle Ages. Most of these cases were decided not by reference to a written law but by a process of reasoning based on the needs of ordered liberty. Certain principles, such as security of possession of private property and the enforcement of contracts, can be applied to a multitude of disputes. Application yields results, which then serve as models or **precedents** for later cases. The courts generally observe the rule of *stare decisis*, "to stand by what is decided"—that is, to follow precedent. Adherence to the example of past decisions allows the law to grow in an orderly and predictable way. By studying prior cases, one can gain a fair idea of how future disputes will be decided. This is how an enforceable body of law can develop over centuries without ever having been issued as general commands. It is judge-made law, although "made" is perhaps not the best word. It might be better to speak of *finding* the common law, as was done in the Middle Ages. The law, or abstract rule, is gradually discovered through experience with a number of concrete cases.

The great advantage of common law is its flexibility, in the sense that it can forever be applied to new situations. It need never become obsolete so long as judges are reasonably free to follow precedents. For example, the law faced a novel situation when radio waves began to be used commercially early in this century. Questions arose, such as whether one could broadcast on a frequency already used by another transmitter. Judges immediately began to cope with these problems, reasoning by analogy with other forms of property.

Common law, having been developed in England, was transported to the British colonies and is still very much alive in Canada, the United States, Australia, and New Zealand. It has a big impact on our lives in areas such as personal property, contracts, and family relationships. But valuable as it is, it has certain inherent limitations. At any given time, it is liable to contain conflicting precedents on unsettled points of law, and conflict means uncertainty. It may become very complex as precedents multiply over the centuries, and complexity is another source of uncertainty. Finally, there is no guarantee that the common law process produces desirable results. Judges may box themselves in through a series of undesirable decisions and in doing so create an impasse that may take decades or centuries to resolve.

LEGISLATION

One solution to these problems is to codify an existing body of customary law in a way that reveals its principles in greater clarity. An example of this is Justinian's Code, produced in the sixth century by order of Justinian, emperor of the surviving eastern half of the Roman Empire. This code systematized the results of a thousand years of Roman customary law. In the early years of the nineteenth century, Justinian's Code served as a model for the French lawyers whom Napoleon had summoned to codify the complex body of French customary law. The Napoleonic Code is an all-encompassing system that forms the basis of law in France as well as in Italy, Spain, and most other European countries.[3]

The production of legal codes is a final step toward deliberate control of law. This conscious creation of law is legislation. It may result in a **statute,** which is a particular piece of legislation, or in a **code of law,** which is a comprehensive set of interrelated rules.

In the common law countries, codification, although important, has not gone as far as it has in Continental Europe, especially in the realm of **private law,** which controls relations between individuals and is different from **public law,** which creates agencies of the state and controls the relations between the state and its subjects. Public law includes constitutional, administrative, and criminal law; private law controls such matters as contracts and family relationships. Statutes in Britain were most often passed in the domain of public law to define political crimes such as treason, to create police forces, navies, government departments, and other state agencies, and to provide for revenue through taxation. There was relatively little legislation in the field of private law; here the state's role was to enforce the rules that gradually emerged from judicial precedents, but not directly to create rules by legislation. Exceptions occurred but were relatively infrequent. In contrast, in legal systems based on the Napoleonic Code, both public and private law are comprehensively codified.

As might be expected, Canada, deriving from two colonial powers, has a mixed legal system. The private law of the province of Quebec was systematized in the *code civil* of 1866;[4] private law in the other nine provinces remains an uncodified extension of the common law. In effect, there are two systems of private law in Canada, which means that three judges on the Supreme Court of Canada must be from Quebec in order to deal with appeals from that province. The criminal law, in contrast, is unified in the Criminal Code, an Act of Parliament passed in 1892 to replace the common law in those matters.

While the concept of legislation has been understood since antiquity, until the last two centuries it played only a restricted role in governmental affairs. However, the modern state now legislates freely in private as well as public law. The general rule is that common law retains its validity until the state displaces it with statutory law. In Canada, large sections of common law have been replaced by legislative statutes or codes. One good example is labour relations. In the nineteenth century, relations between employer and employee were regulated by the common law of contracts, employment being considered the contractual exchange of money for work. But all the provinces of Canada, as well as the federal government, have now replaced the common law with comprehensive labour-relations codes. They have established a framework for collective bargaining—negotiations, strikes, arbitration, certification of bargaining agents, and so forth—which is far different from what existed under the common law.

The expansion of legislation has certain advantages. Legislators can foresee situations and try to prevent conflicts. In contrast, common law adjudication must wait for conflicts to arise. Also, legislation can be created or changed in a relatively short time; in common law it may take decades for solutions to evolve. As well, legislation generally offers greater certainty because the law is not inferred from precedent but is clearly laid down.

This certainty, however, is somewhat illusory. However perfectly designed statutes may be, ambiguity of language can never be completely avoided. Also, statutes are soon overtaken by the course of events and need to be adapted to new situations. Continual legislative amendment is not practical; the statutes must be interpreted in particular disputes as they are brought before the courts. A sequence of cases will arise in which the courts will usually follow precedent according to the rule of *stare decisis*. In this way, legislation becomes subject to the same sort of evolutionary forces that guide the development of common law.

᠍᠍᠍᠍᠍᠍᠍

LEGAL POSITIVISM VERSUS NATURAL LAW

The flowering of legislation in this century has been based on prior developments in the field of **jurisprudence,** or the philosophy of law. The early theorists of sovereignty tended to define law as simply the command of the sovereign. Thomas Hobbes wrote in *Leviathan* (1651) that law "is to every subject, those rules, which the commonwealth hath commanded him, by word, writing, or other sufficient sign of the will, to make use of, for the distinction of right and wrong."[5] To make matters perfectly clear, Hobbes added, "the sovereign is the sole legislator."[6] His view was later developed into the doctrine of **legal positivism** by the English writers Jeremy Bentham and John Austin.

In one sense, legal positivism was directed against common law; Bentham argued that common law was not really law in the true sense and should be replaced by legislated codes. But it was also directed against the broader idea of natural law. Since the time of the Stoics in late antiquity, many writers on law and government have argued that a natural law exists that transcends the state and the will of the sovereign. These writers have held that there is an order in the universe that creates certain principles of conduct binding on all human beings, at all times, wherever they live. There are many versions of natural law theory. Some have an explicitly religious foundation, like that of the thirteenth-century theologian Saint Thomas Aquinas; others are totally secular, like that of the eighteenth-century philosopher

David Hume. All versions agree that a higher law that can be used as a criterion to judge laws made by the state exists, and that in certain cases disobedience to the law of the state can be justified by appeal to this higher law. Thus, Thomas Jefferson invoked "the laws of nature and of nature's God" in the American Declaration of Independence; this was how he justified the rebellion of the thirteen colonies against laws made by Parliament.

The terminology of natural law is infrequently used in twentieth-century political discourse, except at the academic level; however, exactly the same idea has taken strong new root in the contemporary field of human rights. **Human rights** are the rights that all human beings are supposed to enjoy simply by virtue of being human. Freedom of religion, freedom to marry and have children, and freedom from torture and arbitrary imprisonment are examples of human rights that are widely accepted in theory (though often violated in practice). These and other such rights are held up in the international community as standards against which the laws and practices of nations are evaluated, and governments that violate them come under pressure to conform. The idea that a constitution is a proper restraint upon the lawmaking ability of the state—this issue will be explored in depth in the next chapter—is also rooted in the tradition of natural law and human rights.

Even if one has doubts about natural law—and there are many difficulties associated with the concept—it is possible to make a more restricted argument that law does in fact emerge from society rather than the state.

As shown in Figure 7.1, common law and legislation are two different expressions of social ideas about right conduct. The former emerges from conflicts of action, and the latter is created according to deliberate plan, but both rest on the people's conception of what is just. Legal positivism, in contrast, threatens to put the state above society, to treat the state not as a special agency within society but as a power ruling over it. This view holds that laws are rules imposed upon society by force rather than expressions of social morality. This corresponds in real life to the situation of conquest, where a state has imposed itself on unwilling subjects and maintains its rule by coercion. In such circumstances, the absence of legitimate authority has to be compensated for by sheer force. Remember, however, that conquest is not the normal condition of politics, and law is not normally maintained by brute force. Yet legal positivism, as Hobbes understood perfectly well, puts the sovereign above the law, as the source of law rather than the means by which law is enforced or proclaimed.

LAW AND SOCIAL CHANGE

The preceding discussion sheds some light on the much-debated question of whether law should lead or follow social change. Any answer must take into account

FIGURE 7.1 The Social Origins of Law

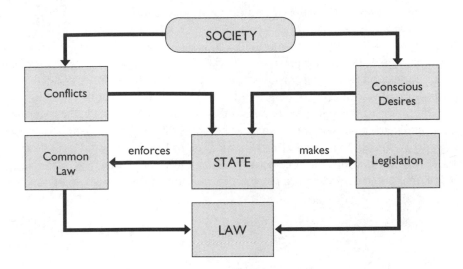

the distinction between judge-made law and legislation. Normally, judges are a conservative force in society, both in developing common law and in interpreting legislation. The rule of *stare decisis* tends to make them look to the past for guidance. While in office they are deliberately (and with good reason) insulated from political pressure and public opinion, and this may partly blind them to social change. For example, the common law acted as a brake on organized labour long after the labour movement had become so powerful that it needed more adequate legal recognition. The solution of collective bargaining finally came through legislation rather than through the evolution of common law. In this instance social change clearly ran ahead of the law until remedial legislation was introduced.

However, the judiciary can also be an innovating force ahead of public opinion. For example, the Ontario Court of Appeal held in 1992 that "sexual orientation" is protected by Section 15(1) of the Charter of Rights and Freedoms, even though these words are not found in the text, and that the Canadian Human Rights Act must be interpreted so as to conform to this reading of the Charter.[7] Groups advocating the rights and interests of gays and lesbians thus won a victory that had long been denied them in Parliament.

At that time, the Progressive Conservative government of Brian Mulroney had not yet delivered on its 1986 promise to amend the Canadian Human Rights Act to cover sexual orientation. This was partly out of fear of the political consequences, not least among Conservative MPs. Shortly after the 1992 decision, Kim Campbell, then minister of justice, announced that the government would accept the decision and not appeal to the Supreme Court of Canada. Thus it would no longer be necessary to amend the act in Parliament, and the government would be delivered from a tricky political dilemma. A few weeks later, she decided to introduce amending legislation to put sexual orientation into the act, but to accompany it with a legal definition of marriage as a union of two people of the opposite sex; the point of this was to head off claims that homosexuals ought to have the legal right to marry. However, when that compromise was attacked by some members of her own party as too innovative, and by gay activists as too restrictive, the cabinet decided not to push it, and it was not passed before Parliament was dissolved for the 1993 election.

The point of this convoluted story is that judges, who are deliberately insulated from public opinion, were willing to make decisions that politicians, who must be sensitive to public opinion, kept trying to avoid. Political ratification did not come until 1996, when, under the Liberal government of Jean Chrétien, Parliament passed legislation to make sexual orientation a protected criterion under the Human Rights Act.

GAY RIGHTS AND THE CHARTER

Section 15(1) of the Canadian Charter of Rights and Freedoms reads:

> Every individual is equal before and under the law and has the right to the equal protection and equal benefit of the law without discrimination and, in particular, without discrimination based on race, national or ethnic origin, colour, religion, sex, age or mental or physical disability.

The text does not mention sexual orientation; in fact, the drafters deliberately decided to omit it, fearing that controversy might jeopardize ratification of the Charter. Note, however, that the wording "without discrimination and, in particular, without discrimination based on ..." is open-ended; that is, the nine explicitly prohibited grounds of discrimination are to be construed as examples, not as an exhaustive list. Gay-rights organizations have been successful in persuading the Supreme Court of Canada that sexual orientation is implied in the phrase "without discrimination" even though it is not included in the list of prohibited grounds of discrimination.

If judges can be either behind or ahead of public opinion, so can legislators. In Canada, the Lord's Day Act remained on the books until 1985, when the Supreme Court held that it conflicted with the Canadian Charter of Rights and Freedoms.[8] For a number of years it had been apparent that the law had become so anachronistic that it was scarcely enforceable and was routinely being ignored by many otherwise law-abiding citizens. But legislators refused to act, preferring to leave this emotional issue to the courts.

Yet, at the same time, legislators sometimes race ahead of public opinion, for example, when capital punishment was abolished in Canada. There has been a long-term trend toward less-physical forms of punishment, and Canadians may eventually turn decisively against the death penalty, as they have against torture and flogging. But in the meantime, if opinion polls can be believed, a majority—about 55 percent of the population—wish that capital punishment had not been abolished and would vote to reinstate it.[9]

Experience suggests that law may be a little behind or a little ahead of popular feeling without causing much trouble; but if the discrepancy becomes great, signs of distress will appear. The law will be widely disobeyed, and escalating levels of coercion will be needed for enforcement. This shows that law does indeed come from society and is not just the command of the sovereign. Neither legislators nor judges are immune to the danger of losing touch with citizens; but in a sense, the two groups can act to balance each other. Legislators can replace outmoded common law, while judges can help adjust legislation to social change.

FURTHER READING

Bogart, W.A. *Courts and Country: The Limits of Litigation and the Social and Political Life of Canada*. Toronto: Oxford University Press, 1994.

Bork, Robert. *The Tempting of America: The Political Seduction of the Law*. New York: Simon and Schuster, 1990.

Brierly, John E.C. "Quebec's Civil Law Codification Viewed and Reviewed," *McGill Law Journal* 14, 1968, pp. 521–89.

Friedland, Martin L. *A Place Apart: Judicial Independence and Accountability in Canada*. Ottawa: Canadian Judicial Council, 1995.

Fuller, Lon L. *The Morality of Law*, 2nd ed. New Haven, Conn.: Yale University Press, 1975.

Hart, H.L.A. *The Concept of Law*. London: Oxford University Press, 1961.

Marshall, T. David. *Judicial Conduct and Accountability*. Scarborough, Ont.: Carswell, 1995.

Merryman, John Henry. *The Civil Law Tradition: An Introduction to the Legal Systems of Western Europe and Latin America*. Palo Alto, Calif.: Stanford University Press, 1969.

Morton, F.L. *Law, Politics and the Judicial Process in Canada*, 2nd edition. Calgary: University of Calgary Press, 1992.

Waddams, S.M. *Introduction to the Study of Law*, 3rd ed. Toronto: Carswell, 1987.

CONSTITUTIONALISM

CHAPTER 8

A **constitution** is a set of fundamental rules and principles by which a state is organized. These rules and principles generally:

a. establish the powers and responsibilities of the legislative, executive, and judicial branches of government,

b. allocate powers to different levels of government, such as federal, provincial, and local,

c. enumerate the rights of citizens in relationship to each other and to the government, as in a bill of rights, and

d. stipulate a procedure for amending the constitution.

The term *fundamental rules* is used advisedly, because a constitution comprises not only laws that are enforceable in the courts but also customs, or conventions, that are enforceable chiefly in the sense that a government may lose political support by violating them. A **convention** is a practice or custom that is consistently followed by those in government even though it is not legally required. According to a leading authority, a convention is not just any custom that happens to be observed. To be considered a convention, a practice must exist for a good reason and those who follow it must be aware that they are following a rational rule.[1]

A recent analysis points out that conventions exist at several different levels; there are strong ones that are essential to the constitution, and weak ones that are really no more than usages. For example, it is essential in a parliamentary democracy that the head of state confide the task of forming a government to a politician who commands a working majority in the representative assembly; otherwise the democratic principle of majority rule would be jeopardized. This convention is of the strongest type. In contrast, there is little or no intrinsic importance to the practice, rigorously followed in Canada, of the Commons adjourning to the Senate to witness royal assent to legislation. The head of state could just as well perform this function in private, as is done in Quebec and Australia. This convention is of the weakest type and could be changed on short notice without damage to the Constitution.[2]

Although useful, the distinction between law and convention is not as solid as it appears, because courts have no power to enforce anything unless they are obeyed by those who control the coercive apparatus of the state. This obedience is itself no more than a convention (albeit of the strongest type) based upon politicians' belief that public opinion wishes the courts to be obeyed.[3] In the last analysis, law and convention are two related manifestations of the same spirit of constitutionalism and the rule of law.

THE UNWRITTEN BRITISH CONSTITUTION

The older type of constitution, which used to be very common but now survives in only a few countries such as Great Britain and New Zealand, is usually called **unwritten.** It is essential for Canadians to have some understanding of the unwritten British Constitution, for it is the source of our own. The term *unwritten* is not quite exact, for most of the British Constitution is written down. But it is not written down in a single place; rather, it must be pieced together from many different sources. "Unwritten" in this context really means uncodified. Also, there exist as part of the British Constitution many conventions that are not written down at all.

Much of the British Constitution consists of statutes of the King-in-Parliament. The oldest such text is the *Magna Carta* (Great Charter), which King John was forced to sign in 1215, before Parliament even existed, and which was later adopted by Parliament in statutory form. It established the principle that the sovereign had to rule within the law of the land. Further restrictions on royal power were established in the Bill of Rights (1689), which, among many other provisions, prevented the Crown from levying taxes without the consent of Parliament. The Act of Settlement (1701), as well as fixing the succession to the throne, protected the independence of judges by making it impossible for the king to dismiss them without cause. The Parliament Act (1911) imposed several restrictions on the powers of the House of Lords and in doing so strengthened the Commons.

These, and many other statutes passed over hundreds of years, make up the legal framework of the British Constitution. But more than statutory law is involved. Since statutes always raise problems of interpretation when they are applied, the body of case law that has developed around the statutes must be considered part of the constitution. Also, the very existence of Parliament rests not on statutes but on the common law or prerogative powers of the kings who first established the practice of calling Parliaments for consultation. In an important sense, the statutory structure of the British Constitution has a common law foundation.

Many of the most important institutions of British government rest not on law but on convention. The cabinet and prime minister are mentioned briefly in some statutes, but the offices have never been deliberately created by legislation. Similarly, it is conventional that the Crown not refuse assent to a bill passed by Parliament, that the leader of the majority party be invited to form a cabinet, and so on.

This short sketch of the British Constitution suggests one of its important characteristics—flexibility. The written part—that is, the constitutional law—is no different from any other type of law; all law, constitutional or otherwise, may be changed by an act of Parliament. An act of Parliament cannot be unconstitutional as long as specified procedures are adhered to, and Parliament could even free itself from existing procedures if it chose. The conventions are even more flexible, since they are essentially usages that are constantly evolving. This peculiar flexibility of the British unwritten constitution has led some observers to say that it is not a constitution at all; and indeed it may be thought of as a synonym for the ensemble of governmental institutions at any given moment.

THE AMERICAN WRITTEN CONSTITUTION

The British Constitution differs strikingly from the American one, which is the world's oldest surviving written constitution. The U.S. Constitution consists of one systematic, deliberately designed document that was drawn up at the constitutional convention in Philadelphia in 1787. In a few pages this text arranges the legislative, executive, and judicial powers of the state; divides government into federal and state levels; and deals with some other necessary matters. The rights of the individual are enumerated in the Bill of Rights, which are the first ten amendments to the Constitution after the adoption of the Constitution. The amending process was intentionally made arduous, so that the constitution could not be lightly changed by the transitory desire of whoever happened to be in power. Amendments must be approved by a two-thirds majority in both houses of Congress and subsequently ratified by three-quarters of the states. Not surprisingly, this very difficult procedure has been used successfully only twenty-six times since 1787.

The difficulty of the process is illustrated by the strange history of the proposed Equal Rights Amendment (ERA): "Equality of rights under the law shall not be denied or abridged by the United States or by any State on account of sex." Congress approved the ERA in 1972 and set a period of seven years for ratification by three-quarters of the states. When only 35 of the 50 states had ratified the amendment by 1978, Congress extended the deadline to 1982;[4] but even with the extension, the approval of the requisite 38 state legislatures was never obtained, thus killing the ERA.

This rather rigid amending process has not hampered constitutional evolution in the United States as much as might be expected, because the courts have taken on the function of declaring the meaning of the constitution in specific applications. A large body of case law has grown up that is indispensable to understanding the constitution; this case law is flexible in much the same way as common law. For example, the U.S. Supreme Court held in 1896 in *Plessy v. Ferguson* that it did not conflict with the constitution for states to require racially segregated coaches on railway trains.[5] According to the court, as long as the facilities were "separate but equal," the situation did not violate the equal protection clause of the Fourteenth Amendment. But in 1954, the same court departed from this precedent in the famous case of *Brown v. Board of Education*, holding that segregated schools were necessarily injurious to the minority and thus contrary to the fourteenth amendment principle of equal protection of the law.[6] Strictly speaking, the Supreme Court did not overrule *Plessy v. Ferguson*; rather, it distinguished *Brown v. Board* because it dealt with education rather than transportation. But the political effect was the same as a change in the constitution. The point here is that the U.S. Constitution is, to a large extent, what the courts say it is.

Although *convention* is not used as a technical term in American constitutional law, there is inevitably something like it in the U.S. Constitution. The power of the courts to declare legislation unconstitutional is not mentioned in the text of 1787. Chief Justice John Marshall first claimed this right in the seminal case of *Marbury v. Madison* (1803); it ultimately rests on the acquiescence of Congress.[7] Another example was the practice established by George Washington, the first president, that no chief executive should serve more than two terms. This precedent was followed until World War II, when Franklin Roosevelt, citing the dangerous international situation, chose to run for a third and then a fourth term. His violation of the practice touched off such a reaction that the twenty-second amendment, ratified in 1951, officially wrote the two-term principle into the constitution. Usage, having proved insufficient, was translated into constitutional law.

The contrast between the British and American Constitutions is instructive. The former is unwritten and flexible, the latter written and rigid. The former can be amended by simple statute, the latter only by an elaborate amending process. Judicial decisions play a role in both, but a far larger role in the American model, where they supply the flexibility that is missing in the constitutional text.

THE CANADIAN HYBRID

The Canadian Constitution may be seen as a blend of the written and unwritten models. Although there is no central, systematic document of the American type, the Canadian Constitution has a substantial written core. As with the British model, this core consists of a series of statutes enacted over a long period of time; but contrary to the British Constitution, these statutes can no longer be amended or repealed by a simple act of Parliament.

The starting point for finding the written constitution is now the Constitution Act, 1982. Schedule I to the Act lists thirty statutes and **orders-in-council** (i.e., formal decisions of Cabinet), some Canadian and some British in origin, that are now assured of constitutional status and can therefore be amended only by approved procedures. The most important of these thirty items is the British North America (BNA) Act, 1867, since renamed the Constitution Act, 1867. This British statute created the Dominion of Canada in 1867, and set up the federal system as well as the legislative, executive, and judicial institutions of government, all of which exist today. Many of the thirty items consist of amendments to the BNA Act made by the British Parliament at the request of Canada between 1867 and 1982. These amendments have all been restyled the Constitution Act, 1871, or 1940, or whichever year applies. Other scheduled items include the statutes and orders-in-council by which Canada was enlarged to its present boundaries, for example, the Manitoba Act, the British Columbia Terms of Union, and the Alberta and Saskatchewan Acts. These have all retained their original names. Finally, there is the Statute of Westminster, 1931, a piece of British legislation by which Britain renounced the right to legislate for Canada except to amend the Canadian constitution—a duty that Britain retained by necessity until 1981, when the federal government and all provinces except Quebec reached agreement on an amending formula.

The Constitution Act, 1982, not only lists and confirms the pre-existing parts of the written constitution but also introduces important new substance, particularly in the first thirty-four sections, known as the Canadian Charter of Rights and Freedoms. In establishing limits to the powers of the federal and provincial legislatures and governments, the Charter has radically transformed the nature of the Constitution, which previously did not contain any statement of the fundamental rights of Canadians. Civil liberties such as freedom of religion and speech, and political rights such as the right to vote and run for office, are now enumerated and entrenched in the Constitution. This in turn has enhanced the political power of the courts, which are the natural interpreters of the Constitution.

The rest of the Constitution Act, 1982, addresses aboriginal and treaty rights of Native peoples, future constitutional conferences, ownership and control of natural resources, and—most importantly for this discussion—the process to be followed in amending the Constitution. Before 1982, those parts of the written constitution that were British statutes (the most important parts) could only be amended by the British Parliament. The normal procedure was for a joint address of the Senate and House of Commons to request that the king or queen have the British Cabinet introduce the needed amendment into Parliament—a request that was never refused. Although the mechanics of the procedure were under federal control, it became a matter of convention to seek provincial agreement to amendments affecting the provinces. This usually but not always meant getting the unanimous consent of the provincial governments.

The Act has now transferred constitutional amendment from the realm of convention to that of law. (See Sections 38–49 of the Act in Appendix B of this book.) There are now three main ways of changing the Canadian Constitution:

1. For certain fundamental matters, such as the existence of the monarchy and the composition of the Supreme Court, the agreement of all provincial legislative assemblies must be added to that of the Senate and the House of Commons; this is the **unanimous procedure.**

2. Most other questions fall under the **general procedure**—there need only be resolutions of the legislatures of at least two-thirds of the provinces, containing among themselves 50 percent of the population of the provinces, and the consent of the Senate and House of Commons.

3. A third option, sometimes called the **bilateral procedure,** exists for situations that affect only one province. In such a case, approval is required from the legislature of the province in question as well as from the House of Commons and the Senate. The bilateral procedure was used in 1993 to entrench official bilingualism in New Brunswick, and again in 1997 to remove the constitutionally guaranteed rights of the Newfoundland public school system's church-administered schools. In the spring of 1997, the government of Quebec asked Ottawa to invoke the bilateral procedure to change religious rights in that province's school system, but Parliament was dissolved and a federal election called before action could be taken. Presumably, however, action will be taken sometime in the future.

In all three procedures, the Senate has only a suspensory veto. In other words, if the Senate does not agree to the resolution, it can be proclaimed by the Governor General if it is passed again by the House of Commons after a waiting period. This happened in the above-mentioned 1996–97 case of the Newfoundland schools amendment. The amendment had been rejected in the Senate the first time around, but then passed a second time in the House of Commons after the required six-month waiting period, so it acquired constitutional force without ever being passed by the Senate.

Quebec refused to ratify the 1982 constitutional amendments for several reasons. It was not in the interest of the Parti Québécois, which governed Quebec at the time, to sign on to any form of "renewed federalism," for that would have conflicted with its own hopes for separation. But opposition in Quebec went far beyond Parti Québécois circles. At the procedural level, many Quebeckers claimed (although the Supreme Court of Canada disagreed) that their province held a veto under a constitutional convention requiring unanimous provincial consent. At the substantive level, many francophones objected to the fact that the Charter, by guaranteeing certain rights of official-language minorities, reduced traditional provincial powers over education and language.

THE MEECH LAKE AND CHARLOTTETOWN ACCORDS

Quebec's refusal to ratify the Constitution in 1982 touched off a decade of gruelling constitutional conflict in Canada. In a legal sense, the Constitution Act, 1982, applied to Quebec, but in a political sense Quebec was left "outside the Constitution." The Progressive Conservatives incorporated this fact into their 1984 electoral strategy in Quebec, offering to obtain further constitutional amendments that would satisfy the demands of the francophone majority for more provincial power. The first result was the Meech Lake Accord of June 23, 1987, which responded to a list of demands submitted by Premier Robert Bourassa of Quebec. In addition to recognizing Quebec as a "distinct society," which presumably would have enlarged that province's jurisdiction over language, culture, and perhaps other areas, the Accord acceded to several other demands from Quebec, not the least of these being a broadening of the unanimity rule so that Quebec had a veto over further changes to national institutions such as the Senate and House of Commons. Initially, Meech Lake seemed certain to gain the approval of all provinces, but opposition gradually developed, especially after former prime minister Pierre Trudeau condemned it. In the end, the Accord failed when Manitoba and Newfoundland did not ratify it within the required three years.

Bourassa then took several dramatic steps. He announced that Quebec would not participate in further constitutional conferences and demanded that Ottawa and the other nine provinces prepare an offer to Quebec. Then, as a threat to spur the rest of Canada into action, he had the Quebec National Assembly pass a law requiring the province to hold a referendum in the two-week period October 12–26, 1992. If the offer from the rest of Canada was considered satisfactory by a legislative committee, the referendum could be on acceptance or rejection of that offer; if the offer was unsatisfactory in terms of meeting Quebec's demands, the referendum would be on sovereignty (i.e., some form of separation from Canada).[8]

After a long and arduous process of public consultation followed by negotiations among the governments of the rest of Canada, Bourassa consented to return to the table with the prime minister and the other provincial premiers. The result was the Charlottetown Accord of August 28, 1992, an immensely complicated package of constitutional amendments that responded to demands from many regions and special interests within the country as well as from Quebec. The package's complexity resulted from the federal strategy of trying to give something to many groups in order to build political support for the result—the "large package" strategy.

In prior decades, ratification by Parliament and the provincial legislatures of the agreement reached at Charlottetown would have been automatic, but the failure of Meech Lake had changed all that. One of the main indictments of the Meech Lake agreement was that it had been negotiated by "eleven men in a closed room," that is, without public consultation. It now seemed that the only politically feasible way to approve the Charlottetown Accord was by a national referendum. Legally, the referendum would be advisory rather than binding, but the prime minister and premiers promised that they would abide by the referendum's results.

The referendum on the Charlottetown Accord was held on October 26, 1992. Quebec held a separate referendum under its own rules on the same day, but the question was the same everywhere. The Accord was defeated in six provinces (British Columbia, Alberta, Saskatchewan, Manitoba, Quebec, and Nova Scotia), with 55 percent of Canadians voting no. This result was surprising, because the Accord was supported by the federal government, the three main federal political parties, all ten provincial governments, the major aboriginal organizations, and most of the big corporations, labour unions, and newspapers in Canada.

The Accord was defeated partly because outside Quebec it was perceived as being too generous to Quebec, and in Quebec as not being generous enough. If those had been the only reasons, Canada might now be dangerously polarized and on the verge of breaking apart. But it also seems that many voters, both in and outside of Quebec, were put off by the nature of the Accord. Its length and complexity made it almost impossible to understand; moreover, it was in many respects incomplete—an agenda for further negotiations rather than a conclusive agreement. This is a problem inherent in "large package" strategies; giving something to everyone is bound to produce an unwieldy end-product. And, of course, even though the Accord was supported by all three major federal parties, it was perceived as primarily the creation of Brian Mulroney, who had by then become a very unpopular prime minister.

The main result of this decade of constitutional politics (1982–92) was the introduction of the popular referendum as an additional means of ratifying constitutional amendments. Although it is not legally required at the federal level, it is now mandatory in the provinces of Alberta and British Columbia; and it seems unlikely that Parliament and the provincial legislatures will ever again attempt to ratify major amendments without first getting approval in a referendum. This will make formal amendment of the Constitution more difficult, because, as shown by the fate of the Charlottetown Accord, even when the political class can agree among itself, the Canadian people will not necessarily accept the results of that agreement.

With the formal amending process now in gridlock, it seems likely that Canada will have to rediscover the virtues of the British tradition, which allows for substantial constitutional evolution through legislation, adjudication, and convention. This is not necessarily a bad development, for much of the Charlottetown Accord consisted of details that did not really require constitutional entrenchment and would never be found in the constitutions of other countries. They got in there simply because provincial governments and interest groups, seeing that the Constitution was open for review, thought that they could take advantage of the situation to get some of their cherished objectives "carved in stone," that is, entrenched in the constitution.

Whatever happens to the formal amending procedures, the most important mechanism of constitutional change in Canada now is judicial interpretation. This has been true since 1867 with respect to the allocation of powers between the federal and provincial governments as set forth in Sections 91 to 95 of the Constitution Act, 1867. It is only by virtue of court decisions that we know, for example, that the federal government has the power to legislate a national system of wage and price controls under conditions of economic emergency.[9] This is the case even though such power is not specifically mentioned in the Act itself. Since 1982, the interpretive function of the courts in constitutional matters has become much wider because the Canadian Charter of Rights and Freedoms, which is a constitutional text, covers so much territory. The courts now not only allocate power (i.e., rule whether the federal or provincial government has the right to legislate on a particular matter) but also deny power (i.e., rule whether a federal or provincial government may abridge freedom of the press, or take away the right to vote, and so on).[10] Canada is now very close to the United States, and far from Great Britain, in the extraordinary importance of the courts in defining what the Constitution means.

In another way, however, we remain close to Great Britain. The Preamble to the Constitution Act, 1867, states that Canada desires to have "a Constitution similar in Principle to that of the United Kingdom." These words have imported into Canada a large body of British constitutional convention relating to the use of the royal prerogative, the appointment of a prime minister and cabinet, the need to maintain support in the House of Commons, and many other matters. The working machinery of parliamentary government in Canada is largely based on these conventions. The Constitution Act, 1867, does not even mention the words *prime minister* and *cabinet;* an uninformed reader of the Act would assume that the governor general and the Queen's privy council for Canada were the chief executive authorities in Canada. Even in 1867 that was far from true, and it is not at all true today. But the outmoded language of the written constitution is meaningful because it is supported by many conventions, such as the existence of cabinet as the working committee of the privy council and the reliance of the governor general upon the advice of cabinet ministers.

CONSTITUTIONALISM

All constitutions, whether of the British unwritten, the American written, or the Canadian hybrid type, ultimately manifest an underlying attitude or spirit of **constitutionalism**. This is the belief that government is not in control of society but an instrument within it. It exercises the powers of authority and coercion for the general welfare by doing things that other agencies cannot do; but it is still part of society, not elevated above it. It is, to use another common expression, a **limited state**. The constitution expresses government's limitations by stipulating which powers will be exercised by which person or body. Perhaps more importantly, it also states which powers are not to be exercised by anyone in government but are to be left to the people, such as the power to decide how God will be worshipped. The constitution of an unlimited state would be mere camouflage, for if government could do whatever it chose, its actions would not be restricted by rules and its discretion would be complete.

᠍᠍᠍᠍᠍᠍

RULE OF LAW

Closely related to constitutionalism and the limited state is the concept of the **rule of law**. This phrase is more readily understood when it is approached as a shortened form of the ancient expression, "the rule of law, not of men." It means that to the greatest extent possible, people should not be subject to the unhindered discretion of others, but that all—rulers and ruled alike—should obey known, predictable, and impartial rules of conduct. It is a shield that protects citizens against the abuse of power "by laying down a set of procedures governing the use and alleged misuse of coercive power."[11] It has always been part of the Canadian constitution to the extent that the Constitution was "similar in Principle to that of the United Kingdom," and it has now been made explicit in the short preamble to the Charter: "Whereas Canada is founded upon principles that recognize the supremacy of God and the rule of law." We can distinguish several layers of meaning in the idea of the rule of law.

Maintenance of Law and Order

At the most elementary level, the government must maintain law and order so that people are, as much as possible, prevented from attacking each other. The enforcement of law in this sense allows us to count on security of person and property. Yet it is not enough for sovereigns to restrain us from despoiling each other if they themselves are not so restrained. Simple law and order must be complemented by restrictions upon government itself. The ideal of the rule of law leads logically to constitutionalism and the limited state.

No Punishment Without Law

The subject should be liable to punishment by government only for violation of law. "No punishment without law" *(nulla poena sine lege)* is an old maxim of English common law. It prevents rulers from using their coercive power arbitrarily against those who are the object of their dislike. People cannot be punished just for who they are; they must commit specified acts that violate known laws. This aspect of the rule of law is an important safeguard of individual freedoms because it means that people are free to do anything not explicitly forbidden by law. The opposite of this principle is exemplified in the following 1935 law of the German Nazi regime:

Any person who commits an act which the law declares to be punishable or which is deserving of penalty according to the fundamental conceptions of a penal law and sound popular feeling, shall be punished. If there is no penal law directly covering such an act it shall be punished under the law of which the fundamental conception applies most nearly to the said act[12]

Under such broadly drawn provisions, one could be punished for any action disliked by someone in authority. The meaning of the rule of law is entirely subverted, even if the form of legislation is preserved.

Discretion

Not all government activity can be reduced to impartial enforcement of rules. There is also the large and important element of **discretion**. This flexibility to decide something within the broader framework of rules appears in law enforcement when the judge assigns a sentence to a convicted offender, and is even more prominent in the service activities of the state. If government is to defend the country from external enemies, it must have discretion to locate military bases in suitable spots, choose effective weaponry, and promote capable officers. If government is to build roads, it must plan their location, acquire land, and let contracts for grading and construction; none of these things can be achieved without discretion.

But discretion need not be complete; it can and must be hedged with limiting rules. Government, for example, must have the discretion to acquire land; but there can be rules ensuring that owners will be compensated at fair market value and that they may appeal to the courts if they are dissatisfied with the state's offer. Similarly, government's discretion in letting contracts can be controlled by requiring contractors to tender bids in an open competition. The rule of law requires that where governmental discretion is necessary, it should be exercised within a framework of rules that discourage arbitrary decisions and offer recourse if such decisions are made.

Government Subject to Law

Government and its employees must be as subject to law as the people who are ruled. This is the great principle that was established in the English-speaking world by the Magna Carta. It means today that the powers of government must be founded on either common law or legislation. For example, it may seem necessary in the interests of national security to open the mail of individuals suspected of treasonous or seditious activities. This is a power that common law gives neither to government nor to private citizens. If it is to be exercised at all, the rule of law requires that it be explicitly approved by legislation setting forth the appropriate conditions. If postal surveillance is carried on without legislative authorization, government employees are in effect acting outside the law, and this is contrary to the rule of law.

This aspect of the rule of law was stated in Canada in the celebrated case of *Roncarelli v. Duplessis.*[13] In 1946, when Maurice Duplessis was premier and attorney general of Quebec, he ordered the Quebec Liquor Commission to revoke the liquor licence of Frank Roncarelli, who owned a small restaurant in Montreal. The only reason given was that Roncarelli, an active Jehovah's Witness, had furnished bail money for other Witnesses who had run afoul of Quebec's laws against distribution of religious literature. The Supreme Court of Canada ultimately concluded that Duplessis had acted without legal authority, because Roncarelli's religious activities were unconnected with the statute under which his liquor licence had been granted. Duplessis was required to pay financial compensation to Roncarelli for the damage caused to his business. His position as premier did not confer on him any immunity for actions taken outside the law.

The 1985 *Operation Dismantle* case extended judicial enforcement of the rule of law even further.[14] A coalition of peace groups known as Operation Dismantle tried to use the courts to prevent testing of cruise missiles in Canadian airspace, arguing that such testing violated the "security of the person" guaranteed by Section 7 of the Charter, in that it made war and attack on Canada more likely. The testing took place under an order-in-council pursuant to Canada's participation in NATO. Although the Supreme Court of Canada refused Operation Dismantle's request for an injunction to halt the cruise tests, it ruled that orders-in-council are governed by the rule of law and must conform to the Constitution, as interpreted in judicial review.

This was an important ruling, for orders-in-council are the chief means by which the political executive acts in a parliamentary democracy. Thousands are passed every year in Canada in the course of meetings of federal and provincial cabinets. Operation Dismantle reaffirmed the principle that those who control the government are not above or beyond the law.

Recognized Procedure

Law itself must be made by known and accepted procedures and is binding only if these procedures are followed. In the common law system, if a judge violates accepted rules of procedure—for example, by not allowing one side to speak—the resulting decision will be reversed on appeal and will not become a precedent contributing to the law. Similarly, legislation can be created only if Parliament follows all its rules of procedure. An attempt by the House of Commons to legislate without the assent of the Senate and the governor general would be contrary to the rule of law. Of course, these legislative procedures are not immutable; they are contained in the Constitution, which can be amended. But amendment itself requires that fixed procedures be followed, as illustrated by the Parliament Act (1911) in Great Britain.

This statute was introduced at the time of a political stalemate created when the Conservative-dominated House of Lords repeatedly rejected economic-reform legislation introduced by the Liberal government of David Lloyd George and passed in the House of Commons. The Act proposed to reduce the power of the House of Lords in approving legislation to a suspensory veto; this amounted to a fundamental amendment to the British Constitution. The House of Commons initiated the change, but it could not become effective until it had been approved by the House of Lords itself. If the Lords had not acquiesced, King George V, on the advice of the cabinet, would have appointed to that House enough new members committed to the change to tilt the balance in favour of the Act. In so doing, the king would have been acting legally, as the power of appointment is among the British monarch's discretionary powers. The point is this: a constitution may be changed in virtually any direction, but the rule of law requires that the amendment be made according to recognized procedures.

Freedom and the Rule of Law

The rule of law as described above is tightly connected to the individual freedom so highly prized in the Western world. A free society is possible only if the rule of law is more or less adhered to. Although it may seem paradoxical, freedom is the consequence of law, not its opposite. "We are all slaves of the law," said Cicero, "that we may be free."[15] Rules of conduct make possible a stable, ordered society in which we can plan our lives with reasonable expectations about how others will respond to our initiatives. Freedom to drive a car depends on a complex set of rules of the road, control of property depends on rules of ownership, and so on.

Normally we think of law in a negative way—as a restraint on our behaviour—but law also has its positive side. It restricts the behaviour of some to violate social rules but enables the rest of us to maximize our freedom of action. If lawbreakers were not restrained, they would use fear and intimidation to limit the freedom of others. A society that lives under the rule of law uses coercion selectively in order to prevent individuals from coercing each other. The result is enhanced freedom for all who abide by the laws.

The protection of liberty under law is not complete until the protecting power, the sovereign, is itself bound by constitutional restraints. James Madison, who drafted the American Constitution, wrote that "in framing a government which is to be administered by men over men, the great difficulty lies in this: you must first enable the government to control the governed; and in the next place oblige it to control itself."[16] Hence the maintenance of a free society depends ultimately on deference to the constitution and a refusal to amend it except by a procedure that is itself part of that same constitution.

Of course, no society manages to live up to the ideal of the rule of law at all times. Perpetrators of crimes sometimes go unpunished, and innocent people may be punished for actions they did not commit, as happened in Canada to Donald Marshall, David Milgaard, and Guy Paul Morin. The wealthy or the well placed may succeed in skirting the law by exerting personal influence. Those in government may use their position to obtain special privileges for themselves. But an ideal is no less important if it is not fully adhered to; things, after all, would be much worse if no one even tried to live up to it. An ideal still retains its validity as a means of judging the performance of government.

It is also important that the rule of law offer means to redress injustices. Roncarelli finally received payment for damages from Duplessis; Milgaard, Marshall, and Morin were finally released from prison, and the latter two received financial compensation; the Japanese Canadians who were interned during World War II finally received an apology and compensation. It would have been better if these injustices had never taken place, but it is asking too much of human institutions to expect that grave mistakes will never be made. At least, when the rule of law is honoured as a principle, it is possible to correct those mistakes.

🔲🔲🔲🔲🔲🔲🔲

FURTHER READING

Beatty, David. *Talking Heads and the Supremes: The Canadian Production of Constitutional Review.* Toronto: Carswell, 1990.

Canada. *Our Future Together: An Agreement for Constitutional Renewal.* Ottawa: Canada. Supply and Services Canada, 1992.

Cook, Curtis, ed. *Constitutional Predicament: Canada After the Referendum of 1992.* Montreal: McGill-Queen's University Press, 1994.

Daley, Timothy Thomas. *The Duties of the Chief Judges of Provincial and Territorial Courts and Their Impact on Judicial Independence.* Halifax: Dalhousie University, Faculty of Law, 1994.

Dicey, A.V. *Introduction to the Study of the Law of the Constitution*, 10th ed. London: Macmillan, 1959.

Heard, Andrew. *Canadian Constitutional Conventions: The Marriage of Law and Politics.* Toronto: Oxford, 1991.

Hurley, James Ross. *Amending Canada's Constitution: History, Processes, Problems and Prospects.* Ottawa: Canada Communication Group, 1996.

Hutchinson, Allan C., and Patrick Monahan, eds. *The Rule of Law: Ideal or Ideology.* Toronto: Carswell, 1987.

Jennings, W. Ivor. *The British Constitution*, 4th ed. Cambridge: Cambridge University Press, 1961.

Knopff, R., and F.L. Morton. *Charter Politics.* Scarborough, Ont.: Nelson Canada, 1992.

Laponce, Jean and John Meisel, eds. *Debating the Constitution: Proceedings of a Conference Held in May 1993 Under the Auspices of the Royal Society of Canada.* Ottawa: University of Ottawa Press, 1994.

Licht, Robert A., ed. *Is the Supreme Court the Guardian of the Constitution?* Washington, D.C.: AEI Press, 1993.

Mandel, Michael. *The Charter of Rights and the Legalization of Politics in Canada.* Toronto: Wall and Thomson, 1989.

———. *The Charter of Rights and the Legalization of Politics in Canada,* rev. edition. Toronto: Thompson Educational Publishing, 1994.

Manfredi, Christopher. *Judicial Power and the Charter: Canada and the Paradox of Liberal Constitutionalism.* Toronto: McClelland and Stewart, 1993.

McWhinney, Edward. *Constitution-Making: Principles, Process, Practice.* Toronto: University of Toronto Press, 1981.

Milne, David. *The Canadian Constitution,* rev. ed. Toronto: James Lorimer, 1991.

Monahan, Patrick. *Meech Lake: The Inside Story.* Toronto: University of Toronto Press, 1991.

Pennock, James Roland, and John William Chapman. *Constitutionalism.* New York: New York University Press, 1979.

Perry, Michael J. *The Constitution in the Courts: Law or Politics?* New York: Oxford University Press, 1994.

Webber, Jeremy H.A. *Reimagining Canada: Language, Culture, Community and the Canadian Constitution.* Kingston, Ont.: McGill-Queen's University Press, 1994.

INTERNATIONAL ORDER

CHAPTER 9

by James F. Keeley and Terry Terriff

U p to this point, the focus of the text has been on politics within states. However, states exist within a larger system consisting of many actors. With the collapse of the Soviet Union, there are now about 190 states in the world. Other types of actors also play a part in international affairs, for example, multinational corporations, political groups (such as the Palestine Liberation Organization), religious groups (such as the Roman Catholic Church), labour unions, political parties, non-governmental organizations (such as Amnesty International), and intergovernmental organizations, such as the United Nations (UN), the Organization of African Unity (OAU), and the World Trade Organization (WTO).

In world politics, the sovereign state is generally considered the dominant unit. Many students of international relations see independent states as central to the nature and workings of the world. Approaches to international politics that take this perspective are called **state-centric**. They may acknowledge the existence and even the relevance of other types of actors; but they also presume that states should remain the focus for understanding the international system. Other analysts have argued that nonstate actors are increasing in importance and that international politics is now too complex to be dealt with satisfactorily through a simple state-centric approach.

We see, then, that there are at least three ways to organize our understanding of world politics: the **realist, liberal,** and **structuralist** positions. Realists, and some liberals, tend to be state-centric. Realists stress military security issues, and argue in general that states are very sensitive to relative gains and losses (thus to the distribution of costs and benefits) in their interactions. They see the world as highly competitive. Liberals generally stress the possibility of cooperation in realizing joint benefits (where everyone can gain, as in the world economy) and the necessity of avoiding joint losses (where everybody can be worse off, as in environmental degradation). While structuralists focus on economic factors, they tend to stress how the world economy may have harmful effects on the political, social, cultural, and economic systems—especially of developing countries.

In this chapter, we will begin with the sovereign state and gradually introduce a number of complications that accompany that concept. Focusing on the sovereign state as the main actor in international politics necessarily implies a decentralized or **anarchic** international system. The word *anarchy* is derived from the Greek words *arche*, which means "rule," and *an*, a negative prefix. In popular speech, anarchy means disorder or chaos; in political science, it refers to the special type of order that can result from mutual coordination in the absence of a higher authority. In calling the international system "anarchic," we mean that it is a political system with no central legal authority that is greater than the individual states. Because sovereignty, by definition, implies the absence of a higher legal authority, a system of sovereign states must be anarchic in this sense. Even the existence of the UN and of international law does not alter this, for the UN, and international law in general, are premised on the existence of sovereign states that voluntarily undertake obligations.

A simple model of international politics takes as its starting point sovereign states in a decentralized or anarchic system. In such a system, each state can rely only on itself to secure its global interests. Realists therefore often use the vocabulary of the philosopher Thomas Hobbes to talk about international politics as if it were a war of all against all. In this view, states might do anything and everything they believe necessary to pursue their policy objectives. The instruments available to them range from the peaceful, such as diplomacy, to the violent, such as war. In pursuing its interests, each state acts as it sees fit, usually relying on diplomacy and bargaining, with war as a measure of last resort.

This view of international politics is suggested by the anarchic nature of the international system. But reality is more complex. "Sovereignty" does not mean that a state is not influenced or affected by others, only that it is not legally subordinated to others. At an extreme, a state may be so strongly influenced by other states that its legal independence is irrelevant. More generally, however, all sovereign states are interdependent—they influence and are influenced by other states, purposefully or not.

Usually, states find that they neither can nor want to ignore, destroy, or dominate other states. They must then find ways to manage their interdependence in order to make co-existence less difficult and to avoid war. To do this, they devise those understandings, rules, and mechanisms that, together with the major actors and decision-making procedures, make up the **international order**. International organizations and international law—the latter including the treaties that states make with each other—are important formal components of this order. The interactions and activities of nonstate actors are, in the liberal and structuralist views, the actual foundations of this order, the basis on which states act and even exist.

These understandings, rules, and mechanisms place some limits on states. If accepted, these limits provide assurance against extreme or unpredictable behaviour. They also provide means for states to coordinate their actions for the benefit of all;

Canada, for example, coordinated its defence policy with other Western states in the North Atlantic Treaty Organization (NATO) in order to meet the threat posed by the Soviet Union during the Cold War. Law, in the form of the North Atlantic Treaty, facilitated this cooperation. In effect, states may cede a little of their sovereignty as the basis for securing an agreement among themselves.

Sometimes, of course, states have disputes. Usually these are either resolved peacefully through legal or political means or allowed to continue without poisoning the states' broader relations. Sometimes, however, the disputes may become violent. According to realists, the possibility that states may resort to armed conflict gives global affairs its special, dangerous, and unforgiving flavour. Key to this notion is not the necessity for fighting but the widely acknowledged *possibility* of fighting. Other theorists, however, argue that war is always an extreme situation. The possibility of war and the anarchic character of the international system may be what sets international politics apart; it is equally true, however, that an analysis confined to the possibility of war ignores, or distorts our understanding of, much that goes on in the modern world.

States pursue differing policies, have differing ideas of what they want or are prepared to accept, and have differing preferences regarding the nature of the international order. States also differ in their ability to pursue their preferred policies—that is, in the amount of power they enjoy in international affairs. The actors in the international system, and the ways in which power is distributed among the actors, are key variables determining the structure of the system. The distribution of power among states tends to be unequal: some states, such as the United States, have a wide range of significant capabilities; others, such as Canada, have a smaller range and/or a lower level of capabilities; still others, such as the smaller countries of the Third World, are practically powerless. The most powerful actors dominate in establishing the understandings, rules, and mechanisms of the international order, if only because their agreement is most important to the maintenance of that order. Others have less influence and may find that the international order is not as they would prefer—perhaps very substantially other than what they would prefer.

In some approaches to the study of international politics, states are viewed as responding to external forces in deciding on and pursuing their policy goals. This approach assumes that every state is a unified actor with a clear and compelling **national interest**, which its policies must serve if it is to survive in a harsh and competitive world. Realism is particularly marked by this. But the ways a state defines its national interest in any given situation, and the means it has and uses to pursue that interest, also depend in part on domestic factors. Who defines that interest and how? This question challenges the assumption that states are unified actors. What domestic resources—money, manpower, and so on—may be mobilized to support a state's foreign policy? Liberal and structuralist theories may give a better answer to these questions than realist theories. Although some theories treat foreign policy as distinct from domestic politics, ultimately the two connect, though in a complex manner.

Some liberals argue, based on the historical record, that liberal democratic states seldom fight each other and that the incidence of war should decline as liberal democracy spreads. This suggests that a direct, powerful, and significant relationship exists between domestic politics and foreign policy. In purely quantitative terms, this observation is correct: no liberal democracies have gone to war against each other in the last one hundred years. What is less clear is the reason why: are democracies really reluctant to fight each other, or have they merely been too busy fighting other states?

⛩⛩⛩⛩⛩⛩⛩

REALMS OF INTERDEPENDENCE

International politics deals with the interactions among states in a wide variety of situations. Traditionally, military security has been the key area of concern; however, other issues are also important in the modern world: for example, the world economy, the environment, and "human issues" such as human rights and immigration. Many theorists therefore distinguish between the "high politics" of traditional security issues and the "low politics" of other international interactions. Realists argue that high political issues and concerns will, as matters of survival, tend to overshadow low political issues and concerns. Liberals question whether this hierarchy of issues always exists. We will now touch briefly on each of these areas of interdependence.

Military Security

States seek to protect themselves from the military power of other states, and sometimes try to impose their military power, or even their rule, on others. The preservation or expansion of sovereignty has always depended on the ability to prevail in battle against an armed enemy. In this area, then, power means military strength—sufficient weaponry and manpower, and the economic, technological, and resource bases needed to maintain this strength. In this context, the distribution of power refers to the distribution of military capabilities among states.

In a **multipolar** system there are several (sometimes five or more) strong states, with none clearly dominating. The international system before World War II was multipolar: the United States, Japan, Germany, Britain, France, Italy, and the Soviet Union were all counted as leading powers. After World War II, because the other major states either had been defeated or had exhausted themselves in winning, the United States and the Soviet Union became the dominant actors: the system was **bipolar**. With the collapse of the Soviet Union in 1991, the claim is sometimes made that the world is now **unipolar**, with the United States as the dominant actor. It is true that the United States is the single strongest state in existence, but this does not mean that its advantage and influence over the rest of the world is so great that the system is strongly unipolar.

In this sort of thinking, the concept of the **balance of power** is very important. This can refer simply to the distribution of power in the system but can also refer to a particular type of international system, in which no state is strong enough to overwhelm the others. If the major powers in such a system actively seek to prevent any one of their number from becoming too strong, they are said to be following a **balance of power policy.** Britain has generally followed such a policy, throwing its weight to one side or the other to prevent any one state from dominating Europe.

The balance of power, as a fact or as a policy, is a key concept in European history: the wars against France in the seventeenth, eighteenth, and early nineteenth centuries, and the two world wars against Germany, are illustrations of this. But balances do not always occur, nor are balance policies always successful—otherwise the Roman Empire would never have arisen. As well, the balancing activities of major powers do not always benefit lesser states. In the late eighteenth and early nineteenth centuries, Poland was dismembered by the Austrian, Prussian, and Russian Empires, which balanced power by sharing the spoils. Finally, preserving the balance—restraining rising or ambitious states—may require the use of force. The balance of power may help to preserve peace if an ambitious state recognizes that it may face an overwhelming coalition if it tries to dominate the system, and therefore avoids provoking a struggle. Nonetheless, the threat and the intermittent reality of war lurk in the background.

In pursuing policies of military security—trying to meet the threats or challenges presented by other states—states face difficult problems. The idea that a state should acquire all the military means necessary to protect itself from others seems relatively simple; the reality is not. The actions that one state takes to protect itself may arouse fear in others and lead them to take countermeasures even when no threat was initially intended. The first state sees these countermeasures as a threat and responds accordingly, and the others respond yet again in an upward spiral of preparations and tension. This situation, known as the **security dilemma**, is a variation on the prisoner's dilemma game, in which ruthless pursuit of self-interest actually makes players worse off. By stimulating an undesired response in others, who see your actions as threatening, your efforts to increase your security may actually decrease it. In such situations, all would be better off if they broke out of this spiral of action and reaction. Arms races are often seen in these terms: the competition between two states feeds on itself. If both stopped, both would feel more secure. Unfortunately, there is always the possibility that one party really *is* "out to get" the other party. Both realists and liberals note the possibility of security dilemmas. But liberals argue the desirability of breaking out of them, while realists wonder if it is possible, or whether the one party is really "out to get" the other. As in prisoner's dilemma situations generally, cooperation is not a realistic alternative unless there are mechanisms to develop trust between the competitors. Bilateral arms control and disarmament agreements, such as SALT and START I between the United States and the Soviet Union, and multilateral agreements such as the Nuclear Nonproliferation Treaty and the Chemical Weapons Prohibition Treaty, are efforts to break out of such spirals.

The idea that military force is a normal and acceptable instrument of foreign policy has been challenged repeatedly since the bloodbath of World War I. Still, the use of force is not uncommon in the world. Most states retain armed forces even if their main purpose is to maintain domestic order, or to keep a government in power, or serve as a symbol of sovereignty. A state's military capability varies with its manpower and economic base. Modern weapons, whether conventional or nuclear, are very expensive to build and maintain, and are used up rapidly in combat. This means that only large and/or economically strong states are able to maintain military forces armed with large numbers of modern, sophisticated weapons.

Also worth noting is that the successful use of military force can depend on domestic politics. To wage large-scale warfare, states must persuade their peoples to make major sacrifices at home, to sustain war-related production, and perhaps to die on the battlefield. This is only possible if populations are strongly united behind their states' policies. The Japanese surprise attack on the U.S. naval base at Pearl Harbor in World War II united the American people, which helped their government to mobilize for the war. In the Vietnam War, however, once the United States began deploying large numbers of ground troops, serious domestic political discord undermined American effectiveness. Similarly, the Soviet Union faced growing internal dissatisfaction when it became bogged down in the fighting in Afghanistan and its casualties mounted. When the United States led a UN-sanctioned intervention force in Somalia, it found that the American people were unconvinced that American national interests justified the casualties it suffered there at the hands of the struggling factions, and it withdrew its forces. Obviously, military power as an instrument of foreign policy is intimately tied to domestic political considerations.

International Economics

In discussions of military security, economic factors are generally treated as elements of national power. Can the state's economy support its military power? Is it vulnerable in strategic resources? Can it control lines of communication and trade? Can it use economic tools (such as blockades) as instruments of coercion? Different questions arise when we consider the development of economic exchanges among states at peace with one another. Liberals and structuralists generally put far more stress on the international economy as a factor in international relations than do realists.

Most states in the modern world are strongly linked to the global economic system: they trade a substantial portion of their gross national product, as importers or exporters; they borrow from and lend to the world capital market; they are affected by fluctuations in the world currency system. The impact on the West of the 1973 and 1979 oil crises, the international debt crisis in the 1980s, and the world stock market crisis of October 1987 shows the importance of the international economy for most states. In Canada, the United States, and Mexico, the debates over the North American Free Trade Agreement clearly illustrate the hopes and fears that influence foreign economic policies. Similarly, the future of Europe depends on the economic health of the European Union of states.

Participation in the international economy allows states to develop and prosper in ways that would be difficult or impossible if they had to rely only on domestic sources and markets. Yet this openness to the international economy also complicates the pursuit of legitimate objectives of domestic economic policy. Thus, although France may want to reduce an unemployment rate it finds unacceptable, it may still have to keep its interest rates relatively high to prevent an outflow of capital to Germany, which is historically more sensitive to the dangers of inflation and thus usually maintains high interest rates. For Japan to meet long-standing American and European demands that it reduce its chronic trade surplus by more effectively opening its markets to their goods, its fragile governments may have to risk electoral defeat—for example, by eroding the protected position of Japanese rice farmers. In the realm of economics, domestic and foreign policies are strongly connected.

Governments may face serious policy difficulties in this complex environment. Foreigners do not vote, so governments tend to be responsive to the desires of their nationals to be protected from the more harmful consequences of foreign competition. Often, declining or uncompetitive industries with large labour forces are given protection from foreign products, especially if these industries are located in politically important regions. These protectionist measures impose costs on consumers of products. Americans pay billions more for cars—and Canadians millions more for beer—than would be the case if free foreign competition were permitted. On the other hand, foreigners are not obliged to lend money to us or to buy our goods if they dislike or distrust our policies. Refusals to lend or buy can place intolerable pressures on governments, which must then risk alienating powerful domestic interests in order to regain access to foreign markets and lenders.

A key concept in understanding the international economy is the **balance of payments**. This is a running account of a state's transactions with the rest of the world, and includes its holdings of assets that the rest of the world will accept as payment for goods and services. Anything bringing money into a country (the exporting of goods and services, public or private borrowing, receipt of foreign aid) is a **credit**; anything sending money out (the importing of goods and services, public or private lending, donation of foreign aid) is a **debit**. A state running a **surplus** on its balance of payments is selling more to the world than it is buying, and/or borrowing more than it is lending. A state running a **deficit** is buying more than it is selling, and/or lending more than it is borrowing. Note that surpluses and deficits on a balance of payments account should not be confused with a government's budget surplus or deficit.

If we think of a state's holdings of foreign-exchange reserves—assets that other states will accept as payment—as a bank account, we see that states running balance-of-payments deficits may face serious policy problems. You may be able to borrow the money to cover a deficit, but if that deficit is large or persistent you may have to cut back your expenditures. At the end of the month, college students living away from home may eat a lot of macaroni and cheese. In terms of national economies, governments may have to raise taxes to discourage spending, or lower inflation and raise interest rates to make their country's goods more competitive internationally and attract lenders (by offering them a higher return). Such measures may not be popular at home, but the alternative—trying to block the import of foreign goods and services—will be unpopular abroad and perhaps bring retaliation from other countries. This retaliation may set in motion a spiral of action and reaction ending in harm to all. During the Great Depression of the 1930s, states sought to protect domestic employment by stimulating exports and blocking imports. The result was a catastrophic collapse of world trade, widespread unrest, and the rise of extremist governments in Europe supported by despairing voters in search of hope.

As World War II came to an end, the victorious states, led by the United States and Britain, sought to establish a world trade and monetary system—a world economic order—that would prevent another collapse. The result was the creation of the **International Monetary Fund** and the **General Agreement on Tariffs and Trade**. The GATT has recently been replaced by a new body, the **World Trade Organization.** These institutions seek to balance the desire of states to pursue independent domestic economic policies with the perceived benefits of a relatively open world economy. It has been a difficult task, and success has not yet been achieved. Nonetheless, the international economy is a perfect example of states trying hard to cooperate in an interdependent world.

The difficulties inherent in economic cooperation are considerable because, even when states agree on the importance of the global economy in achieving domestic prosperity, they may not agree on how this can or should be done. The developed states of the West, with their advanced, broadly capitalistic economies, tend to favour freer movement of goods, services, and capital—although not without very important exceptions. For developing states, however, foreign capital, especially from multinational corporations, may seem threatening. Having obtained their independence recently or having suffered foreign intervention in the past, these states are sensitive to possible losses of national authority to foreign actors. We can look to the debt crisis of the 1980s to see how the international economy may be seen as a threat by such countries. They generally depend on foreign capital to finance economic development. Loans must be paid back, however. Thus, when Argentina (for example) ran into difficulties in selling its goods abroad because of a gathering recession in the developed states, and faced an increase in the interest it had to pay on its loans, a serious domestic crisis was triggered. The government had to cut its spending on domestic development, services, and infrastructure very significantly in order to get its economic house in order and attract more capital from foreign lenders. These sorts of difficulties are at the heart of the structuralist critique of the international economic system. Structuralists see the world economy as serving the interests of wealthy states, and of wealthy individuals and groups within these states. They question whether the benefits pointed to by liberals are really enjoyed equitably by all states and by everyone within them.

States also vary in their power to influence the international economic order. The United States played an overwhelmingly important role in restructuring the world economy after World War II because it had the productive potential, the markets, and the assets to support this effort. Some observers argue that the stability of the international economic system requires the domination of a single state; in their view, the international economic disorder of the last two decades results from the relative decline of American economic power and the economic recovery of the states devastated by World War II. More generally, the major buyers and sellers, and lenders and borrowers, in an economic system will be the most influential in defining the character of that system. What they think are problems will likely be the topics that get addressed; what they think are acceptable solutions will largely be the policies implemented.

Other, weaker actors may not like the results. Many Third World states perceive the international economic system as dominated by the industrialized countries and hindering, if not actively discouraging, their economic development. They have in the past demanded a **new international economic order** that would better address their interests and concerns. They want better access for their manufactured goods to the markets of developed states, better prices for their raw materials, and more advantageous terms of access to technology and capital. While there was some slight movement on such issues in the 1960s, it was only when these states wielded the oil weapon—during the crisis of 1973 in particular—that they were really able to place their concerns at the centre of "world" (i.e., Western) attention. However, it was still difficult to force the Western states to move, except at their own speed and in their own choice of direction. The major oil producers within the Organization of Petroleum Exporting Countries (OPEC) benefited because they offered ready markets for Western goods and services and invested their earnings in Western banks and countries. But the other Third World states, which generally had little influence on the West's actions, were in fact harmed by the rise in oil prices even more than the Western states. Once the oil crisis began to fade, and especially as recession gathered in the developed states, the leverage of the Third World declined radically, except among major debtors, who could threaten to default on their loans and thereby drive their creditors into bankruptcy.

The international economy presents several interesting challenges to the traditional analysis of international relations. First, as we have noted, it breaks down distinctions between foreign and domestic politics in the economic realm. Second, we find a wide range of actors and interactions that might otherwise go unnoticed. Multinational corporations, international banks, intergovernmental economic institutions, global markets for capital, goods, and currencies, and even powerful domestic economic and political actors become relevant to the analysis. Their transactions can have powerful effects on both domestic economies and on the international economy more generally. The Mexican currency crisis of December

1994–January 1995, for example, was caused in the long run by a large, persistent balance of payments deficit and triggered in the short run by massive outflows of capital invested in Mexico. As well as affecting Mexico, however, it also had an impact on other economies in Latin America, which also found it more difficult to borrow foreign capital from now-wary lenders. Some observers suggest that such actors are replacing the state in importance; others do not go that far but note that national policymaking is more complex than it used to be. Some might even ask whether anyone in particular controls the international economic system: has it passed beyond the ability of states acting nationally, and can states coordinate their efforts to guide that system and cope with its consequences?

A third challenge arises from the liberal argument that economic relations between states are a force for peace: you cannot both trade and fight with someone at the same time. Disrupting mutually beneficial economic exchanges, war carries a cost that increases with the degree of economic interdependence. But interdependence also makes it more difficult for states to pursue their domestic objectives. They may find the costs of interdependence so great that they decide to look for ways to reduce it, or seek to extend their control over their trading partners by developing trading blocs or even formal empires. Competition among these blocs could then become a source of disputes or conflicts. Also, states that are suffering in the current international economic order may seek ways to redefine that order if they think it is sufficiently unacceptable and they believe they have the means to reopen the issues.

The Environment

The environment is another important area of international interdependence. Recognition of this has increased in the past few decades because the implications of environmental degradation are becoming clearer and more significant. This degradation does not respect state boundaries; the world is one vast, complex ecosystem linked by intricate processes. Some environmental resources, such as the atmosphere and the oceans, are shared by the entire planet; others, such as rivers and lakes, may be shared by neighbouring states; still others, such as rain forests, are found within one state, but their future is of global concern. The environment, in other words, is a global commons, a resource that everyone shares and depends on.

It is feared that some environmental changes may have imminent and grave effects. Depletion of the ozone layer may result in massive crop failures, as plants have a relatively limited tolerance for radiation. Global warming caused by the release of "greenhouse gases" such as carbon dioxide and methane may change rainfall and temperature patterns, and raise the sea level. This would lead to coastal flooding, desertification, changing storm patterns, shifts in agricultural zones, decreased farm production, increases in human deaths, and movements of populations. The overuse or pollution of critical resources such as fresh water could reduce the carrying capacity of land (the ability of land to support life).

The search for solutions to these problems is complicated by their transnational nature: no state, acting on its own, can solve them, but activities by one state may have adverse effects on others. Efforts to restore Canada's East Coast fisheries will not succeed if other states do not similarly regulate their catch in international waters. In the 1970s, the United States and Canada sought to limit the release of chlorofluorocarbons (CFCs), which were contributing significantly to the degradation of the ozone layer. States in Europe and elsewhere did not cooperate at that time, so these measures initially had little effect.

Unless all states cooperate on environmental concerns, all will suffer the consequences. The environment poses a unique problem of cooperation and coordination that challenges old notions of international politics. Solving transnational problems requires transnational—not just national—solutions. The liberal notion that only by cooperating can everyone avoid suffering the adverse repercussions thus has considerable force. Yet developing the necessary cooperation may be difficult even when the problem—be it global warming, acid rain, ozone loss, or loss of biodiversity—is clearly international in scope. As realists argue, individual states differ in their interests and perspectives. Canada, the United States, and other countries compete for declining fish stocks around the world. States like Thailand and Indonesia, with valuable tropical forests, may see the export of timber and the clearing of land for farming as important to their economic development. Any international agreement to preserve forests—one was attempted at the 1992 United Nations Conference on the Environment and Development (UNCED)—would require these states to lower their economic ambitions and accept some loss of sovereignty—in this case, the right to use their resources as they see fit. As well, environmental changes affect different states differently, and the industrialized world may be better able to cope with the consequences than would less-developed states. Thus developing states, even when they are hit harder by environmental degradation, may see attempts to preserve the environment as coming at their expense.

Despite these differences, the implications of environmental change are of sufficient importance that some agreements have been reached. In 1987, in a real breakthrough, the Montreal Protocol on Substances that Deplete the Ozone Layer was adopted; it was revised in 1990. But the differences between states must also be accommodated. At the UNCED meeting, some states refused to sign agreements, compromises had to be made that significantly weakened agreements, and there was no agreement on how to obtain compliance with the obligations created by the agreements. In certain instances, such as the case of forests, the differences between developed and developing states were so great that no agreement was possible. What the developed states saw as necessary measures of environmental protection seemed to some Third World governments like intolerable roadblocks in the way of economic development. Thus, although the nature of the environmental problems seems to call for cooperative action, the costs (especially domestic costs) of cooperation can be so great that the required restrictions on state behaviour will not be readily accepted.

Human Issues

States also interact on a range of "human issues" relating to the place of individuals and groups in the international system. The most important of these issues are population movements and human rights.

Civil and international wars, environmental change, and the desire of people to seek freedom or improve their lot in life have generated large population movements within and between states in the twentieth century. These movements, whether they are immigration through normal channels or flows of refugees, can present considerable problems for states. Countries absorbing large numbers of newcomers may be worried about the resulting social impact. Immigrants may have a different religious, ethnic, and cultural background, and so may change the character of a society; where they do not fully assimilate, or are perceived as being a burden on society, tensions may arise, and intolerance and even violence may increase. Immigrants are a common target of unrest, especially during economic recessions, even though the argument that they "take jobs away" is often false: in countries where the domestic birthrate is low and the population is aging, immigration helps to replenish the workforce. States often seek to control the number of people seeking entry as immigrants by establishing quotas as well as conditions that prospective immigrants must meet. Controlling illegal immigrants is more difficult and costly, since states must prevent covert entry and develop procedures to detect them and return them to their place of origin. These measures can have implications that are offensive to civil libertarians and to immigration support groups within their borders.

States from which people depart in large numbers are often concerned about the loss of manpower, especially if it is highly trained and desperately needed at home. Less-developed states in particular may suffer a "brain drain" of the most highly educated and productive—precisely the people most likely to be welcomed elsewhere. This means that states sometimes also seek to prevent certain people from leaving. In extreme cases a state may prevent all but a few of its citizens from travelling freely for political as well as economic reasons. The former communist states of Eastern Europe and the Soviet Union did this. The Berlin Wall, built in 1961 to stop a debilitating outflow of people from what was then East Germany, was the most notorious example of an attempt to stop a loss of population.

People fleeing persecution, war, or natural catastrophe pose special problems. Most states accept the principle that legitimate refugees should be protected, especially if returning them to their country of origin would probably mean their death. However, they also set strict standards for what they will consider a reasonable claim to refugee status. But enforcing such standards is not always possible; wars and disasters can provoke a mass exodus of people from one state to another. During the war in Afghanistan, over three million Afghanis fled to neighbouring Pakistan, and almost one million more went to Iran. Hundreds of thousands of Cambodians fled to Thailand to escape a bloody civil war at home. It is estimated that there are 20 to 30 million refugees in the world, and this number is expected to grow. The international community, through such organizations as the Red Cross and the United Nations High Commission for Refugees, accepts some responsibility for improving the plight of refugees, but the demands placed on them exceed the resources they have available.

Caring for such huge waves of refugees can strain a country's services to the breaking point. Also, a large refugee community can be a destabilizing influence: it may arouse local resentment and provide sanctuary or assistance to combatants in its home state. These in turn can lead to domestic unrest or even civil war in the state of refuge: the case of the Palestinians in Lebanon is an example. As well, flows of refugees may motivate states to intervene in the state of origin. When Bangladesh separated from Pakistan in 1971, India intervened on its behalf, in part to halt the flood of people to India seeking safety from the civil war. U.S. intervention in Haiti, under a UN mandate, was driven in part by domestic political considerations arising from the movement of desperate people from Haiti to the United States. The flight of refugees from Rwanda was a factor in the toppling of the government of Mobutu Sese Seko in Zaire (now the Democratic Republic of Congo) in 1997.

The issue of human rights has also gained importance in international politics. Traditionally, a state's treatment of its own nationals was a matter of domestic rather than international concern; other states tried to protect their nationals who were travelling abroad, but the treatment of local people was left up to the local government. This recognized the sovereignty of the local state. This approach is consistent with realist thought, which argues that states are amoral, and cannot be expected to take moral stances when so doing may adversely affect other important national interests. Especially after World War II, however, efforts to protect the rights of all people—even from their own governments—began to increase. This happened for many reasons, but the two main ones were principle (i.e., the view that all persons must enjoy certain basic rights) and expediency (i.e., a recognition that persistent human rights abuses create internal instabilities that can spill across borders). Some nongovernmental organizations, such as Amnesty International, have been successful in monitoring abuses and organizing embarrassing pressure on states to correct their behaviour.

States vary significantly in how they define and protect human rights. Sometimes they have legitimate reasons to resist the loss of sovereignty that the intrusion of international conventions entails. These may introduce concepts at odds with local cultures or legal systems, though we in the West may think of them as universal in scope. This makes progress on human rights difficult to achieve. It is not surprising, therefore, that the broadest consensus on what "human rights" are, and the strongest machinery to protect them, is found where states share a similar cultural, social, and political background. The principles adhered to in Western Europe, in the European Convention on Human Rights, are the most advanced. Those associated with the more universal International Covenant on Civil and Political Rights are much weaker.

An important aspect of human rights is that individuals are not really "persons" in the eyes of international law; they lack the full capacity to claim their rights, on their own behalf, before an international tribunal. Someone else—usually their state—must speak and claim rights for them. States are the only full **international legal persons** in international law, which is sometimes called a "law between states." Machinery that allows individuals to raise complaints about their own governments exists under the Optional Protocol to the International Covenant on Civil and Political Rights, and to a somewhat more effective degree under the European Convention. These bodies may have little power to do anything, such as make a finding of abuse and enforce it, but the fact that these mechanisms exist is significant.

The gross human rights abuses, amounting to genocide (the destruction or attempted destruction of a people), in Bosnia and Rwanda led to the creation of special international tribunals to punish war crimes in these two countries. These tribunals mark a significant development in legal efforts to protect human rights. Both tribunals, however, have been plagued by difficulties in apprehending, trying, and convicting individuals suspected of war crimes. The Dayton Accord, which ended the conflict in Bosnia, provided for the apprehension and bringing to trial of indicted war criminals, but NATO's Implementation Force (I-FOR) and follow-on Stabilization Force (S-FOR) have been unwilling actively to seek to arrest Bosnian war criminals because of concerns about risks to the lives of soldiers and NATO's position as a neutral force. In the case of Rwanda, progress in the UN War Crimes Tribunal has been handicapped by insufficient resources and a lack of access to areas where crimes were committed, while Rwanda's own efforts to try war criminals have been hampered by the destruction of its justice system during the civil war and by the ongoing intimidation and killing of witnesses.

Some liberal democratic states, such as the United States and Canada, have sought to incorporate human rights concerns into their foreign policy. They hope to use their influence to convince nonliberal states to improve their treatment of their citizens, and to adopt liberal human rights policies like those in the developed democratic states of the West. In philosophical terms, such efforts underline the question of whether human rights are universal, or whether they are simply products of Western culture. Many Asian states, attacked for their lack of human rights, complain that Asian concepts of human rights differ from those of the West. Attempts to force them to adopt Western notions are, they complain, a form of cultural and political imperialism, and violate the principle of noninterference in the internal affairs of sovereign states.

The willingness of states to raise questions about human rights abuses in other states may be balanced in practice against their desire for friendly, and profitable, relations. Canada and the United States often cite China for its human rights abuses, yet neither is willing to back its disapproval with forceful diplomatic action because they do not wish to isolate China politically or harm their beneficial bilateral economic relations with it. As a result, some abuses by some states will go largely unaddressed by the community of states, although nongovernmental organizations may try to raise them as issues.

Sustained and general attention to human rights issues is a relatively new development in international relations, one that liberals find a hopeful sign. Nevertheless, there are still significant problems in and disputes arising from these efforts.

᭄᭄᭄᭄᭄᭄᭄᭄

INTERNATIONAL ORDER

Because of the interdependent nature of the world, states have a powerful incentive to cooperate, or at least to restrain their behaviour in the expectation that others will, too. What begins as mutual restraint may become a regular and recognized pattern of cooperation governed by implicit or explicit expectations. These patterns between two or more states are called **international regimes**. International regimes create order in international relations by regulating and coordinating states' behaviour so that policymakers in one state have some idea of how other states are likely to act regarding a given issue or area. Because states can create international regimes, interstate relations are not necessarily a war of all against all even though the international system is anarchic. There is order in this anarchy: as Hedley Bull has suggested, the international system is an "anarchic society."[1]

International regimes usually focus on a specific area of common interest to a group of states; they do not involve other areas or other states. The World Trade Organization is a regime dealing with global trade issues; the Canada–United States Automotive Products Trade Agreement of 1965 created a bilateral regime between those two countries. International regimes do not have to be codified by treaties; they may simply exist as a pattern of behaviour to which all members of a group of states are expected to conform. Thus, the network of international regimes is itself complex and decentralized.

Regimes may exist in virtually all the areas of interdependence that we have touched on, including, in a limited and tentative way, traditional military security. Thus, while we may expect to find regimes in "low political" areas, we also find them in the security issue areas of "high politics." Indeed, one of the most important efforts made by the UN has been to create an international regime of **collective security**. By this term we mean a commitment by a number of states to join in common action against states that threaten the peace or commit acts of aggression. It differs from an alliance, or a **collective defence organization**, in that whereas the threats it tries to meet are from *within* the group, alliances are directed against *external* threats. Thus, the UN tries to check conflicts among its members, which include virtually all the states of the world (collective security), while NATO was formed to meet the perceived common threat to the West from the former Soviet Union (collective defence).

The first modern effort to form a collective security organization came after World War I, with the creation of the League of Nations; its member states sought to preserve peace without using the balance of power. When the League failed to establish collective security, the international community made another effort, creating the UN in 1945. For the first forty years of its existence, the UN had little better luck in implementing collective security. Only once did it respond collectively to aggression (the Korean War, 1950–53), and then only because the Soviet Union was boycotting the Security Council and thus could not use its veto to block the Korean action. Generally, during the Cold War between the United States and the Soviet Union, the UN was paralyzed in terms of its collective security function. It must be understood that the UN, as an organization, is an association of sovereign states, not an independent body that somehow stands over and above its members. The UN can only do what its member states want it to do, and only with the resources they are willing to grant it. These legal and resource limitations severely restrict the UN's powers and ability to act.

But the UN was not entirely without achievements in its first forty years. In particular, its **peacekeeping** operations were useful in maintaining ceasefires between combatants. Peacekeeping involves the interposition of lightly armed military forces between two combatants that have agreed to stop fighting. Typically, peacekeeping forces monitor ceasefires and serve as a buffer between the combatants. They are deployed only with the consent of the combatant states and use force only as a last resort and for self-defence. Until recently, peacekeeping forces were usually provided to the UN only by smaller states. Canada has participated in every UN peacekeeping mission since 1948. Although not as ambitious as collective security, peacekeeping serves many useful functions: it helps to suspend conflicts, keeps the major powers out of direct involvement on one side or another, wins time for possible negotiations that could reduce the level of hostility, and prevents further bloodshed.

The shift in Soviet–American relations from competition toward greater cooperation, even before the collapse of the Soviet Union in 1991, created the opportunity for a more significant role for the UN in maintaining international peace and security. Since 1988, the UN has been involved in military operations both qualitatively and quantitatively different from those it undertook earlier. In the Gulf War of 1990–91, a UN-approved and American-led coalition reversed Iraq's invasion and annexation of Kuwait. A UN operation took over the administration of Cambodia and tried to restore security and conduct a national election. In Bosnia, UN forces attempted to protect populations and to provide humanitarian assistance. In Somalia, the UN authorized American and other forces to protect international relief efforts in conditions of civil war.

These operations are so large, and so different from most of what the UN did before, that "peacekeeping" no longer describes them. The Cambodian and

Somalian operations could be called **peace-building**, in that their goal was to consolidate peace by such steps as disarming warring parties, restoring order, taking custody of and possibly destroying weapons, repatriating refugees, advising and training security personnel, monitoring elections, protecting human rights, and promoting political participation by the local population. The Gulf War and, in part, the Somalia operation can be called **peacemaking**, in that the goal was to bring hostile parties to agreement by peaceful means if possible, but military means if necessary. The UN authorized the American-led coalition to act in the Gulf War because Iraq's invasion of Kuwait was a gross violation of international law as embodied in the UN Charter; it authorized intervention in Somalia because the great suffering resulting from the civil war there was widely seen as intolerable.

The heavy demands placed on the UN are seen by some as presaging the development of a true collective security system.[2] Much will depend on every state's willingness to act against international lawbreakers regardless of its particular or immediate interests. Collective security depends on the group's ability to mobilize a wide coalition of like-minded states against an aggressor. As the failure of the League of Nations and the record of the UN during the Cold War suggest, we cannot assume that states will act as they should. If the costs of collective security are high relative to the perceived gains, or the order being defended is seen as illegitimate, states may be unwilling to act as required. The likely high costs of a major intervention in Bosnia constituted one reason members of the international community, despite having sent troops to provide humanitarian assistance, were unwilling to provide the force needed to stop the fighting by military means. Even instances of apparent collective security action, such as the Korean War and the Gulf War, have depended vitally on major states (the United States in both instances) having strong, particular national interests that led them to act. (We have already noted a domestic political factor—the flow of refugees—which affected U.S./UN action in Haiti.) In the case of UN peacekeeping, the reluctance of states to support significant UN action at an early stage, and the slow UN response when the slaughter began, were factors in the Rwandan genocide. Although some states, such as Canada, have suggested measures to improve the speed with which the UN can react to situations requiring peacekeeping, the adequacy of these measures has yet to be tested.

International law, the body of rules that states observe among themselves, is another important component of the international order. For many, the term seems contradictory: they look at the violence in the world and ask if this is evidence of law. They look for the institutions associated with law in domestic societies—courts, legislatures, and police—and, not finding them, conclude that law does not really exist in the international realm. Both of these points, while arguable, are based on a misconception of both law and international law. Being decentralized, the international system cannot function in the same legal terms as a domestic society. Instead, other mechanisms must be found to serve equivalent functions. States can create and change laws through their agreements, such as treaties, and their actions. They can also enforce the law—the decentralized system is a self-help system. This may seem to weaken the law, but in fact most states do observe international law as a matter of simple self-interest: a law-abiding world is less uncertain and less threatening. States use international law to settle disputes among themselves, for example, by resorting to arbitration or to the International Court of Justice. While neither of these is precisely the same as a domestic court, international law does provide mechanisms to settle disputes. Even the outbreak of wars does not necessarily disprove the existence or effectiveness of international law. Most disputes among states are settled peacefully, and even wartime conduct is governed to some extent by law: There are laws of combat, and the status of prisoners of war, for example, is legally protected.

International law helps to give order to international society by setting up some formal rules and conditions that help the actors pursue their objectives and regulate their interactions. It ascribes formal status to the actors (for example, whether or not an actor is an "international legal person" and, if so, to what degree), states their rights and duties, and lays down the procedures by which they may conduct their business, including the making of binding promises to each other. It provides a mutually intelligible set of concepts by which disputes may be set forth and sometimes resolved. International law is not simply a set of commands—it also offers the actors means by which they can carry on orderly relations with each other.

Diplomacy is a system of formal, regularized communication that allows states to conduct their business with each other more readily. States exchange diplomatic missions, create consulates to help their citizens travelling abroad, and hold international conferences to discuss common problems and to negotiate multilateral solutions. The rules and practices of diplomacy make it easier for states to deal with each other, in this case by setting out guidelines for communication. The existence of highly developed systems of diplomacy and of international law is fundamental to the existence of the general international order, as well as to the creation and management of specific international regimes within this general order.

UNDERSTANDING INTERNATIONAL POLITICS

Because international politics is so vast and complex, we often try to simplify it, to discover and then focus on what we believe are its most important aspects. Traditionally, most thinking about international relations has focused on the issues of sovereignty, decentralization, and military security. Many theorists, particularly realists, still argue that these issues are crucial in international politics, and regard the world in terms of a state of nature that tends strongly to a state of war; they stress the uncertain and potentially threatening character of international politics.

As liberals and structuralists suggest, however, this is not the only way we can approach the subject. Although we have stressed the state in our discussion, one can look at other, nonstate actors and argue that they are becoming more important, and that states are less sovereign and less dominant than before. Some observers stress economic factors over military ones. Some argue that interdependence either can or must lead to a more peaceful world of cooperating actors. We have noted, in a departure from the traditional military-security view of many realists but consistent with the views of many liberals, that there is a great deal of interdependence among states and that increased cooperation is possible if states are able to agree on a united course of action, or if necessity or the domination of one of their number can drive them to it. States try to manage their interdependence in ways that the idea of a state of war tends to ignore. However, interdependence alone does not imply or necessarily produce agreement; it can, instead, produce bitter disagreements, as well as struggles among the actors to reshape the international order in ways that would better serve their perceived individual interests. Thus, while many of the aspects of international politics we have pointed to briefly here seriously challenge traditional and realist understandings, they do not necessarily or automatically sustain the liberal or structuralist positions.

FURTHER READING

Burhenne, Wolfgang E., and Nicholas A. Robinson, eds. *International Protection of the Environment: Conservation in Sustainable Development.* Dobbs Ferry, N.Y.: Oceana Publications, 1995.

Damrosch, Lori Fisler, Gennady M. Danilenko, and Rein Mullerson. *Beyond Confrontation: International Law for the Post-Cold War Era.* Boulder, Colo.: Westview Press, 1995.

Falk, Richard A. *On Humane Governance: Toward a New Global Politics. The World Order Models Project Report of the Global Civilization Initiative.* Cambridge: Polity Press, 1995.

Fawcett, Louise, and Andrew Hurrell, eds. *Regionalism in World Politics: Regional Organization and International Order.* New York: Oxford University Press, 1995.

Frederick, Howard H. *Global Communication and International Relations.* Belmont, Calif.: Wadsworth, 1993.

Halliday, Fred. *Rethinking International Relations.* Vancouver: UBC Press, 1994.

Hay, Robin. *Military and Security Institutions: Challenges in Development and Democratization.* Kingston, Ont.: Centre for International Relations, Queen's University, 1994.

Jackson, Robert H., and Alan James. *States in a Changing World: A Contemporary Analysis.* Oxford: Clarendon Press, 1993.

Kegley, Charles W., Jr., and Eugene R. Wittkopf. *World Politics: Trend and Transformation,* 5th ed. New York: St. Martin's Press, 1995.

Klare, Michael T., and Daniel C. Thomas, eds. *World Security: Challenges for a New Century.* New York: St. Martin's Press, 1994.

Lapid, Yosef, and Friedrich V. Kratochwil, eds. *The Return of Culture and Identity in IR Theory.* Boulder, Colo.: Lynne Rienner Publishers, 1996.

Nierop, Tom. *Systems and Regions in Global Politics: An Empirical Study of Diplomacy, International Organization and Trade, 1950–1991.* Chichester, England: Wiley, 1994.

Neufeld, Mark A. *The Restructuring of International Relations Theory.* New York: Cambridge University Press, 1995.

Palin, Roger H. *Multinational Military Forces: Problems and Prospects.* Oxford: Oxford University Press, 1995.

Roche, Douglas J. *A Bargain for Humanity: Global Security by 2000.* Edmonton: University of Alberta Press, 1993.

Williams, Howard, Moorhead Wright, and Tony Evans. *A Reader in International Relations and Political Theory.* Vancouver: UBC Press, 1993.

Ideology
PART 2

IDEOLOGY

P art One showed that government's authority and legitimacy rest on a network of beliefs about human nature, society, and the purpose of government. Speculation about these matters—known as political philosophy or political theory—was the first aspect of political science to emerge, having been cultivated by the Greek thinkers of classical antiquity. What is said of philosophy in general—that "all philosophy is a footnote to Plato"—is equally true of the special field of political philosophy. All the great issues were already addressed in the writings of Plato and his pupil Aristotle.

Plato (ca. 429–347 B.C.) made a distinction that is still crucial to the study of political beliefs. He distinguished between *episteme*, which we might translate as true, well-founded knowledge, and *doxa*, or opinion. **Episteme** is knowledge that can be demonstrated by logical argument from first principles; **doxa** is an opinion that may be at least partly true but that believers cannot fully expound. They accept it because they have confidence in its source. To take a nonpolitical example, consider the proposition that the earth revolves around the sun. We all know this to be true, but few of us can justify our belief except by referring to the authority from whom we learned it. Only a scientifically instructed minority can develop the proposition from the first principles of physics; the rest of us accept it as *doxa*.

Political philosophy deals with both *episteme* and *doxa*. It tries to achieve *episteme* by uncovering and deducing from valid first principles. It also studies the *doxai* found in society to determine whether they are logically coherent and whether they stem from a more disciplined form of knowledge. The studies of *episteme* and of *doxa* are not wholly separate and generally reinforce each other, since analyzing the opinions that philosophers encounter is a first step in the pursuit of higher levels of understanding.

The usual contemporary word for political *doxa* is **ideology**, which is described in a well-known textbook in the following terms:

An ideology is a value or belief system that is accepted as fact or truth by some group. It is composed of sets of attitudes towards the various institutions and processes of society. It provides the believer with a picture of the world both as it is and as it should be, and, in so doing, it organizes the tremendous complexity of the world into something fairly simple and understandable ... An ideology must be a more or less connected set of beliefs that provide the believer with a fairly thorough picture of the world.[1]

Remember that we have defined politics as the activity of gathering and maintaining support for collective projects. Support might be obtained by offering bribes or making threats, but in the long run it has to rest on conviction. Ideology furnishes a basis for political persuasion by providing certain assumptions and values that may be held in common. More specifically, it has the following attributes:

1. Ideology is not a mere personal opinion, but a social belief accepted by large numbers of people and passed on by the normal channels of cultural transmission.

2. Ideology always involves a mixture of factual and moral beliefs. Because governmental legitimacy is an inherently ethical problem, ideology always includes beliefs about how people should act and what they should consider right and wrong.

3. Ideology, as a mass belief, is somewhat simplified. It reduces the infinite complexity of the world to simpler ideas that can be understood by large numbers of people who, after all, must devote most of their time to concerns other than the study of politics.

4. An ideology is not a random collection of opinions but a more or less organized system of beliefs that fit together logically. It is important to say "more or less," for the integration is never perfect. All of us have some surprising contradictions in our opinions. However, there is a big difference between an orderly, interrelated set of ideas and an assortment of unrelated opinions.

In this sense, ideologies are espoused by intellectuals in politics: by lawyers, teachers, journalists, and politicians who carry on public debate in ideological terms. It is doubtful whether many ordinary people, even among a well-educated populace, can be said to have ideologies.[2] They are more likely to believe in an assortment of somewhat conflicting ideological fragments—to be liberal on some points, socialist on others, and so forth. It does not bother them to be inconsistent in this way because they probably spend relatively little time pondering social and political questions. Examples of contradictory thinking frequently turn up in public-opinion polls. It is routine, for example, for respondents to say that taxes are too high while simultaneously demanding higher levels of public spending on roads, schools, and old-age pensions.

One interesting aspect of the term *ideology* is the negative connotations it carries. The word is often used as a weapon to degrade ideas with which one disagrees. Dismissing ideas as "mere" ideology is a common tactic in argument. It is worth knowing why this is possible.

The word *ideology* was coined in 1796 by the French philosopher Antoine Destutt de Tracy, who gave it a meaning quite different from the one it bears today. For him, ideology was to be the name of a new science—the study of human consciousness in all its aspects. Destutt de Tracy had once supported Napoleon; when he began to criticize him, the emperor responded by ridiculing his new science as an obscure doctrine and branding those who espoused it as ideologues. The concept of ideology probably would have died out if Marx and Engels had not rescued it and redefined it to bolster their theory that all human thought has an economic basis— that art, science, literature, law, and political thought reflect the underlying economic conditions of their creators. Marx wrote that one should always distinguish between the "economic conditions of production," which are the essence of class conflict, and "the legal, political, religious, aesthetic, or philosophic—in short, ideological—forms in which men become conscious of this conflict and fight it out." Economic relations are the "foundation, on which rise legal and political superstructures and to which correspond definite forms of social consciousness."[3]

Marx's view was bound to give the concept of ideology a bad name, because he regarded his own theory not as ideology but as science—scientific socialism. The beliefs of others were ideology, whereas his were science. Marx had a profound, although debatable, reason for thinking this, but it is easy to see how the word could become a mere polemical weapon in the hands of others. Moreover, there is much that is obviously true in Marx's insight. The intellectual world clearly does have some relation to its economic milieu. Marx's insight is so significant that the term he used to express it was bound to become popular.

However, as often happens, the word has become detached from the particular theory that gave it currency. Today, when a belief system is branded an ideology, the detractors might mean any of several things. They might be implying that the beliefs have not really been thought through and would not withstand comparison to a well-developed philosophy (like their own!). Or they might mean that the beliefs are a not very subtle expression of self-interest on the part of some group that is trying to assert itself. Or, following the sociologist Karl Mannheim, they might mean that the beliefs are a rationalization of the status quo, and inherently conservative in function.[4]

Our use of the term is not intended to have any of these special implications. We use ideology simply as a convenient, contemporary word for political ideas in action—ideas not as they are found in the philosopher's study but as they motivate large numbers of people. However, students should be aware of the many other connotations of the term that they will certainly encounter elsewhere.

Part Two will emphasize the four main ideologies that have dominated politics throughout the nineteenth and twentieth centuries: liberalism, conservatism, socialism, and nationalism. It will also take a briefer look at two more recent ideologies—environmentalism and feminism—that have acquired global significance in the latter part of the twentieth century. Ideologies are never static, and it is essential to have some sense of their rise and decline.

Up to a point, it is useful to analyze ideologies as systems of ideas or beliefs. But remember that all ideologies are abstractions. They do not really exist; real people with their individual thoughts, and organizations that adopt statements or programs, are what exist. It is unlikely that the beliefs of any person or organization perfectly fit any of the descriptions given here of particular ideologies. Yet common tendencies and common concerns unite diverse thinkers, even if they do not agree on every point. Think of ideologies as broad tendencies of thought existing over long periods of time. No two people identified as liberal or socialist or feminist think identically, but there are certainly recognizable patterns in their ideas. Above all, do not think of ideologies as fixed creeds, from which a thinker who varies on any point is excommunicated. Ideologies are more like families of ideas; as in any real family, resemblances are strong but disagreements can be heated. When this proviso is kept in mind, the concept of structured ideologies can be a helpful device for showing how ideas are connected to each other.

The six ideological families to be discussed in this book are all peculiarly modern systems of thought. Although they have earlier roots, they have taken on their distinctive forms only in the last two hundred years. The terms liberalism, conservatism, socialism, and nationalism were never used to denote systems of thought before the early decades of the nineteenth century. And, of course, environmentalism and feminism have only crystallized as comprehensive doctrines in the past two decades. These "isms" provide the terms of discourse about politics in the modern world, but they are not a universal and permanent vocabulary of political discourse.

All six ideologies are secular in orientation. Belief in God can be and has been combined with each of them, but it is not essential. All modern ideologies (except for some varieties of environmentalism) are humanistic—not in the sentimental sense of kindness or generosity but in the philosophical sense of being human-centred. They thus take human happiness on earth as an unquestioned goal. Although each has a different way of arriving, the goal remains the same. Jeremy Bentham (1748–1832), an early liberal, expressed the goal when he said, "The business of government is to promote the happiness of the society, by punishing and rewarding,"[5] not to fulfil the will of God or to prepare people for the next life. Marx was even more aggressive in his humanism, stating that belief in God was a hindrance to humanity's struggle to create happiness. "Religion," wrote Marx, "is only the illusory sun about which man revolves so long as he does not revolve about himself."[6] The humanism of the other ideologies is not always as forceful as in Marx's teachings, but it is a common trait. This means that the arguments among them focus on the best means of achieving the agreed-upon goal, which is human happiness on earth. On this point, the only dissent among the ideologies is found in the "ecocentric" varieties of environmentalism, which hold that humanity has no special claim to the planet, that all species have equal rights under the principle of "biocentric equality."[7]

Also, all the ideologies we study presuppose that society is something that people can change, reform, or mould according to their desires. All except conservatism have programs or agendas of social change for government to undertake. Conservatism differs in that it believes that society is too complex to be easily improved by human design. However, conservatism would not exist as a self-conscious ideology except for the challenges posed by the other ideologies. If it had never occurred to anyone that we could take charge of and deliberately improve society, there would have been no occasion to develop a conservative ideology that argues against such a possibility. In this sense the modern confidence in social improvement is the backdrop to all contemporary ideologies.

The four older ideologies stem from the same historical situation, symbolized by the French Revolution: the transition from traditional to legal authority and legitimacy. We can see the central values of these ideologies in the famous slogan of that revolution—*liberté* (liberalism), *égalité* (socialism), *fraternité* (nationalism). Broadly speaking, liberalism celebrates the onset of legal authority as human emancipation from bondage. Socialism is ambiguous about it, welcoming the demise of traditional authority, but also fearing that the freedom created by legal authority will produce a new aristocracy of wealth even more oppressive than the old aristocracy of inherited privilege. Nationalism also welcomes the transition to legal authority but seeks to establish a new form of political identity to replace traditional ones. Conservatism is suspicious of pure legal authority, fearing that the accumulated wisdom of the past will be lost if the transition from traditional authority is too abrupt.

It is no accident that the great ideologies of our age appeared on the political scene almost simultaneously at the end of the eighteenth century. The French Revolution and the Napoleonic Wars were the most visible signs of a vast social change. These events in Europe proved to be a rehearsal for similar changes throughout the world. This is the unifying theme of our era, often called the Age of Ideology.

FURTHER READING

Baldwin, Douglas. *Ideologies*. Scarborough, Ont.: McGraw-Hill Ryerson, 1992.

Ball, Terence, and Richard Dagger. *Political Ideologies and the Democratic Ideal*, 2nd ed. New York: HarperCollins, 1995.

Baradat, Leon P. *Political Ideologies: Their Origins and Impact.* Englewood Cliffs, N.J.: Prentice-Hall, 1979.

Christenson, Reo M., et al. *Ideologies and Modern Politics,* 2nd ed. New York: Dodd, Mead, 1975.

Christian, William, and Colin Campbell. *Political Parties and Ideologies in Canada,* 3rd ed. Toronto: McGraw-Hill Ryerson, 1989.

Eagleton, Terry. *Ideology: An Introduction.* London: Verso, 1991.

Ebenstein, William, and Edwin Fogelman. *Today's Isms,* 8th ed. Englewood Cliffs, N.J.: Prentice-Hall, 1980.

Feuer, Lewis S. *Ideology and the Ideologists.* New York: Harper and Row, 1975.

Gibbins, Roger, and Loleen Youngman. *Mindscapes: Political Ideologies Towards the 21st Century.* Toronto: McGraw-Hill Ryerson, 1996.

Hallowell, John H. and Jene Porter. *Political Philosophy: The Search for Humanity and Order.* Scarborough, Ont.: Prentice-Hall Canada, 1997.

Hinich, Melvin J. and Michael C. Munger. *Ideology and the Theory of Political Choice.* Ann Arbor: University of Michigan Press, 1994.

Hunter, Lynette. *Outsider Notes: Feminist Approaches to Nation State Ideology.* Vancouver: Talonbooks, 1996.

Larrain, Jorge. *The Concept of Ideology.* London: Hutchinson, 1979.

Love, Nancy Sue. *Dogmas and Dreams: Political Ideologies in the Modern World.* Chatham, N.J.: Chatham House Publishers, 1991.

McLellan, David. *Ideology.* Milton Keynes, U.K.: Open University Press, 1986.

Minogue, Kenneth R. *Alien Power: The Pure Theory of Ideology.* London: Weidenfeld and Nicolson, 1985.

Plamenatz, John. *Ideology.* London: Pall Mall Press, 1970.

Sargent, Lyman T. *Contemporary Political Ideologies,* 9th ed. Homewood, Ill.: Wadsworth, 1993.

Seliger, Martin. *Ideology and Politics.* London: George Allen and Unwin, 1976.

LIBERALISM

CHAPTER 11

The word *liberal* comes from the Latin *liber*, meaning "free." Before it became a political word, it had well-established usages, such as a liberal (generous) giver and the liberal arts—that is, the studies worthy of a free person. It was first used as a political term in Spain during the Napoleonic Wars and became common later in the nineteenth century with the establishment of the Liberal Party in Britain. The ideas of liberalism, however, are older than the name. Broadly speaking, liberalism is a product of the constitutional tradition of the West. More specifically, it grew out of the English Whig tradition of liberty under law. Prominent Whig thinkers were John Locke (1637–1704) in England, Adam Smith (1723–90) and David Hume (1711–74) in Scotland, and Thomas Jefferson (1743–1826) and James Madison (1751–1836) in America. These men never called themselves liberals, but they elaborated the principles later known as liberalism. They were followed by such writers as John Stuart Mill (1806–73) and his French contemporary Alexis de Tocqueville (1805–59), who consciously thought of themselves as liberals.

The history of **liberalism** reveals four principles, all of which relate to the broad concept of freedom: personal freedom, limited government, equality of right, and consent of the governed. These principles, which were all mentioned earlier in our discussion of constitutionalism, can be briefly recalled here:

1. **Personal freedom**, as understood by liberals, refers to the absence of coercion in the various realms of life. It includes free speech, religious liberty, the right of private property, and the right of political opposition.

2. **Limited government** means that the state is an instrument serving a particular function in society and is not in general charge of all society.

3. **Equality of right** implies that all must abide by the same laws, which the state enforces with impartiality.

4. **Consent of the governed** means that government emanates from the people, is responsible to them, and may be changed by them; it is a moderate and practical statement of the doctrine of popular sovereignty.

These four principles mark the entire liberal tradition from Locke to the twentieth century. Indeed, there is such wide acceptance of these principles today that almost everyone in the Western world at least pays lip service to them. However, there is also a deep division within liberalism that must be carefully examined. From this point on we will distinguish the older classical liberalism from the newer reform liberalism.

Classical liberalism was the dominant ideology in the nineteenth century in North America, Britain, and much of Western Europe. It accepted the four principles in a straightforward and literal way. In particular, it identified personal freedom with a free-market or laissez-faire economy. **Reform liberalism**, which began as a reform movement within the British Liberal Party at the end of the nineteenth century, was dominant throughout much of the twentieth century. It favours using the state to modify the market system without abolishing it altogether and advocates a larger role for the state in providing equality of opportunity. The differences between classical liberalism and reform liberalism are summarized below in terms of the four principles.

PERSONAL FREEDOM

For classical liberals, freedom is simply the absence of coercion. Without totally rejecting this definition, reform liberals try to add another dimension. They usually think of freedom in terms of our capacity to achieve our goals in life, arguing that freedom from coercion means little unless the means of attaining a decent life are provided. The Canadian journalist Pierre Berton expressed this position in his book *The Smug Minority*:

> A poor man is not free and a destitute man is as much a prisoner as a convict; indeed a convict generally eats better. A man who can't afford a streetcar ticket, let alone real travel, who can exercise no real choice in matters of food, clothing, and shelter, who cannot follow the siren song of the TV commercials, who can scarcely afford bus fare to the library let alone a proper education for himself or his children—is such a man free in an affluent nation?[1]

Berton is saying that the poor man is not really free, even though he is not actively coerced. The lack of financial means limits his opportunities in life as effectively as if he were kept down by force.

This difference in understanding of freedom is not a trivial matter; it is at the heart of the difference between the old and the new liberalism. Classical liberals emphasize the absence of coercion—freedom in the sense of being left alone to do as one wishes, as long as it does not infringe on the freedom of others to do likewise. Reform liberals, on the other hand, wish to use governmental power to reduce the freedom of some in order to provide opportunities for others. They justify this in terms of freedom, arguing that they are increasing the amount of real liberty in society by furnishing people with the means to achieve their goals. The two kinds of liberals use the same words but do not speak the same language. Their differing conceptions of freedom have resulted in differing ideas about the role of the state in economic life. In particular, economic freedom and the market system are not accorded the same primacy in reform liberalism as in classical liberalism.

While reform liberalism now differs significantly from classical liberalism, the former can be seen as a logical outgrowth of the latter. If freedom is the absence of coercion, the primacy of the individual will—the right to do what you want—must be fundamental to freedom. Reform liberalism purports to be a more effective way of enabling more people to obtain the objects of their desire, using the power of the limited state if necessary. Both versions of liberalism agree (and differ from other ideologies) in celebrating the fulfillment of individual desire as the highest good.[2]

LIMITED GOVERNMENT

Classical liberals see the state in negative terms: its role is primarily to prevent people from harming each other through force or fraud. To this end, it accepts the use of force to protect the community from external attack and to punish those who commit acts of aggression or deception against others. Beyond these functions, the state should do relatively little, leaving people to work out their own destinies within society. The classical liberal idea of government has been caricatured as the night-watchman state, as merely the caretaker of society.

Reform liberals accept that the state has caretaking functions, but wish to add to them the interventionist role of promoting freedom in the additional sense of capacity. They want the state to be a positive force that ensures social welfare in the broad sense, that ensures the availability of leisure, knowledge, and security for those who might not otherwise acquire them. The two different views of freedom lead to two different conceptions of the duties of the state.

EQUALITY OF RIGHT

For classical liberals, equality of right means only that all abide by the same rules. It definitely does not imply **equality of result** in the outcomes of social and economic processes. Classical liberals accept that there will always be inequality of wealth, status, and power. One might even say that for them, equality of right is the right to become unequal.[3] Reform liberals, while not committed to a wholesale equalization of results, wish to reduce economic and social differences. They have often adopted what was originally a socialist formula, **equality of opportunity**.

It is easy to see that equality of right and equality of result are two different things—one corresponds to a negative, the other to a positive use of the state. But equality of opportunity is an elusive concept; it seems at first glance to call upon the state only to ensure that no one is prevented by others from having a chance to achieve success. If that were all, it would be little different from equality of right. However, equality of opportunity in today's vocabulary usually implies a claim for positive state action to equalize people's starting points in life.

Opportunities, by themselves, are never equal. One child is born to wealthy parents, another to poor. One child is born to parents who encourage diligence in school, while another is born to parents who care nothing for learning. One child is born with high intelligence, another is not. Obviously, the state can do little about many of these inequalities; but if equality of opportunity is to have any meaning, the state must take positive steps to address those circumstances that cannot reasonably be blamed on the child. Thus, government may provide public schools, trying to ensure that all children start with the same sort of education, and offer low-interest loans to help young people obtain professional training that their parents might not have been able to provide. Such measures go much farther than the classical liberal conception of equality of right.

🝔🝔🝔🝔🝔🝔🝔

CONSENT OF THE GOVERNED

Consent of the governed, to classical liberals, did not necessarily entail democracy in the sense of universal suffrage. It was enough if government was accountable to a sizable section of the population. Classical liberals in the nineteenth century often favoured a **property franchise**, which required citizens to own a stipulated amount of property before receiving the right to vote. Viewing government as based largely on the protection of property, they felt it was reasonable to entrust government to those who possessed substantial amounts of property and who paid most of the taxes supporting the state. Reform liberals, in contrast, are strongly democratic. Since they put so much emphasis on using the state positively to provide for the common welfare, they naturally feel it is important that everyone have a share of political power.

Reform liberalism has much in common with democratic socialism. It differs from socialism in that it uses the liberal rhetoric of freedom rather than the socialist rhetoric of planning, but the specific ideas about the role of the state in society are similar in the two ideologies. For historical reasons, the term *socialist* has been unpopular in North America, whereas it is more respected in Europe. Many who are known as liberals in contemporary North America would be called socialists or social democrats if they lived in Europe.

One final note: the two types of liberalism discussed in this text as ideologies are only loosely connected with the "capital-L" Liberal Party of modern Canada. Over its long history, the Liberal Party has sometimes inclined to one side, sometimes to the other. Under the leadership of Pierre Trudeau (1968–84), the party clearly tilted toward reform liberalism and became quite interventionist in its economic policies; but the Liberal government of Jean Chrétien (1993–) has moved some distance back toward classical liberalism and has downsized or even dismantled many of the interventionist creations of the Trudeau era.

CLASSICAL LIBERALISM

The ideology of classical liberalism calls for a policy of freedom, defined as the absence of coercion, in all areas of human life—social and economic as well as political. This notion of extending freedom consistently to all aspects of life was gradually worked out by a series of important English, Scottish, and American thinkers, from John Locke to John Stuart Mill. A brief sketch of this development is useful to emphasize that ideologies are not static, timeless systems of ideas. They are more like a conversation carried on across generations in which ideas are generated, amplified, modified, and sometimes discarded. An overriding concern with freedom gives classical liberalism coherence, but no two thinkers within the tradition have had precisely the same opinions.

Liberalism grew out of the struggle of Parliament with the Stuart kings in seventeenth-century England. At the level of political power, the Glorious Revolution of 1688 established the supremacy of Parliament over the monarchy. At the level of ideas, the Revolution established that public authority is not derived directly from God, as the Stuarts had tried to maintain, but ultimately resides in the people themselves, who delegate it to the sovereign. Rule is a trust that can be removed if it is abused. The sovereign must rule within the law of the land, as made by Parliament and interpreted by the courts. Arbitrary government is unconstitutional and cause for opposition. The people have a moral right to rise in arms to overthrow an arbitrary government and re-establish the rule of law. In Weberian terms, this is the triumph of legal over traditional authority.

The ideas animating the Glorious Revolution were given classic expression by John Locke in *The Second Treatise of Government* (1690). Locke argued that the people deliberately create government by agreement among themselves in order to achieve a reliable, impartial enforcement of law. The purpose of government is fundamentally to protect them in their "life, health, liberty, or possessions."[4] Government is not authorized "to destroy, enslave, or designedly to impoverish the subject."[5] Arbitrary rule by the Stuarts had just this result, so the English were right to resist and depose them:

> Wherever law ends, tyranny begins if the law be transgressed to another's harm. And whosoever in authority exceeds the power given him by the law, and makes use of the force he has under his command to compass that upon the subject which the law allows not, ceases in that to be a magistrate and, acting without authority, may be opposed as any other man who by force invades the right of another.[6]

Locke's arguments were repeated in the American Declaration of Independence of 1776. This text, which was drafted by Thomas Jefferson, is the most concise and memorable statement of the political theory of classical liberalism:

> We hold these truths to be self-evident, that all men are created equal, that they are endowed by their creator with certain unalienable rights; that among these are life, liberty and the pursuit of happiness; that to secure these rights governments are instituted among men, deriving their just powers from the consent of the governed; that whenever any form of government becomes destructive of these ends, it is the right of the people to alter or to abolish it, and to institute new government.[7]

Similar ideals animated the early days of the French Revolution of 1789. In August of that year, the National Assembly adopted the Declaration of the Rights of Man and of the Citizen, which stated:

> The end of all political associations is the preservation of the natural and imprescriptible rights of man; and these rights are liberty, property, security, and resistance of oppression.
>
> The nation is essentially the source of all sovereignty; nor can any individual, or any body of men, be entitled to any authority which is not expressly derived from it.[8]

These quotations portray the ideals of the rule of law and the consent of the governed, but strictly speaking, they are not democratic in the sense of saying that all people should have an equal voice in choosing their rulers. The political theory of classical liberalism called for equality before the law and equality of right in respect to person and property, but not equality of political participation. In the early stages of the French Revolution, a distinction was made between passive citizens (who had full legal and civil rights but not political rights) and active citizens (who could also vote and hold elective office). The incorporation of democracy into liberalism occurred later and will be discussed in the section on reform liberalism.

The demand that government be bound by law was part of a larger concern for freedom of the individual. The idea was that people ought to be surrounded by a private sphere into which government would not intrude. This was worked out first in the area of religion; many of the disputes between Parliament and the Stuarts had a religious basis. Locke's *Letter Concerning Toleration* (1689) held religion to be a private matter:

> The care of souls cannot belong to the civil magistrate because his power consists only in outward force; but true and saving religion consists in the inward persuasions of the mind, without which nothing can be acceptable to God.[9]

His conclusion was that the state should tolerate all religions as long as they did not disturb civil peace by meddling in politics.

Regarding religion as a private matter was congenial to the increasingly secular outlook of the Enlightenment. It also coincided with a growing feeling that communication ought to be as free as possible. The first amendment to the American Constitution (1791) established a wide freedom of speech and press:

> Congress shall make no law respecting an establishment of religion, or prohibiting the free exercise thereof; or abridging the freedom of speech or of the press; or the right of the people peaceably to assemble, and to petition the government for a redress of grievances.[10]

At about the same time, the Declaration of the Rights of Man and of the Citizen enunciated an even broader principle: that not only thought and speech, but also conduct, should be left alone by the state as long as it did not coercively invade the rights of others:

> Political liberty consists in the power of doing whatever does not injure another. The exercise of the natural rights of every man, has no other limits than those which are necessary to secure to every other man the free exercise of the same rights; and these limits are determinable only by law.[11]

John Stuart Mill brought all these themes together in his book *On Liberty* (1859), which is perhaps the best-known statement in the English language of the value of freedom. *On Liberty* asserted "one very simple principle":

> The only purpose for which power can be rightfully exercised over any member of a civilized community, against his will, is to prevent harm to others. His own good, either physical or moral, is not a sufficient warrant.[12]

Mill tried to prove in his book that in the long run we would all be better off if the state was restrained from prohibiting "experiments in living," provided they were not coercive of others. Freedom to experiment with new ideas and new ways of doing things would encourage progress through discovery of better alternatives to present practices.

In the economic sphere, classical liberalism is identified with the free market. Locke did not have a fully developed theory of the market, but he helped lay the foundations for one by stressing that a major purpose of government is the protection of private property. The principles of the market were brought to light in the eighteenth century by numerous writers, of whom the most famous was Adam Smith. His book *The Wealth of Nations* (1776) used the metaphorical term "invisible hand" to describe what happens when an individual seeks to promote his own self-interest:

> He intends only his own security; and by directing that industry in such a manner as its produce may be of the greatest value, he intends only his own gain, and he is in this, as in many other cases, led by an invisible hand to promote an end which was no part of his intention. Nor is it always the worse for the society that it was no part of it. By pursuing his own interest he frequently promotes that of the society more effectually than when he really intends to promote it.[13]

Smith articulated in this passage a central belief of classical liberalism: that the common good can be served in the economic sphere by individual initiative without state direction. Much the same thing was meant by Anne-Robert-Jacques Turgot, a French contemporary of Smith, who coined the term *laissez faire* (let alone). The terms *invisible hand* and *laissez faire* both imply that human needs are best served by free competition in the economic marketplace. Government has to enforce the rules of property and agreements that make competition possible, but it need not otherwise direct the process.

These thinkers of the Enlightenment did not develop their ideas in a vacuum. They were trying to get governments to end many restrictive practices that were hampering market competition. Under the then prevailing economic philosophy of mercantilism, governments typically set high tariffs to discourage the import of certain goods, conceded monopolies to favoured interests, attempted to fix prices, and in other ways meddled in the market.

Over the course of time, Smith's advice was taken, at least in North America and Western Europe, and governments largely disentangled themselves from the cruder forms of direct intervention in the market. John Stuart Mill supported the doctrine of free trade and open competition in *Principles of Political Economy* (1848), which became the single most widely read textbook of economics in the second half of the nineteenth century. On this issue, Smith and Mill, and many lesser writers, had a great impact on public opinion.

Let us turn to a more systematic exposition of classical liberalism and its leading idea, freedom as the absence of coercion. Locke and Jefferson derived their view of freedom from assumptions about natural rights; but we will not follow their line of thought here, as it rests upon certain metaphysical and theological premises that are no longer universally shared. Rather, we will follow the thinking of those who defend freedom in terms of its utility to human society. This instrumental approach, which was taken by John Stuart Mill, has been espoused in our time by two of the most distinguished advocates of classical liberalism, the economists Milton Friedman and Friedrich Hayek (Nobel Prize winners in 1974 and 1976, respectively).[14] Their argument for freedom runs approximately as follows.

People must live in communities in order to survive and to live well. The efforts of each contribute to the welfare of all. How can all these individual efforts best be coordinated for the common good? One obvious answer is to set up a central source of direction. But liberals believe that people make better use of their talents if they are left to solve their own problems in their own way. Society is so complex that no central power can direct it efficiently; individuals can do better through mutual adjustment to one another's initiatives. While freedom may seem inefficient, in the long run it is the most effective basis for social life, for there is no intelligence that can look after people's affairs better than they themselves can. This becomes more evident the more advanced and complicated society becomes. A single mind might succeed in directing a small clan or tribe with a few basic wants, but it could hardly begin to cope with the demands of our complex civilization.

Individual initiative does not preclude cooperation. As David Hume pointed out in a famous example, two men would quickly discover how to row a boat across a river. Trial and error would show them how to work the oars together.[15] Society is a great self-regulating order whose parts are continually adjusting to each other through processes of communication and exchange. Cooperation exists, but it is decentralized cooperation achieved through mutual consent, not directed from above. Order emerges as the many members of society, pursuing their own good in their own way, respond to the initiatives of others. Following Hayek, we will call this emergent, decentralized, voluntary order **spontaneous order** to distinguish it from a pattern deliberately imposed by authority, which we will call **organization.**[16]

Classical liberalism holds that spontaneous order is more effective than organization in dealing with situations that involve vast amounts of information. An organization, being a structure under deliberate control, is limited by the wisdom of those who run it; spontaneous order, being a decentralized network of mutual coordination, does not limit the information that can be used by the participants. Concrete examples will help to make this argument clear.

The economic marketplace is a spontaneous order since it is not under the control of any one individual or committee. Freely moving prices are the signals by which participants communicate to each other the relative abundance or scarcity of commodities. The science of economics is centred around the ability of the market to clear itself—that is, to bring supply and demand into equilibrium. Producers and consumers use the information conveyed by prices to adjust their expectations so that the quantity produced equals the quantity desired. Classical liberals say that no central planning agency or other organized authority can perform this matching function as well as a self-ordering market. As proof, they point to the shortages and surpluses of essential commodities that used to be a fact of life in the state-managed economies of Eastern Europe.

This view of markets assumes, at a minimum, that there are many buyers and sellers who are trading freely without coercion and who know what they want and what goods and services are available; that entry to the market is relatively open, so that new participants can always undermine any collusion among present participants; and further, that there is a legal framework to protect property and enforce contracts. Under these conditions, it is argued, all exchanges are mutually beneficial: because participants have a variety of choices, they do not engage in transactions unless they find them more worthwhile than the available alternatives. As we will see later, those who criticize the spontaneous market order often do so not because they oppose its intrinsic logic but because they believe that one or more of these assumptions are, in practice, false.

The market order requires that behaviour be limited by rules of conduct to prevent mutual coercion. Such rules include, at a minimum, respect for individuals and their property as well as for agreements and contracts. These rules are necessary for the general welfare; but it will always be in the interest of some individuals to violate them, as long as others abide by them, because by doing so the violators will gain an advantage over the cooperators.

Those who violate rules while expecting others to abide by them are known in the jargon of contemporary economics as **free riders**. Tax evasion, for example, is usually free riding because it is not a protest against government as such, but merely an attempt to enjoy the benefits of government without paying for them. Hence government is necessary to spontaneous order as the means of enforcing those rules without which order breaks down.

In a large and complex society where most transactions are impersonal, coercion is necessary to discourage and punish free riders. Society can live with a few such individuals, but others may soon imitate them. Once that happens, the rules of conduct collapse and with them the possibility of a cooperative spontaneous order. It is the essential role of government to make spontaneous order possible by enforcing those general rules of conduct that are necessary to it. According to classical liberalism, government should otherwise allow individuals to pursue their own interests as they understand them.

This is not a rose-coloured view of society. There is no guarantee that individuals properly understand their own best interests or how to attain them. But, as Mill argued in *On Liberty*, it is unlikely that the state knows better than the individuals themselves. This is why reliance on the individual is thought to be the most effective general policy, even though it may fail in particular cases. Freedom means failed experiments and frustrated expectations, but failure and frustration are the roads to learning and improvement.

Adam Smith's description of the duties of government has never been surpassed as a statement of classical liberalism:

> According to the system of natural liberty, the sovereign has only three duties to attend to; three duties of great importance, indeed, but plain and intelligible to common understandings: first, the duty of protecting the society from the violence and invasion of other independent societies; secondly, the duty of protecting, as far as possible, every member of the society from the injustice or oppression of every other member of it, or the duty of establishing an exact administration of justice; and, thirdly, the duty of erecting and maintaining certain public works and certain public institutions, which it can never be for the interest of any individual, or small number of individuals, to erect and maintain; because the profit could never repay the expense to any individual or small group of individuals, though it may frequently do much more than repay it to a great society.[17]

The first two points should be clear, but the third requires some comment. Smith was thinking of certain activities that are not profitable in a free market because it is difficult to charge for them. For example, it would not pay an entrepreneur to beautify a city because it is difficult if not impossible to charge people for looking; similarly, it seldom pays an entrepreneur to subsidize basic scientific research because profitable application is so uncertain.

In contemporary economics, such things are known as **collective** (or **public**) **goods**. They are defined as goods and services that are not divisible among individuals but are enjoyed in common, and from which it is difficult to exclude consumers. A traffic light, for example, shines for all who are near the intersection. The fact that one person sees the light does not make it less available for others. Contrast this with food or clothing, which cannot be used simultaneously by more than one person.

Collective goods have an inherent free-rider problem. When people feed and clothe themselves, they have to pay for what they consume; but it is tempting for them to hold back their share of the cost of a collective good, in the hope that others will pay for it and that they will be able to enjoy the benefits free of charge. How many streetlights would there be if they were supported by voluntary contributions?[18] The state helps to provide collective goods through ensuring that we all pay our fair share. The state's monopoly on coercion can be used to collect taxes to pay for harbours, roads, scientific research, urban beautification, and many other desirable things. The liberal justification of this procedure is that, in providing collective goods, government is being used to help people attain what they actually want, not to impose goals upon them that are contrary to their own desires.

Classical liberals have always recognized the category of collective goods, but they have not usually been eager to provide many of them through the state. Adam Smith, certainly, had only a few such items in mind when he wrote *The Wealth of Nations*. The problem is that collective goods must be financed by taxation. Revenue transferred from individuals to government leaves that much less available for private decisions in the market. Classical liberals have generally been confident that private ingenuity will find ways to offer in the market the goods and services that substitute for government provision of collective goods. For example, a movie is a sort of collective good, since many people can enjoy it at once, but it can be marketed by the simple expedient of selling the right to a seat.[19]

One crucial tenet of classical liberalism is that, beyond the three functions of government mentioned by Smith, the state has no mandate to correct the results of the marketplace by transferring wealth or income from rich to poor. Classical liberals see a degree of inequality as an inevitable result of free competition. In the long run, they think, it will benefit even the poor, as capital is reinvested to create new opportunities for employment and production. The classical liberal believes that economic advances may initially benefit only a restricted few, but that over time those benefits will become more widely disseminated. Such innovations as television and computers were at first expensive luxuries but eventually became articles of mass consumption.

Classical liberals object to state **redistribution** of wealth and income because they believe it is economically inefficient. For the market to work properly, the agreements made in it must be based on the data about supply and demand that prices furnish. An individual who gains wealth by responding to these price signals is regarded as contributing to the welfare of others, not as taking away from them wealth that must be repossessed by the state. The prospect of gaining wealth is an important incentive, in that it encourages self-interested people to contribute to the common good by providing what is profitable in the marketplace.

Classical liberals also object to coercive redistribution for another reason: they believe it clashes with equality of right, which to them means, among other things, that the property of each will be equally protected, regardless of its size. They see the essence of redistribution as taking from the rich because they are rich and giving to the poor because they are poor; and they think such a policy means that the two classes are not equally treated before the law.

Classical liberalism was certainly not egalitarian in the sense of equality of result. However, it was an important force for promoting equality before the law. Typically, classical liberals agitated for the abolition of the special privileges given to some groups by the state. They fought against both slavery and the privileges of the nobility; against discrimination imposed on ethnic or religious minorities; against monopolies and tariffs that favoured corporations and producer cartels; and against government patronage in employment and public works. Since many of these goals have now been largely achieved in the Western democracies, classical liberalism today seems conservative, a force for preserving the status quo; indeed, classical liberals in this century are often called, and call themselves, conservatives (more on this later). But in the early nineteenth century, classical liberals were a reforming force, and very much in favour of great changes in the existing order.

The economic, social, and political aspects of classical liberalism are closely related. They all support basically the same proposition, which is that people should be left free to lead their own lives within a framework of universal laws that apply equally to all and have the sole purpose of preventing the coercion of others. Society, they think, is a game played fairly according to accepted rules. As in any game, there will be winners and losers, but that does not justify a sudden change of rules at halftime to handicap the winners and help the losers. In any case, society is not really one game but many games played simultaneously, so losers may seek out games at which they are more adept. The function of government is to make sure that all players abide by the rules of the various games. Government is not a coach but an umpire or referee—limited in task, but nonetheless indispensable.

Although classical liberalism is logically consistent in its views on government, it seems to many observers to lack concern for those who are not favoured by ability or good fortune. It is all very well, say the critics, to draw comparisons with athletic events, but losing a football game does not have the same pervasive effects on one's life as does a low economic position. The classical liberal's confidence that, in the long run, free enterprise and the market system will raise the living standards of all does not do much now for those who are less well off. Even those who concede the wealth-creating potential of classical liberalism may dislike the unequal distribution of wealth that seems to accompany it. And even if the economic inequalities generated by the market system are no greater than in other systems, many critics object to classical liberalism's willingness to accept these inequalities as inescapable. It should be possible, they say, to do better—to keep the admittedly useful aspects of the market while using government to ensure that all citizens have a decent standard of living, adequate medical care, and education for their children; and that there is financial security for the injured, the sick, the unemployed, and the old. Sentiments like these have encouraged reform-minded liberals to develop a more activist conception of government's role in society.

🎚🎚🎚🎚🎚🎚🎚

REFORM LIBERALISM

John Stuart Mill, who was perhaps the best-known exponent of classical liberalism, was also in retrospect one of the pioneers of reform liberalism. One aspect of his thought that pointed toward the future was its emphasis on democracy. His father, James Mill, had been the first prominent thinker in England to openly espouse representative democracy as the only acceptable form of government. J.S. Mill was somewhat less enthusiastic about democracy than his father, but he still advocated the extension of voting rights to all adults—men and women alike. Fearful that this new mass of uninstructed voters might use the franchise for selfish purposes such as the confiscation of property, he proposed that the educated be entitled to multiple votes; however, in historical perspective his support of democracy was on the whole more politically significant than his reservations about it.

The democratization of liberalism begins, but does not end, with the expansion of the right to vote; the consequences of this right have transformed the political system in a multitude of ways. Here are mentioned only a few: The ballot has been made secret so that ordinary voters cannot be pressured or intimidated by their employers, creditors, or landlords. Salaries of elected officials have been raised so that one does not have to be independently wealthy to run for office. Entry to careers in the public service now depends on ability rather than on family connections. Limits have been placed on campaign expenditures by political parties so that a "plutocracy" of big donors cannot simply buy an election.

Inevitably, democratization of the political system also transforms the economy. The vote is a form of political power. Once ordinary people gain access to that power, they naturally want to use it to improve their economic status. Though J.S. Mill remained committed to the free market, he was deeply pained by economic inequalities. In 1848 he wrote in *Principles of Political Economy*:

> If the institution of private property necessarily carried with it as a consequence, that the produce of labour should be apportioned as we now see it, almost in an inverse ratio to the labour—the largest portions to those who have never worked at all, the next largest to those whose work is almost nominal, and so in a descending scale, the remuneration dwindling as the work grows harder and more disagreeable, until the most fatiguing and exhausting bodily labour cannot count with certainty on being able to earn even the necessaries of life; if this or Communism were the alternative, all the difficulties, great or small, of Communism would be but as dust in the balance.[20]

Mill flirted with socialism as a way of redressing these inequalities, but ultimately rejected it on the grounds that property could be made more equal within the market system. He thought that taxes on large inheritances and the encouragement of enterprise ownership by workers could produce the best of both worlds: a reformed system of competition that preserved the market's ability to solve complex problems of allocation without perpetuating its great inequalities. Though he remained a classical liberal in outlook, Mill helped to popularize the view that the unequal conditions within the market system of his day were intolerably large.

The decisive step toward reform liberalism in Britain was taken by T.H. Green (1836–82), a professor of philosophy at Oxford University. It was Green who redefined the concept of freedom to include not only the absence of coercion but also the presence of means or capacity:

> When we speak of freedom, we should consider carefully what we mean by it. We do not mean merely freedom from restraint or compulsion … we mean a positive power or capacity of doing or enjoying something worth doing or enjoying and that, too, something that we do or enjoy in common with others.[21]

The context of this new definition of positive freedom was Green's argument that the state would have to regulate liberty of contract in order to secure a higher standard of living for the less fortunate. Green achieved lasting influence by explaining the quest for equality of result in terms of the attainment of freedom. In doing so, he made it possible for liberalism to incorporate equality of result, which previously had been seen as a socialist issue.

Although Green was an academic philosopher, his ideas had considerable practical effect. He and like-minded professors at English universities educated a generation of students who later rose to prominence in the Liberal Party of Great Britain. Imbued with the spirit of reform in Green's egalitarian sense, they laid the foundations of the **welfare state** when they came to power in the first decade of the twentieth century. They adopted the income tax as a means of redistribution; involved the state in unemployment insurance, old-age pensions, and other social-insurance programs; and encouraged, through permissive legislation, the rise of organized labour.

In Canada, William Lyon Mackenzie King was nourished on the same ideas. While he chose to move slowly through the complexities of Canadian federalism, by the time he retired as prime minister, in 1948, he had launched the welfare state. Other Liberal prime ministers, notably Lester Pearson and Pierre Trudeau, built on and expanded his reforms. Their governments expanded unemployment insurance and welfare payments and initiated a national medical-insurance scheme. The thrust of these reforms was to guarantee, through state action, the financial security of all residents of Canada. The welfare state is often described as a safety net that establishes a minimum standard of living below which no one needs to fall, a minimum financial capacity for people to pursue their goals in the marketplace.

Another vital player in the development of reform liberalism was the British economist John Maynard Keynes. His *General Theory of Employment, Interest and Income* (1936) argued that the spontaneous order of the market had a fatal flaw. Because of this flaw, the economy could fall into a permanent depression characterized by high unemployment of labour and underuse of other resources. Government could compensate for this flaw by applying appropriate fiscal and monetary measures. Keynes's theory, which is much too complex to explain here in full, did not make government the central planner demanded by socialism, but it did call for it to be much more than the rule enforcer of classical liberalism. It was now responsible for maintaining prosperity and full employment through fiscal and monetary policy, duties that were explicitly accepted by the governments of Britain, Canada, and the United States at the close of World War II.

A striking feature of reform liberalism is that, while it no longer promotes the *laissez-faire* economic freedom of classical liberalism, it has preserved and even intensified its commitment to freedom in other spheres of life. Contemporary liberals tend to be strongly in favour of freedom of expression, even of legalizing blasphemous and pornographic materials that earlier liberals might have rejected on grounds of public decency. Similarly, reform liberals today often advocate loosening many restrictions on behaviour—for example, legalizing mind-altering drugs and all sexual relations between consenting adults. Pierre Trudeau's famous remark that "the state has no place in the bedrooms of the nation" is a fair statement of the attitude of reform liberals in these matters.

This apparent paradox in reform liberalism can perhaps be explained as a function of the individualistic character of all liberal thought, classical or reform. All liberals see society as essentially a means for enabling individuals to do what they want without preventing others from doing likewise. Reform liberals believe that their economic interventions will help individuals to satisfy their desires. Their general outlook remains individualistic and libertarian even when they advocate increased state involvement in the economy.

In summary, reform liberalism is more democratic than classical liberalism, though the difference is more of degree than of kind. Reform liberalism preserves and even enhances the general commitment of classical liberalism to freedom, except in the realm of economics, where a definite break has occurred. There reform liberals call for an expanded, activist state role to reduce inequalities of result and to guarantee a minimum standard of living for all.

Ideologies do not undergo such profound changes without cause. The rise of reform liberalism was chiefly motivated by concern about the new working class during the Industrial Revolution. The rural poor flocked to cities such as Birmingham, Manchester, and London to work in factories. It is a much-debated question whether their standard of living as industrial workers was lower or higher than it had been as agricultural labourers, but the objective fact is perhaps not as important as the subjective perception.[22] The new working class, concentrated as it was in industrial towns and cities, was far more visible than the rural poor. Extensive urban slums created a widespread belief that the market system caused poverty and wretched living conditions. The new developments in liberalism were an attempt to share the wealth more widely and, in the minds of some, to stave off the socialist revolution that was going to occur if the condition of the working class did not improve.

Another development encouraging the ascendancy of reform liberalism was the growth of large corporations and the reduction of the number of competitors in key markets. Many industries—automobiles, airlines, steel, and petrochemicals, for example—are now dominated by a few giant firms. Reform liberals argue that oligopolies such as these substantially release firms from the constraints of market discipline by weakening competition. Many of them take the position that the factual presuppositions of effective competition no longer exist, and that government must play a regulatory role to protect society from exploitation by corporate giants.[23] Classical liberals dispute this analysis, arguing that, for example, while there may be only a few automobile makers in North America, there are foreign firms able to offer stiff competition now that improved transportation has unified the world market. They also argue that a dynamic and advanced economy offers many alternative products. There may be only a few steel companies, but competition still exists because steel is challenged for many purposes by wood, glass, cement, aluminum, plastics, and other structural materials.[24] This rejoinder does have its supporters, but the reform liberals' attitude toward large corporations has been extremely influential in shaping regulatory legislation.

Reform liberalism was the dominant ideology of the Western world throughout much of the twentieth century, with adherents in parties of all labels. However, the reform liberal consensus that had prevailed since the end of World War II broke down in the 1980s. Keynesianism became discredited in practice because politicians used it to legitimize recurrent deficit spending that had inflationary effects. There was a revival of classical liberalism in both the United Kingdom and the United States under the governments of Margaret Thatcher and Ronald Reagan, respectively. Thatcher and her advisers were particularly influenced by the writings of Friedrich Hayek, Reagan and his advisers by the works of Milton Friedman. Both administrations spoke of reducing the size of government and deregulating the economy, of privatizing government-owned enterprises, of inaugurating a new era of free-market growth, and of lessening our preoccupation with social security and equality of result.

The revival of market-oriented classical liberalism came later in Canada and was enacted less enthusiastically. Pierre Trudeau's last government (1980–84) was highly interventionist in economic affairs. Brian Mulroney's government (1984–93) took steps in the direction of deregulating the economy and privatizing or downsizing government operations, but his initiatives were cautious compared with those in the United States, the United Kingdom, Australia, and New Zealand.[25] The Liberal government of Jean Chrétien, elected in 1993, returned even further to classical liberalism by accepting that the federal budget must be balanced. Repudiation of deficit financing caused the Chrétien government to reduce spending on many government programs, such as unemployment insurance (renamed "employment insurance") and social assistance, that reform liberals had thought indispensable.

The main conflict raised by reform liberalism is the one between freedom (in the classical liberal sense) and state action. Reform liberals must use the state to provide collective goods and to promote egalitarian redistribution, or positive freedom. This conflict often arises in the various domains of government policy.

As we have already seen, classical liberals recognized government's responsibility to provide collective goods but were rather cautious when it came to the scope of such operations. Reform liberals are much more eager to supply collective goods through the state. "Private affluence, public squalor" was the slogan coined in the 1950s by John Kenneth Galbraith, a leading North American liberal.[26] By it he meant that the public sector was starved in comparison with the private. In his view, much more should be spent on collective goods such as urban beautification, scientific research and education, the fine arts, and protection of the environment. Provision of such collective goods increases our standard of living in some respects, but because such programs must be supported by taxation, they reduce individual freedom by taking away the choices people would otherwise be able to make about how to spend their money.

JUSTICE VERSUS SOCIAL JUSTICE

A topic of lively debate between classical and reform liberals focuses on the proper understanding of justice. To the classical liberal, **justice** is not a difficult concept: it is simply the virtue of protecting individuals in the possession of everything they have accumulated within the acknowledged rules of conduct. The most famous definition of justice comes from Justinian's Code: "Justice is a firm and unceasing determination to render to every man his due."[27] As an old proverb has it, "To each his own." Justice does not say anything about the relative size of holdings; it simply says that holdings must be respected, regardless of their size. Equal justice under law means that small holdings are as much protected as large holdings, not that holdings will be equalized. But reform liberals typically talk about **social justice**, which is not the protection of property as such but the partial equalization of wealth and income to reach some conception of a desirable range of outcomes. The fundamental idea is that the outcome of free action in a spontaneous order should not be allowed to result in too great a degree of inequality. Extremes of wealth and poverty are criticized as violations of social justice, even if they have arisen without violation of law.[28]

Demands that the state enforce social justice amount to a call for redistribution—that is, taking property from those who have more and giving it to those who have less. This must clash with the classical liberal's conception of justice, which would not permit the state to take such action. In classical liberalism, governmental redistribution to achieve social justice is theft—a violation of the freedom of some in order to increase the income of others. This differs in principle from the state provision of collective goods, which is intended to be a restriction of the freedom of all for the benefit of all.[29]

The main vehicle of redistribution is the progressive income tax. A **progressive tax** is one whose rate rises as the amount to be taxed increases. It is not just a matter of "the more you earn, the more you pay," for that would also be true if everyone paid, for example, a flat 10 percent of income as tax: someone who earned $10,000 would pay a tax of $1000, $20,000 of earnings would mean a tax of $2000, and so on. A progressive tax means that "the more you earn, the higher rate you pay." The reform liberal praises this as a way of implementing social justice and a means of achieving equality of condition; the classical liberal decries it as a coercive violation of the equality of right.

Since the revival of classical liberalism in the 1980s, there has been a tendency to make systems of personal income tax less progressive. In the United Kingdom, the United States, and Canada, tax reform has reduced the number of tax brackets and lowered the highest marginal rate of taxation. The federal income tax in Canada is now arranged as follows (1996 figures):

up to $29,590	17 percent
next $29,500	26 percent
over $59,180	29 percent

Provincial income tax, calculated as a percentage of the federal amount, varied in 1996 from 45.5 percent in Alberta to 64.5 percent in Newfoundland. This system of calculating provincial tax magnifies the impact of progressive taxation. Both levels of government also impose special surtaxes on high-income earners. When all these taxes are added together, the highest marginal rate of taxation, that is, the rate paid on each additional dollar of income, is over 50 percent. That is, those with a taxable income of over $59,180 keep less than half of every dollar they earn beyond that amount.

However, in assessing the impact of the progressive income tax, one must remember that it is only one among many taxes. We also pay property tax to city governments and school boards, sales tax in all provinces except Alberta, and a variety of both visible and hidden taxes to the federal government (e.g., 7 percent for the goods and services tax). Most taxes other than the income tax are applied at a flat rate; and since they are generally levied on consumption, they tend to be **regressive** in their effect—that is, to weigh more heavily on lower-income earners, who spend a greater proportion of their income on necessities.

A recent example of this is furnished by the changes to the Canada Pension Plan announced early in 1997. The joint employer-employee contribution is now scheduled to rise, by the year 2003, to 9.9 percent from 5.85 percent of the first $35,800 of income. Since the rate is the same for everyone, but applies only to the first part of income, the new schedule in fact weighs more heavily on low-income earners than on high-income earners. Thus, the net impact of all forms of taxation in Canada and most other countries is not nearly as progressive as would appear from the structure of the income tax alone.

Classical and reform liberalism are extreme ideal types within the liberal family of ideas. For intellectual purposes, it is useful to organize ideologies into coherent and consistent positions; but in the actual world of politics, many people see merit in both positions and try to combine them in one way or another, or stake out some intermediate position. The portraits of classical and reform liberalism presented in this chapter can be used as tools for analyzing what people say in political discourse, but do not expect to find such clarity and consistency in real life.

FURTHER READING

Anderson, Charles W. *Pragmatic Liberalism*. Chicago: University of Chicago Press, 1990.

Berlin, Isaiah. *Four Essays on Liberty*. London: Oxford University Press, 1969.

Bramsted, E.K., and K.J. Melhuish. *Western Liberalism: A History in Documents from Locke to Croce*. London: Longman, 1978.

Girvetz, Harry K. *The Evolution of Liberalism*. New York: Collier, 1963.

Gray, John. *Liberalisms*. Milton Keynes, U.K.: Open University Press, 1986.

Hartz, Louis. *The Liberal Tradition in America*. New York: Harcourt, Brace, 1955.

Held, Virginia. *Liberalism and the Ethics of Care*. Toronto: University of Toronto, Faculty of Law, 1997.

Hellsten, Sirkku. *In Defense of Moral Individualism*. Helsinki: Philosophical Society of Finland, 1997.

Hobhouse, L.T. *Liberalism*. New York: Oxford University Press, 1964. First published in 1911.

Jenkins, T.A. *The Liberal Ascendancy, 1830–1886*. New York: St. Martin's Press, 1994.

Laski, Harold J. *The Rise of European Liberalism*. London: George Allen and Unwin, 1936.

Lowi, Theodore J. *The End of Liberalism*. New York: W.W. Norton, 1969.

Minogue, Kenneth. *The Liberal Mind*. London: Methuen, 1963.

Mulhall, Stephen. *Liberals and Communitarians*, 2nd ed. Oxford: Blackwell, 1996.

Rawls, John. *Political Liberalism*. New York: Columbia University Press, 1993.

Ruggiero, Guido da. *The History of European Liberalism*. Boston: Beacon Press, 1959. First English edition 1927.

Schapiro, J. Salwyn. *Liberalism: Its Meaning and History*. New York: Van Nostrand Reinhold, 1958.

Spitz, David. *The Real World of Liberalism*. Chicago: University of Chicago Press, 1982.

CONSERVATISM

To conserve means to save or preserve. Thus we would expect a conservative to be a person who wishes to keep society as it is and who is sceptical about change. **Conservatism** in this sense is a disposition "to prefer the familiar to the unknown … the tried to the untried, fact to mystery, the actual to the possible, the limited to the unbounded, the near to the distant, the sufficient to the superabundant, the convenient to the perfect, present laughter to utopian bliss," stated Michael Oakeshott, a twentieth-century British political theorist and a well-known conservative.[1] Or, as critics of conservatism have said with a touch of exaggeration, a conservative is a person who never wants to do anything for the first time.

This preference for the existing present over the conjectural future rests upon a sober assessment of human nature. The Canadian historian W.L. Morton put it this way:

> To the theologian, this is the belief in original sin, the belief that man is by nature imperfect and may be made perfect only by redemption and grace. In philosophic terms, it is a denial of the fundamental liberal and Marxist belief that human nature is inherently perfectible, and that man may realize the perfection that is in him if only the right environment is created.[2]

According to conservative thinking, the limitations of human nature make it imprudent for society to embark on large-scale ventures of social transformation. Much that is good may be lost with little likelihood of reaching "utopian bliss."

This attitude can also be defended with arguments drawn from social science, particularly from the idea of spontaneous order. The main point is that spontaneous order acts as a vast filter for selecting desirable and discarding undesirable innovations. Such an order consists of millions of intelligences freely cooperating under suitable rules. Any innovation—a new theory in science, a new trend in art, or a new product in business—is subjected to the repeated, independent scrutiny of countless individuals who must decide whether to accept, imitate, or purchase. Any individual may make a poor decision, but there is a strong presumption that in time the right decision or course of action will emerge. This is especially true since the testing process continues over generations.

So there is some reason to assume that the present way of doing things is socially useful. If a better way existed, the chances are that it would already have been adopted. But this is only a probability, not a certainty. The fact that progress occurs shows that some innovations do have value, even if most do not. This is why the conservative tends to adopt a cautious attitude toward changes, waiting to see their usefulness demonstrated before adopting them. This is not hostility to change or improvement as such, but rather respect for wisdom inherited from the past combined with caution in the face of an unknown future.

Social reformers, whose proposals seem so obviously beneficial in their own eyes, are naturally impatient with this conservative attitude. Conservatives reply in their own defence that existing institutions already have the tacit approval of millions of minds over generations. That is a strong counterweight to the reformers' confidence in their own ideas. They may in fact be correct, but they must bear the burden of proof.

An interesting facet of conservatism is respect for habits and customs whose rationale may not be immediately apparent. Conservatives assume that there is tacit wisdom in inherited patterns of behaviour. People may not understand all the reasons for what they do, but they may still be doing the right thing in following custom. Reformers, in contrast, are often quick to condemn what they do not understand, preferring conscious reason to inarticulate habit.

The conservative theory of change is closely associated with the ideas of the Anglo-Irish parliamentarian Edmund Burke (1729–97), who was moved to reflect on change by the outbreak of the French Revolution. In 1789, Louis XVI convened the Estates-General, a medieval type of consultative body that had not met since 1614. His goal was to raise new taxes, but events quickly escaped from his control. The Estates-General converted itself into a National Assembly and declared France a constitutional monarchy. Change followed change with dizzying rapidity. The National Assembly adopted the Declaration of the Rights of Man and of the Citizen, created a form of representative government, abolished the last remnants of feudalism, nationalized the property of the Roman Catholic Church, and replaced the old provinces with geometrically drawn *départements*. Even weights and measures were affected: the National Assembly commissioned the preparation of what became the metric system. All this, as well as much more, was quickly done in an exalted spirit of reform: the rationalism of the Enlightenment, finally put into practice, would remodel society.

The results were not what had been expected. Within four years, France was under the dictatorship of Maximilien Robespierre and the Revolution had entered a phase later known as the Terror. France was also at war with the rest of Europe.

Louis XVI and Marie Antoinette had been put to death by the guillotine, a new form of execution. Thousands of other opponents of Robespierre also went to the guillotine, and the dictator himself was finally removed from power in the same way. Political stability was restored only by Napoleon, who ruled at least as autocratically as any of the Bourbon kings had done, though far more effectively.

Burke wrote *Reflections on the Revolution in France* (1790) before the worst excesses began, but he correctly predicted that turmoil and despotism would grow out of such a radical break with the past. We are not wise enough to remake society all at once, he asserted; we must rely on the accumulated wisdom of the past, contained in customs, traditions, and practices:

> We are afraid to put men to live and trade each on his own private stock of reason; because we suspect that this stock in each man is small, and that the individuals would do better to avail themselves of the general bank and capital of nations and ages. Many of our men of speculation, instead of exploding general prejudices, employ their sagacity to discover the latent wisdom which prevails in them. If they find what they seek, and they seldom fail, they think it more wise to continue the prejudice, with the reason involved, than to cast away the coat of prejudice, and to leave nothing but the naked reason; because prejudice, with its reason, has a motive to give action to that reason, and an affection which will give it permanence.[3]

The contemporary reader is struck by Burke's praise of prejudice, which is today a negative word implying unfair discrimination. For Burke, prejudice meant literally the sort of "prejudgment" that contains the latent wisdom of past experience. People are not able to think their way through each new situation, so they must fall back on rules of thumb that have served them well in the past. Take the modern example of a landlord who may refuse to rent to tenants under 21 years of age, citing several unhappy experiences with young tenants who gave noisy parties, were delinquent in their rent payments, and did not take care of the premises. The landlord's prejudgment against a category of people is, in a sense, unfair and irrational because not all members of the category behave in the same way. Yet, is it irrational for the landlord to rely on prejudice if he has no better way of predicting behaviour? Past experience, limited as it may be, is better than nothing as a guide to the future. The conservative view expressed by Burke is that prejudice is not just an irrational closing of the mind but a necessary way of dealing with a world in which complete information is rarely available.

As the psychologist Gordon Allport has pointed out, "the human mind must think with the aid of categories … Once formed, categories are the basis for normal prejudgment."[4] Such prejudgments are necessary and useful; they "become prejudices [in the pejorative sense] only if they are not reversible when exposed to new knowledge."[5] The challenge for conservatism is to combine open-mindedness about new developments with attachment to traditional values.

Burke did not oppose change as such—he had earlier spoken in defence of the American Revolution—but he wanted it to be gradual, so that the inherited wisdom of the past would not be lost:

> We must all obey the great law of change. It is the most powerful law of nature, and the means perhaps of its conservation. All we can do, and that human wisdom can do, is to provide that the change shall proceed by insensible degrees. This has all the benefits which may be in change, without any of the inconveniences of mutation. This mode will, on the one hand, prevent the unfixing old interests at once: a thing which is apt to breed a black and sullen discontent in those who are at once dispossessed of all their influence and consideration. This gradual course, on the other hand, will prevent men, long under depression, from being intoxicated with a large draught of new power, which they always abuse with a licentious insolence.[6]

The conservative attitude toward change is perhaps best expressed in the old adage, "If it is not necessary to change, it is necessary not to change." In the absence of some compelling reason for innovation, it is desirable not to tamper with the status quo, which has at least shown some degree of viability. Alternatives that are attractive in theory may turn out to be much worse in practice. In evaluating proposed reforms, conservatives are aware that they are comparing things that exist and whose faults are therefore apparent with ideas that have not yet been tested and whose faults may be unsuspected.

Conservatism is a prejudice (in Burke's sense) against using the state's coercive power to sponsor large-scale experiments in social change. The conservative will eventually give grudging approval to change that has occurred spontaneously through the cautious accumulation of many individual decisions, but to use the state as an agency of rapid reform short-circuits this process and may commit society to beautiful but unworkable visions.

Conservatism is conveniently described as an attachment to the present or status quo, but that is an oversimplification in one important respect. Conservatives are often highly critical of present trends, comparing them unfavourably with their image of the past. This is not incompatible with their view of gradual change, for the testing period of complex innovations may well extend over decades or generations. Conservatives often feel that we are heading in the wrong direction and should return to the ways of the past before it is too late. Therefore, they can find themselves in the position of making proposals that are themselves innovative vis-à-vis present arrangements. Burke, for example, wanted to overthrow the revolutionary government of France and restore the monarchy. When we refer to the status quo, we mean the present seen not as an isolated moment in time but as an extension of a long past. It is the prolonged experience of the past that the conservative values, not the mere present existence of a custom, practice, or institution. Where the state has not forcibly induced social changes, the conservative is satisfied with the present as an organic outgrowth of the past.

Burke expressed this unity of past, present, and future by metaphorically speaking of the state as a partnership across generations:

> It is a partnership in all science; a partnership in all art; a partnership in every virtue and in all perfection. As the ends of such a partnership cannot be obtained in many generations, it becomes a partnership not only between those who are living, but between those who are living, those who are dead, and those who are to be born.[7]

No one since has more clearly stated the conservative's sense of continuity. For Burke, this continuity was further buttressed by a belief in divine order as the foundation of social order. Other conservatives have reversed this relationship, seeing religion more as a useful support of society than as its basis. But whatever their differences of religious faith, conservatives all revere the social order as something larger and more important than the individual. They are always mistrustful of the rationalistic intellectual's confidence in individual judgment. Conservatives put more trust in the collective wisdom of society as expressed in customs, usages, and institutions.

As presented here, conservatism is an attitude, not a full-fledged ideology with a whole set of beliefs about human nature, society, and government. By the conservative's own admission, the status quo is always changing and is never the same from year to year. Paradoxically, conservatism's commitment to the status quo entails gradual acceptance of new principles as the present reality changes. In this way, conservatism differs markedly from liberalism and socialism, both of which are built around certain ideas regarded as universal truths. Classical liberals believe that the market is the most effective means of meeting human wants; socialists believe the same of state planning. They defend their systems where they exist and work for their introduction where they do not. They regard the status quo as a secondary factor that merely affects the speed with which desired goals may be achieved; they derive the goals themselves from principles, and have no commitment to what exists simply because it does exist.

All of this means that there is no single unchanging body of doctrine that can be identified as conservative. Those who are so identified, or who so identify themselves, have had varying opinions at varying times and places about the major issues of government. This means that, to understand conservatism as it exists today, we must take into account its long encounter with liberalism.

Here we must confine our view largely to the Anglo-American tradition.[8] In continental Europe during the past two centuries, conservatism has often referred to the ideology of those who have not accepted the legal type of authority and legitimacy, who have wished to cling to the practices that were widespread in Europe before the French Revolution: a hereditary aristocracy, established religion, and a monarchy unchecked by representative government—in general terms, to a traditional society of inherited status. Though Anglo-American conservatism also began with the reaction against the French Revolution, that reaction was not as total and violent, because the status quo in England in 1789 was far removed from that in Europe. The revolution of 1688 had established parliamentary supremacy and religious toleration. Although a powerful aristocracy existed, it was closely tied to the business or mercantile class. In the newly independent American colonies, there was no aristocracy at all, the monarchy had been abolished, and religious freedom was nearly absolute. England and America in 1789 already were, to a great extent, what the early reformers of the French Revolution wished to create. Anglo-American conservatism, epitomized by Burke, rejected sudden, state-directed change, but could not have rejected many of the aspirations of these reformers without rejecting itself.

A brief look at some of Burke's opinions suggests the complexities of being a conservative in a society whose traditions are largely liberal. Burke's economic views were almost identical to those of Adam Smith. He praised the market in these terms: "Nobody, I believe, has observed with any reflexion what market is, without being astonished at the truth, the correctness, the celerity, the general equity, with which the balance of wants is settled."[9] Correspondingly, Burke strongly advocated private property and totally rejected the redistributive state. Politically, Burke was a Whig— that is, a member of the party that, in broad terms, supported the rights of Parliament. He revered the memory of the Glorious Revolution, and he spoke in favour of the American colonies in their dispute with England because he thought they were being deprived of the traditional English right of self-government. All of these positions sound very liberal, seeming to support freedom, constitutionalism, and the rule of law. On the other hand, Burke was a strong advocate of hereditary aristocracy, though he himself was not of that class. To ensure that the nobility together with merchants of great property retained control of English government, he opposed any extension of the right to vote, which in his day was quite narrowly restricted. His conception of equality before the law did not imply that literally the same laws would apply to all. He thought that society was necessarily divided into hierarchical levels and that this was something for government to protect because of the hierarchy's contribution to social stability.

Burke's "conservatism" (we put the term in quotation marks because he did not apply that label to his own thinking) was a combination of economic liberalism and social conservatism. The precise nature of that combination is intelligible only in the context of the issues of his day. Since then, Anglo-American conservatives have held various ideas, depending on when and where they lived, but they have generally followed Burke's example in combining market economics with respect for the past. Two of the chief founders of Canada—John A. Macdonald and George-Étienne Cartier—fit this description exactly. Both were thoroughly committed to the market system. Macdonald eventually adopted a protective tariff—which violates the concept of free trade—but only because he could not conclude a reciprocity agreement with the United States. Both were opposed to universal suffrage and regarded the United States as an instructive example of democracy run amok. Both were strong supporters of the British Empire and the Crown, seeing a constitutional monarchy as a valuable source of social stability. It has been said of these two statesmen:

> It was not that the founders of the Canadian nation despised freedom; indeed, they revered it. But, for them, freedom arises from order, from restraint, not from unconstrained passions. The world they desired was the Burkean world, the world of order, restraint, sterner virtues and prudence.[10]

In comparison with American conservatism, the Canadian variety is less imbued with the virtues of free enterprise and more willing to resort to collectivist economic schemes. By any measure, American society and American thought are more individualistic than their Canadian counterparts, and Canadian conservatism reflects this general difference. Also, there is in Canada a tradition of conservatism that is rather sceptical of the competitive market philosophy of classical liberalism. Thinkers in this vein are often called **Red Tories** because they combine some traditionalist views with others that may seem interventionist or even socialist. The best-known Red Tory is probably the philosopher George Grant, whose 1965 book *Lament for a Nation* has become a classic of Canadian political thought. Grant was stirred to write his book by the collapse of John Diefenbaker's government over the issue of whether Canada should accept American nuclear warheads on its soil. In Grant's view, Lester Pearson's subsequent decision to accept the weapons showed that Canada had been pulled irretrievably into the American orbit. Grant's objection was not based merely on sentiments of Canadian nationalism but also on philosophical considerations:

> The impossibility of conservatism in our era is the impossibility of Canada. As Canadians we attempted a ridiculous task in trying to build a conservative nation in the age of progress, on a continent we share with the most dynamic nation on earth. The current of modern history was against us.[11]

The dynamism to which Grant referred is the individualistic market orientation of American society. He touched here upon a profound truth—that the market is the great dissolver of customs, traditions, and all the things to which conservatives are temperamentally attached. The profit-and-loss psychology of the market tends to promote universal homogeneity and break down local particularity, thus undermining the heritage of the past.

No ideology is ever free of internal contradictions. The characteristic contradiction of conservatism is that in accepting the competitive market, which is really a classical liberal idea, it threatens many of its own values, such as the ones relating to tradition, stability, and social cohesion. Nonetheless, contemporary conservatism as a practical, real-world ideology does try to ride both horses, so to speak; it accepts the *laissez-faire* economic policy of classical liberalism along with a traditionalist view of social customs and morality.

ΠΕΟCΟΠSΕΡΨΑΤΙSΜ: RISE AND FALL?

There was a marked conservative tide during the 1980s in the Western democracies. After the Great Depression and World War II, the state had become generally accepted as a force for implementing a more just and equitable society. But a counter-movement started with the election of Margaret Thatcher in Great Britain in 1979, Ronald Reagan in the United States in 1980, and Brian Mulroney in Canada in 1984. Parties espousing conservative ideology also governed Japan, Italy, and West Germany for most of the 1980s; and other nominally liberal or social-demo-cratic governments, such as those in Australia and New Zealand, followed economic policies similar to those of conservative governments.

It became common to refer to this conservative revival as **neoconservatism,** a term first used in the 1970s by a circle of writers in the United States who had once identified themselves as liberals or even socialists but had become disenchanted with developments at the time in reform liberalism. In this chapter we will continue to use the traditional term *conservatism* because we see no fundamental change in ideology, even though there was at least a temporary increase in popular support for conservative views.

While many welfare-liberal policies have undeniable political appeal, the record in Western societies suggests that it is impossible for a centrally run bureaucracy to respond effectively to all claims made on it. Many policies—such as old-age pensions and medicare—are still highly popular, but there is a growing demand for more selectivity in the scope of the welfare state. Politically powerful conservatives in the 1980s seemed to advocate neither absolute individualism nor absolute collectivism, but a balance between the two.

Conservatism in power in Britain, Canada, and the United States exhibited a number of beliefs derived from classical liberalism. First is the conviction that the public sector had become too large and was crowding out the private sector, and that government must therefore be **downsized**. Conservative governments tried to achieve this with wage freezes and rollbacks in the public service, across-the-board cuts in programs, and selective reductions in sectors thought to be particularly over-funded. The main obstacle to reducing the size of government is that most of the budget of the modern state consists of either transfer payments or services that are popular with large groups of voters, such as education, pensions, health care, and unemployment insurance. Electors may agree in the abstract that government is too large and may vote for a conservative party that promises to do something about it, but they become irate when they see their favourite services cut back.

The Progressive Conservative government of Brian Mulroney had only modest success in downsizing the operations of the federal government. By 1993 it had reduced the size of the federal civil service from about 230,000 to about 220,000 employees, roughly the same number as in 1973.[12] But during Mulroney's first government, the overall federal budget continued to grow faster than the rate of inflation, in spite of highly publicized austerity measures in a few departments and agencies, such as the CBC. The reason is that, before 1989, the government made no serious effort to reduce the size of the transfer payments that make up the core of the welfare state. The prime minister backed away from this aspect of budget-cutting in 1985, after a proposed minor reduction in the rate of increase of old-age pensions brought vociferous political opposition.

In 1989, however, after it was re-elected, the Mulroney government introduced a budget that proposed to reduce the federal contribution to unemployment insurance and to "tax back" family-allowance and old-age income security payments from the highest-income earners. This was the beginning of Mulroney's retreat from his position that Canada's social programs were "a sacred trust not to be tampered with."[13] These moves were quickly followed by changes in the way transfer payments to provinces were calculated, the goal being to reduce the growth of federal contributions to medical care, higher education, and social assistance. This had the effect of "downloading" additional financial pressure onto the provinces, who have the constitutional responsibility for hospitals and medical care, universities and colleges, and welfare services.

In spite of these steps, the Mulroney government made only modest progress in tackling the double challenge confronting politicians in Canada and most other Western governments: the accumulated public **debt** and the annual **deficit**. The promises of the welfare state and reform liberalism, realized in Canada as part of Pierre Trudeau's "just society," have proved expensive to keep. The federal government has run a deficit every year since 1975—that is, it has had to borrow money in order to pay its bills. The biggest expenditures by far are the transfer payments that underpin the welfare state. The accumulated debt (about $600 billion in 1997) is now so large that more than one-third of federal tax revenues goes to interest payments.

The burden of interest payments has become a serious impediment to the government's ability to undertake new policy initiatives. In 1989, for example, the government drastically reduced funding for the purchase of new weapons systems and cancelled a proposed national child-care plan, even though both programs had been important promises in the 1988 Conservative election campaign. After 1989 the Mulroney government repackaged or redesigned some social programs but did not introduce anything that could really be called new.

A second typical conservative belief is that government controls hamper and restrict the private sector. The typical outgrowth of this line of thought is **deregulation**—that is, the lifting of governmental controls on market activity. This was an important theme of the Reagan administration in the United States from 1980 to 1988. During Reagan's two terms in office, the economic (but not safety) aspects of passenger air travel were deregulated, which allowed airlines to determine fares and services competitively, without government approval. (This was in fact the completion of an initiative begun under President Jimmy Carter.) Telecommunications were also partially deregulated, creating competition for long-distance telephone services in the United States.

The Canadian Conservatives also pursued an agenda of deregulation. Shortly after taking office in 1984, they effectively removed the power of the Foreign Investment Review Agency to block or otherwise regulate external takeovers of Canadian businesses. They dismantled the National Energy Program, allowing the price of oil to be set by world markets, and followed the United States in deregulating airline passenger services. In 1992, long-distance telephone services also began to be deregulated.

In the Canadian context, the Free Trade Agreement with the United States might also be considered a form of deregulation. Protective tariffs amount to macroregulation in that they guide the flow of labour and capital toward protected industries. The decision to lower or even abandon such tariffs is by implication a decision to rely more on market forces to determine patterns of investment and economic growth. Under heavy attack from the Liberals and New Democrats, the Conservatives made free trade their main issue in the 1988 election and renewed their mandate. Whatever their ultimate assessment of its results, historians will probably regard the negotiation of the Free Trade Agreement as the most important event of Mulroney's first term in office.

A third conservative watchword is **privatization**—the sale of government-owned assets or activities to the private sector. In the United States, where the federal government has not been a major owner of enterprises, at least in comparison with other countries, privatization has mainly taken the form of **contracting out** at the local level for garbage pickup and disposal, fire protection, street paving, and other public services. Advocates of privatization and contracting out believe that local government can be reduced to little more than an office and staff to set tax rates and receive bids from private contractors, who provide the services desired by the taxpayers. The city of La Mirada, California, operates this way. For a population of 41,000 in 1986, it had only 59 employees to negotiate and monitor the performance of 89 contracts.[14] By way of comparison, Lethbridge, Alberta, had 892 full-time employees for a population of 66,000 in 1997. Resistance from public-sector unions, which are stronger in Canada than in the United States, has slowed the advance of local privatization in Canada.

Privatization in the form of the sale of state-owned corporations has become a global trend. The most spectacular steps were taken by the Thatcher government in Great Britain, which organized many sales of companies that had previously been nationalized. One of the most notable was the sale of the entire telephone system through a public share offering. In their first two terms in office (1979–87), the Conservatives in Britain reduced the share of the industrial and trading economy controlled by the state, going from 10 to 5 percent,[15] and since then there have been further sales.

In Canada, the Mulroney government completely or partly privatized sixteen Crown corporations or other major federally controlled assets in the years 1984–89. Some of these were small and virtually invisible to the public, but others were major economic actors, such as de Havilland Aircraft, Canadair, Air Canada, and the hotel division of Canadian National Railways.[16] After that, the pace slowed, although the government did sell 20 percent of Petro-Canada during its second term.

The Mulroney government's handling of privatization exemplifies the paradoxes of Canadian conservatism in power. There was clearly a substantial shift in a conservative direction, in that the federal government decreased its operating role in the economy. Yet a conservative rationale was never clearly articulated for the privatization program. Rather, the former prime minister and other cabinet members made statements of this type: "Our approach to government ownership is pragmatic. It is not our intention to eliminate all government ownership—when it is the best way to serve the public interest we shall certainly use it."[17] Mulroney added to the confusion by asserting categorically in 1985 that Air Canada was not for sale because Canada needed a public airline, and then privatizing it less than three years later. Perhaps as a result of this ideological equivocation, the Conservatives did not get full credit for their privatization efforts—not even from ideological conservatives, who should have welcomed it.

The main social issue for conservatives is the protection of traditional institutions and practices in an era of rapid social change. Conservatives wish to defend the traditional family. This may imply a number of political positions, such as making abortions difficult to obtain, discouraging youthful sexual activity, and preventing value-free sex education in the public schools. Conservatives also want the state to help maintain traditional standards of conduct by inflicting harsher criminal penalties, including capital punishment, and by enforcing stricter discipline in schools. Conservatives are generally against legalization of such drugs as marijuana and cocaine, on the grounds that they promote a life devoted to pleasure rather than to the fulfillment of responsibilities toward others. Similar reasoning accounts for conservatives' opposition to pornography in films and in print. The common denominator in all these positions is a belief that a good society cannot be merely a collection of pleasure-seeking individuals. Social existence demands that human behaviour be restrained by institutions such as the family, the church, the school, and—if all else fails—the state.

Conservatives are particularly outraged by certain activities of the state that they interpret as weakening other institutions. For example, they see government sponsorship of homosexual rights as an attack on family values, and government-mandated bussing of children to achieve racial balance as an attack on neighbourhood schools.

These social aspects of conservatism have been more prominent in the United States than elsewhere, probably because organizations of evangelical and fundamentalist Protestants are an important part of the conservative Republican coalition in that country. In Canada, where evangelical Protestantism is much less of a political factor, the federal parties have all shied away from an American-style agenda of conservative social policy. Even the new Reform Party (founded in 1987), which is clearly the most conservative of Canada's political parties, has sidestepped these issues. Its policy manual promises to submit contentious moral issues such as abortion and capital punishment to national referendums; the party itself has not taken a collective stand on these issues.

Before the collapse of the Soviet Union, another important issue for conservatives was resistance against the expansion of communism and related forms of revolutionary socialism. Conservatives viewed the world in terms of the East–West split, and saw communism as a threat to the social order of the Western world. Ronald Reagan embraced this issue when, early in his first term, he called the Soviet Union an "evil empire." He matched his words with actions, spending large amounts to build American military strength and sending arms and money to opponents of Marxist regimes in Afghanistan, Angola, Ethiopia, and Nicaragua.

America's military buildup and aggressive foreign policy of the early 1980s may well have been instrumental in bringing the Soviet Union to its knees, because the Soviets could not afford to match the expensive American arms buildup. But this victory in the international sphere had ironic consequences for American conservatives. Freed of concern about the threat of international communism, American voters switched their focus to the domestic ills of recession and unemployment. This led to the defeat of the conservative Republican George Bush in the presidential election of 1992.

In one sense, the conservative revival of the 1980s petered out in the 1990s. In Britain, Margaret Thatcher was forced to resign in 1991 when she lost the support of her caucus. Her successor, John Major, won a majority Conservative government in the election that followed, but he was much less ideological than Thatcher. He was then defeated in the 1997 British election. In the United States, George Bush, Ronald Reagan's successor, was defeated when he sought re-election in 1992; and the new Democratic president, Bill Clinton, won a second term in 1996. And in Canada, the Liberal Party, led by Jean Chrétien, was returned to power in the election of 1993 and held on to it in the election of 1997.

But even if conservative parties are now out of power, the ideological effects of conservatism are still being felt. The Liberals in Canada, the Labour Party in Great Britain, and the Democrats in the United States have all been pulled substantially to the right and have had to adopt large parts of the conservative agenda in order to defeat their conservative competitors. Bill Clinton showed the way in 1992; many of the themes that carried him to victory that year resonated well with conservatives: cutting the deficit, better education and job training, investment in infrastructure, replacing welfare with "workfare." Conservatives might argue about the methods or the amount of money to be spent, but they had no fundamental quarrel with the objectives.

In this context, the record of the Chrétien government is particularly striking. Although as an opposition party the Liberals had criticized all the Mulroney government's initiatives, once they were in power they maintained most of them and indeed took some of them further than Mulroney had done. Specifically, the Chrétien government

- adhered to the Tories' tight-money, low-inflation policy,
- left in place the goods and services tax, which is a flat-rate (7 percent) rather than a progressive tax,
- continued free trade with the United States and extended it to Mexico by signing the North American Free Trade Agreement (NAFTA),
- reduced federal spending so much that the deficit is expected to be eliminated by 1999,
- cut 40,000 positions from the federal civil service,
- reduced fiscal transfers to the provinces for health care, welfare, and advanced education,
- reduced the generosity of federally controlled social programs such as pensions and employment insurance,
- privatized Canadian National Railways, and
- extended deregulation in the field of telecommunications.

The Liberals did not govern in every respect as a conservative party would have done. They took a number of liberal initiatives, particularly in areas where not much money was involved, such as stricter gun control and putting sexual orientation into the human rights code. But they were clearly a much different party from the Liberals of the 1960s and 1970s, who had dramatically expanded the Canadian welfare state.

Similarly, the Labour Party was able to win the 1997 election in Britain only by promising to leave untouched the major policy innovations of the Thatcher years. And in the United States, President Clinton has cooperated with the Republican-controlled Congress on measures such as welfare reform and a plan to balance the federal budget.

The real test of an ideology's influence is the extent to which it influences the thinking even of those who do not consider themselves adherents of that ideology. Conservatism, at least in its economic aspects, became a consensus doctrine in the 1990s and now exercises great influence on parties and leaders who call themselves liberal or social democratic. It is an ironic reversal of the pattern that prevailed in the 1960s and 1970s, when parties that called themselves conservatives were heavily influenced in practice by Keynesian economics and reform liberal ideology.

FURTHER READING

Betz, Hans-Georg. *Radical Right-Wing Populism in Western Europe*. New York: St. Martin's Press, 1994.

Cooper, Barry, Allan Kornberg, and William Mishler, eds. *The Resurgence of Conservatism in Anglo-American Democracies*. Durham, N.C.: Duke University Press, 1988.

Devigne, Robert. *Recasting Conservatism: Oakeshott, Strauss, and the Response to Postmodernism.* New Haven, Conn.: Yale University Press, 1994.

Diamond, Sara. *Roads to Dominion: Right-Wing Movements and Political Power in the United States.* New York: Guilford Press, 1995.

Dorrien, Gary. *The Neoconservative Mind.* Philadelphia: Temple University Press, 1993.

Frum, David. *What's Right: The New Conservatism and What It Means for Canada.* Mississauga, Ont.: Random House of Canada, 1997.

———. *Dead Right.* New York: Basic Books, 1994.

Harbour, William R. *The Foundations of Conservative Thought.* Notre Dame, Ind.: University of Notre Dame Press, 1982.

Hogg, Quintin M. (Lord Hailsham). *The Case for Conservatism.* Harmondsworth: Penguin Books, 1947.

Honderich, Ted. *Conservatism.* London: H. Hamilton, 1990.

Kendall, Willmoore. *The Conservative Affirmation.* Chicago: Henry Regnery, 1963.

Kirk, Russell. *The Conservative Mind,* 7th. ed. Chicago: Henry Regnery, 1986.

Kristol, Irving. *Reflections of a Neoconservative.* New York: Basic Books, 1983.

———. *Neoconservatism: The Autobiography of an Idea.* New York: Free Press, 1995.

Lakoff, George. *Moral Politics: What Conservatives Know that Liberals Don't.* Chicago: University of Chicago Press, 1996.

Lora, Ronald. *Conservative Minds in America.* Westport, Conn.: Greenwood Press, 1979. First published in 1971.

O'Sullivan, Noel. *Conservatism.* London: Dent, 1976.

Rossiter, Clinton. *Conservatism in America: The Thankless Persuasion,* rev. ed. New York: Knopf, 1962.

Scruton, Roger. *The Meaning of Conservatism,* 2nd ed. Harmondsworth: Penguin Books, 1984.

SOCIALISM AND COMMUNISM

Like liberalism and conservatism, **socialism** is not a single ideology. We use the term here as a global concept that includes communism, democratic socialism, social democracy, anarchism, syndicalism, and other ideologies bearing a family resemblance to each other. Four of their common traits are particularly important. We state them here in unqualified form, although it will become obvious that the several socialist schools accept them in varying degrees. It should also be mentioned that members of the socialist family have often waged political battles against each other with deadly ferocity. When we point out common ideological elements, it is not to suggest that there ever has been, or is now, a unified world socialist movement.

COMMON ELEMENTS OF SOCIALIST IDEOLOGIES

Planning

Socialists repudiate the profit-motivated market economy, believing that society can emancipate itself from impersonal market processes and take conscious control of its economic affairs by deliberately planning them to maximize human happiness.

Common Ownership

Socialists dislike private ownership of productive property such as land, factories, stores, and the means of transportation and communication. They believe that such assets should be owned by the community, supposing that the benefits will then flow to all, not just to a restricted circle of private owners.

Equality of Result

Socialists aspire to a high degree of equality of result. While recognizing that people cannot be literally equal in all respects, they believe that much can be done to reduce major inequalities of wealth, income, social position, and political power. They see a planned economy and common ownership as important means to this end.

Selflessness

Socialists regard selfishness not as an innate human characteristic but as the product of flawed social institutions. They are convinced that appropriate social change can produce a new "socialist man" who is less self-interested and more concerned about the welfare of the collectivity.[1] This overall change in human behaviour will result from, and at the same time support, the first three objectives.

HISTORICAL OVERVIEW

The biggest source of disagreement among socialists is the political question of how to obtain and maintain the power necessary to effect such changes in society. At one time or another they have resorted to almost every conceivable strategy: rational persuasion, teaching by the example of a working commune, winning democratic elections, a general strike of organized labour, insurrection of armed workers in major cities, and protracted guerrilla warfare in rural areas. We will explore these political approaches as we sketch a history of the socialist family tree (see Figure 13.1).

Common ownership of property is an ancient topic of philosophical speculation. Plato's *Republic* (ca. 380 B.C.) portrayed a **polis** in which the intellectual and military classes shared property and wives, although the ordinary people continued to have private property and families. Thomas More's *Utopia* (1516) went further and extended common property to an entire society, but it was a satire on the England of his day, not a serious proposal for implementation. Other philosophers toyed with socialism from time to time, but it was not viewed as realistic until the nineteenth century.

There is also a long religious history to socialism. The Acts of the Apostles reports that in the first Christian community of Jerusalem, "the whole body of believers was united in heart and soul. Not a man of them claimed any of his possessions as his own, but everything was held in common."[2] Community of goods has repeatedly been reintroduced by Christian sects, particularly those who believe that the second coming of Christ to earth is imminent. The selfishness of private property does not fit well with the Kingdom of the Saints. In Canada today, this

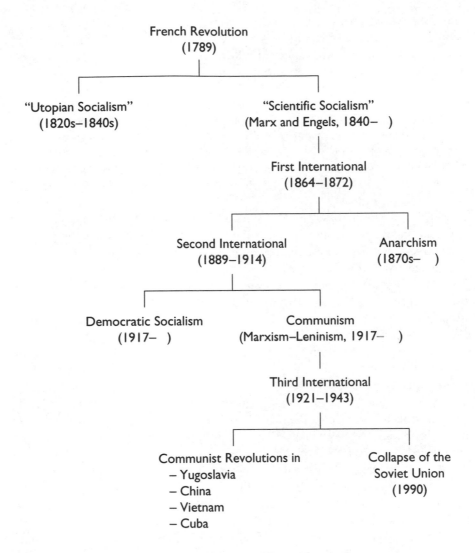

FIGURE 13.1 Socialist Family Tree

French Revolution
(1789)

"Utopian Socialism"
(1820s–1840s)

"Scientific Socialism"
(Marx and Engels, 1840–   )

First International
(1864–1872)

Second International
(1889–1914)

Anarchism
(1870s–   )

Democratic Socialism
(1917–   )

Communism
(Marxism–Leninism, 1917–   )

Third International
(1921–1943)

Communist Revolutions in
 – Yugoslavia
 – China
 – Vietnam
 – Cuba

Collapse of the
Soviet Union
(1990)

kind of Christian socialism is represented by the Hutterites, who collectively own and operate large farms in the western provinces. But our interest is in socialism as a secular, political ideology, not as part of a religious doctrine.

Like so much else in modern politics, secular, political socialism made its debut during the French Revolution. A journalist named François-Noël Babeuf organized an abortive communist uprising in 1796.[3] Its practical significance at the time was nil—the police broke up the plot and Babeuf was sentenced to death. But the events, and particularly the speech Babeuf made at his trial, begin the story that leads to Marx, Lenin, and the socialist revolutions of our time.

Babeuf's plan was for a short, successful insurrection in Paris on the model of several that had been attempted since 1789. Having seized the French state at the centre, he would institute a provisional government to crush the enemies of the people. Private property would be confiscated, and a "Grand National Economy" would replace the market system of allocation with a central storehouse where goods would be deposited, then distributed to all as needed:

> It will be composed of all in complete equality—all rich, all poor, all free, all brothers. The first law will be a ban on private property. We will deposit the fruits of our toil in the public stores. This will be the wealth of the state and the property of all. Every year the heads of families will select stewards whose task will be the distribution of goods to each in accordance with his needs, the allotment of tasks to be performed by each, and the maintenance of public order.[4]

Babeuf did not desire or expect this system to create great wealth. He quoted with approval the words of Rousseau that "all luxury is superfluous—everything is superfluous above and beyond the sheerest of physical necessities."[5] To ensure that luxury did not creep into this Spartan society, money and foreign trade would be banned.

Babeuf's conspiratorial and insurrectionary approach survived his death, but was complemented in the first decades of the nineteenth century by the **utopian socialism** of writers like Robert Owen (1771–1858) and Charles Fourier (1772–1837). They proposed not to seize the state by force but to teach by example— to found small-scale communities in which productive property would be jointly owned, all would share the necessary labour, and living standards would be more or less equalized. Unlike Babeuf, they did not seek to impose a regime of universal poverty; they believed that their communes would allow everyone to enjoy the luxuries previously reserved for the rich. Literally hundreds of these communes, based on various models, have been tried out. Some of these experiments are quite famous, such as New Harmony, in Indiana, which was run by Robert Owen, and Brook Farm, in Massachusetts, which was modelled on the ideas of Fourier.[6] The utopian strategy of showing the world the merits of socialism on a small scale has not been fully successful, but neither has it been without effect. The Israeli kibbutz, for instance, is a lineal descendant of these early experiments.

Karl Marx (1818–83) and Friedrich Engels (1820–95) gave the ideology of socialism its classic formulation. Their greatest innovation was to transform socialism into the doctrine of a single class, the industrial working class, which they renamed the **proletariat**. They labelled their predecessors as utopian for having aimed at the betterment of humanity through appeals to reason. For Marx and Engels, socialism could only be created by the political victory of the working class. The proletariat, as the "universal class," embodied the future hopes of humanity; its political struggle would furnish the "material weapons" needed by socialist philosophy.[7]

Marx's emphasis on the working class gives the impression that for him the central issues were poverty, equality, and living standards; but the discovery of unpublished manuscripts written in his youth has put the matter in a different light. "An enforced increase in wages," wrote Marx in 1843, "would be nothing more than *a better remuneration of slaves*, and would not restore, either to the worker or to the work, their human significance and worth."[8] To Marx, the true issue was what he called alienation. A market system, he argued, reverses the right order of human priorities. Work, which ought to be people's highest activity, the expression of their creative powers, becomes in such a system merely a means for people to keep themselves alive. Instead of valuing human activity for its own sake, they become acquisitive, storing up purchasing power. They lose control over what they produce as their products are bought and sold on the market. Property owners are equally dehumanized, even if they escape the impoverished condition of the proletariat. The social alienation between owners—the **bourgeoisie** in Marx's vocabulary—and workers was only one aspect of the larger alienation of all people from their human essence. Of course, that did not make class differentials less odious, and Marx depicted them with all his rhetorical power:

> Labour certainly produces marvels for the rich but it produces privation for the worker. It produces palaces, but hovels for the worker. It produces beauty, but deformity for the worker. It replaces labour by machinery, but it casts some of the workers back into a barbarous kind of work and turns the others into machines. It produces intelligence, but also stupidity and cretinism for the workers.[9]

Marx offered not only a principled critique of society but also an analysis of the course of history. He wanted to show not just that capitalism ought to be destroyed, but that it would destroy itself through its internal contradictions. Marx and Engels called their doctrine **scientific socialism** because they thought it was not only a morally attractive alternative but also a guide to what was bound to happen. Most of their writings do not in fact deal with socialism; rather, they analyze the capitalist or market system to find the mechanism of its self-destruction. The class-divided market society would, through the victory of the proletariat in the class struggle, give way to a classless society. With the collective ownership of property, there would no longer be a meaningful distinction between proletarians, who live by selling their labour, and bourgeois owners of industry, who become wealthy by employing labour.

Although the subject is much too complex to summarize here, we can indicate the main lines of the capitalist breakdown that Marx foresaw.[10] One salient fact was the polarization of society. Capitalism would create a large working class, who would be the "gravediggers" of the system. The proletariat was doomed to impoverishment—perhaps not in absolute terms, but in comparison with the rapidly increasing affluence of the bourgeoisie. The working class, led by socialist intellectuals such as Marx himself, would eventually seize the state and use it to abolish capitalism. Indeed, when the proletariat came to power, it would find that the system had already virtually abolished itself. The market process would have generated industrial monopolies, as only a few giant firms would have survived the rigours of competition. Without many competitors, the market would not work, even on its own terms. The new proletarian state would simply have to confiscate these monopolies from their bourgeois owners and set them to work under central planning.

Marx thought the rising up of the working class would probably come at the bottom of the business cycle, when unemployment with all its attendant distress was high among the proletariat. He had several reasons for thinking these cycles could not be avoided. From earlier economists, he borrowed speculation about the long-term tendency of the rate of profit to fall and added to it some ideas about overproduction. The full train of reasoning is too technical to pursue here, but his conclusion is relevant: capitalism would destroy itself in a great crash.

Marx held that the ultimate victory of socialism was certain but not automatic; it also required a deliberate political struggle. He proposed (and helped to bring about) the representation of the working class by organized political parties. He saw two means by which the workers' party could come to power: evolution or revolution. In constitutional states with a parliamentary system, the workers might struggle for the universal franchise. Once the vote was achieved for all, socialists could expect to be elected to power, for the proletariat would be a majority of the electorate; in other words, socialism would be a natural outgrowth of democracy. Simultaneously, Marx also proposed a revolutionary seizure of power, particularly where constitutionalism and the rule of law did not exist. In this he was influenced by the insurrectionary tradition that had begun with Babeuf. Such a rising would produce a workers' government, the **dictatorship of the proletariat**. In a situation equivalent to civil war, the proletarian dictatorship would have to ignore the niceties of the rule of law, at least until its power was secure. This dual approach to gaining power was to prove fateful for the subsequent history of socialism. The two approaches, united in Marx, would eventually split into the two mutually antagonistic movements known as socialism and communism.

Because of their emphasis on the collapse of capitalism and the proletarian seizure of power, neither Marx nor Engels wrote much about socialism itself. What one mostly finds are theoretical passages, such as this one:

> With the seizing of the means of production by society, production of commodities is done away with, and, simultaneously, the mastery of the product over the producer. Anarchy in social production is replaced by systematic, definite organisation. The struggle for individual existence disappears. Then for the first time man, in a certain sense, is finally marked off from the rest of the animal kingdom, and emerges from mere animal conditions of existence into really human ones. The whole sphere of the conditions of life which environ man, and which have hitherto ruled man, now comes under the dominion and control of man, who for the first time becomes the real, conscious lord of Nature, because he has now become master of his own social organisation. The laws of his own social action, hitherto standing face to face with man as laws of

Nature foreign to, and dominating him, will then be used with full understanding, and so mastered by him. Man's own social organisation, hitherto confronting him as a necessity imposed by Nature and history, now becomes the result of his own free action. The extraneous objective forces that have hitherto governed history pass under the control of man himself. Only from that time will man himself, more and more consciously, make his own history—only from that time will the social causes set in movement by him have, in the main and in a constantly growing measure, the results intended by him. It is the ascent of man from the kingdom of necessity to the kingdom of freedom.[11]

However, some scattered passages from Marx and Engels give a rough idea of what they expected to happen after the workers came to power. There would have to be a transitional period during which the state would gain control of property and put itself in a position to plan the whole economy. It is striking to read the list of transitional measures given in the *Communist Manifesto* (1848), in that several of them have been implemented by liberal and even conservative governments. The ones marked with an asterisk are at least partly implemented today in most Western democracies:

1. Abolition of property in land and application of all rents of land to public purposes.
2. A heavy progressive or graduated income tax.*
3. Abolition of all right of inheritance.
4. Confiscation of the property of all emigrants and rebels.
5. Centralization of credit in the hands of the State, by means of a national bank with State capital and an exclusive monopoly.*
6. Centralization of the means of communication and transport in the hands of the State.*
7. Extension of factories and instruments of production owned by the State; the bringing into cultivation of wastelands, and the improvement of the soil generally in accordance with a common plan.*
8. Equal liability to all to labour. Establishment of industrial armies, especially for agriculture.
9. Combination of agriculture with manufacturing industries; gradual abolition of the distinction between town and country, by a more equable distribution of the population over the country.
10. Free education for all children in public schools. Abolition of children's factory labour in its present form. Combination of education with industrial production.*[12]

Accomplishing these and other measures would supposedly make the state master of the economy, able to conduct central planning. But full equality of result would take a long time to achieve. There would have to be an interim period during which equality meant, in effect, "equal pay for equal work." All workers would be employed by the state, and ownership of property would no longer allow the wealthy to escape labour; but some would work more effectively and diligently than others, and they would be rewarded for doing so.

Beyond this stage, Marx's thoughts on the future become visionary. The state, even though it would have to be large and powerful in order to conduct central planning, would lose its coercive character. This makes sense if we accept the premise that human quarrels are fundamentally caused by private property; a class-less society would therefore not need a state to maintain civil peace. It was also Marx's view that the state was always the tool that one class used to dominate others, so by definition a classless society would be a stateless society. As Engels put it in a biological metaphor, the state would "wither away." Marx preferred to say that the state would be "transcended"—that people would learn to conduct their affairs without a centralized apparatus of coercion.

The transcendence of the state was linked to what Marx called the "higher phase of communist society," where "equal work for equal pay" would give way to a nobler form of equality:

> In a higher phase of communist society, after the enslaving subordination of the individual to the division of labour, and therewith also the antithesis between mental and physical labor, has vanished; after labor has become not only a means of life but life's prime want; after the productive forces have also increased with the all-round development of the individual, and all the springs of cooperative wealth flow more abundantly—only then can the narrow horizon of bourgeois right be crossed in its entirety and society inscribe on its banners: "From each according to his ability, to each according to his needs."[13]

At this advanced stage of development, the alienation of labour would finally be transcended. Work would become a freely creative activity performed for its own sake, not to be bought and sold. People would express themselves in all directions, utilizing their repertoire of human powers; there would be no economic necessity in the "kingdom of freedom" that forced them to be narrow specialists. In an almost lyrical passage, Marx and Engels wrote:

> For as soon as the distribution of labour comes into being, each man has a par-ticular, exclusive sphere of activity, which is forced upon him and from which he cannot escape. He is a hunter, a fisherman, a shepherd, or a critical critic, and must remain so if he does not want to lose his means of livelihood; while in communist society, where nobody has one exclusive sphere of activity but each can become accomplished in any branch he wishes, society regulates the general production and thus makes it possible for me to do one thing today and another tomorrow, to hunt in the morning, fish in the afternoon, rear cattle in

the evening, criticize after dinner, just as I have a mind, without ever becoming hunter, fisherman, shepherd or critic.[14]

In addition to being theorists, Marx and Engels were also political activists who contributed to the political struggle of the working class. Their first organization, the Communist League, is remembered chiefly because Marx and Engels wrote the *Communist Manifesto* to be its program. More important was the International Workingmen's Association (1864–72), commonly known as the **First International**, in which Marx and Engels were deeply involved. A loose association of socialist parties and labour unions in Western Europe, with headquarters in London, it split into hostile wings in 1872 when old factional differences became too strong to contain. The split was partly a clash of personalities between Marx and the Russian Mikhail Bakunin, but there was also an important ideological issue. Bakunin and his followers, who subsequently became known as **anarchists**, thought that Marx was infatuated with the state. They believed that the state could be destroyed fairly quickly in the aftermath of the workers' revolution, whereas Marx envisioned a period of state socialism leading up to the true classless society and the higher phase of communism. The anarchists feared, with considerable foresight, that the Marxian socialist state might turn out to be permanent rather than temporary.[15]

Although the First International collapsed, socialist parties continued to exist in various European states. They were reunited, excluding the anarchists, in the **Second International**, which was founded in Paris in 1889 to celebrate the centennial of the French Revolution.[16] Marx had died in 1883; it was Engels who became the elder statesman of the new organization, and Marxism that became its ideology. With the Second International, socialism came of age in Europe. Socialist and labour parties thrived by following Marx's evolutionary strategy. None ever won a majority in an election, but all succeeded in electing substantial blocs of representatives wherever liberal and constitutional values kept politics open. Some socialist politicians even served as ministers in coalition governments. The Second International expressed itself in revolutionary rhetoric, but its political practices were overwhelmingly evolutionary and constitutional.[17]

The Russian Empire, however, was ruled autocratically by the Czar; the absence of a parliament and constitution there made the evolutionary strategy inapplicable. The Russian Social Democratic Party was forced to work illegally, secretly, and conspiratorially. Vladimir Ilyich Lenin (1870–1924), leader of the wing of the party known as the Bolsheviks, was led by these conditions, so different from those in Western Europe, to create a new style and a new theory of party leadership. Marx had expected the revolution to grow from the spontaneous class consciousness of the workers; the role of bourgeois intellectuals was not to create this revolutionary state of mind but to lend it theoretical precision. Lenin, faced with a backward country and a small working class, tended to think of revolutionary consciousness as something transmitted by bourgeois intellectuals to the workers. This seemingly minor difference implied a new approach to the problems of party organization. The party had to be firmly controlled from the top because the leadership could not rely on the workers' spontaneity. Lenin's theory of the disciplined party—**democratic centralism**—moulded the party into an effective revolutionary weapon that was especially suited to survival in the autocratic Russian setting.[18]

Lenin, incidentally, is associated with another major innovation in socialist ideology. Marx had always insisted that the socialist revolution would be a world revolution. His view of the world was centred on Western Europe, and he apparently thought that the European nations would drag their empires with them into socialism. Because he emphasized Europe, Marx thought that the revolution would occur soon because capitalism, which was fated to put an end to itself, was well advanced on that continent. Marx certainly expected a proletarian victory in his own lifetime. But when World War I broke out, he had been dead for thirty years and the socialists still had not come to power anywhere.

Lenin spent most of the war in exile in Switzerland and used this period of enforced leisure to write a pamphlet explaining the delay. *Imperialism: The Highest Stage of Capitalism* (1917) argued that the advanced nations had managed to postpone the revolution by amassing colonial empires. Overseas investments counteracted the falling tendency of the rate of profit, while colonial markets temporarily solved the problem of overproduction. Merciless exploitation of the colonies could buy off the proletariat at home, creating a "labour aristocracy" of well-paid workers at the centre of the empire. But the imperialist solution could only be temporary because the world was finite and now totally subdivided. World War I showed that the imperialists had begun to quarrel with each other. The socialist revolution would arise not from a business crash, as Marx had been inclined to believe, but out of the turmoil of war. Lenin thus decisively broadened the scope of socialism from a European to a global movement, and in doing so bolstered his own revolutionary optimism. "Capitalism," he wrote, "has grown into a world system of colonial oppression and of the financial strangulation of the overwhelming population of the world by a handful of 'advanced' countries."[19]

World War I sounded the death knell for the Second International. Although socialists had prided themselves on their internationalism, national loyalties prevailed in wartime. Most of the workers in the combatant states supported the war effort, effectively pitting the International against itself.

The successful socialist revolution in Russia delivered the *coup de grâce* to the International. In February 1917, the Czar was toppled and a constitutional democracy created. In October of the same year, the Bolsheviks, led by Lenin, seized control of the state through insurrections of armed workers in St. Petersburg and Moscow. The Bolsheviks then created a dictatorship of the proletariat in which their party played the dominant role. They outlawed political opposition—even socialist opposition. These events were an agonizing test for the socialists of Western Europe, who had yearned for a revolution for generations. Now they were witnessing a successful one, and they were appalled by its undemocratic aspects.

The eventual result of the Russian Revolution was an irreparable split in the world socialist movement. Those who approved of Lenin and his methods formed **communist** parties in every country and gathered themselves in the **Third International**, or **Comintern** (short for "Communist International"). The official ideology of these parties was now Marxism as modified by Lenin, or Marxism–Leninism. In practice, the Comintern soon became an extension of the Soviet state for foreign-policy purposes. It was dissolved in 1943 by Stalin as a gesture of cooperation with the Allies during World War II. The individual communist parties continued to be closely tied to Moscow, but the organizational emphasis shifted to the Soviet satellite states. In 1947 these were bound together into the **Cominform** (Communist Information Bureau), which in 1956 was in turn replaced by the Warsaw Treaty Organization. The latter was dissolved in 1991 as part of the general decommunization of Eastern Europe. Today, the term *communist* is rarely encountered. The organizations that used to call themselves communist parties still exist, but they have adopted new names emphasizing concepts such as labour or democracy. For example, the Communist Party of Italy has renamed itself the Party of the Democratic Left.

Those who opposed Lenin regrouped under the general name of **social democrats**, often merging with Christian and other moderate socialists who had been outside the Marxist consensus of the Second International. These social-democratic parties still exist as the Labour Party of Great Britain, the Social Democratic Party of Germany, and so on. They have kept to the course of constitutionalism and are well integrated with their respective political systems. They form governments when they win elections and resign from office when they lose.

Socialism, in the form of social democracy, is a familiar part of contemporary politics. Its ideology has over decades become considerably diluted, relative to the Marxist thought from which it sprang, so that social democrats today are hard to distinguish from reform liberals. Both espouse, to a limited degree, the typical socialist goals of central planning, common ownership, and equality of result. Social democrats call for government to guide the economy by pulling the levers of spending, taxation, and regulation; they do not wish to replace the market by comprehensive planning. They wish some major enterprises to be publicly owned—that is, they call for a **mixed economy**—but they do not advocate wholesale nationalization of all business. They approve of redistribution of income in the direction of social justice, but not of thoroughgoing, egalitarian levelling.

Several small socialist parties existed in Canada before the great split between communists and social democrats, but none was ever very significant. The first important party of the social-democratic type was the Co-operative Commonwealth Federation (CCF), founded in Calgary in 1932. It drew together remnants of the old socialist parties, trade unionists, farmer activists, and certain intellectuals who had been educated in Britain or influenced by British socialist thought. The party's first platform was the Regina Manifesto, adopted in 1933. It repudiated "change by violence" and promised to promote the socialist cause "solely by constitutional methods." Although the means would be peaceful, the end was declared to be far-reaching:

> We aim to replace the present capitalist system, with its inherent injustice and inhumanity, by a social order from which the domination and exploitation of one class by another will be eliminated, in which economic planning will supersede unregulated private enterprise and competition, and in which genuine democratic self-government, based upon economic equality, will be possible ... We aim at a planned and socialized economy in which our natural resources and the principal means of production and distribution are owned, controlled and operated by the people.[20]

The CCF achieved some political successes, most notably the election of the first socialist government in North America in Saskatchewan in 1944, but its electoral support eroded badly during the 1950s. In 1961 it restructured itself as the New Democratic Party and greatly strengthened its ties to organized labour. Tellingly, the word *socialism* did not appear in the New Party Declaration it adopted.[21] As in other countries, social democracy in Canada had relaxed its ideology considerably since the Depression. It now presented itself not as a full alternative to the market system, but rather as a means of using the state as a reforming agency.

Ed Broadbent expressed the rapprochement of social democracy with the market when he announced his resignation as federal leader of the NDP in 1989:

> The serious debate about the future is not about the desirability of a market economy. For most thoughtful people that debate is now closed ... We New Democrats believe in the marketplace including private investment decisions, reduced tariffs, private property, the free disposal of assets, the right to make a profit, decentralized decision making ... As the world evolves so must our policies.[22]

From this perspective, social democracy, like reform liberalism, consists of government efforts to "correct" the market—to change some of its results rather than to replace it outright.

In certain ways, socialism has turned out almost the opposite of the expectations of Marx, who saw it as the successor to capitalism. He had a grudging admiration for the market system as a means of accumulating wealth but regarded it as a temporary phase of human development. Socialism, he thought, would be able to make much more humane use of the productive powers unleashed by capitalism. But in fact, socialism has been least successful in precisely those countries that have been most capitalistic and, by Marx's reasoning, most ready for socialism. In the industrialized countries, socialism has been most effective in a diluted form—that is, as social democracy; in such cases it represents a reformist impulse within the system, not a polar alternative. The stronger form of communism came to dominance in the economically backward Russian Empire, and the Soviet Union imposed it by force on the nations of Eastern Europe. Authentic communist revolutions (i.e., that were not the result of Soviet initiatives) have also taken place in Yugoslavia, China, and Vietnam. The latter two revolutions were almost the opposite of what Marx would have anticipated: they happened in preindustrial societies in which capitalism had hardly gotten under way.

Very generally, we can see that socialism has become not the successor to liberalism but an alternative to it as a modernizing force. Socialism found its greatest success in societies that had begun but not yet completed the transition from traditional to legal authority. Much of the Third World claimed at one time to be socialist. One source of socialism's popularity in the Third World is that, because it is anticapitalist, it can become an ideological weapon against the Western powers. Also, great disparities of wealth typical of many traditional societies seem to cry out for state-initiated redistribution. Common ownership and central planning have great appeal in those societies where large portions of arable land are held by a few owners and where great disparities of wealth exist between the land-owning elite and the masses who work that land. Most profoundly, there is a certain congruence between socialist collectivism and the communal institutions that still exist in much of the Third World. This was clearly formulated by Julius Nyerere, former president of Tanzania and a leading theorist of Third World socialism. Nyerere translated the word *socialism* into Swahili as *ujamaa*, which literally means "familyhood." He claimed that in Tanzania, where society is still largely tribal, a socialist state could grow organically out of the family and tribe:

> Traditional Tanzanian society had many socialist characteristics. The people did not call themselves socialists, and they were not socialists by deliberate design. But all people were workers, there was no living off the sweat of others. There was no very great difference in the amount of goods available to the different members of the society ... traditional African society was in practice organized on a basis which was in accordance with socialist principles.[23]

We now move on to a more conceptual analysis of socialism as an ideology.

᠊᠊᠊᠊᠊᠊᠊

PLANNING

In varying degrees, socialists are generally hostile to the market, condemning it as anarchic, inefficient, and inequitable. Even contemporary social democrats, who have accepted the market in principle, think it needs a good deal of correction in practice. Socialists particularly condemn the pursuit of profit; in the words of the Regina Manifesto, the principle of a socialist society "will be the supplying of human needs and not the making of profits."[24] Unfortunately, this formulation obscures the problem. Profit in the market system is not antithetical to need; it is rather the means by which needs are met. That people need food, clothing, shelter, and recreation and are willing to pay for them induces entrepreneurs to seek a profit by offering these goods for sale. The central issue is not need versus profit, but the most effective means of discovering and satisfying human needs. Is it the market system with competition, floating prices, and the profit motive, or is it a **planning** system, in which a central authority decides what to produce and allocates products to consumers?

The market, while hardly a perfect system, demonstrably performs a job of matching production and consumption across a large number of commodities. Early socialists were quite naive about how difficult this task is. Babeuf's central storehouses could scarcely have coped with the problem, but he probably would not have cared because he wanted all to live in Spartan simplicity. Marx simply ignored the problem by refusing to speculate on the practical consequences of a socialist society. Through the pain of much trial and error, the Soviet Union and other socialist states worked out a state planning machinery that was actually a hybrid of the planning principle and the market principle. The State Planning Committee, as it was called in the Soviet Union, developed and continually updated a national plan that specified tonnes of coal and steel of various grades, kilowatt hours of electricity, litres of oil, tonnes of wheat, and other production quantities to be produced by the various industries. One industry supplied another as part of this plan rather than by market auction. But markets connected the industrial complex to the inhabitants of the country, who purchased the output at retail stores owned by the state and sold their labour to the state as employer. By this partial use of markets, the state refrained from trying to directly control the daily affairs of hundreds of millions of people.

These markets, however, were heavily controlled by the state. The labour market was restricted by lack of mobility; for example, a worker on a collective farm was not allowed to leave that farm to seek work in the city. Also, prices in markets for both labour and consumer goods did not float according to supply and demand but were administered by the state. As might be expected, this led to shortages and surpluses of commodities. When price is not used to ration scarce commodities, other forms of rationing must intervene. One is direct assignment by authority, as was used to distribute housing. Another is queuing: the ability to spend time waiting replaced the ability to spend money as a means of acquiring goods. Still another form of rationing was evasion of the law. Those with more money than time frequently resorted to bribery and black marketeering. Indeed, existence in Eastern Europe would scarcely have been possible without the black market, because many goods and services needed in daily life were not available at any price in the state stores.

Returning to a Market Economy

Although it produced a low standard of living in comparison with the Western market economy, the communist-planned economy did work after its own fashion and, in the Soviet Union, brought many people a considerable improvement in living standards relative to czarist days. Jobs were guaranteed for all, inflation was repressed, and food, clothing, shelter, and other basic commodities were available at low prices. Education was universal and in some ways of excellent quality; low-tech medical care was generally accessible; and retired people could count on modest state pensions. Taxes were low because the state derived most of its revenue from its ownership of the economy. Daily life was often uncomfortable, inconvenient, and monotonous, but at least it was predictable. Now that marketization is under way in Eastern Europe, people are often nostalgic about the planned economy, for it is proving more difficult than anyone had anticipated to make the transition to a market economy.

Analytically, it is easy to specify the main changes that have to take place:

- decontrol or "liberalization" of prices, so that they arise in a competitive market rather than being set by administrative command;
- privatization of the means of production, so that the elements of the economy come under private ownership and control;
- disinvestment in inefficient enterprises that existed for political or military reasons;
- opening of the economy to foreign trade and investment, so that modern techniques of production can be adopted; and
- attainment of a stable currency that is "convertible," that is, freely exchangeable against Western currencies.

Of all the countries undergoing decommunization, Czechoslovakia had the quickest success in attaining these objectives. Under the leadership of Václav Klaus, an economist educated at Western universities, prices were liberalized while the money supply was strictly controlled, thus avoiding the hyperinflation that has ravaged much of Eastern Europe.[25] Small enterprises such as restaurants and shops were sold at auction to private buyers, who were often the workers and managers under the previous regime; larger enterprises were privatized through a scheme of vouchers issued to the whole adult population. Foreign investment was wholeheartedly encouraged. Volkswagen bought into the Skoda automobile company; and Bata Shoes, founded in Prague though now headquartered in Toronto, got back its Czech stores and factories with a promise of new investment. Helping this whole process was a unique tourism boom caused by the fact that the baroque architecture of Prague survived World War II virtually undamaged. Today the city is a living museum that attracts tens of millions of tourists annually from Western Europe, all of them spending hard currency.

On the whole, this is a remarkable success story, but even so, there has been a high price to pay. The eastern part of the country was unhappy about this headlong rush into a market economy, mainly because it was home to much of Czechoslovakia's heavy industry (particularly munitions), which the country's leaders, who said it was no longer profitable, planned to phase out. As a result, the country peacefully divided itself at the end of 1992 into two new republics, Slovakia and the Czech Republic. Economic rationalization, even when successful in its own terms, can have great social and political costs.

Elsewhere in Eastern Europe, the picture is very mixed. East Germany was absorbed by West Germany and will enter the market economy by that route; but even there the cost is higher than anyone would have predicted and is making a mockery of German Chancellor Helmut Kohl's prediction that reunification could be accomplished without raising taxes. Hungary and Poland are making measurable progress. In Albania, Bulgaria, Romania, and most of what used to be the Soviet Union, the transition is turning out to be immensely slow and difficult. Few farms, factories, and stores have been transferred to private hands, and there has been limited foreign investment apart from a few well-publicized ventures such as McDonald's and Pizza Hut in Moscow. Price liberalization was accompanied by inflation that wiped out the value of salaries and pensions and created great hardship for many ordinary people; at the same time, a new and unloved class of speculators, profiteers, and extortionists has emerged. Many of these people are former party bosses suddenly doing what the Russians call *biznes*. Industrial productivity has slumped badly because central planning has not yet been replaced by an effective price and payment system to coordinate production efforts. In short, to use Hayek's distinction, the end of the centrally planned and organized economy has resulted in chaos rather than in the spontaneous order of a functioning market economy.

The former East Germany, the Czech Republic, Hungary, Poland, and Slovenia will surely make the transition to capitalism one way or the other and integrate themselves with the economy of Western Europe; the future is more uncertain for the other newly independent states. Most are still ruled by former communists (under different party labels) whose democratic convictions are sometimes suspect. All that is certain for now is that the region will experience years of economic hardship, compounded by political conflicts between ethnic groups.

In the People's Republic of China, the situation is rather different. The Communist Party still exercises firm political control but has largely privatized agriculture, which the overwhelming majority of China's people are still engaged in. Moreover, it has allowed massive foreign investment in enterprise zones in the provinces bordering on Hong Kong. By some estimates, the economy of China is now more than half capitalist, even though the regime is still nominally communist.[26] At the present time, the Chinese economy is undergoing rapid growth.

It may be that China is undergoing a revolution in substance, as opposed to form, and will follow the same path as South Korea and Taiwan, where authoritarian governments backed by overwhelming military force presided over a prolonged period of rapid growth in a capitalist economy. If that is the case, it must be considered encouraging, for both South Korea and Taiwan made some progress toward political democracy in the 1980s and 1990s. If the same happens some day in China, it will amount to the reverse of what took place in the Soviet Union. There, political democracy came before economic liberalization, and the result was virtual economic collapse. If China follows the path of South Korea and Taiwan, economic liberalization and rapid growth may pave the way for a degree of democratization. But all countries are unique and there is no way to be certain about China's future. As of 1997, the Communist Party was still firmly in control and there were no signs of political liberalization.

Social democrats in the Western world made a retreat from full-scale central planning much earlier than the Chinese and Russians. *Social Planning for Canada*, written in 1935 by the leading intellectuals in the CCF, called for a national planning commission modelled on the Soviet example.[27] Today, neither the NDP nor other social democratic parties advocate full-scale planning. Instead, they see the state as a means for guiding the market toward particular objectives such as full employment, location of industry in depressed areas, and advancement of disadvantaged minorities. To achieve these goals, the state may employ taxation, subsidies, monopoly concessions, regulatory legislation, price controls, adjustments in interest rates, and other interventionist tools. A program of such interventions is sometimes called a plan, but it is not planning in the original sense of the term.

COMMON OWNERSHIP

Except in times of war or other emergency, central planning cannot work without a high degree of common ownership. Presumably, the central plan will require investment decisions other than those that private owners would spontaneously make; otherwise there would be no need for the plan. To avoid creating a whole new class of potential criminals, productive property has to be publicly owned to remove any conflicts between the plan and property rights.

Common ownership can be achieved in a number of ways. In the Third World, it can be appended to existing communal traditions. If a peasant village already holds grazing, timber, or water rights in common, collective ownership of the surrounding arable land may not be a drastic step. Another approach to common ownership is the voluntary cooperative, which can be utilized to organize either producers or consumers. A great many cooperatives—credit unions, wheat pools, housing co-ops—already exist in Canada, where they function as part of the market economy; but they could also become part of a socialist economy. Another possibility is for the workers to own their own factory or other workplace. A variant of socialism known as **syndicalism** (from the French *syndicat*, "association") takes this approach. No one has ever tried a fully syndicalist economy, but there were elements of syndicalism in the Yugoslavian version of socialism, in which workers' councils had some say in the running of enterprises.

These options are interesting and important, but in the mainstream of socialism, common ownership has meant state ownership. Socialization or nationalization of property means a takeover by the state, which then owns and administers the property as the agent of the people. This ownership can be direct (as in the case of the Canadian armed forces, which are operated as a government department under ministerial supervision) or indirect (as in the case of Canada Post and the Canadian Broadcasting Corporation, which are Crown corporations owned by the state but operating more or less autonomously under their own boards of directors).

The Soviet Union exemplified state ownership carried out consistently. The state owned all factories, railways, and other means of production, as well as all schools, hospitals, and retail stores. It also owned all natural resources and all land, which it leased to entities such as collective farms and housing cooperatives. Private ownership was almost entirely confined to consumer goods. The other communist states of Eastern Europe did not go this far; for example, in Poland there was always an independent peasantry, as most farmland was never nationalized. But the general principle of state ownership was, until 1989, dominant in Eastern Europe. The same was true for China, Vietnam, North Korea, and Cuba. However, in China and Vietnam the introduction of market-inspired reforms has led to private ownership of small enterprises such as restaurants, boutiques, and personal-service businesses in those countries.

Social democracy retreated long ago from its commitment to complete nationalization. The Regina Manifesto exempted farms from public ownership but called for nationalization of the entire financial industry, as well as the transportation, communications, and electric-power sectors, "and all other industries and services essential to social planning."[28] These latter would have included many firms in the resource sector. The logic of the list was that these industries represented "the commanding heights of the economy."[29] All other businesses—manufacturing, wholesaling, retailing, personal services, and so on—need access to credit, transportation, communications, energy, and natural resources. If the government owned and controlled these indispensable industries, it would be able to compel or induce other industries to work toward politically chosen goals. Manufacturing firms, for example, could be persuaded to locate in depressed areas by offers of low-interest loans or cheap transportation.

᭼᭼᭼᭼᭼᭼᭼᭼

EQUALITY OF RESULT

One of the attractive goals of socialism has been to reduce the material inequalities that are part of a market economy. These inequalities are unseemly to socialists (as well as to many others), who have sought to overcome them through a planned economy and public ownership of property. However, while it is easy to call for equality of result, it is much harder to state precisely what it means. We differ so much in our aptitudes, needs, and desires that it would be absurd to say we should all have the same number of shoes or square metres of housing.

One approach is equality of opportunity: using the state to ensure that everyone can have certain chances in life, but allowing individuals to keep the rewards of their own efforts. This social democratic idea, now widely accepted by reform liberals, fits in well with the contemporary welfare state, which is supposed to educate us as children and protect us against contingencies as adults. Its safety net allows us to bounce back from sickness, accidents, and unemployment but does not in itself guarantee a very desirable standard of living. We have to achieve that on our own initiative.

A related approach to equality is to reduce the range of inequality by raising the floor and lowering the ceiling, so that extremes of wealth and poverty vanish but some variation remains. This partial egalitarianism is widely accepted today, not just by socialists but by reform liberals and many others who have no definable ideology. It can be attempted in the market system through progressive taxation, redistribution, and the abundant services of the welfare state. Or, as in the Soviet style of planned economy, it can be approached by setting wages and salaries on an egalitarian basis.

By some statistical indices the communist states appeared to equalize living standards remarkably. Published data on incomes showed smaller differentials between manual workers and professionals than in the West, and of course large pools of capital no longer existed in private hands. Statistics, however, do not tell the whole story because the communist systems instituted significant forms of non-monetary privilege. For example, high officials of the Communist Party, as well as leading scientists, athletes, managers, and artists, had access to special housing, shopping, and medical care; could often avoid waiting lists for things such as automobiles; and had the privilege of foreign travel.[30]

The most provocative analysis of this inequality came from the Yugoslav communist Milovan Djilas. Once a high official in party and state, he became disillusioned with communism and turned to social democracy, arguing that communism as practised in Eastern Europe was the very opposite of a classless society.[31] The essence of his view was that a "new class" of party officials and managers had created a privileged position for itself, based not on ownership of property but on domination of the state.

The ultimate in equality is still as stated in this Marxian slogan: "From each according to his ability, to each according to his needs." This noble sentiment expresses the operating principle of a happy family, one in which parents assess the needs and abilities of their children—but can an entire society of adults operate like a single family? If we let people assess their own needs and set their own contributions, is it not likely that they will estimate the former on the high side, and reduce the latter below what is reasonable? It seems hard to avoid the requirement for a central authority to decide such things (as, indeed, parents are almost all-powerful in relation to their children). This casts serious doubt on the premise that the state will wither away, which is what is supposed to occur in the highest stage of communism. Who except those who run the state could adjudicate the disputes about abilities and needs that would arise under Marx's famous slogan?

𝕾𝕾𝕾𝕾𝕾𝕾𝕾

SELFLESSNESS

The discussion in the preceding paragraph assumes that human behaviour will remain self-interested. The situation would be different if selfishness arose only from the effects of a market economy, which encourages people to put their own interests first. Socialists have often assumed that conflict is typical of capitalism and that cooperation would be typical of a socialist system. However, to contrast cooperation with conflict is a little misleading. Spontaneous order depends on cooperation voluntarily achieved through mutual pursuit of self-interest, as in Adam Smith's metaphor of the invisible hand. A planned economy calls for cooperation directed from above. The important question is not whether we shall have cooperation, for obviously we must; it is whether mutual coordination is a more effective means of achieving it than authoritative direction.[32]

In contrast to socialism, both liberalism and conservatism accept human beings as they are, with all their flaws, and seek to understand the social order that inevitably follows. They assume that society is and will always be composed of individuals and groups in conflict with one another. They hope to contain that conflict within a peaceful framework, not abolish it altogether. Socialists in the twentieth century, to the extent that they have reduced some of their earlier and more visionary expectations about planning, public ownership, and equality, have also become pessimistic about an easy, quick change in human nature.

𝕾𝕾𝕾𝕾𝕾𝕾𝕾

GOVERNING

We have discussed at some length the differences between communists and social democrats in their approach to obtaining power. The distinction between constitutional and unconstitutional methods is also reflected in the way socialist states are governed. Social democrats in their rapprochement with liberalism have adopted the constitutional philosophy of the limited state and the rule of law. Communists, in contrast, used constitutionalism as a means of achieving power but did not demonstrate any abiding attachment to it; indeed, the Leninist principle of democratic centralism, when made the working theory of the state, seems incompatible with liberal constitutionalism.

Communist states were more than mere absolute or unlimited governments, of which the world has seen many, because central planning and state ownership of the means of production put the entire economy at the disposal of the government. This produced such an unparalleled concentration of power that observers had to invent a new term, *totalitarianism*, to describe the resulting system (see Chapter 19). This expansion of the state posed thorny problems for the ideologists of Marxism–Leninism. Marx's dictatorship of the proletariat was, to be sure, an absolute, unlimited government; but it was clearly meant to be a transitional device, even if Marx did not say how long it would last. Marx, a classically educated man, borrowed the term *dictatorship* from the Romans; a **dictator** in Roman law was an individual appointed for six months at a time to guide the state through emergencies. Marx's dictatorship of the proletariat was supposed to preside over the dissolution of social classes, thereby rendering itself unnecessary; a permanent dictatorship of the proletariat would have been a contradiction in terms.[33]

Soviet thinkers maintained that the Soviet state was "a state of the whole people." In the words of Nikita Khrushchev to the Twenty-second Congress of the Communist Party of the Soviet Union (1961):

> With the victory of socialism and the country's entry into the period of full-scale communist construction, the working class of the Soviet Union has on its own initiative, consistent with the tasks of communist construction, transformed the state of proletarian dictatorship into a state of the whole people. That, comrades, is a fact unparalleled in history! Until now the state has always been an instrument of dictatorship by this or that class. In our country, for the first time in history, a state has taken shape which is not a dictatorship of any one class, but an instrument of society as a whole, of the entire people.[34]

This solved one problem but created others, in that it contradicted Marx's view that all states are means by which one class rules over others and undercut his idea of a state that could be unlimited because it was temporary and transitional.

᭄᭄᭄᭄᭄᭄᭄

CONCLUSION

As was true of liberalism, the general family of socialism gave rise to a number of different movements, the two most important being communism and social democracy. The definitive split between these two branches of socialism in the 1920s led to very real differences in ideology, of which the five listed below are particularly significant.

Social Democrats
1. See socialism as an evolutionary process.
2. Achieve power through constitutional means; accept the limited state and the rule of law.
3. Advocate a mixed economy.
4. Accept a pluralistic society of self-interested individuals and groups.
5. Advocate the competition of political parties.

Communists
1. See socialism as a revolutionary process.
2. Achieve power unconstitutionally; reject the limited state and the rule of law as a bourgeois mystification.
3. Advocate a state-owned and -directed economy.
4. Envision a future harmonious society of selfless individuals.
5. Advocate a one-party state.

These fundamental differences mean that social democracy and communism amount to separate ideologies in the contemporary world, even though they have grown from common roots.

FURTHER READING

Avakumovic, Ivan. *Socialism in Canada.* Toronto: McClelland and Stewart, 1978.

Beilharz, Peter. *Labour's Utopias: Bolshevism, Fabianism, Social Democracy.* London: Routledge, 1992.

Blackburn, Robin. *After the Fall: The Failure of Communism and the Future of Socialism.* London: Verso, 1991.

Cohen, Arthur A. *The Communism of Mao Tse-tung.* Chicago: University of Chicago Press, 1964.

Cole, G.D.H. *A History of Socialist Thought,* 5 vols. London: Macmillan, 1953–1960.

Crowder, George. *Classical Anarchism.* Oxford: Clarendon Press, 1991.

Draper, Hal. *Socialism from Below.* Atlantic Highlands, N.J.: Humanities Press, 1992.

Gidden, Anthony. *A Contemporary Critique of Historical Materialism,* 2nd ed. Basingstoke, England: Macmillan, 1995.

Gwertzman, Bernard. *The Collapse of Communism.* New York: Times Books, 1992.

Hunt, R.N. Carew. *The Theory and Practice of Communism.* Harmondsworth: Penguin Books, 1963. First published in 1950.

Joll, James. *The Anarchists*, 2nd ed. London: Eyre and Spottiswoode, 1979.

Kitschelt, Herbert. *The Transformation of European Social Democracy*. Cambridge: Cambridge University Press, 1994.

Le Blanc, Paul. *From Marx to Gramsci: A Reader in Revolutionary Marxist Politics: Historical Overview and Selection*. Atlantic Highlands, N.J.: Humanities Press, 1996.

Lichtheim, George. *A Short History of Socialism*. New York: Praeger, 1970.

McLellan, David. *Karl Marx: His Life and Thought*. London: Macmillan, 1973.

Meyer, Alfred G. *Leninism*. New York: Praeger, 1962. First published in 1957.

_____. *Marxism: The Unity of Theory and Practice*. Ann Arbor: University of Michigan Press, 1963. First published in 1954.

Ralston, Richard E. *Communism, Its Rise and Fall in the 20th Century*. Boston, Mass.: Christian Science Publishing Society, 1991.

Roberts, Joseph. *Socialism in Crisis: Canadian Perspectives*. Winnipeg: Society for Socialist Studies, 1992.

Steger, Manfred B. *The Quest for Evolutionary Socialism: Eduard Bernstein and Social Democracy*. New York: Cambridge University Press, 1997.

Tucker, Robert. *The Marxian Revolutionary Idea*. New York: W.W. Norton, 1970.

Woodcock, George. *Anarchism and Anarchists*. Kingston, Ont.: Quarry Press, 1992.

Yunker, James A. *Socialism Revised and Modernized: The Case for Pragmatic Market Socialism*. New York: Praeger, 1992.

NATIONALISM

CHAPTER 14

The nation, it will be remembered, is a specific type of political community that evolved out of feudal Europe. The decline of universal institutions—the Roman Catholic Church and the Holy Roman Empire—coupled with the erosion of parochial or regional loyalties to manor, village, city, or province, resulted in large aggregates of people sharing a common identity. The nation, which arose in Western Europe, has now become the model of community for the rest of the world as well.

Nationalism, at the level of emotions, is a feeling of loyalty to one's nation, a recognition of ties with other members of one's group. The pride Canadians feel when a Canadian wins a medal at the Olympics, and the sense of recognition that Canadians may experience when they happen to meet other Canadians in a foreign land, are manifestations of nationalism. Writing about the *polis*, Aristotle said that "friendship ... seems to hold states together."[1] Nationalism is the equivalent of friendship in communities that are so large that we can never actually know more than a tiny proportion of the other members. A common national identity helps us to care about people with whom we are personally unacquainted.

NATIONAL MYTHOLOGY

Loyalty to a nation rests on the fundamental human need for group identification. It is fostered by a sort of national mythology, that is, by stories about the common history and destiny of the nation. The model for such national myths in the Western world is the historical self-awareness of the Hebrews. Their understanding of themselves as a chosen people, bound to God by a special covenant, recurs in the myths by which other nations justify their existence. No nation has a single myth or story;

rather, each has a complex mythology or set of stories existing at different levels ranging from folklore to deliberate creations by intellectuals writing history in order to further national consciousness.

A fine example of the latter is the book by Monseigneur Laflèche, Bishop of Trois-Rivières, *Quelques considérations sur les rapports de la société civile avec la religion et la famille* (1866). Laflèche wrote that "Providence has allotted each and every nation its own mission to fulfil."[2] The French-Canadian people, in his view, were a nation among the human family of nations, with their homeland in the valley of the St. Lawrence. Their special calling was "basically religious in nature … to convert the unfortunate infidel local population to Catholicism, and to expand the Kingdom of God by developing a predominantly Catholic nationality."[3]

Laflèche's sketch of the history of French Canada emphasized missionary work among the Indians. With that period largely past, he wrote, the new calling was to be a devout Catholic enclave in Protestant North America, setting an example that might lead others to Rome. The Catholic faith would be reinforced by adherence to the French language. The historical theory was well suited to preserving the identity of a minority, with its call for an intertwining of language, religion, and customs into a protective whole.

Laflèche did not create French-Canadian nationalism; rather, he articulated historical symbols to express more clearly what the people already felt. His myth entered the wider mythology, to which many other writers also contributed. Of course, mythologies change over time. Today the religious formulation of Laflèche would not express very well the aspirations of Québécois nationalists, who speak about the unique value of their culture and language rather than about religion. But the underlying idea is still the same: the nation has a special role to play in the drama of human history.

This national mythology is likely to be challenged by the effect of current demographic trends in Quebec. As the birthrate has fallen, the government of Quebec has encouraged immigrants from many parts of the Third World to come to the province. Even when they are francophone, as are those from Haiti, they have no natural feeling for the uniquely French-Canadian sense of historical mission. Paradoxically, the new immigration is especially threatening to French-Canadian nationalism because of Quebec's attempt to assimilate the immigrants into the French language and culture. Earlier waves of European immigrants to Quebec— Scots, Irish, Jews, Italians—largely assimilated into the English community and so did not exercise much influence upon the Québécois. It is possible that present demographic realities may in the long run encourage French-Canadian nationalism to become more open and outward looking and, in that respect, more similar to English-Canadian nationalism.

The national mythology of English Canada is more diffuse than that of French Canada because the community itself is less well defined. English-speaking Canada is not a single entity but an alliance of several communities founded in different circumstances. Massive immigration has further complicated an already complex situation. However, there is one constant theme in the interpretations Canadians give to their collective existence: to be Canadian is to be not American. Initially, of course, there was no Canada and no Canadian identity, only several British colonies in North America that shared, for ideological reasons, in the rejection of the American Revolution. Indeed, these colonies were largely populated by the descendants of the United Empire Loyalists, who had left the United States during or shortly after the American Revolution. The union of these separate colonies was impelled less by positive feelings of friendship for one another than by a collective fear that if they remained separate, they would inevitably fall into the orbit of the United States.

Not surprisingly, statements about the meaning of Canada almost always involve a comparison with the United States. During the nineteenth century and much of the twentieth, these comparisons usually interpreted Canada as a more conservative, orderly, and peaceful country than its neighbour. Common themes of self-congratulation were the superiority of constitutional monarchy over republicanism, the British tradition of social deference, an orderly frontier protected by the North-West Mounted Police, and generous treatment of Canada's aboriginal peoples. Today, the topics of comparison are different, but the mental process is much the same.[4] Canadians repeatedly stress that they are fortunate to have less crime than the United States, less racial hostility, a more pristine natural environment, and a more compassionate society. Particular stress is given to Canadian public policies (the key one being national health insurance) that do not exist in the United States. Again, it is obvious that the structure of Canadian national mythology serves to protect the group's distinctiveness by discouraging absorption into a larger neighbour. The logic of the situation compels both English- and French-Canadian national mythologies to be defensive in nature.

The character of American nationalism differs from both Canadian nationalisms. The American national identity rests on the political ideas that animated the Revolution of 1776. Ever since that time, Americans have interpreted themselves as participants in a social experiment of vast importance to all humanity—testing the limits of liberty. Thomas Jefferson wrote in 1802:

> It is impossible not to be sensible that we are acting for all mankind; that circumstances denied to others, but indulged to us, have imposed on us the duty of proving what is the degree of freedom and self-government in which a society may venture to leave its individual members.[5]

American national mythology plays endlessly on the theme of freedom and interprets everything else in relation to it. In this perspective, modern mass democracy, which first appeared in the United States, is not just majority rule, and capitalism is not just a form of economic organization; both are the means by which a free people conducts its affairs. The Declaration of Independence, the Constitution, and the Bill of Rights are not just political documents; they are sacred texts for the inspiration of all humanity.

This characteristic of American national mythology perhaps helps to explain why American ventures in international politics often tend to become crusades: in contests with other nations, freedom itself is at stake. Woodrow Wilson brought the United States into World War I "to make the world safe for democracy." Franklin Roosevelt interpreted American participation in World War II in a similar way. Cold War rivalry with the Soviet Union was not just an exercise in power politics; it was the defence of the "free world." Americans are entirely serious about these slogans, even when they amuse or bewilder observers in other nations.

The point, of course, is not that one nation's myths are false while another's are true. It is that each nation worthy of the name has a mythology that supports its national identity by lending meaning to its collective history. Without such a source of meaning, the nation, which is ultimately a psychological reality, could not exist. Space has permitted only a brief look at a few examples, but similar myths exist for all nations.

This means that nationalism is not a single ideology. The details of each nationalism are unique because each nation is unique. However, there are common factors in the various structures of belief because the national mythologies serve similar purposes for the various nations. Most broadly, nationalism is "the making of claims in the name, or on behalf, of the nation."[6] The claims commonly arise under two headings: loyalty to the nation, and the quest for the nation-state.

Loyalty to the Nation

In the nationalist worldview, loyalty to the nation should transcend other loyalties—for example, allegiance to one's family, region, or ethnic group. The nation is taken to be the primary social group, outranking all others. This presupposition is so deeply entrenched today that we often do not recognize its significance. Why, for example, do we keep economic statistics on a national basis? In fact, economic relationships do not necessarily coincide with national sentiments. To say that the unemployment rate in Canada is 9.7 percent obscures the fact that it may be 18 percent in one province and 6 percent in another. What the national figures mean is rather unclear, yet we religiously compute them. Similarly, athletes can compete in the Olympic games only as members of a national team; they cannot represent themselves, a city, or a club. Yet sport has intrinsically as little to do with the nation as does economics.

Quest for the Nation-State

That the nation and the state should coincide in the nation-state is not a universal belief of nationalism. The traditional posture of French-Canadian nationalism, for example, was defence of the French-Canadian nation within the Canadian binational state, which in practice often meant heavy emphasis on provincial autonomy. That being said, the demand for the nation-state tends to be a recurring one. Thus, French-Canadian nationalism became separatist in the early 1960s. Interestingly, René Lévesque, the first separatist premier of Quebec, once defended separatism by saying that it was "natural" for a nation to aspire to statehood. The word *natural* reflects the predominance of the nation-state in contemporary thinking.

Opinion about the inevitability of the nation-state is divided. Because freedom depends on the voluntary acceptance of legitimate authority, John Stuart Mill argued that in the long run a free society is possible only in a nation-state. He wrote in *Considerations on Representative Government* (1861):

> Free institutions are next to impossible in a country made up of different nationalities. Among a people without fellow-feeling, especially if they read and speak different languages, the united public opinion, necessary to the working of representative government, cannot exist.[7]

Mill feared that in a multinational state one nation would always end up coercively oppressing the others. National antagonism would require such a strong government that individual freedom would be impossible. Indeed, the problem that Mill perceived destroyed the Soviet Union. The reform program introduced by Mikhail Gorbachev allowed for the reassertion of national identities that had long been politically suppressed, first by the Russian Empire and then by the Soviet state. Lithuanians, Latvians, Estonians, Ukrainians, and many other nationalities demanded political independence, until nothing was left of the Soviet Union.

A contrary view was maintained by Mill's younger contemporary, Lord Acton (1834–1902), who wrote that "those states are substantially the most perfect which, like the British and Austrian Empires, include various distinct nationalities without oppressing them."[8] The existence of different nationalities was a positive blessing, according to Acton, because it provided a bulwark against too much state domination of society. Smaller nations within the state, fearful that the government would be controlled by the larger nations, would be reluctant to assign too many functions to the central authorities. Sensitive matters such as education and culture would tend to remain with local governments or perhaps even in private hands.

Acton's beliefs greatly influenced the political thought of Pierre Trudeau and formed the philosophical basis of his linguistic and constitutional policies, which had the intention of making Canada a pluralistic state in which neither the French nor the English would feel oppressed by each other. Trudeau's vision of Canada as a culturally pluralistic state was expressed in his often-quoted essay "The New Treason of the Intellectuals":

> Without backsliding to the ridiculous and reactionary idea of national sovereignty, how can we protect our French-Canadian national qualities? ... We must

separate once and for all the concepts of state and of nation, and make of Canada a truly pluralistic and polyethnic society. Now in order for this to come about, the different regions within the country must be assured of a wide range of local autonomy, such that each national group, with an increasing background of experience in self-government, may be able to develop the body of laws and institutions essential to the fullest expression and development of their national characteristics.[9]

Official bilingualism and multiculturalism became for Trudeau the institutional means of allowing Canada's peoples to co-exist under a political condominium.

TYPICAL FORMS OF NATIONALISM

The two general concerns of nationalism—loyalty to the nation and the quest for the nation-state—manifest themselves in a bewildering variety of complex phenomena. We will draw attention to a few of the typical situations in which we speak of nationalism, commenting first and at greater length on one—Aboriginal nationalism and the demand for self-government—because of its increasing importance in Canadian politics.

Aboriginal Nationalism

A particular form of nationalism involves Aboriginal peoples, now usually known in Canada as "first nations." The first stage in Aboriginal nationalism, now largely concluded in Canada, is a redefining of the group as a nation rather than a tribe or ethnic minority. Native people have achieved this and now claim an inherent right of self-government within Canadian federalism. At this point it is not clear if this legal status will be constitutional or merely statutory—that is, if it will be entrenched in the Constitution or rooted in legislative enactments that are easier to change. Whatever the case, Aboriginal leaders across Canada are pushing for greater political power with which to govern about 500,000 status Indians (about 2 percent of our population) in over 600 bands, as well as more than 200,000 Métis and nonstatus Indians and about 40,000 Inuit.

One must understand what is meant by **self-government**. The term itself is not new in Canadian politics. In the past, municipal governments have often sought greater powers for self-government vis-à-vis provincial governments. When Alberta and Saskatchewan were seeking provincial status before 1905, this goal was expressed in terms of the power of "self-government" and greater "autonomy."[10] Thus, the basic meaning of the term for Aboriginal peoples relates to the right of greater control over one's own affairs.[11] Self-government involves increasing a group's decision-making powers: giving that group the jurisdiction to deal directly with its problems rather than having them dealt with by federal or territorial administrators.

There are, however, very different ideas about self-government within Aboriginal communities. Some groups seek a great deal of power, equivalent or even superior to that of a provincial government; others are striving for powers very similar to the powers of municipal governments. These differences should not pose an insoluble problem. As Pierre Trudeau said some years ago, "between the unacceptable extremes of assimilation or absolute sovereignty there is a broad range of negotiable possibilities."[12]

Aboriginal peoples want self-government partly so they can break with the paternalism of the past. For a long time, status Indians and Inuit were the responsibility of the federal government; authority had long been vested in a minister and delegated to officials in the Department of Indian and Northern Affairs. This paternalistic system began to change when the Indian Act was revised in 1951. Greater powers were **devolved** to elected band councils, but in most cases these powers were still not equivalent to municipal government powers in the provinces, and the minister retained the authority to veto band legislation. Aboriginal peoples, by seeking self-government, are striving for the kind of political power that other Canadians have long enjoyed through their provincial or municipal governments.

A second reason Aboriginal peoples desire greater self-governing power is to avoid cultural assimilation in order to preserve the traditions and values unique to them. While most Aboriginal peoples see themselves as Canadian, they also see themselves as Canada's first peoples. This is not to say they want to return to some vanished traditional lifestyle—on the contrary, they enjoy as much as any Canadians the amenities of modern life. At the same time, however, they do not want to lose those characteristics that make them Aboriginal. In short, Aboriginal peoples would like to live in two worlds, with one foot in modern Canadian society and the other in Aboriginal society. Whether they can succeed at this is not clear, but it is important that they try. The results will also say much about the effectiveness of the Canadian multicultural experiment.

Aboriginal peoples want to be responsible for themselves. Having more control over decisions concerning education, health care, housing, social services, economic development, and criminal justice is crucial to this goal. In the past, most such decisions were made by administrators far from where the lives affected were lived and far from where the attendant problems occurred. Canada's Aboriginal peoples are now saying they can, if given the power, deal more successfully than can outsiders with the chronic problems that affect them including substance abuse, family violence, high dropout rates among students, and unemployment. It is time, they say, to let Aboriginal people devise their own solutions because the European ones haven't worked.

The federal government, with its fiduciary responsibility for Aboriginal affairs, has taken some steps toward this type of devolution. The Cree and Naskapi people in northern Quebec and the Sechelt band in British Columbia already have self-government, and other Native groups are in various stages of negotiations. At the present time, the biggest Indian experiment is in Manitoba, where sixty bands have signed a so-called "framework agreement" to dismantle all functions of the federal

FIGURE 14.1 Nunavut Territory

Date of creation: Formally, April 1, 1999

Area: 1,931,511 km^2; approximately 19 percent of Canada

Population: 25,000, almost 85 percent of whom are Inuit

Communities: Population resides in 27 remote communities, with only about 20 kilometres of maintained roads. Serviced by air and water transport

Land Claim Agreement: Inuit have title to 354,357 km^2 and subsurface rights on 35,633 km^2

Government: Power of the Nunavut government will be similar to those of the Northwest Territories and Yukon

Department of Indian Affairs in that province and transfer them to band governments, either alone or in cooperation with each other.

Another major experiment in self-government is the case of Nunavut. In 1999 a new territory will be created in the central and eastern Arctic. Almost 85 percent of the roughly 25,000 people who live there are Inuit. Formally, Nunavut will not be a Native government, but the Inuit majority is so overwhelming that it will amount to almost the same thing. The people are now in the process of developing their institutions to prepare for 1999.

All of this, however, is being done mainly on a statutory rather than a constitutional basis. An important wing of Aboriginal opinion rejects the statutory approach because it makes Aboriginal governments subordinate to Parliament; these people want to deal with Canada on a "nation to nation" basis. Thus they continue to demand that an "inherent right of self-government" be explicitly entrenched in the Constitution, although they also argue that it is already implied in Section 35 of the Constitution Act, 1982, which says, "The existing aboriginal and treaty rights of the aboriginal peoples of Canada are hereby recognized and affirmed." And a few Aboriginal groups, such as the Iroquois, do not consider themselves part of Canada at all and insist that they possess sovereignty in the full international sense.

Separatism

A national minority may seek to separate from the state that now rules it in order to establish a nation-state, as illustrated by separatist movements in Quebec and among the Welsh and Scots in Great Britain. Sometimes the minority would have to separate from two or more states; examples of this are the Basques, who are now ruled by France and Spain, and the Kurds, who are divided among Turkey, Iraq, Iran, and various states of the former Soviet Union.

Oppression of Minorities

A national majority that controls the government may use its political power to suppress, assimilate, or expel minorities that do not fit the nation-state's image of itself. In the early 1970s, the African states of Uganda, Kenya, and Tanzania expelled most of their substantial East Indian minorities. These people were vilified as alien exploiters who had been given an unfair position of economic advantage by the British colonialists.

Irredentism

A nation-state may claim fragments of territory adjacent to its borders on the grounds that they constitute a historical part of the nation. The constitution of the Republic of Ireland (Eire) specifically mentions the six counties of Ulster (Northern

Ireland) as forming part of its national territory. The government of Ireland does not at the moment press its claim by force, but it hopes that some day Ireland will be unified under its control. Similarly, the preamble to the 1978 constitution of the People's Republic of China states that "Taiwan is China's Sacred Territory. We are determined to liberate Taiwan and accomplish the great cause of unifying our motherland."[13] The technical name for this sort of claim is **irredentism**. A recent example was the Serbian attempt to control parts of Croatia and Bosnia that have significant Serbian minorities.

Imperialism

A large and powerful nation may create an empire by imposing itself on its neighbours. German nationalism between the two world wars began with irredentist claims to territories, such as the Sudetenland in Czechoslovakia, that had once been part of the Austrian Empire but had been taken away by the Treaty of Versailles. From there it went on to demand *Lebensraum*, "living space," and to subjugate the neighbouring states of Central and Eastern Europe. Nationalism can thus transcend the nation-state and lead to a multinational empire under the rule of a dominant nation.

Protectionism

The nation-state may try to insulate itself from external influences perceived as threatening it in some way. This can mean blockading ideas, for example, censoring foreign publications or jamming broadcast signals. It can also mean erecting barriers against the movement of goods, such as import quotas or protective tariffs, the belief being that such measures not only stimulate the domestic economy but also protect the integrity of the nation. During the 1988 federal election in Canada, opponents of the Free Trade Agreement with the United States expressed many fears for Canada's future. They claimed that free trade would not only harm Canadian industries but would also reduce the autonomy of the Canadian state, force Canada to adopt American social policies, and destroy Canada's cultural distinctiveness.[14] Such fears may have been only tenuously founded, but they were understandable in the context of the long-term defensive posture of nationalism in Canada.

HISTORICAL OVERVIEW

The relationship between nationalism and other ideologies is complicated. History shows that one can be a nationalist while simultaneously being liberal, conservative, or socialist. This is because nationalism has a different fundamental concern than these three other ideologies. They focus on the question of what the role of government in society should be, whereas nationalism addresses itself to the question of what the proper limits of the political community are. Three French nationalists can agree that France ought to be a sovereign nation-state *une et indivisible*, while adhering otherwise to conservative, liberal, or socialist views about the functions of government. The relationship between nationalism and other ideologies is not merely a matter of chance but is structured, as Hans Kohn has shown, according to the course of historical development in the last two centuries.[15]

Initially, nationalism and liberalism seemed to be natural allies. Great Britain, the first modern nation to emerge, was also the home of liberal constitutionalism. The United States, the first European colony to achieve independence, was constituted in 1776 in a reaffirmation of the principles of the Glorious Revolution. France proclaimed the concept of nationhood in 1789 as part of the liberal freedoms enunciated in the Declaration of the Rights of Man and of the Citizen.

The political situation in the first half of the nineteenth century strengthened the assumption that nationalism and liberalism were two sides of the same coin. Nationalism chiefly meant struggles to liberate small European nations from rule by large empires: the Irish from the British Empire, the Greeks from the Ottoman Empire, the Poles and Finns from the Russian Empire. With the notable exception of the British Empire, all European empires were based on traditional authority rather than legal constitutionalism. Those who struggled for national emancipation had to struggle at the same time for elected parliaments, freedom of the press, religious toleration, and other liberal goals. It was assumed that the peoples of the earth, once liberated from alien rule, would compose a family of nations living peacefully and freely side by side.

The alliance between liberalism and nationalism reached its peak in 1848, when a wave of attempted revolutions swept across Europe, all having the same goal of creating liberally governed nation-states. But the empires were able to reassert themselves, not least by playing the different nationalities against each other, and the liberal nationalist dream did not become reality.

Liberal nationalism continued to exist after 1848, but it was increasingly displaced by a more militaristic, state-oriented kind of nationalism. The national unification of Italy (1861) and of Germany (1871), long a goal of liberal nationalism, was achieved less by liberal methods of voluntary agreement than by military conquest. The new nation-states of Italy and Germany almost immediately began acquiring colonial empires, especially in Africa, where Britain and France, which had long possessed overseas empires, also joined in. Even the United States, which had always been critical of European imperialism, acquired overseas colonies—Puerto Rico, Cuba, and the Philippines—after a war with Spain in 1898. By the end of the nineteenth century, nationalism had come to imply much less the liberation of small nations than the imperial aggrandizement of powerful nations. Numerous writers extolled the virtues of military service and loyalty to the state. This was also the period when racial theories became allied with nationalism. Writers of the various large nations justified their policies of imperial expansion by claiming biological superiority for Anglo-Saxons, French, or Germans, who had to rule the "coloured" races for their own good as well as that of humanity in general.

This aggressive form of nationalism fostered the growth of anti-Semitism. Jews, who lived dispersed in many European states, were attacked as alien elements in the national community. The German composer Richard Wagner wrote:

> The Jew speaks the language of the nation in whose midst he dwells from generation to generation, but he always speaks it as an alien ... Our whole European art and civilization, however, have remained to the Jew as a foreign tongue; for, just as he has taken no part in the evolution of the one, so he has taken none in that of the other; but at most the homeless wight has been a cold, nay more, a hostile on-looker.[16]

One of the most important expressions of this mood of anti-Semitism was *The Protocols of the Elders of Zion*, a forged document first published in 1903 and often reprinted thereafter.[17] Forged by an agent of the czarist secret police in order to encourage anti-Semitism in Russia, it purported to prove there was a Jewish conspiracy to degrade and enslave the entire world. It interpreted Jewish achievements in science, international finance, and the socialist movement not as unrelated developments but as part of a calculated plot to gain ascendancy over the gentiles (non-Jews). The *Protocols* were to have a fateful influence on Adolf Hitler later in the twentieth century. The myth of an international Jewish conspiracy continues to this day to lead a subterranean existence, surfacing from time to time, as in the 1980s, when Ernst Zundel and Jim Keegstra were prosecuted in Canada for fomenting hatred against Jews. Both men attracted attention for asserting that the Holocaust—the murder of about six million Jews during World War II—had never taken place and was a creation of Jewish propaganda. This assertion was based on the notion of the *Protocols* that there existed a supremely powerful Jewish cabal that could perpetrate such a massive hoax upon the world.[18]

In the late nineteenth century, European Jews reacted to the growing wave of anti-Semitism by developing their own form of nationalism. **Zionism** taught that the Jews would never achieve respect until they became a nation-state and that the Jewish population must therefore gather itself onto a single territory under the control of a sovereign Jewish state.

The aggressive nationalism of the late nineteenth and early twentieth centuries culminated in World War I, when Britain, France, Russia, and Italy fought in alliance against the German, Austro–Hungarian, and Ottoman Empires. At first, the outcome of this bloody war seemed to be a revival of liberal nationalism. The Treaty of Versailles dismembered the empires that had ruled Central and Eastern Europe and replaced them with nation-states equipped with liberal constitutions. Poles, Czechs, Hungarians, Lithuanians, Finns, and other peoples emerged with their own states for the first time in modern history. But nationalism and liberalism soon parted company.

Each of these new nation-states had important national minorities—for example, the Germans in Czechoslovakia and the Hungarians in Romania. Nationalistic conflict and irredentism raised the temperature of politics to the point where individual freedoms seemed of minor concern relative to the security of the national community. In the 1920s and 1930s, constitutional government was overthrown in almost all these new states of Europe, from Italy and Germany eastward. Nationalism then made an even more aggressive appearance in the new ideology of fascism.

It is not easy to describe **fascism** briefly, for it was intimately bound to conditions in Central Europe in the years *entre deux guerres*. A communist takeover, as had occurred in the Russian Empire in 1917, seemed like a very real possibility in many of these countries. Liberal constitutionalism appeared unable to combat this threat or to deal with postwar inflation and unemployment. Benito Mussolini, who had been an ardent socialist but who had rallied to the support of Italy in the Great War, created the alternative of fascism. After the war, he began a political movement with a unique mixture of ideological themes. Rejection of liberal individualism and constitutional government was paramount. There would no longer be a private sphere of life exempt from governmental intrusion. He extolled the state as the highest expression of the nation and praised war as bringing "all human energies to their highest tension and setting a seal of nobility on the peoples who have the virtue to face it."[19]

The symbol of Mussolini's movement, and the source of its name, was the *fasces*, a bundle of rods containing an axe with the blade projecting, which had been a Roman symbol of authority. The rods and axe represented the threatening power of coercion (i.e., beating or beheading); the fact they were bound together symbolized the unity of the nation. For the third time, Italy would emerge as the leader of humanity. After the Rome of the Caesars and the Rome of the Popes would come the "Third Rome," the "Rome of the People." To these nationalist motifs, Mussolini added elements of socialism. The state, while not nationalizing property, would guide the economy for collective purposes. Mussolini had also learned from Lenin that an elite, disciplined party could seize power in a constitutional state and maintain its hold thereafter by ruthlessly suppressing opposition. Conspicuously absent were the egalitarian ideals of socialism, except in the sense that all were equally exhorted to follow the charismatic leadership of the *duce* (leader).

Hitler's doctrine of national socialism was similar to Mussolini's fascism, except that he substituted German for Italian nationalism. His goal was to create the Third Reich, a new German Empire to succeed the medieval Holy Roman Empire and the empire Bismarck had created in 1871. Also, while Mussolini was not anti-Semitic, Hitler made anti-Semitism the centre of his ideology by blaming the German defeat in World War I on the Jews—the "stab in the back" theory—and by promising to make Germany *Judenrein* (free from Jews). Similar ideologies sprang up elsewhere in Europe. Their adherents came to power in Spain, with the help of Italian and German intervention, and became influential in such Central European countries as Hungary and Romania.[20]

Fascism is difficult to categorize. The fact that it is certainly not liberal has led some writers to regard it as a form of conservatism; and indeed, it did play on conservative sentiments by promising to prevent the triumph of communism. But futuristic symbols like the Third Rome and Third Reich express an attitude quite foreign to the conservative reverence for continuity with the past. Fascism was in fact a promise of radical change, a conscious break with the past to produce what Mussolini called "fascist man." On balance, fascism is probably best understood as an extreme form of nationalism that played on fears of communism while incorporating certain elements of socialism to strengthen the state. Some writers have sought to apply the label of fascist to the anticommunist military regimes that until recently ruled such nations as South Korea, the Philippines, and Chile. However, those regimes lacked the futuristic ideology and mass parties that characterized fascism in the 1920s and 1930s. On balance, European fascism was so much a unique product of historical circumstances that it is probably better to restrict the term to Hitler and Mussolini and their contemporaries, and to regard it as a specific phase of nationalism rather than a separate ideology.

One consequence of World War II was that it ushered in a historical period in which nationalism was truly a worldwide force. The British, French, Italian, Portuguese, American, Dutch, and Japanese colonial holdings all attained independence; this left the Russian Empire (i.e., the Soviet Union and its sphere of influence) as the last of the great multinational empires until it dissolved itself in 1991. The world is now a society of nation-states, even if many of the new nations are still rather tentative aggregations of tribal, ethnic, and regional groups. The most important new manifestation of nationalism in the postwar period was the struggle of these new nations for independence. In several instances—for example, in Vietnam, Algeria, Angola, and Mozambique—the colonial power was reluctant to surrender its sovereignty and did so only after a prolonged war of national liberation.

In the Third World, the mentality of national liberation is still strong, and its symbolism is still potent. The new nations have achieved political sovereignty, but in economic terms, most of them are in difficult straits. They commonly blame their low standard of living not only on the colonial past but also on what they perceive as continuing economic domination by the capitalist nations of the Western world, especially the United States. Not surprisingly, since they believe their problems to be caused by the market system, many of the new nations have turned to socialism (see Chapter 13).

However, with some exceptions, they have not turned to orthodox communism. Many leaders in the Third World rejected both the capitalist and communist models as blueprints for rapid social, economic, and political change. Their criticism was that capitalist and communist solutions were devised for situations and experiences unlike those found in developing nations today. The authoritarianism found in communism stifles the initiative and innovation so desperately needed to stimulate development, while the lack of government intervention in capitalism enables the rich in developing nations to maintain a stratified society with little or no social and economic mobility. Developing nations, they argued, must seek their own solutions to their problems of development. Celso Furtado, a Brazilian economist, was critical of communist methods:

> Historical experience has demonstrated that whenever a revolution of the Marxist–Leninist type has been imposed on a complex social structure—as in the case of certain European countries—socialism as a form of humanism becomes perverted. As there is no possibility of converting an open society into a dictatorship without creating a climate of frustration, there is a deterioration of social values. Since the dictatorial regime does not permit the individual to play his proper part in society, a series of social myths is put forward in order to replace genuine human values. Thus, material development can take place at the same time that the dictatorship is consolidating itself upon principles which are the antithesis of humanistic revolutionary ideals.[21]

Eduardo Frei, former president of Chile (1964–70), perceived a flaw in the capitalist system:

> There is something that we should understand. Capitalism as a system dehumanizes the economy, although, in its first stage, it meant an enormous expansion of economic development and the creation of wealth. Yet there is no doubt that it tended to concentrate economic power in a few hands, to allow the great monopolistic powers to control the market so that, by a fierce dialectical process within its own structure, it led to the disappearance of economic freedom. In the productive process, it separated labor from management and, more than that, from the concept of property and the exercise of that right.[22]

Both men sought indigenous solutions to their problems of development in some form of noncommunist socialism.

Concrete manifestations of this socialist nationalism include nationalization of the subsidiaries of multinational firms, or heavy regulation of their business activities; attempts to cartelize production of essential commodities sold on world markets; demands for higher levels of foreign aid with no strings attached; and proposals for an international income tax by which the Third World could claim as a matter of right a share of the wealth of the more advanced nations. Such proposals are often summarized under the heading of the "new world economic order," which is what advocates for the Third World demand. This vision seemed most plausible in the heyday of the Organization of Petroleum Exporting Countries (OPEC) in the late 1970s. If Third World oil producers could bring the West to its knees, why not Third World producers of bauxite or coffee? But it became obvious to everyone in the 1980s that OPEC no longer controlled the price of oil, and no equivalent cartels for other commodities have been organized.

The alliance between nationalism and socialism may prove itself very long-lasting because the two ideologies have one important affinity: both see the state as the central institution in society. For socialists it is the planner of society, and for nationalists it is the expression of national identity; whereas for liberals and conservatives it is only a limited instrument with special purposes. Socialist and nationalist uses of the state are not incompatible and, indeed, can reinforce each other, as when nationalization of a multinational corporation is touted as an assertion of sovereignty as well as a measure to benefit the local working class.

This rapprochement between nationalism and socialism is mildly ironic, in that the early socialists had little use for the nation-state. Marx sympathized with the national aspirations of the Irish and the Poles not for their own sake, but because he thought national liberation would weaken the political system that helped maintain capitalism. Marx believed that all states, including nation-states, would ultimately disappear. The socialist parties of the Second International were also antinationalistic, believing that aggressive nationalism distracted proletarians from the true issue of the class struggle. But the global proliferation of nation-states in this century is a political fact to which ideologies must adjust if they are to survive. Socialists have managed to make the transition by focusing on the state rather than on those parts of their original doctrine that anticipated the passing away of the state.

Nationalism today is critical to the process of building a sense of loyalty and identity among diverse ethnic groups in a given nation-state. At the same time, rabid nationalism can be a very destructive force, as can be seen in the three-sided war in the former Yugoslavia, the repression of the Kurds in Iraq and Turkey, and the war between Azeris and Armenians over control of the enclave of Nagorno-Karabakh in Azerbaijan. In each case, old animosities have triggered atrocities on all sides. These incidents point out the ugly side of nationalism and the enormous problems involved in reconciling differences through politics.

FURTHER READING

Bremmer, Ian, and Ray Taras, eds. *New States, New Politics: Building the Post-Soviet Nations*, rev. 2nd ed. Cambridge, England: Cambridge University Press, 1997.

Brubaker, Rogers. *Nationalism Reframed: Nationhood and the National Question in the New Europe.* Cambridge, England, and New York: Cambridge University Press, 1996.

Canovan, Margaret. *Nationhood and Political Theory.* Cheltenham, England, and Brookfield, Vt.: Edward Elgar, 1996.

Carsten, F.L. *The Rise of Fascism.* London: Methuen, 1967.

Cassels, Alan. *Fascism.* New York: Crowell, 1975.

Comaroff, John L., and Paul C. Stern, eds. *Perspectives on Nationalism and War.* Amsterdam: Gordon and Breach, 1995.

Cook, Ramsay. *French-Canadian Nationalism.* Toronto: Macmillan, 1969.

———. *Canada, Quebec, and the Uses of Nationalism*, 2nd ed. Toronto: McClelland and Stewart, 1995.

Dahbour, Omar, and Micheline R. Ishay. *The Nationalism Reader*. Atlantic Highlands, N.J.: Humanities Press, 1995.

Eley, Geoff, and Ronald Grigor Suny, eds. *Becoming National: A Reader*. New York: Oxford University Press, 1996.

Emerson, Rupert. *From Empire to Nation*. Cambridge, Mass.: Harvard University Press, 1960.

Granatstein, J. *Yankee Go Home: Canadians and Anti-Americanism*. Scarborough, Ont.: Harper Collins Canada, 1996.

Gwyn, Richard. *Nationalism Without Walls: The Unbearable Lightness of Being Canadian*. Toronto: McClelland and Stewart, 1995.

Hayes, Carlton J.H. *Nationalism: A Religion*. New York: Macmillan, 1960.

Ignatieff, George. *Blood and Belonging*. Toronto: Penguin Books Canada, 1993.

Kedourie, Elie. *Nationalism*. New York: Praeger, 1960.

Kellas, James. *The Politics of Nationalism and Ethnicity*. London: Macmillan, 1991.

Kitchen, Martin. *Fascism*. London: Macmillan, 1976.

Kohn, Hans. *The Idea of Nationalism*. New York: Macmillan, 1944.

———. *Nationalism: Its Meaning and History*. New York: Van Nostrand Reinhold, 1965.

Minahan, James. *Nations Without States: A Historical Dictionary of Contemporary National Movements*. Westport, Conn.: Greenwood Press, 1996.

O'Sullivan, Noel. *Fascism*. London: Dent, 1983.

Shafer, Boyd C. *Nationalism: Myth and Reality*. New York: Harcourt, Brace, 1955.

Shapiro, Ian, and Will Kymlicka, eds. *Ethnicity and Group Rights*. New York: New York University Press, 1997.

Smith, Anthony D. *Theories of Nationalism*. London: Duckworth, 1983.

———. *Ethnicity and Nationalism*. The Netherlands: Brill, 1992.

Tully, James. *Strange Multiplicity: Constitutionalism in an Age of Diversity*. Cambridge, England, New York: Cambridge University Press, 1995.

Van Den Berghe, Pierre L. *The Ethnic Phenomenon*. New York: Praeger, 1981.

Watson, Michael. *Contemporary Minority Nationalism*. London: Routledge, 1990.

NEW IDEOLOGIES? FEMINISM AND ENVIRONMENTALISM

In the past quarter-century, the ideological picture has become increasingly complex with the rise to prominence of new systems of thought, especially feminism and environmentalism. Liberalism, socialism, conservatism, and nationalism are all primarily concerned with questions of power, such as who is going to control human communities, and to what end? **Feminism** adds a new dimension to this debate by focusing on power relationships between men and women; **environmentalism**, at least in its most consistent form, transcends it by focusing on the relationships between human beings and the nonhuman universe.

The current prominence of these new ideologies is often seen as a result of **postmaterialism**, a term coined by the American political scientist Ronald Inglehart. According to Inglehart, the years after World War II have seen a gradual but profound shift of values. While there have been periods of recession and some peripheral military conflicts, the general climate in the Western world since the late 1940s has been one of peace and prosperity. Thus, new generations have grown up taking physical and economic security for granted and have achieved higher levels of formal education, and this has produced an electorate more concerned with self-expression and other postmaterialist values.[1] The result is a favourable climate for ideologies that go beyond concerns of public order and material prosperity.

FEMINISM

Feminism is derived from the Latin *femina*, which means "woman" or "female." As the name suggests, the ideology is centred on the position of women in human society. It should be noted in passing that the word *feminist* is a label for certain ideas, or for people who hold such ideas. It is not a synonym for woman. Some men are feminists (John Stuart Mill was one of the most influential feminists of the nineteenth century), and not all women are feminists (in a 1992 poll, only 32 percent of Canadian women answered yes to the question, "Do you consider yourself to be a feminist?").[2]

Feminism is not an entirely new ideology. Its roots go back to the seventeenth century; and, like liberalism, socialism, conservatism, and nationalism, it belongs to the family of ideologies produced by the French Revolution. It may, however, have seemed new when the feminist movement burst on the political stage in the late 1960s. But in fact this was the "second wave" of active feminism. An earlier feminist movement in the second half of the nineteenth century had had as one of its main goals women's suffrage, which was attained in most Western countries by the end of World War I. The "new" ideology of feminism is the rekindling of a fire that had once burned brightly and had never gone out.

As with all ideological trends, there were objective reasons for the "second wave" revival of feminism. A crucial factor was the birthrate, which had peaked in the late 1950s and declined rapidly throughout the 1960s. This decline was associated with, though not entirely due to, the introduction of effective oral contraceptives. Lower birthrates meant smaller families, which in turn meant that women were starting to spend more of their adult lives working in the paid labour force and engaging in public activities such as politics. These objective developments made it pressing to re-examine sex roles in society because laws and social institutions had traditionally assumed that women's lives would be private and domestic, centred on home and family, while men would predominate in the public sphere of the economy and politics.

Like other ideologies, feminism is a family of belief systems with certain concerns and ideas in common but with many internal differences. The central concern is easily stated: whatever their other disagreements, all feminists begin from the belief that society is disadvantageous to women, systematically depriving them of individual choice, political power, economic opportunity, and intellectual recognition. Within this broad perspective are many schools of thought about the causes of and remedies for this situation. We will look at three varieties of feminism often mentioned in the literature: liberal feminism, Marxist feminism, and radical feminism.

Liberal Feminism

Starting in the late seventeenth century, books and pamphlets began to appear arguing that women had the same intellectual and moral capacities as men and should have the same legal rights. The best known of these early works is *A Vindication of the Rights of Woman* (1792) by Mary Wollstonecraft. A largely self-educated schoolteacher and author, Wollstonecraft is also known for being the mother of Mary Wollstonecraft Shelley, who wrote the novel *Frankenstein*.

The context of the *Rights of Woman* is significant. It was printed very soon after Wollstonecraft's earlier pamphlet *The Rights of Men* (1790), which was an attack on Edmund Burke's *Reflections on the Revolution in France*. Wollstonecraft was an ardent defender of the French Revolution, particularly its egalitarian aspects. In her view, equality for women was the logical corollary of the attempt to create a political system based on equality before the law. She argued that women should have the right to vote, to own property, and to pursue whatever profession they chose, and also to be educated in the liberal arts and sciences like men, not just in the arts of running a household. Like feminists ever since, she argued that political and legal equality had to be rooted in equality within the family. Yet, unlike some contemporary radical feminists, she did not challenge the traditional procreative role of women. "Make women rational creatures and free citizens," she wrote, "and they will quickly become good wives and mothers."[3]

The general theme of **liberal feminism** is equality of rights, or the extension of men's rights to women. This is vividly expressed in the Declaration of Sentiments (1848), drafted by Elizabeth Cady Stanton and modelled closely on the American Declaration of Independence:

> When, in the course of human events, it becomes necessary for one portion of the family of man to assume among the peoples of the earth a position different from that which they have hitherto occupied, but one to which the laws of nature and of nature's God entitle them, a decent respect for the opinions of mankind requires that they should declare the causes that impel them to such a course. We hold these truths to be self-evident; that all men and women are created equal; that they are endowed by their Creator with certain inalienable rights; that among these are life, liberty and the pursuit of happiness; that to secure these rights governments are instituted, deriving their just powers from the consent of the governed.[4]

The underlying presupposition of this text and others in the tradition of liberal feminism is that liberalism would be an adequate ideology if it took itself seriously and extended its view to include both halves of the human race on equal terms.

The liberal feminist view was systematically worked out in John Stuart Mill's essay *The Subjection of Women* (1869). The subordination of women, wrote Mill, "ought to be replaced by a principle of perfect equality, admitting no power or privilege on the one side, nor disability on the other."[5] The dependence of women was nothing but "the primitive state of slavery lasting on";[6] and just as men had been liberated from slavery, so should women. The subjection of women might appear natural, but "was there ever any domination which did not appear natural to those who possessed it?"[7]

The emancipation of women, argued Mill, was in everyone's interest, for "any limitation of the field of selection deprives society of some chances of being served by the competent, without ever saving it from the incompetent."[8] That is, everyone, men and women alike, would profit if women were given a fair chance to develop their abilities and put them to use. Although it might indeed be true that there are great natural differences between men and women, Mill claimed that we could not know this for certain because of the dependence in which women had been kept. But that did not matter:

> One thing we may be certain of—that what is contrary to women's nature to do, they never will be made to do by simply giving their nature free play. The anxiety of mankind to interfere in behalf of nature, for fear lest nature should not succeed in effecting its purpose, is an altogether unnecessary solicitude. What women by nature cannot do, it is quite superfluous to forbid them from doing. What they can do, but not so well as the men who are their competitors, competition suffices to exclude them from; since nobody asks for protective duties and bounties in favor of women.[9]

This quotation clearly illustrates the liberal character of Mill's approach, which amounts to a kind of *laissez-faire* argument applied to the relationship between the sexes.

Mill advocated complete legal equality for women. He also thought marriage should be an equal partnership, and was eloquent about how this would increase the happiness of men as well as women. Yet, typical of early liberal feminists, he seems to have taken for granted that the traditional division of labour between the sexes would continue as the social, although not the legal, norm. Men would continue to be more concerned with public life, married women with the household and private life. Individual women should be perfectly free to devote themselves to the public life of work and government, but it would not be the normal state of affairs:

> When the support of the family depends not on property but on earnings, the common arrangement, by which the man earns the income and the wife superintends the domestic expenditure, seems to me in general the most suitable division of labor between the two persons. If, in addition to the physical suffering of bearing children, and the whole responsibility of their care and education in early years, the wife undertakes the careful and economical application of the husband's earnings to the general comfort of the family; she takes not only her fair share, but usually the larger share, of the bodily and mental exertion required by their joint existence ... In an otherwise just state of things, it is not, therefore, I think, a desirable custom, that the wife should contribute by her labor to the income of the family.[10]

Mill's words illustrate the paradox of the early phase of liberal feminism. It advocated equality of rights for women in a legal sense and accepted the validity of individual women choosing to pursue careers in the public domain; but it also took for granted a sexual division of labour in which women, even if with exceptions, would freely choose to devote themselves primarily to childbearing and child rearing for most of their adult lives. Thus reappeared the typical classical-liberal tension between equality of right and equality of outcome: men and women would have equal rights, but the conditions of their lives would be very different; and it is men who would continue in fact to have greater access to wealth and power in the public realm, while most women would remain in the private sphere of the household.

When Mill wrote *The Subjection of Women*, there was already an active political movement of women, usually known as **suffragism** because of its emphasis on attaining the suffrage, or right to vote, for women. But women's emancipation was much broader than this issue; it included the struggle for legal and political equality in all forms, such as the right to hold public office, to attend university and enter the learned professions, to own property in marriage, and to receive custody of children in cases of divorce or separation. These goals were gradually attained in most Western countries toward the end of the nineteenth and the beginning of the twentieth centuries. Some leading Canadian feminists of that era were Dr. Emily Howard Stowe, Canada's first female physician, who founded the Canadian Women's Suffrage Movement in Toronto in 1876; Emily Murphy, a journalist who was appointed police magistrate in Edmonton in 1916, the first such appointment in the British Empire; and Nellie McClung, also a journalist, who was elected to the Alberta legislature in 1921.[11] The sidebar below lists some important milestones in the political progress of Canadian women.

CANADIAN WOMEN'S POLITICAL MILESTONES

1897	Clara Brett Martin is admitted to the Law Society of Upper Canada.
1916	Manitoba, Alberta, and Saskatchewan grant women the right to vote in provincial elections.
1918	Women obtain the right to vote in federal elections.
1929	In the *Persons* case, the Judicial Committee of the Privy Council rules that women are legal persons and may be appointed to the Senate.
1930	Cairine Wilson is appointed to the Senate.
1940	Women get the right to vote in Quebec provincial elections.
1957	Ellen Fairclough becomes the first woman to serve in the federal Cabinet.
1982	Bertha Wilson becomes the first woman appointed to the Supreme Court of Canada.
1989	Audrey McLaughlin is elected leader of the New Democratic Party, the first woman to lead a federal party.
1993	Kim Campbell becomes the first woman prime minister of Canada.
1995	Alexa McDonough succeeds Audrey McLaughlin as leader of the New Democratic Party.

The contemporary phase of liberal feminism was signalled by the publication in 1963 of Betty Friedan's best-selling book, *The Feminine Mystique*. Friedan, an American journalist, devoted her book to "the problem that has no name," namely

> a strange stirring, a sense of dissatisfaction, a yearning that women suffered in the middle of the twentieth century in the United States. Each suburban wife struggled with it alone. As she made the beds, shopped for groceries, matched slipcover material, ate peanut butter sandwiches with her children, chauffeured Cub Scouts and Brownies, lay beside her husband at night—she was afraid to ask even of herself the silent question—"Is this all?"[12]

Friedan's answer at that time was unambiguous: no, domestic life was not enough; women had to become complete participants in the public world of politics and the economy:

> There is only one way for women to reach full human potential—by participating in the mainstream of society, by exercising their own voice in all the decisions shaping that society. For women to have full identity and freedom, they must have economic independence.[13]

In her pursuit of these goals, Friedan went on to become the founder and first president of the National Organization of Women (NOW) and a leading figure in the American women's movement.

Her book *The Second Stage*, published in 1981, examined some of the difficulties arising out of women's attempts to play a full role in economic and political life. In the book, she quotes a young woman who is attending Harvard Medical School:

> "I'm going to be surgeon. I'll never be a trapped housewife like my mother. But I would like to get married and have children, I think. They say we can have it all. But how? I work thirty-six hours in the hospital, twelve off. How am I going to have a relationship, much less kids, with hours like that? I'm not sure I can be a superwoman."[14]

Friedan's answer to this dilemma was "the restructuring of our institutions on a basis of real equality for women and men."[15] Concretely, this would mean changes in sex roles within the family, with both men and women working outside the home while sharing the tasks of housework and child care. It would also require innovations in public policy, such as public support for day care to facilitate women's participation in the workforce.

This approach sits comfortably within the tradition of reform liberalism. If government can provide old-age pensions and medical care in the name of equality, why not day care as well? But such demands collided with the conservative revival of the 1980s and the fiscal pressures of the 1990s, and many aspects of the contemporary liberal feminist agenda have never been fulfilled in North America.

Marxist Feminism

Feminism has always been an important theme in socialist thought. Many of the utopian socialists believed in restructuring the relationships between the sexes. Charles Fourier wrote:

> It is known that the best nations have always been those which concede the greatest amount of liberty to women. As a general proposition: Social progress and changes of period are brought about by virtue of the progress of women towards liberty, and social retrogression occurs as a result of a diminution in the liberty of women.[16]

The Israeli *kibbutz*, remotely based on the ideas of Fourier, tried to revolutionize the status of women by introducing collective housekeeping and child rearing arrangements. Another early utopian, Robert Owen, also proposed easier divorce and other reforms of the family. Philosophically, Owen's great theme was the malleability of human nature, by which he meant that individual behaviour could be changed by alterations in the social environment:

> the character of man is, without a single exception, always formed for him ... it may be, and is, chiefly, created by his predecessors ... they give him, or may give him, his ideas and habits, which are the powers that govern and direct his conduct. Man, therefore, never did, nor is it possible he ever can, form his own character.[17]

If this is true, the relationship between the sexes can be put on the table for social reform along with everything else; there is nothing natural about any particular family structure.

Marx did not write a great deal about the position of women in society, but a few passages show that he made a connection between the family and private property. In *The German Ideology* (1845), he referred to the family as a kind of "latent slavery"—as the first form of property in that it gave the husband "the power of disposing of the labour-power of others" (i.e., of the wife and children).[18] In *The Communist Manifesto*, Marx and Engels predicted that the family would be revolutionized under communism:

> With the transfer of the means of production into common ownership, the single family ceases to be the economic unit of society. Private housekeeping is transformed into a social industry. The care and education of children becomes a public affair; society looks after all children alike, whether they are legitimate or not.[19]

After Marx's death, Engels explored the theme of the family further in *The Origin of the Family, Private Property and the State* (1884), in which he tried to integrate recent anthropological research into his Marxist ideology. Among his conclusions were that:

> The modern individual family is founded on the open or concealed domestic slavery of the wife, and modern society as a mass is composed of these individual families as its molecules … Within the family, he is the bourgeois, and the wife represents the proletariat … the peculiar character of the supremacy of the husband over the wife in the modern family, the necessity of creating real social equality between them and the way to do it, will only be seen in the clear light of day when both possess legally complete equality of rights. Then it will be plain that the first condition for the liberation of the wife is to bring the whole female sex back into public industry, and that this in turn demands that the characteristic of the monogamous family as the economic unit of society be abolished.[20]

Thus arose the standard Marxist position on what the nineteenth century called "the woman question": that the legal equality so beloved of liberal feminists like Mill was essential but insufficient. The true emancipation of women could only be achieved through communist revolution. To change the relationship between the sexes in a thoroughgoing way would necessitate socializing the means of production and abolishing the economic system of capitalism. As August Bebel, a leading German Social Democrat, put it in *Women under Socialism* (1883), "the solution of the woman question [would be] identical with the solution of the social question."[21]

There is a somewhat paradoxical quality to Marxist feminism. On the one hand, it is very sweeping in its ultimate objectives—far more so than liberal feminism—because it envisions not just legal equality but also major transformations relating to property, work, and the raising of children. On the other hand, it saddles feminism with a secondary role in the revolutionary movement by making women's liberation a consequence of the liberation of the proletariat. So, in practice, while women such as Rosa Luxemburg became leading Marxist revolutionaries, there was never an independent women's movement operating on Marxist principles. The female revolutionaries were integrated with, and under the ultimate control of, the male-dominated socialist parties.

Communist regimes in the Soviet Union and elsewhere acted on the implications of Marxist theory. Quickly after coming to power, communist governments legislated legal equality between men and women and also made efforts to destroy "the monogamous family as the economic unit of society." Women were encouraged, indeed virtually required, to take paid employment outside the home. Inexpensive and publicly operated day-care facilities were made easily available to facilitate women's entry into the labour force. Under most communist regimes, divorce, birth control, and abortion were also readily available, which encouraged a sharp drop in the birthrate—this, in what before the revolution had been largely agrarian societies with high birthrates.

These were real and significant changes, and many Western feminists were initially enthusiastic about the effect of communism upon women's lives. Doubts arose, however, as the decades went by. Communism brought women into the labour market, but it did not liberate them from housework, and the lives of ordinary women were filled with overwork and exhaustion. Women entered and even came to dominate certain prestigious professions, such as medicine; but in those professions they earned less than (largely male) factory workers. The climb of women up the administrative and political hierarchies also seemed to stall. No communist regime ever had a female head of state, head of government, or head of the communist party. Women were always represented on the highest committees, but in a token way; never did they exercise controlling power. And while the communist states sponsored mass political organizations for women, these were always carefully controlled; no independent women's movement was allowed to emerge.

For all of these reasons, Marxist feminism of the traditional type has little weight today in North America. There are still individual Marxist theorists of feminism, but most of them are academics. While their writings continue to exercise some influence among intellectuals, traditional Marxists do not dominate any of the women's organizations that are so prominent in contemporary politics. Yet Marxist feminism did not die without leaving heirs; a sort of transmuted Marxist feminism, usually called radical feminism, is the most provocative force on today's intellectual scene and exercises a remarkable influence on contemporary politics and public policy.

Radical Feminism

The ideology of **radical feminism** was created by women writing at the end of the 1960s and beginning of the 1970s. Most had participated in the New Left movement of the 1960s, which was a noncommunist, anti-authoritarian revival of Marxism. The radical feminists broke with the New Left because they felt that the men in that movement regarded women as subordinate and did not take their concerns seriously. When they departed, they gave up orthodox Marxism but took with them a certain Marxist style of thought that served as a framework for their new categories.

In the radical feminist analysis, women and men constitute separate "sexual classes." History is the story of class struggle between these two sexual classes, not, as the Marxists would have it, between the economic classes of owners and employees. The central concept in radical feminism is not capitalism but **patriarchy**. In the words of Kate Millet, the author of *Sexual Politics*:

> When one group rules another, the relationship between the two is political. When such an arrangement is carried out over a long period of time it develops an ideology (feudalism, racism, etc.). All historical civilizations are patriarchies: their ideology is male supremacy.[22]

In one way this was a definite break with Marxism because it no longer saw property relations as the fundamental variable in human history. The New York Radical Feminists stated in a manifesto that "we do not believe that capitalism, or any economic system, is the cause of female oppression, nor do we believe that female oppression will disappear as a result of a purely economic revolution."[23] But in another way the concepts of sexual class and patriarchy carried forward the Marxian view of history as the story of oppression unfolding toward an ultimate liberation.

In contrast to Marxists, who see the wage relationship as the chief means of exploitation, radical feminists focus on personal, face-to-face relationships between men and women. "Women have very little idea of how much men hate them," wrote Germaine Greer in *The Female Eunuch* (1971).[24] Hence the famous feminist slogan, "The personal is the political."

Specifically, radical feminists analyze certain behaviours, usually regarded previously as social pathologies, as typical forms of male control over females. In *Against our Will: Men, Women and Rape* (1975), Susan Brownmiller wrote that rape is "nothing more or less than a conscious process of intimidation by which all men keep all women in a state of intimidation."[25] Radical feminists see rape as well as sexual harassment and violence against women as widespread, almost universal means of social control. They also apply a similar analysis to pornography, which they condemn not because it openly portrays sexual conduct but because it degrades women. "Pornography is the undiluted essence of anti-female propaganda," in Brownmiller's words.[26]

The problem is not just male misconduct but the family itself. "The tyranny of the biological family" must be ended, according to Shulamith Firestone in *The Dialectic of Sex* (1971).[27] For Ti-Grace Atkinson, "the phenomenon of love is the psychological pivot in the persecution of women,"[28] because it leads them to define themselves in relation to men. For a number of leading radical feminists, emancipation from male domination leads directly to lesbianism, which is a political statement, not just a sexual preference. Adrienne Rich wrote:

> It is the lesbian in every woman who is compelled by female energy, who gravitates toward strong women, who seeks a literature that will express that energy and strength … It is the lesbian in us who is creative, for the dutiful daughter of the fathers in us is only a hack.[29]

Firestone's *Dialectic of Sex* goes farthest in developing the idea of revolution against supposedly "natural" sex roles. Whereas orthodox Marxists emphasize the importance of production, Firestone makes reproduction the key issue. Women will never obtain their liberation until they can give up the "barbaric" function of pregnancy. Childbearing must be rejected in favour of a combination of test-tube fertilization and artificial placentas, or perhaps the implantation of human fetuses in an animal host uterus. Responsibility for child rearing must be transferred from biological families to groups of "contracting" adults not necessarily related to the child.

With the end of the biological family, the incest taboo could be dropped, and "humanity could finally revert to its natural polymorphous sexuality—all forms of sexuality would be allowed and indulged."[30]

Firestone's ideas about reproduction, child rearing, and incest may strike many readers as extreme, as may some other notions of radical feminism, such as the equation of heterosexual intercourse with rape. Opponents of feminism often cite them in an attempt to discredit the whole ideology of feminism. These views, however, are by no means typical of the women's movement or of all feminist thinkers; they lie at the far end of a broad spectrum of opinions about women's place in society. But because in social movements the energy often comes from the extreme, the radical analysis has powerfully affected the feminist agenda in the last two decades. Before the rise of radical feminism, discussion mostly revolved around the liberal agenda of legal equality for women who wanted to take their place in the world of work and politics; typical issues were discrimination in employment, admission to professional schools, and nomination as candidates for political parties. While radical feminism did not reject the importance of such issues, it added a new dimension of "sexual politics." The key issues now became rape, violence against women, the sexual abuse of children, sexual harassment, pornography, and the rights of gays and lesbians.

In Canada, as in many other countries, radical feminism has already had a significant impact on public policy. Human-rights law has been amended to incorporate sexual harassment as a form of discrimination—a conceptual merger between the liberal and radical views. Rape-crisis shelters have been established, and Parliament has changed the law and procedures relating to sexual assault to make convictions easier to obtain. The Supreme Court has removed the statute of limitations on incest and child abuse, again increasing the possibility of convictions; and in the *Butler* case it also accepted the radical feminist position that pornography is harmful because it is degrading to women, not because it is sexually explicit. No political observer writing before the emergence of radical feminism would have predicted these legal and political trends.

Perennial Questions of feminism

It is typical of ideologies that their most central questions seem to have no final answers. Liberals have disagreed for centuries over what freedom "really" means, and there is no general consensus among nationalists as to which groups are "really" nations. Similarly, certain issues in the feminist movement have never been resolved. Two of these are discussed below.

1. *How different are men and women?* Liberal and socialist feminists have generally emphasized the fundamental similarity of men and women as human beings, arguing that the two sexes have the same mental and moral capacities and can do the same kinds of work. They generally regard physical differences

of size and strength as not very important in an increasingly technological world. To the extent that there are more important physical differences associated with reproductive biology, they have often proposed to ameliorate the effects of these differences by changing social arrangements. Relevant examples are the provision of day-care facilities to encourage women's participation in the paid labour force and the recent policy of some law firms to reduce the "billable hours" expectation for female lawyers in the years when they have young children. The purpose of these and similar proposals is to allow women to compete on as equal terms as possible in fields of endeavour that have long been dominated by men. The underlying assumption is that clearing the field of obstacles will allow all players to compete and be judged on the basis of individual performance.

In the 1970s, in the first years of the contemporary feminist movement, the emphasis was largely on the similarity of men and women and their integration across a wide spectrum of activities. But since the publication of Friedan's *The Second Stage* in 1981, feminists have increasingly emphasized the ways in which women differ from men. Carol Gilligan's *In a Different Voice* (1983) argued that men and women approach moral questions differently (men allegedly think in terms of abstract rights and rules, women in terms of networks and mutual support). Another widely read book is Deborah Tannen's *You Just Don't Understand* (1990), which documents the different conversational styles of women and men. Others go even further in arguing that women are not only different from men, but morally superior to them, and therefore must develop their differences in a separate "womanculture."

This "feminism of difference," as it has been called, poses difficult problems for the liberal strategy of integration that is based on the assumption of a fundamental similarity between men and women. If there really are subtle and deep-seated differences in areas such as moral reasoning and conversational style, it may be much harder than liberal feminists originally assumed for women and men to play the same roles in the public world of work and government. Different solutions are conceivable—perhaps women need to change, perhaps men need to change, perhaps the two sexes will become more like each other, perhaps the differences will remain and ways will be found to make them more complementary and harmonious—but this will obviously be more complex than the simple legislating of equal opportunity.

2. *What is the origin of the differences?* Are they biological or cultural? Feminists have given different answers to these questions. For Shulamith Firestone, the difference is essentially biological, and women can never be emancipated until they no longer have to bear children. Other radical feminists, however, insist that the differences are fundamentally cultural and as such can be overcome by social and political action:

By destroying the present society, and building a society based on feminist principles, men will be forced to live in the human community on terms very different from the present. For that to happen, feminism must be asserted by women, as the basis of revolutionary social change.[31]

In this view, women are oppressed by male culture, but they also have their own (now subordinated) "womanculture," which can be asserted through political activism and which will eventually reshape society.

No one would deny that there are cultural differences between men and women related to their upbringing, and the way they are educated in school, depicted in the media, treated by employers, and so on. And no one would deny that these cultural differences can be affected by cultural means. Clearly, women can and do learn to be plumbers and men can and do learn to be nurses. But what if men and women tend to learn some things more readily than other things? That is, it may be that the members of either sex can learn to play almost any role; but left to their own devices, they may tend to learn some roles more readily than others. If that is true, any program of eradicating or minimizing gender differences may require degrees of compulsion that will make at least liberal feminists uncomfortable.

ENVIRONMENTALISM

Like feminism, environmentalism is not a single belief system but a family of ideologies riven by profound internal differences. Also like feminism, environmentalism has old roots, although it has become a major political force only since the 1970s. Some versions of environmentalism can be traced back about a century. There are even older antecedents, such as the speculations of Thomas Malthus about the inevitability of overpopulation; but these are probably best interpreted as environmental reflections within a liberal context rather than the beginning of a new ideology. The genuine tradition of environmentalism began about a century ago with the conservationist movement.

Conservationism

Conservationism is the attempt to manage natural resources so that human users, including future generations, derive maximum benefit over a long period of time. The emergence of the discipline of forestry in the last century was an important development in conservationism. In 1872 the U.S. Congress passed the Yellowstone Park Act to create the first national park. Canada followed suit in 1885 with the creation of Banff National Park. Human use was clearly the driving force in the national parks movement; for example, the Banff park was established around hot springs that were being promoted by the Canadian Pacific Railway as a tourist destination and health resort.

Conservationism has continued to be an important political movement. In 1938, for example, the Government of Alberta created the Oil and Gas Conservation Board with the goal of maximizing petroleum output over time by allocating production among producers drawing from the same oilfields. When too much oil is extracted too quickly, pressure drops in the reservoir to the detriment of long-term yields. All producers are better off in the long run when they control their present output. Other aspects of the conservation movement include flood control, reforestation, soil reclamation, and wildlife management and habitat enhancement. The use of resources by humans is the common aim of all these efforts. For instance, many hunters contribute time and money to Ducks Unlimited in an effort to conserve and restore prairie wetlands, with the long-term goal of improving duck hunting.

Human Welfare Ecology

The rise of **human welfare ecology** began, most observers agree, in 1962, when Rachel Carson's book *Silent Spring* publicized the effects of pesticides, particularly DDT, on the reproduction of birds. This movement began as an extension of conservationism, in that it originally focused on wildlife management. At the same time, it transcended the economic dimension of traditional conservationism; instead, it directly addressed the value to human health and happiness of the environment. Since *Silent Spring*, environmental concerns have broadened out till they now embrace an infinity of issues—air and water quality, carcinogens, the ozone layer, global warming, overpopulation, solid-waste disposal, nuclear radiation, and so on—but in all cases the theme is the effect of environmental degradation on humans. For example, human welfare ecologists fear that the thinning of the ozone layer may lead to an increase in the incidence of skin cancers, and that global warming may cause flooding of coastal cities as well as desertification of presently productive agricultural lands. Like conservationism, human welfare ecology is basically "anthropocentric" (i.e., human-centred).[32]

In practical political terms, the human welfare brand of ecology has led to the passage of environmental legislation, the creation of departments of the environment, and the rise of new regulatory processes, such as impact studies and public hearings on the construction of dams, pulp mills, and other major projects. It has also led to the formation of political parties whose programs are constructed around environmental issues. The first of these "Green" parties was the Values Party of New Zealand (1972); it was followed quickly by similar parties in Europe, Australia, and North America.

Both conservationism and human welfare ecology are best understood in ideological terms as extensions of liberalism. They are chiefly concerned with phenomena that we discussed earlier under the heading of public goods. They typically see problems such as the waste of resources or the pollution of the environment as resulting from "market failure." A famous essay along this line is "The Tragedy of the Commons" (1968) by Garret Hardin. The title comes from an illustration Hardin uses: that of a common pasture that is bound to be overgrazed as long as the livestock owners pursue their individual self-interest without coordination. It is in the interest of each to allow his livestock to graze as much as possible on the pasture; a herder who holds his flock back will not get any benefit because others will simply let their animals graze even more. The herders would like to conserve the pasture but cannot do so without a mechanism to prevent free riding. It is in your interest to limit your own herd's grazing only if you can count on others to do likewise.

This approach places environmental issues squarely within the liberal tradition, with its focus on individual action, profit incentives, and enforcement of rights. The remedies that arise within this perspective correspond roughly to the distinction between classical and reform liberalism. One school of thought, analogous to classical liberalism, is known as **free-market environmentalism**. It argues that the underlying problem in public-goods situations is the failure to assign property rights. There would be no "tragedy of the commons" if the commons were divided up into many individually owned pastures. According to this view, a problem such as air pollution arises because no one owns the atmosphere and has an interest in protecting it from degradation. As a result, manufacturers, power producers, drivers of automobiles—all consumers of goods and services—use the atmosphere as a seemingly free way to get rid of waste products. Free-market environmentalists believe that, while it is not feasible to create literal owners of the atmosphere, a similar result can be achieved by other means. For example, public regulatory authorities could issue licences to emit limited amounts of air pollution, and these licences could subsequently be bought and sold in the market. In this way, atmospheric waste disposal, instead of appearing free as it does at present, would acquire a cost; and as a costly good, users would seek ways to economize on it. The market's invisible hand would thus produce the "right" amount of air pollution, that is, the amount that can be absorbed without causing unacceptable deterioration of human amenities. This approach has been adopted in recent American air-quality legislation and will bear watching to see how it performs in practice.

Other thinkers believe that "the tragedy of the commons" can only be resolved by government direction. This view, which is closer to reform liberalism, typically leads to legislation that limits or prohibits certain acts, for example, the production of chlorofluorocarbons (which damage the ozone layer) or the use of chlorine compounds in the production of paper. Environmental debates over issues of this type expand the agenda of liberalism but do not fundamentally break with it. They are similar in principle to the myriad of other debates going on all the time about whether human purposes are better served by the market or by governmental provision.

Deep Ecology

Deep ecology represents a fundamental break with liberalism, and indeed with all other ideologies, because it is "ecocentric"—that is, it posits the entire natural order, not human happiness, as its highest value. As formulated by Arne Naess and George Sessions in 1974, the basic principles of deep ecology are:

1. The well-being and flourishing of human and nonhuman Life on Earth have value in themselves (synonyms: intrinsic value, inherent value). These values are independent of the usefulness of the nonhuman world for human purposes.

2. Richness and diversity of life forms contribute to the realization of these values and are also values in themselves.

3. Humans have no right to reduce this richness and diversity except to satisfy vital needs.

4. The flourishing of human life and cultures is compatible with a substantial decrease of the human population. The flourishing of nonhuman life requires such a decrease.

5. Present human interference with the nonhuman world is excessive, and the situation is rapidly worsening.

6. Policies must therefore be changed. These policies affect basic economic, technological, and ideological structures. The resulting state of affairs will be deeply different from the present.

7. The ideological change is mainly that of appreciating life quality (dwelling in situations of inherent value) rather than adhering to an increasingly higher standard of living. There will be a profound awareness of the difference between big and great.

8. Those who subscribe to the foregoing points have an obligation directly or indirectly to try to implement the necessary changes.[33]

In such an uncompromising form, deep ecology has few adherents. However, two related views have become important political forces. One is **wilderness preservation**, as manifested in, for example, the movements to save the earth's rain forests, both tropical (the Amazon) and temperate (British Columbia). Adherents of preservationist movements sometimes put forward arguments relating to human advantage (e.g., that the tropical rain forest may be a source of useful medicines); but their case rests mainly on the intrinsic importance of wilderness, whether or not humans use it. The preservationist perspective, however, is usually anthropocentric to some degree, because it tends to focus on environments that appeal strongly to the human sense of beauty and grandeur.

Another variant of deep ecology is the **animal liberation** movement, which proposes to ban hunting, the raising of domestic livestock for food and other economic purposes (although not the keeping of pets), and the use of animals in laboratory experiments. An influential exponent of this movement is the philosopher Peter Singer. In *Animal Liberation* (1975), he argued that all creatures have interests to the extent that they can feel pain, which all the higher animals clearly can do. The cutoff line is difficult to draw, but "somewhere between a shrimp and an oyster seems as good a place to draw the line as any, and better than most."[34] The animal liberation movement is limited because it does not consider the interests of the lower animals, plants, and microorganisms. Using the ability to suffer as a criterion is still anthropocentric, at least by analogy, since it starts from the human desire to avoid pain and extends it to other species. Even so, whatever the logical problems may be, wilderness preservation and animal liberation both point in the direction of deep ecology.

It may be a bit misleading to call deep ecology an ideology, for it is a radical challenge to the civilization that has generated all other ideologies. To the extent that it posits inherent values outside human experience, it has some resemblance to a religious revival; but if deep ecology posits a divinity, it exists in the immanent order of the universe, not in a transcendent God. In fact, deep ecologists are keenly interested in pre-Christian native religious traditions and have tried to develop political alliances with native peoples to protest against commercial development of wilderness areas. The alliance, however, is somewhat fragile, because leaders of native communities are often interested in getting control over development projects, not in blocking them altogether.

🔲🔲🔲🔲🔲🔲🔲

FURTHER READING

Anderson, Terry L., and Donald R. Leal. *Free Market Environmentalism*. San Francisco: Pacific Research Institute for Public Policy, 1991.

Backhouse, Constance. *Challenging Times: The Women's Movement in Canada and the U.S.* Montreal: McGill-Queen's University Press, 1992.

Beauvoir, Simone de. *The Second Sex*. New York: Vintage Books, 1989.

Beckerman, Wilfred. *Through Green-Colored Glasses: Environmentalism Reconsidered*. Washington, D.C.: Cato Institute, 1996.

Block, Walter E., ed. *Economics and the Environment: A Reconciliation*. Vancouver: Fraser Institute, 1990.

Boles, Janet. *American Feminism*. Newbury Park, Calif.: Sage, 1991.

Bouchier, David. *The Feminist Challenge: The Movement for Women's Liberation in Britain and the U.S.A.* London: Macmillan, 1983.

Brodie. M. Janine. *Politics on the Margins: Restructuring and the Canadian Women's Movement*. Halifax, N.S.: Fernwood, 1995.

Brown, L. Susan. *The Politics of Individualism: Liberalism, Liberal Feminism and Anarchism.* Montreal: Black Rose Books, 1993.

Burt, Sandra, Lorraine Code, and Lindsay Dorney, eds. *Changing Patterns: Women in Canada.* Toronto: McClelland and Stewart, 1993.

Carty, Linda, ed. *And Still We Rise: Feminist Political Mobilizing in Contemporary Canada.* Toronto: Women's Press, 1993.

Castro, Ginette. *American Feminism: A Contemporary History.* New York: New York University Press, 1990.

Chafėz, Janet Saltzman. *Women's Movement in World and Historical Perspectives.* Totowa, N.J.: Rowman and Allanheld, 1986.

Devall, Bill. *Deep Ecology: Living as if Nature Mattered.* Salt Lake City: Gibb Smith, 1985.

Donovan, Josephine. *Feminist Theory: The Intellectual Traditions of American Feminism.* New York: Ungar, 1985.

Drury, Shadia B. *Alexandre Kojeve: The Roots of Postmodern Politics.* New York: St. Martin's Press, 1994.

Dunn, James R. *Conservative Environmentalism: Reassessing the Means, Redefining the Ends.* Westport, Conn.: Quorum, 1996.

Eckersley, Robyn. *Environmentalism and Political Theory.* Albany: State University Press, 1992.

Ehrlich, Paul R. *Betrayal of Science and Reason: How Anti-Environmental Rhetoric Threatens Our Future.* Washington, D.C.: Island Press, 1996.

Faludi, Susan. *Backlash: The Undeclared War Against American Women.* New York: Crown, 1991.

Firestone, Shulamith. *The Dialectic of Sex.* London: Cape, 1971.

Friedan, Betty. *The Feminine Mystique.* New York: Dell, 1983.

———. *The Second Stage.* New York: Summit Books, 1981.

Gottlieb, Roger S. *The Ecological Community: Environmental Challenges for Philosophy, Politics and Morality.* New York: Routledge, 1997.

Herndl, Carl G., and Stuart C. Brown, eds. *Green Culture: Environmental Rhetoric in Contemporary America.* Madison, Wis.: University of Wisconsin Press, 1996.

Hirsh, Marianne. *Conflicts in Feminism.* New York: Routledge, 1990.

Hunt, Karen. *Equivocal Feminists: The Social Democratic Federation and the Woman Question, 1884–1911.* New York: Cambridge University Press, 1996.

Jaggar, Alison. *Feminist Politics and Human Nature.* Totowa, N.J.: Rowman and Allanheld, 1983.

Jackman, Mary R. *The Velvet Glove: Paternalism and Conflict in Gender, Class, and Race Relations.* Berkeley, Calif.: University of California Press, 1994.

Lipschutz, Ronnie D., with Judith Mayer. *Global Civil Society and Global Environmental Governance: The Politics of Nature from Place to Planet.* Albany: State University of New York Press, 1996.

Lovenduski, Joni, and Pippa Norris, eds. *Gender and Party Politics.* London: Sage, 1993.

Miles, Angela Rose. *Feminism in Canada.* Montreal: Black Rose Books, 1982.

Mill, John Stuart. *The Subjection of Women.* Arlington Heights, Ill.: AHM Publishing, 1980.

Mitchell, J., and Ann Oakley, eds. *What Is Feminism?* New York: Pantheon Books, 1986.

Nash, Roderick. *American Environmentalism: Readings in Conservation History.* New York: McGraw-Hill, 1990.

Pal, Leslie A. *Interests of State: The Politics of Language, Multiculturalism and Feminism in Canada.* Montreal: McGill-Queen's University Press, 1993.

Pepper, David. *The Roots of Modern Environmentalism.* London: Routledge, 1984.

Pierson, Ruth Roach. *Canadian Women's Issues.* Toronto: Lorimer, 1993–1995.

Rebick, Judy. *Politically Speaking.* Vancouver: Douglas & McIntyre, 1996.

Rendall, Janet. *The Origins of Modern Feminism.* London: Macmillan, 1985.

Scheffer, Victor B. *The Shaping of Environmentalism in America.* Seattle: University of Washington Press, 1991.

Sharpe, Sydney. *The Gilded Ghetto: Women and Political Power in Canada.* Toronto: HarperCollins, 1994.

Sommers, Christina Hoff. *Who Stole Feminism? How Women Have Betrayed Women.* New York: Simon and Schuster, 1994.

Spender, Dale. *Feminist Theorists: Three Centuries of Women's Intellectual Traditions.* London: Women's Press, 1983.

Steinem, Gloria. *Outrageous Acts and Everyday Rebellions.* New York: Holt, Rinehart and Winston, 1983.

Tong, Rosemarie. *Feminist Thought.* Boulder, Colo.: Westview Press, 1989.

Worster, Donald. *American Environmentalism: The Formative Period, 1860–1915.* New York: Wiley, 1973.

LEFT, RIGHT, AND CENTRE

CHAPTER 16

Are ideologies related to each other in a sufficiently systematic way that we can array them along a single dimension? The answer is a qualified yes as far as conservatism, liberalism, and socialism are concerned; this becomes much more complicated when nationalism, feminism, and environmentalism are considered.

Conservatism, liberalism, and socialism are often depicted as lying along a spectrum whose ends are designated *left* and *right*. Many observers would agree more or less on the following construction:

Left		Centre		Right	
	Social	Reform	Classical		
Communism	Democracy	Liberalism	Liberalism	Conservatism	Fascism

Although this spectrum corresponds to common perception, it is not easy to say precisely what it means. Is the left for, and the right against, change? That simplistic explanation will hardly do, for everything depends on who is in power. In a communist state, classical liberalism is an ideology of radical change. In constitutional democracies, both communism and fascism represent radical change. As a yardstick, freedom is not much help either. All ideologies, even fascism, claim to be for freedom, but they define it in different ways. Nor does using democracy as a measure solve the problem, because the democratic centralism of Marxism–Leninism is in reality just as antithetical to popular government as fascism is.

Considering the circumstances in which the words left and right first began to be used as political labels sheds some light on the subject. The custom arose shortly after 1789 in the French National Assembly. Those factions that favoured retaining substantial powers for the monarchy, such as the right to appoint judges and to veto legislation, sat to the right of the chairman of the Assembly. Those that favoured reducing the monarch to a purely symbolic figure and letting the elected representatives of the people exercise all political power sat to the left of the chairman. The basic issue was popular sovereignty. The extreme left held that all political power emanated from the people; the extreme right believed that political power was conferred by God on the king through inheritance, and the centre sought a compromise or balance of these two principles.[1]

This political difference between left and right soon took on an economic dimension as socialism assumed a prominent role in European politics. The term "left" was applied to those who favoured equalization of property through political action. Socialists proposed to replace the market process, which is not under the control of any identifiable individual or group, with a system of state planning. Socialism thus extended popular sovereignty from the political to the economic sphere.

Many ambiguities of the left–right terminology arise from this double origin. Advocates of popular sovereignty do not inevitably favour socialist planning; they may be sincerely convinced that the market principle will in the long run be of more benefit to ordinary working people. It is also not inevitable that advocates of socialist planning will support popular sovereignty with equal warmth, for the desires of the real, existing people (as opposed to the hypothetical, reformed people) may obstruct the plan. In short, the political and the economic left often but do not necessarily coincide.

In contemporary usage, the economic factor predominates, though not entirely. Going back to our commonsense listing of ideologies on the left–right spectrum, we can now give an approximate interpretation in terms of the meanings of equality that have been discussed. Let us now redraw the spectrum, adding the various forms of equality and inequality that the ideologies claim as their own:

Left		Centre		Right	
Equality of Condition	Equality of Opportunity	Equality of Right	Aristocracy	Hierarchy
Communism	Social Democracy	Reform Liberalism	Classical Liberalism	Conservatism	Fascism

This picture could be seriously misleading without appropriate qualifications. Communists advocate long-run equality of result in the sense of the equality of happiness that would be produced by implementing the motto, "From each according to his ability, to each according to his needs." In the short run, they claim to equalize conditions somewhat but not absolutely. Social democrats and reform liberals are not exclusively wedded to equality of opportunity. Their use of the progressive income tax as a levelling measure is also an approach to equality of result. The classical liberal commitment to equality of right is not especially problematic in this context, but the conservative position easily causes confusion. Early conservatives such as Edmund Burke saw hereditary aristocracy as a socially useful institution. Twentieth-century conservatives no longer defend the hereditary principle but may argue that the wealthy will perform some of the same useful functions as a hereditary aristocracy—philanthropy, public service, and so on. Obviously, this position shades into classical liberalism; the difference is only a matter of whether we emphasize the equality of universal rules or the unequal results arising from them. Finally, fascists tended to think of hierarchy not as social transmission through legal inheritance, but as biological transmission of racial qualities. For Hitler, Germans were the master race (*Herrenvolk*), while Jews and Slavs were subhuman (*Untermenschen*). This is the most absolute type of inequality that can be imagined, because there is no conceivable way of altering it. Fascists also completely rejected the constitutional principle of rule of law, which is another formulation of equality of right.

This underlying dimension of egalitarianism is not an absolute scale of measurement that allows us to assign a precise value to an ideology from any time or place. "Leftness" is not a measurable attitude like height or weight. However, it does make a limited amount of sense to say of two ideologies at a certain place and time that one is to the left or right of the other. The same applies to the adherents of ideologies. Thus, it is reasonable to say that in recent Canadian politics, the NDP, as a party of social democracy, is usually to the left of the Liberal Party. Yet the difference is chiefly one of degree. Prime Minister Louis St. Laurent said of the CCF, the predecessor of the NDP, that they were only "Liberals in a hurry." That numerous quasi-socialist measures, such as national health insurance and a publicly owned oil company, were proposed by the CCF/NDP and ultimately legislated by the Liberal Party shows the kinship between the two parties. Similarly, the Liberals, as a reformist party, are generally to the left of the Progressive Conservatives. But again there is much overlapping. In the federal election campaign of 1984, the Conservative leader, Brian Mulroney, proclaimed that medicare was a "sacred trust," even though it had been created by a Liberal government. The Conservatives may have been less enthusiastic in the first instance about the various programs of the welfare state, but they seem reluctant to dismantle them. Finally, the new Reform Party is generally considered to be ideologically to the right of the Conservatives; but most of its main policies (a balanced budget, privatization and deregulation, opposition to official bilingualism and multiculturalism) have also been espoused by many within the Conservative Party, so that Reformers have sometimes been called "Tories in a hurry." It is, therefore, best to think of parties as occupying overlapping positions on the ideological spectrum:

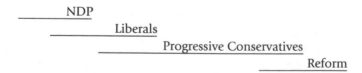

Note that, except for fascism, we have not attempted to place nationalism on the left–right scale. As explained earlier, nationalism has at different times been allied with liberalism, conservatism, and socialism. Commitment to the nation-state does not automatically dictate a position on issues of equality. It is worth noting here that in times of war, normal political differences are suspended. Parties of the left and right often come together in a coalition government of national unity to carry out the war effort. This shows that support for the nation is on a different level than other political issues. When the threat to the nation is past, the distinction between left and right reasserts itself, and governments of national unity soon fall apart (as happened in France and Italy after World War II).

The Bloc Québécois furnishes another example of how nationalism does not fit onto the standard left–right spectrum. The Bloc, formed in 1989 by the former Progressive Conservative Lucien Bouchard as a protest against delays in ratifying the Meech Lake Accord, is essentially a single-issue movement devoted to the goal of turning Quebec into a sovereign state. The MPs who joined the Bloc defected from both the Conservative and the Liberal Parties; and they were joined in the 1993 election by candidates who had previously worked for other parties in Quebec, such as the NDP. The present leader, Gilles Duceppe, was a communist in his youth. Although the party takes positions from time to time on various issues, it really has no program except the independence of Quebec and thus cannot be placed on the same dimension as other Canadian federal parties.

The varieties of feminism can be aligned partially, though not completely, with the left–right spectrum. Liberal feminists and socialist feminists can without too much distortion be seen as liberals and socialists who happen to be particularly concerned with a certain set of problems. Overall, their thinking fits into familiar liberal and socialist categories. Radical feminism, however, is much more difficult to place. As a transformation of Marxism, it seems to belong on the left; and when radical feminists get involved in electoral politics, they usually do so with parties of the left. But their overriding concern with patriarchy is fundamentally different from the concerns with popular sovereignty and economic equality that characterize positions on the left–right spectrum, so that we might think of radical feminism as belonging on a dimension that cuts perpendicularly across the left–right dimension. This helps to explain what otherwise might be seen as some strange political coalitions. For example, radical feminists have frequently worked together with conservatives in law-enforcement agencies on issues such as pornography, sexual abuse, and violence against women. The two groups conceptualize the issues in totally different ways, but they agree on the desirability of harsher criminal penalties. Liberals who are thought of as quite left-wing—for example, members of the Canadian Civil Liberties Association—can find themselves on the opposite side on these issues even though they may think of themselves as quite favourable to feminism.

The situation with environmentalism is similar. Generally, we can comfortably sort out environmentalists by examining the means they advocate to achieve their ends. Free-market environmentalists clearly belong with the classical liberals, while many advocates of human welfare ecology just as clearly prefer the more interventionist tools of reform liberalism and social democracy. But deep ecology, like radical feminism, is really on a different dimension because it rejects the materialist goals of the other ideologies.

The left–right spectrum, though often useful, is unidimensional. Real-world ideologies are multidimensional—that is, they are concerned not only with inequality and equality but with many other political values. For example, it would be possible to map ideologies on a continuum according to their views on the scope of state control of society:

Maximum ⟶		Minimum
Communism	Social Democracy	Classical Liberalism
Fascism	Reform Liberalism	Conservatism	Anarchism

Communists and fascists favour the total identification of state and society. Social democrats and reform liberals favour active government regulation and intervention but do not wish to subject all of society to state control. Conservatives and classical liberals desire a very limited state to carry out certain restricted functions; otherwise, they want society to evolve according to its own laws. Anarchists believe that society can exist without any government at all.

The above is as valid as the conventional left–right approach, but it expresses another aspect of the reality of ideologies, and thus does not coincide with the left–right spectrum. To speak of left and right is a useful shorthand way of referring to ideologies as long as the limitations of this approach are kept in mind. Left and right are only convenient labels; they are no substitute for a detailed understanding of a point of view. Difficulties quickly become apparent when we try to apply the notion of a left–right continuum to concrete issues. To illustrate, let us look at several issues from the realms of economics, politics, and society.

Among economic issues, the left–right spectrum fits very well the debate about progressive taxation. Those furthest to the left are the most vociferous in their desire to "make the rich pay," as the Communist Party of Canada used to put it. Those in the centre accept the principle of progressive taxation but may worry that the marginal rate is so high as to interfere with productivity; they wish the state to act in a redistributive way, but not to "kill the goose that lays the golden eggs." Those on the right reject progressive taxation in favour of a flat tax, that is, one whose rate is the same for all. The issue of taxation can be readily mapped onto the left–right continuum because the underlying question is one of egalitarianism.

On social issues, the left seems to favour a position of individual libertarianism—abortion on demand, legalization of marijuana, abolition of movie censorship—and the right seems to uphold traditional standards of morality. But this seeming unidimensionality exists only in liberal democracies where the extreme left is weak, as in North America. Communists and other revolutionary leftists are in fact rather puritanical in their outlook on many moral questions. Marijuana and other mind-altering drugs are rigorously forbidden in communist countries, as are many mildly obscene books and movies that would hardly raise an eyebrow in the Western world. Freedom of individual choice is not a high priority for the revolutionary left.

Even with all these nuances and exceptions, the terms left and right are convenient for categorizing ideological tendencies. Most of the inconsistencies disappear if we restrict the application of the terms to stable constitutional democracies in which the extreme right and extreme left are weak or nonexistent. Under these conditions, left and right stand for relatively coherent ideological positions—reform liberalism and social democracy on the one side, classical liberalism and conservatism on the other. The more moderate forms of feminism and environmentalism can be fitted into this tableau without too much strain; but if radical feminism and deep ecology ever become dominant ideologies, left and right will have to be either redefined or abandoned altogether as practical labels.

FURTHER READING

Ball, Terence, and Richard Dagger, eds. *Ideals and Ideologies: A Reader*. New York: HarperCollins, 1991.

Boaz, David. *Libertarianism: A Primer*. New York: Free Press, 1997.

Caute, David. *The Left in Europe since 1789*. New York: McGraw-Hill, 1966.

Cheles, Luciano, Ronnie Ferguson, and Michalina Vaughan, eds. *The Far Right in Western and Eastern Europe*. White Plains, N.Y.: Longman, 1995.

Clement, Wallace, and Rianne Mahon, eds. *Swedish Social Democracy: A Model in Transition*. Toronto: Canadian Scholars' Press, 1994.

Cormack, Mike. *Ideology*. London: Batsford, 1992.

Eatwell, Roger, and Anthony Wright, eds. *Contemporary Political Ideologies*. London: Pinter Pubs, 1993.

Hockenos, Paul. *Free to Hate: The Rise of the Right in Post-Communist Eastern Europe*. New York: Routledge, 1993.

Holmes, Stephen. *The Anatomy of Antiliberalism*. Cambridge, Mass.: Harvard University Press, 1993.

Kaase, Max, and Kenneth Nentin, *Beliefs in Government*. Oxford: Oxford University Press, 1995.

Ostry, Sylvia, and Richard R. Nelson. *Techno-Nationalism and Techno-Globalism: Conflict and Cooperation*. Washington: Brookings Institution, 1995.

Waddan, Alex. *The Politics of Social Welfare: The Collapse of the Centre and the Rise of the Right*. Cheltenham, England: Edward Elgar Pub. Co., 1997.

Waller, Michael, Bruno Coppieters, and Kris Deschouwer, eds. *Social Democracy in a Post-Communist Europe*. Ilford, England: Frank Cass, 1994.

Forms of Government

PART 3

CLASSIFICATION OF POLITICAL SYSTEMS

The review of ideologies completed in Part Two leads naturally to a study of forms of government. Ideologies are not just abstract ideas; they reflect the experience of people who live under one form of government or another. This experience may express itself ideologically as acceptance of a governmental form, or as rejection of it, or as a combination—partial acceptance with proposals for modification. Also, as Marx saw, ideology is at least in part determined by the social milieu, in which government is an important factor. Finally, ideology is a determining factor of government because it establishes goals toward which people strive. For example, liberals try to fashion governmental machinery to enhance individual freedom, however they may define it, while socialists enhance the power of the state through central planning and the nationalization of industry. All this means that government and ideology are reciprocally related—each causes and is caused by the other. Part Three of this book examines the chief forms of government in relation to the ideological climate of the late twentieth century.

Before one can understand a complicated set of facts, one must be able to classify them—to sort them into groups based on their position along some dimension. This process of organizing factual information about governmental systems produces broad schemes of classification usually known as **typologies**. Once such typologies are formed, one can formulate and test generalizations about the similarities and differences among the various categories.

🔁🔁🔁🔁🔁🔁🔁

THE CLASSICAL TYPOLOGY

One of the oldest, and still one of the best, typologies of governments dates back to the founders of political science, Plato and Aristotle. They classified governments with two questions in mind: *Who rules?* and *In whose interest?* Possible answers to the first question were simple: rule may be exercised by a single person, by a minority ("the few"), or by a majority of the whole people ("the many"). The second question, concerning whose interests are served, is more difficult and requires a longer answer.

Plato held that there are two basic ways in which rule may be conducted: lawfully and lawlessly. Either the governors are bound by constitutional rules that they are not free to set aside, or they rule according to unchecked whims and emotional desires. The first possibility corresponds to what we have called the rule of law, the second to the arbitrary rule of individuals. In the words of Aristotle:

> He who bids the law rule may be deemed to bid God and Reason alone rule, but he who bids man rule adds an element of the beast; for desire is a wild beast, and passion perverts the minds of rulers, even when they are the best of men. The law is reason unaffected by desire.[1]

Aristotle added that rule by law is in the general interest of the entire community, whereas arbitrary rule represents exploitation of the ruled for the special interest of the governors. He also pointed out that rule in the common interest tends to be seen as legitimate, and gives rulers authority that the ruled will obey voluntarily; while selfish government does not seem legitimate to those who are oppressed, and therefore has to be sustained by coercion and fear. In sum, we have two kinds of regimes: lawful authority seeking the common good, and lawless coercion seeking private interest. Combining these two dimensions of "who" and "how" yields a sixfold typology, illustrated in Figure 17.1.

FIGURE 17.1 Platonic/Aristotelian Typology of Government

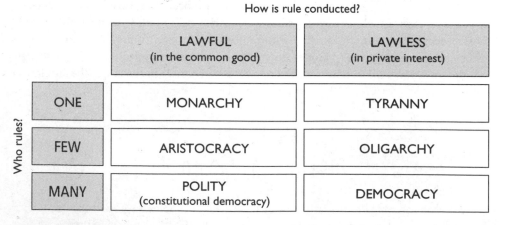

A **monarchy** for Plato and Aristotle was a regime in which sovereign authority was vested in one person, who ruled within the laws of the *polis*. Its corrupt counterpart was a **tyranny**, in which one person ruled arbitrarily. An **aristocracy** was a system in which political power was held by a restricted class—usually the wealthy and those of noble ancestry—that ruled in the general interest under law. An **oligarchy**, in contrast, was a regime where the wealthy minority used its power to exploit and oppress the impoverished majority. **Democracy**, in the Greek sense of the term, was also an exploitative form of government, in the sense that the many used their political power to obtain for themselves the wealth of the rich—a majority oppressing a minority. It was the rule of the common people unchecked by legal restraints. The positive counterpart of democracy was **polity**, which today we might call constitutional democracy. This word is derived from *politeia*, the Greek word for constitution. It expresses the idea that the rule of the many is good only if it is exercised within a fixed constitutional framework that prevents the majority from oppressing minorities. It represents the balance of public and private interests through the political process.

This raises a more general point: to the Greek philosophers, democracy or popular government was not necessarily a good thing. Any lawful regime was preferable to any lawless one. The question of numbers, though not unimportant, was secondary to the question of lawfulness. This insight—that who rules is less important than how rule is conducted—has almost been forgotten because of the twentieth-century habit of regarding democracy as something good in itself. Plato and Aristotle would have said that while a polity or constitutional democracy is a good form of government, unchecked democracy is only mob rule, little different in principle from tyranny or oligarchy. The nineteenth-century writers Alexis de Tocqueville and John Stuart Mill made the same point when they expressed the fear that democracy could become a "tyranny of the majority."[2]

Plato and Aristotle left us a body of thought that emphasizes the rule of law—yet paradoxically, Plato believed there was an even higher form of rule. In his famous book *The Republic*, he sketched the ideal of rule by a **philosopher-king**, a man so preeminent in wisdom and moral virtue that he could rule by personal judgment rather than by the constraint of law. He would not be arbitrary or oppressive, because his philosophic wisdom would protect him from the temptations of power. The people would consent to this form of rule because it would be in their own interest.

Plato never completely renounced his belief in the philosopher–king, but he became rather pessimistic about the possibility of finding such a man. In a later dialogue, *The Statesman*, he suggested that the rule of law was an acceptable, second-best alternative in the absence of a philosopher–king. And in his last work, *The Laws*, the philosopher-king is nowhere to be found.

Thus Plato, along with his pupil Aristotle, came to see the law as the best political solution likely to be attained by imperfect human beings. Rule of law is second-best in terms of what might be imagined, but best in terms of what human beings, with their limited knowledge, can probably achieve. Yet the image of the philosopher–king, who rules above law in the common good, has never ceased to haunt history. Many totalitarian and authoritarian regimes claiming superiority to the law have been based on it.

One other important point must be made. Aristotle was always careful to point out that the conflict between the few and the many was as much one of wealth as of numbers, since in practice the many are usually poor relative to the wealthy few. In his view, the besetting vice of democracy was that the majority used the state's power to confiscate the property of the wealthy minority; the parallel failing of oligarchy was that the wealthy few manipulated the laws to bring about easier exploitation of the masses.

Aristotle's preference was for a polity or constitutional democracy where the rights of property would be protected by law. In a sense, polity is a compromise between two negative governmental forms: democracy and oligarchy. If both the wealthy and the poor, the few and the many, hold a share of power in the state, but neither faction is supreme, they will check each other. Thus, in a negative way, we come back to the desired situation of the rule of law, because the counterpoised factions will watch each other to make sure that neither begins to manipulate the laws to its own advantage. However, Aristotle also pointed out that the balance would probably be unstable if society were polarized into camps of extreme wealth and poverty. It would be best to have a large middle class, as this in a sense would unite numbers and property within itself. Such a class, though not itself rich, would have a stake in protecting the property of the rich—for if the rich could be despoiled, the middle class itself might be next. Aristotle's words have lost none of their wisdom after 2300 years:

> Great then is the good fortune of a state in which the citizens have a moderate and sufficient property; for where some possess much, and others nothing there may arise an extreme democracy, or a pure oligarchy; or a tyranny may grow out of either extreme.[3]

MODERN TYPOLOGIES

The classical typology of the six forms of government was the beginning of political science and is still useful today, but it is not the only approach to classification. Indeed, there can never be a definitive or final typology, because classification depends on which aspect of reality we wish to emphasize. As forms of government evolve through history, schemes of classification evolve with them. The remainder of Part Three uses three different typologies, which correspond to three aspects of government in the twentieth century.

First, we classify governments according to the relationship between state and society on which they are based. The three types that appear in this classification are liberal–democratic, totalitarian, and authoritarian. Second, we classify governments according to the relationship between the executive and legislative powers of government. The chief distinction here is between parliamentary and presidential systems. Third, we classify governments according to their degree of centralization or decentralization. This was not a major concern of Plato and Aristotle, who thought of government chiefly in the context of the small, independent polis; but it is a big problem for the large states of modern times. The major types in this context are the unitary state, devolution, federalism, and confederation.

Our three classification schemes are not mutually exclusive; rather, they can be applied together for a multidimensional description of any particular government. Thus Canada would be described as a liberal–democratic, parliamentary, and federal state; and Indonesia would be authoritarian, presidential, and federal. There are no longer many obvious cases of totalitarianism today—at least, no cases as extreme as Stalin's Soviet Union, Hitler's Germany, or Mao's China in the early years of the People's Republic. Perhaps North Korea and Cuba would qualify, although considerable change has been taking place in Cuba as a result of the loss of Soviet support. There are inevitably many borderline cases that tend to straddle categories; for example, even though political reforms are under way, Mexico still combines certain aspects of both the liberal–democratic and authoritarian forms, while France represents a unique combination of parliamentary and presidential systems, and federalism in the former Soviet Union was largely overridden in practice by the overwhelming power of the Communist Party. Also, due to political transitions occurring in many countries today, nation-states can change quickly from one classification to another. Over the past decade, for example, Chile (a case discussed more extensively in Chapter 20) has moved from an authoritarian military dictatorship to a more liberal–democratic system of government. But, even though all typologies involve intermediate or ill-fitting cases, we can use these classifications as a first approach to the phenomena we wish to study.

FURTHER READING

Almond, Gabriel A., and G. Bingham Powell, Jr., eds. *Comparative Politics Today: A World View*, 6th ed. New York: HarperCollins, 1996.

Andrain, Charles F. *Comparative Political Systems: Policy Performance and Social Change*. Armonk, N.Y.: M.E. Sharpe, 1994.

Blondel, Jean. *Comparative Government: An Introduction*. New York: Phillip Allan, 1990.

———. *The Organization of Government*. London: Sage, 1982.

Crick, Bernard. *Basic Forms of Government: A Sketch and a Model*. London: Macmillan, 1973.

Davis, Morton R., and Vaughan A. Lewis. *Models of Political Systems*. London: Macmillan, 1971.

Diamond, Larry, et al. *Politics in Developing Countries: Comparing Experiences with Democracy*. Boulder, Colo.: Lynne Rienner Publishers, 1990.

Jackson, Robert J., and Doreen Jackson. *Contemporary Government and Politics: Democracy and Authoritarianism*. Scarborough, Ont.: Prentice-Hall, 1993.

Kamrava, Mehran. *Politics and Society in the Third World*. London: Routledge, 1993.

Macridis, Roy C. *Introduction to Comparative Politics: Regimes and Change*. New York: Harper Collins, 1991.

Mayer, Lawrence C. *Comparative Politics: Nations and Theories in a Changing World*, 2nd ed. Upper Saddle River, N.J.: Prentice-Hall, 1996.

Rustow, Dankwart, and Kenneth Paul Erikson, eds. *Comparative Political Dynamics: Global Research Perspectives*. New York: Harper Collins, 1991.

Wiarda, Howard J., ed. *New Directions in Comparative Politics*, 2nd ed. Boulder, Colo.: Westview Press, 1990.

Wilson, Frank Lee. *Concepts and Issues in Comparative Politics: An Introduction to Comparative Analysis*. Upper Saddle River, N.J.: Prentice-Hall, 1996.

LIBERAL DEMOCRACY

In today's world, virtually every government claims to be democratic; certainly, Canadians claim to have a democratic system. And when we criticize a government, it is often for not being democratic enough. But democracy was not always so popular. Its universal acceptance stems only from the years of World War I, which was fought, in the famous words of the American president Woodrow Wilson, "to make the world safe for democracy." Opinion was divided in the nineteenth century; and before then, almost everyone who had ever written anything on politics was sceptical about democracy.

Democracy in itself is simply a technique, a way of making certain decisions by accepting the will of the majority. For us it becomes a legitimate form of government only when it is united with the traditional Western ideals of constitutionalism, rule of law, liberty under law, and the limited state. And conversely, it is not the only legitimate form of government. Although only a relatively small number of people could vote, aristocratic rule was not always considered oppressive. Our current democratic government carries on British constitutionalism while bringing the common people into the political realm.

The most basic conceptual problem today is that the two dimensions of the "how" and the "who" of government have become blurred in the single term *democracy*. Its current usage suggests not only majority rule, but also a condition of freedom in which a limited state respects people's rights. Freedoms of speech, religion, and so on are commonly identified as democratic liberties, though they aren't necessarily found in a democracy. To cloud the issue even further, democracy outside the Western world often means government allegedly for the many, but conducted by a ruling elite, such as a communist vanguard party or a military *junta* (Spanish for a group of individuals forming a government, especially after a revolution) that faces few constitutional limitations. All of this raises so many problems that we will restrict ourselves for the moment to a discussion of Western democracy, which in itself is extremely complex. As one writer has stated:

In the nineteenth century, democratic government was seen mainly in terms of equality of political and legal rights, of the right to vote, to express differing political opinions and to organise political opinion through political parties, of the right of elected representatives to supervise or control the activities of the government of the day. Today, much more stress is laid upon the need for the State to guarantee to everybody certain economic and social rights, involving the elimination of educational and social inequalities.[1]

Over the past century, the concept of democracy has been expanded. As Giovanni Sartori has written:

Up until the 1940s people knew what democracy was and either liked or rejected it; since then we all claim to like democracy but no longer know (understand, agree) what it is. We characteristically live, then, in an age of confused democracy. That "democracy" obtains several meanings is something we can live with. But if "democracy" can mean just anything, that is too much.[2]

Democracy has now come to imply freedom—encompassing political, economic, and social rights—as well as the rule of the many.

Brief reflection is enough to show that these two dimensions are quite different and that there is no necessary connection between them. Freedom is usually made possible by the rule of law, which minimizes arbitrary coercion and maximizes universal submission to equal laws. Yet the rule of the many, as Aristotle saw, may or may not be lawful. Specifically, a majority might take away the property, language, or religious rights of a minority unless the majority itself is restrained by the constitution. Democracy *requires* freedom only in the limited and partial sense that a certain amount of political freedom is necessary if the people are to choose officials: they must have a chance to nominate candidates, discuss issues, cast ballots, and so on. But beyond this necessary minimum, democracy in other realms of life could be quite oppressive.

For example, in the southern United States white employers sometimes refused to hire blacks. And in Canada, employers have sometimes refused to hire aboriginals. Such job discrimination can limit freedom in that the denial of a job possibility may be the denial of an opportunity to improve one's lot in life. In most democracies today, the definition of democracy includes the assumption that all individuals have an equal legal right to be considered for employment.

From now on, we will use the term **constitutional** or **liberal democracy** to denote a system in which the majority chooses rulers, who must then govern within the rule of law. This is exactly what Plato and Aristotle meant by polity.

The term *liberal democracy* must be carefully interpreted. It refers to liberalism in the broadest sense, without distinguishing between classical and reform liberalism. Whatever their disagreements about *laissez faire*, social justice, redistribution, or government intervention, classical and reform liberals are united in their support of constitutional procedures, the limited state, and a private sphere of personal freedom. Liberal democracy, based on this common ground, is broad enough to encompass different experiments in economic policy. The moderate form of socialism that we have called social democracy is also compatible with liberal democracy as a system of government. The limited amounts of nationalization, central planning, and egalitarianism advocated by social democrats are subordinated to majority rule and respect for constitutional procedure.

Communism, however, was never compatible with liberal democracy. In the people's democracies of Eastern Europe, the Leninist theory of democratic centralism, as converted into the operating philosophy of the communist state, did not allow for political freedom and the right of constitutional opposition. The uncontested elections that were the hallmark of communism in power were sharply different from the practice of liberal democracy. When democratization began in Eastern Europe in 1989, those countries repudiated communism and democratic centralism as quickly as they could. From the West they imported the entire apparatus of liberal democracy, including competitive elections, multiple political parties, an executive answerable to an elected legislature, and an independent judiciary. Based on the historical record thus far, we can say that there is only one kind of democracy—liberal democracy—that is worthy of the name.

Liberal democracy can be briefly defined as a system of government in which the people rule themselves, either directly or indirectly (through chosen officials) but in either case subject to constitutional restraints on the power of the majority. This definition can be expanded through an examination of four operating principles of liberal democracy: equality of political rights, majority rule, political participation, and political freedom. Let us look at these one by one.

EQUALITY OF POLITICAL RIGHTS

Equality of political rights means that every individual has the same right to vote, run for office, serve on a jury, speak on public issues, and carry out other public functions. Obviously, political rights are a matter of degree, and it is only in this century, with women and ethnic minorities attaining these rights, that full equality has been approached in most Western systems. There is no hard-and-fast means for determining how much political equality is enough for democracy to exist; that being said, universal adult male suffrage was an important threshold because it broke through the barrier of socioeconomic class. Once all (or almost all) men could vote, granting the franchise to women doubled the electorate. This was certainly a significant change; but women, like men, belong to all classes and do not constitute a class or voting bloc in themselves. (Of course, women as voters are on average more interested in certain types of issues that directly affect them, so their obtaining the right to vote has had an important influence on the political agenda.)

By this criterion, the United States was the first democracy of modern times. Equality of political rights was not attained all at once because the constitution of 1787 let the individual states determine the franchise. In the first decades of the nineteenth century, the states one by one adopted universal manhood suffrage, except in the South, where slaves were excluded. The emancipated slaves were theoretically enfranchised after the Civil War, but most were prevented from voting by various tactics until the 1960s. Women received the right to vote in federal elections at a single stroke, through the Nineteenth Amendment (1920).

Great Britain was somewhat behind the United States in providing equality of political rights. At the beginning of the nineteenth century, there was still a restrictive franchise that allowed only about 200,000 male property owners to vote in elections for the House of Commons. The parliamentary Reform Acts of 1832, 1867, and 1884 gradually extended the franchise to include the middle class and the more prosperous elements of the working class. The remaining men, as well as women aged 30 and older, received the vote in 1918; women were granted suffrage on equal terms with men in 1928. The growth curve of the British electorate is illustrated in Figure 18.1.

The expansion of the franchise in Canada is more difficult to describe because it was intricately involved in federal–provincial relations. Before 1885, qualifications to vote in parliamentary elections had been determined by the provinces. In that year, Sir John A. Macdonald pushed a uniform Electoral Franchise Act through Parliament, in part because he did not like the tendency of provinces to abolish the property franchise.[3] The Act of 1885 established a moderate property qualification that remained until 1898, when the government of Sir Wilfrid Laurier returned the franchise to the domain of the provinces. Most property qualifications disappeared around that time.

FIGURE 18.1 Number of Persons Having Right to Vote per 100 Adults

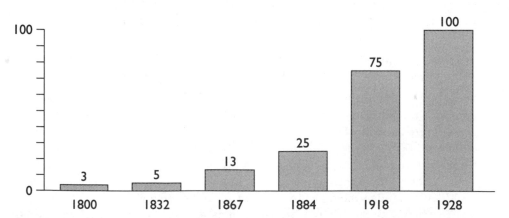

Source: J. Harvey and L. Bather, *The British Constitution*, 2nd ed. (London: Macmillan, 1968), p. 51.

From 1898 to 1917, the provinces controlled the federal franchise, but they could not disenfranchise particular groups of people: if people could vote in provincial elections, they could also vote in federal elections. In other words, provinces could not, through legislation, isolate certain groups demographically and deny them the right to vote in federal elections. In the Military Voters Act and the Wartime Elections Act (1917), the federal government was selective in extending and restricting the suffrage. Under the former, all men and women on active service were permitted to vote. Under the latter, conscientious objectors and those of enemy alien birth were denied the franchise, while wives, widows, and female relatives of men overseas were enfranchised.[4] In 1920, with the passage of the Dominion Elections Act, the federal government resumed control of qualifications for voting in federal elections, while qualifications for voting in provincial elections remained the responsibility of provincial governments. In 1918 women aged 21 and older gained the right to vote in federal elections. Provincially, women were first enfranchised in Manitoba, in 1916; not until 1940 were they allowed to vote in Quebec.[5] Indians were enfranchised in 1960.

Although each country's history is unique, the general pattern in the Western world has been a step-by-step extension of the franchise, with universal adult male suffrage being reached at the end of the nineteenth or beginning of the twentieth century. In most countries, women were given the vote during or shortly after World War I. Switzerland was one exception; women received the right to vote in that country's federal elections only in 1971, and even later in some cantonal (provincial) elections. Indeed, the men of one laggard canton did not agree to grant the franchise to women until 1989.

Today, the franchise can hardly be extended further in most liberal–democratic countries except by giving it to noncitizens, children, prisoners, those with no fixed address, and the mentally disabled. The latter received the right to vote at the federal level in Canada beginning with the election of 1988. The right of prisoners to vote was affirmed in 1993 by the Supreme Court of Canada, when it held that the legislation depriving prisoners of the franchise conflicted with Section 3 of the Canadian Charter of Rights and Freedoms, which states that "every citizen has the right to vote in an election of members of the House of Commons or of a legislative assembly."[6] We have virtually reached the end of a process that has transformed the vote from a trust exercised by property owners or heads of families into a universal right of adult citizens.

꜖꜖꜖꜖꜖꜖꜖

MAJORITY RULE

Majority rule is the normal working principle of decision making in democracies. It can be derived logically from the prior principle of political equality. If each vote is to be counted equally, the decision of the majority must be accepted. Any other procedure must inevitably weigh some votes more heavily than others.

Yet in some circumstances democracies depart from majority rule. Election to public office in Canada, Britain, and the United States is normally by **plurality** rather than **majority**. The candidate with the largest number of votes is declared victorious, even if the number is less than the "50 percent plus one" that constitutes a majority. This easing of the majority criterion is for purposes of economy. If candidates for office were always required to receive a majority, there would have to be an expensive series of runoffs to reduce the candidates to two; only then could it be guaranteed that a plurality would also be a majority of votes cast. In fact, some countries—France, for example—do employ runoff elections. The French president must receive an absolute majority of votes cast, which in practice means a two-stage election.

The majority requirement is also sometimes raised (for example, to three-fifths, or two-thirds, or three-fourths) in what is known as a **qualified majority**. This is done to protect the rights of minorities. Because a qualified majority is obviously harder to obtain than a simple majority, it becomes more difficult for the larger group to act against the rights of the smaller.

The qualified majority, while a constraint upon democracy, is within the spirit of the rule of law. It is incorporated in most modern democracies as part of the process of constitutional amendment, on the assumption that the fundamental laws of the state are so important that they should not be easily altered by a simple majority. A constitutional amendment in the United States, after being passed by two-thirds of the Senate and House of Representatives, must be ratified by three-fourths of the states. In Canada, amending most parts of the Constitution requires ratification by the Senate, the House of Commons, and the legislative assemblies of "at least two-thirds of the provinces that have, in the aggregate, according to the latest general census, at least fifty per cent of the population of all the provinces." On certain matters of fundamental importance, such as recognition of the monarchy, the consent of all provinces is required.[7]

A variation of the qualified majority is the **concurrent majority**, which was sometimes used in the legislature of the old united province of Canada (1840–67). In that specific case, laws had to receive a majority of votes from representatives of both Canada East (Quebec) and Canada West (Ontario). This was supposed to prevent the two regions, one English and one French, from oppressing each other. A special form of the concurrent majority is **bicameralism**, the practice of dividing the legislature into two chambers. The requirement that a bill be passed in two different houses of the assembly is meant to be a safeguard against precipitous action. John A. Macdonald called the Canadian Senate "the sober second thought in legislation." He also supported the requirement, entrenched in Section 23(4) of the Constitution Act, 1867, that a senator's "Real and Personal Property shall be together worth Four thousand Dollars over and above his Debts and Liabilities," a substantial amount at that time. According to Macdonald, "a large property qualification should be necessary for membership in the Upper House, in order to represent the principle of property. The rights of the minority must be protected, and the rich are always fewer in number than the poor."[8]

While the Senate no longer plays the role Macdonald envisioned for it, its continued existence illustrates the principle that liberal democracy sometimes accepts restraints on the will of popular majorities in order to protect the legal rights of potentially unpopular minorities. A requirement for unanimity would be the ultimate in protection for minorities, because then no one could be required to do anything against his or her will. But the practical task of getting unanimous agreement is so formidable that political systems have had to settle for a qualified or concurrent majority as a restraint on popular powers.

POLITICAL PARTICIPATION

Democratic institutions are founded on mass participation. The two great varieties of democracy, which differ in the nature of this participation, are **direct democracy**, the only kind known to the ancient world, and **representative democracy** (or indirect democracy, as it is sometimes called), the predominant form in modern times.

In the city-states of Greece, direct democracy was practised. The highest authority was the assembly of all male citizens (slaves were not citizens and could not vote). Executive officers were either elected by this body or chosen by lot—a procedure that was considered superbly democratic because it gave everyone an equal chance to serve. In either case, terms of office were very short—usually a year or less. Citizens were paid to hold office and even to attend assembly meetings, so that poverty would not prevent participation.

Assembly-style direct democracy faces two obvious problems. One involves the practical difficulty of assembling more than a few thousand individuals to discuss public issues. If direct democracy was just barely possible in the Greek city-state, how could it exist in the modern nation-state, which is so much larger? The other problem concerns the quality of decisions made at large meetings, where emotional rhetoric and demagoguery can easily sway votes. The democracy of Athens destroyed itself by enthusiastically voting for a disastrous military campaign against Syracuse. The best minds of antiquity, including Plato and Aristotle, were so unimpressed with direct democracy in action that they turned decisively against it.[9]

Representative democracy seems to address both problems. It overcomes the obstacles of population and distance while providing the means for choosing rulers whose talents are presumably superior to those of the people at large. These rulers are then kept in check, and directed by the majority, through the machinery of elections. A ruler elected for life would be effectively insulated from the popular will. This is why democracy requires regular elections that those in power cannot indefinitely postpone.

The rationale behind representative government was clearly stated in 1825 by James Mill, the first important political philosopher to argue in favour of what we would today call democracy. "The people as a body," he wrote, "cannot perform the business of government for themselves."[10] What was required, he continued, was the creation of a system of "checks" that would induce rulers to act for the general benefit. These checks would be established by electing representatives of the community for a limited period. Limiting the duration of rule was, according to Mill, "an old and approved method of identifying as nearly as possible the interests of those who rule with the interests of those who are ruled."[11]

It cannot be emphasized too strongly that democratic elections do not and cannot decide questions of policy. Citizens vote for representatives but do not make policy decisions; elected representatives make those decisions for the society. Citizens probably agree with some opinions of their favourite candidates and disagree with others. Also, neither voters nor candidates can be sure of what the future will bring. Politicians are notorious for breaking campaign promises not because they are especially dishonest, but because things look different a year or two after the election, particularly when seen from the perspective of public responsibility. Elections are much more a judgment on recent policies than a decision about the future. If the voters know they are dissatisfied with the past record of the incumbent government, they have the chance to install another government. It is not much, but it is enough to keep representative democracy working.

Many contemporary critics of representative democracy focus on the idea that elected officials have their own political agendas and disregard the wishes of the public. Such critics advocate a move toward some form of direct democracy, or at least more public involvement in the policy-making process. One way to do this would be to institutionalize direct-democratic practices such as the referendum, the initiative, and the recall.

In a **referendum**, electors are asked to vote directly on a constitutional amendment, piece of legislation, or other policy proposal such as a bond issue. Some authors use the term **plebiscite** for a nonbinding, advisory referendum,[12] but we will not follow this usage because it is not universal. Both binding and nonbinding referendums are common around the world.

Referendums are used frequently in Switzerland at all levels of government, and in the United States at the state and local levels (though not the federal one). They are required in Australia for the approval of all constitutional amendments. All Canadian provinces provide for advisory referendums in some circumstances at the local and provincial levels, and there have been three federal referendums: one in 1898 on the prohibition of alcohol, one in 1942 to release Prime Minister William Lyon Mackenzie King from his promise not to send conscripted soldiers overseas, and one in 1992 on the Charlottetown Accord. The Reform Party proposes that referendums be used more frequently in the federal legislative process, but the longer-established parties have not yet shown any enthusiasm for this. It should be noted that Canadian referendums are only advisory—the actual decision is reserved for Parliament or the provincial legislature. The attachment to parliamentary sovereignty explains this reluctance to let the referendum become more than a consultative device.

In Switzerland, however, the vote in a referendum legally determines the legislative outcome of an issue. In France, the president can call a binding national referendum. President Charles de Gaulle (in office 1959–69) used this power on six occasions as a way of circumventing a legislature that would not cooperate on his policy proposals. François Mitterand called a referendum in 1992 on the Maastricht Treaty (which was barely approved).

The British government has used the consultative referendum to clear the air on divisive issues. In 1975 the government called a national referendum on membership in the European Economic Community. It was the first ever held in Britain. The Conservatives had decided on membership three years earlier, but many Labour Party members remained opposed to the decision. So the newly elected Labour government of Prime Minister Harold Wilson called a referendum in hopes of laying the matter to rest. British voters in fact endorsed membership by slightly more than a two-thirds majority. In 1979, referendums were held in Scotland and Wales as a way of deciding the issue of devolution. Voters in both regions delivered a blow to ethnic nationalism by rejecting proposals for regional parliaments, but they later accepted regional parliaments in referendums held in 1997 after Tony Blair's Labour Party came to power.

A second form of direct democracy is the **initiative**. If X voters (the number being spelled out in the constitution, statute, or city by-law) sign a petition on a particular issue, the government is required to act on it. The required action may be either that the legislative body enact the proposal outlined in the petition or that it submit the proposal to voters in a referendum. A referendum originates in the legislative body and is "referred" to the electorate; an initiative moves from the people to the legislature.

In Switzerland, 50,000 voters are enough to force the government to hold a referendum. Initiatives have also been used often in California. The famous Proposition 13 was committed to a statewide referendum in 1978 as a result of an initiative signed by 1.5 million voters. The voters of California proceeded to endorse a forced limit on local property taxes—a move that naturally was unpopular with politicians but very popular with the electorate.[13]

Several standard arguments are made against referendums and initiatives—that legislation is too complex, that voters become fatigued when asked to decide too many issues, and that there is a danger of whipping up antagonism against unpopular minorities. There is undoubtedly some truth in these contentions, and, therefore, the routine use of referendums and initiatives as instruments of governance is probably ruled out. However, voters do not seem to rule out direct democracy as an occasional supplement to representative democracy. Of the arguments in favour of direct democracy, the most interesting comes from former Conservative MP Patrick

Boyer, Canada's leading authority on and advocate for referendums. Boyer argues that referendums are particularly useful in a parliamentary system of disciplined parties where the legislative agenda is controlled by politicians who believe that electoral victory has given them a mandate to legislate as they please.[14] Mechanisms of direct democracy would be a way for special-interest legislation—whether favourable to business, labour, or any other group—to be tested against the judgment of the public. To date, referendums and initiatives have been used sparingly in Western democracies, but the development of electronic communications may soon make these consultative processes more cost effective and lead to their increased use.

A third element of direct democracy is the **recall**, which enables voters in a constituency (riding) to remove their elected representative from office. This practice was introduced in the United States at the turn of the century. Its purpose was to rid constituencies of representatives controlled by "political machines" (i.e., party organizations dominated by a few backroom leaders). Provisions for recall usually require a petition signed by a substantial number of voters, and a successful recall vote requires at least a simple majority of those voting. These provisions are designed to protect representatives from a minority of voters who may not like a particular stand. Recall is used in cities and states in the United States, though less frequently today than in the 1920s. Voters in Wisconsin introduced a recall of the controversial Red-hunting senator Joseph McCarthy in 1954; it was unsuccessful.[15]

An interesting episode involving recall took place in Alberta during the first Social Credit government (1935–40). Premier William Aberhart had the legislature pass a recall act as part of a reform package, but then had the act repealed when a petition for his own recall was circulated in his constituency. He charged that the recall petition had been circulated by the oil companies and other business interests, who were using intimidation to gather signatures.

In Canada, there is less support for a recall mechanism than for other forms of direct democracy. At the present time, only the province of British Columbia has recall legislation, which has been deliberately designed to be difficult to use. The Reform Party is the only federal party to advocate the principle of recall. The recall may be a fine idea in the United States, where elected officials serve fixed terms and are judged as individuals because party discipline is weak or nonexistent. But in a parliamentary system such as Canada's, elected officials are always members of a team that functions collectively—the Cabinet and caucus in the case of the government, the caucus in the case of the Opposition. In 1992, Joe Clark spent all his time as a cabinet minister on the constitutional negotiations that led to the Charlottetown Accord, and then on trying to get the Accord passed in the referendum. Now it is clear that the voters in his Alberta riding (Yellowhead) did not like the Accord: almost 70 percent voted no on October 26. But should they have had the right to recall their hardworking MP because he was working on a project of which they disapproved? The answer may be yes if we think of MPs primarily as representatives of their constituencies, but it is probably no if we think of them as members of a team pursuing national policies.

Today, public opinion polls also play an important advisory role in all democratic countries. An enthusiast for direct democracy will periodically remind us that it is now technically possible to wire all citizens into one computer system and let them decide questions of public policy. But even if such a nonstop referendum were possible, it is doubtful that it would be a good idea. Complex questions of public policy need the attention and deliberation of informed minds, and both legislators and the public need time to digest various views. Representative democracy is not just a second-best substitute for direct democracy, made necessary by the size of modern states; rather, it is a mechanism for achieving the consensus that is essential to good government. However, direct-democratic devices could be a useful supplement when such wisdom does not emerge from representative institutions.

Democratic participation involves far more than the election of representatives. It also involves influencing government policy either through public debate or by making submissions to elected representatives. Governments today often consult extensively with the public before passing major legislation. A general policy statement may be published, followed by a draft of the statute. Often there are public hearings at which interested parties express their views. In fact, participation has expanded so much in recent years, particularly at the level of local government, that it is sometimes seen as unduly slowing decision making and offering too much influence to vocal and well-organized minorities.

Even when they possess a strong parliamentary majority, governments will occasionally withdraw or modify policy proposals in the face of public criticism. Public participation and consultation is now an ongoing process in democratic government. Elections punctuate the process; when governments are not responsive, voters change the participants.

Access to the decision makers is a major problem in contemporary democracies; this issue will be discussed in more detail in Part Four. Critics of democracy say that powerful interests dominate the political process and that groups more marginal to the system have difficulty in influencing decisions. For example, women's and environmental groups claim they have been shut out of the process in the past. However, the existence of elections as open contests at least offers a possibility, if not the certainty, that previously marginalized groups will be able to exert more influence on decision makers.

POLITICAL FREEDOM

Meaningful participation is possible only if political freedom prevails. Limited participation or directed mobilization of the masses is characteristic not of genuine democracy but of totalitarian pseudodemocracy. An infallible test for political freedom is the legitimacy of opposition: freedom is meaningful only if it extends to those whose opinions differ from the opinions of those in authority. Freedom only to agree is no freedom at all. If freedom does not exist, public support or opposition can only be speculative, and this uncertainty can be very convenient for manipulative rulers. At the same time, the opposition in a liberal democracy must operate within the rule of law. When it resorts to unlawful means—for example, if it connives with a foreign power or plots an insurrection—its actions are not compatible with political freedom in a liberal democracy.

Political freedom has numerous aspects: the right to speak freely, even to criticize the government; the right to form associations, including political parties, that may oppose the government; the right to run for office; and the right to vote without intimidation and to choose from a slate of at least two candidates. Without these rights, democracy might be "for the people," but it is certainly not "by the people."

Extensive and important as it is, political freedom is only a part of the whole range of personal freedoms. For instance, it does not include the right to own property or to use one's chosen language. It is quite possible for very wide political freedom to coexist with, and even be the cause of, reduced freedom in other areas. An example can be taken from Quebec: all citizens have full political freedom in that province, but businesses have been restricted by legislation from posting signs in languages other than French. In 1989 the provincial government used its override power, as provided by Section 33 of the Canadian Charter of Rights and Freedoms, to reinstate its language legislation after the Supreme Court of Canada had ruled that the law violated the freedom of expression guaranteed by the Charter.[16] Both the legislation and the use of the notwithstanding clause (as Section 33 is often called) were popular at the time with the francophone majority in Quebec. In this instance, a majority used its political freedom to reduce the linguistic freedom of minorities. However, the abrogation of freedom proved to be temporary because, in 1993, the province's Liberal government introduced amendments to the legislation that left more scope for commercial signs in languages other than French.

This example highlights what is sometimes seen as a general problem of constitutional democracy. Can the power of the majority be restrained by law so that it does not use its political freedom to take away other freedoms from unpopular minorities? The tension between democracy and the rule of law is illustrated in this passage from Xenophon, a pupil of Socrates. It had just been proposed to the Athenian Assembly—the democratic gathering of all male citizens—that certain alleged enemies of the regime be arrested:

> Great numbers cried out that it was monstrous if the people were to be prevented from doing whatever they wished ... Then the Prytanes [the executive committee of the Assembly], stricken with fear, agreed to put the question [to a vote]—all of them except Socrates ... he said that in no case would he act except in accordance with the law.[17]

Socrates was ultimately put to death by a democracy that ignored the rule of law and heeded only its own will.

A fear first voiced by Aristotle, and echoed since by countless other writers, is that in a democracy, the many would use their political power to expropriate and distribute the wealth of the few. In the words of John Adams, the second American president, "Debts would be abolished first; taxes laid heavy on the rich, and not at all on the others; and at last a downright equal division of everything be demanded and voted."[18] In fact, the record of liberal democracy does not bear out this gloomy prediction of a dramatic clash of rich and poor, probably because in those countries where liberal democracy has been successful, society has not been polarized into extremes of wealth and poverty.

A more realistic danger for liberal democracy arises from interest-group competition, which is a powerful force in modern democratic politics. The freedom to participate that is part of liberal democracy encourages the formation of organized groups that promote the interests of their members. One result of universal suffrage and majority rule is that politicians must appeal to these groups in order to build electoral coalitions. In return for their support, these groups often demand concessions or privileges from government that are contrary to the general interest. Manufacturers demand import quotas and protective tariffs; unions work for laws that will promote their ability to extract concessions from employers; the organized professions seek rules of licensing and accreditation to keep out "unqualified" practitioners; dependent groups like pensioners and welfare recipients agitate for higher transfer payments; environmentalists seek to block economic development projects, while developers seek lax environmental policies. Democratic politics may as a result degenerate into an auction in which state power is "sold" to the highest-bidding groups. Over time, this may lead to an accumulation of restrictions and special privileges contrary to the spirit of liberal democracy.[19]

One result of such **auction politics** in Canada was a chronic difficulty experienced by both federal and provincial governments in balancing their budgets. Groups clamoured for benefits from government, and politicians competed with each other to win office by satisfying these demands. Because conferring benefits is always more popular than levying taxes, overcommitted politicians resorted to deficit financing to pay for past and future promises. But the resilience of liberal democracy was illustrated in the second half of the 1990s when governments of several different parties recognized the seriousness of the problem and brought their budgets into balance.

All forms of government are capable of pursuing potentially ruinous policies; what distinguishes liberal democracy is its ability to correct mistakes. Political freedom is crucial in this regard. The freedom to criticize and to run for office on an alternative platform means that bad policies can be pointed out and, hopefully, corrected before they do irreparable damage.

ꜟOBLEMS OF LIBERAL DEMOCRACY

᠁ Winston Churchill, liberal democracy is not the perfect form of gov-
‿ out it remains the best devised to date. For discussion purposes, we will
‿der three basic problems inherent in all liberal democracies: elite rule, majority
᠁rsus minority rights, and public versus private interests.

Elites

Cabinet minister decide what is to be done influenced by rich companies prime

One common, and serious, criticism of liberal democracy is that it is elitist—that
such democracies are, in effect, ruled by elites and therefore undemocratic. It is true
that representative democracy is a form of elite rule, if by an **elite** we mean "a
minority of the population which takes the major decisions in the society."[20] But to
see the place of political elites in modern politics, one must compare them with the
elites that were found in traditional societies of earlier centuries. In the latter, a tiny
and interlocking group of families dominated the social, economic, and political life
of society. In most instances, these families owned large estates, which their children
inherited along with all the wealth and responsibilities that went with their status.

Traditional societies were highly stratified; that is, there was a large gap between
the elite and the masses. This simple, dichotomized society was perpetuated as the
children of the elite inherited their positions, while opportunities for the masses were
restricted. There was little if any social mobility between the elite and the masses.

In most Western countries this situation has gradually been transformed. The
Industrial Revolution broke the hold of the landed aristocracy and created new
sources of wealth and employment; mass education created opportunities for many
in the lower classes; guilds and unions helped artisans and workers to get better
working conditions and wages; urban centres served as the base for dynamic marketing systems; and new attitudes about equality and freedom led to more participatory politics. Modern society is characterized by a large middle class, not by
polarization between wealth and poverty. Opportunities for education and jobs are
extensive, and this promotes social mobility between classes. Politics is charged with
new sources of authority and legitimacy. In short, the old dualism of the traditional
society has given way to a complex and dynamic modern social order.

Correspondingly, the old idea of a traditional elite was replaced by the concept
of pluralism. New elites began to spring up and challenge the agrarian aristocracy.
An industrial elite, a commercial elite, a financial elite, a military elite, and even a
political elite emerged; and each had a degree of wealth and power that posed a
threat to the old guard with its roots in the land. In modern societies, elites have not
disappeared; rather, they have become more numerous and more diverse. Many
Marxists tend to deny that this change has really affected societies much. They still

see a simple dichotomy—the rulers and the ruled. The two-class situation dominates their frame of reference; except in socialist societies, rulers are thought to exploit the masses. But other observers recognize that modern societies have become pluralistic, and that so have their politics. As the French author Raymond Aron has written:

> Democratic societies, which I would rather call pluralistic societies, are full of the noise of public strife between the owners of the means of production, trade union leaders and politicians. As all are entitled to form associations, professional and political organizations abound, each one defending its members' interests with passionate ardour. Government becomes a business of compromises.[21]

In democracies, those who aspire to rule must build a power base. They must first of all be chosen by the electorate; then, if they are to remain in office, their policies must be responsive to the needs of some coalition of groups. Contemporary theorists of democracy emphasize the competition of these diverse elites. They see the representative system as an instrument for insuring that no single elite can attain power unless it reflects the desires of some fraction of the ordinary people. If elections are working as they should, there is not necessarily a contradiction between liberal democracy and elite rule.

Majority Versus Minority Rights

Liberal democracies operate on the majoritarian principle. Political party nominations, elections to office, and legislative decisions are decided on the basis of a majoritarian vote. But how do minorities fare under majoritarian government? Is it true, as the proponents of liberal democracy claim, that minority rights can be reconciled with majority rule? For example, in a multicultural society, when one or two ethnic groups (or nationalities) occupy a dominant position, can it be guaranteed that the rights of minority cultures will be protected? Can the rights of Native peoples in Canada be protected when they make up less than 4 percent of the total population? How can the rights of cultural minorities such as the Chinese or West Indians, or the political rights of gays and lesbians, be guaranteed when the vast majority of Canadians are European, English- or French-speaking, and heterosexual?

One argument is that all majority and minority rights are protected on the floor of the House of Commons and the Senate. This argument revolves around the assumption that most elected representatives want to be re-elected and so must appeal to a broad coalition of groups in their constituencies. They try not to alienate any voters— and certainly as few as possible—if they have to legislate in a way that will alienate any. But the fact remains that winning coalitions need not be, and probably will not be, all-inclusive. Some minorities, particularly small ones, are likely to be left out, which opens up the possibility that an elected assembly could become a "tyranny of the majority" that consistently votes to override minority rights.

A second way of protecting minority rights is through a constitution and the judicial process. Since the passage of the Canadian Charter of Rights and Freedoms in 1982, individual rights for all Canadians have been spelled out in the Constitution. If the rights of a minority may have been violated by a legislative assembly, representatives of that minority are entitled to challenge the constitutionality of the legislation in the courts. If members of a legislative assembly choose to ignore the rights of a certain segment of society, the citizens affected have recourse through the courts. While there is no guarantee that court rulings will satisfy either the majority or the minority, the judicial system is another possible venue for reconciling majority rule with minority rights.

Public Versus Private Interests

Another very difficult problem to resolve in liberal democracies relates to the conflict between public and private interests. Ideally, the public interest involves the well-being of all individuals or all groups in society. It is difficult, however, to find an interest that is equally shared by everyone. In practice, therefore, the term *public interest* refers to interests that are relatively broadly shared, such as national defence, enforcement of the law, protection of life and property, stable prices, low taxation, public education, accessible health care, and a social safety net. *Private interests* include the interests of specific groups such as businesspeople, unionized workers, farmers, and students and professors. Most such groups attempt to achieve certain ends through the political process. They may seek concessions of some kind from governments, and these concessions may or may not be in the public interest. For example, postsecondary students may want to have free college or university training. Most colleges and universities are public institutions in Canada, so the taxpayers would have to provide every dollar to maintain these institutions, and taxes would have to be increased accordingly. Since college and university graduates usually get better-paying jobs than nongraduates, it seems reasonable that these students should pay at least some tuition. However, society (public interest) benefits from the presence of educated young people (private interest), so it pays most of the costs of higher education.

Few conflicts between public and private interest are as easy to reconcile. Often such conflicts centre on definitions of the public interest and the presence or absence of a level playing field. Disputes between developers and environmentalists are notoriously difficult to resolve. Private interests will push for what they see as a healthy economic-development project. It might be a water-storage project for irrigation, or a timber-cutting licence for a pulp mill. In either case, it will be argued that private industrial activity will, through capital investment and job creation, also serve the broader public interest by enhancing the local or regional economy. Developers often make the case, particularly in times of recession, that a softening of environmental regulations would reduce the cost of the project. The argument is usually that increased costs will make the project uncompetitive and that investment and jobs will for that reason be lost.

At the same time, governments are also pressured by those who want to preserve the quality of the air and water in the region. These people argue that poor air and water quality affects the health not only of local residents but also of the environment itself. They argue, as well, that a healthy environment will attract environmentally "clean" industries. In effect, there is a political clash not only between private interests but also between differing conceptions of the public interest. Whichever side the government comes down on, it will claim that its decision is in the public interest.

When legislators write lax environmental regulations, or loosen existing regulations to lure industry, environmentalists claim that private interests have prevailed at the expense of the public interest—that the playing field has been tipped to favour developers. When legislators support strict environmental regulations, industrialists claim that narrow but powerful environmental interests have thwarted the public interest, which is for more jobs and increased investment—that the field was tipped to favour environmentalists. Here again, the challenge facing public decision makers is to balance the demands of conflicting private interests, with their different conceptions of the public interest.

ORGANIZING LIBERAL DEMOCRACIES

Organization within liberal democracies does not adhere to a single pattern. There are a number of ways that the relationship between society and the state can be structured. For example, within a liberal–democratic society, interest groups such as business organizations, labour unions, and farmers' associations may have a great deal of political autonomy—that is, a great deal of freedom to pursue political objectives without interference from the state. At the same time, interest groups in other liberal democracies may be restricted in their political activity by a powerful regulatory state. We can classify variations in liberal democracies according to their organizational characteristics as pluralist, corporatist, or consociational.

Pluralism

Liberal democracies in which individuals and groups compete freely and openly in the political process are labelled **pluralist**. Robert Dahl's term for this pluralist form of liberal democracy is **polyarchy**, which means many different sources of power. For Dahl, "the characteristics of polyarchy greatly extend the number, size, and diversity of the minorities whose preferences will influence the outcome of governmental decision."[22] In a polyarchy, control of the governmental process may change hands frequently as different groups compete for political power. Or, as with the Liberal Democratic Party in Japan, voters may continue to support a coalition of business leaders and politicians that has dominated the system for decades.

In pluralist societies, highly autonomous interest groups lobby governments to further their own political ends. Or they work the electoral process, either directly or within interest-group coalitions, with the goal of increasing their influence or control over the state. In effect, pluralism involves a wide variety of political interests competing in the political process for control of political resources. Political power is not necessarily concentrated in any one group of individuals; rather, it is widely dispersed throughout society and brought together periodically through a powerful coalition of interests.

Features of pluralist liberal democracies include:

a. a high degree of autonomy for political interests in society to pursue their political ends;

b. equality of all groups in the political process—ideally, there is a level playing field on which political interests compete; and

c. an absence of monopoly control of government or state power by any one group. The power of groups ebbs and flows with societal conditions, as coalitions are accepted or rejected by the voters.

Corporatism

Another way of organizing state–society relations in liberal democracies is **corporatism**. Whereas pluralism is marked by the autonomy of interests in the political process, corporatism is marked by the lack of such autonomy. In the corporatist pattern, the state is the dominant force in society and the activities of all interests in society are subordinate to that force. One of the principal writers on corporatism, Philippe C. Schmitter, has defined the concept as follows:

> Corporatism can be defined as a system of interests representation in which the constituent units are organized into a limited number of singular, compulsory, non-competitive, hierarchically ordered and functionally differentiated categories, recognized or licensed (if not created) by the state and granted a deliberate representational monopoly within their respective categories in exchange for observing certain controls on their selection of leaders and articulation of demands and supports.[23]

The term corporatism is derived from the Latin word *corpus*, meaning "body." The corporatist political process is analogous to the human body. All parts of the body—the skin, bones, heart, brain, and so on—constitute an organic whole, and each component makes a specific contribution to the body's functioning. The various parts are interdependent; when they work together, the system as a whole can function. For example, the heart and lungs provide the means for distributing blood and oxygen to the extremities of the body. But the brain is the most vital component: without it, the other parts of the body cannot function.

The idea of corporatism grew out of the teachings of medieval Roman Catholicism. The corporate body of the church represented a hierarchy in which church leaders dictated law and parishioners were expected to obey.

For corporatists, the political process is seen as an organic whole. The various components of that process (e.g., interest groups, political parties, the executive or legislature, the courts, and the constitution) are parts of a whole. Each component makes a specific contribution to the political process. But the state is the dominant organ in the process: it is equivalent to the brain in the body. The state stands above the various parts of the political process. It is supreme; the components are not autonomous but subordinate to the state and thus dependent on it. In the corporatist scheme, then:

a. the components of the political process are arranged in a hierarchy and are not equal;

b. the components have limited autonomy, with the state restricting their actions;

c. competition is limited, in the sense that the various components are not free to compete with each other for political ends;

d. the components in the process are dependent on the state; and

e. the relative power of different components may vary, depending on their relationship to the state.

The National Socialist (Nazi) Party in Germany, and the Fascist parties in Italy and Spain, embraced corporatist ideas in their efforts to justify government by a controlling elite. Corporatism, however, is not confined to dictatorial systems. Canadian political scientist Leo Panitch makes a strong case for the argument that corporatist tendencies exist in liberal democracies, where they pose considerable problems for modern capitalism.[24] To the extent that the state undertakes to organize a hierarchy of interest groups, and to grant special funding and access to some while denying these privileges to others, and to take an active role in channelling interest-group pressures rather than waiting passively for such pressures to be applied, corporatism is found in liberal democracies. In practice, most such democracies are probably a mixture of the pluralist and corporatist types.

Consociationalism

In the form of democracy known as **consociationalism**, elites and organized interests play a special and distinctive role. This form is found in several countries, including the Netherlands, Switzerland, and (to a degree) Canada. The basis for consociationalism is a society so sharply divided along linguistic, ethnic, or religious lines that the segments have their own social institutions and live largely apart from one another. The Netherlands is a classic case: although everyone speaks Dutch, the society is divided into Roman Catholic, neo-Calvinist, liberal, and socialist "spiritual families," each of which has its own schools and universities; newspapers, and radio and television programs; and labour unions and recreational associations. Switzerland is similarly divided, by language as well as by religion and ideology.

Consociational democracy, which has evolved as a way for such segmented societies to maintain internal peace and self-government, is a pattern of institutions in which:[25]

a. each social segment has a high degree of autonomy over its internal affairs, particularly language, culture, religion, and education;

b. a rule of proportionality is followed in allocating government jobs, expenditures, and benefits among the segments;

c. all important segments have the power to veto major changes affecting their vital interests; and

d. government is carried on through a "grand coalition" of political representatives of all the main segments.

The last point is of most interest here. Generally speaking, the logic of democracy is majoritarian; at any given time, those who can coalesce to form a majority will be the winners, and those winners will conduct the government. But in Switzerland and the Netherlands, cabinets are deliberately composed of representatives of all the main social segments more or less in proportion to their voting strength. This "grand coalition" approach to running a democratic system requires a cooperative ethic among political elites and a deferential ethic among the population at large. Ordinary people of all social segments must be willing to give the political elite a fairly free hand to make the elaborately balanced deals that keep the consociational ship afloat.

Canada has some of the hallmarks of a consociational democracy: high segmentation between the English and French language groups; relative autonomy of the segments, at least as far as Quebec's role in the federal system is concerned; a tradition of proportionality in the distribution of government benefits (alternation of English and French Governors General, three Quebec seats on the Supreme Court, a proportionate share of Quebec members in the Cabinet, working bilingualism in the federal public service); and, to some extent, a veto over constitutional change for the French minority as represented by the government of Quebec.

Canada, however, has operated all along with the British model of parliamentary democracy, which is inherently majoritarian. Yet the "winner take all" effects of this model have been softened by the fact that Quebec voters have usually contrived to be part of the victorious electoral coalition and thus have seldom found themselves outnumbered and friendless in a head-to-head confrontation with the country's English majority.

There are different patterns of politics in liberal democracies, patterns that seem to follow particular cultural attributes of societies. For example, politics in the United States, a country with a strong liberal, antistate tradition, comes close to the pluralist process Dahl describes as polyarchy. In Canada and Great Britain, where elites have played a greater role in the political process, one finds traces of corporatist and consociational thinking and institutions. And in countries like Mexico and Brazil, the corporatist tradition is very strong, to the point that one can rightly ask whether these political systems are liberal democratic or authoritarian. The lines of demarcation between political systems can be just as porous as those between political ideologies.

CONTEMPORARY CRITICISMS OF DEMOCRACY

Up to this point, our discussion of liberal democracy has been mainly theoretical, with a review of some of the problems encountered in this particular form of government. However, we should not give the impression that all is well with liberal democracies. Any perceptive person today knows that nothing could be further from the truth. In most Western democracies, criticisms abound. And most of those criticisms are justified. People feel that political leaders are unresponsive, that they have their own agendas. There is a common perception that the relationship between the Cabinet, high administrative officials, and powerful lobbyists is too cozy, that governments are ignoring the demands and expectations of large segments of the population. As a result, there is a great deal of cynicism about modern politics; people feel manipulated by the media and politicians, and powerless in a decision-making process in which, theoretically, citizen participation is valued. Never have people had so many opportunities to participate in politics; yet, paradoxically, never have more people been so critical of the political process.

The polls verify this sense of disillusionment. The public nowadays has far less faith in the system and in politicians than it did twenty years ago. Yet individuals still expect a great deal from politicians. Nowhere was this made clearer than in the report of the Citizens Forum on Canada's Future, or the Spicer Commission (1991). The commission heard from more than 350,000 adult Canadians, and the message they sent to Ottawa was emphatic: representatives must become "more responsive to the wishes of their constituents." This is a clear indication that modern democracies are in trouble. We can identify at least three major reasons why: the overall performance of the system, the workings of cabinet government, and the changing nature of society itself.

With respect to the first issue, for the past fifty years Canadian governments have followed a highly interventionist course under the assumption that the state can: guide the economy; solve social problems such as unemployment, poverty, and prejudice; care for the aged and infirm; and inspire loyalty to and support for the nation-state. A vast amount of legislation has been passed in those fifty years relating to unemployment insurance, welfare payments, old-age pensions, health care, family allowances, civil rights, and government assistance to businesses. Multiculturalism has been strengthened. Even our flag and our anthem date from this time. In effect, the state has been intervening to regulate society and to provide services to create a more just society. Throughout, most people have supported these actions, in part because most have benefited from them in one way or another.

These programs have been both extensive and expensive. Between the 1960s and the 1990s, government was a growth industry. Budgets and bureaucracies grew, but because public-sector expansion was undertaken at a time when the economy was also expanding rapidly, governments could, and did, increase taxes to pay for the increased services and regulations. Canadians were earning enough discretionary income that most middle-income citizens could pay more taxes and still maintain their standard of living. As government expenditures rose, revenues could be increased to sustain the policies and programs. When the economy faltered, however, and revenues levelled off, governments began to borrow in order to maintain their services and programs, under the assumption that the economy would soon return to a growth cycle, at which time taxes could again be increased. The result has been high and rising levels of public debt (see Figure 18.2). The Canadian federal budget now includes an item of about $40 billion for debt-service charges, amounting to about

FIGURE 18.2 Net Debt from March 31, 1985, to 1998, as a Percentage of GDP

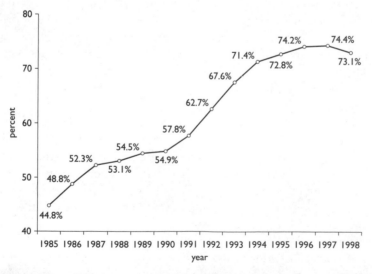

Source: Canadian Tax Foundation, *The National Finances*, 1994; *Finances of the Nation*, 1995 and 1996 (Toronto: Canadian Tax Foundation, 1994, 1995, 1996); and Department of Finance, "Budget Plan, 997," p. 44.

one-third of all tax revenues collected. The necessity to pay so much in interest on past loans cannot help but squeeze expenditures on social programs.

The heavy burden of taxation, coupled with the debt legacy that the present generation is leaving for the future, has led to an outcry against politicians and their recent performance. Citizens now expect better fiscal management; and because they do not feel they are getting it, there are questions about how "representative" our system is.

A second reason that citizens are criticizing the democratic process relates to the parliamentary process with its cabinet government and disciplined political parties. This system grew up in the nineteenth century, before universal suffrage was introduced and social relationships were democratized. Cabinet ministers still cling to this elitist system; they claim it cannot work without party discipline because changes in government could lead to political instability. Their argument is that a strong executive is vital to the parliamentary system. But this executive-dominated process has now given rise to a populist reaction, as illustrated in the widespread opposition to the Meech Lake and Charlottetown Accords. That opposition did not focus entirely on proposed changes to the Constitution; much of it stemmed from the fact that citizens felt the country's first ministers were imposing these changes on the people. Thus, with the heavy hand of the executive strengthened by political-party discipline, many people question whether their representatives can truly represent them.

A third cause of widespread criticism of the present democratic process has to do with changes that have occurred in Canadian society. Many writers and analysts today are talking about a "new politics." What they mean by the phrase is that beliefs and values have changed considerably over the past half century. There is much less deference now toward all social authorities, and especially toward politicians. Many citizens are highly educated; have had a great deal of business, professional, and political experience; and are quite willing to challenge any direction public leaders are embarking on. Many people view it as their "right" not only to vote for their political leaders but also to be involved in the process by which their leaders choose particular policies.

Such people are not willing to permit a Cabinet to sit down in its wisdom and dictate public policy. They know that Cabinets have their biases, and that to counter these biases, they must hear arguments from a cross-section of the population. Governments cannot afford to be indifferent to the "new politics": as recent election results in France, the United Kingdom, Japan, and Canada show, they are not likely to remain in office if they do not take account of the new developments in public opinion.

Can changes be made to restore Canadians' faith in the democratic process? In general, there are two alternatives in this age-old debate: find "better" people to rule or change the system itself. We believe that systemic change is the better solution to the problem of good government.

As mentioned earlier, mechanisms of direct democracy would involve the public more directly in decision making. While these mechanisms are not without their problems, they do provide a means by which the public, if mobilized, can initiate action. In that sense, they may provide a safety valve when governments become paralyzed and are unable to respond.

Another approach might be to develop more opportunities for the public to influence the policymaking process. As mentioned earlier, governments often follow elaborate consultative procedures when formulating policies on particular issues. Cabinets consult with major interests; there are royal commissions; and parliamentary committees sometimes have elaborate cross-country hearings. But these devices, valuable and necessary as they may be, do not appear to be enough. Politicians are now experimenting with new forms of consultation, such as televised town-hall meetings and electronic forums. Such mechanisms require a great deal of time on the part of political leaders, but the dividends in terms of rapport with the people may be great. And given the cynical view people now have about the process, such mechanisms may help to break down the feeling many Canadians have that elected officials are cloistered, unresponsive, and unavailable to the public they are supposed to serve.

THE PROSPECTS FOR DEMOCRACY

A liberal–democratic political system, then, is one in which, on the basis of universal adult suffrage, citizens select their governors (representatives); these representatives can be changed by the electorate through periodic elections; individual or group opinions can be discussed freely without fear of retaliation by public officials or private individuals; a legal opposition is free to criticize; and an independent judiciary resolves disputes between citizens, between citizens and government, and between levels of government. If this seems excessively long for a definition, that is because it is not easy to characterize in fewer words a form of government that seeks to reconcile freedom with majority rule.

Liberal democracy is an expression of the political experience of the Western world. It is now practised in every country of Western Europe, although Spain and Portugal did not emerge from authoritarian rule until the 1970s, and Greece underwent a period of military dictatorship in the same decade. Liberal democracy is also strongly entrenched in countries that are essentially transplanted European states: for example, Canada, the United States, Australia, New Zealand, and Israel.

While liberal democracy is a product of Western European traditions and culture, democrats believe that it can be adopted successfully outside that milieu. Two good examples are Japan and India. Both countries have ancient cultural traditions that are quite distinct from those of Western Europe, yet they have successfully operated reasonable approximations of liberal democracy for over forty years. There was an initial period of transplantation, to be sure—from the American occupation in Japan, and from the British Raj in India—but since those times, liberal democracy has continued successfully on its own. The economic contrast between Japan and India is also significant. Both countries are heavily populated. Japan is now wealthy, with a standard of living similar to Canada's. India is still poor, with a largely agricultural economy. Nonetheless, in spite of severe religious differences, it has been able to make liberal democracy work. This shows that a high standard of living is not absolutely vital for liberal democracy to work. It is probably true, however, that it is more likely to succeed in countries where the economy is highly developed.

Until the 1980s, Japan and India appeared to be exceptional cases. Most former colonies in Asia and Africa had quickly fallen under military dictatorships or other forms of authoritarian rule, even though the Western European colonial powers had equipped them with democratic-looking institutions at the time of decolonization. The 1970s were a particularly bleak period for democracy. Numerous countries in the Third World (Ethiopia, Angola, Mozambique, Nicaragua, and Afghanistan, to name a few) became Marxist client-states of the Soviet Union; on the other side of the political spectrum, right-wing military dictatorships proliferated throughout Latin America and Asia (for example, in Argentina, Brazil, South Korea, and the Philippines).

This trend reversed itself in the 1980s when almost all of Latin America and the Caribbean returned to some approximation of democracy. And, of course, the collapse of communism has brought about a movement toward democracy in Eastern Europe. So far Poland, the Czech Republic, and Hungary have made the smoothest transition.

However, there are still at least five huge challenges for democracy:

1. The world's largest country, the People's Republic of China, with an estimated population of 1.2 billion, remains firmly antidemocratic in politics, though it is experimenting with economic liberalization.

2. Democracy is exceedingly superficial in many of the Soviet successor states in Eastern Europe and Central Asia. In countries such as Russia, Ukraine, and Kazakhstan, recycled communists still hold power and the future of democracy is far from certain. In other new states, such as the fragments of the former Yugoslavia, ethnic hostilities and civil war are constant possibilities, making normal democracy almost impossible to establish.

3. The world of Islam, from Indonesia through the Middle East to North Africa, has never embraced liberal democracy. Turkey, with its strong connections to Europe, is the main exception among the forty-six Islamic states; and even Turkey's democracy has been broken by periods of military rule and is now challenged by Islamic fundamentalism. The Lebanese democratic experiment was torn apart by internal religious rivalries and external political hostilities between Israel and the Arab states. Pakistan's conversion to democracy is promising but too recent to be considered permanent. In many other states, the rise of Islamic fundamentalism has made the adoption of liberal democ-

racy less rather than more probable. For example, the military seized power in Algeria in 1992 to avert a likely victory of Islamic fundamentalists in what was supposed to be the first democratic election in thirty years, and a bitter civil war continues there as of 1997.

4. Democratic experiments in sub-Saharan Africa are in their earliest stages and are beset with difficulties. One of the largest and wealthiest countries in the region, Nigeria, is still ruled by a military dictatorship. Tribal rivalries are a deeply rooted problem, and in the worst cases, such as the Democratic Republic of Congo (formerly Zaire), Rwanda, and Liberia, civil order has completely broken down. However, the successful transition of the Republic of South Africa from apartheid to a multiracial, multiparty democracy is an enormously hopeful development. With its large population and (by African standards) highly developed economy, South Africa can help show other countries the way toward liberal democracy.

5. Liberal democracies do not always "fit" local cultures. Liberal democracy is a value-laden process of government; and if it is going to become universal, ways must be found to resolve conflicts between liberal–democratic values and existing cultural values. For example, in the Islamic world men and women often do not enjoy political equality. And in certain societies throughout the world, traditional elites have governed for centuries. Few of these elites will willingly risk giving up power in free and fair elections. We are not arguing that liberal–democratic values, nurtured in the Western world, should be imposed universally. The adoption of such a value system has to be the choice of the people in each society. When, however, liberal–democratic values are rejected by societies, these societies and their political leaders cannot claim to be liberal–democratic in the full sense.

In spite of these many and grave obstacles facing liberal democracy, those who advocate it are entitled to enjoy some cautious optimism. It is better entrenched in the world than ever before; and though the number of democratic states continues to increase, it still remains true that no two liberal democracies have ever gone to war against each other. The widespread adoption of democracy may be the best available strategy for reducing armed conflict in the world.

᠊᠊᠊᠊᠊᠊᠊

FURTHER READING

Alexander, P.C. *The Perils of Democracy*. Bombay: Somaiya Publications, 1995.

Arthur, John, ed. *Democracy: Theory and Practice*. Belmont, Calif.: Wadsworth Publishing Co., 1992.

Bachrach, Peter. *The Theory of Democratic Elitism*, rev. ed. Washington, D.C.: University Press of America, 1980.

Bauzon, Kenneth E., ed. *Development and Democratization in the Third World: Myths, Hopes and Realities*. New York: Crane Russak, 1992.

Brooks, Stephen. *Canadian Democracy. An Introduction*, 2nd ed. Toronto; New York: Oxford University Press, 1996.

Chapman, John W. and Ian Shapiro. *Democratic Community*. New York: New York University Press, 1993.

Dahl, Robert A. *Democracy and its Critics*. New Haven: Yale University Press, 1989.

———. *Polyarchy: Participation and Opposition*. New Haven, Conn.: Yale University Press, 1971.

Dalton, Russell J. *Citizens, Protest, and Democracy*. Newbury Park, Calif.: Sage, 1993.

Di Palma, Giuseppe. *To Craft Democracies: An Essay on Democratic Transitions*. Berkeley, Calif.: University of California Press, 1990.

Downs, Anthony. *An Economic Theory of Democracy*. New York: Harper and Row, 1957.

Esposito, John L. *Islam and Democracy*. New York: Oxford University Press, 1996.

Evans, Mark, Michael Slovodnik, and Terezia Zoric. *Democracy and Government in Canada: Participating for Change*. Toronto: ITP Nelson, 1996.

Fischer, Mary Ellen. *Establishing Democracies*. Boulder, Colo.: Westview Press, 1996.

Fishkin, James S. *The Voice of the People: Public Opinion and Democracy*. New Haven: Yale University Press, 1995.

Gould, Carol C. *Rethinking Democracy: Freedom and Social Cooperation in Politics, Economy and Society*. Cambridge: Cambridge University Press, 1988.

Grossman, Lawrence K. *The Electronic Republic: Reshaping Democracy in the Information Age*. New York, N.Y.: Viking, 1995.

Huntington, Samuel P. *The Third Wave: Democratization in the Late Twentieth Century*. Norman, Oklahoma: University of Oklahoma Press, 1991.

Keane, John. *Democracy and Civil Society*. London: Verso, 1988.

Kymlicka, Will. *Multicultural Citizenship: A Liberal Theory of Minority Rights*. Oxford: Clarendon Press and New York: Oxford University Press, 1995.

Lijphart, Arend. *Democracies: Patterns of Majoritarian and Consensus Government in Twenty-One Countries*. New Haven, Conn.: Yale University Press, 1984.

———. *Democracy in Plural Societies*. New Haven, Conn.: Yale University Press, 1977.

Lindsay, A.D. *The Modern Democratic State*. New York: Oxford University Press, 1962.

Manji, Irshad. *Risking Utopia: On the Edge of a New Democracy*. Vancouver: Douglas & McIntyre, 1997.

March, James G. and Johan P. Olsen. *Democratic Governance*. New York: Free Press, 1995.

Mouffe, Chantal. *Democracy and Pluralism: A Critique of the Rationalist Approach*. Toronto: Faculty of Law, University of Toronto, 1995.

Parry, Gerraint. *Political Elites*. London: George Allen and Unwin, 1969.

Pateman, Carole. *Participation and Democratic Theory*. Cambridge: Cambridge University Press, 1970.

Pennock, J. Roland, and John W. Chapman, eds. *Liberal Democracy*. New York: New York University Press, 1983.

Sartori, Giovanni. *The Theory of Democracy Revisited: Part I, The Contemporary Debate*. Chatham, N.J.: Chatham House Publications Inc., 1987.

————. *The Theory of Democracy Revisited: Part II, The Classical Issues*. Chatham, N.J.: Chatham House Publications Inc., 1987.

Saul, John Ralston. *The Unconscious Civilization*. Concord, Ont.: Anansi, 1995.

Corporatism

Cawson, Alan. *Organized Interests and the States: Studies in Meso-Corporatism*. London: Sage, 1992.

————. *Corporatism and Political Theory*. New York: Basil Blackwell, 1986.

Harrison, Reginald James. *Pluralism and Corporatism: The Political Evolution of Modern Democracies*. London: George Allen and Unwin, 1980.

Wilensky, Harold, and Lawell Turner. *Democratic Corporatism and Policy Linkages: The Interdependence of Industrial, Labour Market, Incomes and Social Policies in Eight Countries*. Berkeley, Calif.: University of California Press, 1987.

Williamson, Peter J. *Corporatism in Perspective: An Introductory Guide to Corporatist Theory*. London: Sage, 1992.

Zeigler, L. Harman. *Pluralism, Corporatism and Confucianism: Political Associations and Conflict Resolution in the United States, Europe and Taiwan*. Philadelphia: Temple University Press, 1988.

Consociationalism

Lamy, Steven Lewis. *Consociationalism, Decentralization and Ethnic Group Equalization: The Case of Constitutional Engineering in Belgium*. Ann Arbor, Mich.: University of Michigan Press, 1980.

Lijphart, Arend. *The Politics of Accommodation: Pluralism and Democracy in the Netherlands*, 2nd ed. Berkeley, Calif.: University of California Press, 1975.

McRae, Kenneth Douglas, ed. *Consociational Democracy: Political Accommodation in Segmented Societies*. Toronto: McClelland and Stewart, 1974.

TOTALITARIANISM

CHAPTER 19

Aristotle defined tyranny as "the arbitrary power of an individual which is responsible to no one, and governs all alike ... with a view to its own advantage, not to that of its subjects, and therefore against their will."[1] Montesquieu (1689–1755) said much the same thing when he defined **despotism** as one man ruling through fear without regard to law.[2] These and other definitions of tyranny or despotism always point to certain similar and interrelated characteristics:

- Rule is arbitrary and not bound by law.
- Rule is exercised in the interest of the rulers and not in the common interest.
- Rule is based on coercion and fear.

These ideas are logically interlocked. People willingly submit to authority if it is exercised under genuine laws that are universal rules of conduct, and if these rules are binding on government and citizens alike for the common good. When these conditions are not met, fear must substitute for voluntary compliance.

Note that the essence of tyrannical rule is found in the "how" of government, not in the "who." It is not a question of numbers. A single individual who rules under law is a constitutional monarch; someone who rules arbitrarily, according to caprice, is a tyrant.

Tyranny is nothing new. There is little to be added to the description and analysis of it given by classical authors such as Plato, Xenophon, and Aristotle. But many scholars argue that the twentieth century has witnessed a new form of despotic rule: **totalitarianism**. The word was coined by Mussolini to describe his system of government. He summarized his views in a speech in 1925: "Everything in the state, nothing outside the state, nothing against the state."[3] The term was soon accepted by the Nazi regime in Germany and later applied by external observers to the Stalinist regime in the Soviet Union and to the People's Republic of China under Mao Zedong.

Totalitarianism is a way of organizing tyrannical or despotic rule in a modern society. In a perceptive analysis of the way totalitarian leaders manipulate the masses, use political organization and the power of the state, and apply ideology and terror, Hannah Arendt noted that

> totalitarianism differs essentially from other forms of political oppression known to us such as despotism, tyranny, and dictatorship. Wherever it rose to power, it developed entirely new political institutions and destroyed all social, legal, and political traditions of the country.[4]

As a term, totalitarianism was most used immediately after World War II. Usage began to fall as Hitler and Mussolini faded from public memory, as the Soviet regime moderated its practices in some respects after Stalin's death in 1953, and as communist China began to open itself to the rest of the world after the death of Mao in 1976. Some scholars have held that the concept is merely propaganda—that totalitarianism exists more in the minds of analysts who are anticommunist or antifascist than as a real political system. This issue could be debated forever. That being said, the term is still used by politicians, journalists, and scholars; and because totalitarian regimes may arise again in the future, it is important to analyze the principles on which they operate.[5]

Arendt restricts the term *totalitarian* to a small number of regimes—to those that combine an all-powerful political leader and an almost messianic sense of historical mission. Two distinguishing features of totalitarianism are, first, the existence of a revolutionary movement that claims to base itself on nature or history, and second, the use of terror as an integral tactic in maintaining the momentum of a society in transformation. The leader uses systematic terror as a means of atomizing individuals and keeping the entire population off-balance. Arendt describes this use of terror:

> Under conditions of total terror not even fear can any longer serve as an advisor of how to behave, because terror chooses its victims without reference to individual actions or thoughts, exclusively in accordance with the objective necessity of the natural or historical process.[6]

In Arendt's analysis, the arbitrary use of terror on any and all segments of the population becomes an institutionalized way of preventing the development of political forces opposed to the leader's vision of a new society.

Carl Friedrich and Zbigniew Brzezinski offer a broader definition of totalitarianism. To them it is a "syndrome," or "pattern of interrelated traits," which includes the following six elements:

1. an official ideology
2. a single party typically led by one man
3. a terroristic police

4. a communications monopoly

5. a weapons monopoly

6. a centrally directed economy.[7]

One or more of these elements may be found individually in other forms of government; totalitarianism exists when they all come together.

The analysis of totalitarianism presented here is based on the historical reality of fascist regimes (Italy and Germany) and communist regimes (the Soviet Union and its East European satellites; the People's Republic of China; and the smaller communist states of Yugoslavia, Albania, North Korea, Vietnam, Cambodia, Laos, and Cuba). Of course, with the collapse of international communism, much of this description is recent history rather than current politics. The Soviet Union and Yugoslavia no longer exist as multinational communist states. China and Vietnam are still nominally communist, but they are encouraging a market economy and foreign investment to such an extent that it is questionable whether the state still exercises total control over society. Even North Korea and Cuba have undertaken internal changes that represent a departure from the "totalitarian syndrome." But even if it is temporarily in eclipse, totalitarianism is a real and recurrent possibility in the modern world and as such cannot simply be tucked away into the history books along with the descriptions of the Greek *polis* and the Mongol Empire.

Below we describe the "totalitarian syndrome" under eight headings derived from Friedrich and Brzezinski, Arendt, and other writers on the subject.

🔲🔲🔲🔲🔲🔲🔲

ATTEMPT TO REMAKE SOCIETY

Central to totalitarianism, and distinguishing it from simple tyranny, is the attempt to remake society on a grand scale, to produce a condition of utopian perfection. These blueprints for the future are usually a part of the official ideology. Communists, for example, claim to be working toward the classless society and the withering away of the state. This transformational view of history was enshrined in the Soviet constitution, the preamble of which asserted that the Soviet Union was "a developed socialist society" that was "a logically necessary state on the path to communism."[8] Hitler envisioned a new order in which the German master race would create a new empire (the Third Reich) that would last a thousand years. Mussolini proclaimed the age of the Third Rome (the first two being the Roman Empire and the Roman papacy), during which modern Italy would again lead the world to new heights of civilization. Both the communist and fascist visions of the future were sweeping, radical, and above all **monistic** in the sense that they reduced everything to a single factor—class (communism), race (Nazism), or state (Mussolini's fascism). Such monism gives rise to terror as a principle of government because pluralistic societies must be forcibly remoulded to fit the monistic image.

Thus arises the enormous scale of violence that has marked totalitarianism. Hitler was responsible for the death of six million Jews, half a million Gypsies, and several million Slavs—all of them members of allegedly inferior races. As part of the collectivization of agriculture in the early 1930s, Stalin eliminated perhaps fourteen million Ukrainian kulaks (independent peasants) through famine and deportation.[9] Between 1975 and 1979, in an attempt to purify the country of Western and bourgeois influences, the Khmer Rouge may have killed one-sixth of the population of Cambodia. In 1958, at the time of the Great Leap Forward, which was a disastrous attempt to industrialize China almost overnight, Mao expressed the totalitarian outlook in an unforgettable way:

> Apart from their other characteristics, China's 600 million people have two remarkable peculiarities; they are, first of all, poor, and secondly, blank ... A clean sheet of paper has no blotches, and so the newest and most beautiful pictures can be painted on it.[10]

Society, to vary the metaphor, is viewed by totalitarian regimes as raw material to be moulded by the state according to ideological design.

ONE-PARTY STATE

Totalitarianism imposes a single mass political party that penetrates all aspects of state and society, including the army, schools, trade unions, churches, and leisure organizations. This disciplined party, controlled from above, coordinates all sectors of society. Social organizations may be formally distinct from government, but the leaders of all institutions are either members of the party or acceptable to it. All other political parties are either outlawed, as was the case in the Soviet Union, or carefully manipulated in a common front, as was done in East Germany. Never is real opposition tolerated.

The rejection of political pluralism is linked to the transformation of society. If, as in Mao's metaphor, a picture is being painted, the artist must be in control of the materials and cannot allow other artists to sketch rival conceptions on the same canvas. The fundamental difference between this approach and that of liberal democracy lies in the totalitarian assumption that society is united in a single common project directed by the party through the state. In contrast, liberal democrats see society as the field in which individuals and groups pursue projects of their own choosing.

This leading role of the party was a central tenet of communism from the time the Bolsheviks came to power in 1917. The Soviet Union intervened in Czechoslovakia in 1968 precisely because it feared that the Communist Party there was losing its monopoly of political power. The watershed event in the movement away from totalitarianism in Eastern Europe was the decision by the Polish authorities to allow the Solidarity labour movement to contest the parliamentary elections of 1989. The system was still rigged against Solidarity in that large numbers of seats were effectively reserved for the Communists; but the very fact that another party was allowed to contend for power broke the totalitarian mould. Within three years, the rest of Eastern Europe and the Soviet Union had followed the Polish example and legalized political opposition.

ALL-POWERFUL LEADER

At one time, it seemed that domination of the party by an all-powerful, charismatic leader was an integral part of totalitarianism. However, Lenin, Stalin, Mao Zedong, Ho Chi Minh, and Tito passed away without leaving replacements of comparable stature, yet their regimes endured, at least for a time. The only totalitarian leaders today that one might call omnipotent or charismatic are Kim Jong Il of North Korea and Fidel Castro of Cuba. It may be that charismatic leadership is a phenomenon of the early stages of totalitarianism, a requirement for transmitting the energy necessary to seize and consolidate power. The routinization of charisma described by Max Weber in other contexts applies here as well: after the death of the revolutionary leader, power passes into the collective leadership of the party. There may be a reaction against the departed leader, as occurred in the Soviet Union after Stalin's death in 1953, when a new generation of leaders criticized the cult of personality and vowed that it would never arise again. Or, as has taken place in China, the memory of the leader may be revered, while at the same time there is an effective break with many of his policies. In either case, the evidence is that totalitarianism seems able to carry on without charismatic leadership.[11] However, the loss of charismatic authority tends to release demands for democratic reform.

PSEUDODEMOCRATIC RULE

The leader and party maintain their power by force but rationalize their rule with pseudodemocratic arguments. Hitler argued that he represented the people (*Volk*) in such a special way that elections were unnecessary. Until Gorbachev's time, communism relied on Lenin's theory of democratic centralism. Elections took place, but the party nominated or approved all candidates. Usually there was only one candidate per position, and voting was more ratification than selection. The role of an elected representative was not to contest the policies of the leadership but to increase and maintain society's support for the leadership and its policies.

Authoritarian regimes may also use pseudodemocratic devices to legitimize their authority; but when they do so, it is usually in a cynical and transparently obvious way. In contrast, pseudodemocracy is an intrinsic part of totalitarianism. Because society is being remade, it is important to create popular participation while at the same time making sure the people cannot change their rulers. Thus arises the curious situation that political participation, though ineffective and meaningless from a liberal–democratic point of view, is energetically promoted by the state. Voting is made a legal duty. School and university courses in political education are mandatory. Attendance at political meetings and discussion groups is encouraged or even required. Parades and demonstrations are arranged as needed for specific purposes. In contrast, authoritarian regimes are usually happiest if their subjects refrain from criticism and stay out of politics altogether.

CONTROL OF COMMUNICATIONS

The totalitarian state seeks to monopolize the flow of ideas. This means that the physical bases of communication—newspapers, radio stations, publishing houses—are either owned or completely controlled by the state. Before Gorbachev, prepublication censorship in the Soviet Union was rigidly enforced to ensure that public statements followed what communists called "the party line." Photocopying machines and personal computers were considered a potential threat, and access to them was carefully restricted. Foreign books, newspapers, and magazines were not sold freely but were confined to special libraries used by trustworthy researchers. With the means of mass communication so much under state control, dissenting opinions could circulate only by word of mouth or by the laborious process of *samizdat* (self-publication), which involved dissidents typing and retyping their treatises.

The purpose of control over communications is to support an official ideology. In totalitarian states, political doctrine amounts to an official religion. Fascism or Marxism–Leninism is taught in the schools and otherwise made the only publicly acceptable system of belief, while proponents of competing ideologies are subject to persecution.

An important aspect of totalitarianism is that it takes a political doctrine and forces it deep into nonpolitical activities, even the fine arts and natural sciences.

Because of Albert Einstein's Jewish origin, the Nazis rejected the theory of relativity and did not allow it to be taught in German universities. They also banned works of art and literature by Jewish artists and authors. In the Soviet Union in the 1930s, an obscure agronomist named T.D. Lysenko attracted Stalin's attention with the Lamarckian theory of the inheritance of acquired characteristics, a theory long discredited among biologists. Lysenko promised a shortcut to breeding better strains of wheat and cattle; instead of the patient work of selective breeding over generations, he believed that it was necessary to nourish only one generation exceptionally well and let it pass on its vigour to its progeny. This doctrine was officially ratified by the Central Committee of the Communist Party in 1948 and was not repudiated until after the fall of Nikita Khrushchev in 1964. It dealt Soviet agriculture a blow from which it never fully recovered. In China the expansion of ideology merged with the charismatic leadership of Mao Zedong to produce the almost magical "thought of Chairman Mao":

> The thought of Mao Tse-tung is the sun in our heart, is the root of our life, is the source of all our strength. Through this, man becomes unselfish, daring, intelligent, able to do everything … The thought of Mao Tse-tung transforms man's ideology, transforms the Fatherland.[12]

USE OF TERROR

Totalitarian rule is supported by the terroristic activities of a special **political police**. The Nazi Gestapo and the Soviet KGB were two such forces. A political police reports directly to the leader and is under no legal restraint. It may use intimidation, arbitrary arrest, torture, and execution. It infiltrates other coercive agencies of the state, such as the regular police and the armed forces, to ensure their compliance. Stalin and Hitler even used their political police against the party to ensure their personal control of the apparatus. A political police operates as an empire in itself, maintaining its own prisons, mental hospitals, and labour camps outside the supervision of the legal agencies of the state.

Authoritarian regimes also make use of political police, and their methods are equally grim. Brutality, torture, and summary execution are international phenomena, not confined to a single ideology or system. But there is usually a difference in the scale of operations. Authoritarian governments tend to single out overt political opponents for mistreatment; totalitarian regimes may use the political police against almost anyone. This is a logical consequence of remaking society: anyone who does not wholeheartedly embrace the state-sponsored monistic society of the future is a political opponent. The difference could be formulated this way: in a liberal democracy, the only political crime is to attempt or advocate the violent overthrow of the government; in an authoritarian regime, even criticism or peaceful opposition becomes a political crime; in a totalitarian state, literally any word or action that suggests less than complete commitment to the regime can become cause for detention by the political police.

SUBORDINATION OF LAW TO THE STATE

In a totalitarian state, law is a tool. It is only what the state says today, and it may speak differently tomorrow. Law is subordinate to the state, not the other way around; there are no rights in the proper sense of the term, for rights exist only under law.

In the enthusiasm of the first years after the October Revolution, Soviet theorists held that law would disappear altogether in a communist society. Enforceable rules of conduct were required only because of the antagonisms of class society and would no longer be necessary in the classless society of the future. These early notions were soon replaced by the concept of socialist legality, which is a particular form of legal positivism. It holds that the state should follow regularized procedures in dealing with citizens. These legal norms, however, arise less from an existing consensus in the present society than from the desired shape of the future society that is under construction. Because the state, guided by the party, is the only legitimate interpreter of the goal of evolution, it is for all practical purposes the source of all law.

One illustration of this relates to the status of constitutional documents in totalitarian states. All the communist states had constitutions that spelled out civil liberties in admirable terms. What could be clearer than Article 45 of the 1978 Chinese constitution (no longer in force): "Citizens enjoy freedom of speech, correspondence, the press, assembly, association, procession, demonstration and the freedom to strike, and have the right to speak out freely, air their views fully, hold great debates and write big-character posters."[13] In fact, periods of freedom of speech were announced several times in China with great fanfare, for example, in Mao's Hundred Flowers campaign of 1957 ("Let a hundred flowers bloom, let a hundred schools of thought contend"); and after Mao's death in September 1976, when the new leadership suggested the virtue of "four freedoms"; and in 1986, when General Secretary Hu encouraged open criticism of party policies. In each case, the state later intervened to suppress discussion when it threatened to become critical. The tragic events of 1989, when, after having encouraged freer speech for a time, the government used tanks to crush student demonstrations at Tiananmen Square, were only the latest episode in a pattern stretching back more than four decades.

The status of law is a crucial issue in the internal reform of totalitarian regimes. Initially, citizens may be grateful merely to enjoy freedom of speech and voluntary political participation, but they will soon want to see these rights entrenched in the constitution and protected by an independent judiciary. Legal theorists in Eastern Europe are now adopting the liberal idea of rule of law. Movement in this direction is less visible than highly publicized electoral reform, but it is at least as important in restricting the arbitrary power of the state.

🔲🔲🔲🔲🔲🔲🔲

PLANNED ECONOMY

The totalitarian state aspires to control a planned economy. This may entail public ownership, as in communism, or state supervision of private enterprise, as in Nazi Germany or fascist Italy, where the state took a vigorous role in setting prices and production quotas. A controlled economy is vital to the totalitarian state. It cannot allow a liberal economy, in which each individual or group pursues private interests and coordination is left to Adam Smith's invisible hand. Individual interests and goals must be subordinated to the imposed goal of social transformation.

This helps to explain the position of labour unions in totalitarian states. All such states foster unions by making membership compulsory, but these organizations are not autonomous associations of workers. Leadership is controlled by party members, and collective bargaining in the Western sense does not take place. The union is a control over the workers rather than an expression of their interests. This is not surprising; in any economy, labour is the most important factor of production. If the state could not set wages and otherwise direct labour, central planning would be meaningless. This is why the emergence in Poland in 1980 of the Solidarity union as an autonomous force was an event of the highest significance. In December 1981, the Polish government declared martial law, which restricted the activities of Solidarity. Then in October 1982, it banned all unofficial unions and thereby re-established the supremacy of the Communist Party. These moves demonstrated the reluctance of Poland's leaders to accept a relatively autonomous organization in society. Thus the legal recognition of Solidarity in 1989 was a landmark in Poland's gradual rejection of totalitarian rule.

China is now attempting to combine elements of a market economy with the totalitarian apparatus of rule. (On a smaller scale, so is Vietnam.) The initial results of this experiment have been encouraging from the rulers' point of view: production has soared while the Communist Party continues to control the state. However, one may question whether this will be a stable combination in the long run. A rapidly growing market economy will bring about all sorts of challenges to the "totalitarian syndrome," such as ever-increasing exposure to foreign influences, the proliferation of faxes, cell phones, and e-mail outside state control, and an ethic of individual self-fulfillment and self-expression rather than subordination to the collective good as defined by the state. Such sweeping economic change must inevitably result in political transformation.

CONCLUSION

Totalitarianism, then, makes use of the vastly improved technical apparatus of rule that has become available in this century. Innovations in mass communication make it possible to saturate the population with propaganda to an unprecedented degree. Inventions in weapons and new forms of organization provide a means to coerce people on a much vaster scale. Totalitarianism is in one sense a bigger and better despotism, implemented by the most up-to-date means. But it differs from authoritarianism in the importance it places on ideology and in its single-minded urge to remake society according to a utopian vision.

Many aspects of the totalitarian syndrome can also be found in other types of systems. Certainly, many governments use terror to keep themselves in power. The Argentine military regime of 1976–84 was terribly brutal in its treatment of the opposition. And General Augusto Pinochet resorted to horrific methods in attempting to eliminate leftist political parties and other oppositional forces in Chile. Was this not worse than the treatment many totalitarian regimes accorded their citizens? In a sense, yes. But violence is not the only distinguishing characteristic of totalitarian rule.

In all totalitarian systems, one finds in the political leaders a tremendous will to transform society, to mobilize the people in order to achieve that transformation, and to use indiscriminate force against those who might oppose the transformation. This seems to be the telling difference between totalitarian and authoritarian dictatorships. Authoritarian dictators usually try to avoid extensive changes. Indeed, change is seen as disruptive, as something to be avoided, or at least carefully administered. The totalitarian regime, on the other hand, is engrossed in a vision of achieving a new destiny for the society. The means to achieve this end involve rapid and pervasive change. The compelling drive to attain a utopian social order at whatever cost is the mark of a totalitarian system. The distinction between authoritarian and totalitarian rule will be clearer after we discuss authoritarian systems in the next chapter.

FURTHER READING

Arendt, Hannah. *The Origins of Totalitarianism*, rev. ed. Cleveland, Ohio: World Publishing, 1958.

Aron, Raymond. *Democracy and Totalitarianism*. New York: Praeger, 1969.

Beilharz, Peter, Gillian Robinson, and John Rundell, eds. *Between Totalitarianism and Postmodernity: A Thesis Eleven Reader*. Cambridge, Mass.: MIT Press, 1992.

Boesche, Roger. *Theories of Tyranny, From Plato to Arendt*. University Park, Penn.: Pennsylvania State University, 1996.

Brooker, Paul. *Twentieth-Century Dictatorships: The Ideological One-Party States*. New York: New York University Press, 1995.

Curtis, Michael. *Totalitarianism*. New Brunswick, N.J.: Transaction Books, 1980.

Friedrich, Carl J., and Zbigniew K. Brzezinski. *Totalitarian Dictatorship and Autocracy*, 2nd ed. New York: Praeger, 1965.

Friedrich, Carl J., Benjamin Barber, and Michael Curtis. *Totalitarianism: Its Changing Theory and Practice*. New York: Praeger, 1969.

Gleason, Abbott. *Totalitarianism: The Inner History of the Cold War*. New York: Oxford University Press, 1995.

Howe, Irving, ed. *1984 Revisited*. New York: Harper and Row, 1983.

Kershaw, Ian, and Moshe Lewin, eds. *Stalinism and Nazism: Historical Perspectives on Nazism and Stalinism*. New York: Cambridge University Press, 1996.

Menze, Ernest A. *Totalitarianism Reconsidered*. Port Washington, N.Y.: Kennikat Press, 1980.

Soper, Steven Paul. *Totalitarianism: A Conceptual Approach*. Lanham, Md.: University Press of America, 1985.

Talmon, J.L. *The Origins of Totalitarian Democracy*. New York: W.W. Norton, 1970.

Thurston, Robert W. *Life and Terror in Stalin's Russia, 1934–1941*. New Haven: Yale University Press, 1996.

AUTHORITARIANISM

Most contemporary states do not fit comfortably into the categories of either liberal democracy or totalitarianism. The most common word applied to these regimes is authoritarian. In a way, the term is ambiguous, for authority is a universal aspect of politics and is as much a part of liberal democracy as of authoritarian government. The concept of **authoritarianism** implies authority that may or may not rest on wide popular support but that is not put to the test of free elections. Another problem in speaking of authoritarian regimes is that the category includes such a wide diversity of types. Some regimes are civilian (Syria), others military (Nigeria); some are secular (Iraq), others avowedly religious (Iran); some are capitalist (Indonesia), others socialist (Myanmar, formerly Burma).

We cannot pursue all these differences here, but we will draw a distinction between right-wing conservative regimes that interpret their mission as protecting society from harmful (usually communist) influences, and left-wing revolutionary regimes that claim to be building a new society (usually socialist). Current examples of the former are Indonesia and Nigeria; of the latter, Tanzania, Libya, and Iraq.

RIGHT-WING AUTHORITARIANISM

Drawing heavily on the example of Spain under Francisco Franco (1936–75), Juan Linz developed a model of the right-wing authoritarian system of government that emphasizes the following characteristics:

- limited political pluralism,
- no elaborate or guiding ideology,

- no extensive political mobilization, and
- leaders who exercise power within ill-defined yet predictable limits.[1]

One might add to these a bias toward statism and a major political role for the military.

In most right–authoritarian systems there is no idea of a classless society or a master race. A substantial degree of social pluralism is tolerated. As the society grows more complex, a variety of organizations—business associations, labour unions, churches, peasant groups—can function with a minimum of interference by government. In fact, an authoritarian regime may use these organizations to achieve certain goals, such as the production of goods and services, or look to them for political support. These organizations can survive as long as they offer political support or at least remain neutral politically. If, however, they become too critical of government policy or suggest fundamental societal change or a change in political leadership, they are expendable.

Right–authoritarian systems do not have an elaborate blueprint for utopian order. While the authoritarian ruler always advocates economic development, there is usually no doctrinaire plan to totally transform society to achieve this growth. Rather, economic development (the most common objective) is defined in terms of doing more of what is already being done and doing it within the existing structures of society.

The military regime that ruled South Korea from 1961 to 1988 is an excellent example. The government encouraged industrialization by creating favourable conditions for large companies to operate. Within two decades, South Korea became an international force in steel, shipbuilding, automobiles, clothing, electronics, and other industries. The country transformed itself in a very short period of time from a backward agricultural economy into a modern industrial power. Standards of living also rose dramatically, and continue to do so although they are still below those in Japan or North America.

During these years of rapid development, the government tolerated token political opposition but manipulated elections to ensure its continued dominance. Social pluralism was allowed, but organizations that challenged government policy, such as labour unions, were severely repressed. The government often equated opposition to itself with communism—a tactic that retained some credibility because of the belligerence of North Korea. Right-wing authoritarianism in South Korea was typical in its political methods but exceptional in the success of its economic policies; few governments of this type have presided over such rapid and sustained industrial growth.

Another characteristic of the authoritarian model is that there is no great drive to mobilize the society in order to achieve utopian ends. In Chile, for example, all political parties were banned from 1973 until the closing years of General Pinochet's regime; the military government did not even maintain a party of its own, so great was its distaste for mass participation in politics. Mobilizing large numbers of people can nurture political instability by breaking down old patterns of living and stimulating the growth of new institutions. Unless the effects of these changes can be channelled or contained, they can be disastrous for a political leader. This is one of the primary reasons totalitarian leaders employ elaborate controls. Few authoritarian leaders are willing to risk the consequences of drastic change. On the contrary, most cling to the stability of the status quo. However, they may undertake certain reforms, particularly in the interest of economic efficiency. South Korea redistributed much agricultural land—large holdings were appropriated from their owners, divided into smaller pieces, and given to peasants; and the late Shah of Iran confiscated large landholdings of the Islamic clergy. Improvements in nonpolitical areas (for example, technical education) are also not uncommon in conservative authoritarian regimes. However, reform generally stops short of upsetting the balance of political power.

Rightist authoritarianism, even though broadly opposed to socialism, often leans toward **statism**. Rulers are usually unwilling to leave the process of economic development entirely to the private sector. While they may not impose state ownership of the economy, they see the state as a principal instrument in expanding the production of goods and services. The state becomes the driving force, influencing wages, employment, investment, and the development and management of natural resources and international trade. South Korea, for example, controlled exchange rates and restricted imports during its period of highest industrial growth, thus restricting opportunities for consumption and channelling savings into investment.

This particular role of the state seems to be a significant characteristic of many authoritarian systems. Numerous authoritarian governments have used their concentrated political power to control many, if not all, aspects of a market economy. Examples are Taiwan, South Korea, Kenya, Brazil, and Chile. The last case is particularly instructive.

In 1973 a military revolt overthrew the socialist government of President Salvador Allende. The government of General Pinochet, tacitly supported by the United States, soon reversed many of Allende's socialist policies—most notably in the monetary field, where rampant inflation was reduced through application of conservative economic theories. Relative monetary stability resulted in an improved climate for business investment and the development of new industries, such as the production of fruit and wine for export. Yet the military government did not reverse Allende's decision to nationalize the copper industry. This illustrates the general rule that authoritarian rulers are often eclectic with respect to ideologies. They choose ideas from several sources; they don't commit themselves to a doctrine. In this sense, their approach remains statist, for the ultimate choice of policy is determined by the needs of the rulers rather than being left to spontaneous social evolution.

The military is usually the dominant institution in right-wing authoritarianism. Given its weapons and organizational capability, the military can intimidate political parties, interest groups, and the courts. Because authoritarian leaders have to rely on coercion rather than popular support, the military becomes the decisive force in the struggle for power. It often promises a return to civilian rule, but usually the date of free elections is repeatedly postponed until it vanishes into the indefinite future.

There are, however, at least three Latin American cases in which military regimes voluntarily relinquished power. In Brazil (1964), Uruguay (1973), and Argentina (1976), authoritarian military regimes ousted elected civilian governments. In each case they accused the civilian politicians of creating economic chaos and pledged economic stability and development through efficient management. In 1984, each regime took steps to return the government to elected civilians. Interestingly, in each case the economy was in no better shape than it had been when the military seized power. These examples do not support the "efficient authoritarian" hypothesis; generals, like other mortals, do not necessarily have a quick fix for the complex economic problems of development.

That being said, the record of military regimes is not totally devoid of economic success stories. Pinochet's regime in Chile (1973–90) had an abysmal record on human rights, but it also liberalized trade, reduced inflation, and reformed social programs. The result, after some years of austerity, was an export boom that continued through the transition to democracy and gave Chile one of the most dynamic economies in South America. Chile has, in fact, initiated free trade with Mexico, as a step toward entering the North American Free Trade Agreement (NAFTA) along with Canada, Mexico, and the United States. Chile's entry into such a free-trade bloc would help to "lock in" its internal reforms by tying them to external treaty commitments.

Chile is a difficult case to evaluate. Unlike most right–authoritarian regimes, the military regime in Chile did have certain economic successes, which laid the foundation of the present dynamism of the Chilean economy. But those successes have to be measured against the horrifying measures the government took in trying to eradicate the socialist movement as a political force. Chile under the military regime was certainly far from the freedom, open society, and toleration that are the hallmarks of liberal democracy.

LEFT-WING AUTHORITARIANISM

Left–authoritarian regimes seem very different from their right-wing counterparts, at least at first glance. They have an official ideology—usually some variety of socialism other than orthodox Marxism–Leninism, combined with a strong element of nationalism. Tanzania had Nyerere's *ujamaa* socialism—a blend of British Labour ideology and indigenous African traditions. Iraq and Syria, though mortal enemies, both profess *ba'ath* (renaissance) socialism. In Libya, Colonel Kaddafi has propounded a unique mixture of revolutionary socialism and Islamic fundamentalism. His *Green Book*, like the *Little Red Book* of Chairman Mao, is prescribed ideological reading for a whole nation. Another example is the "revolutionary humanism" of the early years of the left-wing military regime that ruled in Peru from 1968 until it voluntarily relinquished power in 1980:

The Peruvian Revolution is an autonomous process of development for changing the political, economic, and social system of the country, and ending our capitalist and oligarchic state of underdevelopment and submissiveness to interests of imperialism, and it is intended to construct a social democracy in which all Peruvians will be able to contribute through full participation in the exercise of social power in a truly sovereign national community. The Peruvian Revolution is defined as Nationalistic or Independent and ideologically it is rooted in a Revolutionary Humanism clearly in opposition to dogmatic and totalitarian systems of social exploitation. Therefore, it rejects the capitalist and communist systems.[2]

Though they differ in detail, the ideologies of all these regimes call for a fundamental social transformation and refer to revolution in all public discussion. In certain other ways, too, they seem more totalitarian than authoritarian, at least at the rhetorical level. Political mobilization of the masses is a continuing theme, as is centralized economic planning under the control of a vanguard party.

Perhaps the difference between these left–authoritarian regimes and true totalitarianism is one of degree rather than of kind. If they lived up to their stated goals, they might well become totalitarian. But their revolutions have not been as thoroughgoing or single-minded in the pursuit of the stated utopian goals; there has been more compromise with present reality, and more autonomy for groups in the society that do not oppose the leadership. In Libya, for example, Kaddafi nationalized the oil reserves previously owned by foreign oil companies, but he did not take the country out of the international network of the oil industry. Large numbers of managers and workers from other countries continue to operate the extraction and refining systems, and the products are exported to Western purchasers. Compare that to the autarchic policies of totalitarian states such as Albania and Cambodia, which excluded Western influences altogether; or to the Soviet Union, which tried to develop major industries, including a petroleum industry, without outside help, although it was willing to export surpluses for hard currency.

Lacking the full intensity of totalitarian regimes, left–authoritarian governments in practice often resemble right–authoritarian ones. Some social pluralism is tolerated as long as it does not become politically dangerous. Police terrorism is used chiefly as a way of retaining power rather than as a means of inducing social change. The rigours of central planning are softened by bribery and corruption. Lip service is paid to ideological goals, but the government does not enforce a monopoly of ideas. Foreign travel is allowed, as are foreign publications, and these things lead to some ideological diversification.

Whether of the left or right, authoritarian leaders tolerate little or no opposition and may do almost anything to remain in power. In virtually every case, they reject the principles of liberal democracy—or the "capitalist state," as they are likely to call it. They regard Western-style liberal democracy as too inefficient for the needs of developing nations. They argue that democracy promotes factions and that a faction-ridden society is unable to attain the mass unity required for social and economic development.

There is, no doubt, a great deal of truth in these criticisms. Liberal democracies are clumsy in their response to crisis and slow to implement public policies when a variety of interests must be considered. Yet the alleged efficiency of authoritarian rulers is often illusory. Their statist mentality often leads them to impose on society vast projects that seem no more productive than the pyramids of the Pharaohs. Or they may embark on reckless international adventures: Iraq's invasion of Iran in 1981 was one of these, as was Argentina's attempt to take the Falkland Islands by force in 1982. When only one will is obeyed, the chances of dramatic error are heightened. The presumed inefficiency of a liberal government is in the long run actually one of its virtues. By fragmenting power, it allows many projects to compete with each other. Some will inevitably fail, but diversity increases the likelihood that solutions to the unexpected problems of the future will be found.

While liberal democracies have worked well for most Western societies, they are not easy to manage, and a certain democratic tradition may be required to make them work. The fact remains, however, that they are not designed to run efficiently. Internal checks are built into them to impede a takeover by a powerful military leader. The processes are set up in such a way that a political leader cannot set a blind course and refuse to hear criticism or consider alternative courses. What seems like inefficiency in the short run may be the most efficient long-run method of governing in an ever-changing and unpredictable world.

Evidence of this can be seen in the fact that many authoritarian rulers enjoy power for only a short time, even when they were first greeted as saviours and later employed various tactics to maintain popular support. Leaders like this are frequently charismatic and often articulate nationalist goals (mostly economic) that have mass appeal. In time, however, enthusiasm wanes as the leader is unable to perform economic miracles. Time seems to erode initial support for authoritarian dictators; to remain in power they begin to rely more on coercion than on popular support. Often they are overthrown in a **coup d'état** organized by a faction within the military or the ruling party. In many authoritarian systems, the *coup d'état* has been virtually institutionalized as a means of changing officeholders and plays a role analogous to elections in a liberal democracy. The system remains authoritarian, but there is rotation of personnel at the top.

TRANSITIONS TO DEMOCRACY?

One of the most interesting aspects of political science today is the analysis of authoritarian regimes in transition. Everywhere in the world, attempts are being made to move political systems toward more democratic processes of governing. As Robert Dahl has noted:

> ... the mature democratic countries and the newer democratic countries together accounted in the mid-1980s for just under forty percent of the world's population. Should the transitions taking place in Eastern Europe eventuate in democratic systems, then over half the population of the world will be governed under relatively democratic systems.[3]

At the same time, he was cautious in his optimism:

> It is important to keep in mind that while today transitions to democracy are very much in the air, it was not long ago that scholars were attempting to describe and account for the breakdown of democracy—in Italy, Germany, Spain, and Austria in the 1920s and 1930s, and in Chile, Uruguay, Brazil, Argentina, and Turkey in the 1970s, not to mention virtually all of the sub-saharan African countries with the exception of Botswana.[4]

Evolution toward democracy is not inevitable, rather, "consolidated democracy is only one among the possible outcomes of the collapse of authoritarian regimes."[5]

If the transition to democracy is not inevitable, in what circumstances is it likely? We will identify at least three important factors. The first is what James N. Rosenau calls the "relocation of authority." For Rosenau, citizen activity in the polity is significant in relocating the "loci of authority" in society. But it is not simply that individuals join the political process. They have learned how to play the game of politics:

> The point is, that while the attitudes and priorities of publics may not differ from those held in the past, their skills in employing, articulating, directing, and implementing their attitudes and priorities have undergone a major transformation.[6]

The pressure these people exert in political life leads to "alterations in the status of states, governments and subgroups."[7]

A second factor influencing the transition to democracy is the "free association" of individuals and groups in society. According to Marcia A. Weigle and Jim Butterfield, "autonomous social values and activism, and thus the seeds of a civil society, developed in post-totalitarian regimes as a result of systemic crisis."[8] And as Michael Bernhard sees it, autonomy and a civil society are preconditions for democracy:

> Modern democracy, as well as the limited forms of representative government that preceded it, have only existed in conjunction with a civil society. It constitutes the sphere of autonomy from which political forces representing constellations of interests in society have contested state power. Civil society has been a necessary condition for the existence of representative forms of government including democracy.[9]

Thus, the development of autonomous political forces that can challenge the state may constitute one important measure of the transition to democracy.

A final factor influencing the transition is economic development. In their seminal work on the democratic experience in developing countries, Larry Diamond, Juan Linz, and Seymour Martin Lipset see political legitimacy as a fundamental component of the democratic process. They envision political legitimacy growing out of the "performance" of the regime:

> Democratic legitimacy derives, when it is most stable and secure, from an intrinsic value commitment rooted in the political culture at all levels of society, but it is also shaped (particularly in the early years of a democracy) by the performance of the democratic regime, both economically and politically.[10]

Individuals in a polity respond to the economic and political conditions around them. If that response is positive over time, it provides the base for building a democracy that can "endure crises and challenges."[11]

With regard to the latter view, we would offer only one comment. The track records of many developing nations over the past several decades are not encouraging. While the average annual GNP per capita for the industrialized nations continues to grow, although more slowly than in the past, the trend line for most developing nations, except in East Asia, is essentially flat. Many of the emerging nations in Africa, Asia, Latin America, the Middle East, and Eastern Europe have not experienced recent economic growth. This means that if Diamond, Linz, and Lipset are right, many developing nations may find it very difficult to make a transition from authoritarianism to democracy. Indeed, it should be obvious that any transition to democracy is a complex process that may not be completed in one try. A society grappling with the problem of building a nation, building a state, and building an economy may have to make a number of attempts before all three ends can be achieved simultaneously. Certainly the ongoing relationship between economic development and political democracy in emerging societies will be a major focus of concern for political scientists in the twenty-first century.

FURTHER READING

Angell, Alan, and Benny Pollack. *The Legacy of Dictatorship: Political, Economic and Social Change in Pinochet's Chile*. Liverpool, England: University of Liverpool, Institute of Latin American Studies, 1993.

Boron, Atilio C. *State, Capitalism, and Democracy in Latin America*. Boulder, Colo.: Lynne Rienner, 1995.

Casper, Gretchen. *Negotiating Democracy: Transitions from Authoritarian Rule.* Pittsburgh, Pa.: University of Pittsburgh Press, 1996.

———. *Fragile Democracies: The Legacies of Authoritarian Rule.* Pittsburgh: University of Pittsburgh Press, 1995.

Collier, David, ed. *The New Authoritarianism in Latin America.* Princeton, N.J.: Princeton University Press, 1979.

Dominguez, Jorge I., ed. *Authoritarian and Democratic Regimes in Latin America.* New York: Garland Pub., 1994.

Germani, Gino. *Authoritarianism, Fascism and National Populism.* New Brunswick, N.J.: Transaction Books, 1978.

Gunther, Richard P., Nikiforos Diamandouros, and Hans-Jurgen Puhle. *The Politics of Democratic Consolidation: Southern Europe in Comparative Perspective.* Baltimore: Johns Hopkins University Press, 1995.

Haggard, Stephen, and Robert R. Kaufman. *The Political Economy of Democratic Transitions.* Princeton: Princeton University Press, 1995.

Hogman, David E. *Neo-Liberalism with a Human Face? The Politics and Economics of the Chilean Model.* Liverpool: University of Liverpool, Institute of Latin American Studies, 1995.

Huntington, Samuel P., and Clement H. Moore, eds. *Authoritarian Politics in Modern Society: The Dynamics of Established One-Party Systems.* New York: Basic Books, 1970.

Jalal, Ayesha. *Democracy and Authoritarianism in South Asia: A Comparative and Historical Perspective.* New York: Cambridge University Press, 1995.

Moore, Barrington, Jr. *Social Origins of Dictatorship and Democracy.* Boston: Beacon Press, 1967.

Nelson, Daniel N., ed. *After Authoritarianism: Democracy or Disorder?* Westport, Conn.: Greenwood Press, 1995.

Neumann, Frantz. *The Democratic and Authoritarian State.* New York: Free Press, 1964.

O'Donnell, Guillermo, et al., eds. *Transitions from Authoritarian Rule: Comparative Perspectives.* Baltimore: Johns Hopkins University Press, 1986.

O'Donnell, Guillermo, and Philippe C. Schmitter. *Transitions From Authoritarian Rule: Tentative Conclusions about Uncertain Democracies.* Baltimore: Johns Hopkins University Press, 1986.

Perlmutter, Amos. *Modern Authoritarianism.* New Haven, Conn.: Yale University Press, 1981.

Pridham, Geoffrey, ed., *Transitions to Democracy: Comparative Perspectives from Southern Europe, Latin America and Eastern Europe.* Aldershot, England: Dartmount, 1995.

Seligman, Adam B. *The Transition from State Socialism in Eastern Europe: The Case of Hungary.* Greenwich, Conn.: JAI Press, 1994.

Shain, Yossi with Juan J. Linz. *Between States: Interim Governments and Democratic Transitions.* Cambridge, England: Cambridge University Press, 1995.

Shapiro, Ian, and Russell Hardin, eds. *Political Order.* New York: New York University Press, 1996.

Wittfogel, Karl A. *Oriental Despotism.* New Haven, Conn.: Yale University Press, 1967.

PARLIAMENTARY AND PRESIDENTIAL SYSTEMS

CHAPTER 21

Of the many possible models for organizing the apparatus of representative government, the two most important are the parliamentary and presidential systems. Both originated in Britain in the seventeenth and eighteenth centuries and are now found everywhere in the world, even in societies that owe relatively little to Anglo-American traditions. They exist in their pure form only in liberal democracies, though many authoritarian or totalitarian systems have "borrowed" them to create a veneer of legitimacy.

The difference between the parliamentary and presidential systems can only be understood in the context of **separation of powers**, a doctrine that has a long history in political science. All governments, no matter how they are organized, have to perform certain functions and exercise certain powers. The most common approach is to divide these powers into three categories: legislative, executive, and judicial. The **legislative** power makes general laws of conduct for members of the community. Included are matters of both private law (such as rules against theft and murder) and public law (such as rules governing voting, military service, and payment of taxes). The **executive** power does not make general rules but proposes policies and administers the state's resources. For example, the executive commands the army (which was created by the legislative power), oversees the monetary system, and raises and spends taxes that the legislative power has authorized. This entails making many discretionary decisions, such as where to locate post offices and military bases. In the area of private law, the executive power enforces the rules of conduct by administering police forces and prisons to ensure that laws are obeyed. The *judicial* power, or **judiciary,** resolves conflicts that arise when laws are not obeyed or when there is disagreement over what the law means.

Early liberals such as John Locke argued that these powers of state should be distributed among different hands rather than concentrated in one institution, because dispersion lessens the temptation to use power arbitrarily: "In all moderated monarchies and well-framed governments," wrote Locke, "the legislative and executive power are in distinct hands."[1] In its simple form, this view tends to equate each power with one branch of government, which specializes in it. In his *Spirit of the Laws* (1748), Montesquieu analyzed British government in this way. He wrote that Parliament constituted the legislative branch, the monarch and ministers the executive branch, and the courts the judicial branch. The separation of powers into distinct branches of government was, in Montesquieu's opinion, the secret of the excellence of the British constitution, which made Britain the freest and most enviable country in Europe. Soon after, the doctrine of separation of powers became an integral part of liberal thinking, providing a structural and legal way of limiting the power of government.

Although certainly true in part, Montesquieu's analysis was simplistic. He overlooked the fact that the courts had a large share of legislative power since the common law evolved through their decisions. This was not deliberate making of law (which was Parliament's function), but it was equally significant as a source of rules of conduct. Even more importantly, Montesquieu did not fully appreciate the custom—increasingly observed since the Glorious Revolution—that ministers of the Crown had to be members of parliament, in either the Commons or the Lords. The executive and legislative branches were more closely connected than Montesquieu thought.

Since the publication of *Spirit of the Laws*, British-style representative government has evolved in two different directions. In the United States, where Montesquieu's philosophical authority was very great at the time of the constitutional convention, the Americans retained institutions modelled on those of Britain, but the division between the president and Congress was made sharper than the one between Crown and Parliament. This American model is the source of most contemporary presidential systems in which the separation of powers is still maintained. In Britain, however, and in colonies such as Canada that stayed within the Empire, political evolution has brought the legislative and executive branches closer together. In modern parliamentary systems, the executive (cabinet) and the legislature work closely together because of the practice of political party discipline. We will discuss the parliamentary system first and then return to the presidential model.

THE PARLIAMENTARY SYSTEM

After the Norman Conquest, all three powers of government were united in the monarchy. The king was the "font of justice" and the supreme military commander and could also legislate by royal proclamation. Parliament, which was first convened by Edward I in 1295, was at first not a legislative body at all. Its major functions were to advise the monarch and to approve the taxes necessary to support government. Over time, Parliament increased its power by refusing to grant revenue unless the monarch fulfilled its desires, which were drawn up in "bills," or lists of requests. This ancient practice is the reason a statute under consideration by Parliament is known today as a **bill**. Another reminder of this early period is that all legislation is still proclaimed by the monarch "with the advice and consent" of Parliament. Though Parliament long ago captured the legislative power, this verbal formula shows that it once belonged to the Crown.

The Glorious Revolution brought about a separation of powers that had till then been united. Parliament made itself a legislative body and also created an independent judiciary by forcing the Crown, which appointed judges, to respect the tenure of those judges. The settlement of 1689, although it made Parliament supreme, still left the monarch with considerable prerogative powers. The King or Queen remained a true chief executive, with the discretionary right to appoint and dismiss officials, declare war, conduct foreign relations, command the armed forces, pardon convicted criminals, and (as a remnant of lost legislative power) withhold assent to legislation.

Further political evolution reunited the legislative and executive powers under the control of a new executive: the prime minister and cabinet. At first this trend seemed to be a further victory of Parliament over the Crown, as the custom grew that ministers had to be members of parliament and had to have the political support of a working majority in the House of Commons. This mechanism of **responsible government** meant that the Crown could act only on the advice of those who had the confidence of Parliament. Parliament, by the middle of the nineteenth century, appeared to have captured the executive power as it had previously captured the legislative. But before long, the new practice of **party discipline** made it clear that the cabinet, led by the prime minister, was the real victor. As long as the supporters of the prime minister in the House of Commons vote as directed, the executive and legislative powers are fused, and separation of powers no longer acts as a check. The check in a parliamentary system comes when the prime minister loses majority support and the opposition can withdraw confidence from the government.

The Westminster Model

The political machinery of the British parliamentary system, referred to as the Westminster model, consists of the Crown, the cabinet, the House of Commons, and the House of Lords. The Crown requests the leader of the majority party or majority coalition to form a government, which consists of cabinet ministers sitting in either house; they govern supported by a majority in the House of Commons. If a majority party does not exist and there is no formal coalition, a party leader with a large bloc of seats will be asked to form a government. Such a situation is referred to as a minority government, and this government is entitled to govern as long as a majority in the Commons supports it, or at least does not defeat it.

Parliament is a bicameral institution consisting of the House of Commons and the House of Lords. The Commons is structured in a pyramidal fashion. The prime minister, who is leader of the majority party, was originally thought to be *primus inter pares*—"first among equals." Now, however, he or she is much more: the first minister of cabinet, the party leader, and the leader of government. Cabinet ministers of the governing party manage the legislative process with some cooperation from opposition parties. Those who do not belong to the cabinet are referred to as **private members,** whether they sit on the side of the government or in the opposition. They are the rank and file: the elected parliamentary members who are not part of the governing party's leadership. Their influence is not substantial. While they may introduce **private members' bills,** few of these bills are ever passed by Parliament.

The House of Lords has over 1000 members, most of whom are hereditary peers. Only about 150 of them are active in conducting the business of the institution. Since 1958, distinguished men and women appointed to life peerages have constituted about one-quarter of the membership of the Lords, and a majority of those active in legislative work. The powers of the two houses of Parliament were originally equal, but since the Parliament Acts of 1911 and 1949 were passed, the Lords has become subservient to the Commons. It may initiate and amend legislation, but it cannot veto acts of the Commons and can only delay bills for approximately one year. The parliamentary system today has become what some observers refer to as cabinet government or prime-ministerial government; for no one—not the monarch, not private members in the Commons, not members of the House of Lords—is as powerful as the prime minister and the cabinet.

Canada was one of the first colonies in modern history to peacefully attain independence from a colonial power. Its Parliament developed within the British tradition. Before 1867, colonial governors representing the Crown existed alongside locally elected legislatures. The Constitution Act, 1867, finally implemented one recommendation from Lord Durham's report of 1839. Durham had been appointed governor in 1838 to reform the colonial system so as to prevent further rebellions like the ones of 1837. He called for the eventual union of the colonies of Upper and Lower Canada, Nova Scotia, and New Brunswick, based on the assumption that a larger polity would be better able to assimilate the restive French-Canadian population.

At the national or federal level, one Parliament was created for all the colonies in 1867. This institution, like the British Parliament, was a bicameral legislature containing two houses, the Senate (which now has 104 seats) being the upper house and the Commons (which now has 301 members) being the lower one. Canada is a federal system; otherwise, the Canadian Parliament operates in principle like the British. The British monarch is our **head of state**. The Crown's representative in Canada is the governor general, who is appointed by the monarch on the advice of the Prime Minister of Canada. Lieutenant governors, who are appointed by the governor general (also on the advice of the prime minister), play the role of head of state in provincial governments. The Queen, governor general, and lieutenant governors together represent the Crown in Canada. The prime minister and the provincial premiers are the **heads of government.**

The heads of state normally do not exercise actual political power; they "reign rather than rule." Most functions of a head of state are symbolic in nature. The duties include selecting or dismissing a head of government; performing certain ceremonial functions—for example, greeting foreign dignitaries; assenting to and proclaiming legislation; formally appointing public officials such as judges; dissolving Parliament and calling elections; and exercising certain emergency powers if and when there is a leadership crisis or when government is deadlocked. In normal circumstances, the representative of the Crown carries out these functions without making real prerogative choices. The monarch or governor general must take the advice of the cabinet as long as there is a government in office. No executive action is taken without the signature of one or more ministers. Even in selecting a new government, the head of state normally has no real choice, because the individual appointed to be head of government has already been determined by the voters.

By constitutional convention, the political party with a majority of seats in the House of Commons is asked by the governor general to form the government of Canada. The prime minister then nominates the rest of the cabinet for appointment by the governor general. If there is no single party with a majority of seats, the party leader with the largest plurality of seats or who has received sufficient indications of support from other parties is asked to form a government. For example, in May 1979, the Progressive Conservatives were asked to form a government with 136 seats. They did not have the 142 seats needed for a clear majority, but they had more seats than any other party and an expectation of being able to get support from other parties on specific measures. In short, they were entitled to form a government as long as they could keep the **confidence** of the House, that is, as long as they could continue to win votes in the House.

An interesting development occurred in Ontario in 1985. The Conservatives, who had been in power since 1943, won only 52 of the 124 seats in the provincial legislature in the April election. The Liberals won 47 seats and the New Democrats 25. Conservative premier Frank Miller continued to govern until June, when he was defeated in the legislature by the Liberal and NDP opposition on a nonconfidence motion. David Peterson, leader of the Liberals, then formed a government supported by the NDP. It was not a coalition, because no ministerial positions were allocated to the NDP. Rather, the two parties signed an "accord," a written agreement that for two years the Liberals would not call an election and the NDP would not defeat the government on a nonconfidence motion. There is a long history in Canada of informal understandings being reached for the purpose of supporting a minority government, but this was the first formal, written agreement. It may also be the last, since the consequences of that agreement suggest that smaller parties have little to gain by entering such accords. The Liberals called an election after two years and won a majority.

The constitution almost always dictates the actions of the Crown. In rare circumstances, there might not be a constitutionally clear course of action—for example, if a prime minister were to unexpectedly die in office and the party had not agreed on a successor. Then the head of state might have to use his or her discretion in asking someone to form an interim government until the majority party could sort out its affairs. In general, the Crown acts unilaterally only if a crisis immobilizes responsible political institutions. In times of emergency, there is a role to be played by the head of state; this has been one of the principal arguments made by those who favour retaining the Crown as an integral part of Canadian government.[2]

A case in point was the course of action taken following the crisis that provoked the American intervention in Grenada in October 1983. Prime Minister Maurice Bishop had seized power in 1979, backed by the New Jewel Movement, which initially enjoyed a great deal of popular support on the island. In October 1983 Bernard Coard, an official in the Bishop government, staged a *coup d'état*. Bishop was ousted and later shot by forces supporting Coard. The United States then intervened militarily at the request of several neighbouring islands. With the prime minister dead and Coard in custody, Governor General Sir Paul Scoon assumed responsibility for governing the island and scheduled national elections for 1984. Thus the head of state governed until the people had an opportunity to choose new leaders to form a government.

The second major component of the parliamentary system is the House of Commons. The House is to the machinery of government what an engine is to an automobile. The government of the day is formed mostly from the House. The leader of the majority party, or of a party that has a working majority, becomes prime minister and chooses ministers from among members of the House or the Senate. Technically, a prime minister may choose an individual who is not a member of either house to become a member of the cabinet, but the practice is rare, and when it is followed, that person is expected to obtain a seat in the House or the Senate within a matter of months. Cabinet ministers, supported by members of their party, have legitimate and legal powers to govern as long as they can command the confidence of the House.

The third component of the Canadian parliamentary system is the Senate. Under the Constitution Act, 1867, the passage of legislation requires the approval not only of the House of Commons but also of the Senate. The Senate has exactly the same legislative power as the House of Commons except that bills involving taxes or expenditures must originate in the House.[3] The Senate, however, is not a confidence chamber. When it rejects a bill from the Commons, the government does not have to resign.

It was long thought that the Senate had faded into insignificance in the Canadian parliamentary system, but events since 1984 have forced observers to modify that view. During the Mulroney years, the large Liberal majority in the Senate repeatedly obstructed the plans of the Conservative government. By refusing to pass legislation until it was amended, the Senate forced several important bills to be changed. The Senate's refusal to pass legislation to implement the Free Trade Agreement in the fall of 1988 led Prime Minister Mulroney to request a dissolution of Parliament and an election—an election that turned into a virtual referendum on free trade. After the Conservatives won the election, the Senate passed the free-trade legislation, even though it still had the constitutional right to reject it.

Senators are chosen by personal decision of the prime minister, and this method of appointment tends to produce a Senate dominated by the opposition party when, as in 1984, power shifts in the House of Commons after one party has been in power for a long period of time. Because the Liberals had been in power almost continuously from 1935 to 1984, Liberal prime ministers had chosen almost all those sitting in the Senate by the time Brian Mulroney became prime minister. Since senators serve until the age of 75, Mulroney had no standard means available to install a Conservative majority in the upper house. In 1989, in order to ensure passage of the GST legislation, which the Liberals were blocking in the Senate, he resorted to an obscure provision of the Constitution that allows the governor general, with the prior approval of the Queen, to appoint eight extra senators.[4]

The shoe was on the other foot when the Liberals returned to power in 1993. Prime Minister Chrétien had at the time to deal with a holdover Conservative majority in the Senate, which succeeded in blocking several pieces of Liberal legislation. By 1996, however, Chrétien had restored the Liberal majority in the Senate by appointing a Liberal every time a vacancy occurred.

Canada's difficulties with the Senate are unique because it is a centrally appointed upper house in a federal system of government, but other parliamentary systems have also experienced problems with an upper house. In 1975, Australia's House of Representatives passed a money bill that the Senate refused to approve. The conflict evolved into a fiscal and constitutional crisis. The government would not budge, nor would the Senate, which is popularly elected in Australia. Finally, the governor general exercised his royal prerogative, dissolved both houses, and issued the writs for a new election. The prime minister was furious and accused the governor general of overstepping his powers and precipitating a constitutional crisis by permitting the upper house to bring down the government. The election that followed resolved the political issue with the defeat of the government, which vindicated the governor general to some degree.

There is general agreement that an upper house with equal power can obstruct the legislative proceedings of a parliament. There is little agreement, however, on the validity of such obstruction. Advocates of unicameralism argue that the final say on bills should rest with a single house in which representation is based on population. They see obstruction by another house as a violation of parliamentary principles. Many advocates of bicameralism in Canada reply to this that an elected second house, with representation based on regions, should be able to veto the bills of a lower house—especially when representation in the lower house may reflect a

'ty of the population concentrated in a single region, which then controls a
.y of seats in the legislature. This is the argument for a "triple-E" Senate,
which is made often by Western Canadians: an elected, equal, and effective Senate
would safeguard regional interests.

Fusion of Powers

In order to understand how Parliament actually runs, one must understand the
fusion of powers between the executive and the legislature. As Figure 21.1 indicates,
the prime minister cannot function without support in the House of Commons, and
ultimately, it is the electorate that provides this support by determining the balance
of partisan power in the House of Commons. Three election outcomes are possible.
One party may win a majority of seats in the House, in which case its leader will form
a **majority government**. If no party wins a majority, the leader of one party—usually
but not necessarily the party with the largest number of seats—will form a **minority
government**. Such a minority government can stay in office only if the other parties
refrain from defeating it. Finally, two or more parties may join forces to form a **coalition government**, dividing ministerial appointments between them. The leader of the
larger partner in the coalition normally becomes prime minister.

There has never been a true coalition government at the national level in
Canada. The "Union Government" that ruled during World War I under Robert
Borden consisted of breakaway Liberals who joined with the Conservatives; it was

FIGURE 21.1 The Canadian Parliamentary System

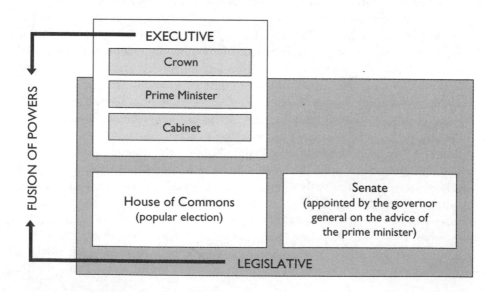

not a genuine coalition of the two parties. However, there have been a number of coalitions at the provincial level.

In forming the federal cabinet, the prime minister chooses the other ministers, who are then officially appointed by the governor general. Thus, after the 1997 federal election, Prime Minister Chrétien recommended 25 other MPs (and one Senator) for appointment as cabinet ministers. The governor general would also dismiss them on the advice of the prime minister, although the usual course is for the prime minister to request and receive a resignation from a minister whose presence is no longer desired in the cabinet. The prime minister and the cabinet ministers, along with the Crown, form the political executive.

The cabinet determines legislative priorities and sets the legislative agenda. Cabinet decisions supported by a majority in Parliament ultimately become the laws and public policies of the land. Cabinet ministers initiate almost all legislative proposals, using the civil service as a primary source of information and ideas. The cabinet has aptly been called "a combining committee—a hyphen which joins, a buckle which fastens, the legislative part of the state to the executive part."[5] It is the institution that most clearly distinguishes the modern parliamentary system from the presidential form of government. It is a true collective decision-making body, although in most circumstances formal votes are not taken. After extensive discussion, the prime minister may summarize the arguments and announce the action to be taken. Once a course is set, the principle of **cabinet solidarity** is supposed to prevent ministers from differing with government policy in public, whatever their private reservations. There are occasional departures from this practice in Canada, but generally not for very long and only on matters of secondary importance.

Private members' bills, which are introduced by members of parliament who are not ministers, may be numerous but are seldom passed. Significant legislation is almost invariably initiated by cabinet ministers. The prime minister, the cabinet, and the leaders of the opposition parties, together with their chief advisers, are the dominant figures in the parliamentary process. However, changes in the rules of procedure of the House of Commons adopted in 1986 have made it possible for a small number of private members' bills to be selected for more extended debate, and a few have actually been passed since then.

The House functions within strict procedures and rules that are observed most of the time by all parties and enforced by a Speaker who is elected by the House. Until recently, it was customary for the prime minister to nominate the Speaker, and party discipline turned the election into a foregone conclusion. Now, however, the Speaker is chosen by free election, without prime-ministerial nomination and party discipline.[6] In Great Britain the Speaker becomes an impartial figure who completely withdraws from party affiliations, runs unopposed for re-election, and serves as Speaker until retirement from the House. In Canada the Speaker is also supposed to conduct the affairs of the House impartially, but the divorce from partisan politics is not so complete. The opposition parties may field candidates in the Speaker's constituency at election time, and a Speaker is selected each time a new Parliament convenes. A change in majority party will certainly result in a new Speaker.

A proposed bill must go through three **readings** in both chambers. At the first reading, the bill's title is introduced; the text of the proposed legislation is then printed and distributed to members. After the second reading, there is a full debate on the bill, with the opposition and government backbenchers having a specified time to address different aspects of it. It may then go to a standing committee, or, more commonly, to a special legislative committee of the House. **Standing committees** are permanent committees appointed to study particular areas of public policy; their membership is proportional to party strength in the House. Examples include committees on agriculture; external affairs and national defence; and finance, trade, and economic affairs. **Special (ad hoc) committees** are established to deal with specific problems and are dissolved when their assignment is finished. Most legislation is now considered by small special committees. Backbenchers can become involved in the legislative process by serving on parliamentary committees, but their power is limited because bloc voting by party prevails. The same party or coalition that forms the government and dominates the House also controls committee proceedings. Committees sometimes produce amendments to government bills, but they do not reject them altogether. The bill then goes through the **report stage,** at which time the House receives the committee report and votes on any proposed amendments.

The bill as amended is then received and voted on by the House in the third reading; no amendment is allowed at this final stage. Normally, the bill is then introduced in the Senate, whose deliberations also may involve committee action. The Senate may suggest changes and send its version of the bill back to the House. Occasionally, the Senate tries to block legislation coming from the House, as described above, but more frequently it functions as a source of technical amendments. It may even finish considering a bill before the Commons does. When this happens, its suggested amendments may be incorporated by the Commons at third reading.

Throughout the whole legislative process, it is the cabinet members—with the support of their party—who determine what sort of legislation is passed. If the minister responsible for the legislation does not like the amendments proposed by the opposition on the floor of the Commons, or in parliamentary committees, or in the Senate, they will probably be rejected. Again, the power of the prime minister and the cabinet, supported by their party majority, represents a strong system of government.

A bill passed by the Commons and the Senate then goes to the governor general for **royal assent** and **proclamation**. Royal assent means that the governor general approves the bill; proclamation involves setting the date on which the new law will take effect. There is often a period of weeks or months—sometimes even years—between royal assent and proclamation.

Throughout the legislative process, the **opposition** parties (i.e., those parties that do not share ministerial appointments) criticize the government and sometimes win concessions from it even though they do not have the voting strength to make their views prevail. The government may feel that points raised by the opposition have merit or public support; or it may yield in order to avoid obstructive or disruptive behaviour.

In Canada and Britain, the largest of the opposition parties is singled out as the **official Opposition** (or, the Opposition). Such status entitles the party to preferential funding and certain privileges during debate. The leader of the Opposition assigns various party members to follow the activities of one or more cabinet ministers with particular attention. For example, there may be an agriculture critic among the Opposition to watch the minister of agriculture. In Britain, the leader of the Opposition and these specialist critics form a cohesive group known as a **shadow cabinet**, ready to assume office if invited to do so by the head of state; but Canadian Opposition parties have not always had this degree of organization. Indeed, it is inconceivable that the Bloc Québécois, which formed the official Opposition from 1993 to 1997, would ever be invited to form the government of Canada. After the 1997 election, the Reform Party, with 60 seats in the House of Commons, formed the official Opposition.

In the parliamentary process, the lifeblood of the government is party loyalty. For its tenure, the government depends not just on the support of the electorate at election time but on its ability to maintain a majority on the floor of the House of Commons. In other words, the exercise of power hinges on the government's ability to maintain the **confidence** of the House. The idea of confidence is rooted in the principle of responsible government, which makes the cabinet responsible to the House of Commons. Every legislative proposal made by the government must go to the floor of the House. As long as these proposals are supported by a majority of those voting, the government enjoys the confidence of the House and is ruling "responsibly."

Note that the term *responsible government* (meaning that the cabinet must enjoy the continued support of the popularly elected house of the legislative assembly in order to remain in office) is a concept associated with parliamentary government. It is an essential aspect of the parliamentary form of representative democracy, but not of representative democracy in general. In the governments of Switzerland and the United States, the cabinet does not need legislative support to remain in power; but these governments are just as democratic as parliamentary ones—they are also responsible or accountable to the people through elections. Our point is that this broader sort of accountability should not be confused with the precise form of responsible government that characterizes the parliamentary system.

In Canada, though not in all parliamentary systems, votes on bills introduced by the government are treated as confidence votes. That is, the government is expected to win every vote and to resign if it is defeated. Exceptions are made when the House decides that a particular motion is not to be treated as a confidence vote (i.e., it will be a "free vote"—discussed in more detail below), or when a defeat occurs in peculiar circumstances, such as the unexpected absence of a large number of government members when a vote is taken. In such cases, a defeat of the government does not indicate a loss of confidence.

The necessity of maintaining a majority has led to the strengthening of party discipline in all parliamentary systems. A member's loyalty to the party may take precedence over personal views or loyalty to constituents. A member who does not support the party position on the floor of the House or in committee can be punished in various ways; for example, travel opportunities or choice committee assignments may be denied. At the extreme, a recalcitrant member may even be expelled from caucus, and the party may deny that individual the right to run in the next election under the party label, as happened to the Liberal MP John Nunziata after he voted against his own government's budget. However, the role of coercion should not be overestimated. Caucus members vote together most of the time more or less voluntarily for three reasons: they want to remain in the good graces of the party's leadership; they would like to benefit from political patronage; and they see themselves as part of a team, and understand that the parliamentary system of responsible government will not work unless parties exhibit some coherence. Contemporary Canadian practice allows members of parliament to deviate from the party line occasionally, but not too often, especially if it might unseat the government.

In Britain, the party system has become more flexible. Government bills are defeated more often, and these defeats no longer constitute grounds for the government to resign. Between 1974 and 1978, governments (both Labour and Conservative) were defeated 123 times in the House of Commons; between 1945 and 1966, this had happened only 11 times.[7] On motions of nonconfidence or when the vote involves a financial bill, government must still resign if defeated. Absolute party discipline appears to be giving way on certain issues, though it is still paramount when confidence is involved. (In Ontario under the 1985–87 accord between the Liberals and the NDP, defeats for the government on ordinary matters were not treated as nonconfidence votes.)

One other variation should be noted. Occasionally the government may allow a **free vote** on certain bills that are of a controversial nature. In this situation, all members of the caucus do not have to vote with the party; they are free to "vote their conscience." The Mulroney government held free votes on the morally supercharged issues of capital punishment and abortion while the Chrétien government allowed free votes on religious educational rights in Newfoundland and Quebec.

Critics of the parliamentary system often complain that members do not have the freedom to vote either their conscience or the will of their constituents. This is true if party discipline is effective, but it does not necessarily mean that **backbenchers**—those who are not in the cabinet or the shadow cabinet and who therefore sit on the rear benches in the House—have no influence on their party leadership. One primary function of the party **caucus** is to give party members an opportunity to be heard by their leaders. A party caucus is a closed meeting of the members of a parliamentary party in the House and Senate. Every party in Parliament has a caucus. At caucus meetings, backbenchers can question their own leaders and suggest alternatives to the party's policies. During these meetings, MPs within a party can argue policy with each other and the leadership can test the pulse of the backbenchers on particular proposals. Party leaders know that the support of backbenchers is required to maintain a majority position and that they must therefore take into account the nature and strength of backbench opinion. In caucus meetings an attempt is made to arrive at a consensus on issues. Unanimity seldom exists, so these meetings can be knockdown-dragout affairs. However, once a given issue is settled and goes to the House, all members are expected to support the government's position. The backbenchers of a majority party can bring down a government by failing to support their own leaders. Although this rarely happens, it does mean that the government's own party provides an important check on political power.

A second check on government is the opposition. The development of an institutionalized practice of loyal opposition in which one can legally challenge the government without fear of repression is one of the significant achievements of liberal democracy. The rationale for an opposition is the liberal view that everyone has limited knowledge and that no government or governor is infallible. The mighty also make mistakes, and there should always be an opportunity to air them in public.

The essence of the parliamentary process is the formal duel between the government and those forces unable to muster sufficient legislative seats to form a government. This opposition has three basic functions: to offer an alternative government, to offer alternative policies, and to question and call attention to controversial legislative proposals or government actions of any kind. If the opposition is a minority, it cannot by itself defeat the government; it does, however, have important opportunities to object to legislation to which it is opposed and to delay and obstruct legislative proposals it wants altered. Time is limited in the House, and parliamentary procedures protect the role of the opposition. Proceedings can be immobilized until the opposition and government come to a compromise agreement. A government that tries to run roughshod over the opposition parties may succeed in passing a particular piece of legislation, but may well find other aspects of its program jeopardized by delaying tactics.

A final check on the government is the electorate. At least every five years, voters have the opportunity to pass judgment on the record of the party in power. This serves to remind us of the liberal–democratic principle that political power emanates from the people and rests upon the consent of the governed. Ideally, the check exercised by elections ensures that government legislation is responsive to the needs of the people. However, in the liberal tradition, there is an unwillingness to assume that governments will automatically act in the best interests of their citizens. So checks also come into play when an unresponsive system needs prodding.

Variations on the Westminster Model

We have used the British and Canadian examples in describing the parliamentary system of government. While there are a number of structural differences between our process and Britain's (federalism, for instance), both systems exemplify the Westminster model. In other countries, that basic model has been modified to meet the needs of different political environments and also, often, to strengthen the role of the executive, especially when it must face a politically fragmented legislative body. The parliamentary process can easily result in minority government; without a majority, governments may change frequently, the result being political instability. In very few instances has Canada or Great Britain had to contend with the problem, but twentieth-century political history in Germany and France illustrates the point.

Under the Weimar constitution, which was adopted in 1919, Germany had something close to the Westminster model of parliamentary government. But representation in the legislative body was badly fragmented among a number of political factions so that no political party commanded a majority. Weak coalition governments, many of them depending on the support of extremist or splinter parties, were unable to deal effectively with political crises. The system found itself unable to combat the economic crash of 1929, with the result that the Third Reich was established by Hitler in 1933.

After World War II, the Germans modified the parliamentary system in order to deal with the problem of instability. The constitution of the Federal Republic of Germany, known as the Basic Law, was adopted in 1949. Those who drafted the document instituted a positive or **constructive vote of confidence**. The chancellor, or prime minister, is the leader of the majority party, or a coalition of parties making up a majority, in the *Bundestag* (the lower house of Parliament). The government can be defeated on a nonconfidence vote in the *Bundestag;* however, the vote defeats the government only if the chancellor's successor is chosen at the same time. In other words, a majority in the *Bundestag* can bring down the government, but not until that majority approves another government. This breaks with the British and Canadian custom of holding an election or forming a new government after defeat on a nonconfidence motion or any major piece of legislation.

France experienced a similar type of political instability during the Fourth Republic (1946–58). Numerous political parties were represented in the National Assembly; none, however, could command a majority of the seats. Governments were founded on loose and generally short-lived coalitions. In the constitution of the Fifth Republic (1958), General Charles de Gaulle remedied the instability by modifying the political executive. In addition to the prime minister and the cabinet, France now has a president who is elected directly by the people for a seven-year term of office. The president is the actual head of government, not just a titular head of state. He appoints the prime minister, who is traditionally the leader of the majority party or of the senior party in a coalition in the National Assembly. The president also appoints the cabinet, although the prime minister can propose candidates for the positions. The National Assembly can still pass a nonconfidence motion—or **vote of censure** as it is called—and defeat the government, but this right can be exercised only once in a year. When the government is censured, only the prime minister and the cabinet must resign; the president has been elected for a specific term of office.

Because the president remains in office in spite of government turnovers, the executive branch of government is stabilized; however, the value of this stability should be weighed against the possibility of deadlock. A French president may belong to a different party than the majority in the National Assembly. This was precisely the case after the 1986 elections to the National Assembly: no party won an absolute majority, but a conservative coalition led by Jacques Chirac was able to muster a working majority. Yet the socialist François Mitterand was still president. He invited Chirac to become prime minister, and for two years the Left and the Right shared power in an uneasy arrangement dubbed "cohabitation." Observers had wondered whether the system could survive such an arrangement, but in fact it worked rather well, with both sides exercising considerable restraint. The standoff was resolved in 1988, when Mitterand was re-elected president and the socialists won enough seats in the National Assembly to regain control. In the 1993 National Assembly elections, however, conservative parties handed the socialists their worst defeat in twenty-five years, thus beginning a second period of "cohabitation."

In 1995, Chirac was elected President of France with a seven-year term. In 1997, he dissolved the National Assembly, anticipating a return of the right-of-centre coalition government. In the election, however, the Socialist Party won 275 of the 577 seats in the Assembly, making it the base of a left-of-centre coalition government. The Socialist leader, Lionel Jospin, was named prime minister, thus commencing a third period of cohabitation, which may well last another five years. Cohabitation is not yet the norm, but it is no longer a rare exception.

Israel has found yet another way of coping with cabinet instability. Because that country uses proportional representation (see Chapter 28), there are so many political parties that all governments have to be coalitions. Israeli governments take coalitions as a fact of life and treat cabinets almost as if they were legislatures. Cabinet secrecy has been abandoned, as has cabinet solidarity; formal votes are taken in cabinet on important issues, and the results are announced to the public. The result is that, having made their opposition to a policy known, coalition partners do not necessarily feel obliged to break up the coalition. Thus, coalitions can survive tensions that would destroy cabinets operating on the Westminster model, and political instability can be avoided despite the proliferation of parties.

Different modifications have been made in other parliamentary systems. However, the basic principle of these systems remains responsible government. A government is not entitled to govern unless it commands a working majority of the seats in the elected portion of the legislature. Regardless of the way in which the machinery is adjusted, this principle remains essential to the parliamentary apparatus.

Assessing Parliamentary Systems

Critics argue that the problem with the parliamentary process is that the executive has become too powerful. In using strong party discipline, the executive has created an imbalance in the legislative process. As the dominant institution in the legislative process, the executive is denying other members of parliament their role as representatives of the people. With reference to executive federalism (i.e., federal politics monopolized by first ministers), Stephen Brooks suggests that:

> It is a process from which legislatures are almost entirely excluded, except when called upon to ratify an agreement reached between executives of the two levels of government.[8]

And, in regard to the policymaking process of the federal government, he says:

> The popular identification of "government" with the individual who occupies the position of prime minister and his team of cabinet colleagues entails an accurate assessment of where the centre of power lies in the state system. In parliamentary systems as different as those of Canada, Belgium, and France the political executive is that part of the state system best able to shape the direction of public policy.[9]

When the executive initiates party policy and caucus members are expected to support it, the executive has become in effect an almost autonomous force at the expense of the legislature.

This is certainly how most of the electorate perceives the process. The cabinet is seen as being cloistered in Ottawa together with top bureaucrats, making public policy for the country with little regard for alternative proposals. Backbenchers are expected to support the party's objectives regardless of the feelings of their constituents. Elected MPs not in the inner circles of government do not have the opportunity to advocate the views of their constituents; they are expected to toe the party line. Such perceptions may not be altogether true, but they exist and have led to a great deal of frustration in the electorate. Many voters are claiming that their representatives have been stifled by party discipline and are calling for reforms of parliament. Some have become supporters of anti-establishment political parties.

All of this highlights one of the paradoxes of the parliamentary system. With a strong majority in the House of Commons, the leadership of a political party can override the petty bickering and the powerful special interests that attempt to thwart the interest of the entire nation. In short, a government with a substantial majority in a parliamentary system represents an extremely powerful liberal–democratic government. If, however, the governing majority pursues its own legislative agenda without regard for popular feeling, a large portion of the public may come to feel alienated from the process of government; and if the government continues on its course, voters may shift to the opposition or to minor parties that they feel represent their interest.

In the system there is thus a need to balance the roles of the legislature and the executive. The executive must not operate as an autonomous force, and there must be a way to involve backbenchers—and the public for that matter—in the process of formulating policy. The question is, how can this be accomplished without rendering the legislative process impotent? How can the process be made more open to differing points of view without bringing it to a grinding halt?

If party discipline does in fact undermine representation, there are ways to relax that discipline, such as increasing the number of free votes, or permitting party members to oppose the government on votes. The result might well be a more open debate on issues within the governing party itself. A reduction of party discipline might also show the electorate that backbenchers are not just puppets of the leadership; the party's rank and file would in fact have an opportunity to more openly represent constituents. Yet too much autonomy of the legislature could lead to gridlock, as is sometimes the case in the presidential system.

᠋᠋᠋᠋᠋᠋᠋᠋

THE PRESIDENTIAL SYSTEM

The presidential system of government was first devised in the United States, as an alternative to the monarchical system. It is chiefly used today in areas of the world where American influence has been particularly strong, as in Latin America, the Philippines, and South Korea. In some cases, it may simply be a guise for an authoritarian dictatorship. Or, like the parliamentary model, it may be adapted to fit particular needs, as in France. Nevertheless, the basic model is distinctive; the principle of separation of powers and the lack of responsible government set it apart from the parliamentary system.

After 1776, the new United States reacted to their experience of a strong British executive by granting an extraordinary amount of political power to the legislative body. This was logical, given their suspicion of strong government as exercised by the British Crown. They felt that the danger of abuse could be minimized if governors were elected and periodically held responsible to the people. These sentiments were demonstrated in the adoption of the first constitution for the new republic—the Articles of Confederation of 1781, which almost eliminated the executive. The legislatures of the several states were supreme. In time, however, it was realized that an executive to supervise the work of government was essential. The fault was corrected with the adoption of the Constitution in 1789. A president was made the chief executive officer of the government, answerable to the legislative branch in certain respects, but not dependent on it for continuation in office.

While the parliamentary system is known for the fusion of powers and for cabinet government, the presidential system is known for the separation of powers and for the congressional committee system. The executive branch, although instrumental in the legislative process, is physically separated from the legislative branch.

While the separation is real (each branch has veto powers), cooperation is required to pass legislation. In this system of government, the committees of both houses of Congress dominate the legislative process. Figure 21.2 depicts the presidential system of the United States.

The customary term used to describe the presidential system—separation of powers—is somewhat misleading. James Madison, the chief draftsman of the American Constitution, explicitly criticized the oversimplified view that the legislative, executive, and judicial powers of government ought to be absolutely separated among the distinct institutions or branches of government. In No. 47 of *The Federalist*, a series of essays he wrote with Alexander Hamilton and John Jay to persuade the American public to ratify the new constitution, Madison outlined the ideal of placing each power in the custody of a branch of government primarily concerned with it, while allowing the other two branches a secondary role in exercising it. This delicate balance of institutions would diminish arbitrary government by preventing unilateral actions. Neither the president, Congress, nor the courts would be able to follow a course of action for very long without the cooperation of the other branches. A modern scholar has suggested that "separated institutions sharing powers" is a more apt description of the Madisonian system than "separation of powers."[10] Figure 21.3 illustrates this complex balance.

The President

The president, who is elected by a national constituency for a four-year term, is both head of state and head of government. As head of state, he greets foreign dignitaries and performs other ceremonial functions. As head of government, he is the chief executive officer. The constitution grants the president powers that are, on the whole, rather similar to the ancient prerogative powers of the British Crown. In Britain these are now wielded by the prime minister with relatively little interference by Parliament as long as party discipline holds; in the United States the president's powers are hemmed in at every step by a Congress of which he is not a member and among whose members he may exercise influence but not authority. Let us look at this complex balance of power in some detail.

The president has the power to appoint the highest officials of government: cabinet secretaries, ambassadors, federal judges, senior civil servants, and members of regulatory commissions. But all these appointments must receive the advice and consent of the Senate, the upper house of Congress. A simple majority suffices. As chief executive, the president directs the manifold business of government, yet he is dependent for revenue on appropriations from Congress. He submits a budget to Congress, but that body can and does alter it freely. Congress also has the power to investigate the administrative activities of government in either closed or public hearings.

The president is responsible for the general conduct of foreign affairs and, in particular, is authorized to negotiate treaties with other states. But these treaties must also receive the advice and consent of the Senate—in this instance a qualified

FIGURE 21.2 The United States Presidential System

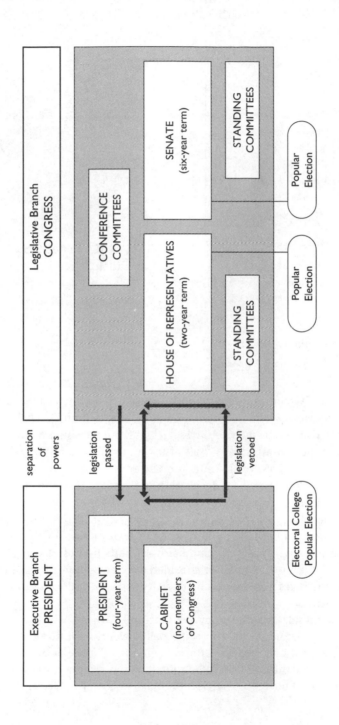

FIGURE 21.3 Balance of Powers in the American Presidential System

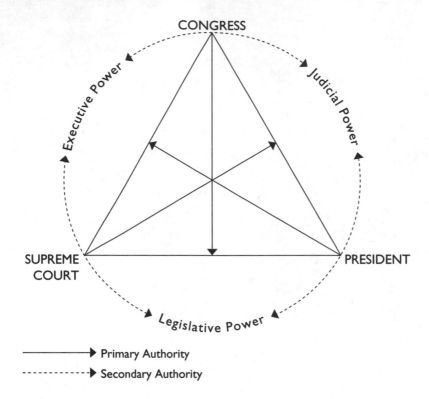

Primary Authority

Secondary Authority

majority of two-thirds. Canadians were reminded in 1981 that the U.S. Senate can and does reject treaties, when President Ronald Reagan had to withdraw a Canadian–American fisheries treaty because he knew the Senate would not ratify it.[11]

The president is the commander-in-chief of the armed forces, but this coercive power is also subject to congressional limitation. The armed forces can be paid only with revenue voted by Congress, and a declaration of war requires approval in both houses of Congress. This constitutional provision has not been invoked since 1941. (The Korean and Vietnam wars were waged as "police actions" under presidential authorization and were not declared by Congress.) In 1990, President George Bush requested and received a resolution of approval from both houses of Congress for the Gulf War with Iraq; but this was not considered a declaration of war because technically the United States was responding to a UN Security Council resolution to come to the aid of Kuwait.

Technically, the president is chosen by the **Electoral College,** which was established in 1787. Some delegates to the constitutional convention of that year wanted the president to be elected by Congress. Others, fearing the demise of state power in the federal system, wanted the president to be chosen by state legislators. A few others considered a more radical move—direct election by all voters. The Electoral College was the compromise. This was a group of electors, each supposedly an upstanding and respected individual of independent mind. They would be chosen by voters within the states and would in turn formally elect the president. The number of electors from each state was determined by adding the number of representatives from the state in the federal House of Representatives (determined by the population of the state) and the number of senators from the state (two). The total Electoral College vote in the United States is now 538: 435 for the members of the House, 100 for the senators, and an additional 3 electors from the District of Columbia.

In each state, each political party selects a slate of electors, who are pledged to cast their votes in the Electoral College for their party's candidate. When voters cast their ballot for president on election day in November, they are, strictly speaking, voting for one of these slates. The electors assemble in Washington, D.C., in December to cast their votes, which remain secret until January, when they are counted by the vice president in the presence of the Speaker of the House of Representatives.

In fact, everyone knows the outcome of the race on election night because members of the Electoral College usually vote according to the popular vote in the state. In some states this is a legal requirement, but in most states it is merely a well-observed practice.

Since the candidate who gets a plurality of popular votes in a state gets all of that state's electoral votes, there is often a marked difference between the percentage of popular votes and the percentage of electoral votes that candidates obtain. Table 21.1 shows how 55 or 60 percent of the popular vote can translate into 80 or 90 percent of the electoral votes.[12]

In the November 1996 election, Bill Clinton, the Democratic candidate for president, won 49.2 percent of the popular vote and 379 electoral college votes; the Republican candidate Bob Dole won 40.8 percent of the popular vote and 159 electoral college votes; and the Reform candidate Ross Perot won 8.5 percent of the popular vote and no electoral college votes. While the Democrats won the presidential election, the Republicans gained a majority of seats in both the Senate and the House of Representatives. Therefore, President Clinton will face a Republican Congress at least until the interim elections of 1998.

TABLE 21.1   Landslide Presidential Elections in the United States

Winner	Year	Popular Vote(%)	Electoral Vote	States Won
Warren G. Harding (R)	1920	60.3	404 (76.1%)	37
Franklin D. Roosevelt (D)	1936	60.8	523 (98.5%)	46
Lyndon B. Johnson (D)	1964	61.1	486 (90.3%)	44
Richard M. Nixon (R)	1972	60.7	520 (96.7%)	49
Ronald Reagan (R)	1984	58.9	525 (97.6%)	49

The Congress

Congress, like the Canadian Parliament, is a bicameral legislature. The House of Representatives has 435 members, all elected in constituencies based on population. Each elected member represents a constituency called a congressional district. The boundaries of these districts are redrawn periodically to reflect population shifts, and attempts are made to keep these districts approximately equal in size. Each state, no matter how small, gets at least one representative.

The term of office of a member of the House is two years. Unlike the parliamentary system, the presidential system does not provide for the government to call elections. Rather, the dates are fixed. Election day in the United States is on the Tuesday after the first Monday in November. At that time, voters select all elected officials at the federal and state levels, as well as many at the local level. This system of fixed dates for elections prevents the president from dissolving the Congress at a politically opportune time and going to the people for a new mandate.

The Senate has 100 members (two from each state), each elected for a six-year term. Senators were originally chosen by state legislatures, but this process was changed in 1913 by the seventeenth amendment, so they are now directly elected. At the constitutional convention in 1787, equal representation of states in the Senate and representation by population in the House represented a compromise. It was a trade-off between the populous states (which wanted to emphasize numbers as the basis of representation) and the thinly populated states (which wanted to emphasize territory). The Senate is considered the upper house and has more functions than the House of Representatives; most notably, it confirms presidential appointments and ratifies treaties. However, all money bills (i.e., those involving revenue or appropriations) must originate in the House of Representatives. This echoes the ancient British practice whereby revenue bills must originate in the House of Commons.

Congress is the chief repository of legislative power; but as Congress checks the president in the executive area, so the president checks Congress in the legislative area. All bills passed by Congress are sent to the president, who then has three options: to sign the bill, at which time it becomes law; not to sign the bill (after ten days it becomes law without the signature); or to **veto** the bill. In the event of a veto, the bill returns to Congress. If the bill passes again with a two-thirds majority in each house, the president's veto is overridden and the bill becomes law. This latter contingency is rather rare; the president's veto is usually final except on occasional highly charged issues.

The veto power is especially important because the president must approve or veto a bill as a whole. Most American state constitutions give the governor an **item veto**—the power to reject only certain clauses within a bill—but the president must approve or reject an entire package. Knowing this, Congress often puts together omnibus legislation, which contains items that the president is known to oppose along with those he is known to like. Such tactics, coupled with the inevitable shortage of legislative time, often manoeuvre the president into signing legislation that he would not otherwise sign. In the mid-1990s, Congress passed legislation giving the president an item veto, but it has never been used, and at the time of writing an American court had declared the legislation unconstitutional. Thus, whatever its intrinsic merits may be, the outlook for the item veto at the federal level does not seem promising.

The president cannot actually introduce a bill into Congress—that task must be performed for him by a senator or representative—but he can have legislation drafted to submit to Congress; and, in fact, a large majority of American legislation originates this way. However, it is subject to amendment as it goes through Congress, and the final result may differ greatly from the original draft.

There are other important ways in which the presidential machinery of government differs from the parliamentary model. Neither the president nor the cabinet secretaries may hold a seat in Congress. In fact, if the president chooses a member of the House or Senate to be a cabinet secretary, the member must resign from Congress. The American cabinet, furthermore, is not a collective decision-making body. The main relationship is between the president and the secretaries individually. Under some presidents, the cabinet seldom or never met as a group. The number of cabinet secretaries varies with the administration; it was 14 under Bush, but Clinton enlarged it to 16 when he took office in 1993 and kept it the same size after being re-elected in 1996.

Another essential feature of the presidential system is that there is no vote of confidence and thus no principle of responsible government. The tenure of office of the president and members of Congress is specified in the constitution. No matter how votes go on the floor of either house, there is nothing comparable to the non-confidence motion or the dissolution of Parliament. Barring death, resignation, or removal for misconduct, the president is in office for four years, members of the House of Representatives for two years, and senators for six years. Since the executive is not responsible to the legislature, there is less need to practise party discipline, and party solidarity is not crucial for survival. A member who chooses to vote against the party's position on a bill will not be disciplined. In such a system, the individual's first loyalty can be to the constituency rather than to the party. Party leaders in Congress try to invoke party discipline on votes, but they simply do not have the power that they would in the parliamentary system.

This generalization admits certain exceptions. Appointments to congressional standing committees are made along party lines at the opening of each session. If, for example, 60 percent of the membership of a chamber is Democratic, the partisan division of members constituting committees will be 60 to 40, Democrats to Republicans. Party positions often, though not invariably, count in these committees. Still, the necessity for strong party ties that exists in the parliamentary system does not hold in the presidential system.

A final feature of the presidential system is the importance of congressional committees. The number of committees may vary slightly, but it is usually around twenty in each house of Congress. Committees in the House include agriculture, armed services, banking and currency, foreign affairs, veterans' affairs, and ways and means. Most of the committees of the Senate are similar in name and jurisdiction, except that there is a finance committee instead of a ways-and-means committee. These committees are almost little legislatures in themselves. After a bill is introduced in either house, it goes immediately to a committee. In most instances, if a bill is to reach the floor of either house, it must first be approved by the committee.

Congressional committees, like the cabinet in the parliamentary system, are powerful organizations for managing the legislative process. A bill that has successfully passed through a committee usually passes on the floor vote in the House or Senate. Conversely, bills can easily be bottled up in committee by influential members such as the chairman of the whole committee or of a powerful subcommittee. A great deal of vote trading, or **logrolling,** develops among committee members in the process of getting legislation passed. Deals arise in committee that, in the parliamentary system, would be hidden in cabinet proceedings.

Legislative committees also exist in parliamentary systems, but they are much weaker because they are controlled by members of the majority party, which in turn is controlled by the cabinet. The cabinet manages the legislative process and does not allow desired bills to die along the way. Committees serve as forums for debate that sometimes produce minor or technical amendments, but rarely substantial changes.

Judicial Review

Although the American constitution does not explicitly mention **judicial review**—the power to declare legislation or executive action unconstitutional—the U.S. Supreme Court quickly claimed this role for itself and the lower courts. Judicial review means that in constitutional matters the courts have, in effect, the power to veto legislation, which amounts to a share of legislative power. As well, they share executive power to the extent that they rule on the legality of administrative actions when these are challenged. This power helps keep executive discretion within the bounds of the law.

Court decisions are final in the short run; in the long run, the judiciary is balanced by the other branches of government. Because federal judges must be appointed by the president and confirmed by the Senate, the political complexion of the courts can be changed gradually as retirements open vacancies on the bench. During his years in office, President Reagan had the opportunity to appoint three new members to the Supreme Court out of a total of nine, and to elevate William Rehnquist from associate justice to chief justice. Even more strikingly, he had appointed more than half of the lower federal judges by the end of his second term. All of this had a noticeable effect on judicial decision making because Reagan, like other presidents, appointed judges whom he considered sympathetic to his own ideology. The result has been a shift in the American federal courts toward conservative judicial restraint and away from liberal judicial activism. President Bush continued this trend with his appointments to the bench, most notably by elevating Clarence Thomas to the Supreme Court, which solidified the conservative majority on that court. President Clinton, for his part, will tend to appoint liberals to the judiciary, as he did in 1993 with his first appointment to the Supreme Court, Ruth Bader Ginzberg.

Even when the courts declare a piece of legislation unconstitutional, their ruling may not be the end of the story. Congress can introduce an amendment to the constitution. The amending process is complex: an amendment must be approved by two-thirds of the members of Congress, then ratified by three-quarters of the state legislatures. Nevertheless, the amending process serves as a potential check on the judiciary by the legislative branch.

Checks and Balances

The system of **checks and balances**, as the Americans call it, gives the many interest groups of a pluralistic society marvellous opportunities to find friends in government. Cotton growers, to select an example at random, make a special effort to have good relations not only with the chairmen of the Senate and House agriculture committees but also with the chairmen and members of the subcommittees that deal primarily with fibre crops. Even if the president or a congressional majority has pledged to do something that may reduce cotton growers' incomes—for example, end a price-support program—they may be able to hold their ground by getting a strategically placed senator or representative to arrange for the bill to die a lingering death in committee. Or if a group cannot get Congress or the president to act upon its demands, as was true of blacks seeking civil rights in the 1950s, it may turn to the courts to accomplish by litigation what it could not achieve by legislation. In the more narrowly focused power configuration of the parliamentary system, it is much harder to influence government in this manner.

Clearly, the presidential system is highly decentralized, almost fragmented. Power, instead of being concentrated in the hands of a prime minister and cabinet, is divided among many offices. The reason for this was explained by Madison in *The Federalist* No. 51:

> Ambition must be made to counteract ambition ... If men were angels, no government would be necessary. If angels were to govern men, neither external nor internal controls on government would be necessary. In framing a government which is to be administered by men over men, the great difficulty lies in this: you must first enable the government to control the governed; and in the next place oblige it to control itself.[13]

Separation of the legislative, executive, and judicial branches is one way of organizing government so as to "oblige it to control itself."

Assessing Presidential Systems

The presidential system is founded on entirely different principles than the parliamentary system. Its critics argue that the legislature is too powerful. The executive initiates policy proposals, but the House of Representatives and the Senate deal with those proposals in their own way. When the Congress and the president are in accord on proposed legislation, the system can work very smoothly in passing bills; but when the president and the Congress are at loggerheads over an issue, the system can go into gridlock. A great deal of vote trading can be done to develop grounds for a compromise; but if the Congress can muster a majority in opposition to the president's policy proposals, there is no way the executive will get what it wants. Inevitably the legislature is much more autonomous in the presidential than in the parliamentary system.

The presidential forms of government used around the world today are not mere carbon copies of the American one. Structural as well as cultural factors influence the way in which forms of government work in other countries. In Mexico, for example, a very powerful president dominates all facets of the political process. He is chosen for a six-year term and is not permitted to serve two terms in a row. While in office, he uses a powerful institution—the Institutionalized Revolutionary Party (PRI)—to control the governmental machinery and coordinate control of the Congress, the bureaucracy, the courts, and even the governments of the states and municipalities. He uses patronage, legislative programs, electoral intimidation, and coercion to achieve personal ends. Who knows what current reforms will bring in Mexico? Through 1997, however, the Mexican system consisted of an authoritarian president using a single dominant party as a power base.

PARLIAMENTARY AND PRESIDENTIAL SYSTEMS

Whether the parliamentary system is preferable to the presidential system as a form of liberal democracy is hardly worth asking. Interestingly, those who live under one system and become critical of it usually wish to make it more like the other. For example, it is often said in Canada that the prime minister's power of appointment is too unrestricted and that there should be a body, like the American Senate, to confirm appointments to the bench or other high office. Or it is suggested that party discipline is too strict, and that members of parliament should be free to vote their conscience or the wishes of their constituents.

But the separation of powers creates problems of its own, as illustrated by the collision that occurred between President Clinton and the Republicans, who had a majority in both houses of Congress in the years 1995–96. Clinton vetoed the Republicans' budget because, he said, the spending cuts were too severe. When the

Republicans refused to pass Clinton's budget, the federal government ran out of money; it did not quite shut down, but it had to curtail some activities for several weeks. Canadians are quite unused to such a degree of disorganization in their national government.

Because of the logic of the presidential system and the lack of party discipline, cooperation can never be taken for granted but must always be maintained through careful practice of the art of politics. Both parties seem to have drawn this conclusion after the 1996 election, in which the Republicans retained control of Congress while President Clinton was also re-elected. In the spring of 1997, the two sides reached agreement on a multiyear plan to bring the budget into balance early in the next century.

Perhaps the conclusion must be drawn that "the grass is always greener" elsewhere. Once a system is solidly established, it has so much inertia and weight of tradition behind it that the benefit of a wholesale change is unlikely to be worth the cost, although piecemeal reforms may transfer to one system some of the advantages of the other.

The two systems, while more or less equally viable, have different strengths and weaknesses, which can be summarized as follows.

Overall, it might be said that, while both are effective forms of liberal democracy, the presidential system is more liberal and the parliamentary system is more democratic. By "more liberal," we mean that the presidential system has more internal checks on the exercise of power, which is in line with the liberal fear of excessive state control of society. By "more democratic," we mean that the parliamentary system is more effective in expressing the will of the majority because it allows the electorate to choose a government that can govern with relatively little hindrance from countervailing power.

This democratic potential of the parliamentary system raises problems for a country such as Canada, in which a national majority is often difficult to form because of regional or linguistic fragmentation. In such situations, the parliamentary system may confer tremendous power on the governing party even though it represents not a true majority, but only the largest single minority. For example, the Conservatives won a solid majority of 169 seats in the House of Commons in the 1988 election, but with only 43 percent of the popular vote. They then used their majority to push through the Free Trade Agreement and the goods and services tax, even though the former might well have been defeated, and the latter certainly would have been defeated, in a popular referendum. Although the government was much criticized by the opposition parties for legislating contrary to the "will of the people," it was not acting any differently than have other governments in the past. It is part of the logic of the parliamentary system that the representatives of the largest voting minority act as if they represented a majority, at least for a period of time.

One of the recurrent themes of Canadian politics is protest by minorities who feel that their rights have been ignored or curtailed by overwhelming parliamentary

PARLIAMENTARY	PRESIDENTIAL
STRENGTHS	
1. With a majority, the government has the power to govern.	1. Separation of powers discourages concentration of power.
2. The nonconfidence vote provides a check on the government.	2. Checks and balances limit the power of branches of government.
3. The lines of responsibility for passage or defeat of legislation are clear. A voter can make decisions on the basis of party stance.	3. Without strict party discipline, members can be more constituency-oriented.
WEAKNESSES	
1. The system may be unstable if a majority is not obtained.	1. Separation of powers fragments the system, often rendering it immobile.
2. The power of a government with a large majority is very great—it is possibly insensitive to public desires.	2. Voters cannot pin responsibility on any one party.
3. Because party loyalty is necessary, individual members may have to vote against the wishes of their constituents.	3. Without a nonconfidence vote, the electorate must wait for an election to unseat an unpopular president or member of Congress.

majorities. One thinks immediately of the resistance of French Canadians against conscription in the two world wars, the demands of Aboriginal peoples for self-government, and the constant struggle of the Western provinces against Ottawa during the Trudeau years. Parallels at the provincial level are the attempts of anglophones in Quebec and francophones in Manitoba to assert linguistic rights in the face of legislation supported by large majorities in the provincial electorate and legislature. These considerations lead to the discussion of the centralization and decentralization of government in the next chapter.

FURTHER READING

Parliamentary Systems

Aydelotte, William O., ed. *The History of Parliamentary Behavior*. Princeton, N.J.: Princeton University Press, 1977.

Courtney, John C. *The Canadian House of Commons: Essays in Honour of Norman Ward*. Calgary: University of Calgary Press, 1985.

D'Aquino, Thomas, G. Bruce Doern, and Cassandra Blair. *Parliamentary Democracy in Canada*. Toronto: Methuen, 1983.

Dodd, L.C. *Coalitions in Parliamentary Government*. Princeton, N.J.: Princeton University Press, 1976.

Franks, C.E.S. *The Parliament of Canada*. Toronto: University of Toronto Press, 1987.

Herman, V. *Parliaments of the World*. London: Macmillan, 1976.

Jennings, W. Ivor. *Parliament*, 2nd ed. Cambridge: Cambridge University Press, 1957.

MacKinnon, Frank. *The Crown in Canada*. Toronto: McClelland and Stewart, 1976.

Mackintosh, John P. *The Government and Politics of Great Britain*, 5th ed. London: Hutchinson, 1982.

March, Roman R. *The Myth of Parliament*. Scarborough, Ont.: Prentice-Hall Canada, 1974.

Marshall, Edmund. *Parliament and the Public*. London: Macmillan, 1982.

Rose, Richard, and Ezra N. Suleiman, eds. *Presidents and Prime Ministers*. Washington, D.C.: American Institute for Public Policy Research, 1980.

Rush, Michael. *Parliamentary Government in Britain*. London: Pitman, 1981.

———. *The Cabinet and Policy Formation*. London: Longman, 1984.

Seidel, F. Leslie, ed. *Rethinking Government: Reform or Reincarnation?* Institute for Research on Public Policy. Ottawa: Renouf Publishing, 1993.

Verney, Douglas V. *British Government and Politics*, 3rd ed. New York: Harper and Row, 1976.

Presidential Systems

Barilleaux, Ryan J. *The Post-Modern Presidency: The Office after Ronald Reagan*. New York: Praeger, 1988.

Bessette, Joseph M., and Jeffrey Tulis, eds. *The Presidency in the Constitutional Order*. Baton Rouge: Louisiana State University Press, 1981.

Burns, James MacGregor. *Presidential Government*. Boston: Houghton Mifflin, 1965.

Califano, Joseph A., Jr. *A Presidential Nation*. New York: W.W. Norton, 1975.

DiBacco, T.V. *Presidential Power in Latin American Politics*. New York: Praeger, 1977.

Elton, David. *Democracy on the Instalment Plan: Electing Senate Nominees*. Calgary: Canada West Foundation, 1989.

Fisher, Louis. *Constitutional Conflicts Between Congress and the President*, 3rd ed. Kansas: University Press of Kansas, 1991.

Gilmour, Robert S., and Alexis A. Halley, eds. *Who Makes Public Policy?: The Struggle for Control Between Congress and the Executive*. Chatham, N.J.: Chatham House, 1994.

Goldwin, Robert A., and Art Kaufman. *Separation of Powers: Does it Still Work?* Washington, D.C.: American Enterprise Institute, 1986.

Heclo, Hugh, and Lester M. Salamon, eds. *The Illusion of Presidential Government*. Boulder, Colo.: Westview Press, 1981.

Lijphart, Arend, ed. *Parliamentary Versus Presidential Government*. Oxford: Oxford University Press, 1992.

McDonald, Forrest. *The American Presidency: An Intellectual History*. Lawrence, Kan.: University Press of Kansas, 1994.

Nwabueze, B.O. *Presidentialism in Commonwealth Africa*. New York: St. Martin's, 1974.

Pfiffner, James P. *The Modern Presidency*. New York: St. Martin's Press, 1994.

Schneier, Edward V. *Congress Today*. New York: St. Martin's Press, 1993.

UNITARY AND FEDERAAL SYSTEMS

Governments can also be classified according to the degree of centralization they exhibit. The two main types applicable to modern circumstances are the **unitary system**, in which a single sovereign government controls all regions of the country, and **federalism**, in which sovereignty is divided between a central government and several regional or provincial governments. Two other types of less practical significance are **devolution** and **confederation**.[1] The former is a variant of the unitary state in which the central government creates regional governments but can override them as it wishes, even to the point of abolishing them. The latter is an inherently unstable arrangement in which sovereign constituent governments create a central government without sovereign power of its own.

These types can be arranged as follows on a continuum of centralization:

Sovereign States	Confederation	Federalism	Devolution	Unitary State
No central government	Central government exists but sovereignty retained by constituent governments	Sovereignty shared between central and constituent governments	Constituent governments exist, but sovereignty monopolized by central government	No constituent governments

As with most other classifications, the types represent points on a continuum, and existing political systems may fall between types. One federal system, for instance, may be so centralized as to approach devolution, while another may be so decentralized that it almost amounts to a confederation. With this qualification in mind, let us discuss the major types.

THE UNITARY SYSTEM

In a unitary system, powers and responsibilities are concentrated within central governmental authorities. Constitutionally, the central government is sovereign. Municipal or county governments may exist, but their responsibilities are delegated by statute from the central government. Their functions are more administrative than legislative, much of their revenue comes from grants made by the central government, and in general they depend heavily on the central government. In a unitary system, no attempt is made to create provinces or states with specific powers established in a constitution. Great Britain has a unitary system of government, and so do France, Spain, Colombia, Japan, Sweden, and almost 150 other contemporary states. In each case, a National Assembly, Congress, Parliament, or Diet is responsible for governing the entire nation. The power of local governments varies considerably, depending on the extent to which central authorities have delegated responsibilities of government and administration.

Devolution—the granting of governmental responsibilities, including limited legislative responsibilities, to regional governments—is a step toward decentralization. The powers of regional governments, however, are not entrenched in the constitution. They are created by statute of the central government and may be modified or abolished in the same way. An example would be the government of Northern Ireland from 1921 to 1972. Under the Government of Ireland Act of 1920, the British established at Stormont a Parliament with local responsibilities. This legislative body had a great deal of autonomy in domestic matters such as housing, services, and public employment. The experiment was terminated in 1972 because violence between the Protestant majority and the Roman Catholic minority rendered the society ungovernable.[2] This example illustrates the utter dependence of regional governments upon the central government in a devolved system. There was no constitutional barrier to the British cabinet's unilateral decision to dissolve the Stormont Parliament and put Northern Ireland under the direct control of a Secretary of State for Northern Ireland.

In the mid-1970s, there was some support for devolution in Scotland and Wales. Advocates suggested that regional Parliaments be formed along the same lines as in Northern Ireland, but the proposals were not implemented because Scottish voters rejected devolution in an advisory referendum (1979). However, devolution will go forward following successful referendums in 1997.

In Spain, the Basques (who make up about 12 percent of the voting population) have for years mounted a strong separatist movement. Since the death of Franco (1975), the Spanish government has decentralized the system, granting greater powers to the regions. Thus, decentralization (or devolution) is one way to counter separatist movements in unitary systems.

FEDERALISM AND CONFEDERATION

In a federal system, powers and responsibilities are divided between a federal (or national) government and various regional governments. The federal government, for example, may be responsible for minting money and raising an army, while the provinces (or states, or cantons, or departments) may be responsible for education and public works. Constitutionally, sovereignty is divided between different levels of government instead of being concentrated in one government. Both levels of government are mentioned in a constitutional document, and neither level can unilaterally modify or abolish the other. In reality, however, it is virtually impossible to divide powers neatly so that the responsibility of one level of government is totally independent of the other. This means that disputes, overlapping jurisdictions, and joint efforts are commonplace in any federal system.

Although Switzerland has a history of confederation dating back to 1291, it was the American constitution of 1789 that created the world's first modern federal system. The model has since been imitated in about twenty states, including Brazil, Mexico, Venezuela, Canada, Australia, Indonesia, India, Germany, and Russia. The invention of federalism was precipitated by the inadequacy of confederation as a form of government. After winning its independence from Britain, the United States adopted in 1781 the Articles of Confederation, the first American constitution. The states retained sovereignty, and the federal Congress was little more than a meeting place for ambassadors of these state governments. Congress could not levy taxes, raise an army, regulate commerce, or enforce law within the states, nor was there a national executive authority. General recognition that this system could not last very long led to the constitutional convention of 1787.

As with many important political innovations, the invention of modern federalism was almost accidental. According to the conventional wisdom of the eighteenth century, sovereignty was indivisible. Those who supported the Articles of Confederation saw sovereignty as lodged in the thirteen sovereign states; those who criticized them wanted to create a new unitary state possessing sovereignty at the centre. Both sides agreed that sovereignty had to be in one place or the other. James Madison broke the deadlock by suggesting that two levels of government could each have legislative authority secured by the constitution. The logical puzzle about sovereignty was solved by declaring that the people were sovereign, and that the state and federal governments were their instruments, created and restrained by the constitution, which the people could alter according to prescribed methods. Few people at the time saw this as a new type of government; most thought of it as a constitutional marriage of two existing and well-understood forms of government: confederation and the unitary state. But it has since become conventional in political science to emphasize the division of sovereignty and to speak of federalism as a distinct form of government rather than a combination of other types.

The rise of federalism has largely driven confederation from the field as a serious alternative, though it still appears occasionally, as in the proposal for sovereignty-association between Quebec and the rest of Canada—which, depending on the details of implementation, might not even reach the level of a confederation. According to the official proposal by the Parti Québécois, Canada and Quebec would be sovereign nations cooperating in selected areas. For example, there might be a common currency supervised by a central bank in which both partners would hold shares. But there would be no central legislature of any kind, not even one like the very weak American Congress of 1781–87.

We may also see a resurgence of confederations as the world economy becomes more tightly interconnected. When the European Union was founded in 1956, it was little more than a free-trade zone. In governmental terms, it represented six sovereign states agreeing to specific forms of cooperation under the Treaty of Rome. But since that treaty was signed, the cooperation has become so massive and complex that use of the term confederation may one day be justified. There is as yet nothing resembling a European cabinet or head of state, but there are European prototypes of the other main governmental institutions—for example, the European Parliament at Strasbourg, a European bureaucracy at Brussels, and a European Court of Justice in Luxembourg—as well as regular meetings of first ministers. There have been attempts to harmonize policy in so many areas, such as labour codes, human rights, consumer standards, and the environment, that the legislative discretion of member states is now substantially reduced. Whether or not we call the European Union a confederation may be only a semantic quibble.

Because of its special relevance to Canadians, let us return to a more extended discussion of federalism. Federal systems emerge for at least three important reasons. First, it has been said that "federalism is one way to resolve the problem of enlarging governments."[3] Federal systems are alternatives to large empires established by imperial force. Decentralization allows far-flung regions to feel that not all decisions are made for them in a distant capital. Not surprisingly, most federal states are geographically large: Russia, Mexico, Australia, India, and so forth. Second, federal systems are often established in societies where a substantial degree of linguistic, religious, or cultural diversity exists. This explains the development of federalism in Switzerland, which is geographically small but linguistically and religiously diverse. Linguistic division is not a factor in Germany, but the circumstances of history have promoted federalism there. Because Germany was not fully united until 1871, some of the German *Länder* (provinces), such as Bavaria, were sovereign states until relatively recently and still have important historical traditions of their own. Federalism can accommodate this sort of diversity. In practice, a large land area and cultural pluralism often go together, which means that federalism has a double *raison d'être* in such countries as India and Canada. Third, federal systems provide one way of checking governmental power. When powers are divided between levels of government, absolute power is not concentrated within a single unit. The logic is much the same as in Madison's justification of the separation of powers—in a federation, government in effect "controls itself" because the ambitions of one group of politicians can never entirely defeat the ambitions of another. When the provinces check the federal government and the federal government checks the provinces, a balance may well result.

There are other advantages to the federal system of government. A larger state probably has greater human and natural resources with which to defend itself against foreign enemies. Also, the larger the nation-state, the greater the economies of scale. It should be cheaper to administer public services on a large scale where costs can be spread among more people. Also, when governments are located at a regional level, people tend to feel closer to the decision-making process, and the decision-makers tend to be more aware of local needs and better able to respond to them. Finally, constituent governments can often establish innovative programs and policies aimed at particular problems. These experiments may prove valuable for the entire country once they are tested. For example, Saskatchewan enacted hospital insurance in 1946 and medical-care insurance in 1961; in each case that province anticipated federal legislation by a decade.

In spite of these advantages, as Garth Stevenson states, "One is tempted to conclude that both the arguments against federalism and the arguments in its favour can be as easily refuted as supported."[4] "Layered" government has financial costs that may outweigh any economies of scale. And while governments at the local or provincial level are closer to the people, this is no guarantee that they are any more responsive to local needs than a federal government would be. And the federal system may foster divisive intergovernmental conflict.

Obviously, the division of sovereignty in a federal system reduces the power of the central government, thus taking away some of its ability to oppress the people. Less obvious, but equally true, is that the existence of two levels of government is a check on tyrannical tendencies in the constituent governments. This was brilliantly pointed out by Madison in his contributions to *The Federalist*. He showed that in a small democracy, there is a strong likelihood of some group gaining the upper hand and practising a tyranny of the majority. A small jurisdiction is usually homogeneous in social composition, and this makes it easy for a majority to form. But in a large country, there is such a diversity of classes and interests—farmers, workers, merchants, and so forth—that there is "in the society so many separate descriptions of citizens as will render an unjust combination of a majority of the whole very improbable."[5] While the following example dates from 150 years later, it indicates that Madison may have had a point. In the 1930s in Alberta, William Aberhart's Social Credit government, elected by a majority including many debtors, passed laws against banks that amounted to confiscation of property. When the newspapers criticized him harshly, he tried to impose a form of censorship on them. The federal government protected the rights of banks and newspapers by disallowing provincial legislation and exercising judicial review.

The situation with blacks in the American South is also a case in point, but from a different perspective. For almost 100 years, state governments in the decentralized American federal system had been able to pass laws that discriminated against blacks. For instance, laws were passed limiting voting rights and segregating schools. By 1965, with the U.S. Supreme Court leading the way, the federal government was finally able to override the legal structure of racial segregation. The point is that in a decentralized federal system, power at the constituent level (in this case, the state level) can be used to restrict the social, economic, and political rights of minorities. Although it took about a century and a great deal of grief for blacks and some whites, Madison's idea of justice finally prevailed. The genius of federalism lies in its recognition that power at any level is subject to abuse and in the way it establishes layers of government with enough power to balance each other.

Structural Features of Federalism

Although each federal system must be uniquely adapted to the pluralistic conditions of its society, certain structural features are universal, or very nearly so. First, there must be a written document that explicitly assigns powers to the two levels of government. In Canada, Section 91 of the Constitution Act, 1867, grants power to the federal government, while Sections 92 and 93 spell out the powers of the provinces. Section 95 assigns concurrent jurisdiction to the two levels of government over agriculture and immigration. The powers of the federal or national Parliament include, for example, control of trade and commerce, maintenance of a postal service, and responsibility for navigation and shipping. Provincial powers under Section 92 include control of the sale of alcoholic beverages, responsibility for the solemnization of marriage, and management of hospitals. Section 93 makes provincial governments responsible for education "in and for each province"; this wording is open enough to allow the federal government to help support universities, whose research role transcends provincial boundaries.

The constitution of a federal system also has to say something about **residual powers**—that is, those powers of government that are not specifically mentioned in the text. No list of functions can ever be complete, if only because situations unforeseen at the time of drafting are bound to arise. In Canada, residual powers were given to the federal government by Section 91 of the Constitution Act, 1867:

> It shall be lawful for the Queen, by and with the Advice and Consent of the Senate and House of Commons, to make Laws for the Peace, Order, and good Government of Canada, in relation to all Matters not coming within the Classes of Subjects by this Act assigned exclusively to the Legislatures of the Provinces.

In contrast, the tenth amendment to the American constitution took the opposite approach: "The powers not delegated to the United States by the Constitution or prohibited by it to the States, are reserved to the States respectively, or to the people."

Practically all federal systems have bicameral legislatures in the central government, although in some the powers of the upper house have atrophied over the years. The rationale behind federal bicameralism is to provide the provinces or regions with a special form of representation within the central government. This is supposed to ensure that regional voices are heard in the capital and to prevent regional interests from being overridden by a numerical majority in the nation as a whole. It is quite frankly a restraint upon the pure democracy of majority rule.

Germany is a good example of federal bicameralism. The upper house or *Bundesrat* is composed of delegates chosen by and responsible to the governments of the *Länder*; the number of delegates is roughly in proportion to the size of the *Land* ("province"). The federal cabinet is responsible only to the lower house or *Bundestag*, but the *Bundesrat*, unlike the Canadian Senate, often exercises its power of refusing to pass legislation. The American Senate is another good example. Senators, now democratically elected, were once chosen by state legislatures and still feel responsible for seeing that their states' interests are respected in Washington. Having two senators per state, regardless of the state's size, guarantees equal state representation.

In comparison, Canada has a weaker form of federal bicameralism, because the power of the Canadian Senate is quite limited in practice. Section 22(4) of the amended Constitution Act, 1867, specifies a certain regional distribution of senators (24 each from Quebec, Ontario, Western Canada, and the Maritimes; 6 from Newfoundland; and one each from Yukon and the Northwest Territories), but this distribution does not make senators true provincial representatives, since they are appointed by the governor general on the advice of the prime minister. From the beginning, the cabinet, which has traditionally included ministers from each province, has been a stronger instrument of federalism in Canada than the Senate.

Not surprisingly, most of the recent proposals to reform the Canadian constitution involve changing the Senate to make it a more active representative of provincial interests. The Meech Lake Accord would have required the prime minister to choose senators from among names submitted by the governments of the provinces, and the Charlottetown Accord would have gone even further by giving each province an equal number of popularly elected senators.

Without reform, Canada's upper house will never really do the job that such bodies in most federal states perform. Even when it is active, as in recent years when Liberals and Conservatives have taken turns in using the Senate to block or delay legislation coming from the House of Commons, it does not effectively represent regional or provincial interests. The fact that the Senate does not speak for the regions undoubtedly contributes to the feeling among such provinces as Newfoundland and Alberta that their interests are not effectively represented in Ottawa. Residents of these provinces often feel they are repeatedly overridden by the majority power of the electors in Ontario and Quebec. To this, many Members of Parliament and some analysts of the Canadian federal system would answer that all provinces are represented in the House of Commons and that, regardless of whether the MP is on the government or the opposition side, this representation is adequate.

Table 22.1 suggests the basis for the regional arguments for a strong Canadian Senate. Ontario and Quebec have 178 of the 301 seats in the House of Commons (151 would be a majority). If a political party can build a strong base in those two provinces, it can dominate Canadian politics.

TABLE 22.1 Canadian House of Commons Regional Breakdown of Seats, 1980–1997

Province	Party	1980	1984	1988	1993	1997
Atlantic	PC	13	25	12	1	13
NF 7	Liberal	19	7	20	31	11
NS 11	NDP	0	0	0	0	8
NB 10						
PEI 4						
TOTAL		32	32	32	32	32
Quebec	PC	1	58	63	1	5
	Liberal	74	17	12	19	26
	NDP	0	0	0	0	0
	Bloc	0	0	0	54	44
	Other	0	0	0	1*	—
TOTAL		75	75	75	75	75
Ontario	PC	38	67	47	0	1
	Liberal	52	14	42	0	101
	NDP	5	13	10	0	—
	Reform	—	—	—	1	—
	Other	0	1*	0	0	1*
TOTAL		95	95	99	99	103
Prairies	PC	33	39	36	0	1
AB 26	Liberal	2	1	5	21	9
MB 14	NDP	14	9	13	6	9
SK 14	Reform	—	—	—	27	35
Total		49	49	54	54	54
British	PC	16	19	12	0	0
Columbia	Liberal	0	1	1	6	6
	NDP	12	8	19	2	3
	Reform	—	—	—	24	25
TOTAL		28	28	32	32	34
NWT	PC	2	0	0	0	0
Yukon	Liberal	0	3	2	2	2
	NDP	1	0	1	1	1
TOTAL		3	3	3	3	3
TOTAL		282	282	295	295	301

*Independent

Those who advocate the primacy of majoritarian party politics in the House of Commons have a point in terms of democratic representation. Many critics, however, argue that federalism requires, by definition, a dual basis for representation. Their position is that an upper house is an integral part of any federal system and should represent the interests of the regions. There have been many suggestions over the past fifteen years relating to how regional interests can be better represented in Ottawa. They range from the "triple-E" proposal to the compromise in the Charlottetown Accord (see Figure 22.1).

Although the abolition of the Senate has been suggested, this position seems a bit facile in that Canada would then be the only federal system in the world without an upper house. Most federalists argue that an upper house is an integral part of our federal system, and that what we need is a Senate that is democratic, has real power vis-à-vis the House of Commons, and represents all provinces and territories without entirely disregarding population differences.

The weakness of regional representation in Ottawa has encouraged Canadian federalism to develop an *interstate* (activity between provinces and the federal government) rather than an *intrastate* (activity within the nation-state) character.[6] Provincial governments have become the main advocates of regional interests and now deal with each other and with the federal government in quasi-diplomatic fashion. The most visible manifestations of this **executive federalism** are the periodic first ministers' conferences, which are conducted very much like international conferences, that is, with public posturing, secret negotiations, and final communiqués. These sessions are only the most visible meetings in the ceaseless round of federal–provincial talks at various levels among cabinet ministers, deputy ministers, and officials. This cycle of negotiations and meetings occurs outside parliamentary government in Ottawa. There is nothing like it in other major federal polities such as Australia, the United States, and Germany.

In federal systems, constituent governments often clash with each other and with the national government, and the courts often become the arbiters of these conflicts. Judicial review, the power to declare legislation unconstitutional, is an important feature of most federal constitutions. Curiously, judicial review in federalism issues is now relatively unimportant in the United States, where federalism originated.[7] But it is still generally true, and certainly true in Canada, that federalism gives the courts a higher profile than in most unitary states. This in turn makes judicial appointments politically sensitive.

In the United States, Senate confirmation of presidential appointments to the bench helps raise the legitimacy of the federal judiciary in the eyes of the states. In Canada, judicial appointments are made by the governor general on the advice of the minister of justice, with the prime minister playing a special role by nominating the members of the Supreme Court of Canada and the chief justices of the other courts. At present, the provinces play no role in appointing judges, even though the Supreme Court's decisions can have a major impact on provincial powers. The

FIGURE 22.1 Proposed Geographical Distribution of Senate Seats

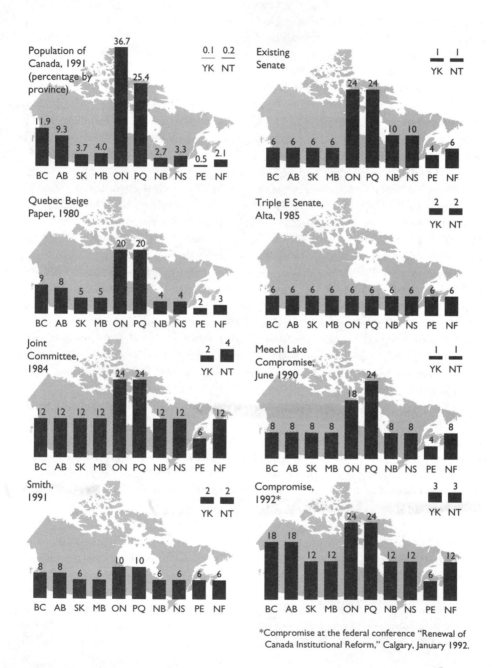

*Compromise at the federal conference "Renewal of Canada Institutional Reform," Calgary, January 1992.

Meech Lake and the Charlottetown Accords tried to address this problem [by] [pro]viding that Supreme Court judges be chosen from lists submitted by the pr[ovinces.] Since the defeat of both amendment packages, the status quo has pre[vailed, and] undoubtedly the provinces will continue to feel that the Supreme Court of Ca[nada is] too much an instrument of the federal government.

Until 1949 the highest Canadian appeals court was the **Judicial Committee of the Privy Council (JCPC)**, a special British court that heard appeals from the whole empire. The provinces had never considered this a problem because in fact, the JCPC rendered a long series of decisions favourable to the provinces in their disputes with Ottawa. But when appeals to the committee were abolished in 1949, the Supreme Court of Canada, appointed solely by federal authorities, became the ultimate interpreter of the Constitution. Since that time, the provinces have increasingly desired a role in choosing judges, and something in this direction will probably happen sooner or later.

Constitutional amendment is another contentious subject in federal systems. There must be some sort of balance between the two levels of government. If the central government can change the constitution at will without the consent of the regional governments, the system is tantamount to devolution, because the central government could modify or even abolish the regional governments by unilateral constitutional amendment. Before 1982, the legal method for amending the Canadian Constitution was for the British Parliament, acting on a joint address from the Canadian Senate and House of Commons, to amend the British North America Act (as it was then called). In most, but not all, instances in which provincial rights were affected, the federal government obtained the prior consent of all the provinces before requesting constitutional amendments. An all-Canadian amending formula was introduced as part of the Constitution Act, 1982. Under the general procedure of Section 38, amendments must be passed by the House, the Senate, and the legislative assemblies of two-thirds of the provinces that have at least 50 percent of the population of all the provinces; and amendments in certain matters require the agreement of all provinces. These provisions institutionalized the roles of the federal and provincial governments in amending the Constitution and excluded Great Britain altogether. In the United States, all constitutional amendments must receive approval from two-thirds of both houses of Congress and three-quarters of state legislatures. Again there is a balance of power between the central and constituent governments.

At the time of Confederation, the Canadian system had a feature that is unusual in federal states: the right of the central government to nullify the legislation of the constituent governments, even when they were acting within their proper constitutional sphere. There are two mechanisms by which this can happen. In the first, known as **reservation**, the lieutenant governor of a province can refuse royal assent to a bill and refer it to the federal cabinet for a final decision. In the second, known as **disallowance**, the federal cabinet can nullify a provincial act within one year of passage, even though it has received royal assent from the lieutenant governor of the province. These powers of the federal government were used frequently in the early years of Confederation, and are still constitutionally alive, though they are now in abeyance. No provincial act has been disallowed since 1943, although Ottawa has sometimes threatened such action. In 1961, Saskatchewan's lieutenant governor reserved a bill without seeking prior advice from Ottawa, much to the embarrassment of Prime Minister John Diefenbaker. Except in that confused episode, neither power has been used recently—an indication of how Canadian federalism has become more decentralized. In practice, court challenges have replaced reservation and disallowance. In the United States, as in most federal systems, there is no parallel to this constitutional dominance by the central government.

This review shows that Canadian federalism was originally so highly centralized as to border on devolution. In other words, a very centralized federal system may resemble very closely a unitary system that has undergone devolution. The federal right to appoint judges and senators, nullify provincial legislation, amend the constitution, and exercise residual powers far outweighed the provincial powers. This was by design. The Fathers of Confederation could not ignore the American Civil War (1861–65). Most believed that the American constitution had granted too much power to the states. Sir John A. Macdonald would have preferred a unitary state, then known as a *legislative union* (only one legislature for all of Canada); but he realized that some form of federalism was required to entice Quebec and the Atlantic provinces into association with Ontario. The solution that emerged was, in legal terms, a strong central government with minimal concessions to the provinces.

The subsequent evolution of Canada has undone much of this work. The forces of decentralization were too strong to be contained within the centralizing constitution of 1867. The JCPC rendered a long series of decisions that circumscribed the legislative powers given Ottawa under Section 91 and expanded provincial powers under Section 92. Ottawa also gradually relinquished the use of centralizing powers such as reservation and disallowance.

There was, to be sure, a centralizing trend that began in World War II and carried on into the postwar period. The federal government acquired the important new jurisdictions of unemployment insurance and old-age pensions through constitutional amendment. It also used its extensive revenues to create national welfare programs such as health-care insurance and the Canada Assistance Plan. But this centralizing thrust in turn gave rise to a counter movement of decentralization. As the provinces expanded their tax base in the late 1950s and 1960s, they became less dependent on the federal government for financial support, which encouraged a new dynamic in the federal system. The Meech Lake and Charlottetown Accords contained provisions that would have enhanced provincial at the expense of federal jurisdiction. Quebec, motivated by linguistic and cultural factors, is at the forefront of provinces seeking more power, but it is not the only such province. The decentralizing trend is likely to continue because the postwar expansion of federal responsibilities rested primarily upon Ottawa's financial resources, but the federal budgetary picture has forced it to cut transfers to the provinces.

Canadian federalism today may be at a significant crossroads. Over the past decade, there have been many proposals for reforming the federal system. Of these, the Meech Lake and Charlottetown Accords, arrived at by the first ministers, received the most attention. But most provinces and a number of high-profile private groups also produced recommendations, such as Quebec's Bélanger–Campeau Report and British Columbia's *The Renewal of the Federation* (the Smith Report).[8] Proposals have dealt with almost every conceivable topic, including multiculturalism, Senate reform, immigration policy, Supreme Court nominations, and the use of referendums. Almost invariably there has been a clear recommendation to expand the role of the provinces in the federation.

One interesting product of these constitutional discussions was the concept of **asymmetrical federalism**, a term used to convey the idea of powers being divided unevenly among provinces, of some provinces choosing to have greater responsibilities or more autonomy than others. Of course, a degree of asymmetry already exists in Canadian federalism. Quebec, for instance, collects its own income tax, operates its own provincial pension plan, and exercises more control over immigration than do the other provinces, which have been content to let Ottawa perform these functions. The transfer of powers to the provinces envisioned in the Meech Lake and Charlottetown Accords would have led to more of these asymmetrical arrangements. Many Canadians feared that, as a result, Canada would be "balkanized," that is, reduced to a patchwork of different programs in different jurisdictions across the country.

Proponents of asymmetrical federalism are willing to run this risk. They believe that greater flexibility in federalism will accommodate the differing needs of the provinces, especially those of Quebec, and thus reduce the threat of separatism. Opponents question whether pushing asymmetry too far might not lead to the disintegration of federalism as we know it. They fear that too much decentralization would so weaken the federal government that Canada would be left with only a very loose confederation. This debate was not really resolved with the rejection of the Charlottetown Accord and continues to bubble beneath the surface of Canadian politics.

Curiously, American political evolution has moved in the direction of greater centralization, with power shifting steadily toward the federal government. International crises—two world wars, the Cold War, and the Korean, Vietnam, and Gulf Wars—and the nationalization of domestic issues, such as racial disparities and inflation, have tended to make all eyes focus on Washington for solutions. The federal government totally overshadows any state or group of states in its ability to confront national issues. An abstract reading of the American and Canadian Constitutions would suggest that American states are far more powerful than Canadian provinces, but this is in fact a highly distorted picture of the current reality.[9] The constitutional allocation of residual powers to the federal government in Canada and to the states in the United States has had little long-run, practical effect.

Assessing Federal Systems

While federal systems have enabled the building of large nation-states, they have not provided the cure for all political ills. Indeed, separatist movements have plagued many countries with a federal form of government. The Civil War in the United States was fought over the South's right to secede from the Union. In Nigeria, Biafrans with their strong tribal identity and oil resources tried in 1967 to secede from the federation. The Chechens have fought Russia to a standstill in their attempt to found an independent republic. Separatists in the Parti Québécois still vow to establish sovereignty in Quebec.

A basic problem with all federal systems is establishing a workable balance that is acceptable to all levels of government. It was once believed that a central government was best suited to cope with national problems. Over the last sixty years, there have been two conflicting trends: one toward centralizing power at the national level because governments have expanded their functions to meet economic crises and have become involved in international conflicts, and the other toward decentralizing power because national and ethnic feeling are running strong and because many people feel that regional governments can best deal with individual citizens. There seems to be much appeal in the thesis that "small is beautiful." Indeed, many federal systems of government are using decentralization as a way of countering separatist movements.

In Canada we are also getting mixed signals about our federation. The provinces have become more powerful in the federal system, and the Meech Lake and Charlottetown Accords were proposals to institutionalize that trend. However, for a variety of reasons, both accords failed to pass. Two issues now appear to be dictating the future of our federal system. One is Quebec sovereignty, which is going to remain high on the national agenda. The other is the fiscal crisis at both levels of government. The fact that the federal and provincial governments have acquired huge debt loads and are short of revenue will force political leaders to take a hard look at the existing division of powers and to try to rationalize government functions within federalism. Federalism will continue to involve tough negotiations over the division of powers. Indeed, this kind of ongoing negotiation over power is what federalism is supposed to be about—flexibility in sharing power. There is no particular division of powers that is carved in stone for all time. Time and circumstances seem to dictate the movement toward a more centralized or decentralized federal system of government.

᠎᠎᠎᠎᠎᠎᠎

FURTHER READING

Bakvis, Herman, and William M. Chandler, eds. *Federalism and the Role of the State*. Toronto: University of Toronto Press, 1987.

Bird, Richard M., ed. *Fiscal Dimensions of Canadian Federalism*. Toronto: Canadian Tax Foundation, 1980.

Burgess, Michael. *Canadian Federalism: Past, Present and Future*. Leicester, England: Leicester University Press, 1990.

Burgess, Michael, and Alain G. Gagnon, eds. *Comparative Federalism and Federations: Competing Traditions and Future Directions*. Toronto: University of Toronto Press, 1993.

Cairns, Alan C. *Charter Versus Federalism: The Dilemmas of Constitutional Reform*. Kingston: McGill-Queen's University Press, 1992.

Courchene, Thomas J. *In Praise of Renewed Federalism*. Toronto: C.D. Howe Institute, 1991.

Duchacek, Ivo D. *Comparative Federalism: The Territorial Dimension of Politics*. New York: Holt, Rinehart and Winston, 1970.

Elazar, Daniel J. *Federalism and the Way to Peace*. Kingston, Ont.: Institute of Intergovernmental Relations, Queen's University, 1994.

——, ed. *Federal Systems of the World: A Handbook of Federal, Confederal and Autonomy Arrangements*. Harlow, England: Longman, 1991.

Gibbins, Roger. *Regionalism: Territorial Politics in Canada and the United States*. Toronto: Butterworths, 1982.

Harrison, Kathryn. *Passing the Buck: Federalism and Canadian Environmental Policy*. Vancouver: UBC Press, 1996.

Hobson, Paul A.R., and France St. Hilaire. *Toward Sustainable Federalism: Reforming Federal-Provincial Fiscal Arrangements*. Montreal: Institute for Research on Public Policy, 1993.

King, Preston. *Federalism and Federation*. London: Croom Helm, 1982.

Knop, Karen, et al. ed., *Rethinking Federalism: Citizens, Markets, and Governments in a Changing World*. Vancouver: UBC Press, 1995.

LaSelva, Samuel V. *The Moral Foundations of Canadian Federalism: Paradoxes, Achievements, and Tragedies of Nationhood*. Montreal: McGill-Queen's University Press, 1996.

Meekison, J. Peter, ed. *Canadian Federalism: Myth or Reality*, 3rd ed. Toronto: Methuen, 1977.

Oates, Wallace E. *Studies in Fiscal Federalism*. Aldershot, England: Elgar, 1991.

Randall, Stephen J., and Roger Gibbins. *Federalism and the New World Order*. Calgary: University of Calgary Press, 1994.

Riker, William H. *Federalism: Origin, Operation, Significance*. Boston: Little, Brown, 1964.

Rocher, François, and Miriam Smith, eds. *New Trends in Canadian Federalism*. Peterborough, Ont. and Orchard Park, N.Y.: Broadview Press, 1995.

Simeon, Richard, and Ian Robinson. *State, Society, and the Development of Canadian Federalism*. Toronto: University of Toronto Press, 1990.

Smiley, D.V. *The Federal Condition in Canada*. Toronto: McGraw-Hill Ryerson, 1987.

Stevenson, Garth. *Unfulfilled Union: Canadian Federalism and National Unity*, 3rd ed. Toronto: Gage, 1989.

Tushnet, Mark V., ed. *Comparative Constitutional Federalism: Europe and America*. New York: Greenwood Press, 1990.

Wheare, K.C. *Federal Government*. New York: Oxford University Press, 1964.

Zimmerman, Joseph Francis. *Contemporary American Federalism: The Growth of National Power*. Leicester, England: Leicester University Press, 1992.

The Political Process

PART 4

THE POLITICAL PROCESS

CHAPTER 23

I n Part One we discussed politics in abstract terms, associating it with functions such as the exercise of authority, the allocation of values, and the settling of disputes. In Part Four we want to move from the level of abstraction to the level of concrete reality and be much more specific about the political process. Our objective is to explain politics as an institutionalized process for making public decisions. Our hope is that politics becomes a vivid and concrete idea in the mind of the student.

The task may be easier to state than to accomplish. While all of us know that the process exists and that it works, it is still difficult to describe in precise terms. The **political process** is the complex activity of making public decisions for a society. It involves the interaction of organized political structures such as interest groups, political parties, executives, legislatures, and the courts. Politics is the interplay of all these components in devising public laws and policies, selecting and rejecting rulers, and shaping public opinion. Finding a successful course of action that can withstand the scrutiny of public dialogue is an art that requires a particular intuitive sense. It is probably true that the greater the freedom in society, the greater the participation in politics; and the greater the participation in politics, the more complex the political process. It is, then, a challenge to be able to understand this dynamic aspect of public life in an open society.

There is in all societies an endless and ongoing political process by which public decisions are made in response to claims and counterclaims from elements of that society. This political process produces not only decisions but also patterns of support for and resistance to these decisions. The process can be conceived as a system. In the cybernetic sense, a system is a connected set of functions that converts inputs into outputs and feeds the results back as data for future rounds of decision making.[1]

POLITICS AS A SYSTEMIC PROCESS

David Easton specifically applied systems analysis to politics in a well-known book, *A Systems Analysis of Political Life* (1965). He showed that the political system in its simplest form was a process of authoritative decision making,[2] as illustrated in Figure 23.1. Consider politics as a systemic flow. Specific inputs (demands and supports) are generated in society. Demands are what people would like government to do for them; supports are the approbation they bestow on a government they consider legitimate. These demands and supports are transformed or converted into outputs: laws and policies. This conversion takes place in what Easton calls the "black box," which is made up of the various branches and layers of government. He calls it the black box because at this point he is not concerned with the internal mechanisms by which conversion is accomplished; he is just noting that conversion occurs and is trying to situate it in a systemic context. The box is black because he does not yet look inside it. The impact of laws and policies on society takes place through feedback, which generates new demands and supports. Easton was one of the first to apply the term *political system*, which is now used extensively in the political science literature to refer to the process of government and politics in any state.

A rather similar approach was taken in an influential book by Gabriel Almond and G.B. Powell, *Comparative Politics* (1966).[3] They also adopted the fundamental notions of input, conversion, output, and feedback. However, they provided a more detailed analysis of the conversion process in the modern democratic state—an analysis that is at the same time compatible with traditional ideas in political science, such as the separation of powers into legislative, executive, and judicial

FIGURE 23.1 The Systemic Flow of Politics

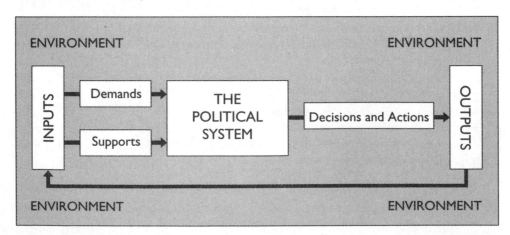

branches. They pointed to six important *structures* that carry out necessary functions: interest groups, political parties, the mass media, legislatures, executives, and the judiciary. The corresponding *functions* in the political process are interest articulation (making the position of the group known), interest aggregation (combining the positions of a number of interests), communication, making laws, administering laws, and adjudicating disputes.

Our model, shown in Figure 23.2, portrays politics as a process in which information flows from left to right. The process begins with the plural society (one composed of many interests) and converts political inputs (demands, expectations, and supports) into political outputs (laws and policies). Institutions, both formal and informal, interact to achieve this conversion and produce laws and public policies. Laws and policies can be classified as **regulative, extractive, distributive,** and **symbolic**. They are regulative when they control individual and group behaviour in society, extractive when they take taxes from citizens to pay for government, distributive when they extend payments and services to individuals, and symbolic when they represent the community with images like a flag or national anthem. Feedback allows the system to adjust spontaneously to ever-changing conditions as outputs are evaluated and give rise to new inputs.

In society, conflicts inevitably develop among groups with different interests, goals, and expectations. For example, the financial problems experienced by Canadian Airlines in 1996 ended up pitting the western provinces of Alberta and British Columbia against Quebec. Canadian's operations are centred in Calgary and Vancouver, while its main competitor, Air Canada, is domiciled in Montreal. Not surprisingly, politicians from the West wanted the federal government to help out with tax concessions; but the Bloc Québécois took the view that help to Canadian Airlines would be unfair competition against Air Canada. In such circumstances, any governmental decision is an output that affects various groups. Even a decision to postpone a decision is in effect an output that ratifies the status quo.

Nothing in the model assumes that all groups will be equally powerful or have an equal chance of advancing their interests. Depending on the social structure, some groups will have command over greater resources or will be more strategically positioned. Rather than being egalitarian, the outcomes of the political process tend to reflect the inequalities of the existing social structure.

Not all political activity is necessarily conflict-oriented; many actions by individuals and groups support the political process. Taxes are paid and speed limits are observed. For society to be orderly, there must be compliance with authority. In fact, without compliance, the entire process would become oppressive. The point is that the political behaviour of individuals and groups involves both demands and supports. For example, people usually pay taxes voluntarily. If, however, tax rates go beyond what people consider a just proportion, tax avoidance and evasion may reduce the amount of revenue collected. Clearly, government cannot function without a basis of support.

FIGURE 23.2 The Political Process

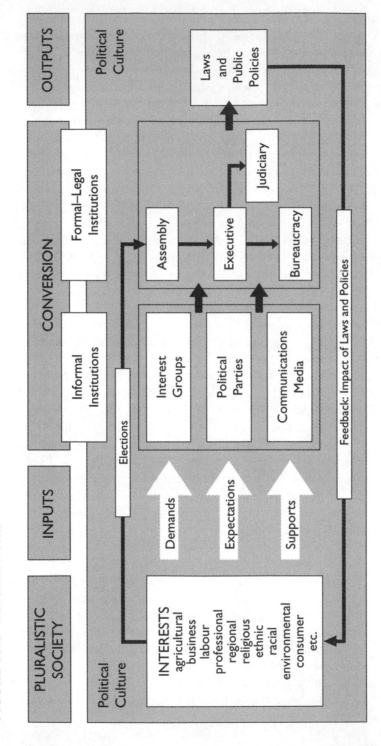

Public participation by individuals and groups in the political process follows certain patterns. Most of it is organized around the various intermediate institutions that link people and their governors: interest groups, political parties, and the media. These are frequently referred to as the **informal institutions** of government. While they are an integral part of the process, they are informal (as opposed to formal–legal) because they are not established by a constitution. Yet they have power because they tend to coordinate and channel the activities of people in a concerted way. The development of these intermediate institutions has facilitated participation by large numbers of people in the modern political process.

Other institutions are **formal–legal**—that is, they are created explicitly by a constitution, which provides the rules of the political game. One of the primary functions of a constitution is to grant power to various institutions that formalize laws and policies for a society. These institutions include elected assemblies, executives, and the judiciary. A final formal–legal institution is, of course, the election—the means by which society's members choose their governors and express their opinion of past governmental performance. The activities of these formal–legal organizations are the most visible part of the political process.

᠍᠍᠍᠍᠍᠍᠍᠍

POLICY COMMUNITIES AND NETWORKS

The political process can also be examined in the context of public policy. Political scientists study topics such as the politics of energy, health care, unemployment insurance, transportation, and defence. Instead of focusing on the role of particular institutions such as interest groups, political parties, the cabinet, the bureaucracy, and the courts, political scientists may analyze the interactions of the major players involved in enacting or rejecting a specific policy or set of policies.

Paul Pross enhanced this approach to political analysis by formulating the idea of a **policy community**. William Coleman and Grace Skogstad suggest that the policy community includes:

> all actors or potential actors with a direct or indirect interest in a policy area or function who share a common "policy focus," and who, with varying degrees of influence shape policy outcomes over the long run.[4]

The policy community forms once a particular policy becomes an issue. Within the policy community there are subgovernment groups and the attentive public. Subgovernments include "government agencies, interest associations, and other societal organization such as business firms." The attentive public includes "relevant media and interested and expert individuals."[5]

The policy community is interactive and dynamic (see Figure 23.3). For example, once the federal government begins to consider a clean-air standards act, an environmental policy community emerges. Agencies of the state involved in this policy decision will include the cabinet, the departments of environment and industry, agencies concerned with interprovincial and international trade, parlia-

FIGURE 23.3 The Policy Community

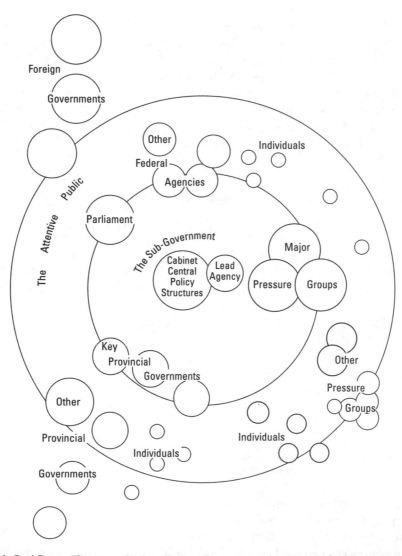

Source: A. Paul Pross, "Pressure Groups: Talking Chameleons." In Michael S. Whittington and Glen Williams, eds. *Canadian Politics in the 1990s*, 3rd ed. (Scarborough: Nelson Canada, 1990), p. 301.

ment, and perhaps the courts. Other groups with a stake in this process will also become involved: environmental groups and provincial governments, as well as actors in the private sector such as business firms and labour unions. Presumably the interaction of these organizations will produce some kind of policy.

In the rest of Part Four, we return to our first way of conceptualizing politics and examine the informal and formal–legal institutions and their role or function in a modern democratic process.

There are two fundamental aspects of the political process—a structural one and a cultural one. The structures include interest groups, political parties, the media, elections, the legislature, the political executive, the administration, and the judiciary. The cultural dimension includes the various attitudes, beliefs, and values that individuals hold regarding government and politics. In the following chapters we describe each of these components and their role in the political process.

᭒᭒᭒᭒᭒᭒᭒᭒

FURTHER READING

Almond, Gabriel A., and G. Bingham Powell, Jr. *Comparative Politics—A Developmental Approach: System, Process and Policy*, 2nd ed. Boston: Little, Brown, 1978.

Andrain, Charles F. *Comparative Political Systems: Policy Performance and Social Change*. Armonk, N.Y.: M.E. Sharpe, 1994.

Bertalanffy, Ludwig von. *General System Theory*. New York: George Braziller, 1968.

Cerny, Philip G. *The Changing Architecture of Politics: Structure, Agency, and the Future of the State*. London: Sage, 1990.

Cummings, Thomas G. *Systems Theory for Organization Development*. England: Chicester Publications, 1980.

Curtis, Richard Kenneth. *Evolution or Extinction*. New York: Pergamon Press, 1982.

Deutsch, Karl W. *The Nerves of Government: Models of Political Communication and Control*, 2nd ed. New York: Free Press, 1966.

Doern, G. Bruce, Leslie A. Pal, and Brian W. Tomlin. *Border Crossings: The Internationalization of Canadian Public Policy*. Toronto: Oxford University Press, 1996.

Dunn, William N. *Public Policy Analysis: An Introduction*, 2nd ed. Englewood Cliffs, N.J.: Prentice–Hall, 1994.

Easton, David. *The Analysis of Political Structures*. New York: Routledge, 1990.

———. *A Systems Analysis of Political Life*. New York: Wiley, 1965.

Gorden, Morton. *Comparative Political Systems*. New York: Macmillan, 1972.

Hill, Michael, ed. *The Policy Process: A Reader*. New York: Harvester Wheatsheaf, 1993.

Pal, Leslie A. *Beyond Policy Analysis: Public Issue Management in Turbulent Times*. Scarborough, Ont.: ITP Nelson, 1997.

Wiseman, H.V. *Political Systems*. New York: Praeger, 1966.

POLITICAL CULTURE

CHAPTER 24

All action within the political system is influenced by the cultural milieu of the actors. Even before beginning to trace the systemic flow of demand and support, we must therefore pay some attention to the concept of culture, and in particular political culture.

Observers have long noticed that the different peoples of the world possess what might be called cultural traits. The Chinese, for example, are thought to be industrious and to maintain close family ties. When Thomas Sowell examined the culture of various ethnic groups after immigration to the United States, he found that the Chinese had become known for their "endurance and frugality" and these characteristics carried over into younger generations in the New World. As children, they were "better behaved and more hard working." All this led to a high percentage of people from Chinese immigrant communities entering the professions, so that by 1959, their average income had surpassed the American national average.[1] People of Latin origin are said to be emotional in speech and action. North Americans are probably more egalitarian in their outlook than any other society, yet they are also materialistic and achievement-oriented. Such traits are considered part of the traditions of a society; they reflect national character and persist over long periods of time and even after migration.

Anthropologically, one might refer to these traits as part of culture. Culture in this sense refers to the total living patterns of a people: the place of the family, the role of religion, and the influence of economics and politics. *Culture* has become an umbrella term that reflects institutional arrangements as well as the attitudes, beliefs, and values that accompany them. The part of a total culture that reflects a people's orientation to politics—that is, the attitudes, beliefs, values, and norms that people have developed toward government and politics—is known as **political culture.**[2]

Popular stereotypes, sometimes containing a good deal of truth, exist about different political cultures. Germans, for example, think of themselves as being, and are thought by others to be, very respectful of public authority. While such a generalization is interesting and perhaps true, it cannot explain all of German politics. For one thing, it is rare indeed that a whole nation can be grouped within a single political culture.

Studies of public opinion reveal that most societies possess a number of political cultures. In a five-nation study constituting one of the seminal works on this subject, Gabriel Almond and Sydney Verba established that there are three basic categories of political culture: parochial, subject, and participatory.[3] In a *parochial culture*, people do not expect any positive action from government. They perceive government as a police officer and tax collector, and wish to keep as much distance as possible between themselves and the authorities. They do not expect to participate individually in politics, which they consider a game for the upper classes. In a *subject culture*, people do expect some positive action from governments. Perhaps influenced by the revolution of rising expectations, they may anticipate a school for the community, a dam to develop an irrigation system and expand crop production, or a paramedical unit for the village. Yet they still do not see themselves involved in politics. They expect the questions of where to put schools, dams, and medical teams to be decided by people with power and influence. In a *participatory culture*, people have high expectations of government and expect to participate in politics, by choosing political leaders and by attempting to influence political action. A participatory political culture is an integral part of liberal democracy.

Political culture represents the psychological dimension of politics.[4] It exists in the minds of individuals and provides the interface between people and the political process. Because it includes attitudes, beliefs, values, and norms regarding government and politics, it is simultaneously rational, emotional, and judgmental. Political culture also encompasses ideology—notions about what government is and what it ought to be.

An example may clarify the relationship between political culture and political ideology. Belief in individual freedom is a fundamental part of the political culture of the Western world. At the same time, within the ideology of liberal democracies, we not only value individual freedom but also believe that maintaining it should be a primary goal of governments. Freedom of political action is the basis on which individuals and groups can become involved in the political process. Without political freedom, there would be little opportunity to participate in politics. Thus the liberal–democratic ideology is an integral part of our political culture.

By way of contrast, Latin American political systems are influenced by Iberic–Latin traditions that include, among other things, a society that is hierarchical, stratified, and authoritarian.[5] These social traits seem to produce a political culture that is less conducive to liberal and participatory democracy. Thus Latin American politics is often characterized as class-based, authoritarian, paternalistic, and elitist.

THE FRAGMENT THEORY

A good deal of energy has gone into discussing the differences in political culture between the United States and Canada. A common denominator for much of this discussion is the fragment theory first formulated by the American historian Louis Hartz. In brief, the **fragment theory** holds that colonial societies such as the United States and Canada originated as fragments of the larger European society and have remained marked throughout their history by the conditions of their origin.

Several of the American colonies began as havens for those seeking refuge from religious and political domination, and the American polity as a whole was formed in an act of revolution against the parliamentary and imperial authority of Great Britain. It is thus not surprising that individual freedom and suspicion of government have remained abiding themes of American political thought.

The origins of Canada were quite different. The first Europeans in Canada were the French settlers of Acadia and New France, who never rebelled against imperial rule but were transferred from one empire to another. Then came the Loyalists, the refugees from the American Revolution, who wanted to leave the United States, or were driven out, because of their continuing allegiance to the British Crown. In western Canada, the story is somewhat different but also nonrevolutionary: the centuries-long dominance of the Hudson's Bay Company created a corporate ethos quite at variance with the individualism of the American frontier.

There are, to be sure, great regional differences in both the United States and Canada; but in general, Canada's distinctive origins have made its culture more corporatist, collectivist, and deferential than the American. This difference is expressed in all the tired clichés of the Canadian identity, which contain an element of truth in spite of being clichés:

- There is less crime in Canada than in the United States.
- Canadians speak more softly than Americans, especially in elevators and restaurants.
- Canadians are more polite and tolerant, and have more respect for authority.

These general cultural differences have led to obvious differences in political culture. Throughout Canadian history, governments have been suspicious of the individualistic market process and have tended to opt for nonmarket solutions to economic and social problems. Interestingly, these approaches can be either more conservative or more socialist than the market solutions typically resorted to in the United States. On the right, Canadian governments have a long history of subsidizing profit-making corporations and protecting them from competition. For example, Canadian anticombines legislation, which is supposed to outlaw price fixing and other conspiracies in restraint of trade, is so weak as to be virtually meaningless. There is nothing in Canadian history corresponding to the government-enforced breakup of large corporations in the oil, steel, sugar, tobacco, and telephone industries that occurred in the United States. On the left, Canadian governments, with the support of politicians from all parties, have created programs of public medical insurance and family benefits that have no counterpart in the United States. The common denominator is greater confidence in government and less confidence in the unaided individual. This is the reverse of the American pattern of suspicion of government and confidence in, even glorification of, the individual.

𝕤𝕤𝕤𝕤𝕤𝕤𝕤𝕤

TRENDS IN POLITICAL CULTURE

Although such cross-national differences are important and long-lasting, there are other trends in political culture that seem to affect many societies simultaneously. A prime example is the growth of postmaterialism in the political culture of the Western world, which we mentioned earlier in the discussion of feminism and environmentalism. According to Ronald Inglehart, who pioneered research on postmaterialism, the years since World War II have seen a gradual but profound shift of values. New generations have grown up that are able to take physical and economic security for granted and are exposed to higher levels of formal education. The result is an electorate more concerned with self-expression and less inclined to leave politics to politicians and to accept the necessity of pragmatic compromises.[6] There have been several political results. One is a decrease in voter loyalty to particular parties and a corresponding increase in vote switching from election to election. Another is the rise of single-issue movements (feminist, pro-choice, pro-life, environmentalist, ethnic, linguistic, gay-rights, rights for the disabled, and so on) that are unwilling to submerge their causes within a single political party.

Establishing the exact connection between political culture and the political process is difficult. One way of visualizing this connection is offered by Almond, who suggests that the political process is "embedded" in the political culture.[7] Attitudes and beliefs that individuals hold about government and politics influence at every step the interaction among the elements of the political process. Political culture is a matrix within which the entire process takes place.

The study of political culture and its precise place in the analysis of politics is a challenging undertaking in any country. Only in the last three decades, however, has the systematic study of political culture become an integral part of the broader study of politics. Obviously, knowledge of the political institutions and how they work is crucial to the study of any political process. Critical also is knowledge of the cultural dimension of that process.

The means by which a political culture is transmitted from generation to generation is known as **political socialization**.[8] A number of socializing agents—the family, schools, peer groups, the media, the workplace—as well as contacts with government itself, transmit the beliefs and values that create patterns of behaviour within the society.

Socializing new generations with values and beliefs is not always an orderly process. Political culture cannot be static, because beliefs and values are forever changing. There may be a significant conflict between generations in a society over which values or beliefs should be revered. Such a conflict can lead to the disintegration of order; or it may be contained by maintaining a public dialogue, without which politics is reduced to mere coercion. Public discussion is the means by which various social groups articulate their interests and demand government action. Thus we come back to social pluralism as the source of inputs for the political system. The next chapter looks at interest groups as an extension of this pluralism.

FURTHER READING

Almond, Gabriel A., and Sidney Verba. *The Civic Culture*. Princeton, N.J.: Princeton University Press, 1963.

——. *The Civic Culture Revisited*. Boston: Little Brown, 1980.

Bashevkin, Sylvia. *True Patriot Love: The Politics of Canadian Nationalism*. Don Mills, Ont.: Oxford University Press, 1991.

Borman, Kathryn M., ed. *The Social Life of Children in a Changing Society*. Hillsdale, N.J.: Lawrence Erlbaum Associates, 1982.

Diamond, Larry Jay, ed. *Political Culture and Democracy in Developing Countries*. Boulder, Colo.: Lynne Rienner, 1993.

Gibbins, John R., ed. *Contemporary Political Culture: Politics in Postmodern Age*. London: Sage, 1989.

Gibbins, Roger, and Neil Nevitte. *New Elites in Old States: Ideologies in the Anglo-American Democracies*. Toronto: Oxford University Press, 1990.

Gutmann, Amy, ed. *Multiculturalism, Examining the Politics of Recognition*. Princeton, N.J: Princeton University Press, 1994.

Hartz, Louis. *The Founding of New Societies*. New York: Harcourt, Brace and World, 1964.

Inglehart, Ronald. *Culture Shift in Advanced Industrial Society*. Princeton, N.J.: Princeton University Press, 1990.

Jaros, Dean. *Socialization to Politics*. New York: Praeger, 1973.

Langton, Kenneth P. *Political Socialization*. New York: Oxford University Press, 1969.

Lipset, Seymour Martin. *Continental Divide: The Values and Institutions of the United States and Canada*. New York: Routledge, 1990.

Merelman, Richard M. *Partial Visions: Culture and Politics in Britain, Canada and the United States*. Madison, Wis.: University of Wisconsin Press, 1991.

Rosenbaum, Walter A. *Political Culture*. New York: Praeger, 1975.

Thompson, Michael, et al. *Cultural Theory*. Boulder, Colo.: Westview Press, 1990.

Wilson, Richard. *Compliance Ideologies: Rethinking Political Culture*. Cambridge, England: Cambridge University Press, 1992.

INTEREST GROUPS

CHAPTER 25

The political process begins with the articulation of demands for action by particular social groups, usually called interest groups. An **interest group** is defined most simply as a collection of individuals who pursue common political goals.[1] It represents people who band together to accomplish specific objectives. Because interest groups exert political pressure to achieve their ends, they may also be called pressure groups. Obviously, not all groups are political; people may organize for any number of reasons. There are social groups such as bridge and dance clubs, sports clubs, community associations, and professional organizations. Most of these voluntary organizations will never become involved in politics; however, if they do, they become interest groups in the political process. As such, they facilitate popular participation in politics. By coordinating political activities, they offer individuals an opportunity to become involved in the complex process of politics. Politics is an endless cycle because there are always new demands, generated by a variety of interests, with which government must deal.

Interest groups do not seek to control the entire machinery of government; they seek merely to influence the political process with the goal of achieving certain legislative or policy ends. Organizations that seek to actually control governments are political parties. Interest groups may work with political parties and may even become affiliated with them—as in the relationship between the New Democratic Party (NDP) and some, but not all, member unions of the Canadian Labour Congress (CLC). Generally, however, parties and interest groups are conceptually distinct, even if their activities sometimes overlap.

The function of a group in politics is to articulate the interest of its members with the goal of changing laws and influencing policies. Interest groups seek to achieve their ends by persuading public officials. Land developers may try to influence a city council's decision on planning and zoning; labour unions may try to persuade the provincial cabinet to amend collective-bargaining legislation; conservation organizations may seek to influence public policies relating to national or provincial parks. Interest groups also address themselves to public opinion; in the Canadian election of 1988, business, labour, and other groups all spoke out vigorously about free trade, although the business community, led by the Business Council on National Issues and the Canadian Manufacturers' Association, had much more money to spend on advertising. In all such cases, citizens with a common goal band together in an effort to shape legislation that they believe affects their lives.

In the second half of the twentieth century, one of the great developments in the political process in Western democracies has been the proliferation of organized interest groups. Before World War II, organized interest groups were relatively few in number and consisted chiefly of economic producer groups with a specific focus: business and industrial associations, labour unions, farmers' associations, and the organized professions, such as doctors, lawyers, and teachers. Because groups had to operate with whatever resources they could collect from their members, those representing a well-to-do clientele tended to be the most effective.

The present-day picture is radically different. First, there are now vastly greater numbers of politically active groups. Second, there are politically effective groups representing not only traditional producers but also diverse consumer interests (consumer associations, environmental protection groups), as well as a host of moral, cultural, and symbolic causes. Movements arise and organizations are created in rapid succession; witness the way in which the original ethnolinguistic liberation movements of the 1960s (black civil rights in the United States, bilingualism in Canada) have been followed by feminist, gay liberation, and animal-rights movements. All have stimulated the growth of organized interest groups that are an integral part of the contemporary political process.

An entire body of research, the "new social movements" literature, has been devoted to exploring the causes of this interest-group proliferation. Here we can mention only a few factors. One is the expansion of formal education. More people now have the skills required to run an organization—public speaking, keeping minutes and financial records, doing research on political issues, writing and submitting briefs to public officials. Another is the ongoing revolution in transportation and communication, which has dramatically lowered the costs of building and maintaining a national organization. With the advent of the jet airplane, the long-distance teleconference call, the fax machine, electronic mail, and so on, people can now create organizations that would not have been able to exist fifty years ago. The same technology has also revolutionized fundraising methods. Even relatively small groups can raise significant amounts of money through telephone solicitation and direct mail driven by computerized lists of target recipients. Finally, the growth of postmaterialism in the political culture has made organizing to achieve specific lifestyle objectives seem more mainstream; and this enhanced acceptability of interest-group activity in the political culture has created new sources of financial support from philanthropists, foundations, and government itself.

Ottawa is not the only Canadian city to witness the proliferation of interest groups. In provincial capitals and even at the municipal level, interest groups have become a key part of the political process. Many community or neighbourhood associations are politically active when city councils consider by-laws or otherwise make decisions that have an impact on their section of the city. As one writer has suggested, interest groups have become "creatures of mass political behavior."[2] With governments becoming more involved in all facets of social life, more groups are trying to influence legislation. The proliferation of interest groups is directly related to the extraordinary expansion of the state's role in the twentieth century.

Within the scope of this activity, how do we classify interest groups? One standard typology is the fourfold division of anomic, associational, institutional, and nonassociational groups.[3]

ANOMIC GROUPS

An **anomic group** forms spontaneously out of concern over a specific issue or issues. If, for example, an official from a foreign country visits Ottawa, and individuals happen to be opposed to government policies in that country, an organization may be formed to protest the visit. Demonstrations may occur at the airport or at meetings the official attends. The group organizes in response to a specific visit and makes its position known, but after the visit there is little reason for the organization to continue. Anomic groups may attract temporary publicity, but they are usually of little real importance, except as indicators of public opinion.

ASSOCIATIONAL GROUPS

An **associational group** has a continuing formal organization and seeks to articulate the interests of its members over long periods of time. Labour, farm, business, and professional groups are examples. They are able to marshal their various resources over time in order to achieve their ends. They are often the political arm of an organized group that already exists for other reasons, such as a trade union or professional association. This extra-political base, when it exists, is a vital source of workers, revenue, and continuity.

An important theoretical analysis by Mancur Olson suggests that the costs in time and money of organizing for political action often outweigh the benefits that an individual can expect to gain by lobbying.[4] This is another aspect of the free-rider problem discussed earlier in the book. Why should I spend my time working, for example, in an environmental association when the benefits of cleaner air and water will be enjoyed by all who live in the community, whether or not they contribute to the movement? It might be rational for me to contribute my time and money if I could be sure that others would do likewise, but how can I obtain that guarantee?

One answer is that when a group is already organized for other reasons, its incremental costs of entry into the political system may be much lower. A group may also provide nonpolitical benefits, such as the recreational activities sponsored by the Sierra Club.[5] In both these ways, pre-existing associations have an advantage in undertaking pressure-group activity. The prediction that pre-existing associations such as labour unions and professional associations should be formidable lobbyists seems to be borne out empirically.

᭙᭙᭙᭙᭙᭙᭙

INSTITUTIONAL GROUPS

An **institutional group** is an organization closely associated with government that acts internally to influence public decisions. Public-service unions and the military establishment are good examples. While these people are a part of government and are in theory politically neutral, they too have interests to articulate and specific ends to seek. The expansion of government's service activities has made these institutional groups far more numerous and influential than they used to be. Like associational groups, they have the advantage of continuity and permanent organization.

There are certain associational groups that, according to this classification, might almost be labelled "institutional" because of their close association with governments. Such ties are usually financial. Aboriginal and Métis associations are examples, as are francophone and anglophone minority-language associations in the provinces and multicultural ethnic societies. All such groups receive substantial financial support from the federal government, mainly through the Department of Canadian Heritage. They would not be nearly so influential, and perhaps would not even exist, without this funding.

Government support of interest groups first became important in Canada as part of Pierre Trudeau's "Just Society." The rationale for it was that Aboriginal peoples, women, and ethnic and linguistic minorities were disadvantaged or even oppressed groups that could not hope to compete on equal terms in the political marketplace. It was thought that giving them financial assistance to form interest groups would enable them to exert political pressure for economic and social reforms and thereby improve their position over the long run. Public support of interest groups was thus a logical corollary of reform liberalism.

Machiavelli once observed that gratitude is the weakest of human emotions. Perhaps it is not surprising that such federally funded interest groups have often become the severest critics of federal policy, sometimes in unexpected ways. For example, the National Action Committee on the Status of Women actively opposed most of the initiatives of the Mulroney government, including the FTA and NAFTA, the Charlottetown Accord, and many changes in social policy. NAC's funding from the federal government tracked downward during Mulroney's tenure but did not totally disappear.

These love–hate ties raise obvious questions about independence. Can these groups really look after the interests of their members when their very existence depends on government? Similarly, can government be expected to fund organizations and still scrupulously refrain from attempting to influence their policies? Such government funding tends to blur the lines between private and public spheres of activity. However, even with all its obvious pitfalls, it is a fact of increasing importance in pressure-group politics.

NONASSOCIATIONAL GROUPS

A **nonassociational group** is made up of individuals who feel close to one another on the basis of class, religion, race, culture, or some other distinctive quality. French Canadians, West Indians, Catholics, and Westerners are examples. Such groups lack formal organization and seldom function as coherent political groups, but all are often considered as if they were organized. The alternative term *latent group* captures their significance. The fact that such blocs are not formally organized does not mean that they will not organize themselves in certain circumstances. Politicians realize this, and take the interests of such groups into their calculations.

POLITICAL CONSULTANTS AND LOBBYING

The expansion of interest-group activity has given rise to a new profession, that of the **political consultant**.[6] Consultants are usually ex-politicians or civil servants who see the opportunity to put their expertise to work in the private sector. For a fee, they keep clients informed of new developments within government and advise them on how to pursue their goals effectively. After consultants have been retired from the public service long enough to avoid charges of conflict of interest, they may also engage in lobbying (see discussion that follows).

An advertisement in *The Globe and Mail* on January 22, 1993, illustrates this new industry. It announces the formation of the "Government Business Consulting Group," which will "provide strategic and government relations counsel to corporate clients." The chairman and chief executive officer is Fred Doucet, a college friend of Brian Mulroney who served a stint as chief of staff in the Prime Minister's Office. Other major figures are Jean-Jacques Blais, a former Liberal cabinet minister; Jack Manion, a retired civil servant who served in some of the highest positions in the federal bureaucracy; Lincoln Alexander, a former Conservative cabinet minister and former lieutenant governor of Ontario; and Judd Buchanan, a former Liberal cabinet minister. Doucet had been in the political consulting business for several years but was now bringing Liberals on board to prepare for the expected return of that party to power in Ottawa. Such interweaving of Liberals and Conservatives, who may have been bitter political opponents earlier in their careers, is not unusual. Consulting companies need to be able to work with governments of any stripe and to serve as wide a range of corporate clients as possible.

The term **lobbying** is derived from the old practice of individuals and groups but-tonholing MPs in the lobby of the British House of Commons. The practice now involves many different methods for influencing decisions: arranging an interview with a cabinet member, submitting a brief to a royal commission or parliamentary committee hearing, writing letters to elected representatives, advertising in the media to generate public pressure over an issue, and offering gifts of various kinds to public officials. In every case, the objective is the same: to influence governors and the public so that they will be favourably disposed to the interest group's position on an issue.

Lobbying has become an accepted part of today's political process. There are now about 2800 registered lobbyists in Canada and an undetermined number of lawyers, accountants, and other professionals who do informal lobbying on an occasional basis.[7] While the term carries certain derogatory connotations, many public officials admit that they depend on lobbyists as a source of information. Typically, elected officials depend on members of the administration or bureaucracy to supply the facts they require to make a political decision. But the administration has its own views and biases, or may not have all the information pertinent to a decision; as a result, resorting to lobbyists for a range of views has become a recognized part of politics. In this sense, interest group lobbying can be seen as a positive part of politics, in that it counters the entrenched views of bureaucrats or cabinet members.

The focus of lobbying depends on the institutional arrangements of government. In the United States, where Congress is a more autonomous body and is not controlled by party discipline, lobbyists concentrate on swaying the minds of individual representatives and senators. Such a strategy would have little payoff in Canada, or in other parliamentary systems in which elected representatives must vote according to party discipline. In those milieux the goal is to influence members of cabinet and the senior advisers of the prime minister. In all systems, however, lobbyists strive to cultivate good relations with the permanent civil servants, who influence government policy while elected politicians come and go. And in countries like the United States and Canada, where judicial review is an important factor in the political process, interest groups may also devote resources to sponsoring litigation.

⑀⑀⑀⑀⑀⑀⑀

DETERMINANTS OF INFLUENCE

An important question is why some groups are more influential in their lobbying than others. What makes an interest group powerful? A number of factors have been suggested: the size and cohesion of the group; its wealth, organizational abilities, and leadership; and the nature of the issue at hand. Let us examine each factor in turn.

Numbers cannot help but count in democratic politics, so legislators have to listen when a group represents a large membership. Groups often try to expand their membership in the hope of gaining more political influence. But numbers do not tell the whole story. For instance, organized labour represents one of the largest segments of our society. If it voted as a bloc, it could elect whomever it wanted in many constituencies and probably lobby better than any opponent. But organized labour has never operated as a fully cohesive body in Canadian politics. Numerical strength is obviously affected by the level of cohesion within the group.

Another adage in politics is that money talks; it requires financial resources to put together an effective interest group. Hiring consultants and lobbyists, maintaining an office, advertising, holding meetings—all these activities require funds on which the group can draw. A modestly funded group such as the National and Provincial Parks Association of Canada may want to undertake an advertising campaign across the country in order to make citizens aware of the value of parks, but putting ads in newspapers in major metropolitan centres is an expensive undertaking. Thus, groups whose supporters are relatively well-to-do start with a natural advantage, although that advantage may be reduced by other factors, such as the Canadian government's policy of funding groups that it considers disadvantaged.

It requires organizational skills to use the human resources of a large group effectively and to translate people's emotions into action. No matter how strongly people feel that taxes are too high, little will be gained by ad hoc and sporadic complaints to public officials. However, if individual responses are coordinated within a national organization such as the Canadian Taxpayers Federation, there is a much greater chance that they will have an impact on public policy. The federation publishes a newspaper that documents what it considers to be wasteful government spending, issues frequent releases to the media, holds conferences to teach its members effective methods of protest, makes submissions to government budget officers and legislative committees across the country, and in general tries to articulate public demands for tax reduction and steer policymakers in that direction. Other organizations proceed in much the same way to exert pressure on behalf of their own favourite causes.

Another factor is leadership. Leaders can inspire and direct the activities of the members by writing letters, donating money, and appearing at public hearings. Leadership often makes the difference between a political group that is effective and one that is not. Would the American consumer movement ever have become so powerful without Ralph Nader?

A final factor is the nature of the issue itself. The issue must have significant appeal to legislators and to the public, or there is little chance of obtaining results in politics. However, support must be interpreted dynamically rather than statically. When the antismoking movement began in the 1970s, it seemed to have little chance of success. More than half of North American adults smoked; and not only was smoking in public taken for granted, it was on the increase. For example, during the 1960s university students were successful in winning the right to smoke in class as part of a larger students' rights movement, and even many secondary schools set aside smoking rooms for their pupils. There was already substantial medical evidence about the harmful effects of smoking, but it made little impact on the public consciousness. Then, as part of wider trends involving diet, fitness, health and the environment, the medical evidence began to register, public opinion began to turn against smoking, and antismoking groups became highly successful lobbyists, achieving higher taxes on tobacco products, limitations on tobacco advertising, and restrictions on smoking in public places.

Invariably, most of these factors register on the positive side in any effective interest group. Provincial medical associations are an example. While their members are few in relation to the larger society, they are cohesive because their members share a common education and body of professional practices. They have great financial resources as well as excellent leaders and organizational capabilities. All this has made them effective lobbyists on the political scene.

INTEREST GROUPS AND THE POLITICAL SYSTEM

Let us make some general observations about the place of interest groups in contemporary liberal democracies. First, there is a correlation between interest-group activity and the guarantee of political freedom in a society. Without constitutional guarantees of free speech, a free press, and the right to assemble, the political activities of interest groups would be seriously jeopardized. Governments seldom cherish criticism, and a good portion of an interest group's activities involves criticizing proposed or existing laws and policies. Without immunity from reprisal, there would be considerably less enthusiasm for this type of public participation. Even in our own relatively free society, governments are sometimes accused of withholding vital information and even using intimidation.

Second, interest-group activity may be good "therapy" in the participatory society. While all groups cannot achieve all their ends in the political process, most of them are successful at least occasionally. The theory of group politics suggests in part that successful participation in the political process through interest-group activity reinforces confidence in the system. Group politics thus has the potential to enhance the legitimacy of the system in the minds of citizens. To deny groups an opportunity to participate in politics would be to undermine this perceived legitimacy.

The increase in the activity of interest groups is a fact, but it is also a fact that only a small number of people become activists in group politics. Are nonparticipants— those not affiliated with an interest group—excluded from the benefits of public decisions? Certainly to some extent, but perhaps not entirely, because the unorganized still have the potential to organize and therefore constitute latent interests.[8] In other words, when public officials distribute benefits through the political process, they cannot afford to bypass unorganized interests totally, because the unorganized are voters and have the potential to become organized into effective groups.

Political freedom has nurtured a great deal of interest-group activity, with the benefits described above; yet there are ways in which interest groups may damage the community. For one thing, interest-group activity is closely interwoven with a distributive approach to politics in which political activity represents an exchange: voters render their support (votes) to politicians, and politicians in turn enact programs and policies for the benefit of those groups that support them. Although this may be an accurate account of much that occurs in the politics of liberal democracy, it is hard to view it without concern. Liberal democracy as a form of government rests ultimately on the notion that these are universal laws that apply equally to all citizens. It is this general equality before the law that justifies equal political rights for all citizens. But aggressive interest-group activity may easily become a pursuit of special privileges, which is inimical to equality before the law. Manufacturers of certain products lobby for protective tariffs to prevent consumers from buying cheaper foreign products. Organized labour uses collective-bargaining legislation to win for itself benefits denied to the rest of the workforce. Organized farmers use their political power to get government to set up marketing boards to raise prices in their favour. As one special-interest group succeeds in its objectives, other interests may be stimulated to organize themselves for entry into the lobbying contest. If this process continues over many decades, a society of equality before the law can transform itself into a society of entrenched privilege, with each interest group jealously defending its special prerogatives.

A related phenomenon is the tendency to politicize issues. Once groups learn that they can use government to their particular advantage, they tend to begin looking for political rather than economic or social solutions to problems. For example, owners of declining industries, faced with severe competition from foreign producers, may seek protective tariffs and quotas rather than new outlets for their

Interest-group politics can be seen positively as part of the tendency toward democratization in modern society. The increase in the number of effective interest groups has probably produced a more nearly level playing field in politics. As more people participate in politics, the number of interest groups grows accordingly. Environmental groups and women's groups are current examples of different segments of the population organizing around new political issues.

But interest-group politics also has a negative aspect. The playing field in the competition of interest groups is not perfectly level. Some have greater financial resources or better access to the levers of power and therefore get more than their fair share of benefits. Yet, imagining modern participatory politics without interest groups would be impossible. So, to curb the possibilities of unfairness in the operations of interest groups, there has been a growing tendency toward public regulation of interest-group activity, including public identification as well as tighter definitions of conflict of interest on the part of politicians and civil servants.

capital. Similarly, the workers in such industries may pressure government to protect their jobs by propping up or even nationalizing faltering companies. What were once economic matters decided in the marketplace can become political issues decided by a preponderance of power. Politicization can jeopardize the fundamental liberal concept of the limited state by injecting government into more and more realms of social activity. If each group single-mindedly pursues its own interests, all groups together may bring about a general situation that none of them would ever have chosen in the first place.

For reasons like this, some analysts see interest-group politics as a long-term threat to liberal democracy. Legislators at all levels of government have voiced the concern that powerful lobbying by special interests can dominate the process for distributing public goods and services. Mancur Olson suggests that small but cohesive organizations with a single purpose have a great capacity for influencing public officials. Because the goals of these groups are usually self-centred, they may create economic inefficiency for the larger society. Privileges granted to these interests may in fact lead to a decline in the well-being of a national economy.

Political thinkers at the dawn of the democratic era were acutely aware of these problems. Rousseau went as far as wishing to outlaw organized groups:

But when cabals and partial associations are formed at the expense of the great association, the will of each such association, though general with regard to its members, is private with regard to the State. It is therefore of the utmost importance for obtaining the expression of the general will, that no partial society should be formed in the State, and that every citizen should speak his opinion entirely from himself.[9]

Rousseau's view was that individuals, taken singly, could exercise their political responsibilities in the spirit of what he called the "general will"—that is, the good of the whole community—but that the formation of groups fostered a selfish spirit of particular advantage.

Rousseau's diagnosis was undoubtedly shrewd, but his remedy of banning private associations was extreme and perhaps totalitarian in its implications. James Madison suggested a more moderate approach in *The Federalist*, where he discussed interest groups, which in his time were called **factions**:

> By a faction, I understand a number of citizens, whether amounting to a majority or minority of the whole, who are united and actuated by some common impulse of passion, or of interest, adverse to the rights of other citizens, or to the permanent aggregate interests of the community.[10]

Madison realized that factions could not be banned without destroying liberty itself. His remedy (which Rousseau had also accepted as a second-best solution) was to promote the existence of a great number and variety of factions, so as to maintain an approximate balance or equilibrium among them. This fundamentally defensive strategy is based on the hope that a drive for special privilege by one group will generate contrary political pressure from other groups that stand to be adversely affected.

FURTHER READING

Ball, Alan R., and Frances Millard. *Pressure Politics in Industrial Societies*. Basingstoke, U.K.: Macmillan, 1986.

Carty, R. Kenneth, ed. *Canadian Political Party Systems: A Reader*. Broadview Press: Peterborough, Ont., 1992.

Coleman, William, and Grace Skogstad. *Policy Communities and Public Policy in Canada: A Structural Approach*. Mississauga, Ont.: Copp Clark Pitman, 1990.

Duverger, Maurice. *Party Politics and Pressure Groups: A Comparative Introduction*. New York: Thomas Y. Crowell, 1972.

Finkle, Peter, et al. *Federal Government Relations with Interest Groups: A Reconsideration*. Ottawa: Supply and Services Canada, 1994.

Greenwood, Justin, et al., eds. *Organized Interests and the European Community*. London: Sage, 1992.

Hayes, Michael T. *Lobbyists and Legislators: A Theory of Political Markets*. New Brunswick, N.J.: Rutgers University Press, 1981.

Knoke, David. *Organizing for Collective Action: The Political Economies of Associations*. New York: Aldine De Gruyter, 1990.

Kwavnick, David. *Organized Labour and Pressure Politics: The Canadian Labour Congress 1956–1968*. Montreal/Kingston: McGill-Queen's University Press, 1972.

Moe, Terry M. *The Organization of Interests*. Chicago: University of Chicago Press, 1980.

Olson, Mancur. *The Logic of Collective Action*, rev. ed. Cambridge, Mass.: Harvard University Press, 1971.

Ornstein, Norman J., and Shirley Elder. *Interest Groups, Lobbying and Policymaking*. Washington, D.C.: Congressional Quarterly Press, 1978.

Petracca, Mark P., ed. *The Politics of Interests: Interest Groups Transformed*. Boulder, Colo.: Westview Press, 1992.

Pross, Paul A. *Group Politics and Public Policy*, 2nd ed. Toronto: Oxford University Press, 1992.

———. *Governing Under Pressure*. Toronto: Institute of Public Administration of Canada, 1982.

———. ed. *Pressure Group Behavior in Canadian Politics*. Toronto: McGraw-Hill Ryerson, 1975.

Richardson, J.J., and A.G. Jordan. *Governing under Pressure: The Policy Process in Post-Parliamentary Democracy*. Oxford: Martin Robertson, 1979.

Rothenberg, Lawrence S. *Linking Citizens to Government: Interest Group Politics at Common Cause*. Cambridge, England: Cambridge University Press, 1992.

Sawatsky, John. *The Insiders: Government, Business, and the Lobbyists*. Toronto: McClelland and Stewart, 1987.

Seidle, F. Leslie, ed. *Interest Groups and Elections in Canada*. Royal Commission on Electoral Reform and Party Financing, vol. 2. Toronto: Dundurn Press, 1991.

Thompson, Fred, and W.T. Stanbury. *The Political Economy of Interest Groups in the Legislative Process in Canada*. Ottawa: Institute for Research on Public Policy, 1979.

Truman, David B. *The Governmental Process*. New York: Knopf, 1958.

Walker, Jack L., Jr. *Mobilizing Interest Groups in America: Patrons, Professions, and Social Movements*. Ann Arbor, Mich.: University of Michigan Press, 1991.

Willetts, Peter, ed. *Pressure Politics in Contemporary Britain*. Lexington, Mass.: D.C. Heath, 1978.

———. *Interest Groups: Policy and Politics in America*. Englewood Cliffs, N.J.: Prentice-Hall, 1985.

Wilson, Graham K. *Interest Groups*. Oxford: Blackwell, 1990.

Wright, John R. *Interest Groups and Congress: Lobbying, Contributions, and Influence*. Boston: Allyn and Bacon, 1996.

POLITICAL PARTIES

Political parties are an essential feature of politics in the modern age of mass participation. In liberal–democratic systems, they help to keep governments accountable to public opinion. In totalitarian or authoritarian governments, they help the government maintain its hold on power. In either case, political parties are an important link between government and the people.

In historical terms, political parties are a rather recent phenomenon, having evolved with the extension of the franchise. In the eighteenth century, the Tories and Whigs dominated the British Parliament as political clubs of the upper class. They had little in the way of strong connections with the general population. But as the Reform Acts of 1832, 1867, and 1884 extended suffrage to most adult males, these clubs were transformed to accommodate the influx of voters, and the Conservative and Liberal Parties were formed. The tendency toward greater mass participation continued with the development of the Labour Party in the late nineteenth century as a party of the working class. By the 1930s, it had replaced the Liberals as the principal competitor to the Conservatives, leaving the Liberals a third and minor party in the British system.

A political party performs so many tasks in the political process that it is difficult to establish a simple definition. However, Joseph LaPalombara's working definition can serve as a point of departure:

> A political party is a formal organization whose self-conscious, primary purpose is to place and maintain in public office persons who will control, alone or in coalition, the machinery of government.[1]

These organizations are not usually part of the formal–legal machinery of government. In most Western nations, they do not derive power from a constitution. Any power they have depends on how the electorate responds in elections. However, there is an increasing tendency in many countries for political parties to be drawn into the formal sphere of government. In Canada, for instance, certain types of donations to parties are tax-deductible, while party finances are regulated by government and subject to disclosure laws. Their very success as informal institutions is pushing them toward formal–legal status.

The first and most important goal of the political party in a democratic system is electoral success. An election win entitles the party to dominate the governmental machinery and perhaps enact some of the proposals to which it is committed. Electoral success short of outright victory may enable it to participate in a coalition government and thus achieve at least some of its aims.

A number of other roles complement the primary objective of winning power. A political party is the mechanism by which candidates are chosen to run for public office. A person may choose to run as an independent, but almost all successful candidates for public office are selected by party machinery. A related role is to influence voters during campaigns. A great deal of the work of a party organization involves trying to get voters to support its candidates.

At the governmental level, the members elected with the support of the party put forward and pass legislative proposals in the assembly. Obviously, in a parliamentary body of 301 members (Canada) or 651 members (United Kingdom), there must be some organization. The cabinet of the governing party determines which legislative proposals are to be considered, drafted, debated, and (the governing party hopes) passed.

The party also acts as an intermediary between elected members and the public, that is, between people and their government. While the bulk of party activity occurs at election time, this continuous interchange between people and government can be an important function of the party.

Finally, the political party provides a training ground for political leaders. The party ranks are a pool from which political leaders are recruited. Party workers in constituency organizations often choose to run for office; if elected, they may work their way up from the backbenches to a ministerial post. In Canada, however, there has been a tendency in recent decades for leaders of the major national parties to be brought in "sideways," as it were. Pierre Trudeau was a university professor and journalist before being invited into the cabinet and was chosen leader after only three years in Parliament. Brian Mulroney had long been a Conservative activist and insider, but had never held an elected office before becoming Conservative leader. John Turner came back from political retirement to lead the Liberals, a feat that Jean Chrétien repeated in 1990. It may be that, in our age of mass media, a new face at the top is more of an advantage than continuity.

The most important function of the democratic political party is the aggregation of demands. Interest groups make a great many demands on government, and it is never possible for a government to meet all of them, mainly because many of the demands are mutually incompatible. For example, organized consumer groups will demand that import quotas on shoes be abolished, while manufacturers will demand that those quotas be made more restrictive. The political party is a forum at which conflicting interests may be at least partially reconciled, where compromises can be reached and then bundled into a program that most party supporters can accept.

In authoritarian or totalitarian systems, the party also aggregates demands to some extent, although because of the lack of political freedom, this must be done behind the scenes. Specialists in Soviet politics often suggested that the monolithic façade of the Communist Party concealed squabbling factions representing such interests as the military and agriculture. More obvious is the totalitarian party's function of promoting support for the regime. The party is the government's instrument for enhancing popular acceptance of its policies. To this end, the party coordinates publicity in the mass media, organizes meetings and demonstrations, and carries out persuasion through its cells in workplaces.

It must be remembered that we are speaking of political parties in general. Not all parties perform all of the above roles, and the roles may be played in different ways. For example, the role of political parties in the Canadian system has changed over time. They remain the primary vehicle through which politicians are recruited, and they continue to mobilize the electorate at election time. But their function has changed in the area of policy formation. Most policy proposals come from the political executive—the prime minister and other cabinet ministers and their personal advisers—or from the permanent administration. The work of developing policy proposals is not so much the effort of the party as it is of the senior people working for members of cabinet, some of whom may not even belong to the party organization. Thus, while local, regional, provincial, and national party organizations meet and make policy recommendations to the party leadership, the policy proposals that emerge from the government may not reflect opinions at the grassroots level of the party. This is why most analysts now agree that the role of political parties in the legislative process has declined and that the executive and bureaucracy are now more influential.

Because no two parties function in the same way, it is necessary to have a scheme of classification. Without pretending to be definitive, the following typology captures some of the main types: pragmatic, ideological, interest, personal, and movement parties.

THE PRAGMATIC PARTY

One of the more common types in Western society is the **pragmatic party.** The dictionary defines pragmatism as a philosophy of action in which "truth is ... tested by the practical consequences of belief."[2] In other words, a pragmatist is not concerned with truth as expressed in a doctrine, but in the consequences of how something works. A pragmatic political party is concerned primarily with programs that the public views as solutions to problems. The pragmatic party gears its campaign promises not to beliefs founded on doctrine, but to programs that it believes have the greatest appeal to the public. It is thus open to the criticism of having no principles and of moving with the wind, and its programs sometimes appear to reflect nothing more than a cynical desire for power.

The mass parties in the Anglo–American tradition are generally classified as pragmatic: Conservatives and Labour in Great Britain, Progressive Conservatives and Liberals in Canada, Republicans and Democrats in the United States. The pragmatism of such parties always generates confusion about where they stand. Brian Mulroney's Conservatives, for example, were attacked by voices on the left for pursuing a "right-wing, neoconservative" agenda; yet organizations on the right, such as the Fraser Institute and the National Citizens' Coalition, condemned Mulroney for failing to implement a conservative agenda. Pragmatic parties sometimes appear more ideological—as the British Conservatives did under Margaret Thatcher—but this usually reflects not so much a fundamental change in the party as the temporary ascendancy of one faction within it. With the passage of time, the party usually reverts to a more pragmatic and less ideological stance, as happened when John Major replaced Thatcher as leader.

When pragmatic parties compete head to head, they characteristically make overlapping proposals, even to the extent of borrowing each other's ideas. For example, when Pierre Trudeau imposed a three-year program of general wage and price controls in 1975, he was implementing an important part of the Conservative platform from the election of 1974, even though he had ridiculed the idea during that campaign. The proposal for a comprehensive Free Trade Agreement with the United States arose from a royal commission appointed by Trudeau and chaired by Donald Macdonald, a former Liberal cabinet minister. Brian Mulroney opposed the idea when he was running for the leadership of the Conservatives, but later adopted it as the most important policy initiative of his first term in office. The Liberals strenuously opposed the Free Trade Agreement while it was being negotiated, but Jean Chrétien's government gave it final approval for implementation.

This mutual borrowing is not confined to particular policies; it also extends to broader party positions. Between the 1950s and the 1970s, the welfare state and government interventionism were dominant ideas, and the pragmatic parties of the right had to accept them or face electoral extinction. "We are all Keynesians now," said Republican Richard Nixon when he was president. But during the 1980s and 1990s, when the fiscal difficulties of the welfare state led to the revival of conservatism, the pragmatic parties of the left had to come to terms with privatization, deregulation, and balanced budgets. Bill Clinton was elected president in 1992 at least partly because he acknowledged the importance of traditional conservative objectives such as reducing the deficit, tightening up welfare programs, and enhancing business competitiveness; indeed, he claimed to be more able than

President Bush to attain these ends, albeit using different means. One reason the Labour Party regained power in the British election of 1997 was its promise to leave Margaret Thatcher's reforms undisturbed.

This is not to say that a Democratic (or Liberal or Labour) government will behave exactly like a Republican (or Conservative) government. There will be many differences in practice because every party represents a different coalition of interests, and this will require different payoffs from the party in power. But it will be difficult to interpret the outcomes in consistent ideological terms.

Ideally, a pragmatic party ought to be able to adapt to changes in the electorate's priorities and demands by shifting its platform accordingly. However, inertia is a factor. When party policies become entrenched over a period of years, it may be very difficult for the leadership to alter programs and priorities to fit voters' new expectations. Instances of this have occurred in Canada, Great Britain, and the United States over the past decade.

In Canada, the federal Liberals and Conservatives have governed since World War II, frequently using deficit spending as a way to stimulate economic growth. But the accumulation of debt provided fertile ground for the Reform Party, which proceeded to make inroads into the system by positioning itself as the most resolute opponent of deficit spending. In Great Britain, the control of the left over the British Labour Party in the early 1980s led to the exit of more moderate elements to form the Social Democrats. In fact, the Labour Party was not able to regain competitive status with the Conservatives until more moderate elements regained control. In the 1992 national election in the United States, the economy was not in good shape, and neither Republicans nor Democrats appeared to be addressing issues perceived to be important in the eyes of the public. That is why Ross Perot's blunt message about attacking deficit spending appealed to a number of voters. His ability to garner 19 percent of the popular vote in the presidential race indicated substantial voter dissatisfaction with the major parties, which were slow to adapt to the politics of the 1990s.

THE IDEOLOGICAL PARTY

The **ideological party,** in contrast, emphasizes ideological purity more than the immediate attainment of power. Party doctrine is even more important than electoral success. Such parties are criticized, of course, for their inflexibility. Often they put doctrine before the wishes of the voters, convinced that in time voters will come around to their way of thinking. The Communist Party is a good example of an ideological party, as are socialist parties and even some social democratic parties. On the right, some conservative parties are as doctrinaire as any on the left.

The New Democratic Party is the most ideological of the traditional Canadian parties, as shown by the clarity of several of its major policy commitments: cancellation of the Free Trade Agreement, abolition of the GST in favour of higher taxes on corporations and high-income earners, reregulation of air passenger travel. The Reform Party is understood by most observers to be an ideological party of the right, in that it also presents a simple, doctrinaire program: balancing of the federal budget, reduction of taxes and government spending, abolition of official bilingualism, the introduction of recall legislation, and so on. More careful observers, however, have noted that Reform Party positions are often phrased with a "calculated ambiguity" that suggests a pragmatic party in waiting.[3] For example, the party's recall proposal requires that the petition to hold a by-election receive the signatures of at least 50 percent of the enumerated voters in a constituency—a threshold high enough to ensure that few recalls will ever take place.[4]

〰〰〰〰〰〰

THE INTEREST PARTY

Another type of party is the **interest party**. Here we find people converting their interest group into a full-fledged political party that runs candidates and attempts to obtain power. Such a group feels that it can best achieve its ends by acting as a party rather than trying to influence existing parties, but its narrow basis of support makes it hard for it to win control of the state. In Australia, the National Party (previously known as the Country Party) began as a farmers' party. There have also been peasants' parties in Eastern Europe and Latin America. In Scandinavia, industrialists have formed conservative parties. And in Great Britain, the Labour Party began as an interest party that focused on the welfare of the working class. In the first half of the twentieth century, labour was the largest single group in British society; if all workers had supported the Labour Party, it would easily have won every election. Workers, however, have never voted as a bloc. To expand its appeal to other segments of society and keep pace with the Conservatives, the party had to become more pragmatic. In Canada, the NDP is sort of a cross between an interest party and an ideological party. Some locals of the Canadian Labour Congress (CLC) are affiliated with the NDP, but they have never completely controlled the party; and the relationship with organized labour was seriously weakened by Ontario NDP premier Bob Rae's "social contract" legislation, which had the effect of revising collective agreements previously negotiated by public-sector unions.

There is vigorous debate about the merits of pragmatic, ideological, and interest parties. Some believe that pragmatic parties contribute to the stability of the political system—that they cover the waterfront, so to speak, in their response to demands made by groups in society. These parties endeavour to include something for everyone in their platforms. They appeal to diverse groups—employers and labour unions, farmers and consumers, conservationists and developers. Many people see pragmatic parties as mechanisms for aggregating interests and mending the fault lines in a pluralistic society.

Those who advocate the virtues of interest and ideological parties make their arguments from the standpoint of representation. They are quite critical of pragmatic parties, suggesting that by making broad appeals to all groups, such parties dilute their platforms so that in the end they represent no one. This is the position taken by Maurice Duverger, the noted authority on political parties, whose comparative work is still basic in the field.[5] An interest or ideological party, according to this view, can make its platform specific by catering to a single interest or a group with a defined ideology. Political parties of this type are able to offer voters a clear choice, and elected members have a responsibility to a specific clientele. But what is made up in representation could be lost in stability. The advocates of pragmatic parties suggest that interest and ideological parties tend to intensify cleavages in society rather than reconcile them. Moreover, when these parties are not willing to compromise at the legislative level, little is accomplished, and governmental instability and inaction may well result.

In fact, both pragmatic parties and interest or ideological parties have shown themselves capable of aggregating interests and reconciling conflicts. In the Anglo–American model of pragmatic parties, the resolution of conflicts takes place within the party. Labour, business, and agricultural organizations come to some sort of compromise with the government of the day, which is almost always formed by a single party. In contrast, in democracies where coalition governments of ideological or interest parties are the norm, interest reconciliation takes place among parties. Parties do not have to surrender their principles internally, but they have to make compromises to keep a coalition cabinet in power. This illustrates the general principle that the necessary functions of the political process may be accomplished in quite different ways in different systems. Any successful political system must resolve conflicts of interest among different social groups; but this task can be carried out within parties, among parties, or by other institutions in the governmental process. The method may not matter very much as long as the job gets done. The advantage of approaching politics as a process is that one becomes sensitive to relationships of this type and learns to look at institutions not in isolation but rather as they relate to other institutions.

᎒᎒᎒᎒᎒᎒᎒

THE PERSONAL PARTY

Another type of party is the **personal party,** which is founded around a single, influential political leader. After World War II, supporters of Charles de Gaulle formed the Gaullist Party, which became the strongest political force in France after de Gaulle established the Fifth Republic in 1958. With the support of this party, called the Union for the Defence of the Republic (UDR), de Gaulle was elected president in 1958 and 1965. The Gaullists, under a variety of party names, survived the general's retirement in 1969 and today represent a coalition of moderate conservatives. Juan Perón of Argentina also developed a political party from his personal following. His supporters elected him president in 1946 and 1951. Perón, however, was removed from office after a *coup d'état* in 1955. The Peronistas were the main force behind the election of President Carlos Menem in 1989, which shows again that personal parties need not die with their founders.

Personal parties are common in the Third World, particularly in Africa. Jomo Kenyatta of Kenya was one of the chief architects of KANU—the Kenya African National Union. KANU provided a base of support for Kenyatta, who attempted to use the party to integrate Kenya's many tribal groups. Kenyatta died in 1978, but his party has remained the dominant force in Kenya. For years Robert Mugabe of Zimbabwe dreamed of establishing his Zimbabwe African National Union–Patriotic Front (ZANU–PF) as the single party under which racial and ethnic groups would be united. This was accomplished in December 1987, when he agreed on a merger with Joshua Nkomo's Zimbabwe African People's Union (ZAPU). Nkomo agreed to take a senior ministerial post and be vice president of the party. A number of political groups, many of which are fragments of old political parties, continue to oppose ZANU-PF, but in 1996 Mugabe was elected president for another six years.

All these examples show that the personal party, like the other types of parties, is not an entirely clear-cut category. All parties have leaders who are usually quite prominent even in a thoroughly democratic party; and even the most dominating leader has to have an organization to be effective. Thus parties that may be considered personal vehicles at the outset often evolve into long-lasting pragmatic, ideological, or interest parties.

THE MOVEMENT PARTY

A **movement party** is a political movement that evolves into a party apparatus. A movement is a union of people that aims at a profound social change, such as national independence, but does not itself aspire to govern. A movement sometimes is converted into a party when the prestige it gains by achieving its goals makes it a logical choice to become the government. The Congress Party in India is a good example. The Indian National Congress, organized in 1885, became the instrument by which Indians sought independence from Great Britain. The party became the focus of nationalist feeling throughout India and mobilized popular pressure against the British. After achieving independence in 1947, it became the dominant political force in the federal Parliament, a position that it long maintained, although it has slipped a good deal during the 1990s. In Canada, the Bloc Québécois could be considered a movement party. Its only real program is the sovereignty of Quebec. If it ever achieves this goal, it will probably break up into ideological factions. In the meantime, it is using the House of Commons as a forum for promoting the independence of Quebec.

POLITICAL PARTY SYSTEMS

Political party systems also influence the manner in which parties carry out their roles. There are basically three types of party systems: one-party, two-party, and multiparty.

The One-Party System

This type includes true **single-party systems** and **one-party-dominant systems**. In the former, there is only one party in the political system, and no political alternative is legally tolerated. The Communist Party of the Soviet Union, whose leading role was guaranteed in the Constitution, was the classic example. Where political leaders are building a utopian order according to an ideological blueprint, political opposition becomes heresy. Under such conditions any political alternative is prohibited. There are also a great many noncommunist single-party systems—for example, in Zimbabwe, Tanzania, and Iraq.

In a one-party-dominant state, a single political party dominates the political process without the official support of the state. While a number of minor parties offer political alternatives, the electorate usually votes overwhelmingly for the dominant party. The Institutionalized Revolutionary Party (PRI) of Mexico is an example. After the Mexican Revolution began in 1910, a fierce struggle occurred during which many leaders, such as Pancho Villa and Emiliano Zapata, fought to gain control of the national government. Plutarco Calles consolidated power in the late 1920s and developed a party organization that in time emerged as the PRI. The party today claims to stand as a symbol of the ongoing revolution. Its critics suggest that the party is more institutionalized than revolutionary. Opposition is not outlawed, but the PRI has maintained power by clever use of the state apparatus, and especially through patronage and corruption. While the PRI has not yet lost a presidential election, electoral reforms initiated under President Ernesto Zedillo will, no doubt, make the electoral process more competitive in the future.

Finally, there are times when one party dominates without in any way using the state machinery to support its position. For whatever reason, voters seem content with a single party for long periods of time. The Democrats dominated the American South for a century after the Civil War. In Canada, the province of Alberta has had the curious habit of endorsing one party for long periods, then suddenly turning to another. Since 1905, no party in Alberta, having once formed a government and then lost an election, has ever returned to power. The result has been a sequence of one-party-dominant situations rather than sustained competition between two or more credible contenders.

Canadian federal politics also seems to have entered a one-party-dominant phase with the election of 1993, as confirmed by the results of the 1997 election. The Liberals are now the only party able to elect MPs in all regions of the country, while each of the other parties has a much narrower geographic and demographic base. The Bloc Québécois appeals only to francophones in Quebec. Reform is strong in the West but unable to win appreciable numbers of seats elsewhere. The NDP has pockets of support in inner-city ridings, in strongholds of organized labour, and, since the 1997 election, for the first time in Atlantic Canada. The Progressive Conservatives won seats in 1997 in Atlantic Canada and rural Quebec, but could add only one seat in Ontario and one in the West to their newfound base (see Chapter 28). In this one-party-plus configuration, the Liberals may remain dominant for a long time unless there is some consolidation among the other parties.

The Two-Party System

A **two-party system** exists when two parties are credible contenders for power and either is capable of winning any election. The United Kingdom and the United States are commonly cited as illustrations, but neither is literally a two-party system.

In Britain, the Conservatives and Labour have been challenged by the Liberal Democrats, plus several regional parties operating in Scotland, Wales, and Northern Ireland respectively. In the American election of 1992, Ross Perot, an independent candidate for president, received 19 percent of the popular vote, although he did not get any electoral votes. Perot then transformed his movement into a more conventional political party, borrowing the name Reform Party from Canada. When he ran for president again in 1996, however, he received only 9 percent of the popular vote and again collected no votes in the Electoral College.

In Britain and the United States, there have been many third parties, but they have rarely gained enough popular support to threaten the two major parties. Thus, when we speak of a two-party system, we mean that victory at the polls is likely to go to the Conservatives or Labour (or to the Democrats or Republicans), even though minor parties may also contest the election. Where there are also minor parties, it might be more accurate to call these systems **two-party-plus systems**, as some observers do.

Germany furnishes an example of two-party-plus politics. The Christian Democrats and Social Democrats there are so evenly matched at the polls that the small Free Democratic Party often determines who will govern by throwing its parliamentary weight to one side or the other.

Canada was close to a strict two-party system in the first fifty years of Confederation. From 1867 to 1917, only the Conservatives and Liberals mattered in federal politics. But from 1921 onwards, there have always been more than two parties represented in the House of Commons. The Progressives were the first successful third party, followed by Social Credit and the CCF, which both entered the House of Commons in 1935. The CCF continues in the form of the NDP, while more recently we have also seen the rise of the Bloc Québécois and the Reform Party. Indeed, as suggested above, the system may now be closer to being a one-party-plus than a two-party-plus system.

The two-party system is widely praised as a source of political stability, especially in parliamentary systems, in which the cabinet must maintain the confidence of an elected assembly. A two-party system is likely to yield majority governments that can hold office for a respectable length of time. Less convincing is the common argument that a two-party system serves the interests of voters by offering them a clear choice between two responsible aspirants to power. Parties in two-party systems are often highly pragmatic, so that for long periods of time their platforms may greatly resemble each other, giving voters little real choice. American and Canadian politics are like this at most elections. This is not to say that the two-party system is necessarily any worse than the multiparty alternative—only that it is not as obviously superior as newspaper editorials in the Anglo–American democracies often maintain.

The Multiparty System

In a **multiparty system**, three or more political parties have a realistic chance of participating in government. In most cases, the parties are either interest parties or ideological parties, which consider the interests of their supporters their first priority. Sweden is a multiparty system. From left to right on the political spectrum, the political parties there are the Communists, Social Democrats, Liberals, Agrarians, Conservatives, and New Democrats. The Communists and Social Democrats are generally backed by workers and intellectuals, the Liberals by professionals and bureaucrats, the Agrarians by farmers, the Conservatives by big business, and the New Democrats by small business and the self-employed.

Cabinet instability is common in parliamentary systems in which there are many parties. When representatives are drawn from a number of parties, majority governments are difficult to come by, and coalition governments may become the norm. Where the parties in a coalition government hold to principle and refuse to compromise, governments tend to change frequently. This was the case in the Fourth Republic of France in the 1950s, which saw thirteen governments in one period of eighteen months. The same is true of Italy, which has averaged about one government a year since the end of World War II.

However, generalizations seldom apply universally in political science. Instability does not occur in all multiparty systems. The multiparty systems of Denmark, Norway, and Sweden, for example, have usually produced durable coalitions that cannot be characterized as unstable. The difference has an interesting and logical explanation. Italy and Portugal have had large extremist parties of both the left and the right. Some of these parties are fundamentally opposed to the constitution and, hence, are not acceptable coalition partners; this restricts the number of possible coalitions. When a working partnership among parties breaks down, there may be no alternative to re-establishing it, except perhaps by replacing the cabinet. The result is a game of political musical chairs in which cabinets succeed each other with monotonous regularity. In contrast, the Scandinavian countries do not have large extremist parties. All important parties are acceptable coalition partners, so there is more room to manoeuvre and create durable coalitions.

It should also be noted that cabinet instability in multiparty systems may be more apparent than real. The Christian Democrats were the senior partner in all the Italian coalitions from the end of World War II to the mid-1990s, and ministers often ended up with the same posts after a new coalition was formed. In addition, the civil service provided administrative continuity even when the cabinet was in transition. In fact, the Italian system was so stable, with no alternation whatsoever of ruling parties, that corruption became endemic and a new electoral law was adopted in 1993 with the goal of making politics more competitive.

𝕤𝕤𝕤𝕤𝕤𝕤𝕤

ASSESSING POLITICAL PARTIES

Political parties developed while the franchise was expanding in the nineteenth and twentieth centuries, and they have helped to legitimize mass democracy. But this does not mean that all political parties are mass organizations with every voter holding a membership; on the contrary, in most Western societies the actual number of party members is very small. In Canada, less than 5 percent of voters belong to any federal or provincial party. Moreover, most of those who do are in the middle and upper-middle income brackets, are relatively well educated, and generally feel they have a great deal at stake in the political process. For this reason, political parties have been criticized as representing not the masses but the social and economic elite in society. Indeed, when one examines a sociological profile of party activists, the criticism may seem valid. Oligarchies of a kind do run political parties.

This point was made early in the century by Roberto Michels in his classic work *Political Parties*. Michels argued that even the parties that talked the most about democracy, such as the social democratic parties of his day, inevitably fell under the control of small, self-perpetuating elites. He went so far as to state that an "iron law of oligarchy" represented the real truth about democracy.[6]

However, the charge of elitism conveys the idea of a group closed off from the rest of society by restricted membership; and this is not really the case with political parties in most Western democracies. While there may be only a few militants, and they may represent the upper echelons of society, the doors of party organizations are not closed. On the contrary, anyone who pays the nominal membership fee is welcomed with open arms, and anyone who volunteers for party work is quickly inundated with tasks. The ranks of political parties are filled by a few middle-class activists because they are the ones who choose to become involved. Many people simply may not have an interest in the mundane tasks that accompany political party membership. In most cases, the individual reward or payoff for party work is relatively small when measured against the effort involved.

It has also been argued that in election-oriented parties, a small elite cannot get away with pursuing its narrow interest.[7] The necessity of winning elections forces political parties to aggregate as many interests as possible under the party banner. The only way to win elections in modern politics is by building a broad political base.

In another sense, however, parties are elitist. Modern political competition depends heavily on public relations, advertising, polling, and fundraising—the so-called "black arts" of politics. These tasks require special skills and connections possessed by only a few insiders. While there may be many ordinary people serving as foot soldiers in the trenches of political warfare, the commanders and strategists are well-paid, well-connected people possessing unusual skills.

Be that as it may, we are seeing a remarkable proliferation of new political parties in Western Europe and North America. On the left, the main entrants are the "Green" parties, which represent environmentalism as a rising political issue. There are also a number of "new" socialist parties, which are actually recycled versions of older communist parties. On the right, the picture is even more complex. New "populist" conservative parties have emerged recently in several countries; for example, the New Democracy in Sweden, the Northern League in Italy, and the Reform Party in Canada. These parties tend to be market-oriented, to advocate direct democracy, to be opposed to large-scale immigration, and to be rather antagonistic to corporations, trade unions, government bureaucracies, and other large organizations. Further to the right are nationalistic, even racist, parties like the National Front of Jean Le Pen in France, the Republican Party in Germany, and the Freedom Party in Austria.

At one level, these new parties are responding to emerging issues. Green parties are responding to environmental concerns; populist conservative parties are driven by the fiscal problems of the welfare state; and nationalist–racist parties represent a backlash against the flood of refugees and other immigrants into Western Europe. But at another level, this does not explain why the established parties have not responded adequately to these new issues, as they have to other emerging issues in previous decades.

Without pretending to give a complete answer to this difficult question, we would draw attention to one factor that is surely involved, namely the rise of post-materialism as discussed in an earlier chapter. Voters influenced by the postmaterialist political culture are more concerned about self-expression and less willing to defer to the compromises engineered by political brokers. This points toward the emergence of new political parties catering to the demands of a more diverse, opinionated, and fractious electorate.

FURTHER READING

Ajzenstat, Janet, and Peter J. Smith, eds. *Canada's Origins: Liberal, Tory, or Republican?* Ottawa: Carleton University Press, 1995.

Archer, Keith, and Alan Whitehorn. *Canadian Trade Unions and the New Democratic Party*. Kingston: Industrial Relations Centre, 1993.

Bakvis, Herman, ed. *Canadian Political Parties: Leaders, Candidates and Organization*. Royal Commission on Electoral Reform and Party Financing, vol. 13. Toronto: Dundurn Press, 1991.

———. *Representation, Integration and Political Parties in Canada*. Royal Commission on Electoral Reform and Party Financing, vol. 14. Toronto: Dundurn Press, 1991.

Bashevkin, Sylvia B. *Toeing the Lines: Women and Party Politics in English Canada*, 2nd ed. Toronto: Oxford University Press, 1993.

Brodie, M. Janine, and Jane Jenson. *Crisis, Challenge and Change: Party and Class in Canada, Revisited*, rev. ed. Ottawa: Carleton University Press, 1988.

Campbell, Colin, and William Christian. *Parties, Leaders, and Ideologies in Canada,*. McGraw-Hill Ryerson, 1996.

Carty, Kenneth R., ed. *Canadian Political Party Systems: A Reader*. Peterborough, Ont.: Broadview Press, 1992.

Carty, Kenneth R., et al., eds. *Leaders and Parties in Canadian Politics: Experiences of the Provinces*. Toronto: Harcourt Brace Jovanovich, 1991.

Christian, William, and Colin Campbell. *Political Parties and Ideologies in Canada*, 3rd ed. Toronto: McGraw-Hill Ryerson, 1990.

Dominguez, Jorge I. *Parties, Elections, and Political Participation in Latin America*. New York: Garland Pub., 1994.

Duverger, Maurice. *Political Parties*, 3rd ed. New York: Wiley, 1978.

Epstein, Leon D. *Political Parties in Western Democracies*. New York: Praeger, 1967.

Flanagan, Tom. *Waiting for the Wave: The Reform Party and Preston Manning*. Toronto: Stoddart, 1995.

Frears, J.R. *Political Parties and Elections in the French Fifth Republic*. London: C. Hurst, 1977.

Goodman, William. *The Party System in America*. Englewood Cliffs, N.J.: Prentice-Hall, 1980.

Katz, Richard S. *A Theory of Parties and Electoral Systems*. Baltimore: Johns Hopkins University Press, 1980.

Klingemann, Hans-Dieter, Richard I. Hofferbert, and Ian Budge. *Parties, Policies, and Democracies*. Boulder, Colo.: Westview Press, 1994.

Kornberg, Allan, Joel Smith, and Harold D. Clarke. *Citizen Politicians—Canada: Party Officials in a Democratic Society*. Durham, N.C.: Carolina Academic Press, 1979.

Laver, Michael, and Ben W. Hunt. *Policy and Party Competition*. New York: Routledge, 1992.

Laver, Michael, and Norman Schofield. *Multiparty Government: The Politics of Coalition in Europe*. New York: Oxford University Press, 1990.

Michels, Robert. *Political Parties*. New York: Free Press, 1962. First published in 1911.

Panebianco, Angelo. *Political Parties*. Cambridge: Cambridge University Press, 1988.

Paterson, William E., and Alastair H. Thomas, eds. *Social Democratic Parties in Western Europe*. London: Croom Helm, 1977.

Piven, Frances Fox, ed. *Labor Parties in Postindustrial Societies*. Cambridge, England: Polity Press, 1991.

Pomper, Gerald M. *Passions and Interests: Political Party Concepts of American Democracy*. Lawrence, Kan.: University Press of Kansas, 1992.

Robins, Lynton, Hilary Blackmore, and Robert Pyper, eds., *Britain's Changing Party System*. London: Leicester University Press, 1994.

Rose, Richard. *Do Parties Make a Difference?*, 2nd ed. London: Macmillan, 1984.

Seidle, Leslie F., ed. *Comparative Issues in Party and Election Finance in Canada*. Royal Commission on Electoral Reform and Party Financing, vol. 4. Toronto: Dundurn Press, 1991.

———. *Issues in Party and Election Finance in Canada*. Royal Commission on Electoral Reform and Party Financing, vol. 5. Toronto: Dundurn Press, 1991.

———. *Provincial Party and Election Finance in Canada*. Royal Commission on Electoral Reform and Party Financing, vol. 3. Toronto: Dundurn Press, 1991.

Sorauf, Frank J. *Party Politics in America*, 4th ed. Boston: Little, Brown, 1980.

Sortari, Giovanni. *Parties and Party Systems: A Framework for Analysis*. Cambridge: Cambridge University Press, 1976.

Thorburn, Hugh G., ed. *Party Politics in Canada*, 6th ed. Scarborough, Ont.: Prentice-Hall Canada, 1991.

Ware, Alan. *Political Parties and Party Systems*. Oxford and New York: Oxford University Press, 1996.

Wearing, Joseph. *Strained Relations: Canadian Parties and Voters*. Toronto: McClelland and Stewart, 1988.

Wolinetz, Steven B., ed. *Parties and Party Systems in Liberal Democracies: Continuity and Change*. London: Routledge, 1988.

Young, Walter D. *Democracy and Discontent: Progressivism, Socialism and Social Credit in the Canadian West*, 2nd ed. Toronto: McGraw-Hill Ryerson, 1978.

COMMUNICATIONS MEDIA

Communications media include newspapers, magazines, pamphlets, books, and direct mail (print media) as well as radio, television, recordings, films, and the Internet (electronic media). These media are not political institutions in the same way as interest groups and political parties, which have an overt political purpose—that is, to influence or control government. The ostensible purpose of the media is to inform or entertain. However, the media have such vast influence on the political process that we must consider them an integral part of it. They are vital transmission channels for both articulating demands and expressing support. Communications media are particularly important if democratic government is to be meaningful. The French political analyst Jean-François Revel has this to say about democracy and the media:

> What purpose do the press and other media serve in this system? To place at the disposal of citizens information, without which they cannot govern themselves wisely or at least pick out and judge those who are to govern them. It is this organic link between self-government and information, without which the citizen's choices would be made blindly, which justifies freedom of the press and makes it so necessary to a democracy.[1]

Most people involved in newspapers, radio, and television would deny that their work is political. Their job, so they claim, involves reporting facts, political events, and circumstances without political bias. Nonetheless, bias is perceived on all sides, though the charges sometimes cancel each other out:

> Some critics do see a consistent bias in the news coverage by the national media. Many conservatives view the major news services and television networks as an arrogant, liberal elite, more interested in advancing their own influ-

ence on society than in promoting the good of the nation. Left-wing critics point to the control of the major media by a shrinking circle of large corporations. They argue that the media distort the news to protect the interests of their corporate owners and government allies. Still other media observers who don't see a conscious conspiracy to distort the news believe the national media unintentionally bias their coverage in favor of government officials and policies. These observers point out that much of what the national media report as news involves government officials and often uses information provided by the government. They argue that the national media provide too much of a forum for government officials and do too little independent investigating and reporting.[2]

Whether or not bias exists, the media are political institutions, not necessarily in partisan terms, but as links between people and government. The media provide the basis for public discussion of issues. Not only do they report political events, but they also provide the means for individuals, groups, and government to state positions that can be aired before the public. Thus, in terms of the total political process, the media are essential to communication on public issues.

We often take the political importance of the media for granted. However, it must be remembered that newspapers have existed for only about two centuries, and the electronic media are even more recent. Representative government, having been established before the age of mass media, was originally based on face-to-face contact between representatives and their electors, who were few in number. Each representative was personally known to almost all who voted for him, and the election was held by a show of hands at a meeting of electors convened for that purpose. Rival candidates would be present at this meeting to speak before the vote was taken. This method of election persisted well into the nineteenth century, until democratic extension of the franchise so expanded the electorate that it became impossible for representatives and electors to know each other personally. The introduction of the secret ballot made the electoral process more anonymous and impersonal, so that images conveyed by the mass media have now almost entirely replaced direct human contact. The consequences for democratic government are complex and cannot be fully discussed here, but it is clear that representative democracy as we know it could not possibly exist without the mass media.

Political communication through the media takes many forms. On one side, governments use the media to transmit information to the public. A prime minister or president may call a press conference or choose to address a national audience via radio or television. The press agents of important ministers make news releases available on particular issues. Governments may use the media as a way of informing people of public hearings or petitions for rezoning. Some of this flow of information is purely factual, but much of it contains implicit or explicit pleas for support of government policy.

Members of society also rely on the media to communicate information to governments. Letters to the editor can express support for or opposition to specific policies. Various interest groups frequently advertise in the media as a way of taking their case to a wider public. Individuals may contribute articles, stories, and interviews with a political slant.

〽〽〽〽〽〽〽〽

CAMPAIGNS AND THE MEDIA

Political parties and election campaigns have been particularly affected by recent developments in the communications media. In all industrial democracies, electoral politics is now conducted primarily, if not exclusively, in the media. One result of this has been the rise to prominence in political parties of media and other technical consultants, who are now indispensable. Four types of activities deserve particular mention.

The first is public relations, as managed by the "spin doctors," whose job is to release news stories to, and answer questions from, print and electronic reporters. Insiders refer to the world of daily news coverage as the unpaid media. Every day there is a tremendous volume of potential free publicity in the form of political news coverage, and political leaders have to ensure that their activities are represented as favourably as possible. Amateurism in this enterprise can be dangerous, since reporters are quick to pounce on any error or misstatement. Thus all major parties now place great emphasis on "quick response" and "damage control" to reduce the negative effects of poorly worded statements.

A special form of unpaid media, and one that is having an increasing effect on political campaigns, is the televised debate among party leaders. In 1984 the debate resulted in the decisive turn from the Liberals to the Conservatives when Brian Mulroney effectively attacked John Turner over patronage appointments. In 1988 Turner "won" the debate by focusing on free trade and produced a large but temporary spike in support for the Liberals. In 1993 there was no clear winner among the five debaters, but Prime Minister Kim Campbell "lost" by being too strident and by being unwilling or unable to answer Lucien Bouchard's question about the size of the deficit. In 1997, Jean Charest spoke most fluently in both the English and French debates and got a temporary boost in the polls, but could not maintain his new support through to the end of the campaign. All these episodes illustrate that these are not debates in the usual sense. The purpose of the exercise is not to produce better arguments overall but to generate powerful short stretches of political theatre that can be played over and over on news programs and be incorporated into advertising. To make sure they generate the right sound bites, leaders prepare for days with their professional advisers.

The second great branch of media politics is the world of paid media or advertising. Political parties advertise in all media during election campaigns, but television now gets the lion's share of expenditures. As in the realm of unpaid media, professionals have come to dominate. Political advertising campaigns are prepared by advertising executives who lend their services to political parties out of a mixture of motives, such as ideology, personal friendship and loyalty, and the hope of future patronage contracts. Ads are carefully tested in focus groups before they are run, and their performance is monitored equally carefully. If they do not seem to be working, they are pulled and replaced.

In spite of this research and development process, disastrous mistakes can occur. Late in the 1993 election campaign, the Conservatives started to run television ads attacking Jean Chrétien's leadership ability. The ads featured close-up pictures of Chrétien that drew attention to the fact that one side of his mouth is partially paralyzed. When the ads had been tested, members of the focus groups had not perceived them as making fun of Chrétien's disability; but they had this effect on the public at large when they were broadcast, and the Conservatives had to pull them amid great embarrassment. A more ambiguous episode occurred with the Reform Party's 1997 attack ad, in which the ability of "Quebec-based" political leaders to deal with the issue of Quebec separatism was questioned. The ad seemed to have increased Reform's support in the West but to have had a neutral, or even negative, effect in Ontario. Since the ad was intended to bring about the long-awaited Reform breakthrough in Ontario, it could be considered a failure. But its effect in the West was Reform's increase to 60 parliamentary seats from 52 in 1993, and the cementing of its status by becoming the official Opposition.

The third activity that has become indispensable to modern politics is public-opinion polling. With the development of survey techniques and computer analysis, it is now possible to get fast and accurate information about the views of the public on any issue. Both public relations and advertising are now driven by polling data, and pollsters have become key figures in most parties' campaign management committees. The goal of such committees is to produce a seamless interface between the party's and politicians' activities as reported in the news and the themes that are repeated in the paid advertising, while at the same time addressing concerns that polling has discovered among the voters. An important development in polling technology is the rolling or tracking poll, which all parties now use during campaigns. The pollster surveys a small new sample every night and averages those data with the results of (usually) the preceding two nights' surveys. The aggregate is large enough to be statistically reliable, and the averaging smooths out day-to-day fluctuations. Those in charge of the campaign get a report every morning and can change course if it suggests that things are not going well.

A final media specialty to be considered is that of direct mail, which has become an irreplaceable fundraising tool in both Canada and the United States. The dominance of the Conservatives in federal politics in the 1980s was to a considerable extent based on the party's decision a decade earlier to launch a direct-mail fundraising program. The Tories began building their list of donors by prospecting, that is, renting membership and subscription lists from other sources and sending out initial appeals. One is lucky to break even on the first round of prospecting. The payoff comes later. Since those who give once are much more likely to give another time, the profitability ratio on subsequent mailings can be much higher. The Liberals had less need of direct mail at the time because they controlled the federal government. Indeed, they have never really mastered the art and as a result were in debt from 1984 until they became the government in 1993. The Reform Party's entry into Canadian politics was also based on direct mail, in this case an in-house operation that did not take the prospecting route but was aimed at the party's mass membership. This approach produced a substantial yield very quickly but also came up against a ceiling because it depended on repeat giving from a limited list of donors.

Some observers are concerned about the overwhelming importance of the media and related technology in contemporary public life, fearing that it makes politics too professionalized, expensive, and manipulative. However, the result of the 1992 referendum campaign shows that money, technology, and professionalism do not always win. The Charlottetown Accord was supported by the three major federal parties, who put some of their best strategists, spin doctors, pollsters, and advertisers at the disposal of the Yes committee. Money was also no problem; the Yes committee had over $7 million to spend. And polls taken when the Accord was announced made it seem almost certain to pass; it was trailing only slightly in Quebec and leading by large margins in all the other provinces.

The only well-funded opponent of the Accord was the No committee in Quebec, which received about $2 million of public money under Quebec law and which could draw on the considerable expertise of the Parti Québécois machine. Outside Quebec there was only an uncoordinated assortment of poorly funded opponents. The players on the No side had to proceed without tracking polls, focus groups, and the other elements of contemporary technology. The Referendum Act did give both sides equal access to a certain amount of free advertising time on radio and television; but against the professionally produced and tested Yes ads, the No ads looked as if they had been made with a camcorder in someone's basement.

It appeared to be a hopelessly unequal contest, and yet technology and money lost decisively because there were certain parts of the Accord, such as the guarantee of 25 percent of House of Commons seats for Quebec, that were very difficult to defend in the rest of Canada. Sophisticated use of the media is obviously an asset to political parties, and they will continue to strive for technological mastery; but the referendum campaign suggests that there are always limitations on what can be achieved.

PRIMING AND AGENDA-SETTING

Besides playing a large—and increasingly larger—role in political campaigns, the media actively participate in the day-to-day dissemination of political information, opinion, and symbolism. To some extent, they do this openly in editorials, where they take explicit stands on various issues. However, people have minds of their own and are not necessarily persuaded by editorials. This was illustrated during the 1992 referendum campaign, when almost every large English newspaper in Canada (including *The Globe and Mail* and the other Thomson papers, *The Toronto Star* and the eighteen papers of the Southam chain, and *The Financial Post* and the four papers of the associated *Sun* chain) supported the Charlottetown Accord, yet the Accord was decisively defeated.

More important than editorials is the "objective" task of factual news reporting. Reporters strive for objectivity, but like the rest of us, they work within intellectual and emotional constraints of which they may not be fully aware. Probably more profound in its effects than personal bias is the media's internal logic. We do not need to subscribe fully to Marshall McLuhan's famous dictum that "the medium is the message" to see that news reporting has certain basic and sometimes conflicting requirements. While appearing to be accurate and objective, it must also be concise, interesting, and even entertaining. If it is too detailed, complex, or subtle, it will lose its mass audience. The audience will also evaporate if news reporting is too far at variance with the fundamental values and opinions of the political culture.

One way for journalists to reconcile these various demands is to focus on conflict. Arguments, debates, fights, strikes, boycotts, wars, and revolutions are far more exciting to report than cooperation, agreement, consensus, and quiet compromise. There is, therefore, an understandable tendency for almost all news to be recast according to a conflict model. Journalists play a great role in setting up conflicts by choosing the authorities whose conflicting opinions they cite. They also heighten conflicts by actively seeking out controversial opinions on matters regarding which there is in fact a high degree of consensus. However, none of this is to say that journalists possess sinister powers of persuasion. Repeated studies of the effects of the mass media on opinion have shown that people tend to pick out reported facts that reinforce their deeply held beliefs. There is no guarantee that even deliberately slanted stories would have the desired effect on their audience.

But if news reporting does not change people's opinions in a direct way, it plays an extremely important role in **agenda-setting**.[3] Attention is a scarce resource; people cannot think about everything at once. The media do not tell people what to think, but they may tell people what to think about. And this is of the highest importance in politics, because interest groups, parties, and ideologists often differ profoundly in their assessment of what constitutes a problem worth thinking about.

Canadian conservatives tend to regard the federal deficit as the country's most serious problem, while social democrats and reform liberals tend to put it further down on their action lists. It was not, therefore, a politically neutral act when the Canadian media started to run stories about the deficit in the early months of 1989. In the very act of reporting the government's budget plans, they were helping establish an agenda for public discussion.

A concept related to agenda-setting is **priming,** which "refers to changes in the standards that people use to make political evaluations."[4] Because political events and personalities are always too complicated to be reported in their totality, journalists must be selective in the portraits they present. Inevitably, they produce stereotypical images by attaching key words to names. For example, it was a matter of considerable political importance whether those who opposed the Sandinista government in Nicaragua were "U.S.-backed contras" or "Nicaraguan freedom fighters," and whether a proposed system of defence against ballistic missiles was called "Strategic Defence Initiative" or "Star Wars." In the same vein, is Dr. Henry Morgentaler best described as an "abortionist" or an "advocate of choice"? Even though reporters usually refrain from open editorializing, the way they prime their messages can have an almost subliminal effect upon public opinion. Two American authors have put it this way:

> In commanding attention and shaping opinion, television is now an authority virtually without peer. Near the close of the twentieth century, in the shadow of Orwell's 1984, it would be both naive and irresponsible to pretend that such an authority could ever be neutral.[5]

Those who engage in politics are quite aware of the ways in which the media actively create rather than passively report news, so they do their best to manipulate the media. Mass public demonstrations that are supposed to be spontaneous expressions of demand or support are usually in fact carefully staged events that depend on the cooperation of the mass media. Organizers invite newspaper and television reporters well in advance. A study of the American news media reports that in the 1960s, when there were many demonstrations against the Vietnam War, "experienced organizers scheduled demonstrations to fit the schedules of camera crews."[6]

Reporters come to such events because mass demonstrations provide an interesting subject. They take photographs and film footage of the most rousing events: the singing, the dramatic speeches, the shouts of affirmation, the violent clashes with the police. They hold interviews with the leading demonstrators, which gives the latter a chance to communicate their prepared messages to the public. When it is all over, newspapers and television stations present to the public the news of an event in which the mass media themselves were the most important participants.

The media also shape political reality through their investigative or watchdog activities. With the help of the opposition, reporters often uncover inconvenient facts that governments or powerful interest groups would like to suppress. The most famous example of this activity is, of course, the Watergate affair, when American reporters uncovered the misdeeds of officials in Richard Nixon's administration. As a result of their efforts, Nixon was forced to resign in 1974. This episode elevated the media to new heights of prestige.

This investigative role is less highly developed in Canada than it is in the United States and Great Britain. One reason is the state of Canadian media law. Laws requiring governments and public corporations to disclose information are so weak in this country that journalists often resort to American sources to discover information about Canada. Also, libel laws are so strong that the rich and powerful can effectively use the legal system to discourage reporters from pursuing controversial stories.[7] Another layer of silence arises in the judicial system itself. There is a strong Canadian tradition, enforced by judicial findings of contempt of court, that limits media discussion of cases being tried. This allows the rich and the powerful to avoid disclosure by launching a libel action and dragging it out for years, during which time the information usually loses its relevance to political action.

INFLUENCE, OWNERSHIP, AND CONTROL

Most of the media are well skilled at continuously reporting a flow of news, but do not involve themselves in a thorough analysis of issues. In many countries, therefore, one or two newspapers have emerged as particularly important in politics because they provide both good coverage and sharp analysis. In Britain, almost everyone involved in government or seriously observing it reads the *Times*, the *Guardian*, or the *Independent*. Letters to the editors of these papers are often carefully thought-out statements by important people meant to be read by other important people. The papers in general serve as a handy means of communication among the political elite of the country. In France, *Le Monde* and *Le Figaro* are read in the same way. In the United States, *The New York Times* and the *Washington Post* have this position in national politics, although many other papers are of regional importance. For years Canada did not really have an equivalent, except for *Le Devoir* in Quebec; however, in English Canada, the Toronto-based *Globe and Mail*, using satellite technology, has now emerged as a national newspaper. Except for the more specialized *Financial Post*, it is the only daily newspaper in Canada that can be purchased in every province and territory. The absence until recent years of a truly national newspaper in Canada may have contributed to the fragmentation of Canadian political culture. Politicians and leaders in other walks of life in different parts of the country often lacked a common frame of reference and fund of information, which might have been supplied in part if they were reading the same paper.

The print media—newspapers, magazines, publishing houses—took shape in the eighteenth and nineteenth centuries, before the socialist idea of state ownership had become influential. These media receive government subsidies in some countries; however, in the Western world they remain almost entirely in private hands and are run as profit-making businesses. Governments do not license or otherwise regulate them, except for enforcing laws against libel, pornography, false advertising, and so on. Underlying this arrangement is the classical liberal philosophy that holds that the public good is best served through the competition of private actors following their own interests. Newspapers, magazines, and books constitute a mass market of profit-seeking interests in the field of ideas, information, and entertainment.

The recent trend toward concentration of ownership poses difficult problems to the classical liberal model. Newspapers, magazines, and publishing houses are now generally owned in chains by large corporations. When the number of owners is drastically reduced, and when the owners are mostly large corporations, does a free market of ideas in the mass media still exist?

The concentration of newspaper ownership has intensified in recent years as Conrad Black has used his Hollinger company to acquire control of the Southam chain. Indirectly or directly, Black now owns about half the newspapers published in Canada, including major metropolitan dailies in Vancouver, Edmonton, Calgary, Saskatoon, Regina, Hamilton, Ottawa, and Halifax. Yet there is still a significant degree of competition. Canada's largest single newspaper, *The Toronto Star*, is independently owned; and there are some independent dailies, such as the *Winnipeg Sun*. *The Globe and Mail* is owned by the Thomson chain; and the *Sun* chain, allied with *The Financial Post*, operates dailies in Toronto, Ottawa, Calgary, and Edmonton.

Those who oppose government intervention in the newspaper business argue that concentration of newspaper ownership, at least at its present level, does not threaten the free market of ideas. Even if a city has only one local daily, its inhabitants can still receive news from many other sources, such as papers from other cities, weekly magazines, radio, and television. The debate is analogous to the one over government regulation of oligopolies (which was touched on earlier in the discussion of liberalism).

The electronic media, born as they were in the twentieth century, when public ownership was becoming a powerful idea, have been involved with government almost from the start. There are technical aspects of broadcasting that invite public regulation. A radio or television signal is a public good, available to anyone with an antenna and a receiver. Broadcasters can seriously interfere with competitors' transmissions unless they respect the concept of reserved frequencies. In many European countries—for example, England, France, and Germany—radio and television are dominated by public corporations. Private enterprise is permitted in some cases but only in a secondary role. In the United States, private ownership is the rule, but unlike the print media, the electronic media are subject to government licensing. Canada combines both models. There are publicly owned English and French networks of radio and television stations (such as the CBC, Radio-Canada, and some smaller provincial networks), but they do not dominate the market, which consists mostly of privately owned, governmentally licensed stations. Advocates of public ownership say that a network supported by taxes rather than advertising revenue is able to offer news and public affairs in greater depth—an argument that surely has some merit. Perhaps there is something to be said for the Canadian arrangement, which provides the benefits of a subsidized, nonprofit system but does not give government a predominant role in the electronic media.

Outside the liberal democracies, almost all mass media, whether print or electronic, are owned or controlled by the state. In totalitarian systems, the mass media are quite simply an instrument used by the state to transform society. Communication with the masses is considered too important to be left to independent organizations in society, so state control is total.

Authoritarian states also supervise the mass media, but not quite to the same extent: their chief concern is usually to ensure that the government is not criticized in public. Criticism may result in the imprisonment or exile of writers or the closing of newspapers, journals, and radio and TV stations. Independent units of the media may exist and operate as long as their political reporting is neutral or complimentary to the government. In both totalitarian and authoritarian systems, the media are viewed more as means of generating support for the regime than as means of articulating demands by the public. As the late Forbes Burnham, former dictator of Guyana, said in 1975, the media must become "an agency for pushing the development of the nation in the context of Government policy."[8]

However, the pace of technological advance is now making it increasingly difficult for any kind of government to maintain monopolistic control over what is reported in the country. Satellite dishes, camcorders, cellphones, and the Internet are now available almost everywhere in the world, making it harder for anyone to control the flow of information. Revolutionary movements, such as the Tupac Amaru guerrillas in Peru, maintain their own Websites. Hostage takers with cellphones can broadcast their demands around the world. A bystander holding a camcorder can videotape examples of police brutality, as in the famous Rodney King affair in Los Angeles. And both rebels and government forces now release videocassettes of themselves torturing and executing their opponents as a way of intimidating others. The new technology can be a tool for whoever wishes to use it.

᭚᭚᭚᭚᭚᭚᭚

FURTHER READING

Bain, George. *Gotcha! How the Media Distort the News*. Toronto: Key Porter, 1994.

Bender, David L., and Bereno Leone, ed. *The Mass Media: Opposing Viewpoints*. San Diego, Calif.: Greenhaven Press, Inc., 1988.

Desbarats, Peter. *Guide to Canadian News Media*. Toronto: Harcourt Brace Jovanovich, 1990.

Ericson, Richard V., et al. *Visualizing Deviance: A Study of News Organization*. Toronto: University of Toronto Press, 1987.

Fletcher, Frederick J., ed. *Election Broadcasting in Canada*. Royal Commission on Electoral Reform and Party Financing, vol. 21. Toronto: Dundurn Press, 1991.

———. *Media and Voters in Election Campaigns*. Royal Commission on Electoral Reform and Party Financing, vol. 18. Toronto: Dundurn Press, 1991.

———. *Media, Elections, and Democracy*. Royal Commission on Electoral Reform and Party Financing, vol. 19. Toronto: Dundurn Press, 1991.

———. *Reporting and the Campaign: Election Coverage in Canada*. Royal Commission on Electoral Reform and Party Financing, vol. 22. Toronto: Dundurn Press, 1991.

Gans, Herbert J. *Deciding What's News*. New York: Pantheon Books, 1979.

Hackett, Rober A., and Yuezhi Zhao. *Sustaining Democracy? Journalism and the Politics of Objectivity*. Toronto: Garamond, 1997.

Homes, H., and David Taras, eds. *Seeing Ourselves: Media Power and Policy in Canada*. Toronto: Harcourt, Brace Jovanovich, 1992.

Iyengar, Shanto. *Is Anyone Responsible? How Television Frames Political Issues*. Chicago: University of Chicago Press, 1991.

Iyengar, Shanto, and Donald R. Kinder. *News that Matters: Television and American Opinion*. Chicago: University of Chicago Press, 1987.

Jamieson, Kathleen Hall, ed. *The Media and Politics*. Thousand Oaks, Calif.: Sage, 1996.

Joslyn, Richard. *Mass Media and Elections*. Reading, Mass.: Addison-Wesley, 1984.

Kellner, Douglas. *Media Culture: Cultural Studies, Identity and Politics Between the Modern and the Postmodern*. London: Routledge, 1995.

Kesterton, Wilfred H. *The Law and the Press in Canada*. Toronto: McClelland and Stewart, 1976.

Lachapelle, Guy. *Polls and the Media in Canadian Elections*. Royal Commission on Electoral Reform and Party Financing, vol. 16. Toronto: Dundurn Press, 1991.

Levine, Allan Gerald. *Scrum Wars: The Prime Ministers and the Media*. Toronto: Dundurn Press, 1993.

Negrine, Ralph M. *Politics and the Mass Media in Britain*, 2nd ed. London: Routledge, 1994.

Neuman, Johanna. *Lights, Camera, War: Is Media Technology Driving Foreign Politics?* New York: St. Martin's Press, 1995.

Paletz, David L. *Media Power Politics*. New York: Free Press, 1981.

Parenti, Michael. *Inventing Reality: The Politics of News Media*, 2nd ed. New York: St. Martin's Press, 1993.

Picard, Robert G. *Media Portrayals of Terrorism: Functions and Meaning of News Coverage*. Ames: Iowa State University Press, 1993.

Righter, Rosemary. *Whose News? Politics, the Press and the Third World*. London: Burnett Books, 1978.

Rosenstiel, Tom. *Strange Bedfellows: How Television and the Presidential Candidates Changed American Politics, 1992*, 1st ed. New York: Hyperion Press, 1993.

Taras, David. *The Newsmakers*. Scarborough, Ont.: Nelson Canada, 1990.

Turpin, Jennifer E. *Reinventing the Soviet Self: Media and Social Change in the Former Soviet Union*. Westport, Conn.: Praeger, 1995.

Wells, Alan. *Mass Media and Society*, 4th ed. Palo Alto, Calif.: Mayfield, 1987.

Winter, James P. *Democracy's Oxygen: How Corporations Control the News*. Montreal: Black Rose Books, 1996.

ELECTIONS AND ELECTORAL SYSTEMS

The process of electing public officials is central to liberal democracy. Elections provide a way of changing rulers without resorting to bloodshed—no small accomplishment in itself, although hereditary selection has achieved the same thing. More profoundly, competitive political elections are the basis of democratic legitimacy. The opportunity to participate in choosing rulers confers on the participants an obligation to obey the laws made by those who are chosen. Citizens are presumed to consent to laws to the extent that they have participated in choosing the lawmakers (see Figure 28.1). Disagreement with the substance of lawmakers' decisions is not normally sufficient reason for disobedience, because there will soon be an opportunity (i.e., another election) to vote for other lawmakers who are willing to alter the disliked rule or policy. Of course, if an elected government repeatedly ignores the will of most citizens on issues of vital concern, it is likely to provoke mass demonstrations and even violent protest. In any case, the replacing of traditional with legal authority results in the collapse of traditional theories of obligation based on the will of God or on inherited position; democratic elections provide an alternative theory of obligation that is compatible with the legal concept of authority.

In the political process, elections are best interpreted as a form of voter reaction. Because elected governors must answer to the public in a future election, the assumption is that they will rule responsively. In other words, elected officials want to be re-elected and will therefore enact laws and policies that meet current desires. As the philosopher John Plamenatz put it, "Elections are important not only for what happens at them but also for what happens because of them."[1]

The most obvious thing that an election does is determine the composition of the representative assembly. Figures 28.2, 28.3, 28.4, and 28.5 give the partisan breakdown for Canada, the United Kingdom, the United States, and France, respectively, after the most recent elections in these countries.

FIGURE 28.1 Elections Legitimize

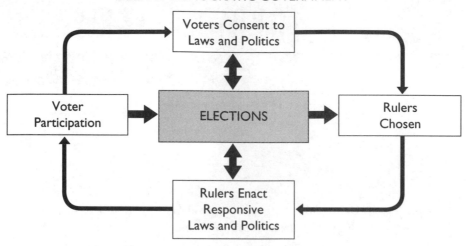

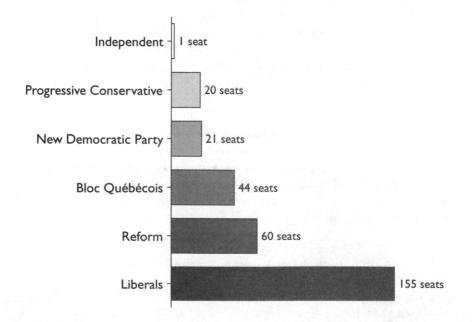

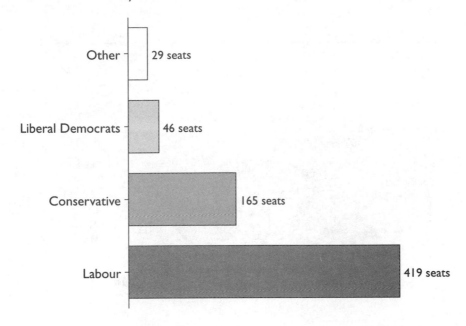

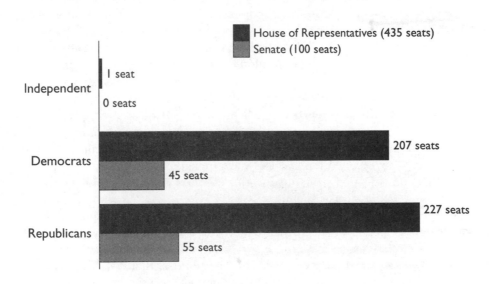

FIGURE 28.5 French National Assembly—577 seats: Distribution After Election, June 1997

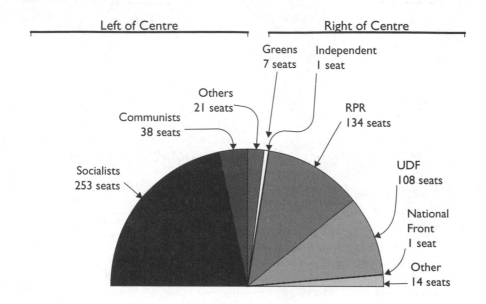

In a simpler world, public officials might be elected with a mandate to do certain things and thus implement popular desires in a direct and unambiguous way. If that were the case, elections could be considered a mechanism for articulating demands. However, elections are more like a judgment of the record of those in office, whose actual performance may have had little to do with the promises they made when elected. If voters like what has happened, they can vote for a continuation; if not, they can vote for a change, without being quite sure what the alternative will be. In this way elections are an ingenious mechanism for coping with an uncertain and ever-changing future. Elected rulers are allowed periods of creativity during which they seek to cope with the unexpected problems that are always presenting themselves; afterward the voters decide whether they will be allowed to continue their efforts. Dealing with dilemmas gradually as they appear is a more supple procedure than trying to work out far in advance the answers to problems that may never arise in their expected form. The greatest strength of liberal democracy may well be the sophistication of its institutions that link the rulers and the ruled. Among these, elections are paramount.

For elections to provide this link, at least three conditions must be present. First, elections must be periodic. Usually their frequency is specified in a constitution and ranges from every two years (the House of Representatives in the United States) to every seven years (the President of France). The point is that elections must be institutionalized so that a head of government cannot arbitrarily cancel or postpone them in order to rule indefinitely. They must be regular and reasonably frequent if they are to be effective in a democratic system. As voters evaluate political outputs, they may decide to choose new governors. If that opportunity is taken away, the democratic system loses its grounds for legitimacy.

Second, there must be wide opportunity for all to run for office so that voters have a genuine choice. If restrictions are placed on who can run for office, elections cannot be democratic. There has been a great deal of discussion about whether elections in one-party systems might be considered democratic. If the process for selecting candidates is rigid, and if this process is controlled by a small party elite, there is little competition for public office and little choice for voters. However, some argue that the one-party system can be democratic if there is competition among factions within the party. If the party nomination process is relatively open, there may be a choice of candidates. But the choice in this case is made by party members, not all voters, so this process is democratic only in a very restricted sense.

Third, there must be a high degree of political freedom. If freedom of speech or of the press is limited, the electoral campaign cannot function as it must, and voters are unable to make fully informed decisions. Restrictions on political freedom inhibit the role of the electoral process.

Even after elections were established as a way of selecting rulers, various devices were sometimes used to limit mass participation. Under the property franchise, for example, an individual was required to own a specified amount of assets before being allowed to vote. Poll taxes, which had to be paid as a prerequisite for voting, also limited participation by the poor. More recently, age and extensive residency requirements have been manipulated to influence voter turnout, and literacy requirements are still used in many developing nations to restrict full participation in elections. This is especially true where educational opportunities are limited. Until after World War I, half the population—the female half—was barred from voting lists. As discussed earlier, the long-term trend of liberal democracy has been to erase or minimize all such restrictions.

In totalitarian and authoritarian governments, elections have little or nothing to do with the give-and-take between rulers and the ruled; rather, they are means of mobilizing support for the regime. Voters ratify lists of selected candidates and often are penalized for not participating in the election. Token opposition is sometimes permitted by authoritarian regimes when they have a firm grip on the government, as a way of enhancing the external legitimacy of the electoral result. This mobilization of support for the government also attaches legitimacy to elections in liberal democracies. National elections are quasi-sacred occasions during which the participants reaffirm their commitment to constitutional procedures. This comparison of liberal–democratic with authoritarian and totalitarian elections again shows how seemingly similar institutions can perform quite different functions in different systems.

An election is a complex procedure, and countries use many different methods to conduct them. A bewildering variety of electoral systems have been tried at one time or another. Below, we describe some of the more common kinds and point out a few of the consequences of each type for the democratic process.

Students of physics may have encountered the Heisenberg uncertainty principle, which states that it is impossible to measure simultaneously the velocity and position of a subatomic particle. The very act of measuring the speed will affect the position, and vice versa, so that complete information is impossible to attain. Recent work has shown the existence of a somewhat analogous situation in the use of electoral procedures in democratic politics. It turns out that the result obtained from an election depends in a very fundamental sense upon the method that is employed. There is no "will of the people" independent of the instrument chosen to measure it. The way votes are counted has a profound effect on the outcome.[2] Political scientists are aware now more than ever that the choice of electoral procedures is a crucial variable in political systems.

Liberals put party in one area PQ scattered

🔲🔲🔲🔲🔲🔲🔲🔲

THE SINGLE-MEMBER-PLURALITY SYSTEM

One of the two great electoral system types, the **single-member-plurality system (SMP)**, popularly known as "first-past-the-post," is familiar from its use in Britain, Canada, and the United States. One candidate is elected in each **constituency**, that is, in each geographical district that has a representative, and each elector has one vote to cast. The winning candidate is the one who receives a plurality of valid ballots. If there are only two candidates, the winner automatically gets a majority; but if there are several candidates who split the vote fairly evenly, the winner's plurality may be far from a majority.

The SMP method is a natural partner to the two-party system because it does not distort electoral results when there are only two candidates. In that case, a plurality is also a majority, and the democratic criterion of majority rule is unambiguously satisfied. However, when social cleavages are such that a two-party system cannot be maintained, adhering to first-past-the-post can have peculiar and even disturbing consequences.

In the 1994 Quebec provincial election, the Parti Québécois (PQ) received 44.7 percent of the vote, and the Liberals 44.3 percent. In spite of being almost tied with the Liberals in popular votes, the PQ won a solid majority of seats (77 out of 125). This happened because the Liberals "wasted" many of their votes running up huge majorities in the anglophone constituencies of Montreal, while the PQ vote was more strategically spread across the francophone ridings in the rest of the province. An even more remarkable result occurred in the British Columbia provincial election of 1996. The Liberals led in popular vote (42 percent), the NDP came second (39

42 out of 100

percent), and the provincial Reform Party came third (9 percent). Yet the NDP took a majority of seats (39 out of 75) and thus formed the government, even though the Liberals won substantially more votes. The Liberals got their numbers by running up big majorities in Vancouver suburbs; but in many rural ridings they split the right-wing vote with the Reform Party, allowing the NDP to "sneak up the middle" and win the seat with a plurality.

The effects of SMP were equally manifest in the 1997 federal election. With 38 percent of the popular vote, the Liberals won a slim but still workable majority of 155 seats. The Reform Party won 19 percent of the vote and 60 seats and became the official Opposition, while the Progressive Conservatives, with a virtually identical share of the popular vote, won only 20 seats. Meanwhile, the Bloc Québécois, with only 11 percent of the popular vote, took 44 seats. The reason for these seemingly odd results is that the Bloc Québécois vote was highly concentrated in the francophone areas of Quebec, and the Reform vote was concentrated in the West. The Conservatives also achieved some territorial concentration in Atlantic Canada and rural Quebec, but not to the same extent as Reform in the West and the BQ in Quebec.

In general, SMP penalizes small parties. Like the Conservatives in 1993, a party might get almost 20 percent of the popular vote but win hardly any seats. The one exception to this relates to small parties that are regionally concentrated, like the Bloc Québécois and the Reform Party. It is thus almost a general law of politics that no new party can break into a system based on first-past-the-post voting unless it achieves territorial concentration. This also explains why Mel Hurtig's new National Party won no seats in 1993. It had a certain amount of support, but it was too scattered across the country to result in victories in any particular constituency.

SMP also magnifies relatively small shifts in the popular vote. In a two-party system, an increase in a party's popular vote from 50 to 60 percent of the total will produce a landslide in parliamentary seats; and if there are three or more competitive parties, anything over 45 percent for one will probably produce a landslide. For example, between 1980 and 1984, the popular vote for the federal Conservatives went from 37.4 to 49.96 percent, while the same party's seats increased from 103 of 282 (36.5 percent) to 211 of 282 (74.8 percent). Such results may be particularly drastic in multiparty situations, in which fragmentation of the opposition can give the governing party an artificially and enormously inflated strength in the elected assembly.

Particularly in ethnically segmented societies, the first-past-the-post method can lead to the permanent underrepresentation of minorities. During the years of the Stormont Parliament, the Catholics of Northern Ireland constituted about one-third of the population, but they never came close to winning one-third of the seats in the assembly. Electoral districts were **gerrymandered**[3]—that is, deliberately drawn to favour one side, in this case the Protestant majority, over the other. Blocks of Catholic voters were divided up so as to form permanent minorities within Protestant-dominated constituencies. Such longstanding underrepresentation can destroy the legitimacy of government in the minds of the aggrieved minority.

Because of these many difficulties, SMP has been falling out of favour over the last hundred years. It was originally used almost everywhere that elections were held, but among the world's stable industrial democracies, it is now used only in Great Britain, the United States, and Canada. New Zealand dropped it in 1992, when its voters decided in a 1992 referendum to replace it with the form of proportional representation known as mixed-member-proportional (see below).

The Runoff System

The **runoff system** resembles SMP except that the winner must obtain a majority of the votes cast. If no candidate receives a majority, additional rounds of balloting are held. Trailing candidates are successively dropped until someone obtains a majority. This system is often used to choose both candidates and party leaders at conventions in Canada and the United States. The candidate with the lowest total is dropped after each ballot, and voting continues until someone gets a majority. All of this ensures that the ultimate winner has a majority of the votes cast on the final ballot, and this helps to preserve party unity. To have a leader chosen by less than a majority would be to invite dissension within the party.

In France's Fifth Republic, a somewhat similar system for parliamentary and presidential elections has been used since 1959, except for one experiment with proportional representation in 1986. There are, however, only two ballots. Trailing candidates are not automatically dropped; rather, parties are given the opportunity to form coalitions in the constituencies during the interval between ballots. Once coalitions are formed, various candidates withdraw in favour of others. Because it is possible for more than two names to be on the final ballot, the system is not technically a runoff; but in practice it functions like one by strongly rewarding those who make coalitions and penalizing those who do not.

The system was introduced in France by Charles de Gaulle to encourage the numerous small parties to form coalitions. De Gaulle envisioned it as a step toward a two-party system. We can now say that, after almost forty years, it has had an influence in that direction but has not been able by itself to do the job. Coalitions have been formed and broken repeatedly because of personal rivalries and ideological differences. Although cooperation among parties continues, there is no sign of the outright mergers that would create a two-party system. It seems that technical changes in the electoral system are not in themselves powerful enough to overcome the social cleavages that produce a multiparty system.

The runoff system is proving popular in some of the countries that have recently turned from totalitarianism or authoritarianism to democracy. When political freedom is first introduced, there is often a plethora of political parties and an obvious need to reduce the number or at least encourage cooperation and coalition-building. Fledgling democracies that have adopted the runoff system at the presidential level include Portugal and Nicaragua.

The Preferential or Alternative Ballot

Another variation on SMP is the **preferential** or **alternative ballot,** which attempts to capture information not only about voters' first choices but also about their second, third, and further choices. Electors are given a form on which they rank candidates in order of preference. If only two candidates are running, this system operates just like SMP. But when there are three or more candidates, the picture changes radically. Voters' first preferences are tabulated on the first count. If no one has a majority, the lowest candidate is dropped and a second count is taken. The eliminated candidate's votes are distributed to the other candidates according to the second preferences expressed on those ballots. The process continues until a majority is reached. The objective of the preferential ballot is similar to that of a runoff: to ensure that the victor has majority support. The difference is that the preferential ballot collects the necessary information in advance and thus dispenses with further rounds of balloting. In a sense, it is a condensed runoff system.

The preferential ballot is used at present in elections for the Australian House of Representatives. Alberta, British Columbia, and Manitoba have also experimented with it at various times. For instance, it was introduced in British Columbia in 1952 by the Liberals in order to hurt the CCF, whose fortunes were then on the rise. It was widely assumed that the Liberals and Conservatives would be each other's second choice, so that CCF candidates would do poorly on the second count. To everyone's surprise, the next election was won by the new Social Credit Party, which no one had considered a serious contender for power. Perhaps the lesson is that electoral methods, like all political institutions, should be based on general principles rather than opportunistic attempts to help or harm a specific party.

In practice, the preferential ballot, like the runoff system, allows parties to retain a separate existence while forming coalitions with each other for electoral advantage. In Australia, the Liberal Party and the National (previously Country) Party have maintained a working coalition for three-quarters of a century, and together they dominate the conservative side of the ideological spectrum. The electoral system favours their coalition because a conservative-minded voter who tilts toward one party or the other can rank the Liberal (or National) candidate first and the National (or Liberal) candidate second. At some point in the vote-counting process, the trailing candidate will be dropped but those votes will be transferred rather than wasted. As a voter on the right, you can vote for your favourite party without fearing that you will "split the right-wing vote" and thus help to elect a left-wing candidate. The same logic would apply on the left, but thus far the large Labour Party has been able to go it alone without a coalition partner.

PROPORTIONAL REPRESENTATION

Proportional representation (PR) is the second great type of electoral system. It is designed to provide representatives for a broad spectrum of interests in a constituency. Proportional representation requires multimember constituencies. The representatives for a constituency reflect not a single majority but a number of minorities (the actual number depending on the number of representatives to be selected). Representation is proportional to the vote that major interests receive in a constituency.

John Stuart Mill was the first important political thinker to popularize proportional representation. He thought that the first-past-the-post system, which was then widely used, gave too much power to the triumphant majority, which might then abuse the rights of minorities. As he explained in *Considerations on Representative Government*, he preferred proportional representation precisely because it would ensure that various minorities would be represented:

> Because the majority ought to prevail over the minority, must the majority have all the votes, the minority none? Is it necessary that the minority should not even be heard? In a really equal democracy, every or any section would be represented, not disproportionately, but proportionately.[4]

There are two main forms of proportional representation: the list system and the single-transferable-vote (STV) system (sometimes called the Hare system after its inventor, Thomas Hare). Both have the same aim: to ensure that representatives are elected in numbers proportional to the share of votes that their parties receive in the balloting.

The List System

The **list system** is the easier of the two to grasp. The elector votes not for individuals but for parties. Each party has a list of as many candidates as there are positions to be filled. If a party gets x percent of the popular vote, then the top x percent of its list is declared elected. This system gives great power to the party leaders, who determine the candidates' positions on the list. Being high on the list of a major party is tantamount to election; being low on the list of any party is tantamount to defeat. Barriers are usually inserted against tiny parties, such as the requirement of a minimum of 5 percent of the popular vote in order to get any seats at all.

The purest examples of the list system in practice are found in Israel and the Netherlands. In each case, the entire country is treated as a single constituency and there is a very low threshold (1 percent of the vote) for obtaining representation in the legislature. The result is a faithful translation of popular vote into the proportion of parliamentary seats, as well as a proliferation of parties and a permanent situation of coalition government. The list system is also widely used, with various modifications, in many other European countries, in both the established democracies of Western Europe and the emerging democracies of Eastern Europe.

Mixed-Member-Proportional System

In a particularly interesting modification of the list system, the list and the first-past-the-post systems are used together. According to this system, invented and used in Germany, on election day the voters cast two ballots, one for a local candidate running in a territorial constituency and the other for a national list of candidates put forward by a political party. The purpose of the second vote is to determine "the total number of seats each party receives in the Bundestag [the German equivalent of the House of Commons] on a basis of proportional representation."[5] After the local constituency winners are known, members from the lists are added to the territorial members in the numbers needed to ensure proportionality. This approach combines the advantages of proportionality with the virtues of having individual representatives for territorially defined constituencies—hence its name, **mixed-member-proportional,** commonly abbreviated as MMP.

MMP has been gaining popularity during the 1990s, as it has been adopted, with minor variations, in New Zealand, Italy, Russia, and Japan. It is often held up as a model of possible electoral reform for Canada because it would allow us to retain our tradition of local representation while mitigating some of the worst defects of the first-past-the-post system.[6]

Single-Transferable-Vote System

The **single-transferable-vote (STV) system** of proportional representation is best understood as an extension of the alternative or preferential ballot from single-member to multimember constituencies. Electors vote for individuals rather than party lists, but they do so preferentially, that is, by ranking the candidates in their order of choice. A formula establishes the quota of votes required to win, and the victors' surplus votes are transferred according to lower preferences. The following formula has been widely used:

$$\frac{\text{Total number of valid ballots} + 1}{\text{Number of seats} + 1} \cong \text{Quota}$$

In a constituency with four seats and 100,000 valid ballots cast, the quota would be calculated as follows (rounding the quota up because there are no fractional votes):

$$\frac{100,000 + 1}{4 + 1} \cong 20,001$$

Any candidate receiving 20,001 or more first preferences would be elected immediately. The remaining positions would be filled by counting procedures that take account of second and lower choices. These procedures are complex, but the basic idea is votes are transferred both from below and from above. From below, they are transferred as trailing candidates are dropped. From above, they are transferred because, when a candidate reaches the quota, there will usually be a surplus to be distributed among other candidates. Suffice it to say that STV produces a more or less proportional result without endowing the party leadership with the extraordinary power given it by the list system. John Stuart Mill advocated the quota system rather than the list system of proportional representation because he disliked the control that centralized and disciplined parties exercised over their members. STV is currently used for elections to the Dáil (lower house) in the Republic of Ireland and to the Senate (upper house) in Australia.

Many debates have been held about proportional representation since Mill stated his case. The main arguments for it may be listed as follows:

- Every vote counts; there are no wasted votes, which there inevitably are in the winner-take-all, first-past-the-post system.
- It is a more democratic system, for it ensures minority representation in the precise ratio of minority votes.
- It is mathematically accurate.
- Every politically active group of any size will, with very few exceptions, have some representation in the legislature.
- It provides greater freedom of choice for voters and thereby raises their interest in the body politic. Turnout at elections tends to be higher under the various forms of proportional representation.
- It tempers the domination of political machines.
- It eliminates the evils of gerrymandering because there are no districts to be gerrymandered.

The main arguments against proportional representation, on the other hand, can be summed up in the following way:

- It creates splinter parties; it balkanizes the party structure.
- It encourages bloc voting and extremism.
- It is divisive; it renders compromise extremely difficult, and may even eliminate it entirely.

- Majority government—government by a single political party with a [   ] of seats in the legislature—is usually impossible to attain; hence, pr[   ] representation militates against government stability.
- It centralizes control by political parties, by strengthening party mach[   ]
- It is mathematically confusing to the voter.
- It weakens the intimate contact with the constituency that is possible under single-member-constituency systems.[7]

How does en courage small parties

Proportional representation in all forms does tend to promote the existence of small parties, although the proliferation of parties can be controlled by using a seat threshold like the 5 percent employed in Germany and New Zealand. It is not necessary to come anywhere close to a majority to attract voters, as in a first-past-the-post situation. A party only has to be able to retain the support of its loyalists. Thus, proportional representation tends to encourage relatively small or medium-sized interest or ideological parties—for example, Catholic parties, farmers' parties, workers' parties, employers' parties. Such alignments can be stable over long periods of time, and this can create a distribution of representatives in the assembly that changes very little from election to election. This is the contemporary situation in most European states.

When distribution is steady, and when no single party commands a majority, the result must be prolonged coalition government. This in itself is not a bad thing, though it is alien to the British tradition. It can work well, as it has in most Scandinavian countries; but in cases such as Italy, where the presence of large extremist parties has severely limited the choice of coalition partners, the result may be cabinet instability.

Proportional representation has often been attacked for encouraging the proliferation of parties, thus balkanizing politics and making majority government impossible. The criticism is not without force. But it is often true that social cleavages exist that will produce a multiparty system regardless of the electoral method. In these circumstances, proportional representation is a way of keeping civil peace by allowing all significant minorities to feel represented. A first-past-the-post system might extinguish the smaller parties and leave certain minorities permanently underrepresented.

TURNOUT

One of the hallmarks of modern democratic systems is the opportunity for all adult citizens to participate in choosing their governors. This political right was a fundamental principle that fired the hearts and minds of our ancestors, some of whom went to the streets to gain the right to vote. However, in many contemporary nation-states that qualify as liberal democracies, the voter turnout rate is far from 100 percent.

In Figure 28.6 election turnout rates since World War II are plotted for Canada and the United States. One can immediately see the difference between the two countries; on average, turnout in Canada was about 10 to 15 percentage points higher than in the United States. Explaining this difference is not easy. Several factors, including political culture, help to explain the difference, but the most important explanation is institutional. Canada actively enumerates eligible voters, whereas the practice in most American states is to require voters to come to an office to register themselves. Since it requires more effort to get on the voters list in the United States than in Canada, fewer people bother to do it, and the turnout rate is lower.

Although the Canadian turnout rate is consistently higher than the American, both countries are in the lower third of voter participation rates throughout the

FIGURE 28.6 Voter Turnout Percentages in Canadian Federal and U.S. Presidential Elections, 1948–1997

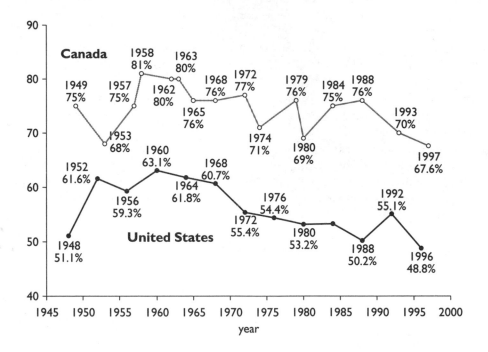

*Percentages are based on numbers of eligible votes.

Sources: John R. Colombo, ed. *The Canadian Global Almanac, 1997* (Toronto: Macmillan Canada, 1997), p. 181; *Globe and Mail*, June 4, 1997, p. A6; *Facts on File*, 56: 2918, Nov. 7, 1996, p. 812.

world. Australia, which has compulsory voting, is first; in the 1980s, turnout in Australia averaged about 94 percent. Germany and France were in the upper third of democratic states with 87 and 86 percent, respectively. Costa Rica, in the middle of the pack with 79 percent, showed that Third World countries can achieve respectable turnout figures.

National averages obscure the fact that there can be considerable variation within countries. Canada has quite a disparity of participation rates among provinces. In the 1997 federal election, Prince Edward Island had the highest turnout rate at 74 percent, while Alberta and Newfoundland brought up the rear with 60 and 56 percent, respectively.

The most important question arising from these figures is why citizens in a democracy today would choose to not exercise their franchise. Why would one-third of Canadian voters and as many as one-half of Swiss and American voters not exercise their right to support or reject their governments?

Some citizens may not vote because they are satisfied with what is going on and, so, do not bother, having decided not to let elections get in the way of their busy lives. If that is the case, there may not be much to worry about. But others may not vote because of **political alienation**; that is, they feel estranged from the process or because they have become quite cynical about it. These feelings often are driven by a sense that voters are not effective in the process; their votes will not make a difference, so why vote? If this is the situation, democracy may be in danger of losing its essential popular support.

Beyond these issues of attitude, which vary greatly from one country to another, political scientists have learned a lot about factors that contribute to higher turnout rates. Below are a few of the findings:

- Voters are less likely to vote when it is troublesome to do so. Bad weather can reduce turnout, as can inconvenient registration systems like the American one.

- Exciting, closely contested elections tend to increase turnout.

- People are more likely to vote in national elections than in local ones. Turnout in Canadian municipal elections is usually well below 50 percent.

- People get tired of having to vote if they are too often asked to do so. Switzerland and the United States, which hold frequent elections and referendums, have low turnout rates.

- Proportional representation tends to be associated with higher turnout rates. Under SMP, many voters apparently feel their ballot is "wasted"; and because they know their preferred candidate has no chance of winning, they do not bother to turn out. That is an important reason Canada and the United States, two of the few democracies that still use SMP, fall into the bottom third of countries for turnout levels.

How is vote wasted

FURTHER READING

Bakvis, Herman. *Voter Turnout in Canada*. Royal Commission on Electoral Reform and Party Financing, vol. 15. Toronto: Dundurn Press, 1991.

Bell, David V.J., and Frederick J. Fletcher, eds. *Reaching the Voter: Constituency Campaigning in Canada*. Royal Commission on Electoral Reform and Party Financing, vol. 20. Toronto: Dundurn Press, 1991.

Blizzard, Christina. *Right Turn: How the Tories Took Ontario*. Toronto: Dundurn Press, 1995.

Boyer, Patrick. *Direct Democracy in Canada: The History and Future of Referendums*. Toronto: Dundurn Press, 1992.

_____. *The People's Mandate: Referendums and a More Democratic Canada*. Toronto: Dundurn Press, 1992.

Brennan, Geoffrey, and Loren E. Lomasky. *Democracy and Decision: The Pure Theory of Electoral Preference*. Cambridge, England: Cambridge University Press, 1993.

Cassidy, Michael, ed. *Democratic Rights and Electoral Reform in Canada*. Royal Commission on Electoral Reform and Party Financing, vol. 10. Toronto: Dundurn Press, 1991.

Clarke, Harold. *Political Choice in Canada*. Toronto: McGraw-Hill Ryerson, 1979.

———, et al. *Absent Mandate: Candidate Electoral Politics*, 3rd ed. Vancouver, B.C.: Gage, 1996.

———, et al. *Absent Mandate: Interpreting Change in Canadian Elections*. Toronto: Gage Educational, 1991.

Courtney, John C. et al., eds. *Drawing Boundaries: Legislatures, Courts and Electoral Values*. Saskatoon: Fifth House, 1992.

Crewe, Ivor, and David Denver. *Electoral Change in Western Democracies: Patterns and Sources of Electoral Volatility*. London: Croon Helm, 1985.

Crotty, William J., ed. *Political Participation and American Democracy*. New York: Greenwood Press, 1991.

Dalton, Russell J., et al. *Electoral Change in Advanced Industrial Democracies: Realignment or Dealignment?* Princeton, N.J.: Princeton University Press, 1984.

Frizzell, Alan, Jon H. Pammett, Anthony Westell, eds. *The Canadian General Election of 1993*. Ottawa: Carleton University Press, 1994.

Ginsburg, Benjamin, and Alan Stone, eds. *Do Elections Matter?* Armank, N.Y.: M.E. Sharpe, 1993.

Holler, Manfred J. Power, *Voting and Voting Power*. Vienna: Physica-Verlag, 1982.

Johnston, Paul J., and Harvey Pasis, eds. *Representation and Electoral Systems: Canadian Perspectives*. Scarborough: Prentice-Hall Canada, 1990.

Johnston, Richard, et al. *Letting the People Decide: Dynamics of a Canadian Election*. Montreal: McGill–Queen's University Press, 1992.

Kavanagh, Dennis, ed. *Electoral Politics*. Oxford: Clarendon Press, 1992.

Kornberg, Allan, and Harold Clarke, eds. *Political Support in Canada*. Durham, N.C.: Duke Press, 1983.

Lijphart, Arend. *Electoral Systems and Party Systems: A Study of Twenty-Seven Democracies.* Oxford: Oxford University Press, 1994.

Lijphart, Arend, and Bernard Grofman, eds. *Choosing an Electoral System: Issues and Alternatives.* New York: Praeger, 1984.

Lipset, Seymour M., and Stein Rokkan, eds. *Party Systems and Voter Alignments: Cross-National Perspectives.* New York: Free Press, 1967.

Loenen, Nick. *Citizenship and Democracy: A Case for Proportional Representation.* Toronto: Dundurn, 1997.

Lyons, W.E. *One Man—One Vote.* Toronto: McGraw-Hill Ryerson, 1970.

McLaughlin, David. *Poisoned Chalice: The Last Campaign of the Progressive Conservative Party?* Toronto: Dundurn Press, 1994.

Mishler, William. *Political Participation in Canada.* Toronto: Macmillan, 1979.

Norris, Pippa. *Political Recruitment: Gender, Race and Class in the British Parliament.* Cambridge, England: Cambridge University Press, 1995.

Parry, Geraint, et al. *Political Participation and Democracy in Britain.* Cambridge, England: Cambridge University Press, 1992.

Pierce, Roy. *Choosing the Chief: Presidential Elections in France and the United States.* Ann Arbor: University of Michigan Press, 1995.

Posado-Carbo Eduardo. *Elections Before Democracy: The History of Elections in Europe and Latin America.* New York: St. Martin's Press, 1996.

Rae, Douglas W. *The Political Consequences of Electoral Laws,* rev. ed. New Haven, Conn.: Yale University Press, 1971.

Reeve, Andrew, and Alan Ware. *Electoral Systems: A Comparative and Theoretical Introduction.* London: Routledge, 1992.

Rose, Richard, ed. *Electoral Participation.* Beverly Hills, Calif.: Sage, 1980.

Seidle, Leslie F., ed. *Comparative Issues in Party and Election Finance.* Royal Commission on Electoral Reform and Party Financing, vol. 4. Toronto: Dundurn Press, 1991.

———. *Issues in Party and Election Finance in Canada.* Royal Commission on Electoral Reform and Party Financing, vol. 5. Toronto: Dundurn Press, 1991.

———. *Provincial Party and Election Finance in Canada.* Royal Commission on Electoral Reform and Party Financing, vol. 3. Toronto: Dundurn Press, 1991.

Small, David, ed. *Drawing the Map: Equality and Efficacy of the Vote: Canadian Electoral Boundary Reform.* Royal Commission on Electoral Reform and Party Financing, vol. 11. Toronto: Dundurn Press, 1991.

Verba, Sidney, Norman H. Nie, and Jae-On Kim. *Participation and Political Equality.* Cambridge: Cambridge University Press, 1978.

Wayne, Stephen J. *The Road to the White House, 1996: The Politics of Presidential Elections.* New York: St. Martin's Press, 1996.

Wearing, Joseph, ed. *The Ballot and Its Message: Voting in Canada.* Toronto: Copp Clark Pitman, 1991.

White, Stephen. *How Russia Votes.* Chatham, N.J.: Chatham House Publishers, 1997.

REPRESENTATIVE ASSEMBLIES

According to liberal–democratic theory, the representative assembly should be the central institution for converting political inputs into outputs. Through the mechanism of elections, the sovereign people have delegated to the assembly their power to rule—that is, to make decisions about public business. In the political system, these decisions constitute conversion. Conversion that takes place in the elected assembly meets the standard of democratic legitimacy because it is performed by representatives of the people.

This ideal, which gives central importance to the assembly, must be heavily qualified in reality, because a great deal of decision making also occurs in the executive and judicial branches of government and this decision making is often beyond the effective control and supervision of the assembly. However, we will discuss the assembly first because of its special importance in the theory of liberal democracy.

The most visible function of the democratic assembly is to legislate. This is so true that a representative assembly is commonly referred to as a **legislature.** This terminology is misleading, however, for two reasons: modern assemblies do much more than legislate; and at least in parliamentary systems, they do not effectively control the content of legislation—such control is in the hands of the executive. In the parliamentary system, as described in Chapter 21, the assembly's role is now mostly to discuss and publicize measures drafted by the executive, while party discipline ensures that the outcome of voting is seldom in doubt.

A well-known book on the Parliament of Canada describes the situation in these terms:

> Four essential functions of parliament in the Canadian system are: first, to make a government, that is, to establish a legitimate government through the electoral process; second, to make a government work, that is, to give the government the authority, funds, and other resources necessary for governing the country; third, to make a government behave, that is, to be a watchdog over the government;

and fourth, to make an alternative government, that is, to enable the opposition to present its case to the public and become a credible choice for replacing the party in power. Parliamentary activities of legislating and policy-making are largely aspects of the function of making a government work, and parliament's role in them is not now, nor has it ever been, the dominant one.[1]

The assembly ensures that the business of government is carried out by the executive branch: that laws are enforced, taxes collected, roads paved, and so forth. The assembly cannot itself perform such tasks, but it can cause them to be performed, investigate the performance, and debate the results. In the parliamentary system, responsible government is the chief mechanism by which the assembly retains some control over the business of government. The highest executive officers of the state must be members of the assembly, must be answerable to their colleagues in the assembly for the conduct of business, and must retain the confidence of a working majority. Members of the assembly may ask questions of the executive, request disclosure of documents, and even conduct special investigations into governmental business. Assemblies in presidential systems do not have such intimate ties with the executive, but they possess other powers of control, such as the power to alter budgets. In various ways, all democratic assemblies seek to influence the administration of public business.

Other functions of the assembly can be more briefly described. One is local representation, which has two aspects. At the collective level, representatives speak in the assembly for the interests of their constituents. Representatives from Newfoundland and coastal British Columbia take a special interest in fisheries, those from Saskatchewan have to be vitally concerned with the Wheat Board, and so on. At the individual level, elected representatives, with the aid of their paid staff, spend a great deal of time acting as virtual ombudsmen for the voters in their constituencies. When citizens experience problems with government services—anything from pension cheques to passports—they may ask their representatives to intervene on their behalf.

Still another function is to provide opposition. Members of the assembly who are not on the government's side of the house criticize policies and programs so that governments cannot sweep issues or incidents under the rug. The organized opposition within the assembly may also be ready to offer an alternative government if necessary, so that changes in power can take place without a period of confusion.

An assembly plays two additional roles. It educates the public in the sense that its debates and discussions draw the public's attention to certain issues. And it also socializes the public: because it attempts to wrestle with public problems, it can stimulate the formation of public opinions, attitudes, and beliefs about the nature of the governmental process.

As the scope of state activity has expanded in this century, the limitations on what the assembly can accomplish by itself have grown. During the period of classical liberalism, government was relatively small and the assembly could debate most legislation at length and monitor all the administrative activities of the state.

But the welfare state has grown so large that this is impossible today. This is why there has been a trend in all countries toward greater responsibility of the executive at the expense of the assembly.

This tendency is particularly noticeable in parliamentary systems. Through party discipline, the modern cabinet exercises a high degree of control over the majority caucus and thus over the assembly as a whole. Under these conditions, individual members of the assembly have little effective control over legislation and particularly over governmental revenues and expenditures. The assembly still links the executive to the electorate, but it has lost much of its power to initiate legislation. This is less true in presidential systems, where the assembly is not so subject to party discipline; but even in the United States, which probably has the most independent assembly of all important democracies, political observers have repeatedly commented on how the president's power has grown at the expense of Congress. Recall the discussion in Chapter 21 about the autonomy of Congress in the presidential system.

To grasp the complexity of the Canadian legislative process and the extent to which it is dominated by the executive, consider Figure 29.1. The chart begins with a minister submitting a legislative proposal to cabinet. Probably, this proposal has already been discussed at length within the minister's department. If the proposal survives consideration in a cabinet committee and receives the formal approval of the whole cabinet, it goes for legal drafting by officials of the Department of Justice. It must then be approved by another cabinet committee and again by the whole cabinet. By this time, members of cabinet will have developed firm views about the draft legislation and will not want to see it greatly altered in Parliament.

There are, of course, opportunities for further discussion and amendment in Parliament. The bill must go through floor debate and committee discussion in both the House of Commons and the Senate, and groups affected by the bill can try to get MPs and senators to introduce amendments that are favourable to their interests. Changes to bills take place, but party discipline generally ensures that these changes are within limits acceptable to the cabinet. The chief power of the opposition is that it can exploit the complexity of the process to create delay and force the government to set priorities on its objectives. A determined government can have virtually anything it wants, but it cannot have everything it wants.

The decline of assemblies has long been noted by political scientists but has perhaps not been fully grasped by the public. Many naive views still exist about how assemblies work. People often visualize the elected assembly as the focal point at which all issues are raised, debated, and voted on. Visitors to Ottawa and to the provincial capitals frequently express disillusionment when they see a single speaker talking to an almost empty House. The fact is that much of the work of the assembly is done elsewhere: in the parliamentary system by cabinet, the bureaucracy, the caucus, and parliamentary committees; in the presidential system by cabinet, the bureaucracy, and congressional committees. Full debates from which significant decisions follow are rare. In many cases, full debates come after most of the wrinkles have been ironed out of legislative proposals and compromises have already been struck. In effect, the assembly is putting its stamp of approval on a bill that has already been subjected to a great deal of discussion and scrutiny; and individual members, by making speeches pro and con, are staking out political turf for possible use in the next election.

It would be impossible for the entire assembly to handle all the intricate details involved in working out a compromise among conflicting interests. This is why the executive is responsible for preparing most of the assembly's business and carrying out the administrative details of bills the assembly passes. But, again, the executive must have the support of a majority of members of the assembly before establishing laws or policies. To that extent, the assembly retains real power in the conversion part of the political process. It remains a check on executive power.

The long-term decline of the assembly relative to the executive arm of government has been accompanied by the decline of bicameralism. Many assemblies today are at least nominally bicameral, as shown by the following list.

COUNTRY	LOWER HOUSE	UPPER HOUSE
United Kingdom	House of Commons	House of Lords
Canada	House of Commons	Senate
Australia	House of Representatives	Senate
United States	House of Representatives	Senate
Japan	House of Representatives	House of Councillors
Germany	*Bundestag*	*Bundesrat*
France	National Assembly	Senate

Unicameral assemblies are less common but not rare. They exist, for example, in Denmark, Finland, New Zealand, Tanzania, and all the Canadian provinces. Unicameralism is more common in homogeneous societies or in societies where a deliberate attempt is made to avoid fragmenting a government when the society is already divided along cultural, regional, or racial lines.

Most commonly, upper houses have been allowed to atrophy rather than be abolished outright. They do not fit well with either the logic of majoritarian democracy or the machinery of responsible government. The experience of Canada's Parliament, which has seen the Senate decline in both power and prestige, is typical of many countries. Generally speaking, the only upper houses that have been able to retain their vitality are in presidential systems, such as the one in the United States, or in federal parliamentary systems, such as the one in Germany. In the former instance, senators are elected by the voters of the states; in the latter, they are appointed by the governments of the *Länder*. In both instances, they are seen to represent important and durable interests of particular regions of the country. This principle, which in the end comes down to protecting the minority rights of different regions, has been able

FIGURE 29.1 Overview of the Legislative Process

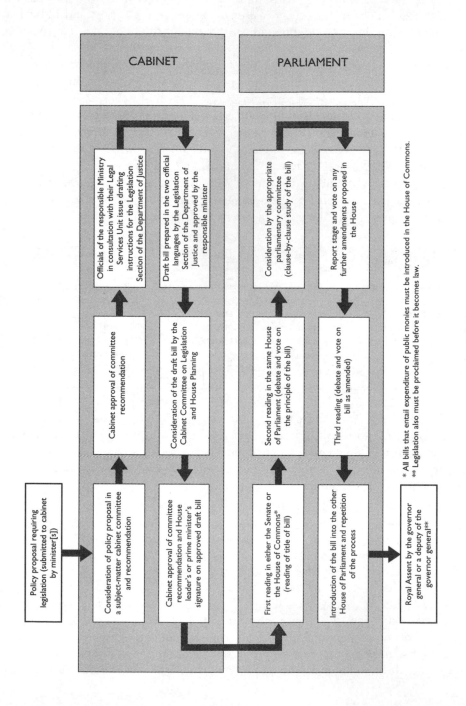

to maintain itself against the democratic legitimacy of majority rule. In contrast, other ways of choosing a second chamber, such as heredity (the House of Lords) or appointment as a reward for service (the House of Lords, the Canadian Senate) provide those bodies so chosen with little force in a direct conflict with democratically elected lower chambers. However, the expertise of an appointed body can make it a legitimate source of technical amendments to legislation.

These considerations lead directly to the much discussed question of how to reform Canada's Senate. Three main options have been put forward in the constitutional debates of the last thirty years. The first is simply to abolish the Senate. This has long been the official position of the NDP, although individuals in that party have sometimes supported other options. In concise terms, the case for abolishing the Senate is that it does not do anything very important, so we should abolish it and save the cost of running it. The second option is to make the Senate a "House of the Provinces," that is, to let senators be appointed by provincial cabinets or elected by provincial legislators and let them serve in Ottawa as acknowledged ambassadors of provincial interests. This model, which is loosely based on the *Bundesrat* model in Germany, would extend the interstate approach to federalism that has characterized recent Canadian political history, as well as legitimize the growing tendency for provinces to deal with each other and with Ottawa almost as though they were sovereign states. The third option is the "triple-E" proposal, which originated in Alberta and has sometimes received support from other provinces. The second chambers in Australia, Switzerland, and the United States serve as models for this approach. In those countries, each constituent government has the same number of representatives (equal); the members are elected by the people, not by the provincial legislatures (elected); and the second chamber has the same, or almost the same, legislative power as the lower house (effective). The triple-E proposal represents the intrastate model of federalism, in which the interests of the various regions of the country are given effective representation within the machinery of the central government as well as through constituent governments. It has been argued that Canadian federalism has veered too much toward the interstate model and that a triple-E Senate would help to restore this country's intrastate character by establishing a federal institution based on provincial interests.

The Charlottetown Accord contained a compromise between the second and third options. Each province was to have the same number of senators, and they were to be popularly elected—except in Quebec, where they were to be chosen by the Quebec National Assembly. The Quebec senators, moreover, were to have a special veto over legislation affecting the French language and culture, thus reinforcing their role as ambassadors of a constituent government rather than equal participants in a federal institution. Opinions differed as to how "effective" this reformed Senate would be. In most cases, its veto could have been overridden in a special joint sitting with the House of Commons, where senators would be greatly outnumbered; but some analysts thought that the power to delay would frequently be equivalent to the power to deny. With the defeat of the Charlottetown Accord, the details are no longer of great importance; but the issue of Senate reform is likely to reappear if and when the larger issue of constitutional change comes back to the political agenda.

※※※※※※※

REPRESENTATION

Before continuing this discussion of representative assemblies, we must re-examine the basic concept of representation.[2] The word *representation* has three different meanings, all of which are relevant to political science:

1. A representative may be a symbol—that is, a sign by which something else is known. A flag or national anthem may be said to represent a country.

2. A representative may be an agent who is empowered to act for a principal, as a lawyer represents a client in the courtroom. In a similar sense, city councillors, members of provincial legislative assemblies, and members of parliament are representatives because they are agents who act on behalf of their electors, who are the principals.

3. A person who shares some of the typical characteristics of a group is sometimes said to represent it. At the collective level, a subset of items is said to be a representative sample if it accurately reflects selected characteristics of the population from which it is drawn. For example, feminists have said that the House of Commons is not truly representative of the Canadian people because only a small minority of its members are women, although more than half of the adult population is female.

We will not concern ourselves further with representation in the symbolic sense. Our focus will be on the latter two meanings, both of which have a bearing on the way people view the role of representatives. Representation is almost a universal fact of politics. Any system, except the smallest and simplest direct democracy, requires that some people act for others. And questions inevitably arise about whether the agents reflect the salient characteristics of their principals.

Theories of representation are as varied as theories of legitimacy. Authoritarian and totalitarian governments of all sorts generally claim to represent their people in some way that does not need to be tested by competitive elections. We will confine ourselves here to discussing representation in liberal democracies.

There are four different ways in which agents represent those who elect them to a representative assembly. Three concern the individual representatives; the fourth concerns representatives as a collective body. To put it another way, representatives may play any one of four different roles.

Trustee

The role of **trustee** demands that representatives rely on their personal judgment when deciding what is in the best interests of the community as a whole. The people elect them and may refuse to re-elect them if they do not like what they do; but in the meantime the representatives act independently. Edmund Burke gave this theory its classic formulation in 1774 in a speech to the electors of Bristol: "Your representative owes you, not his industry only, but his judgement, and he betrays, instead of serving you, if he sacrifices it to your opinion."[3]

Note that Burke was speaking at a time when the right to vote was still extremely limited. Burkean trusteeship is essentially a predemocratic theory of representation. It gives representatives almost *carte blanche* to carry on the business of government, subject to the sole constraint of facing periodic elections. It does not conceive of democracy as an ongoing process in which the people are actively involved in ruling themselves.

In any event, party discipline in parliamentary systems has largely destroyed trusteeship. Canadian MPs are free to use their own judgment only in rare free votes or in behind-the-scenes attempts to influence the party leadership. However, cabinet members might be considered trustees to the extent that they deliberate to determine policy positions that are then imposed on backbenchers. City councillors may act as trustees because parties do not normally function at that level in Canada. American representatives may also act as trustees because party discipline in the United States is rather weak.

Delegate

Representatives are **delegates** if they subordinate their own views to those of their constituents and act as instructed by them. Party discipline largely excludes this role, along with that of trustee. But city councillors often act as delegates when they vote in accord with the wishes of their ward on such issues as road location and the granting of building permits. American representatives also sometimes act as delegates. A famous example was Senator William Fulbright from Arkansas: although he privately claimed to be an integrationist, he voted against civil-rights bills because of the wishes of the majority of his constituents. The delegate model is also used in many private associations, such as trade unions, political parties, and churches; in these cases, representatives chosen to attend national conventions go armed with specific instructions. In Canada, the delegate model has recently been revived by the Reform Party, which has made a big point of claiming that it wants MPs to be free to vote as their constituents wish.

Although the delegate model is attractive to voters in an era when elitism is under attack, there are some major problems in applying it to the running of a large country. Typically, the Parliament of Canada passes dozens of bills every year, some-times more than one hundred. Is it practical for MPs to find out what voters think about all, or even many, of them? And if such consultation is to take place, how should it be organized—town-hall meetings, mail-in ballots, or surveys? And who will interpret the "will" of the constituency? Since there are more than two alterna-tives on most issues of public policy, a majority within the constituency for any par-ticular position may not result. All in all, MPs would have considerable room to create the appearance of consulting their constituents while in fact predetermining the outcome through manipulation of the process.

Note also that the delegate model requires representatives to pursue the special interests of their constituents, not the general good of the community. This limita-tion suggests that representatives cannot always be delegates. There are occasions when the general interest must be paramount over sectional concerns and represen-tatives must rise above the wishes of their electors.

Party Member

Representatives who are party members may vote and act only as loyal members of their caucus, following the instructions of the leadership. The underlying assump-tion is that parties are teams that work together collectively and that people make a choice between these teams when they vote, even though in a legal sense they are voting for individual representatives. Since representatives are team players in this model, they have to vote together in the assembly and be judged on the party's col-lective record at election time. Party discipline has made this the dominant form of representation in parliamentary systems in the twentieth century. However, it is only a minor feature of American politics and does not apply at all to the nonparty sys-tems found in most municipal governments.

The party model assumes that the policy of the party takes account of the gen-eral interest as well as of special interests. In a sense, the party leaders act as trustees, using their own judgment and drawing on their own consciences to determine what is best for the community. Thus, the notion of trusteeship appears somewhere in each of these three models.

The party-member model of representation has become the norm in parliamen-tary systems, particularly in Canada, where party discipline is stronger than in almost any other democracy; and it is generally accepted by politicians and political scientists as indispensable to responsible government. It has never really been accepted by the public, however, and if anything it is growing more unpopular. (Burke, it should be noted, had to leave Bristol and find another riding when he sought re-election.) At the end of 1992, Canadians were asked in a *Maclean's*/CTV poll to express their opinion about the three main theories of representation by answering the question, "How should your Member of Parliament vote on major issues?"[4] The results showed a huge preference for the delegate theory and only tiny support for the party-member model:

- 71 percent said according to the majority view in his or her own riding;
- 21 percent said according to his or her own conscience and beliefs; and
- 7 percent said according to the policies of his or her political party.

Politicians, of course, are aware of the state of public opinion. The Reform Party has gone furthest in trying to exploit the issue by calling on party leaders to allow more free votes in Parliament and on MPs to vote according to the "consensus of the constituency."[5] Many in the other parties have also called for a relaxation of party discipline, but so far nothing much has happened. The brute fact is that the incentives created by the parliamentary system lead inevitably to the party-member model of representation, and the behaviour of MPs will not change without major changes in the system.

The Microcosm

Whatever role representatives play, a qualitatively different question is bound to arise: are they similar to those they represent? In other words, do they reflect the characteristics of race, language, religion, gender, class, income, and occupation that are found in the population at large? A common feeling today is that representatives must be similar to their constituents in order to have their best interests at heart. We can call this the **microcosm theory**—the idea that a governing body should be a miniature replica of those it represents. John Adams, the second president of the United States as well as a political philosopher, wrote 200 years ago that the representative assembly "should be in miniature an exact portrait of the people at large. It should think, feel, reason, and act like them."[6]

Obviously, the microcosm theory cannot be applied too literally. There is an infinity of characteristics that might be considered politically relevant. It is impossible to get a working body of a reasonably small size that will have just the right proportions of all conceivable characteristics. But the theory can be given a more sensible interpretation. While exact proportionality is not important, no significant group of people should be left without a voice. This ties in well with the view of Bernard Crick, discussed in Chapter 2, that politics involves the reconciliation of differences. For example, the precise proportion of French- and English-speaking judges on the Supreme Court of Canada is not critical, but it is important that there be some of each. A more complex example is the Canadian cabinet. In choosing ministers, the prime minister usually tries to select about three-quarters anglophones and one-quarter francophones, including anglophones from inside Quebec and francophones from outside Quebec. In addition, the prime minister wants to have at least one minister from each province, as well as at least token representation for women, ethnic groups, and regions. It is a complicated balancing act with a double purpose: to allow all significant groups to be heard and to convince the population that no sector has been omitted from consideration. Image is as important as reality.

In selecting the ministry (28 cabinet members and eight secretaries of state) after the 1997 election, Prime Minister Chrétien included at least one member from every province plus one from the Northwest Territories. Many minorities were also represented: eight women; four visible-minority representatives, including an Aboriginal person; and an anglophone from Quebec plus two francophones from outside Quebec. Of course, the composition of the cabinet was also affected by the Liberal Party's strong base of support in central Canada; 22 of 28 cabinet ministers came from Ontario and Quebec. Yet, within these political limitations, the prime minister did what he could to send signals to other provinces. He appointed a senator from Nova Scotia, where the Liberals elected no MPs; and he appointed both of the two Liberal MPs from Alberta to the cabinet.

Although microcosmic representation in the cabinet seems necessary in a pluralistic country like Canada, there can be political costs, as illustrated by the story of Brian Mulroney's first cabinet. Because of the long years of Liberal dominance in Quebec, the 58 Conservative MPs from that province were relatively inexperienced when they came to Ottawa in 1984. Many had not been active in politics before or had been associated with other Quebec parties, such as the Union Nationale or the Parti Québécois. In appointing eleven Quebec ministers to his first cabinet, Mulroney had to draw from a less-experienced pool of talent than is usual and desirable. Several of his original appointments did not turn out well, and a few ministers were forced from the cabinet under embarrassing circumstances. All of this contributed substantially to the Mulroney government's image problems in its first term. But the long-term political consequences of underrepresenting Quebec in the cabinet might have been much worse than the effects of these passing embarrassments.

Another problem with the microcosm theory of representation is that, if pushed hard enough, it can conflict with the ordinary democratic understanding of elected representation. Those with the desired demographic characteristics of race or gender may not be those with the ability to get nominated and win an election. This conflict has bedevilled recent discussions about how the proportion of women in the House of Commons can be increased. That proportion has been rising steadily, from less than one percent as recently as 1968 to 18 percent after the election of 1993, to 21 percent after the 1997 election; but it is still much less than the percentage of women in the voting-age population (which is greater than 50 percent because, on average, women live longer than men). The federal Liberals set a goal for the 1997 election of 25 percent women candidates; but in order to reach that goal, the leader had to appoint women to run in some ridings, thus circumventing the normal process of local selection. One can imagine similar problems arising in attempts to fix the gender ratio of elected MPs.

One proposal, however, may at least partially circumvent these difficulties. It has been suggested by the National Action Committee on the Status of Women that single-member constituencies could be turned into dual-member constituencies, and that one member would have to be a woman and the other a man. Voters would have two ballots, one of which they would cast in the women's contest, the other in the men's contest. In this scheme, men and women elected to public office would not just represent their own sex, for each would have been elected by voters of both sexes. In that respect, the proposal would not divide the electorate into opposed camps based on gender. It is true that men would only run against men, and women against women; but that might not be such a grave drawback when we think of the overall contest as one of party against party, for the candidates of all parties would be equally composed of men and women. A proposal similar to this was advanced for the new territory of Nunavut, but it was defeated in a referendum in the spring of 1997.

Each of the four models of representation has its own strengths and weaknesses. Trustees are a bit removed from popular pressure and can thus take a more independent view. The result of the free vote on capital punishment in the House of Commons was that MPs voted to abolish it, even though public-opinion polls showed that most people wanted to reinstate the death penalty. While the trustee role offers an opportunity for independence, it may also lead to representatives voting their own particular biases. Conversely, a close adherence to public opinion, which is the virtue of the delegate role, may blind representatives to the long-range general interest. Party discipline restricts representatives' initiative, but it tends to produce a more coherent and intelligible set of policies. Local politics often degenerates into a name-recognition or popularity contest because councillors act individually as delegates or trustees but rarely as cohesive, identifiable groups. Finally, the microcosm theory has its own special problem: it can clash with efficiency and even with democracy. The person with the right demographic characteristics of gender, language, region, and ethnicity may not be the most able person for the job, or even the person that the voters would choose if they had a choice.

Perhaps there is no simple solution to these problems. It may be that all the modes of representation are useful in varying circumstances and that each can compensate for the drawbacks of the other three. Regardless of what may be best in some abstract sense, the tendency in parliamentary democracies is clear. The roles of trustee and delegate have declined; the party-member role and the microcosm idea now predominate. These latter two are more compatible with the expanded power of the executive that is typical of the welfare state.

FURTHER READING

Arnold, R. Douglas. *The Logic of Congressional Action*. New Haven, Conn.: Yale University Press, 1990.

Birch, A.H. *Representation*. London: Pall Mall Press, 1971.

Campbell, Colin. *The Canadian Senate: A Lobby from Within*. Toronto: Macmillan, 1978.

Close, David, ed. *Legislatures and the New Democracies in Latin America*. Boulder, Colo.: Lynne Rienner, 1995.

Fisher, Louis. *The Politics of Shared Power: Congress and the Executive*. Washington, D.C.: Congressional Quarterly Press, 1981.

Fraser, John A. *The House of Commons at Work*. Montreal: Editions de la Cheneliere, 1993.

Jackson, Robert J., and Michael M. Atkinson. *The Canadian Legislative System*, rev. ed. Toronto: Macmillan, 1980.

Kornberg, Allan. *Canadian Legislative Behaviour: A Study of the 25th Parliament*. Toronto: Macmillan, 1974.

Kornberg, Allan, William Mishler, and Harold D. Clark. *Representative Democracy in the Canadian Provinces*. Scarborough, Ont.: Prentice-Hall Canada, 1982.

Loewenberg, Gerhard, and Samuel C. Patterson. *Comparing Legislatures*. Boston: Little, Brown, 1979.

March, James G., and Johan P. Olsen. *Democratic Governance*. New York: Free Press, 1995.

Mezey, M., *Comparative Legislatures*. Durham, N.C.: Duke University Press, 1979.

Mezey, M.L., and David M. Olson, eds. *Legislatures in the Policy Process: The Dilemmas of Economic Policy*. Cambridge, England: Cambridge University Press, 1991.

Norton, Philip, ed. *Legislatures*. Oxford: Oxford University Press, 1990.

Olson, David M. *Democratic Legislative Institutions: A Comparative View*. Armonk, N.Y.: M.E. Sharpe, 1994.

Ornstein, Norman J., ed. *The Role of the Legislature in Western Democracies*. Washington, D.C.: American Enterprise Institute for Public Policy Research, 1981.

Pitkin, Hanna F. *The Concept of Representation*. Berkeley: University of California Press, 1967.

Sandquist, James L. *The Decline and Resurgence of Congress*. Washington, D.C.: Brookings Institute, 1981.

Schroedel, Jean Reith. *Congress, the President, and Policymaking: A Historical Analysis*. Armonk, N.Y.: M.E. Sharpe, 1994.

Strom, Kaare. *Minority Government and Majority Rule*. Cambridge, England: Cambridge University Press, 1990.

Weaver, R. Kent, and Bert A. Rockman, eds. *Do Institutions Matter? Government Capabilities in the United States and Abroad*. Washington,D.C.: Brookings Institution, 1993.

White, Randall. *Voice of Region: The Long Journey to Senate Reform in Canada*. Toronto: Dundurn Press, 1990.

THE POLITICAL EXECUTIVE

B roadly speaking, the executive branch of government includes not only highly visible officials, such as the prime minister or president, but also the many anonymous officials who labour in the civil service. We will discuss the latter group in the next chapter under the heading of administration; here we will confine our attention to those at the top of the executive pyramid—to those officers of state who are in some sense politically responsible (as opposed to politically neutral, which most public employees are supposed to be). This category includes the head of state, the head of government, and the ministry or cabinet. It also includes the personal advisers and assistants to these officers. We shall refer to all these people as the **political executive.**

THE PARLIAMENTARY EXECUTIVE

We have already discussed the head of state and head of government at some length, but we have said relatively little about other ministers. In Britain, the cabinet is relatively small by Canadian standards; it usually consists of 22 members.[1] However, the British prime minister also appoints dozens of junior ministers, who have specific responsibilities but do not sit in the cabinet. The whole group, which includes but is not limited to cabinet members, is known as the **ministry**.

A century ago, Sir John A. Macdonald could make do with a cabinet of 12, and in the late 1940s, Louis St. Laurent's cabinet had only 19 ministers; but membership grew steadily larger with the expansion of the welfare state. Brian Mulroney governed with 39 or 40 ministers in the cabinet, until he reduced the size to 35 in January 1993.

By that time, the size of the Canadian cabinet had become a political issue in its own right. Comparisons with the American cabinet of 16 are perhaps unfair because of other differences between presidential and parliamentary government; all the same, Canada's cabinets of three dozen or more ministers were very large by the standards of other parliamentary systems. Nations such as Great Britain, Australia, France, and Germany got along perfectly well with about two dozen or even fewer ministers (although in some of these cases junior ministers perform executive functions but do not sit in the cabinet).

Canadian cabinets were oversized for political rather than administrative reasons. The extra appointments were made to put MPs from various regions and demographic categories into positions of prominence and to promote and reward members of caucus whom the prime minister wished to advance because of perceived talent or loyalty.

Canadian cabinets were so big that they almost ceased to function as a whole. The important work was done in cabinet committees and ratified, when necessary, in the increasingly infrequent meetings of the whole cabinet. For a long time the most important cabinet committee (first introduced by Pierre Trudeau) was the Priorities and Planning Committee, which was responsible for setting the agenda of the government. But this body itself tended to grow in size; it reached 19 members by January 1989. At that point, Brian Mulroney created two smaller and more powerful committees: Operations and Expenditure Review.

All of this changed dramatically when Kim Campbell became prime minister in June 1993. She reduced the size of cabinet from 35 to 25, cut the number of cabinet committees in half, and abolished the Priorities and Planning Committee, leaving the Operations Committee as the main inner circle of power. The cabinet was supposed to return, at least to some degree, to the traditional model of doing business as a single body rather than as a collection of committees.

Jean Chrétien initially continued Kim Campbell's reforms by keeping cabinet size at around two dozen, but he increased it to 28 after the 1997 election. He has also appointed another eight or nine (nine in 1993 and eight in 1997) "secretaries of state," which are positions equivalent to British junior ministers (ministers of the Crown exercising specific administrative responsibilities and reporting to senior ministers). The secretaries of state are not paid as much as senior ministers, do not have all the perks, and do not normally attend meetings of the full cabinet, though they may participate in cabinet committees.

Political executives in a liberal democracy perform much the same tasks as executives in any organization—they manage the business of the enterprise. But this is management on a grand scale. The budget of the federal government is larger than that of the twenty largest Canadian corporations combined.

The political executive has two main functions: to initiate policy proposals for the assembly and to supervise the administration of laws passed by the assembly. The first function is a necessity. A session of Parliament would never end if the entire body had to develop its own policy proposals, debate these proposals, consider amendments, and vote on the final versions. Thus, the executive formulates legislative proposals to be submitted to the entire assembly. In parliamentary systems, of course, the executive goes further and actually controls the deliberations of the assembly.

Administration of existing laws is also the responsibility of the executive. Ministers run the different departments in their particular areas of responsibility. A minister of agriculture, for example, is responsible for all federal activities that fall under the department of agriculture. This will include keeping trained agricultural agents in the field, running experimental farms, providing loans to farmers in special situations, and keeping statistics on farm production. The same applies to the fisheries, transport, and labour departments, and so on. Each minister, along with the cabinet collectively, is responsible to the House (and ultimately to the people) for the business of a specific administrative department.

It should be noted again that structural differences exist between parliamentary and presidential executives. Because the executive and the legislature in the parliamentary process are fused, all ministers answer directly to the House for the work of their departments. The institution of Question Period allows backbenchers to pose questions directly to ministers, sometimes putting them under intense political pressure. Steering legislation through the House, and the committees, and so on, is the responsibility of the House Leader, who is also a member of the cabinet. In the presidential system, the president and cabinet secretaries are not members of the legislative assembly, because these institutions are separated. While the executive formulates policy proposals, it is up to the party leaders and committee chairs to manage the flow of legislation. And since cabinet members do not hold seats in the legislature, they cannot be subjected to routine questioning there; no equivalent to Question Period exists in the presidential system.

In the preceding chapter, we noted that the power of the executive has been growing at the expense of the assembly. As governments increase their activities in society, much of the burden of this activity falls on the executive. When governments expand their regulatory role, extend social programs, and generally spend more money on services, the ultimate decision to do all this must be ratified by the legislature. But the executive must formulate proposals and administer those that are passed. This expanding responsibility has, today, placed political executives in the limelight. When people clamour about jobs, inflation, the deficit, and protection of the environment, they aim their comments at the executive. And when governments seem to accomplish something, the executive is the first to take the credit.

The members of the executive also perform symbolic and ceremonial functions, provide party and national political leadership, make government appointments to the judiciary and regulatory agencies, and exercise military power. The expanding role of the political executive has influenced the governmental process in two important ways. First, there has been dramatic growth in the administrative arm of government. Departments, agencies, boards, and commissions have increased in number and size because of the need to carry out more and more administrative responsibilities. This growth is manifested in the size of the civil service at the federal, provincial, and municipal levels. Second, there has developed a very significant organizational tier of advisers to the government. While these advisers are part of the executive, they are separate from the traditional civil service. These personal advisers to the prime minister and the cabinet are important not in terms of numbers, but in terms of their influence on the governmental process.

In Canada, the management of government involves half a dozen so-called **central agencies**, of which four are particularly important: the **Department of Finance;** another government department, the **Treasury Board,** which is supervised by a cabinet committee of the same name; and two staff organizations, the **Prime Minister's Office (PMO)** and the **Privy Council Office (PCO)**. All four are deeply involved in initiating, implementing, and monitoring policy proposals.

The Department of Finance is important because the minister of finance, advised by officials from the Department, prepares the annual budget of the federal government. There may be some discussion in cabinet or in cabinet committees; but, under current practice, the minister of finance will make decisions about how much money each department gets. Only the prime minister can give direction to the minister of finance, and that happens very rarely. That is why, in the Chrétien government of the 1990s, it is Paul Martin, the minister of finance, who has received so much credit for moving toward a balanced budget and who would have received the blame if no progress had been made.

Budgetary allocation elevates the minister of finance over all other cabinet members except the prime minister. Several ministers in the Chrétien government learned to their sorrow that they would have to give up cherished spending projects because they could not get Paul Martin's support. Control of the budget is the single most important management tool that is exercised over the entire range of government activities.

The Treasury Board, which has been separate from the Department of Finance since 1967, is responsible for public administration in general terms. Its minister, known as the President of the Treasury Board, presides over a large bureaucracy, the most important function of which is to provide central control over expenditures. Proposals from departments to spend money must be approved by the Treasury Board, which verifies that they conform to government policy. The Department of Finance prepares the budget and allocates money to the various departments, while the Treasury Board ensures that the money is spent for approved purposes.

The PMO came into its own under Pierre Trudeau and has continued to be important under every prime minister since. Directed by the prime minister's chief of staff or principal secretary, the PMO includes political operatives as well as advisers on special topics such as trade, energy, and regional economic development. These people are hired and fired by the prime minister and serve without the career security of civil servants. In particular, the prime minister relies on the PMO for political advice that neutral public servants should not be asked to give. The highest appointments in the PMO are usually personal friends or political associates of the prime minister; the junior appointments are usually young people who put in a few years of extremely concentrated work before going on to something more regular (and probably less exciting).

The PCO is a special organization designed to serve the cabinet. First, a word about the Privy Council. It is made up of all present and former cabinet ministers, as well as a few other individuals who have received the special honour of membership. However, the cabinet is the only working part of the Privy Council and acts in its name; the council as a whole does not meet. R. MacGregor Dawson explained it this way:

> The Privy Council ... performs no functions as a Council, despite the fact that it is mentioned a number of times in the British North American Act as an advisory body to the Governor. Such functions have been assumed by that small portion of the Council which constitutes the Cabinet of the moment.[2]

The PCO, however, is very much alive; as the secretariat to the cabinet, it is responsible for helping that body to manage overall government priorities and coordinating the process by which these priorities are achieved. Cabinet relies on the PCO as a source of advice independent of the permanent departments, which ministers often perceive as captive to tradition and special interests.

These and other central agencies do not themselves provide services to the public; rather, they are instruments by which the prime minister and cabinet attempt to manage the entire public service. Which organizations play the key role in the process depends to a great extent on the style of the prime minister. Trudeau, for example, relied heavily on the PMO and then on the PCO to assist the executive in setting the agenda for parliamentary sessions. Brian Mulroney was more inclined to listen to the Priorities and Planning Committee of cabinet when setting the agenda of his government. Formally, the lines of responsibility are as follows:

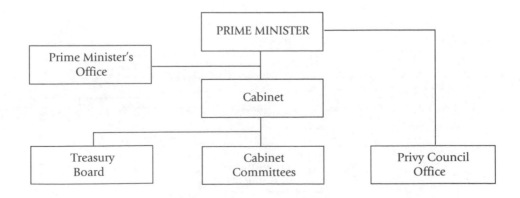

This structure complements the older direct relationship between the prime minister, the cabinet, and the bureaucracy, and also acts as a counterweight to the growing permanent bureaucracy. At the same time, however, it has led critics to suggest that cabinet ministers and senior bureaucratic officials, such as deputy ministers and assistant deputy ministers, have taken a back seat to the prime minister's personal advisers. Critics contend that central agencies have given the prime minister an inordinate amount of power in the legislative arena. With the support of the PMO and PCO, the prime minister can dominate the process by which public policy proposals are developed and priorities assigned. The expansion of these organizations reinforces the argument that the collegiality of cabinet government has given way to prime-ministerial government, which is highly focused on the person of the prime minister.

THE PRESIDENTIAL EXECUTIVE

Comparisons are sometimes drawn between the contemporary situation of the prime minister, who has a phalanx of personal advisers in the PMO and PCO, and that of an American president, who has an admittedly much larger staff. The comparison is worrisome in that the president does not control Congress to the extent that the prime minister controls Parliament. The power of the latter is less balanced by an independent legislative assembly.

The executive branch in the United States also is responsible for initiating legislation. The president has some 4000 staff members who are the organizational network supporting domestic- and foreign-policy initiatives. The president, like the prime minister, is the chief executive officer. He chooses cabinet secretaries to direct the administrative departments of government, such as agriculture, defence, foreign affairs, and transportation. In addition, the president has two offices that assist in setting the policy direction of the government: the **White House Staff** and the **Executive Office.**

Composed of personal advisers to the → president

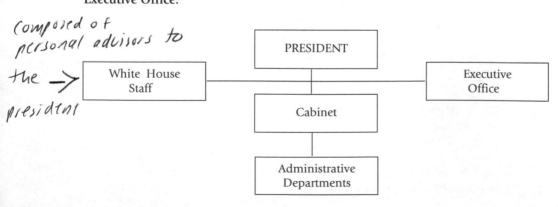

The White House Staff is composed of the personal advisers to the president. The description by two writers on American politics conveys the flavour of this system:

> It is not accidental that journalists have come to popularize the staff of each president with such names as the "Irish Mafia" (Kennedy), the "Georgia Mafia" (Carter), and the "California Mafia" (Reagan). Every modern president has gathered around himself those people who fought most of the battles with him during his long struggle for ultimate political success. These are his trusted political friends, and their value to him has been proven over time. But this group of trusted cronies is now only the small core of a large personal staff, the White House staff.[3]

During the Bush administration, those around the president were often called the "Eastern Establishment" and now of course there is Bill Clinton's "Arkansas Mafia." Prominent figures in the White House staff of any president include the chief of staff, the communications director, and the special legal counsel. The president's wife (until now all presidents have been men and almost all have been married) may also be an influential figure. Clinton put his wife, Hillary Rodham Clinton, more in the public eye by appointing her to head a special task force on health-care issues; but other wives have been highly influential behind the scenes.

The Executive Offices are in the building adjacent to the White House. These offices house a number of agencies that are vital to the president's policy-making role; for example, the Office of Management and Budget, the Council of Economic Advisors, the Office of the United States Trade Representative, and the National Security Council. The president consults the latter organization in times of international crisis. It was in almost constant session just before the decision to launch the Gulf War.

The individuals and organizations that make up the executive in the presidential system do not merely initiate policy—they also have the formidable job of selling the policy proposals to Congress. They must get a majority of those voting in both the House of Representatives and the Senate on their side to get the legislation through Congress. This means that much of their work involves finding ways to get members of Congress of whatever party to support their initiatives. This work is part of the dynamic of "logrolling" or "porkbarrelling," as this kind of politics is sometimes called. By any name, it involves devising tradeoffs that will lead to a majority vote in Congress.

🝆🝆🝆🝆🝆🝆🝆

RESPONSIBLE GOVERNMENT AND MINISTERIAL RESPONSIBILITY

Returning to the parliamentary system, two mechanisms were traditionally thought to make the assembly the ultimate master of the political executive. Under the principle of responsible government, the cabinet is collectively accountable to the House because the prime minister and the cabinet cannot remain in office without the support of a working majority in the popularly elected branch of the assembly. But we have seen how party discipline has weakened, if not completely destroyed, the meaning of responsible government. Recall the discussion in Chapter 21 about the dominance of the executive in the modern parliamentary system.

The second great check on the political executive was supposed to be the individual responsibility of every minister to the assembly. Each minister receives a **portfolio**, which contains one or more departments or agencies. Under the doctrine of **ministerial responsibility**, when there is a serious problem in a department, such as dishonesty, mismanagement, or gross incompetence, a minister should offer to resign. This idea developed in the age of smaller government, when it was reasonable to assume that ministers could keep in touch with everything done by the employees of their departments. It is somewhat unrealistic to expect the same today, given the far-flung activities of departments that may have thousands of employees and budgets of billions of dollars. Thus, ministers in Canada today do not usually offer their resignations unless they are personally implicated in a breach of trust, even if the opposition parties demand that they step down.

All recent ministerial resignations under the doctrine of ministerial responsibility have involved personal actions. During Brian Mulroney's first term, eight ministers resigned from cabinet for personal indiscretions. For example, Robert Coates visited a strip bar in West Germany while on an official trip, and Sinclair Stevens did not insulate himself completely enough from his private business affairs. In contrast, Michael Wilson rejected calls for his resignation as finance minister when the 1989 budget was leaked to the press before it was read to the House of Commons. Wilson, supported by the prime minister, said he could not be expected to resign because of an error by an unknown employee far down the chain of command.

The same pattern prevailed during the term of the Liberal government of Jean Chrétien that came to power in 1993. The prime minister accepted the resignation of Sheila Copps because she had publicly promised to resign if the goods and services tax was not repealed; she then won a hastily called by-election and was reappointed to the cabinet. During the Somalia inquiry, David Collenette's position as minister of defence steadily became more untenable as revelations mounted about military misconduct; but, in spite of many calls from the opposition benches for his resignation, he did not resign over this issue. He did resign, however, after the publication by the press of a letter that went out over his signature. The letter concerned an immigration problem in his own riding and had nothing at all to do with his ministerial responsibilities.

Ministerial responsibility has lost much of its effectiveness because it is now in practice limited to the minister's personal actions and no longer includes the actions of departmental officials. Nonetheless, the assembly still has the power to inquire, expose, and accuse. Ministers do not wish to appear in a bad light; for, even if their jobs are not immediately threatened, their long-term political future could be jeopardized. Thus, most executive functions are tempered by regard for the assembly. In spite of the trend toward executive power, the executive and the assembly remain interdependent. Checks on the executive exist today as they always have. Votes of confidence, the opinions of caucus, and regular elections are only three of these. The power of the executive, while great, is not absolute.

𝕤𝕤𝕤𝕤𝕤𝕤𝕤

FURTHER READING

Bakvis, Herman. *Regional Ministers: Power and Influence in the Canadian Cabinet*. Toronto: University of Toronto Press, 1991.

Band, John R., and Richard Fleisher. *The President in the Legislative Arena*. Chicago: University of Chicago Press, 1990.

Burns, James MacGregor. *Leadership*. New York: Harper and Row, 1978.

Campbell, Colin. *Governments under Stress: Political Executives in Washington, London and Ottawa*. Toronto: University of Toronto Press, 1983.

Campbell, Colin, and M.J. Wyszomirski, eds. *Executive Leadership in Anglo-American Systems*. Pittsburgh: University of Pittsburgh Press, 1991.

Davis, James W. *The President and Party Leader*. New York: Greenwood Press, 1992.

Dunn, Christopher J.C. *The Institutionalized Cabinet: Governing the Western Provinces*. Kingston, Ont.: Institute of Public Administration of Canada, 1995.

French, Richard D. *How Ottawa Decides: Planning and Industrial Policy Making, 1968–1980*. Ottawa: Canadian Institute for Economic Policy, 1980.

Gardner, John William. *On Leadership*. New York: Free Press, 1990.

Hennessy, Peter. *Cabinet*. Oxford: Basil Blackwell, 1986.

Hirschfield, Robert S. *The Power of the Presidency*. New York: Aldine, 1982.

Keyes, John Mark. *Executive Legislation: Delegated Law Making by the Executive Branch*. Toronto: Butterworths, 1992.

Laver, Michael, and Kenneth A. Shepsle. *Making and Breaking Governments: Cabinets and Legislatures in Parliamentary Democracies*. New York: Cambridge University Press, 1996.

———, eds. *Cabinet Ministers and Parliamentary Government*. Cambridge, England: Cambridge University Press, 1994.

Linz, Juan J., and Arturo Valenzuela. *The Failure of Presidential Democracy*. Baltimore: Johns Hopkins University Press, 1994.

Lynn, Lawrence E., Jr. *Managing the Public's Business: The Job of the Government Executive*. New York: Basic Books, 1981.

Mackintosh, John P. *The British Cabinet*, 3rd ed. London: Stevens and Sons, 1977.

Neustadt, Richar, E. *Presidential Power and the Modern Presidents: The Politics of Leadership from Roosevelt to Reagan*. New York: Free Press, 1990.

Pal, Leslie, and David Taras, eds. *Prime Ministers and Premiers: Political Leadership and Public Policy in Canada*. Scarborough, Ont.: Prentice-Hall Canada, 1988.

Punnett, R.M. *Front Bench Opposition: The Role of the Leader of the Opposition, the Shadow Cabinet, and the Shadow Government in British Politics*. London: Heinemann, 1973.

———. *The Prime Minister in Canadian Government and Politics*. Toronto: Macmillan, 1977.

Smith, David E. *The Invisible Crown: The First Principle of Canadian Government*. Toronto: University of Toronto Press, 1995.

Thurber, James A. *Divided Democracy: Cooperation and Conflict Between the President and Congress*. Washington, D.C.: Congressional Quarterly Inc., 1991.

Warwick, Paul. *Government Survival in Parliamentary Democracies*. Cambridge, England: Cambridge University Press, 1994.

THE ADMINISTRATION

CHAPTER 31

The modern state requires a large administrative apparatus to implement its legislation and policies. The assembly and the executive would be powerless without the support of a massive **administration**, a term which is used here interchangeably with **bureaucracy**. The latter word has acquired many negative connotations relating to delay, inflexibility, and red tape; but it has a particular and indispensable meaning in social science. Bureaucracy is a particular kind of social structure for carrying out organized work, a structure that has the following characteristics:

1. The work is divided into impersonal roles or offices that may be filled by different people as the need arises. Bureaucracies always have job descriptions to ensure that the functions of the positions are stable over time.

2. These positions tend to be specialized—another way of saying that there is a high degree of division of labour.

3. This specialization demands a career commitment from employees, because complex roles can be learned only through long experience.

4. Careers are protected by some form of job security or tenure. Usually this means that employees can be dismissed only for designated cause.

5. Positions are filled by **merit recruitment**, which normally means competitive examination. The opposite is recruitment by patronage, which means that jobs are distributed according to kinship, friendship, or personal favour.

6. Ideally, a bureaucracy is supposed to be a neutral instrument in the hands of those who command it; in this regard, it is organized as a hierarchy, with authority flowing from top to bottom.

7. A bureaucracy minimizes the discretion of its employees, who must work within policies and rules laid down by authority. Found in almost every bureaucracy are an administrative manual, a rule book, a policy manual, and extensive written records; all of these help to make administration regular and predictable.

The bureaucratic form of organization is not confined to government. The Roman Catholic Church and large corporations are examples of private bureaucracies. Although bureaucracies were known in ancient empires such as Rome, Egypt, and China, they have been perfected and widely used in the West only in recent times. The absolute monarchs of the eighteenth century created bureaucratic armies, but government administration did not become bureaucratic in general until the late nineteenth and early twentieth centuries. The principle of merit recruitment was not really accepted in Canada until the Civil Service Act of 1908 was passed.

A bureaucracy has many advantages when it runs smoothly—that is why it has been so widely adopted. Ideally, it exhibits honesty, impartiality, stability, predictability, and a measure of competence. It may be short on imagination and innovation, but presumably these qualities can be found elsewhere in the political system. In theory, it should be politically neutral, responding to directions from the assembly and the political executive but not itself making political decisions. As we shall see, this last expectation is not wholly realistic: the bureaucracy must be considered an independent element in the conversion phase of the political process, not just a passive adjunct to the political executive. Moreover, because the bureaucracy tends to become the home of many institutional pressure groups that pursue their own interests while also performing the public business, it is an important source of demands on the political system.

The bureaucracy has two fundamental roles in the governmental process: it advises the political executive, and it administers the laws and policies enacted by the assembly. Under the first heading, whenever the cabinet wishes to introduce legislation, the preparatory work and the drafting will always be done by civil servants. In its administrative role, the bureaucracy is responsible for such matters as distributing child-benefit cheques and veterans' pensions, staffing customs and immigration offices in Canada and abroad, monitoring environmental conditions, and performing a myriad of other tasks in the modern welfare-service state.

TYPES OF STATE AGENCIES

The bureaucratic structure is enormously complex. In the early 1990s, there were about 220,000 employees in the federal public service, excluding the employees of Crown corporations and uniformed military personnel in the Canadian Forces. The budget cuts made by the Chrétien government in the mid-1990s were expected to reduce that total by about 40,000 positions over a period of several years. If one counts the number of people working directly or indirectly for the federal government in departments, agencies, boards, Crown corporations, and the military, the total may be around 500,000. If one includes provincial and municipal employees, the figure is well over one million people.

Canadian governments have created several kinds of bureaucracies. Most completely under government control is the public service in the narrow sense; this includes the departments and other agencies that are directly supervised by ministers, such as the agriculture and transport departments. Less thoroughly controlled are the many autonomous or semiautonomous boards, commissions, and Crown corporations. It is difficult to generalize about these bodies because their structures and responsibilities vary greatly with the statutes by which they were created. Students will be most familiar with those Crown corporations that are essentially business enterprises owned by the government, such as Canada Post, Via Rail, and the Canadian Broadcasting Corporation. Other boards, commissions, and Crown corporations are more regulatory in character—that is, they do not operate large programs of their own, but monitor and control the activities of others. Examples of regulatory bodies are the Canadian Radio–television and Telecommunications Commission and the Canadian Transport Commission. **Regulatory agencies** attempt to impose public policies on the market without resorting to public ownership.

The term **Crown corporation** is unique to Canada, but public corporations can be found in almost every nation-state. They used to be numerous in Great Britain, where a great wave of nationalization of key resource and transport industries occurred after World War II. Between 1946 and 1951, the Labour government created the National Coal Board, the British Railways Board, the National Bus Company, the National Freight Corporation, the British Gas Corporation, and the British Steel Corporation. Between 1971 and 1977, the government also acquired a number of ailing industries: Rolls Royce, British Leyland, British National Oil Corporation, British Shipbuilders, and British Aerospace. By 1976, nationalized public corporations "accounted for 9.6% of GNP and 6.9% of employment."[1] But under Margaret Thatcher's privatization policy, almost all of these corporations, as well as many not named here, were sold to owners in the private sector.

Public corporations in the United States are mostly public utilities—for example, electric companies—managed by independent commissions. These are usually authorized under state law. Amtrak (the national railway-passenger service) and the U.S. Postal Service are two public corporations responsible to the federal government. In all cases, the public corporation, as an alternative to the conventional civil service, is supposed to offer more business flexibility while remaining linked to the political executive.

At the provincial level in Canada, the same distinction exists between the public service in the narrow sense and semi-independent agencies and Crown corporations. For example, most provinces have monopolistic agencies to market alcoholic beverages; from a functional point of view, these are businesses that happen to be owned by government. Provincial governments also own, or have owned in the past, a wide range of businesses such as railways, airlines, natural-resource companies, utilities, and financial institutions. At the provincial and municipal levels, many service agencies have been established by government, and are largely funded by it, but operate more or less autonomously under elected or appointed boards of directors. Public schools, universities, hospitals, and police forces are in this category.

᠍᠍᠍᠍᠍᠍᠍᠍

CONTROL OF THE ADMINISTRATION

The basic principle of control of the public service in a parliamentary system is that the bureaucracy is supposed to be responsible to the political executive and through it to the elected assembly. Each department is headed by a minister of the Crown. Quasi-independent agencies and boards, such as the Canadian Human Rights Commission and the National Parole Board, as well as Crown corporations like Via Rail and the Bank of Canada, are not directly under ministerial authority but must report to a minister. If the operations of a commission or Crown corporation do not please the cabinet or the assembly, different personnel may be appointed to leadership positions, or legislation may be introduced to change the body's terms of reference. The underlying principle is hierarchical control and responsibility, modelled on a pyramid of authority delegated from the sovereign.

This political control of bureaucracy in the public sector contrasts with the competitive balance of bureaucracies in the private sector. Private bureaucracies are to some extent a check on each other, as corporations compete for dollars and churches for souls; but what is to restrain the public bureaucrats who wield the authority of the state? When government offers a nonmonopolistic public service, competition provides some control, as in the case of the CBC; but most governmental services are monopolistic, so that the competitive model is inapplicable. What remains is the model of authoritative hierarchy and responsibility.

In the British parliamentary tradition, Canada has tried to control the public service by ensuring that it is firmly subordinated to Parliament, as illustrated in Figure 31.1. The basis of the Canadian system is that all executive power emanates from the Crown. The Crown acts only through ministers, who in turn are accountable to the House of Commons for their actions. These ministers supervise the machinery of government under their respective portfolios and thus share responsibility for the supervision of the entire public service. The bureaucracy, as a hierarchy, is supposed to respond to direction from above. In this way popular sovereignty is ultimately served and the public service is kept a servant of the people, not its master.

Ministers are politicians, not specialists in the business of their portfolios. They seldom serve in any one position long enough to build up much expertise; in fact, many prime ministers deliberately rotate their ministers to prevent them from becoming too identified with a particular aspect of government. **Deputy ministers**, in contrast, are not politicians but career civil servants (or, occasionally, administrative experts brought in from the private sector). The prime minister's power to appoint deputy ministers is an important lever for controlling the public service.

FIGURE 31.1 Subordination of Bureaucracy to Parliament

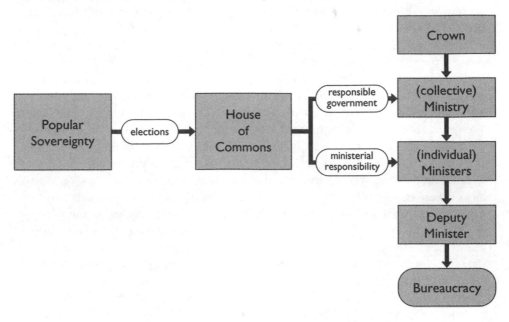

Deputy ministers have reached the apex of the bureaucracy; presumably they have been promoted for competence. They run their departments, issuing instructions through assistant deputy ministers down the whole chain of command. They are also supposed to offer advice to their ministers, explaining what is or is not administratively feasible. Because of this huge responsibility, deputy ministers serve at the pleasure of the Crown and can be dismissed at any time; but it is Canadian practice not to fire deputy ministers very often. They may be transferred from one department to another, but they are seldom dismissed unless they have been politically indiscreet. This is in sharp contrast to the American custom, which is for the incoming president to make wholesale changes in the top ranks of the federal civil service.

By the time Bill Clinton was inaugurated as president on January 20, 1993, his transition team had been busy for months finding ideologically and politically suitable people to fill the more than 3,000 appointments he would make. President Clinton left many of these people in office after he won the 1996 election; but if his opponent, Bob Dole, had won, there would have been a complete housecleaning and the Republican transition team would have been presenting thousands of new faces for appointment. In the American system, the changeover in personnel goes far beyond the equivalent of the deputy-minister level; it reaches down five or six layers into the bureaucracy. To some extent, the American practice is a survival of the nineteenth-century **spoils system** ("To the winners belong the spoils," President Andrew Jackson is reputed to have said); but it represents more than pure patronage. It is based on the assumption that the political executive—which includes the president and the cabinet—cannot really control the bureaucracy unless it has the support of like-minded administrators at the pinnacle of the civil service. The result is a frank and open politicization of the upper levels of the bureaucracy.

In contrast, Canadian civil servants are supposed to be politically neutral and able to work under a minister of any party. After coming to power in 1984, the new Conservative government of Brian Mulroney dismissed very few senior civil servants, a surprise after so many years of Liberal government appointments. The new government did, however, initiate an extensive retirement program for senior civil servants as a way of renewing the administration. Similarly, the government of Jean Chrétien offered generous early retirement incentives, although this was done to reduce the size of the civil service rather than to change its political complexion.

The Canadian model of administrative control assumes that there is a clear distinction between politics and administration. Politics is supposed to be the realm where goals are set and choices are made between options; administration is supposed to be the realm where settled policy is carried into effect. Politics is the business of ministers, and administration is the business of deputy ministers; and the latter are clearly subordinate to the former. But this assumption is only partially true. Politicians in power depend on information and expert advice from the public service. These administrative officials, with their knowledge and experience, wield a great deal of power in the political process. This power may overshadow that of elected officials, who are not expected to have technical expertise. Civil servants can make or break legislative proposals. Furthermore, even when legislation is adopted, it will have to be put into effect by the public service. Much may depend on the way a law is put into practice. Modern legislation is only a broad framework; its impact only becomes clear as administrative decisions accumulate.

The British television series *Yes Minister* derived its popularity from the way it portrayed the efforts of Jim Hacker, a new and bumbling minister, to control Sir Humphrey Appleby, his cunning and experienced **permanent secretary** (the British equivalent of a deputy minister). Hacker loses almost all the battles, for many reasons. He cannot deal directly with the civil service but must work through the permanent secretary. Sir Humphrey is far more experienced and knowledgeable about the affairs of the department than is Hacker, and he knows that Hacker is likely to last no more than a year or two at this particular ministry.

Many observers of politics fear that too much power is vested in the public service and that it is not as subordinate as it should be to cabinet and Parliament. A number of experiments have been made in an effort to address this issue. As mentioned above, prime ministers have greatly enlarged their personal staff in the Prime Minister's Office and the cabinet staff in the Privy Council Office with the goal of depending less on the regular public service for advice. The federal House of Commons has appointed an independent **auditor general** to review the annual expenditures of the public service. The Public Accounts Committee of the House, to which the auditor general reports, is chaired by a member of the Opposition, which gives it greater latitude in investigating possible administrative misuse of funds.

Nine of the ten provinces have established an **ombudsman's** office to deal with complaints from individual citizens who feel that bureaucrats have not treated them properly. Typically, the office does not have the authority to grant relief to a complainant; even so, its power to investigate and expose may be enough to goad the bureaucracy into taking another look at the matter.

These and other reforms may all do something to reduce the power of the public bureaucracy and make it accountable to politicians—and ultimately to the people. Yet it is doubtful whether any true solution to the problem is in sight. The mechanisms of parliamentary control of administration were developed in an era of small government. If people want a large, service-oriented state that does a great deal for them, they will have to live with a powerful bureaucracy, since it is the only means by which such a state can deliver the services people demand of it.

Even the most casual observer of government knows that bureaucratic agencies, once created, are rarely dissolved, and that most seem to grow inexorably despite changes in the political complexion of the cabinet. There is a logical reason for this. Public servants, like other individuals, are self-interested—they seek success and advancement in their chosen careers. In order to advance in a bureaucratic structure, one must supervise more people, run more programs, spend a larger budget, and deliver more services. Thus, those who work within any bureaucracy have powerful incentives to try to expand their own organization.

This tendency is equally strong in private and public bureaucracies, but there are stronger countervailing tendencies in the former than in the latter. Business corporations cannot pursue growth to the neglect of profitability; expansion for its own sake will lead to lower rates of return on investment, declining dividends on shares, falling prices on the stock market, and possibly even bankruptcy. The existence of market competition, to the extent that it is effective, disciplines the internal tendencies of the bureaucracy toward expansion for its own sake. Public bureaucracies, which rarely compute profit and loss and usually enjoy a monopoly position, lack this countervailing force. This tendency toward self-aggrandizement must be checked by political resistance—most often a shortage in the public treasury. Because of the internal incentives built into public administration, the political masters of the bureaucracy will continue to receive advice favouring the growth of the welfare-service state.[2] This was summarized by Sir Humphrey Appleby in *Yes Minister* in the following way:

> There has to be some way to measure success in the Service. British Leyland can measure success by the size of its profits ... However, the Civil Service does not make profits or losses. Ergo, we measure success by the size of our staff and our budget. By definition a big department is more successful than a small one.[3]

While large bureaucracies may be a fact of life in modern governments, they nevertheless are a problem, as articulated in a lecture delivered by a former leader of the Conservative Party, Robert Stanfield:

while the House of Commons has been losing control, so also has the Government. The ministers just do not have the time to run such a vast show and make such a vast range of decisions. Consequently, more and more is for all practical purposes being decided by and implemented by the bureaucracy.[4]

The federal government is the largest employer in the country; effective management of federal employees will never be easy. However, the fact that future governments will not enjoy the same revenue growth as in the past may force better management of the public sector.

In the postwar expansionary period of the Western democracies, when public revenues seemed to be on a permanently upward course, the drive of the civil service to aggrandize itself interlocked neatly with the desire of politicians to win support by offering government services to the voters. These forces worked together to increase the size of government. However, the old rules appear to be changing as politicians compete with each other to reduce deficits. In Canada, as in many other countries, government as measured in the number of employees and the cost of operations has been shrinking in recent years as a percentage of gross domestic product. Faced with difficult choices, politicians opted to cut government operations before touching transfer payments that go directly into the pockets of citizens. The ambitions of civil servants should not be taken as a master explanation for the growth of government; the self-interest of politicians and voters was just as important a factor.

§§§§§§§

FURTHER READING

Bird, Richard M., in collaboration with Meyer W. Bucovetsky and David K. Foot. *The Growth of Public Employment in Canada*. Ottawa: Institute for Research on Public Policy, 1979.

Brown, R.G.S., and D.R. Steel. *The Administrative Process in Britain*, 2nd ed. London: Methuen, 1979.

Campbell, Colin, and George J. Szablowski. *The Superbureaucrats: Structure and Behavior in Central Agencies*. Toronto: Macmillan, 1979.

Campbell, Robert Malcolm, and Leslie A. Pal. *The Real Worlds of Canadian Politics: Cases in Process and Policy*, 3rd ed. Peterborough, Ont.: Broadview Press, 1994.

Dilulio, John J., Jr., ed. *Deregulating the Public Service: Can Government Be Improved?* Washington: Brookings Institution, 1994.

Downs, Anthony. *Inside Bureaucracy*. Boston: Little, Brown, 1967.

Etzioni-Halevy, Eva. *Bureaucracy and Democracy*. London: Routledge and Kegan Paul, 1983.

Granatstein, J.L. *The Ottawa Men*. Toronto: Oxford University Press, 1982.

Hodgetts, J.E. *The Canadian Public Service: A Physiology of Government 1867–1970*. Toronto: University of Toronto Press, 1973.

Johnson, Cathy Marie. *The Dynamics of Conflict Between Bureaucrats and Legislators*. Armonk, N.Y.: M.E. Sharpe, 1993.

Kauffman, Franz-Xavier, ed. *The Public Sector: Challenge for Coordination and Learning*. Berlin: Walter de Gruyter, 1991.

———. *Public Administration in Canada*, 5th ed. Toronto: Methuen, 1987.

Kernaghan, Kenneth, and John W. Langford. *The Responsible Public Servant*. Halifax: Institute for Research on Public Policy, 1990.

Kingdom, John, ed. *The Civil Service in Liberal Democracies: An International Survey*. London: Routledge, 1990.

Levine, Charles H., et al. *Public Administration: Challenges, Choices and Consequences*. Glenview, Ill.: Scott, Foresman/Little, Brown Higher Education, 1990.

Lynn, Naomi B., and Aaron B. Wildavsky, eds. *Public Administration: The State of the Discipline*. Chatham, N.J.: Chatham House, 1990.

Morgan, Nicole S. *Implosion: An Analysis of the Growth of the Federal Public Service in Canada, 1945–1975*. Montreal: Institute for Research on Public Policy, 1986.

Osbaldeston, Gordon F. *Keeping Deputy Ministers Accountable*. Toronto: McGraw-Hill Ryerson, 1988.

Paehlke, Robert, and Douglas Torgerson, eds. *Managing Leviathan: Environmental Politics and the Administrative State*. Broadview Press: Peterborough, Ont., 1990.

Pal, Leslie A. *State, Class and Bureaucracy: Canadian Unemployment Insurance and Public Policy*. Kingston, Ont.: McGill-Queen's University Press, 1988.

Peters, B. Guy. *The Politics of Bureaucracy*, 2nd ed. New York: Longman, 1984.

Rowat, Donald C., ed. *Public Administration in Developed Democracies: A Comparative Study*. New York: Dekker, 1988.

Savoie, Donald. *The Politics of Public Spending in Canada*. Toronto, Ont.: University of Toronto Press, 1990.

Self, Peter. *Administrative Theories and Politics*. Toronto: University of Toronto Press, 1973.

Taylor, James R., and Elizabeth J. Van Every. *The Vulnerable Fortress: Bureaucratic Organization and Management in the Information Age*. Toronto: University of Toronto Press, 1993.

Wilson, Vincent Seymour. *Canadian Public Policy and Administration*. Toronto: McGraw-Hill Ryerson, 1981.

THE JUDICIARY

Although the judicial system was originally intended to be apolitical, it has now become a key part of the political process. Political actors now see the courts as an alternative (usually the last alternative) to the legislature, the political executive, and the bureaucracy in matters of achieving policy objectives. We will describe some of the less political functions of the judiciary before returning to its role in political decision making.

JUDICIAL STRUCTURES

The rule of law is a cornerstone of civilized life. Institutionalized rules (laws), when applied equally, discourage both public authorities and private individuals from arbitrarily using power. An extension of the rule of law is the court system, where legal disputes are adjudicated. The adjudication of disputes between individuals, between individuals and the state, and between different levels of government within the state takes place within the boundaries of a single country. There are also disputes involving two or more states, and individuals or corporations and other states, that concern breaches of international law. Such disputes may be brought before the International Court of Justice, but the decisions of that body are not binding because no power exists to enforce them; compliance in such cases is voluntary. In this chapter we will not look further at international courts, but will confine ourselves to a discussion of domestic law and court systems.

There is no single model for a system of courts; rather, every country seems to adopt a structure of courts in response to its particular needs. In particular, court systems tend to vary between federal and unitary states. In a unitary system, there is typically a single set of laws passed by the national legislature and a single system of courts administering justice. In a federal system, in which laws are made by different levels of government, there may be more than one tier of courts: federal courts with responsibility for federal laws, and provincial or state courts for provincial or state laws. Moreover, specialized courts may be established to deal with specific laws. For example, tax, labour, family, and juvenile courts can be found in many countries.

The British courts are an example of court organization in a unitary state. There is a single unified system, and all judges are appointed by the Crown on the advice of the prime minister and/or the Lord Chancellor. The highest court of appeal is the House of Lords, but by custom the whole house does not hear cases. This work is left to a special committee of the Lords with legal expertise. An interesting feature of the British system is that there are separate courts for criminal and civil matters, although appeals from both divisions go ultimately to the Law Lords.

The American system makes an instructive contrast to the British because federalism has had such a strong impact on how American courts are organized. As shown in Figure 32.1, the United States has a dual system of courts. Disputes under federal law go before a system of federal courts; federal judges are appointed by the

FIGURE 32.1 The American Court System

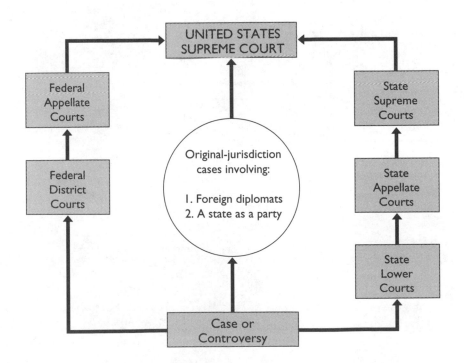

president, subject to the advice and consent of the Senate. In addition, each of the fifty states maintains its own system of courts with a state Supreme Court at the top. There is great diversity among these systems: in some, judges are appointed by the state governor; in others, they are popularly elected. Although federal and state courts are organizationally distinct, they are not completely isolated from each other. For one thing, many cases can go to either federal or state court, because federal and state laws overlap. Kidnapping, for example, is an offence in all states, and also becomes a federal crime if state lines are crossed, so that an accused kidnapper may be tried in either system. Also, the federal Supreme Court exercises appellate jurisdiction over the supreme courts of the states if federal or constitutional questions are involved.

The Canadian arrangement falls between the British and the American. Figure 32.2 shows that the system is fundamentally unified. The Federal Court of Canada deals with certain specialized matters of federal administrative law: claims against the Crown, taxation, customs duties, immigration, and so on. All other cases are

FIGURE 32.2 The Canadian System

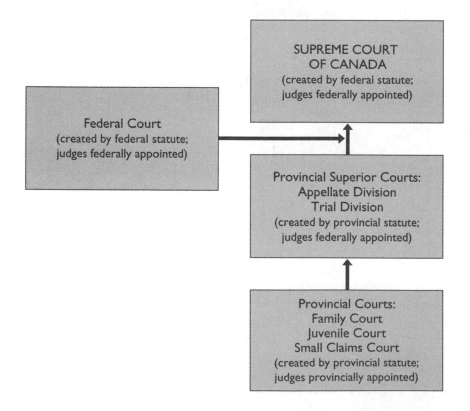

heard in the provincially organized courts at one level or another. The provinces maintain their own **provincial courts** for such matters as small claims and minor criminal offences. The judges of the **superior courts** are all appointed by the governor general on the advice of the cabinet. By long-standing practice, the prime minister personally selects the members of the Supreme Court of Canada and the chief justices of the other courts, and the minister of justice selects all other federally appointed judges.

Each province organizes its superior courts in a distinctive way. The provinces also provide the support personnel and services required by the courts. Canada's courts are thus a practical compromise between the unitary and federal approaches to court organization. The power of the provinces to organize the provincial and superior courts as they wish recognizes the diversity of local conditions; but the system is pushed toward uniformity of interpretation by the federal power of appointment and by the overall appellate jurisdiction of the Supreme Court of Canada.

The apex of the Canadian court system is the Supreme Court of Canada, which is the highest court of appeal. This does not mean that every appeal will be heard by the Supreme Court, for the justices often deny leave to appeal, allowing the decisions of lower courts to stand. The Supreme Court has not always been the highest court of appellate jurisdiction. Before 1949, court decisions could be appealed to the Judicial Committee of the Privy Council in Britain, the highest court of appeal for the British Empire and Commonwealth. The removal of the Judicial Committee's appellate jurisdiction over Canadian cases was another step in Canada's gradual emancipation from British institutions of government.

The Supreme Court is made up of nine justices, of whom one is the chief justice. Three of the justices must be from Quebec, a stipulation that reflects a previously discussed peculiarity in that province's legal system: while other provinces rely on the British common law tradition, Quebec has its own *code civil* for matters of private law.

INDEPENDENCE AND ACCESS

The professed object of a court system in a liberal democracy is to administer justice equally to all citizens. Unequal treatment before the law constitutes a violation of one of the fundamental principles of liberal democracy. Here we can mention some of the main factors that determine whether equality before the law is realized in practice.

There must be judicial independence from direct political interference; this can be guaranteed in a number of ways. The principle of tenure in office (serving "during good behaviour") ensures that judges cannot be discharged except for violation of law or gross impropriety of conduct. In the United States, Congress is constitutionally barred from lowering judges' salaries while they are in office (although neglecting to grant periodic raises may have the same effect in an inflationary age). In spite of such safeguards, politicians may still try to influence judges, either by criticizing them in public or through more subtle private communications. In Canada in the 1970s and 1980s, several ministers had to resign from the federal cabinet after trying to influence judges. Judicial independence, probably the single greatest institutional support of the rule of law, can never be taken for granted.

The courts must be efficient. Cases before the courts must be handled expeditiously. Lives can be ruined if individuals are held in custody for a long period of time awaiting a criminal trial, or if payment of compensation in a civil suit is indefinitely postponed by legal manoeuvres.

Court rulings must be consistent, so that similar punishment is imposed for similar crimes. The sentencing practices of judges have long been debated by law reform commissions. There is no way to guarantee that judges in Halifax and in Toronto, or even two judges in the same city, will apply the same penalty for similar crimes. Penalties written into the law contain some latitude, and for a good reason: judges usually take account of the particular circumstances surrounding a crime, and their interpretations of the severity of a crime vary greatly. We will undoubtedly never find uniformity when punishing violators of the law, but there must be some common denominator, or again, the system will be questioned.

A final problem involves the cost of obtaining justice in the court system. Lawyers, especially good ones, are expensive—often too expensive for many people in society. Because of this, our legal system is criticized for having a double standard—one for the rich and one for the poor. This criticism is at least partly met by providing free or inexpensive legal services through legal aid; but this helps only the very poor while leaving ordinary people of modest resources facing a legal system that is often far too costly for their use.

THE JUDICIARY IN THE POLITICAL PROCESS

Canadian courts are strictly neutral in partisan politics, but they still play an important role in the political process. Their decisions about cases sometimes have the same effect as legislative outputs from Parliament, or policy outputs from the executive or bureaucracy, or even amendments to the Constitution. Of course, most cases that come before the courts do not have such sweeping implications; they merely require the application of a known principle of law to a particular situation. But occasionally, there may be no **precedent** that really applies to the case; or perhaps the dispute hinges on the interpretation of the wording of statutory or constitutional language. In such instances, the court's decision, in that it becomes a precedent for subsequent decisions of other courts, is a source of law just as if a statute were passed or amended.

A good example of the potential importance of statutory construction is furnished by a series of court decisions in Manitoba in the late 1970s and early 1980s that had the effect of abolishing mandatory retirement in that province. The courts held that the way the prohibition of age discrimination in the Manitoba Human Rights Act was worded made it illegal for employers and unions to negotiate contracts with a fixed age of retirement. Public statements from members of the cabinet who brought in the legislation made it clear that they had not intended it to have any effect on retirement plans, but courts construe the words of statutes, not the statements of politicians. The effect was a major change in public policy brought about without any of the normal processes of study by experts and debate in the legislature.[1]

An important example of constitutional interpretation is the celebrated *Persons* case of 1929. Section 24 of the Constitution Act, 1867, allows "qualified persons" to be appointed to the Senate. At the time the Act was passed, "persons" was a technical legal term that generally referred only to adult males. When William Lyon Mackenzie King wanted to appoint Emily Murphy of Edmonton to be the first woman in the Senate, it was not clear whether the words "qualified persons" included women; but the Judicial Committee of the Privy Council held that women were persons within the meaning of the Act.[2] The case was political in at least two ways: because it changed law and policy to allow women to sit in the Senate, it was virtually the equivalent of a constitutional amendment; and because it signalled a remarkable victory for women as a group, it helped lead to subsequent improvements in their status. In this instance, a judicial decision provided an easier means than formal constitutional amendment for recognizing the emerging social consensus in favour of equal political rights for women.

An even more spectacular political role of the courts is judicial review. Essentially, judicial review is a court ruling on the constitutionality of legislation or executive action. The concept was mentioned in our earlier discussion of federalism because disputes often arise in federal systems, where legislative powers are granted to different levels of government. Because the distribution of powers is often not absolutely clear, or there may be overlapping responsibilities, jurisdictional disputes invariably arise between levels of government.

Judicial review exists in both Canada and the United States, as in most federal systems. However, it has had a different character in the two countries; at least, it did before the adoption of the Canadian Charter of Rights and Freedoms. Before 1982, judicial review in Canada mainly involved the courts deciding which assembly, provincial or federal, possessed legislative power under the Constitution Act, 1867. Having decided which was the appropriate legislature, the Canadian courts seldom used judicial review to challenge legislative wisdom. Also before 1982, there was no Canadian equivalent to a constitutional Bill of Rights placing limits on what any legislature, provincial or federal, could do.[3] The United States has long had such an entrenched document, and it has made American courts more self-confident in ruling legislation *ultra vires,* that is, beyond the constitutional power of a legislature to enact.

The power of the courts to interpret and even set aside legislation, coupled with their relative independence from the assembly and the executive, makes them an attractive alternative for interest groups that lack influence with other decision-making bodies. In the United States, the National Association for the Advancement of Colored People (NAACP) pursued litigation for decades to challenge legal segregation of the races; the case of *Brown v. Board of Education* (1954), in which the Supreme Court held segregated schools to be unconstitutional, is the most famous result of their work. Similar strategies have also paid off in Canada. In Manitoba, the trivial matter of a parking ticket became the case of *Forest v. the Queen,* which led to the ruling that Manitoba, established as an officially bilingual province by the Manitoba Act, 1870, must publish all its statutes in both English and French—an extraordinary victory that the francophone minority of that province could never have won in the legislature.[4]

Interest groups now pursue strategies of litigation as calculatingly as they lobby the assembly for legislation. The four basic steps of such strategic litigation are described in a document produced by the Canadian Advisory Council on the Status of Women:

1. defining a goal in terms of the desired principle of law to be established;
2. plotting how the principle of law can be established from case to case in incremental, logical, and clear steps;
3. selecting winnable cases suitable for each stage taken to achieve the goal;
4. consolidating wins of each stage by bringing similar cases to create a cluster of cases in support of the principle established.[5]

The most successful practitioner of strategic litigation in Canada has undoubtedly been the Legal Education and Action Fund (LEAF), a feminist organization that receives substantial federal money from the Court Challenges Program. LEAF has been associated with most of the major cases involving the legal rights of women in areas such as abortion, employment opportunities, and protection against violence. In some cases, LEAF has actually sponsored the litigation, that is, paid for legal representation; in others, it has **intervened**, that is, with the permission of the court, it presented its views on the law without actually representing a client. LEAF has also supported research useful in its cause and offered orientation sessions to judges to sensitize them to women's issues.

Aboriginal people are also making sophisticated use of strategic litigation. Native bands in British Columbia have brought several cases designed to increase their share of the salmon and other fisheries. One major success was the *Sparrow* case, which established their constitutionally protected right to fish for food.[6] Largely as a result of this case, the Department of Fisheries and Oceans introduced a new policy in 1992 that allowed bands to take a greater share of the Fraser River salmon run. It is unlikely that the bands would have achieved this political success without winning first in the courts. No one case can be considered typical of the wide range of land claims and treaty issues that aboriginal people have attempted to litigate, but *Sparrow* does illustrate how strategic litigation can work toward the achievement of larger political goals.

Strategic litigation dovetails well with the growing activism of courts. **Judicial activism**, defined as the willingness of judges to overturn legislation or executive action, has been a feature of American politics for the past half-century. In the 1930s, the U.S. Supreme Court initially ruled much of Franklin Roosevelt's New Deal legislation unconstitutional. In one period from 1935 to 1937, the court held twelve acts of Congress *ultra vires*. There was then a sudden shift in the court's decisions after the president threatened to "pack" it by expanding its size and appointing members who shared his ideology of reform liberalism. In this instance, judicial activism favoured the ideological right, but it can be used equally to forward the aims of the left.

The U.S. Supreme Court was particularly active between 1954 and 1969, while Earl Warren was chief justice. The Warren court struck down racial segregation, compelled the states to draw constituency lines to approximate "one man, one vote," greatly enhanced the rights of those accused of crimes, outlawed prayer in public schools, and in many other ways wrought unprecedented changes in the social fabric of the United States. When courts begin to decide so many questions of policy, they have plainly become politicized. There is in all of this a difficult question of democratic theory, for judges, after all, are appointed, not elected. Is it compatible with the idea of representative government to have so many questions settled by appointed officials who serve for life and never have to confront the voters?[7]

This is not a problem in Great Britain because judicial review in the technical sense does not exist in that system of parliamentary supremacy. If elected politicians in Britain do not like the way that the courts have interpreted a law, they are, at least in theory, free to change the law. British courts can interpret acts of Parliament but they cannot strike them down as being in conflict with the written constitution because there is no written constitution. The potential conflict between judicial review and democratic government is, however, a very real problem in both the United States and Canada.

In the United States, the problem is addressed in part by the constitutional requirement that the Senate approve the federal judges nominated by the president. Because of the acknowledged policymaking role of the courts, and particularly of the Supreme Court, it is now commonly accepted that nominees to that body will be carefully interrogated by the Senate about their political philosophy as well as about their legal competence and personal character. In 1987, the Senate rejected Ronald Reagan's nomination of Robert Bork to the Supreme Court. No one could impugn Bork's character or competence, but the Senate found him to be too conservative.

George Bush's nomination of Clarence Thomas precipitated yet another bitter Senate hearing; Thomas's character and competence were challenged along with his conservative ideology. Ironically, Thomas was confirmed and Bork was not, at least partly because Bork's prolific writings had made his views abundantly clear, whereas Thomas's were less well documented. Whatever one may think of these hearings, they at least draw attention to the political consequences of judicial appointments and bring political factors into the process.

No equivalent process exists in Canada, where judges are chosen by the minister of justice and the prime minister without public hearings and confirmation votes. However, there is another form of political balance in Canada, namely Section 33 of the Charter, the **notwithstanding clause**. This clause allows Parliament and the provincial legislatures to enact legislation even if the courts hold it to be in conflict with certain sections of the Charter (Sections 2 and 7–15). This "legislative review of judicial review," as Peter Russell has called it, is a unique way of elevating democratic government over the decisions of unelected judges. However, this tool has not been used very frequently. Also, the override can only be applied for five years at a time, after which it will expire unless it is passed again by the legislature.

In 1989 Quebec's National Assembly invoked the notwithstanding clause to protect Bill 178 from judicial review. The Supreme Court had held that the province's language legislation violated freedom of speech inasmuch as it prohibited the posting of commercial signs in languages other than French. In response, Premier Robert Bourassa's government introduced Bill 178 to allow commercial signs inside buildings in languages other than French, as long as French signs were present and at least equally prominent; it then invoked the notwithstanding clause to make sure that this "inside–outside" legislation would not be upset in the courts.

In 1993, Bourassa introduced more permissive legislation, hoping that it would survive judicial challenges so that use of the notwithstanding clause would not be necessary. This illustrates the importance of the five-year limitation. If there had been no such limitation, it would have been easier for the Quebec government to leave Bill 178 on the books; but under Section 33 it was forced to review the matter.

LIFE IN CHARTERLAND

The adoption in 1982 of the Canadian Charter of Rights and Freedoms as part of the Constitution accelerated the growth of judicial activism. The guarantee of individual rights and freedoms now depends on the Constitution and on the courts' protection of the Charter's principles. Constitutional sovereignty has replaced parliamentary sovereignty, except in the rare cases when Parliament or a provincial legislature invokes the notwithstanding clause. This fundamental change in constitutional law in Canada will by no means work itself out overnight. Individuals and groups are now frequently using the courts to challenge the constitutionality of particular federal and provincial laws.

The reason for adopting the Charter, it was explained to the Canadian public, was to advance toward the ideal of rule of law in a liberal democracy. The Charter would prevent governments, no matter how strong their majority support, from violating the rights of individuals or minorities. While this is undoubtedly true, there is another aspect of the Charter that cannot be overlooked: it involves an extensive transfer of decision-making power from legislatures to the courts.

The rights enunciated in the Charter are necessarily described in such broad language that they become meaningful only through judicial interpretation. To take one example, Section 10 of the Charter reads in part:

> 10. Everyone has the right on arrest or detention ... (b) to retain and instruct counsel without delay and to be informed of that right.

The *Therens* case, which was decided in 1985 by the Supreme Court, hinged on the precise meaning of the word *detention*.[8] After an automobile accident in Moose Jaw, Saskatchewan, Therens was requested by a police officer to come to the police station to take a breathalyzer test. (To refuse this request is itself a violation of the Criminal Code.) Therens complied and was later prosecuted for driving while impaired. At the trial, Therens's counsel moved for dismissal of the breathalyzer evidence because the police constable had not informed Therens of his right to retain counsel. The legal question, ultimately decided in the affirmative by the Supreme Court, was whether being asked to go to the police station to give a breath sample amounted to detention.

A related question was whether evidence obtained in violation of Section 10(b) might be introduced anyway. Section 24(2) of the Charter states:

> the evidence shall be excluded if it is established that, having regard to all the circumstances, the admission of it in the proceedings would bring the administration of justice into disrepute.

Again, the courts were required to interpret abstract words. The Supreme Court upheld the view of the lower courts that to admit such evidence would in fact bring the administration of justice into disrepute.

The point here is not whether the decision was right or wrong, but where decision-making power is located. Parliament, in providing for check-stop procedures under the Criminal Code, had not explicitly said that those requested to "breathe into the box" should be informed of their right to retain counsel. By interpreting the generalized language of the Charter, the courts have now laid down this rule, which is just as binding as if it had been legislated by Parliament.

After its proclamation on April 17, 1982, the Charter's effects were at first felt largely in the field of criminal law. Most frequently litigated in the early years were such rights as the right to security against unreasonable search or seizure and the right to counsel. Numerically, the main groups resorting to Charter arguments in the courts were those accused either of driving while impaired or of selling illegal drugs.[9] Because the courts obviously have great expertise in criminal law, the transfer of decision-making power from government and Parliament did not seem problematic. Outside the field of criminal law, only a few early Supreme Court decisions based on the Charter had broad consequences.

This situation, however, has been gradually changing since the proclamation on April 17, 1985, of the **equality rights** section of the Charter, Section 15(1), which reads:

> Every individual is equal before and under the law and has the right to the equal protection and equal benefit of the law without discrimination and, in particular, without discrimination based on race, national or ethnic origin, colour, religion, sex, age or mental or physical disability.

Federal and provincial statute books contain literally thousands of clauses authorizing differential treatment based on the criteria mentioned in Section 15(1). To mention only a few examples: one generally has to be 16 to obtain a driver's licence and 18 to vote; publicly supported athletic competitions are usually divided into classes by sex; physically and mentally disabled children are subject to special treatment of many kinds in the public schools. Proclamation of Section 15 was delayed for three years, from 1982 to 1985, in order to give Parliament and the provincial legislatures time to amend such laws so that they conformed to the Charter; but many of them remain on the books because they seem reasonably justifiable. (Is it really age discrimination to require a minimum age to obtain a driver's licence?) However, now that Section 15 has been proclaimed, the courts are inevitably drawn into deciding whether particular rules or policies are discriminatory. In the long run, the effects of the Charter in this regard may profoundly transform the Canadian political process.

Peter Russell, the dean of Canadian political scientists who study the judicial process, sees the effect of the Charter as moderate up to this point, and probably into the foreseeable future. He stresses that there was an initial period of activism in which the Supreme Court of Canada decided in favour of Charter litigants 60 percent of the time, but points out that the success rate of Charter complaints before that court has since fallen dramatically. He also emphasizes that most of the statutes invalidated by the Supreme Court have dealt with criminal matters, in which judicial expertise is self-evident and widely acknowledged.[10]

A different view emerges, however, if one considers all appellate courts, not just the Supreme Court. Table 32.1 reproduces the data of F.L. Morton and his associates on the nullification of statutes by the twelve appellate courts (the Supreme Court, the Federal Court of Appeal, and the ten provincial courts of appeal) during the first ten years of the Charter's life.[11]

These data are important because most cases never get to the Supreme Court; the decisions of the various courts of appeal are generally allowed to stand. Taking appellate courts as a whole, the tendency to nullify statutes because of Charter challenges showed a steady rise throughout the 1980s. Moreover, the federal statutes that were invalidated related mainly to legal rights under the Criminal Code or related statutes such as the Narcotic Control Act. Most such decisions dealt with procedural matters, such as how the police carry out searches and interrogations. Even the highly publicized *Morgentaler* decision was essentially procedural. It held that the existing system of therapeutic abortion committees violated the security of the person guaranteed to all persons, including women, by Section 7 of the Charter; it did not, however, prohibit Parliament from passing further legislation on this issue.

TABLE 32.1   Total of Nullified Statutes by Year of Decision

YEAR	PROVINCIAL	FEDERAL	TOTAL
1982	0	0	0
1983	1	3	4
1984	4	3	7
1985	5	5	10
1986	3	2	5
1987	4	9	13
1988	14	10	24
1989	4	4	8
1990	5	2	7
1991	3	12	15

The impact of Charter jurisprudence tends to be different at the provincial level, where substantive matters of social policy are often under attack. Charter decisions have nullified language laws in Quebec, mandatory-retirement legislation in British Columbia and Nova Scotia, British Columbia's attempts to require physicians to practice in remote regions of the province, and other provincial enactments in the field of social policy.[12] The political relevance of the judicial process is likely to increase as interest groups learn to use systematic litigation in pursuit of their goals, and as they learn to exploit the almost boundless possibilities of Section 15 of the Charter.

The Charter clearly provides a new political option for a number of groups who felt marginalized in traditional Canadian politics. Women's organizations, gays and lesbians, environmentalists, and official language minorities have all scored important victories through litigation. Their involvement in the judicial process has, as Rainer Knopff and F.L. Morton note:

made the courtroom a more pervasive and visible arena of politics and imposed the form of legal disputation on more of our public life. By the same token, it has focused attention on the judges themselves as political actors.[13]

Not everyone would agree that this role of judicial review is necessarily a good thing for liberal democracies. Giving appointed judges a crucial role in the policy process is sometimes criticized as antidemocratic, although others hail it as an advance for groups previously excluded from power. This debate will continue as the judiciary becomes even more central to the political process in Canada.

🙪🙪🙪🙪🙪🙪🙪

FURTHER READING

Abraham, Henry J. *The Judicial Process: An Introductory Analysis of the Courts of the United States, England and France*, 5th ed. New York: Oxford University Press, 1986.

Bogart, W.A. *Courts and Country: The Limits of Litigation and the Social and Political Life of Canada*. Toronto: Oxford University Press, 1994.

Cairns, Alan C. *Disruptions: Constitutional Struggles, From the Charter to Meech Lake*. Toronto: McClelland and Stewart, 1991.

Daley, Timothy Thomas. *The Duties of the Chief Judges of Provincial and Territorial Courts and Their Impact on Judicial Independence*. Halifax: Dalhousie University, Faculty of Law, 1994.

Gall, Gerald L. *The Canadian Legal System*. 2nd ed. Toronto: Carswell, 1983.

Horowitz, Donald. *The Courts and Social Policy*. Washington, D.C.: Brookings Institution, 1977.

Kulchyski, Peter, ed. *Unjust Relations: Aboriginal Rights in Canadian Courts*. Toronto: Oxford University Press, 1994.

Manfredi, Christopher P. *Judicial Power and the Charter: Canada and the Paradox of Liberal Constitutionalism*. Toronto: McClelland and Stewart, 1992.

McCormick, Peter. *Canada's Courts: A Social Scientist's Ground-Breaking Account of the Canadian Judicial System*. Toronto: James Lorimer, 1994.

McCormick, Peter, and Ian Greene. *Judges and Judging: Inside the Canadian Judicial System*. Toronto: James Lorimer, 1990.

McWhinney, Edward. *Judicial Review in the English-Speaking World*, 3rd ed. Toronto: University of Toronto Press, 1965.

———. *Constitutional Tribunals and Judicial Law-Making*. Dordrecht, Netherlands: Nijhoff, 1986.

Morton, F.L. *Law, Politics and the Judicial Process in Canada*, 2nd ed. Calgary: University of Calgary Press, 1992.

———. *Morgentaler v. Borowski: Abortion, the Charter, and the Courts*. Toronto: McClelland and Stewart, 1992.

Murphy, Walter, and C. Herman Pritchett. *Courts, Judges, and Politics*, 4th ed. New York: Random House, 1986.

Perry, Michael J. *The Constitution in the Courts: Law or Politics?* New York: Oxford University Press, 1994.

Russell, Peter H. *The Judiciary in Canada: The Third Branch of Government.* Toronto: McGraw-Hill Ryerson, 1987.

Schubert, Glendon. *Judicial Policy Making*, rev. ed. Glenview, Ill.: Scott, Foresman, 1974.

Shapiro, Martin M. *Courts: A Comparative and Political Analysis.* Chicago: University of Chicago Press, 1981.

Strayer, Barry Lee. *The Canadian Constitution and the Courts*, rev. ed. Toronto: Butterworths, 1988.

Theberg, Leonard J., ed. *The Judiciary in a Democratic Society.* Lexington, Mass.: D.C. Heath, 1979.

GLOSSARY

administration. The organized apparatus of the state for the preparation and implementation of legislation and policies, also called the bureaucracy.

agenda-setting. Controlling the focus of attention by establishing the issues for public discussion.

anarchic order. Order resulting from mutual coordination in the absence of a higher authority.

anarchism. A stateless society that allows total individual freedom.

animal liberation. A movement that proposes to ban hunting, the raising of domestic livestock for food and other economic purposes, and the use of animals in laboratory experiments.

anomic group. Spontaneously formed interest group with concern over a specific issue.

aristocracy. A form of government in which a minority rules under the law.

associational group. Formally organized group that articulates the interests of its members over long periods of time.

asymmetrical federalism. A federal system of government in which powers are unevenly divided among provinces (i.e., some provinces have greater responsibilities or more autonomy than others).

auction politics. A danger in democratic politics in which state power may be "sold" to the highest-bidding groups.

auditor general. An official of Parliament whose staff audits the expenditures of government departments and who provides an annual report on instances of funds being unlawfully or unwisely spent.

authoritarianism. A system of government in which leaders are not subjected to the test of free elections.

authority. A form of power based on consensus regarding the right to issue commands and make decisions.

backbencher. Members of parliament on the government side who sit on the backbenches and are not in cabinet, or those similarly distant from shadow cabinet posts in opposition parties.

balance of payments. A state's running account of economic transactions (exports and imports) with the rest of the world.

balance of power. The distribution of power in a system such that no one state may overwhelm others.

balance of power policy. The active prevention of any one state from becoming too strong by the major powers in the system.

behavioural revolution. The introduction of more empirical analysis into the study of government and politics.

bicameralism. A system of government in which the legislature is divided into two chambers, an upper and a lower house.

bill. A piece of legislation under consideration by a legislative body.

binational state. Two nations co-existing within one state.

bipolar. An international system in which there are two dominant nation-states.

bourgeoisie. A Marxist term referring to those who own the means of production.

bureaucracy. A type of administration characterized by specialization, professionalism, and security of tenure.

caucus. A meeting of legislators of any one party to discuss parliamentary strategy and party policy.

central agencies. Government agencies such as the PMO, the PCO, the Treasury Board, and the Finance Department that have certain coordinating functions across the whole federal public service.

charismatic authority. Authority based on the admiration of personal qualities of an individual.

checks and balances. A system of government in which power is divided between the executive, legislative, and judicial branches of government, and these powers check and balance each other.

citizenship. Legal membership in a community known as a nation-state.

classical liberalism. A liberal ideology entailing a minimal role for government in order to maximize individual freedom.

coalition. An alliance between two or more political units in response to opposing forces.

coalition government. A parliamentary government in which the cabinet is composed of members of more than one party.

code civil. The unique system of civil law used in Quebec.

code of law. A comprehensive set of interrelated legal rules.

coercion. A form of power based on forced compliance through fear and intimidation.

collective defence organization. An alliance among states against external threats.

collective (public) goods. Goods and services enjoyed in common and not divisible among individuals.

collective security. A commitment by a number of states to join in an alliance against member states that threaten the peace.

Cominform. "Communist Information Bureau"; an international communist organization formed after World War II.

Comintern. "Communist International"; also known as the Third International, the communist international organization between the two World Wars.

common law. The accumulation of judicial precedents as the basis for court decisions.

communications (mass) media. A general term for all modern means of conveying information.

communism. A political ideology characterized by a belief in eliminating exploitation through public ownership and central planning of the economy.

comparative politics. An area of political study concerned with the relative similarities and differences among political systems.

concurrent majority. Approval by a majority vote in two or more bodies, such as two houses of parliament or multiple provincial legislatures.

confederation. A federal system of government in which sovereign constituent governments create a central government but balance of power remains with constituent governments.

confidence. Support for the government by the majority of the members of parliament.

consent of the governed. People's acceptance of the form of government under which they live.

conservationism. The attempt to manage natural resources in order to maximize benefits over a long period of time.

conservatism. A political ideology generally characterized by a belief in individualism and minimal government intervention in the economy and society; also a belief in the virtue of the status quo and general acceptance of traditional morality.

consociationalism. A form of democracy in which harmony in segmented societies is maintained through the distinctive roles of elites and the autonomy of organized interests.

constituency. An electoral district with a body of electors who vote for a representative in an elected assembly.

constitution. The fundamental rules and principles by which a state is organized.

constitutional democracy. See liberal democracy.

constitutionalism. The belief that governments will defer to the rules and principles enshrined in a constitution and uphold the rule of law.

constructive vote of confidence. A system in which the majority in the lower house can bring down the government, but not until that majority approves another government (e.g., in Germany).

contracting out. The hiring of private organizations to provide public services.

convention. A practice or custom followed by those in government, although not explicitly written in the constitution or in legislation.

corporatism. The organization of liberal democracies in such a way that the state is the dominant force in society and the activities of all interests in society are subordinate to that force.

coup d'état. A forcible and unconstitutional change of government, often by a faction within the military or the ruling party.

credit. Any transaction that brings money into a country (e.g., payments for the export of goods).

Crown corporations. Corporations owned by the government that assume a structure similar to that of a private company and that operate semi-independently of the cabinet.

current accounts surplus. A state selling more to the world than it is buying.

custom. A generally accepted practice or behaviour developed over time.

customary law. Rules of conduct developed over time and enforceable in court.

debit. Any transaction that sends money out of a country (e.g., payments for the import of goods).

deep ecology. A form of environmentalism holding that nature and the natural order should be valued over individual human happiness.

deficit. In international trade, occurs when the value of a state's imports is more than the value of its exports.

delegate. A representative role in which the individual subordinates his or her views to those of his or her constituents.

democracy. In the original sense of the term, a system of government in which the majority rules without legal restraint. Compare liberal democracy.

democratic centralism. The concentration of power in the leadership of the Communist Party, which in theory acts in the interests of the people.

Department of Finance. The government department that has overall responsibility for the government's finances and its role in the economy.

deputy minister. A Canadian public servant who heads a government department, manages the department, and advises the minister.

deregulation. A government policy designed to remove regulations on market activity.

despotism. An individual ruling through fear without regard to law and not answerable to the people.

devolution. A system of government in which the sovereign central government devolves (delegates) power to regional governments, subject to its overriding control.

dictator. In Roman Law, an appointed individual given exceptional powers in times of crisis.

dictatorship of the proletariat. A revolutionary seizure of power by the "vanguard" of society, the communist party, which then rules in the name of the working class.

diplomacy. A system of formal, regularized communication that allows states to peacefully conduct their business with each other.

direct democracy. A system of government based on public decisions made by citizens meeting in an assembly or voting by ballot.

disallowance. A power given to the federal government in the Constitution Act, 1867, under which the cabinet can nullify any provincial law, even though it has received royal assent from the lieutenant governor of the province.

discretion. The flexibility afforded government to decide something within the broader framework of rules.

distributive laws. Laws designed to distribute public goods and services to individuals in society.

downsizing. Reduction of the size and scope of government.

doxa. Greek word for an opinion that may be at least partly true but cannot be fully expounded.

Electoral College. The body which formally chooses the president of the United States.

elite. A small group of people with a disproportionate amount of public decision-making power.

empirical. Political analysis based on factual and observable data in contrast to thoughts or ideas.

environmentalism. A family of idelogies in which human damage to the natural world is the central concern.

episteme. Greek word for knowledge that can be demonstrated by logical argument from first principles.

equality of opportunity. The equalization of life chances for all individuals in society, regardless of economic position.

equality of result. The equaliz comes of social and economi

equality of right. Applicatior the same way to all.

equality rights. A section of the Rights and Freedoms (s. 15) that prohibits governments from discriminating against certain categories of people.

ethnic group. A subgroup within a nation based on common descent.

executive. A small group of elected officials who direct the policy process and oversee the vast array of departments and agencies of government.

executive federalism. A federal process directed by extensive federal-provincial interaction at the level of first ministers, departmental ministers, and deputy ministers.

extractive laws. Laws designed to collect taxes from citizens to pay for governing society.

faction. An association of individuals organized for the purpose of influencing government actions favourable to their interests, now known as interest groups.

fascism. An extreme form of nationalism that played on fears of communism and rejected individual freedom, liberal individualism, democracy, and limitations on the state.

federalism. A system of government in which sovereignty is divided between a central government and several provincial or state governments.

feminism. The belief that society is disadvantageous to women, systematically depriving them of individual choice, political power, economic opportunity, and intellectual recognition.

First International. A loose association of socialist parties and labour unions in Western Europe, organized in 1864.

formal–legal institutions. Institutions that are explicitly created by a constitution.

fragment theory. A theory (proposed by Louis Hartz) according to which colonial societies such as Canada originated as fragments of the larger European society and these societies have remained marked throughout their history by the conditions of their origin.

free-market environmentalism. The view that environmental problems are best solved by property rights and markets.

free riders. Those who enjoy a collective good without helping to pay for it.

free vote. A legislative vote in which members are not required to toe the party line.

functions. The special activity or purpose structures serve in the political process; for example, interest groups to articulate interests.

General Agreement on Tariffs and Trade. See World Trade Organization.

gerrymander. Manipulating constituency boundaries for partisan election purposes.

government. A specialized group of individuals, institutions, and agencies that make and enforce public decisions.

habit. A personal rule of conduct.

head of government. The person in effective charge of the executive branch of government; the prime minister in a parliamentary system.

head of state. An individual who represents the state but does not exercise political power.

human rights. Rights thought to belong to all people simply because they are human beings.

human welfare ecology. Offshoot of conservation movement that addresses the value to human health and happiness of the environment.

ideological party. A type of political party that emphasizes ideological purity over the attainment of power.

ideology. A system of beliefs and values that explains society and prescribes the role of government.

influence. A form of power based on the ability to persuade others to share in a desired objective.

informal institutions. Institutions that are an integral part of the political process, but that are not established by a constitution.

initiative. The initiation of legislative action on a particular issue by way of a voters' petition.

institutional group. Groups that are closely associated with the government and that act internally to influence public decisions.

interest party. A political party with a single interest or purpose, such as the Green Party.

interest (pressure) group. Organizations whose members act together to influence public policy in order to promote their common interest.

international law. The body of rules governing the relationships of states with each other.

International Monetary Fund. An international organization created to prevent another collapse in the world monetary system through the stabilization of national currencies throughout the world.

international order. The combination of major actors, rules, mechanisms, and understandings that manage the co-existence and interdependence of states.

international regimes. The pattern of regular cooperation governed by implicit and explicit expectations between two or more states.

international relations. An area of political study concerned with the interaction of independent states.

intervention. In a court case, the presentation of a view on the law without representing one of the parties in the litigation.

irredentism. Nationalistic desire to recover lost territory adjacent to the boundaries of the state.

item veto. The power of an American president or state governor to veto particular components of a bill rather than reject the entire legislation.

judicial activism. The willingness and inclination of judges to overturn legislation or executive action.

Judicial Committee of the Privy Council (JCPC). A British Court that functioned as Canada's final court of appeal until 1949.

judicial review. The power of the courts to declare legislation unconstitutional (*ultra vires*).

judiciary. The branch of government with the power to resolve legal conflicts that arise between citizens, between citizens and governments, or between levels of government.

junta. A Spanish word meaning a group of individuals forming a government, especially after a revolution or *coup d'état*.

jurisprudence. The philosophy and analysis of law.

justice. The virtue of protecting individuals' possessions within the acknowledged rules of conduct.

laissez-faire. The nonintervention of the state in the economy.

law. Enforceable rules of conduct.

legal authority. System of authority based on general rules rather than inheritance or personal qualities.

legal positivism. A theory holding that law is the command of the sovereign.

legislation. Consciously formulated and deliberately constructed law.

legislative. The branch of government responsible for making laws for society.

legislature. A representative assembly responsible for making laws for society.

legitimacy. Belief in the "rightness" of rule.

liberal democracy. A system of government characterized by universal adult suffrage, political equality, majority rule, and constitutionalism.

liberal feminism. The advocacy of equal rights between men and women.

liberalism. A family of ideologies that emphasizes individual freedom, a limited state, constitutionalism, and the rule of law.

liberalism between states. A theory (in international relations) that stresses the rule of law in dealings between states.

limited government. A state restricted in its exercise of power by the constitution and the rule of law.

limited state. See limited government.

list system. A form of proportional representation in which the elector votes not for individuals but for parties, which have lists of candidates running for office.

lobbying. Activities of interest groups aimed at influencing governors and the public to achieve favourable policy decisions.

logrolling. The act of vote trading among legislators in the process of getting legislation passed.

Magna Carta. (Great Charter) A document signed by King John in 1215, conceding that the king is subject to law.

majority. Fifty percent plus one of those voting. Also called "simple majority."

majority government. A parliamentary government in which the party in power has more than 50 percent of the seats in the legislature.

merit recruitment. A system of hiring public servants on the basis of qualifications rather than on party preference or other considerations.

microcosm theory. The idea that a governing body should be a miniature replica of the society it represents.

ministerial responsibility. The principle that cabinet ministers are individually responsible to the House of Commons for everything that happens in their department.

ministry. The entire group of MPs appointed by the prime minister to specific ministerial responsibilities.

minority government. A parliamentary government in which the government party has less than 50 percent of the seats in the legislature.

mixed economy. An economy based on both private and public (government-controlled) enterprises.

mixed-member-proportional (MMP) system. Electoral system in which voters cast two ballots, one for a local candidate running in a territorial constituency (first-past-the-post) and the other for a list of candidates put forward by a political party (list system).

modernization. The gradual replacement of traditional authority with legal authority.

monarchy. Form of government in which a single person rules under the law.

monism. Exclusive emphasis on a single principle or interest.

movement party. A type of political party that emerges from a political movement, such as a national liberation movement.

multinational state. Three or more nations co-existing under one sovereign government.

multiparty system. A party system in which there are three or more major contenders for power.

multipolar. A system of actions involving several states.

nation. Individuals whose common identity creates a psychological bond and a political community.

national interest. Interests specific to a nation-state, including especially survival and maintenance of power.

nationalism. The feeling of loyalty and attachment to one's nation or nation-state, and strong support for its interests.

nation-state. A state with a single predominant national identity.

natural authority. Authority based on spontaneous deference to an individual's knowledge or social position.

natural law. Rules of conduct binding by virtue of human rationality alone.

neoconservatism. An ideological term characterizing parties or politicians who not only advocate an end to government expansion, but believe in reducing its role via downsizing, privatization, and deregulation.

new international economic order. A revision of the international economic system in favour of Third World countries.

nonassociational (latent) group. A group that lacks formal organization but has the potential for mobilizing politically.

normative. Political analysis based on values, commitments, and ideas.

notwithstanding clause. Section 33 of the Charter of Rights and Freedoms, which allows federal or provincial legislatures to pass laws that may violate certain sections of the Charter.

official Opposition. In a parliamentary system, the largest of the opposition parties, given a special role to play in the legislative process.

oligarchy. A form of government in which a minority rules outside the law.

ombudsman. An official with the power to investigate complaints against government administration.

one-party-dominant system. A party system in which there are political alternatives but a single political party dominates the political process as a result of the overwhelming support of the electorate.

opposition. Those members of parliament who are not part of the government of the day.

order-in-council. Decision by Cabinet that carries legal force.

parliamentary sovereignty. The supreme authority of parliament to make or repeal laws.

party discipline. The convention that all MPs within any party vote together, as pre-determined in the party caucus and enforced by the party whip.

patriarchy. The domination of society by men.

peace-building. A process for working toward objectives associated with peaceful coexistence of combatants.

peacekeeping. The interposition of lightly armed military forces between combatants who have agreed to stop fighting.

peacemaking. A process for bringing hostile parties to agreement by peaceful means if possible, but military means if necessary.

permanent secretary. The British equivalent of a Canadian deputy minister.

personal freedom. The absence of coercion in various aspects of life.

personal party. A type of political party founded around a single, overwhelmingly influential political leader.

philosopher–king. Plato's view of the ideal individual who rules in the common interest and is directed by wisdom and virtue rather than the constraint of law.

planning. Production and allocation of resources determined by a central authority.

plebiscite. Another term for an advisory referendum.

pluralism. The open competition of political interests.

plurality. A voting decision based on assigning victory to the largest number of votes, not necessarily a majority.

policy community. The network of individuals and organizations deeply involved in a particular area of public policy.

polis. Greek city-state.

political alienation. The sense of estrangement from political power.

political consultant. A professional adviser who puts his or her political expertise to work in the private and public sectors.

political culture. Attitudes, values, beliefs, and orientations that individuals in a society hold regarding their political system.

political economy. The study of the involvement by the state in the economy of the nation-state.

political executive. The politically accountable heads of government.

political party. An organized group that makes nominations and contests elections in the hope of gaining control of government.

political patronage. Government appointments made as a payoff for loyal partisan activity.

political philosophy. An area of political study based on historical, reflective, and conceptual methods.

political police. Forces reporting directly to a political leader who uses them for political purposes rather than law enforcement.

political process. The interaction of organized political structures in making and administering public decisions for a society.

political science. The systematic study of government and politics.

political socialization. The process by which political culture is transmitted from generation to generation.

politics. A process of conflict resolution in which support is mobilized and maintained for collective action.

polity. A form of government characterized by popular sovereignty but exercised within a constitutional framework to prevent the oppression of the minority by the majority rule.

polyarchy. Robert Dahl's term for pluralist forms of liberal democracy, in which many different interests complete.

popular sovereignty. Supreme authority residing in the consent of the people.

portfolio. The administrative responsibility carried by a minister, usually some combinations of departments and other agencies.

postmaterialism. The shift in values since the late 1940s from public order and material prosperity to self-fulfillment.

power. The ability to get other individuals to do as one wants them to do.

pragmatic party. A type of political party concerned primarily with winning elections.

precedent. A previous judicial case used as an example for deciding the case at hand.

preferential (alternative) ballot. Electoral system in which voters rank the candidates.

prerogative. The residual powers of the Crown that can be exercised at its own discretion.

Prime Minister's Office (PMO). Support staff appointed by the prime minister to carry out political functions.

priming. The selective portrayal of political events and personalities by the media, which in turn affects public opinion.

primus inter pares. Latin phrase meaning "first among equals."

private law. Laws controlling relations between individuals.

private member's bill. Public bill introduced in the legislature by a member who is not in the cabinet.

privatization. The sale of government-owned assets or activities to the private sector.

Privy Council. A ceremonial body made up of all present and former cabinet ministers.

Privy Council Office (PCO). A governmental department that supports the prime minister, cabinet, and cabinet committees in devising government policy.

proclamation. The announcement of the official date a new law will take effect.

progressive tax. A tax rate that increases as the amount of one's income increases.

proletariat. A Marxist term referring to those who sell their labour to the bourgeoisie; the working class.

property franchise (suffrage). The requirement that citizens own a stipulated amount of property to receive the right to vote.

proportional representation (PR). An electoral system in which the share of seats won closely matches the share of popular votes received.

provincial courts. Courts created by provincial statute, staffed by judges appointed by the province to deal with matters such as small claims and minor criminal offences.

public authority. Authority based on institutional officeholding.

public debt. The accumulated sum owed by the government to its creditors.

public law. Laws controlling the relations between the state and individuals in society.

qualified majority. The raising of the simple majority requirement of "50 percent plus one" to a higher level, in order to protect the rights of the minorities.

race. A group of individuals differentiated through distinct physical characteristics and common ancestry.

radical feminism. A belief that men and women constitute "sexual classes" and that women's subordinated status is the result of a system which is controlled by men.

readings. First, second, and third readings representing the introduction and debate of proposed bills in the legislative chambers.

realism. A theory of international relations that holds that struggles are resolved on the basis of power of conflicting parties.

recall. The ability of voters in a constituency to remove their elected representative from office by means of a petition.

redistribution. The process of reallocating wealth and income to achieve an economic or social objective.

Red Tory. A conservative with collectivist leanings.

referendum. A decision on policy proposals by a direct vote of the electorate.

reform liberalism. A liberal ideology that advocates a larger role for the state in providing equality of opportunity.

regressive tax. A tax that weighs more heavily on those with low incomes.

regulative laws. Laws that control individual and organizational behaviour.

regulatory agencies. Government agencies established to administer regulative laws in certain fields, for example, the Canadian Human Rights Commission.

report stage. The stage in the legislative process after the second reading when the House debates the committee's report on a proposed bill.

representative democracy. A system of government based on the election of decision makers by the people.

reservation. Mechanism by which the lieutenant governor of a province can refuse royal assent to a bill and refer it to the federal cabinet for a decision.

residual powers. Those powers in a federal system of government not explicitly allocated in a constitution.

responsible government. A form of government in which the political executive must retain the confidence of a majority of the elected legislature or assembly, and must resign or call an election if and when it is defeated on a vote of nonconfidence.

royal assent. The approval of a bill by the Crown.

rule of law. Belief that all actions, of individuals and governments, are subject to an institutionalized set of rules and regulations.

runoff system. An electoral system in which additional rounds of balloting are held (with trailing candidates dropped) until a candidate receives a majority of the votes cast.

scientific socialism. The term Marx and Engels used to stress that their ideology was based on an analysis of class conflict.

Second International. The organization of socialist and labour parties in Europe, with the absence of anarchists, established in 1889.

security dilemma. The spiral of preparations and tensions that emerges when the protective actions of one state lead to countermeasures by another state.

self-government. The right of members of a group to control their own collective affairs.

separation of powers. The separation of powers between executive, legislative, and judicial branches of government.

shadow cabinet. The cohesive group of specialized critics in the official Opposition party.

single-member-plurality (SMP) system. An electoral system in which the candidate with the most votes wins, even though that win may not represent 51 percent of the votes.

single-party system. A party system in which there is only one party, and no political alternatives are legally tolerated.

single-transferable-vote (STV) system. A form of proportional representation in which electors vote for individuals rather than party lists, but they do so by ranking the candidates in their order of choice.

social democrats. Socialists emphasizing popular consent, peaceful change, political pluralism, and constitutional government.

socialism. A leftist political ideology that emphasizes the principle of equality and usually prescribes a large role for government to intervene in society and the economy via taxation, regulation, redistribution, and public ownership.

social justice. The partial equalization of wealth and income to reach a more desirable outcome.

society. A self-sufficient group of individuals living together under common rules of conduct.

sovereign. The highest or supreme political authority.

special (ad hoc) committee. Legislative committees appointed for special, temporary purposes, such as to investigate a problem before the government prepares legislation on the subject.

spoils system. The assumption that, after successfully winning an election, the political executive is entitled to appoint large numbers of supporters to the bureaucracy.

spontaneous order. The pattern of mutual coordination that emerges as individuals pursue their own interests in society.

standing committee. Legislative committees that are set up permanently and parallel government functions.

stare decisis. The legal principle that precedents are binding on similar subsequent cases; the basis of the common law system.

state. Combination of people, territory, and sovereign government.

state-centric. An approach to international relations positing sovereign states as the focus for understanding the nature and workings of the international system.

stateless society. A society without a sovereign government.

statism. The heavy intervention of the state in societal affairs, especially in the economic system.

statute. A specific piece of legislation.

structure. In social-science jargon, an organization or an organized pattern of behaviour.

structuralism. A theory of international relations that stresses the impact of world economic structures on the political, social, cultural, and economic systems of countries.

subjects. Members of a society who are not involved in the political process of that society.

suffragism. A political movement by women to obtain the right to vote in an election.

superior courts. In Canada, courts organized by provincial statute and staffed by judges appointed by the federal government.

surplus. In international trade, a positive balance of payments.

symbolic laws. Laws designed to create special meaning for society, such as the adoption of a national anthem.

syndicalism. A variation of socialism in which the workers own or control the factory or workplace.

Third International. The political organization in which the official ideology was Marxist-Leninism or communism, established in 1921.

totalitarianism. A modern form of despotic rule in which the state undertakes to remake society according to an ideological design.

traditional authority. Authority based on birthright and custom.

Treasury Board. A cabinet committee and government department whose primary responsibility is to oversee government spending.

tribe. A community of people tied together by a myth of common ancestry.

trustee. A representative who acts independently in deciding what is in the best interests of his or her constituents.

two-party-plus system. A party system in which there are two major contenders for power of approximately equal strength plus one or more minor parties able to win seats but not to control the government.

two-party system. A party system in which there are two credible contenders for power and either is capable of winning any election.

typology. A broad classification scheme of governmental systems.

tyranny. A form of government in which one person rules arbitrarily.

ultra vires. Term used to describe an action which exceeds the conferred constitutional powers of the actor. Literally, "beyond the power."

unipolar. An international system with only one dominant state.

unitary system. A system of government in which a single sovereign government rules the country.

unwritten constitution. An uncodified constitution established through traditional practice.

utopian socialism. Early-nineteenth-century socialism based on a universal appeal to reason.

veto. The authorized power of a president to reject legislation passed by Congress.

violence. The utilization of physical force or power as a means of achieving ends.

vote of censure. A motion of nonconfidence requiring the prime minister and the cabinet to resign.

welfare state. The provision for redistributed benefits such as education and health services by the state.

White House Staff. Special advisers to the U.S. president; part of the Executive Office and similar to the Canadian Prime Minister's Office.

wilderness preservationism. A form of environmentalism positing the intrinsic importance of wilderness for humankind.

World Trade Organization. An international organization created to provide the ground rules for international trade and commerce.

Zionism. Jewish nationalist movement advocating establishment of a Jewish nation-state.

APPENDIX A

Constitution Act, 1867
(formerly British North America Act, 1867)

Below are a few sections of the Act of particular interest to Canadian students of political science at the introductory level.

. . . .

Preamble

WHEREAS the Provinces of Canada, Nova Scotia and New Brunswick have expressed their Desire to be federally united into One Dominion under the Crown of the United Kingdom of Great Britain and Ireland, with a Constitution similar in Principle to that of the United Kingdom:

And whereas such a Union would conduce to the Welfare of the Provinces and promote the Interests of the British Empire:

And whereas on the Establishment of the Union by Authority of Parliament it is expedient, not only that the Constitution of the Legislative Authority in the Dominion be provided for, but also that the Nature of the Executive Government therein be declared:

And whereas it is expedient that Provision be made for the eventual Admission into the Union of other Parts of British North America:

. . . .

VI. DISTRIBUTION OF LEGISLATIVE POWERS.

Powers of the Parliament

Legislative Authority of Parliament of Canada.

91. It shall be lawful for the Queen, by and with the Advice and Consent of the Senate and House of Commons, to make Laws for the Peace, Order, and good Government of Canada, in relation to all Matters not coming within the Classes of Subjects by this Act assigned exclusively to the Legislatures of the Provinces; and for greater Certainty, but not so as to restrict the Generality of the foregoing Terms of this Section, it is hereby declared that (notwithstanding anything in this Act) the exclusive Legislative Authority of the Parliament of Canada extends to all Matters coming within the Classes of Subjects next herein-after enumerated; that is to say,—

1. The amendment from time to time of the Constitution of Canada, except as regards matters coming within the classes of subjects by this Act assigned exclusively to the Legislatures of the provinces, or

as regards rights or privileges by this or any other Constitutional Act granted or secured to the Legislature or the Government of a province, or to any class of persons with respect to schools or as regards the use of English or the French language or as regards the requirements that there shall be a session of the Parliament of Canada at least once each year, and that no House of Commons shall continue for more than five years from the day of the return of the Writs for choosing the House: provided, however, that a House of Commons may in time of real or apprehended war, invasion or insurrection be continued by the Parliament of Canada if such continuation is not opposed by the votes of more than one-third of the members of such House.

1A. The Public Debt and Property.
2. The regulation of Trade and Commerce.
2A. Unemployment insurance.
3. The raising of Money by any Mode or System of Taxation.
4. The borrowing of Money on the Public Credit.
5. Postal Service.
6. The Census and Statistics.
7. Militia, Military and Naval Service, and Defence.
8. The fixing of and providing for the Salaries and Allowances of Civil and other Officers of the Government of Canada.
9. Beacons, Buoys, Lighthouses, and Sable Island.
10. Navigation and Shipping.
11. Quarantine and the Establishment and Maintenance of Marine Hospitals.
12. Sea Coast and Inland Fisheries.
13. Ferries between a Province and any British or Foreign Country or between Two Provinces.
14. Currency and Coinage.
15. Banking, Incorporation of Banks, and the Issue of Paper Money.
16. Savings Banks.
17. Weights and Measures.
18. Bills of Exchange and Promissory Notes.
19. Interest.
20. Legal Tender.
21. Bankruptcy and Insolvency.
22. Patents of Invention and Discovery.
23. Copyrights.
24. Indians, and Lands reserved for the Indians.
25. Naturalization and Aliens.
26. Marriage and Divorce.

27. The Criminal Law, except the Constitution of Courts of Criminal Jurisdiction, but including the Procedure in Criminal Matters.
28. The Establishment, Maintenance, and Management of Penitentiaries.
29. Such Classes of Subjects as are expressly excepted in the Enumeration of the Classes of Subjects by this Act assigned exclusively to the Legislatures of the Provinces.

And any Matter coming within any of the Classes of Subjects enumerated in this Section shall not be deemed to come within the Class of Matters of a local or private Nature comprised in the Enumeration of the Classes of Subjects by this Act assigned exclusively to the Legislatures of the Provinces.

Exclusive Powers of Provincial Legislatures

Subjects of exclusive Provincial Legislation

92. In each Province the Legislature may exclusively make Laws in relation to Matters coming within the Classes of Subject next herein-after enumerated; that is to say,—

1. The Amendment from Time to Time, not withstanding anything in this Act, of the Constitution of the Province, except as regards the Office of Lieutenant Governor.

2. Direct Taxation within the Province in order to the raising of a Revenue for Provincial Purposes.

3. The borrowing of Money on the sole Credit of the Province.

4. The Establishment and Tenure of Provincial Offices and the Appointment and Payment of Provincial Officers.

5. The Management and Sale of the Public Lands belonging to the Province and of the Timber and Wood thereon.

6. The Establishment, Maintenance, and Management of Public and Reformatory Prisons in and for the Province.

7. The Establishment, Maintenance, and Management of Hospitals, Asylums, Charities and Eleemosynary Institutions in and for the Province, other than Marine Hospitals.

8. Municipal Institutions in the Province.

9. Shop, Saloon, Tavern, Auctioneer, and other Licences in order to the raising of a Revenue for Provincial, Local, or Municipal Purposes.

10. Local Works and Undertakings other than such as are of the following Classes:—

(a) Lines of Steam or other Ships, Railways, Canals, Telegraphs, and other Works and Undertakings connecting the Province with any other or others of the Provinces, or extending beyond the Limits of the Province;

(b) Lines of Steam Ships between the Province and any British or Foreign Country;

(c) Such Works as, although wholly situate within the Province, are before or after their Execution declared by the Parliament of Canada to be for the general Advantage of Canada or for the Advantage of Two or more of the Provinces.

11. The Incorporation of Companies with Provincial Objects.

12. The Solemnization of Marriage in the Province.

13. Property and Civil Rights in the Province.

14. The Administration of Justice in the Province, including the Constitution, Maintenance, and Organization of Provincial Courts, both of Civil and of Criminal Jurisdiction, and including Procedure in Civil Matters in those Courts.

15. The Imposition of Punishment by Fine, Penalty, or Imprisonment for enforcing any Law of the Province made in relation to any Matter coming within any of the Classes of Subjects enumerated in this Section.

16. Generally all Matters of a merely local or private Nature in the Province.

. . . .

For section 92A, see section 50 and 51 of the Constitution Act, 1982, in Appendix B in this volume.

. . . .

Education

Legislation respecting Education

93. In and for each Province the Legislature may exclusively make Laws in relation to Education, subject and according to the following Provisions:—

(1) Nothing in any such Law shall prejudicially affect any Right or Privilege with respect to Denominational Schools which any Class of Persons have by Law in the Province at the Union:

(2) All the Powers, Privileges, and Duties at the Union by Law conferred and imposed in Upper Canada on the Separate Schools and School Trustees of the Queen's Roman Catholic Subjects shall be and the same are hereby extended to the Dissentient Schools of the Queen's Protestant and Roman Catholic Subjects in Quebec:

(3) Where in any Province a System of Separate or Dissentient Schools exists by Law at the Union or is thereafter established by the Legislature of the Province, an Appeal shall lie to the Governor General in Council from any Act or Decision of any Provincial Authority affecting

any Right or Privilege of the Protestant or Roman Catholic Minority of the Queen's Subjects in relation to Education:

(4) In case any such Provincial Law as from Time to Time seems to the Governor General in Council requisite for the due Execution of the Provisions of this Section is not made, or in case any Decision of the Governor General in Council on any Appeal under this section is not duly executed by the proper Provincial Authority in that Behalf, then and in every such Case, and as far only as the Circumstances of each Case require, the Parliament of Canada may make remedial Laws for the due Execution of the Provisions of this Section and of any Decision of the Governor-General in Council under this Section.

. . . .

Old Age Pensions

Legislation respecting old age pensions and supplementary

94A. The Parliament of Canada may make laws in relation to old age pensions and supplementary benefits, including survivors and disability benefits irrespective of age, but no such law shall affect the operation of any law present or future of a provincial legislature in relation to any such matter.

. . . .

Agriculture and Immigration

Concurrent Power of Legislation respecting Agriculture, etc.

95. In each Province the Legislature may make Laws in relation to Agriculture in the Province, and to Immigration into the Province, and it is hereby declared that the Parliament of Canada may from Time to Time make Laws in relation to Agriculture in all or any of the Provinces, and to Immigration into all or any of the Provinces; and any Law of the Legislature of a province relative to Agriculture or to Immigration shall have effect in and for the Province as long and as far only as it is not repugnant to any Act of the Parliament of Canada.

. . . .

Use of English and French Languages

133. Either the English or the French Language may be used by any Person in the Debates of the Houses of the Parliament of Canada and of the Legislature of Quebec; and both those Languages shall be used in the respective Records and Journals of those Houses; and either of those Languages may be used by any Person or in any Pleading or Process in or issuing from any Court of Canada established under this Act, and in or from all or any of the Courts of Quebec.

The Acts of the Parliament of Canada and of the Legislature of Quebec shall be printed and published in both those languages.

APPENDIX B

Constitution Act, 1982
Schedule B to Canada Act 1982 (U.K.)

PART I
CANADIAN CHARTER OF RIGHTS AND FREEDOMS

Whereas Canada is founded upon principles that recognize the supremacy of God and the rule of law:

Guarantee of Rights and Freedoms

Rights and
Freedoms
in Canada

1. The *Canadian Charter of Rights and Freedoms* guarantees the rights and freedoms set out in it subject only to such reasonable limits prescribed by law as can be demonstrably justified in a free and democratic society.

Fundamental Freedoms

Fundamental
freedoms

2. Everyone has the following fundamental freedoms:
(a) freedom of conscience and religion;
(b) freedom of thought, belief, opinion and expression, including freedom of the press and other media of communication;
(c) freedom of peaceful assembly; and
(d) freedom of association.

Democratic Rights

Democratic righs
of citizens

3. Every citizen of Canada has the right to vote in an election of members of the House of Commons or of a legislative assembly and to be qualified for membership therein.

Maximum
duration of
legislative bodies

4. (1) No House of Commons and no legislative assembly shall continue for longer than five years from the date fixed for the return of the writs at a general election of its members.

Continuation
in special
circumstances

(2) In time of real or apprehended war, invasion or insurrection, a House of Commons may be continued by Parliament and a legislative assembly may be continued by the legislature beyond five years if such continuation is not opposed by the votes of more than one-third of the members of the House of Commons or the legislative assembly, as the case may be.

Annual sitting of
legislative bodies

5. There shall be a sitting of Parliament and of each legislature at least once every twelve months.

Mobility Rights

Mobility of citizens

6. (1) Every citizen of Canada has the right to enter, remain in and leave Canada.

Rights to move and gain livelihood

(2) Every citizen of Canada and every person who has the status of a permanent resident of Canada has the right

(a) to move to and take up residence in any province; and

(b) to pursue the gaining of a livelihood in any province.

Limitation

(3) The rights specified in subsection (2) are subject to

(a) any laws or practices of general application in force in a province other than those that discriminate among persons primarily on the basis of province of present or previous residence; and

(b) any laws providing for reasonable residency requirements as a qualification for the receipt of publicly provided social services.

Affirmative action programs

(4) Subsections (2) and (3) do not preclude any law, program or activity that has as its object the amelioration in a province of conditions of individuals in that province who are socially or economically disadvantaged if the rate of employment in that province is below the rate of employment in Canada.

Legal Rights

Life, liberty and security of person

7. Everyone has the right to life, liberty, and security of the person and the right not to be deprived thereof except in accordance with the principles of fundamental justice.

Search or seizure

8. Everyone has the right to be secure against unreasonable search or seizure.

Detention or imprisonment

9. Everyone has the right not to be arbitrarily detained or imprisoned.

Arrest or detention

10. Everyone has the right on arrest or detention

(a) to be informed promptly of the reasons therefore;

(b) to retain and instruct counsel without delay and to be informed of that right; and

(c) to have the validity of the detention determined by way of *habeas corpus* and to be released if the detention is not lawful.

Proceedings in criminal and penal matters

11. Any person charged with an offence has the right

(a) to be informed without unreasonable delay of the specific offence;

(b) to be tried within a reasonable time;

(c) not to be compelled to be a witness in proceedings against that person in respect of the offence;

(d) to be presumed innocent until proven guilty according to law in a fair and public hearing by an independent and impartial tribunal;

(e)   not to be denied reasonable bail without just cause;

(f)   except in the case of an offence under military law tried before a military tribunal, to the benefit of trial by jury where the maximum punishment for the offence is imprisonment for five years or a more severe punishment;

(g)   not to be found guilty on account of any act or omission unless, at the time of the act or omission, it constituted an offence under Canadian or international law or was criminal according to the general principles of law recognized by the community of nations;

(h)   if finally acquitted of the offence, not to be tried for it again and, if finally found guilty and punished for the offence, not to be tried or punished for it again; and

(i)   if found guilty of the offence and if the punishment for the offence has been varied between the time of commission and the time of sentencing, to the benefit of the lesser punishment.

Treatment or punishment

12.   Everyone has the right not to be subjected to any cruel and unusual treatment or punishment.

Self-crimination

13.   A witness who testifies in any proceedings has the right not to have any incriminating evidence so given used to incriminate that witness in any other proceedings, except in a prosecution for perjury or for the giving of contradictory evidence.

Interpreter

14.   A party or witness in any proceedings who does not understand or speak the language in which the proceedings are conducted or who is deaf has the right to the assistance of an interpreter.

Equality Rights

Equality before and under law and equal protection and benefit of law

15.   (1) Every individual is equal before and under the law and has the right to the equal protection and equal benefit of the law without discrimination and, in particular, without discrimination based on race, national or ethnic origin, colour, religion, sex, age or mental or physical disability.

Affirmative action programs

(2)   Subsection (1) does not preclude any law, program or activity that has as its object the amelioration of conditions of disadvantaged individuals or groups including those that are disadvantaged because of race, national or ethnic origin, colour, religion, sex, age or mental or physical disability.

Official Languages of Canada

Official languages of Canada

16.   (1) English and French are the official languages of Canada and have equality of status and equal rights and privileges as to their use in all instructions of the Parliament and government of Canada.

Official languages in New Brunswick

(2) English and French are the official languages of New Brunswick and have equality of status and equal rights and privileges as to their use in all institutions of the legislature and government of New Brunswick.

Advancement of status and use

(3) Nothing in this Charter limits the authority of Parliament or a legislature to advance the equality of status or use of English and French.

Proceedings of Parliament

17. (1) Everyone has the right to use English or French in any debates and other proceedings of Parliament.

Proceedings of New Brunswick legislature

(2) Everyone has the right to use English or French in any debates and other proceedings of the legislature of New Brunswick.

Parliamentary statuses and records

18. (1) The statutes, records and journals of Parliament shall be printed and published in English and French and both language versions are equally authoritative.

New Bruswick statutes and records

(2) The statutes, records and journals of the legislature of New Brunswick shall be printed and published in English and French and both language versions are equally authoritative.

Proceedings in courts established by Parliament

19. (1) Either English or French may be used by any person in, or in any pleading in or process issuing from, any court established by Parliament.

Proceedings in New Brunswick courts

(2) Either English or French may be used by any person in, or in any pleading in or process issuing from, any court of New Brunswick.

Communications by public with federal institutions

20. (1) Any member of the public in Canada has the right to communicate with, and to receive available services from, any head or central office of an institution of the Parliament or government of Canada in English or French, and has the same right with respect to any other office of any such institution where

(a) there is a significant demand for communications with and services from that office in such language; or

(b) due to the nature of the office, it is reasonable that communications with and services from that office be available in both English and French.

Communications by public with New Brunswick institutions

(2) Any member of the public in New Brunswick has the right to communicate with, and to receive available services from, any office of an institution of the legislature or government of New Brunswick in English or French.

Continuation of existing constitutional provisions

21. Nothing in sections 16 to 20 abrogates or derogates from any right, privilege or obligation with respect to the English and French languages, or either of them, that exists or is continued by virtue of any other provision of the Constitution of Canada.

Rights and privileges preserved

22. Nothing in sections 16 to 20 abrogates or derogates from any legal or customary right or privilege acquired or enjoyed either before or

after the coming into force of this Charter with respect to any language that is not English or French.

Minority Language Educational Rights

Language of instruction

23. (1) Citizens of Canada

(a) whose first language learned and still understood is that of the English or French linguistic minority population of the province in which they reside, or

(b) who have received their primary school instruction in Canada in English or French and reside in a province where the language in which they received that instruction is the language of the English or French linguistic minority population of the province, have the right to have their children receive primary and secondary school instruction in that language in that province.

Continuity of language instruction

(2) Citizens of Canada of whom any child has received or is receiving primary or secondary school instruction in English or French in Canada, have the right to have all their children receive primary and secondary school instruction in the same language.

Applications where numbers warrant

(3) The right of citizens of Canada under subsections (1) and (2) to have their children receive primary and secondary school instruction in the language of the English or French linguistic minority population of a province

(a) applies wherever in the province the number of children citizens who have such a right is sufficient to warrant the provision to them out of public funds of minority language instruction; and

(b) includes, where the number of those children so warrants, the right to have them receive that instruction in minority language educational facilities provided out of public funds.

Enforcement

Enforcement of guaranteed rights and freedoms

24. (1) Anyone whose rights or freedoms, as guaranteed by this Charter, have been infringed or denied may apply to a court of competent jurisdiction to obtain such remedy as the court considers appropriate and just in the circumstances.

Exclusion of evidence bringing administration of justice into disrepute

(2) Where, in proceedings under subsection (1), a court concludes that evidence was obtained in a manner that infringed or denied any rights or freedoms guaranteed by this Charter, the evidence shall be excluded if it is established that, having regard to all the circumstances, the admission of it in the proceedings would bring the administration of justice into disrepute.

General

Aboriginal rights and freedoms not affected by Charter

25. The guarantee in this Charter of certain rights and freedoms shall not be construed so as to abrogate or derogate from any aboriginal treaty or other rights or freedoms that pertain to the aboriginal peoples of Canada including

(a) any rights or freedoms that have been recognized by the Royal Proclamation of October 7, 1763; and

(b) any rights or freedoms that now exist by way of land claims agreements or may be so acquired.[1]

Other rights and freedoms not affected by Charter

26. The guarantee in this Charter of certain rights and freedoms shall not be construed as denying the existence of any other rights or freedoms that exist in Canada..

Multicultural heritage

27. This Charter shall be interpreted in a manner consistent with the preservation and enhancement of the multicultural heritage of Canadians.

Rights guaranteed equally to both sexes

28. Notwithstanding anything in this Charter, the rights and freedoms referred to in it are guaranteed equally to male and female persons.

Rights respecting certain schools preserved

29. Nothing in this Charter abrogates or derogates from any rights or privileges guaranteed by or under the Constitution of Canada in respect of denomination, separate or dissentient schools.

Application to territories and territorial authorities

30. A reference in this Charter to a province or to the legislative assembly or legislature of a province shall be deemed to include a reference to the Yukon Territory and the Northwest Territories, or to the appropriate legislative authority thereof, as the case may be.

Legislative powers not extended

31. Nothing in this Charter extends the legislative powers of any body or authority.

Application of Charter

Application of Charter

32. (1) This Charter applies

(a) to the Parliament and government of Canada in respect of all matters within the authority of Parliament including all matters relating to the Yukon Territory and Northwest Territories; and

(b) to the legislature and government of each province in respect of all matters within the authority of the legislature of each province.

Exception

(2) Notwithstanding subsection (1), section 15 shall not have effect until three years after this section comes into force.

Exception where express declaration

33. (1) Parliament or the legislature of a province may expressly declare in an Act of Parliament or of the legislature, as the case may be, that the Act or a provision thereof shall operate notwithstanding a provision in section 2 or sections 7 to 15 of this Charter.

Operation of exception	(2) An Act or a provision of an Act in respect of which a declaration made under this section is in effect shall have such operation as it would have but for the provision of this Charter referred to in the declaration.
Five year limitation	(3) A declaration made under subsection (1) shall cease to have effect five years after it comes into force or on such earlier date as may be specified in the declaration.
Re-enactment	(4) Parliament or the legislature of a province may re-enact a declaration made under subsection (1).
Five year limitation	(5) Subsection (3) applies in respect of a re-enactment made under subsection (4).

Citation

Citation	**34.** This Part may be cited as the *Canadian Charter of Rights and Freedoms*.

PART II
RIGHTS OF THE ABORIGINAL PEOPLES OF CANADA

Recognition of existing aboriginal and treaty rights	**35.** (1) The existing aboriginal and treaty rights of the aboriginal peoples of Canada are hereby recognized and affirmed.
Definition of "aboriginal peoples of Canada"	(2) In this Act, "aboriginal peoples of Canada" includes the Indian, Inuit and Métis peoples of Canada.
Land claims agreement	(3) For greater certainty, in subsection (1) "treaty rights" includes rights that now exist by way of land claims agreements or may be so acquired.
Aboriginal and treaty rights are guaranteed equally to both sexes	(4) Notwithstanding any other provision of this Act, the aboriginal and treaty rights referred to in subsection (1) are guaranteed equally to male and female persons.[2]
Commitment to participation in constitutional conference	**35.1** The government of Canada and the provincial governments are committed to the principle that, before any amendment is made to Class 24 of section 91 of the *"Constitution Act, 1867,"* to section 25 of this Act or to this Part,

(a) a constitutional conference that includes in its agenda an item relating to the proposed amendment, composed of the Prime Minister of Canada and the first ministers of the provinces, will be convened by the Prime Minister of Canada; and

(b) the Prime Minister of Canada will invite representatives of the aboriginal peoples of Canada to participate in the discussion on that item.[3]

PART III
EQUALIZATION AND REGIONAL DISPARITIES

Commitment to promote equal opportunities

36. (1) Without altering the legislative authority of Parliament or of the provincial legislatures, or the rights of any of them with respect to the exercise of their legislative authority, Parliament and the legislatures, together with the government of Canada and the provincial governments, are committed to

(a) promoting equal opportunities for the well-being of Canadians;

(b) furthering economic development to reduce disparity in opportunities; and

(c) providing essential public services of reasonable quality to all Canadians.

Commitment respecting public services

(2) Parliament and the government of Canada are committed to the principle of making equalization payments to ensure that provincial governments have sufficient revenues to provide reasonably comparable levels of public services at reasonably comparable levels of taxation.

PART IV
CONSTITUTIONAL CONFERENCE

Constitutional conference

37. (1) A constitutional conference composed of the Prime Minister of Canada and the first ministers of the provinces shall be convened by the Prime Minister of Canada within one year after this Part comes into force.

Participation of aboriginal peoples

(2) The conference convened under subsection (1) shall have included in its agenda an item respecting constitutional matters that directly affect the aboriginal peoples of Canada, including the identification and definition of the rights of those peoples to be included in the Constitution of Canada, and the Prime Minister of Canada shall invite representatives of those peoples to participate in the discussions on that item.

Participation of territories

(3) The Prime Minister of Canada shall invite elected representatives of the governments of the Yukon Territory and the Northwest Territories to participate in the discussion on any item on the agenda of the conference convened under subsection (1) that, in the opinion of the Prime Minister, directly affects the Yukon Territory and the Northwest Territories.

PART IV.1
CONSTITUTIONAL CONFERENCES

Constitutional conferences

37.1 (1) In addition to the conference convened in March 1983, at least two constitutional conferences composed of the Prime Minister of

Canada and the first ministers of the provinces shall be convened by the Prime Minister of Canada, the first within three years after April 17, 1982 and the second within five years after that date.

Participation of aboriginal peoples

(2) Each conference convened under subsection (1) shall have included in its agenda constitutional matters that directly affect the aboriginal peoples of Canada, and the Prime Minister of Canada shall invite representatives of those peoples to participate in the discussions on those matters.

Participation of territories

(3) The Prime Minister of Canada shall invite elected representatives of the governments of the Yukon Territory and the Northwest Territories to participate in the discussions on any item on the agenda of a conference convened under subsection (1) that, in the opinion of the Prime Minister, directly affects the Yukon Territory and the Northwest Territories.

Subsection 35(1) not affected

(4) Nothing in this section shall be construed so as to derogate from subsection 35(1).[4]

PART V
PROCEDURE FOR AMENDING CONSTITUTION OF CANADA

General procedure for amending Constitution of Canada

38. (1) An amendment to the Constitution of Canada may be made by proclamation issued by the Governor General under the Great Seal of Canada where so authorized by

    (a) resolutions of the Senate and House of Commons; and

    (b) resolutions of the legislative assemblies of at least two-thirds of the provinces that have, in the aggregate, according to the then latest general census, at least fifty per cent of the population of all the provinces.

Majority of members

(2) An amendment made under subsection (1) that derogates from the legislative powers, the proprietary rights or any other rights or privileges of the legislature or government of a province shall require a resolution supported by a majority of the members of each of the Senate, the House of Commons and the legislative assemblies required under subsection (1).

Expression of dissent

(3) An amendment referred to in subsection (2) shall not have effect in a province the legislative assembly of which has expressed its dissent thereto by resolution supported by a majority of its members prior to the issue of the proclamation to which the amendment relates unless that legislative assembly, subsequently, by resolution supported by a majority of its members, revokes its dissent and authorizes the amendment.

Revocation of dissent

(4) A resolution of dissent made for the purposes of subsection (3) may be revoked at any time before or after the issue of the proclamation to which it relates.

Restriction on proclamation

39. (1) A proclamation shall not be issued under subsection 38(1) before the expiration of one year from the adoption of the resolution initiating the amendment procedure thereunder, unless the legislative assembly of each province has previously adopted a resolution of assent or dissent.

Idem

(2) A proclamation shall not be issued under subsection 38(1) after the expiration of three years from the adoption of the resolution initiating the amendment procedure thereunder.

Compensation

40. Where an amendment is made under subsection 38(1) that transfers provincial legislative powers relating to education or other cultural matters from provincial legislatures to Parliament, Canada shall provide reasonable compensation to any province to which the amendment does not apply.

Amendment by unanimous consent

41. An amendment to the Constitution of Canada in relation to the following matters may be made by proclamation issued by the Governor General under the Great Seal of Canada only where authorized by resolutions of the Senate and House of Commons and of the legislative assembly of each province:

(a) the office of the Queen, the Governor General and the Lieutenant Governor of a province;

(b) the right of a province to a number of members in the House of Commons not less than the number of Senators by which the province is entitled to be represented at the time this Part comes into force;

(c) subject to section 43, the use of the English or the French language;

(d) the composition of the Supreme Court of Canada; and

(e) an amendment to this Part.

Amendment by general procedure

42. (1) An amendment to the Constitution of Canada in relation to the following matters may be made only in accordance with subsection 38(1):

(a) the principle of proportionate representation of the provinces in the House of Commons prescribed by the Constitution of Canada;

(b) the powers of the Senate and the method of selecting Senators;

(c) the number of members by which a province is entitled to be represented in the Senate and the residence qualifications of Senators;

(d) subject to paragraph 41(d), the Supreme Court of Canada;

(e) the extension of existing provinces into the territories; and

(f) notwithstanding any other law of practice, the establishment of new provinces.

Exception

(2) Subsections 38(2) to (4) do not apply in respect of amendments in relation to matters referred to in subsection (1).

Amendment of provisions relating to some but not all provinces

43. An amendment to the Constitution of Canada in relation to any provision that applies to one or more, but not all, provinces, including

(a) any alteration to boundaries between provinces, and

(b) any amendment to any provision that relates to the use of the English or the French language within a province, may be made by proclamation issued by the Governor General under the Great Seal of Canada only where so authorized by resolutions of the Senate and House of Commons and of the legislative assembly of each province to which the amendment applies.

Amendments by Parliament

44. Subject to sections 41 and 42, Parliament may exclusively make laws amending the Constitution of Canada in relation to the executive government of Canada or the Senate and House of Commons.

Amendments by provincial legislatures
Initiation of amendment procedures

45. Subject to section 41, the legislature of each province may exclusively make laws amending the constitution of the province.

46. (1) The procedures for amendment under sections 38, 41, 42 and 43 may be initiated either by the Senate or the House of Commons or by the legislative assembly of a province.

Revocation of authorization

(2) A resolution of assent made for the purposes of this Part may be revoked at any time before the issue of a proclamation authorized by it.

Amendments without Senate resolution

47. (1) An amendment to the Constitution of Canada made by proclamation under section 38, 41, 42 or 43 may be made without a resolution of the Senate authorizing the issue of the proclamation if, within one hundred and eighty days after the adoption by the House of Commons of a resolution authorizing its issue, the Senate has not adopted such a resolution and if, at any time after the expiration of that period, the House of Commons again adopts the resolution.

Computation of period

(2) Any period when Parliament is prorogued or dissolved shall not be counted in computing the one hundred and eighty day period referred to in subsection (1).

Advice to issue proclamation

48. The Queen's Privy Council for Canada shall advise the Governor General to issue a proclamation under this Part forthwith on the adoption of the resolutions required for an amendment made by proclamation under this Part.

Constitutional conference

49. A constitutional conference composed of the Prime Minister of Canada and the first ministers of the provinces shall be convened by the Prime Minister of Canada within fifteen years after this Part comes into force to review the provisions of this Part.

PART VI
AMENDMENT TO THE CONSTITUTION ACT, 1867

Amendment to
Constitution Act, 1867

50. The Constitution Act, 1867 (formerly named the British North America Act, 1867) is amended by adding thereto, immediately after section 92 thereof, the following heading and section:

"Non-Renewable Natural Resources, Forestry Resources and Electrical Energy

Laws respecting non-renewable natural resources, forestry resources and electrical energy

92A.(1) In each province, the legislature may exclusively make laws in relation to

(a) exploration for non-renewable natural resources in the province;

(b) development, conservation and management of non-renewable natural resources and forestry resources in the province, including laws in relation to the rate of primary production therefrom; and

(c) development, conservation and management of sites and facilities in the province for the generation and production of electrical energy.

Export from provinces of resources

(2) In each province, the legislature may make laws in relation to the export from the province to another part of Canada of the primary production from non-renewable natural resources and forestry resources in the province and the production from facilities in the province for the generation of electrical energy, but such laws may not authorize or provide for discrimination in prices or in supplies exported to another part of Canada.

Authority of Parliament

(3) Nothing in subsection (2) derogates from the authority of Parliament to enact laws in relation to the matters referred to in that subsection and, where such a law of Parliament and a law of a province conflict, the law of Parliament prevails to the extent of the conflict.

Taxation of resources

(4) In each province, the legislature may make laws in relation to the raising of money by any mode or system of taxation in respect of

(a) non-renewable natural resources and forestry resources in the province and the primary production therefrom, and

(b) sites and facilities in the province for the generation of electrical energy and the production therefrom, whether or not production is exported in whole or in part from the province, but such laws may not authorize or provide for taxation that differentiates between production exported to another part of Canada and production not exported from the province.

"Primary production"

(5) The expression "primary production" has the meaning assigned by the Sixth Schedule.

(6) Nothing in subsections (1) to (5) derogates from any powers or rights that a legislature or government of a province had immediately before the coming into force of this section."

51. The said Act is further amended by adding thereto the following Schedule:

"THE SIXTH SCHEDULE

Primary Production from Non-Renewable Natural Resources and Forestry Resources

1. For the purposes of section 92A of this Act,

(a) production from a non-renewable natural resource is primary production therefrom if

(i) it is in the form in which it exists upon its recovery or severance from its natural state, or

(ii) it is a product resulting from processing or refining the resource, and is not a manufactured product or a product resulting from refining crude oil, refining upgraded heavy crude oil, refining gases or liquids derived from coal or refining a synthetic equivalent of crude oil; and

(b) production from a forestry resource is primary production therefrom if it consists of sawlogs, poles, lumber, wood chips, sawdust or any other primary wood product, or wood pulp, and is not a product manufactured from wood."

PART VII
GENERAL

52. (1) The Constitution of Canada is the supreme law of Canada, and any law that is inconsistent with the provisions of the Constitution is, to the extent of the inconsistency, of no force or effect.

(2) The Constitution of Canada includes

(a) The *Canada Act 1982*, including this Act;

(b) the Acts and orders referred to in the schedule; and

(c) any amendment to any Act or order referred to in paragraph (a) or (b).

(3) Amendments to the Constitution of Canada shall be made only in accordance with the authority contained in the Constitution of Canada.

53. (1) The enactments referred to in Column I of the schedule are hereby repealed or amended to the extent indicated in Column II thereof and, unless repealed, shall continue as law in Canada under the names set out in Column III thereof.

(2) Every enactment, except the *Canada Act 1982*, that refers to an enactment referred to in the schedule by the name in Column I thereof is hereby amended by substituting for that name the corresponding name in Column III thereof, and any British North America Act not referred to in the schedule may be cited as the *Constitution Act* followed by the year and number, if any, of its enactment.

54. Part IV is repealed on the day that is one year after this Part comes into force and this section may be repealed and this Act renumbered, consequentially upon the repeal of Part IV and this section, by proclamation issued by the Governor General under the Great Seal of Canada.

54.1 Part IV.1 and this section are repealed on April 18, 1987.[5]

55. A French version of the portions of the Constitution of Canada referred to in the schedule shall be prepared by the Minister of Justice of Canada as expeditiously as possible and, when any portion thereof sufficient to warrant action being taken has been so prepared, it shall be put forward for enactment by proclamation issued by the Governor General under the Great Seal of Canada pursuant to the procedure then applicable to an amendment of the same provisions of the Constitution of Canada.

56. Where any portion of the Constitution of Canada has been or is enacted in English and French or where a French version of any portion of the Constitution is enacted pursuant to section 55, the English and French versions of that portion of the Constitution are equally authoritative.

57. The English and French versions of this Act are equally authoritative.

58. Subject to section 59, this Act shall come into force on a day to be fixed by proclamation issued by the Queen or the Governor General under the Great Seal of Canada.

59. (1) Paragraph 23(1)(a) shall come into force in respect of Quebec on a day to be fixed by proclamation issued by the Queen or the Governor General under the Great Seal of Canada.

(2) A proclamation under subsection (1) shall be issued only where authorized by the legislative assembly or government of Quebec.

(3) This section may be repealed on the day paragraph 23(1)(a) comes into force in respect of Quebec and this Act amended and renumbered, consequentially upon the repeal of this section, by proclamation issued by the Queen or the Governor General under the Great Seal of Canada.

60. This Act may be cited as the *Constitution Act*, 1982, and the Constitution Acts 1867 to 1975 (No. 2) and this Act may be cited together as the *Constitution Acts, 1867 to 1982*.

61. A reference to the *"Constitution Acts, 1867 to 1982"* shall be deemed to include a reference to the *"Constitution Amendment Proclamation, 1983."*[6]

---

[1]Paragraph 25(b) was repealed and the present paragraph 25(b) was substituted by the Constitution Amendment Proclamation, 1983.

[2]Subsections (3) and (4) of s. 35 were added by the Constitution Amendment Proclamation, 1983.

[3]Section 35.1 was added by the Constitution Amendment Proclamation, 1983.

[4]Part IV.1, consisting of s. 37.1, was added by the Constitution Amendment Proclamation, 1983.

[5]Section 54.1 was added by the Constitution Amendment Proclamation, 1983.

[6]Section 61 was added by the Constitution Amendment Proclamation, 1983.

SCHEDULE
to the

Constitution Act, 1982
Modernization of the Constitution

Item	Column I Act Affected	Column II Amendment	Column III New Name
1.	British North America Act, 1867, 30–31 Vict., c. 3 (U.K.)	(1) Section is repealed and the following substituted therefor: "1. This Act may be cited as the *Constitution Act, 1867*." (2) Section 20 is repealed. (3) Class 1 of section 91 is repealed. (4) Class 1 of section 92 is repealed.	Constitution Act, 1867
2.	An Act to amend and continue the Act 32–33 Victoria chapter 3; and to establish and provide for the Government of the Province of Manitoba, 1870, 33 Vict., c. 3 (Can.)	(1) The long title is repealed and the following substituted therefor: "*Manitoba Act, 1870*." (2) Section 20 is repealed.	Manitoba Act, 1879
3.	Order of Her Majesty in Council admitting Rupert's Land and the North-Western Territory into the union, dated the 23rd day of June 1870		Rupert's Land and North-Western Territory Order
4.	Order of Her Majesty in Council admitting British Columbia into the Union, dated the 16th day of May, 1871		British Columbia Terms of Union

SCHEDULE
to the

Constitution Act, 1982 (continued)

5.	British North America Act, 1871, 34–35 Vict., c. 28 (U.K.)	Section 1 is repealed and the following substituted therefor: "1. This Act may be cited as the *Constitution Act, 1871.*"	Constitution Act, 1871
6.	Order of Her Majesty in Council admitting Prince Edward Island into the Union, dated the 26th day of June, 1873		Prince Edward Island Terms of Union
7.	Parliament of Canada Act, 1875, 38–39 Vict., c. 38 (U.K.)		Parliament of Canada Act, 1875
8.	Order of Her Majesty in Council admitting all British possessions and Territories in North America and islands adjacent thereto into the Union, dated the 31st day of July, 1880		Adjacent Territories Order
9.	British North America Act, 1886, 49–50 Vict., c. 35 (U.K.)	Section 3 is repealed and the following substituted therefor: "3. This Act may be cited as the *Constitution Act, 1886.*"	Constitution Act, 1886
10.	Canada (Ontario Boundary) Act, 1889, 52–53 Vict., c. 28 (U.K.)		Canada (Ontario Boundary) Act, 1989
11.	Canadian Speaker (Appointment of Deputy) Act, 1895, 2nd Sess., 59 Vict., c. 3 (U.K.)	The Act is repealed.	

SCHEDULE
to the

Constitution Act, 1982 (continued)

12.	The Alberta Act, 1905, 4–5 Edw. VII, c. 3 (Can.) Alberta Act		Alberta Act
13.	The Saskatchewan Act, 1905, 4–5 Edw. VII, c. 42 (Can.)		Saskatchewan Act
14.	British North America Act, 1907, 7 Edw. VII, c. 11 (U.K.)	Section 2 is repealed and the following substituted therefor: "2. This Act may be cited as the *Constitution Act, 1907.*"	Constitution Act, 1907
15.	British North America Act, 1915, 5–6 Geo. V, c. 45 (U.K.)	Section 3 is repealed and the following substituted therefor: "3. This Act may be cited as the Constitution Act, 1915."	Constitution Act, 1915
16.	British North America Act, 1930, 20–21 Geo. V, c. 26 (U.K.)	Section 3 is repealed and the following substituted therefor: "3. This Act may be cited as the *Constitution Act, 1930.*"	Constitution Act, 1930
17.	Statute of Westminster 1931, 22 Geo. V, c. 4 (U.K.)	In so far as they apply to Canada, (a) section 4 is repealed; and (b) subsection 7 (1) is repealed.	Statute of Wesstminster, 1931
18.	British North America Act, 1940, 3–4 Geo. VI, c. 36 (U.K.)	Section 2 is repealed and the following substituted therefor: "2. This Act may be cited as the *Constitution Act, 1940.*"	Constitution Act, 1940

SCHEDULE
to the

Constitution Act, 1982 (continued)

19.	British North America Act, 1943, 6–7 Geo. VI, c. 30 (U.K.)	The Act is repealed.
20.	British North America Act, 1946, 9–10 Geo. VI, c. 63 (U.K.)	The Act is repealed. (U.K.)
21.	British North America Act, 1949, 12–13 Geo. VI, c. 22 (U.K.)	Section 3 is repealed and the following substituted therefor: "3. This Act may be cited as the *Newfoundland Act.*"	Newfoundaland Act
22.	British North America (No. 2) Act, 1949, 13 Geo. VI, c. 81 (U.K.)	The Act is repealed.
23.	British North America Act, 1951, 14–15 Geo. VI, c. 32 (U.K.)	The Act is repealed.
24.	British North America Act, 1952, 1 Eliz. II, c. 15 (Can.)	The Act is repealed.
25.	British North America Act, 1960, 9 Eliz. II, c. 2 (U.K.)	Section 2 is repealed and the following substituted therefor: "2. This Act may be cited as the *Constitution Act, 1960.*"	Constitution Act, 1960
26	British North America Act, 1964, 12–13 Eliz. II, c. 73 (U.K.)	Section 2 is repealed and the following substituted therefor: "2. This Act may be cited as the *Constitution Act, 1964.*"	Constitution Act, 1960

SCHEDULE
to the

Constitution Act, 1982 (continued)

27.	British North America Act, 1965, 14 Eliz. II, c. 4, Part I (Can.)	Section 2 is repealed and the following substituted therefor: "2. This Part may be cited as the *Constitution Act, 1965.*"	
28.	British North America Act, 1974, 23 Eliz. II, c. 13, Part I (Can.)	Section 3, as amended by 25–26 Eliz. II, c. 28, s. 31 (Can.), is repealed and the following substituted therefor: "3. This Part may be cited as the *Constitution Act (No. 1), 1974.*"	Constitution Act, 1974
29.	British North America Act, 1975, 23–24 Eliz. II, c. 28, Part I (Can.)	Section 3, as amended by 25–26 Eliz. II, c. 28, s. 31 (Can.), is repealed and the following substituted therefor: "3. This Part may be cited as the *Constitution Act (No. 1), 1975.*"	Constitution Act, (No. 1), 1975
30.	British North America Act (No. 2), 1975, 23–24 Eliz. II, c. 53 (Can.)	Section 3 is repealed and the following substituted therefor: "3. This Act may be cited as the Constitution Act (No. 2), 1975." *Constitution Act (No. 2), 1975*	Constitutional Act (No, 2), 1975

NOTES

Preface

1. E.D. Hirsch, Jr., *The Schools We Need: And Why We Don't Have Them* (New York: Doubleday, 1996), p. 156.

PART ONE
Chapter 1

1. David M. Ricci, *The Tragedy of Political Science: Politics, Scholarship, and Democracy* (New Haven: Yale University Press, 1984), pp. 60–61.
2. Alan C. Cairns, "Political Science in Canada and the Americanization Issue," *Canadian Journal of Political Science* 8 (1975), p. 196.

Chapter 2

1. Edward I. Hall, *The Hidden Dimension* (Garden City, N.Y.: Doubleday Anchor, 1969), pp. 121, 161.
2. A seminal work is Edward O. Wilson, *Sociobiology: The New Synthesis* (Cambridge: Belknap Press of Harvard University Press, 1975). An overview for a popular audience is David P. Barash, *The Hare and the Tortoise* (New York: Viking, 1986).
3. Marcel Giraud, *Le Métis canadien* (Paris: Institut d'Ethnologie, 1945), pp. 57–61.
4. Bertrand de Jouvenel, *The Pure Theory of Politics* (New Haven: Yale University Press, 1963), p. 30.
5. J.D.B. Miller, *The Nature of Politics* (Harmondsworth: Penguin, 1965), p. 14.
6. Alan R. Ball, *Modern Politics and Government* (London: Macmillan, 1971), p. 20.
7. Harold D. Lasswell, *Politics, Who Gets What, When, How* (New York: Peter Smith, 1950). First published in 1936.
8. David Easton, *A Systems Analysis of Political Life* (New York: John Wiley and Sons, 1965), p. 21.
9. Jouvenel, *Pure Theory of Politics*, pp. 204–12.
10. Bernard Crick, *In Defence of Politics*, rev. ed. (Chicago: University of Chicago Press, 1972), p. 22.
11. Alexander H. Harcourt and Frans B.M. de Waal, eds., *Coalitions and Alliances in Humans and Other Animals* (Oxford: Oxford University Press, 1992), p. 3.

12. Norman Cohn, *The Pursuit of the Millennium*, rev. ed. (New York: Oxford University Press, 1970).

13. V.I. Lenin, "The State and Revolution," in *Selected Works* (Moscow: Progress Publishers, 1967), vol. 2, p. 345.

14. Marx himself did not use the term "withering away of the state." It was popularized by his collaborator Friedrich Engels. See his "Socialism: Utopian and Scientific," ch. 3, in Karl Marx and Friedrich Engels, *Selected Works* (Moscow: Progress Publishers, 1968), pp. 417–36.

15. Robert Axelrod, *The Evolution of Cooperation* (New York: Basic Books, 1984).

Chapter 3

1. Liberal democracies define political crimes narrowly as the use of force, or the advocacy of such use, against the state. Totalitarian and authoritarian regimes extend the definition to include peaceful opposition to or criticism of the state. The definition of a political crime is an almost infallible test for the genuineness of liberal democracy.

2. Stuart Schram, ed., *The Political Thought of Mao Tse-tung* (New York: Praeger, 1963), p. 209.

3. R.M. MacIver, *The Web of Government*, rev. ed. (New York: Free Press, 1965), p. 64.

Chapter 4

1. Carl J. Friedrich, *Man and His Government: An Empirical Theory of Politics* (New York: McGraw-Hill, 1963), p. 225.

2. H.H. Gerth and C.W. Mills, ed. and trans., *From Max Weber* (New York: Oxford University Press, 1950), Part II.

3. Alexis de Tocqueville, *Democracy in America*, Andrew Hacker, ed. (New York: Washington Square Press, 1964), pp. 9–10.

4. Cited in Reinhard Bendix, *Max Weber: An Intellectual Portrait* (Garden City, N.Y.: Doubleday, 1960), p. 88, note 15.

5. Thomas Flanagan, *Louis "David" Riel: "Prophet of the New World,"* rev. ed. (Toronto: University of Toronto Press, 1996).

6. Cited in J.G. Ismael and T.Y. Ismael, "Social Change in Islamic Society: The Political Thought of Ayatollah Khomeini," *Social Problems* 27 (1980), p. 614.

7. Gerth and Mills, *From Max Weber*, p. 297.

Chapter 5

1. Cited in Jacques Maritain, "The Concept of Sovereignty," in W.J. Stankiewicz, ed., *In Defence of Sovereignty* (New York: Oxford University Press, 1969), pp. 44–46.

2. Jean-Jacques Rousseau, *The Social Contract* (New York: Hafner, 1947), p. 85.

3. Robert L. Carneiro, "A Theory of the Origin of the State," *Science* 169 (21 August 1970), pp. 733–38.

4. The literature is summarized in Fred H. Wilhoite, Jr., "Political Evolution and Legitimacy: The Biocultural Origins of Hierarchical Organizations," in Elliot White and Joseph Losco, eds., *Biology and Bureaucracy: Public Administration and Public Policy from the Perspective of Evolutionary, Genetic, and Neurobiological Theory* (University Press of America, 1986), pp. 193–231.

5. I Kings 11:3.

6. France, Secrétariat d'état chargé des relations culturelles internationales, *1789: Exposition* (Paris: Axiom Graphic, 1988), no. 24.

Chapter 6

1. Cited in Hans Kohn, ed., *Nationalism: Its Meaning and History* (New York: Van Nostrand Reinhold, 1965), p. 1.

2. Louis L. Snyder, *Global Mini-Nationalism: Autonomy or Independence* (Westport, Conn.: Greenwood Press, 1982).

3. Pierre L. van den Berghe, *The Ethnic Phenomenon* (New York: Praeger, 1981), pp. 15–36.

4. Theodore Draper, *The Rediscovery of Black Nationalism* (New York: Viking Press, 1969), ch. 5.

5. Mel Watkins, ed., *Dene Nation: The Colony Within* (Toronto: University of Toronto Press, 1977), p. 3.

6. Menno Boldt and J. Anthony Long, "Tribal Traditions and European–Western Political Ideologies: The Dilemma of Canada's Native Indians," *Canadian Journal of Political Science* 17 (1984), pp. 537–53; Thomas Flanagan, "Indian Sovereignty and Nationhood: A Comment on Boldt and Long," *Canadian Journal of Political Science* 18 (1985), pp. 367–74.

7. *Renewal: A Twenty-Year Commitment*, vol. 5, Report of the Royal Commission on Aboriginal Peoples (Ottawa: Minister of Supply and Services Canada, 1996), p. 5.

8. Michael Asch, *Home and Native Land* (Toronto: Methuen, 1984), p. 34.

9. P.B. Waite, *The Confederation Debates in the Province of Canada/1865* (Toronto: McClelland & Stewart, 1963), p. 50.

Chapter 7

1. Exodus 34:27–33.

2. F.A. Hayek, *Law, Legislation and Liberty*, 3 vols. (Chicago: University of Chicago Press, 1973–9), vol. I, p. 81.

3. John Henry Merryman, *The Civil Law Tradition: An Introduction to the Legal Systems of Western Europe and Latin America* (Palo Alto, Calif.: Stanford University Press, 1969).

4. John E.C. Brierly, "Quebec's Civil Law Codification Viewed and Reviewed," *McGill Law Journal* 14 (1968), pp. 521–89.

5. Thomas Hobbes, *Leviathan* (New York: E.P. Dutton, 1950), p. 226.

6. Ibid.

7. Michelle Falardeau-Ramsay, "The Changing Face of Human Rights in Canada," *Constitutional Forum* 4 (1993), p. 64.

8. *R. v. Big M Drug Mart*, [1985] 1 S.C.R. 295.

9. The Gallup Report, March 18, 1996.

Chapter 8

1. Ivor Jennings, *The Law of the Constitution*, 5th ed. (London: University of London Press, 1959), p. 136.

2. Andrew D. Heard, "Recognizing the Variety among Constitutional Conventions," *Canadian Journal of Political Science* 22 (1989), pp. 63–82.

3. Rainer Knopff, "Legal Theory and the 'Patriation' Debate," *Queen's Law Journal* 7 (1981), p. 54.

4. J.N. Peltason, *Corwin and Peltason's Understanding the Constitution*, 8th ed. (New York: Holt, Rinehart and Winston, 1979), p. 236.

5. *Plessy v. Ferguson*, 163 U.S. 537 (1896).

6. *Brown v. Board of Education*, 437 U.S. 483 (1954).

7. *Marbury v. Madison*, 1 Cranch 137 (1803).

8. Statutes of Quebec, 1990, c. 150, popularly known as Bill 150.

9. Peter Russell, "The Anti-Inflation Case: The Anatomy of a Constitutional Decision," *Canadian Public Administration* 20 (1977), pp. 635–65.

10. F.L. Morton, ed., *Law, Politics and the Judicial Process in Canada* (Calgary: University of Calgary Press, 1984), pp. 262–67.

11. J.R. Lucas, *The Principles of Politics* (Oxford: Clarendon Press, 1966), p. 106.

12. Jennings, *The Law of the Constitution*, p. 52.

13. *Roncarelli v. Duplessis*, [1959] S.C.R. 121.

14. *Operation Dismantle v. the Queen*, [1985] 1 S.C.R. 441.

15. Cited in F.A. Hayek, *The Constitution of Liberty* (Chicago: Henry Regnery, 1968), p. 462.

16. Alexander Hamilton, John Jay, and James Madison, *The Federalist* (New York: Modern Library, n.d.), p. 337.

Chapter 9

1. Hedley Bull, *The Anarchical Society* (London: Macmillan, 1977).

2. Boutros Boutros-Ghali, Secretary-General of the United Nations, *An Agenda for Peace* (New York: United Nations, 1992).

PART TWO
Chapter 10

1. Lyman Tower Sargent, *Contemporary Political Ideologies*, 4th ed. (Homewood, Ill.: Dorsey Press, 1978), p. 3.

2. Philip Converse, "The Nature of Belief Systems in Mass Publics," in David Apter, ed., *Ideology and Discontent* (Glencoe: Free Press, 1964), pp. 206–61.

3. Karl Marx, "A Contribution to the Critique of Political Economy" (1859), in Lewis S. Feuer, ed., *Marx and Engels: Basic Writings on Politics and Philosophy* (Garden City, N.Y.: Doubleday, 1959), p. 44.

4. Karl Mannheim, *Ideology and Utopia* (New York: Harcourt, Brace and World, n.d.). First published 1936.

5. Jeremy Bentham, "An Introduction to the Principles of Morals and Legislation" (1789), in Jeremy Bentham and John Stuart Mill, *The Utilitarians* (Garden City, N.Y.: Anchor Books, 1973), p. 73.

6. Karl Marx, "Introduction to the Critique of Hegel's Philosophy of Right" (1843), in T.B. Bottomore, ed., *Karl Marx: Early Writings* (New York: McGraw-Hill, 1963), p. 44.

7. Bill Devall, *Deep Ecology: Living as If Nature Mattered* (Salt Lake City: Peregrine Smith Books, 1985), p. 67.

Chapter 11

1. Pierre Berton, *The Smug Minority* (Toronto: McClelland & Stewart, 1968), pp. 42–43. Reprinted by permission of McClelland & Stewart.

2. Bertrand de Jouvenel, *Sovereignty: An Inquiry into the Political Good*, trans. J.F. Huntington (Chicago: University of Chicago Press, 1957), pp. 247–59.

3. John H. Schaar, "Equality of Opportunity and Beyond," in J. Roland Pennock and John W. Chapman, eds. *Equality* (New York: Atherton, 1967), p. 242.

4. John Locke, *The Second Treatise of Government* (Indianapolis: Bobbs-Merrill, 1952), p. 5.

5. Ibid., p. 76.

6. Ibid., p. 114.

7. Carl L. Becker, *The Declaration of Independence*, 2nd ed. (New York: Random House, 1942), p. 8.

8. J. Salwyn Schapiro, ed., *Liberalism: Its Meaning and History* (New York: Van Nostrand Reinhold, 1958), p. 129.

9. John Locke, *A Letter Concerning Toleration*, 2nd ed. (Indianapolis: Bobbs-Merrill, 1955), p. 18.

10. Schapiro, *Liberalism*, p. 126.

11. Ibid., p. 129.

12. John Stuart Mill, *On Liberty* (Indianapolis: Bobbs-Merrill, 1956), p. 13.

13. Adam Smith, *The Wealth of Nations* (Chicago: University of Chicago Press, 1976), vol. 1, pp. 477–78.

14. See especially Milton and Rose Friedman, *Free to Choose* (New York: Harcourt Brace Jovanovich, 1970); and Friedrich A. Hayek, *The Constitution of Liberty* (Chicago: University of Chicago Press, 1960).

15. David Hume, A Treatise of Human Nature (1739), cited in James Moore, "Hume's Theory of Justice and Property," *Political Studies* 24 (1976), p. 108.

16. Friedrich A. Hayek, *Law, Legislation and Liberty* (Chicago: University of Chicago Press, 1973–79), vol. 1, pp. 35–54.

17. Smith, *The Wealth of Nations*, vol. 2, pp. 208–9.

18. The discerning reader will see that the streetlight is a collective good because streets are publicly owned. If the streets were turned over to an entrepreneur who could find an appropriate way of charging for their use, lighting could be furnished as part of the overall service.

19. It is now recognized that many collective goods can be offered in some way in the market. See the essays in Tyler Cowen, ed., *The Theory of Market Failure* (Fairfax, Va.: George Mason University Press, 1988).

20. John Stuart Mill, *Principles of Political Economy*, vol. 2 of *The Collected Works of John Stuart Mill* (Toronto: University of Toronto Press, 1965), p. 207.

21. T.H. Green, "Liberal Legislation and Freedom of Contract" (1881), in John R. Rodman, ed., *The Political Theory of T.H. Green* (New York: Appleton-Century-Crofts, 1964), pp. 51–52.

22. F.A. Hayek, ed., *Capitalism and the Historians* (Chicago: University of Chicago Press, 1954).

23. John Kenneth Galbraith, *The New Industrial State* (Boston: Houghton Mifflin, 1967).

24. Neil H. Jacoby, *Corporate Power and Social Responsibility* (New York: Macmillan, 1973), ch. 6.

25. Barry Cooper, Allan Kornberg, and William Mishler, *The Resurgence of Conservatism in Anglo-American Democracies* (Durham, N.C.: Duke University Press, 1988).

26. John Kenneth Galbraith, *The Affluent Society*, 3rd ed. (Boston: Houghton Mifflin, 1976).

27. Jouvenel, *Sovereignty*, p. 139.

28. W.G. Runciman, *Relative Deprivation and Social Justice* (sponsored by the Institute of Community Studies, London: University of California Press, 1966).

29. Good critiques are Jouvenel, *Sovereignty*, ch. 9; and Hayek, *The Mirage of Social Justice*, vol. 2 of *Law, Legislation and Liberty*, ch. 9.

Chapter 12

1. Michael Oakeshott, *Rationalism in Politics and Other Essays* (London: Methuen, 1962), p. 169.

2. W.L. Morton, "Canadian Conservatism Now" (1959), in Paul W. Fox, ed., *Politics Canada*, 3rd ed. (Toronto: McGraw-Hill, 1970), p. 233.

3. Edmund Burke, *Reflections on the Revolution in France* (Indianapolis: Liberal Arts Press, 1955), p. 99.

4. Gordon W. Allport, *The Nature of Prejudice* (Reading, Mass.: Addison-Wesley, 1954), p. 20.

5. Ibid., p. 9.

6. Edmund Burke, "Letter to Sir Hercules Langrische on the Catholics" (1792), cited in Russell Kirk, *The Conservative Mind* (Chicago: Henry Regnery, 1960), p. 99.

7. Burke, *Reflections on the Revolution in France*, p. 110.

8. Clinton Rossiter, "Conservatism," in David L. Sils, ed., *International Encyclopedia of the Social Sciences* (New York: Macmillan and The Free Press, 1968), vol. 3, p. 294.

9. Edmund Burke, "Thoughts and Details on Scarcity" (1795), cited in C.B. Macpherson, *Burke* (Oxford: Oxford University Press, 1980), p. 58.

10. Rod Preece, "The Political Wisdom of Sir John A. Macdonald," *Canadian Journal of Political Science* 17 (1984), p. 479.

11. George Grant, *Lament for a Nation: The Defeat of Canadian Nationalism* (Toronto: McClelland & Stewart, 1965), p. 68.

12. This represents the civil service in the narrow sense, that is, those controlled by the Treasury Board and the Public Service Commission. Inclusion of uniformed soldiers, the RCMP, and employees of Crown corporations raises the total to about half a million.

13. David Bercuson, J.L. Granatstein, and W.R. Young, *Sacred Trust? Brian Mulroney and the Conservative Party in Power* (Toronto: Doubleday Canada, 1986), p. 94.

14. Randall Fitzgerald, *When Government Goes Private: Successful Alternatives to Public Services* (New York: Universe Books, 1988), p. 57.

15. Steve H. Hanke, *Privatization and Development* (San Francisco: Institute for Contemporary Studies, 1987), pp. 184–85.

16. N.J. Baxter-Moore, "Ideology or Pragmatism? The Politics and Management of the Mulroney Government's Privatization Programme," *British Journal of Canadian Studies* 7 (1992), pp. 290–325.

17. John McDermid, Minister of State for Privatization and Regulatory Affairs, May 1989, quoted in Baxter-Moore, "Ideology or Pragmatism?" p. 290.

Chapter 13

1. Mikhail Heller, *Cogs in the Wheel: The Formation of Soviet Man* (New York: Alfred A. Knopf, 1988). As far as we know, Marx first used the phrase "socialist man" in 1844 in "Economic and Philosophical Manuscripts," in Bottomore, *Karl Marx: Early Writings*, p. 166.

2. Acts of the Apostles 4:32–33.

3. J.L. Talmon, *The Origins of Totalitarian Democracy* (New York: Praeger, 1960), pp. 167–247.

4. John Anthony Scott, ed., *The Defense of Gracchus Babeuf* (New York: Schocken Books, 1972), p. 68. Copyright 1967 by University of Massachusetts Press.

5. Ibid., pp. 62–63.

6. Mark Holloway, *Heavens on Earth: Utopian Communities in America 1680–1880*, 2nd ed. (New York: Dover, 1966).

7. Karl Marx, "Contribution to the Critique of Hegel's Philosophy of Right" (1843), in Bottomore, *Karl Marx: Early Writings*, pp. 58–59.

8. Marx, "Economic and Philosophical Manuscripts" (1844), p. 132.

9. Ibid., p. 124.

10. M.M. Bober, *Karl Marx's Interpretation of History*, 2nd ed. (New York: W.W. Norton, 1965), ch. 12.

11. Friedrich Engels, "Socialism: Utopian and Scientific" (1892), in Karl Marx and Friedrich Engels, *Selected Works* (Moscow: Progress Publishers, 1968), p. 432.

12. Karl Marx and Friedrich Engels, *The Communist Manifesto* (Harmondsworth: Penguin Books, 1967), pp. 104–5.

13. Karl Marx, "Critique of the Gotha Programme" (1875), in Lewis S. Feuer, ed., *Marx and Engels: Basic Writings on Politics and Philosophy* (Garden City, N.Y.: Doubleday, 1959), p. 119.

14. Karl Marx and Friedrich Engels, *The German Ideology* (Moscow: Progress Publishers, 1968), p. 45.

15. On anarchism, see James Joll, *The Anarchists* (London: Methuen, 1964).

16. James Joll, *The Second International* (London: Routledge and Kegan Paul, 1955).

17. Alfred G. Meyer, *Marxism: The Unity of Theory and Practice* (Ann Arbor: University of Michigan Press, 1963), pp. 122–26.

18. Lenin's seminal work on party organization is *What Is to Be Done?* (1902). On democratic centralism see Alfred G. Meyer, *Leninism* (New York: Praeger, 1962), pp. 92–103.

19. Lenin, *Selected Works*, vol. 1, p. 680.

20. Michael S. Cross, ed., *The Decline and Fall of a Good Idea: CCF–NDP Manifestoes 1932–1969* (Toronto: New Hogtown Press, 1974), p. 19.

21. Ibid., pp. 33–42.

22. Quoted in Charlotte Gray, "Designer Socialism," *Saturday Night*, August 1989, p. 8.

23. Julius K. Nyerere, *Nyerere on Socialism* (Dar es Salaam: Oxford University Press, 1969), p. 42.

24. Cross, *Decline and Fall of a Good Idea*, p. 19.

25. Václav Klaus, *Dismantling Socialism: A Preliminary Report (A Road to Market Economy II)* (Prague: TOP Agency, 1992).

26. Gregory C. Chow, "The Integration of China and Other Asian Countries into the World Economy," Mont Pèlerin Society, Vancouver, B.C., August 31, 1992.

27. Research Committee of the League for Social Reconstruction, *Social Planning for Canada* (Toronto: University of Toronto Press, 1975). First published in 1935. The League for Social Reconstruction was an intellectual study group, founded in 1932 on the model of the British Fabian Society. It was not, strictly speaking, affiliated with the CCF, but members of the LSR were usually CCF activists.

28. Cross, *Decline and Fall of a Good Idea*, p. 20.

29. The "Waffle Manifesto" (1969), in Cross, *Decline and Fall of a Good Idea*, p. 45.

30. David Lane, *The End of Inequality? Stratification under State Socialism* (Harmondsworth: Penguin, 1971); and Mervyn Matthews, *Privilege in the Soviet Union* (London: George Allen and Unwin, 1978), ch. 2.

31. Milovan Djilas, *The New Class: An Analysis of the Communist System* (New York: Praeger, 1957).

32. Charles E. Lindblom, *Politics and Markets: The World's Political–Economic Systems* (New York: Basic Books, 1977). Lindblom adds a third alternative, exhortation, which does not seem to be even close to the other two in long-term effectiveness.

33. See Richard N. Hunt, *The Political Ideas of Marx and Engels* (Pittsburgh: University of Pittsburgh Press, 1974), vol. 1, ch. 9.

34. N.S. Khrushchev, "Report on the Program of the Communist Party of the Soviet Union, October 17, 1961," in *Documents of the 22nd Congress of the CPSU* (New York: Crosscurrents Press, 1961), vol. 2.

Chapter 14

1. Aristotle, *Nicomachean Ethics*, 1155a, in Richard McKeon, ed., *The Basic Works of Aristotle* (New York: Random House, 1941), p. 1058.

2. Ramsay Cook, ed., *French-Canadian Nationalism: An Anthology* (Toronto: Macmillan, 1969), p. 95.

3. Ibid., p. 98.

4. Seymour Martin Lipset, "Canada and the United States: The Cultural Dimension," in Charles F. Doran and John H. Sigler, eds., *Canada and the United States* (Englewood Cliffs, N.J., and Scarborough, Ont.: Prentice-Hall, 1985).

5. Letter to Joseph Priestley, June 19, 1802, cited in Saul K. Padover, ed., *Thomas Jefferson and the Foundations of American Freedom* (Princeton, N.J.: D. Van Nostrand, 1965), pp. 120–21.

6. Edward A. Tiryakian and Neil Nevitte, "Nationalism and Modernity," in Edward A. Tiryakian and Ronald Rogowski, *New Nationalisms of the Developed West* (Boston: Allen and Unwin, 1985), p. 67.

7. John Stuart Mill, *Considerations on Representative Government* (Chicago: Henry Regnery, 1962), p. 309.

8. Lord Acton, "Nationality" (1862), in Gertrude Himmelfarb, ed., *Essays on Freedom and Power* (New York: The Free Press, 1949), p. 193.

9. Pierre Elliott Trudeau, "The New Treason of the Intellectuals," in *Federalism and the French Canadians* (Toronto: Macmillan, 1968), pp. 177–78.

10. See, for example, C.C. Lingard, *Territorial Government in Canada: The Autonomy Question in the Old North-West Territories* (Toronto: University of Toronto Press, 1946); Lewis Herbert Thomas, *The Struggle for Responsible Government in the Northwest Territories*, 2nd ed. (Toronto: University of Toronto Press, 1978).

11. Frank Cassidy, "Introduction," in Frank Cassidy, ed., *Aboriginal Self-Determination* (Montreal: The Institute for Research on Public Policy, 1991), p. 1.

12. Canada, Indian and Northern Affairs, Communiqué, 3–8304, "Notes Prepared for The Honourable John C. Munro, Minister of Indian Affairs and Northern Development For the Debate in the House of Commons on the Motion to Ratify the Constitutional Accord," Ottawa, 1983, p. 7.

13. Edward McWhinney, *Constitution-Making* (Toronto: University of Toronto Press, 1981), p. 206.

14. Kenneth Woodside, "The Canada–United States Free Trade Agreement," *Canadian Journal of Political Science* 22 (1989), pp. 155–70.

15. Hans Kohn, ed., *Nationalism: Its Meaning and History*, 2nd ed. (Princeton, N.J.: D. Van Nostrand, 1965).

16. Richard Wagner, "Judaism in Music" (1850), in Hans Kohn, ed., *Nationalism*, p. 165.

17. On the Protocols, see Norman Cohn, *Warrant for Genocide*, 2nd ed. (New York: Harper and Row, 1969).

18. An elaborate exposition of "Holocaust revisionism" is Arthur Butz, *The Hoax of the Twentieth Century* (Brighton, England: Historical Review Press, 1977).

19. Benito Mussolini, "The Doctrine of Fascism" (1932), in Department of Philosophy, University of Colorado, *Readings on Fascism and National Socialism* (Denver: Alan Swallow, n.d.), p. 15.

20. A convenient overview of fascism is Eugen Weber, *Varieties of Fascism* (New York: Van Nostrand Reinhold, 1964).

21. Reprinted in Paul E. Sigmund, ed., *The Ideologies of the Developing Nations*, rev. ed. (New York: Praeger, 1967), p. 415.

22. Ibid., p. 384.

Chapter 15

1. For a summary, see Neil Nevitte, "New Politics," in Dickerson, Flanagan, and Nevitte, *Introductory Readings in Politics and Government*, pp. 161–70.

2. Environics Focus Canada, February/March 1992.

3. Quoted in Margaret Tims, *Mary Wollstonecraft: A Social Pioneer* (London: Millington, 1976), pp. 135–36.

4. Quoted in Josephine Donovan, *Feminist Theory: The Intellectual Traditions of American Feminism* (New York: Frederick Ungar, 1985), p. 6.

5. John Stuart Mill, *The Subjection of Women*, Sue Mansfield, ed. (Arlington Heights, Ill., AHM Publishing, 1980), p. 1.

6. Ibid., p. 5.

7. Ibid., p. 11.

8. Ibid., p. 18.

9. Ibid., p. 26.

10. Ibid., p. 47.

11. Betty Steele, *The Feminist Takeover* (Toronto: Simon & Pierre, 1987), pp. 36–37.

12. Betty Friedan, *The Feminine Mystique*, 2nd ed. (New York: Dell, 1983), p. 15.

13. Ibid., pp. 384–85.

14. Betty Friedan, *The Second Stage* (New York: Summit Books, 1981), p. 16.

15. Ibid., p. 41.

16. Jonathan Beecher and Richard Bienvenu, eds., *The Utopian Vision of Charles Fourier* (Boston: Beacon Press, 1971), p. 195.

17. Robert Owen, *A New View of Society and Other Writings* (London: Dent, 1927), p. 45.

18. Quoted in Donovan, *Feminist Theory*, p. 70.

19. Quoted in ibid., p. 75.

20. Frederick Engels, *The Origin of the Family, Private Property and the State* (New York: International Publishers, 1972), pp. 137–38.

21. Quoted in Donovan, *Feminist Theory*, p. 76.

22. Quoted in ibid., p. 145.

23. Quoted in ibid., p. 144.

24. Quoted in Elaine Storkey, *What's Right with Feminism* (London: SPCK, 1985), p. 94.

25. Quoted in ibid., p. 100.

26. Quoted in Donovan, *Feminist Theory*, p. 146.

27. Quoted in ibid., p. 147.

28. Quoted in ibid., p. 152.

29. Quoted in ibid., p. 163.

30. Donovan, *Feminist Theory*, p. 147; Storkey, *What's Right with Feminism*, pp. 98–99.

31. Roxanne Dunbar, quoted in Donovan, *Feminist Theory*, p. 142.

32. Robyn Eckersley, *Environmentalism and Political Theory: Toward an Ecocentric Approach* (Albany: State University of New York Press, 1992), p. 38.

33. Quoted in Devall, *Deep Ecology*, p. 70.

34. Quoted in Eckersley, *Environmentalism and Political Theory*, p. 43.

Chapter 16

1. David Caute, *The Left in Europe since 1789* (New York: McGraw-Hill, 1966), chs. 1 and 2.

PART THREE
Chapter 17

1. Aristotle, *Politics*, iii, 16, in McKeon, *The Basic Works of Aristotle*, p. 1202.
2. Mill, *On Liberty*, p. 7; de Tocqueville, *Democracy in America*, p. 102.
3. Aristotle, *Politics*, iv, 11, p. 1221.

Chapter 18

1. Dorothy Pickles, *Democracy* (London: B.T. Batsford, 1970), p. 11.
2. Giovanni Sartori, *The Theory of Democracy Revisited, Part One: The Contemporary Debate* (Chatham, N.J.: Chatham House, 1987), p. 6.
3. R. MacGregor Dawson, *The Government of Canada*, 4th ed., rev. by Norman Ward (Toronto: University of Toronto Press, 1963), p. 351.
4. Ibid. p., 351.
5. Terence H. Qualter, *The Election Process in Canada* (Toronto: McGraw-Hill, 1970), p. 9.
6. *A.G. Canada v. Sauvé and R. v. Belczowski*, Supreme Court of Canada, 1993, unreported.
7. The Constitution Act, 1982, ss. 38, 41.
8. Speech of October 11, 1864, in Joseph Pope, ed., *Confederation* (Toronto: Carswell, 1895), p. 58.
9. J.A.O. Larsen, "The Judgment of Antiquity on Democracy," *Classical Philology* 49 (1954), pp. 1–14.
10. James Mill, *An Essay on Government* (Indianapolis: Bobbs-Merrill, 1955), p. 66.
11. Mill, *An Essay on Government*, p. 70.
12. Patrick Boyer, *The People's Mandate: Referendums and a More Democratic Canada* (Toronto: Dundurn, 1992), pp. 23–26. See also David Butler and Austin Ranney, eds., *Referendums* (Washington, D.C.: American Enterprise Institute, 1978).
13. Alvin Rabushka and Pauline Ryan, *The Tax Revolt* (Stanford, Calif.: Hoover Institution, 1982).
14. Boyer, *The People's Mandate*, pp. 113–16. The argument actually comes from A.V. Dicey.
15. Particulars of the initiative, referendum, and recall can be found in J.A. Corry and Henry J. Abraham, *Elements of Democratic Government*, 4th ed. (New York: Oxford University Press, 1964), pp. 410–22.
16. *Quebec v. Ford*, [1988] 2 S.C.R. 712.
17. Cited in Hayek, *Law, Legislation and Liberty*, vol. 3, p. 1.
18. John Adams, "A Defense of the American Constitutions" (1787), in George A. Peek, ed., *The Political Writings of John Adams* (Indianapolis: Bobbs-Merrill, 1954), p. 148.

19. On this theme, see Samuel H. Beer, *Britain Against Herself: The Political Contradictions of Collectivism* (New York: W.W. Norton, 1982); and Mancur Olson, *The Rise and Decline of Nations: Economic Growth, Stagflation, and Social Rigidities* (New Haven: Yale University Press, 1982).

20. Geraint Parry, *Political Elites* (London: George Allen and Unwin, 1969), p. 30.

21. Raymond Aron, "Social Structure and the Ruling Class," *British Journal of Sociology* 1 (1950), p. 10, quoted in T.B. Bottomore, *Elites and Society* (Harmondsworth, U.K.: Penguin, 1966), p. 115.

22. Robert A. Dahl, *A Preface to Democratic Theory* (Chicago: University of Chicago Press), 1956, p. 133.

23. Philippe C. Schmitter, "Still the Century of Corporatism," Philippe C. Schmitter and Gerhard Lehmbruch, eds., *Trends Toward Corporatist Intermediation* (Beverly Hills, Calif.: Sage Publications, 1979), p. 13.

24. Leo Panitch, "The Development of Corporatism in Liberal Democracies," in Schmitter and Lehmbruch, *Trends Toward Corporatist Intermediation*, pp. 63–94.

25. Arend Lijphart, *Democracy in Plural Societies: A Comparative Exploration* (New Haven: Yale University Press, 1977), p. 25.

Chapter 19

1. Aristotle, *Politics*, iv, 10, p. 1219.

2. Baron de Montesquieu, *The Spirit of the Laws* (New York: Hafner, 1949), p. 26.

3. Giorgio Pini, *The Official Life of Benito Mussolini* (London: Hutchinson, 1939), p. 149.

4. Hannah Arendt, *The Origins of Totalitarianism*, 2nd ed. (New York: World Publishing, 1958), p. 460.

5. Carl J. Friedrich and Zbigniew K. Brzezinski, *Totalitarian Dictatorship and Autocracy*, 2nd ed. (New York: Praeger, 1965); Waldemar Gurian, "The Totalitarian State," *The Review of Politics* 40 (1978), pp. 514–27.

6. Arendt, *The Origins of Totalitarianism*, p. 467.

7. Friedrich and Brzezinski, *Totalitarian Dictatorship and Autocracy*, p. 9.

8. Edward McWhinney, *Constitution-Making* (Toronto: University of Toronto Press, 1981), p. 190.

9. Robert Conquest, *The Harvest of Sorrow: Soviet Collectivization and the Terror-Famine* (Edmonton: University of Alberta Press, 1986), p. 306.

10. Schram, *The Political Thought of Mao Tse-tung*, p. 253.

11. Richard Lowenthal, "Beyond Totalitarianism?" in Irving Howe, ed., *1984 Revisited: Totalitarianism in Our Century* (New York: Harper and Row, 1983), pp. 209–67.

12. Robert Jay Lifton, *Revolutionary Immortality* (New York: Random House, 1968), p. 73.

13. McWhinney, *Constitution-Making*, p. 210.

Chapter 20

1. Juan J. Linz, "An Authoritarian Regime: Spain," in Erik Allardt and Stein Rokkan, eds., *Mass Politics: Studies in Political Sociology* (New York: The Free Press, 1970), p. 255.

2. *La Prensa* (Lima), 26 February 1975.

3. Robert A. Dahl, "Transitions to Democracy," a keynote address to the Symposium, "Voices of Democracy," The University of Dayton Center for International Studies, March 16–17, 1990, p. 3.

4. Ibid.

5. Adam Przeworski, *Democracy and the Market: Political and Economic Reforms in Eastern Europe and Latin America* (Cambridge: Cambridge University Press, 1991), p. 37.

6. James N. Rosenau, "The Relocation of Authority in a Shrinking World," *Comparative Politics* 24 (1992), p. 269.

7. Ibid., p. 255.

8. Marcia W. Weigle and Jim Butterfield, "Civil Society in Reforming Communist Regimes: The Logic of Emergence," *Comparative Politics* 5 (1992), p. 5.

9. Michael Bernhard, "Civil Society and Democratic Transition in East Central Europe," *Political Science Quarterly* 108 (1993), p. 307.

10. Larry Diamond, Juan J. Linz, and Seymour Martin Lipset, "Introduction: Comparing Experiences with Democracy," in Larry Diamond, Juan J. Linz, and Seymour Martin Lipset, eds., *Politics in Developing Countries, Comparing Experiences with Democracy* (Boulder, Col.: Lynne Rienner, 1990), p. 9.

11. Ibid.

Chapter 21

1. Locke, *The Second Treatise of Government*, p. 91.

2. Frank MacKinnon, *The Crown in Canada* (Toronto: McClelland & Stewart, 1976).

3. Constitution Act, 1867, s. 53.

4. Constitution Act, 1867, s. 26.

5. Walter Bagehot, cited in R. MacGregor Dawson and Norman Ward, *The Government of Canada*, 5th ed. (Toronto: University of Toronto Press, 1970), p. 168.

6. C.E.S. Franks, *The Parliament of Canada* (Toronto: University of Toronto Press, 1987), p. 122.

7. John E. Schwarz, "Exploring a New Role in Policy Making: The British House of Commons in the 1970s," *The American Political Science Review* 74 (1980), pp. 23–27; Jon B. Johnson, "Testy U.K. Backbenchers Cloud the Patriation Issue," *The Globe and Mail*, 25 February 1981.

8. Stephen Brooks, *Public Policy in Canada: An Introduction* (Toronto: McClelland & Stewart, 1989), p. 135.

9. Ibid., p. 136.

10. Richard Neustadt, *Presidential Power*, 2nd ed. (New York: Wiley, 1964), p. 42.

11. Stephen Clarkson, *Canada and the Reagan Challenge* (Toronto: James Lorimer, 1982), p. 211.

12. *Congressional Quarterly Almanac* 40 (1985), p. 48.

13. Alexander Hamilton, John Jay, and James Madison, *The Federalist*, No. 51 (New York: Modern Library, n.d.), p. 337.

Chapter 22

1. Canadian Confederation (with a capital *C*) is an example of federalism. The general term confederation (with a small *c*) is an abstract concept of political science not particularly associated with Canada.

2. Vernon Bogdanor, *Devolution* (New York: Oxford University Press, 1979), ch. 3.

3. William H. Riker, *Federalism: Origin, Operation, Significance* (Boston: Little, Brown, 1964), p. 2.

4. Garth Stevenson, *Unfulfilled Union: Canadian Federalism and National Unity* (Toronto: Macmillan, 1979), p. 23.

5. Hamilton, Jay, and Madison, *The Federalist*, p. 339.

6. Alan Cairns, "From Interstate to Intrastate Federalism," *Bulletin of Canadian Studies* 2 (1979), pp. 13–34.

7. Robert C. Vipond, *"From National League of Cities to Garcia:* The Framers' Intentions and the Rhetoric of Rights," Conference on Adaptive Federalism, Dartmouth College, June 1989.

8. Commission on the Political and Constitutional Future of Quebec, The Political and Constitutional Future of Quebec (Quebec: Secretariat of the Commission, 1991); Melvin H. Smith, *The Renewal of the Federation: A British Columbia Perspective* (Victoria: Queen's Printer, 1991).

9. Roger Gibbins, *Regionalism: Territorial Politics in Canada and the U.S.* (Scarborough, Ont.: Butterworths, 1982).

PART FOUR
Chapter 23

1. Ludwig von Bertalanffy, *General System Theory* (New York: George Braziller, 1968). James A. Bill and Robert L. Hardgrave, *Comparative Politics: The Quest for Theory* (Columbus, Ohio: Charles E. Merrill, 1973), ch. 4.

2. Easton, *A Systems Analysis of Political Life*, p. 32.

3. Gabriel A. Almond and G. Bingham Powell, Jr., *Comparative Politics: A Developmental Approach* (Boston: Little, Brown, 1966), pp. 16–41.

4. William D. Coleman and Grace Skogstad, eds., *Policy Communities and Public Policy in Canada: A Structural Approach* (Mississauga: Copp Clark Pitman, 1990), p. 25.

5. Ibid.

Chapter 24

1. Thomas Sowell, *The Economics and Politics of Race* (New York: William Morrow, 1983), pp. 47, 49.

2. Gabriel A. Almond and Sidney Verba, *The Civic Culture: Political Attitudes and Democracy in Five Nations* (Boston: Little, Brown, 1963), ch. 1.

3. Almond and Powell, *Comparative Politics*, p. 23.

4. Almond and Verba, *The Civic Culture*, ch. 1.

5. Howard J. Wiarda, "Toward a Framework for the Study of Political Change in the Iberic-Latin Tradition: The Comparative Model," *World Politics* 25 (1973), pp. 206–35.

6. For a summary, see Neil Nevitte, "New Politics," in Mark O. Dickerson, Thomas Flanagan, and Neil Nevitte, *Introductory Readings in Politics and Government*, 3rd ed. (Toronto: Nelson Canada, 1991), pp. 161–70.

7. Gabriel A. Almond, "A Comparative Study of Interest Groups and the Political Process," *The American Political Science Review* 52 (1958), pp. 270–82.

8. Bill and Hardgrave, *Comparative Politics: The Quest for Theory*, ch. 4.

Chapter 25

1. Bill and Hardgrave, *Comparative Politics: The Quest for Theory*, ch. 4; Hamilton, Jay, and Madison, *The Federalist*, p. 54.

2. Joseph LaPalombara, *Politics within Nations* (Englewood Cliffs, N.J.: Prentice-Hall, 1974), p. 323.

3. Gabriel A. Almond and James S. Coleman, eds., *The Politics of Developing Nations* (Princeton, N.J.: Princeton University Press, 1960), pp. 33–34.

4. Mancur Olson, *The Logic of Collective Action* (Cambridge, Mass.: Harvard University Press, 1965).

5. Russell Hardin, *Collective Action* (Baltimore: Johns Hopkins University Press, 1982).

6. John Sawatsky, *The Insiders: Government, Business, and the Lobbyists* (Toronto: McClelland & Stewart, 1987).

7. *The Globe and Mail*, February 17, 1993.

8. David B. Truman, *The Governmental Process* (New York: Alfred A. Knopf, 1951).

9. Jean-Jacques Rousseau, *The Social Contract* (New York: Hafner, 1947), pp. 26–27.

10. Hamilton, Jay, and Madison, *The Federalist*, p. 54.

Chapter 26

1. LaPalombara, *Politics within Nations*, p. 509.

2. *Webster's Seventh New Collegiate Dictionary* (Springfield, Mass.: Merriam Webster, 1969), p. 667.

3. Murray Dobbin, *Preston Manning and the Reform Party* (Toronto: James Lorimer, 1991), p. 215.

4. Private member's bill introduced in December 1992 by Reform MP Deborah Grey.

5. Maurice Duverger, *Political Parties*, 3rd ed. (New York: Wiley, 1978).

6. Robert Michels, *Political Parties* (New York: Free Press, 1962; first published 1911).

7. Leon D. Epstein, *Political Parties in Western Democracies* (New York: Praeger, 1962).

Chapter 27

1. Jean-François Revel, *The Flight from Truth: The Reign of Deceit in the Age of Information*, cited in Kimberley Noble, *Bound and Gagged: Libel Chill and the Right to Publish* (Toronto: HarperCollins, 1992), p. 14.

2. Neal Bernards, ed., *The Mass Media: Opposing Viewpoints* (San Diego: Greenhaven Press, 1988), p. 16.

3. Shanto Iyengar and Donald R. Kinder, *News That Matters: Television and American Opinion* (Chicago: University of Chicago Press, 1987).

4. Ibid., p. 63.

5. Ibid., p. 133.

6. Herbert J. Gans, *Deciding What's News* (New York: Pantheon Books, 1979), p. 88.

7. Noble, *Bound and Gagged*.

8. Rosemary Righter, *Whose News? Politics, the Press and the Third World* (London: Burnett Books, 1978), p. 190.

Chapter 28

1. John Plamenatz, "Electoral Studies and Democratic Theory," *Political Studies* 6 (February 1958), p. 9.

2. William H. Riker, *Liberalism Against Populism: A Confrontation Between the Theory of Democracy and the Theory of Social Choice* (Prospect Heights, Ill.: Waveland Press, 1988).

3. The term *gerrymander*, which means to draw constituency lines so as to achieve a deliberate result, comes from Elbridge Gerry, governor of Massachusetts in 1812, who tried to favour his party at the time of redistricting.

4. Mill, *Considerations on Representative Government*, p. 141.

5. Michael Cassiday, "Fairness and Stability: How a New Electoral System Would Affect Canada," *Parliamentary Government* 42 (August 1992), p. 14.

6. Ibid.

7. Much of this material on electoral systems is taken from J.S. Corry and Henry J. Abraham, *Elements of Democratic Government*, 4th ed. (New York: Oxford University Press, 1964), ch. 11; and John C. Wahlke and Alex N. Dragnich, eds., *Government and Politics*, 2nd ed. (New York: Random House, 1971), pp. 540–73.

Chapter 29

1. C.E.S. Franks, *The Parliament of Canada* (Toronto: University of Toronto Press, 1987), pp. 4–5.

2. See, in general, Hanna Pitkin, *The Concept of Representation* (Berkeley: University of California Press, 1967); and A.H. Birch, *Representation* (London: Macmillan, 1971).

3. Edmund Burke, *Burke's Speeches and Letters on American Affairs* (London: E.P. Dutton, 1908), p. 73.

4. *Maclean's*, January 4, 1993, p. 19.

5. Reform Party of Canada, *Principles and Policies*, 1991, p. 39.

6. Adams, "Thoughts on Government," in *The Political Writings of John Adams*, p. 86.

Chapter 30

1. Peter Hennessy, *Cabinet* (Oxford: Basil Blackwell, 1986).

2. R. MacGregor Dawson, *The Government of Canada*, 4th ed. (Toronto: University of Toronto Press, 1963), p. 185.

3. Theodore Lowi and Benjamin Gindsberg, *American Government: Freedom and Power* (New York: W.W. Norton, 1990), p. 273.

Chapter 31

1. Colin Leys, *Politics in Britain* (Toronto: University of Toronto Press, 1983), p. 269.

2. William A. Niskanen, Jr., *Bureaucracy and Representative Government* (Chicago: Aldine–Atherton, 1971), pp. 36–42.

3. Jonathan Lynn and Antony Jay, *The Complete Yes Minister* (New York: Harper and Row, 1981), p. 59.

4. Quoted in Kenneth Kernaghan and David Biegel, *Public Administration in Canada*, 2nd ed. (Toronto: Nelson Canada, 1991), p. 293.

Chapter 32

1. Thomas Flanagan, "Policy-Making by Exegesis: The Abolition of 'Mandatory Retirement' in Manitoba," *Canadian Public Policy* 11(1985), pp. 40–53.

2. *Edwards et al. v. Attorney General of Canada et al.*, [1930] A.C. 124.

3. Originally, the Bill of Rights applied only to the federal Congress, but the Supreme Court held that it was extended through the Fourteenth Amendment to the state legislatures.

4. [1979] 2 S.C.R. 1032.

5. M. Elizabeth Atcheson, Mary Eberts, and Beth Symes, *Women and Legal Action: Precedents, Resources and Strategies for the Future* (Ottawa: Canadian Advisory Council on the Status of Women, 1984), pp. 166–67.

6. *R. v. Sparrow*, [1990] 1 S.C.R. 1075.

7. See, for example, Theodore J. Lowi, *The End of Liberalism*, 2nd ed. (New York: W.W. Norton, 1979), ch. 11.

8. *R. v. Therens*, [1985] 1 S.C.R. 613.

9. F.L. Morton and M.J. Withey, "Charting the Charter, 1982–1985: A Statistical Analysis," *Canadian Human Rights Yearbook*, 1987.

10. Peter H. Russell, "Canada's Charter of Rights and Freedoms: A Political Report," *Public Law* (autumn 1988), pp. 385–401.

11. F.L. Morton et al., "Judicial Nullification of Statutes under the Charter of Rights and Freedoms, 1982–1988," University of Calgary, Faculty of Social Sciences, Research Unit for Socio-Legal Studies, Research Study 4.3, Table 6, n.p. Data updated courtesy of the authors.

12. Ted [F.L.] Morton, "Insight: Federal Character of Canada Being Eroded by Charter Rulings," *Financial Post*, June 5, 1989.

13. Rainer Knopff and F.L. Morton, *Charter Politics* (Scarborough, Ont.: Nelson Canada, 1992), p. 3.

INDEX

Kenyatta, Jomo, 345
Keynes, John Maynard, 123
KGB, 251
Khmer Rouge, 248
Khomeini, Ayatollah, 35, 36
Khrushchev, Nikita, 163, 251
Kibbutzim, 146, 189
Kim Jong Il, 249
King, William Lyon Mackenzie, 123, 224,
    419
King, Rodney, 362
Kinship, 52
Klaus, Vaclav, 157
Knopff, Rainer, 425
Kohl, Helmut, 158
Kohn, Hans, 176
Korea, 53. *See also* North Korea; South Korea
Korean War, 96, 97, 284
Kurds, 174, 181
Kuwait, 96, 97

Labour Party (Australia), 373
Labour Party (Britain), 140, 141, 153, 225,
    229, 338, 341, 342, 347
Labour relations, 25–26, 60
Laflèche, Monseigneur, 167–68
Laissez faire, 116, 123

Lamarckian theory, 251
Laos, 247
LaPalombara, Joseph, 338
Lasswell, Harold, 16
Latent group, 330
Laurier, Wilfrid, 220
Law
    common, 58–59, 60–62
    and convention, 66–67
    customary, 58
    defined, 56
    enforcement of, 56–57
    and government, 75–79
    and human rights, 62, 63–64
    international, 82, 94, 97–98
    natural, 61–62
    private, 60
    public, 60
    Roman, 38, 43, 58, 60
    and social change, 62–65
    social origins of, 62
    in totalitarianism, 252–53

LEAF (Legal Education and Action Fund),
    420
League of Nations, 96
Lebanon, 51, 241
Lebensraum, 175
Le Devoir, 360
Le Figaro, 360
Left, political, 202–207
Legal authority, 32–34
Legal positivism, 61–62
Legislation, 58, 59–62
Legislative power, 265
Legislative union, 306
Legislature, 382
Legitimacy, 28, 30–31
Le Monde, 360
Lenin, Vladimir Ilyich, 20, 151–53, 163,
    249, 250
Le Pen, Jean, 350
Lesbianism, 192
Lesbians, 63–64
Lévesque, René, 170
Liberal approach, 81
Liberal democracy. *See* Democracy
Liberal Democratic Party (Japan), 234
Liberal Democrats (Britain), 347
Liberal feminism, 184–88, 205
Liberalism
    classical, 113–21, 204
    and conservatism, 197
    development of, 109–10, 113–16
    and nationalism, 176–77
    reform, 121–26, 203
Liberal Party (Australia), 373
Liberal Party (Britain), 109, 110, 123, 338
Liberal Party (Canada), 19, 113, 123,
    140–41, 204, 341, 342, 347, 357,
    371, 392
Liberia, 242
Libya, 256, 259, 260
Lieutenant governor, 268–69
Limited government, 109, 111
Limited state, 74
Linz, Juan, 256, 263
Lipset, Seymour Martin, 263
List system, 374–75
Lloyd George, David, 77
Lobbying, 331–32
Locke, John, 109, 113–16, 265–66
Logrolling, 288

Nixon, Richard M., 285, 341, 360
Nkomo, Joshua, 345
Nonassociational groups, 330
North American Free Trade Agreement.
    See NAFTA
Northern League (Italy), 350
North Korea, 160, 247, 257
North–West Rebellion, 35, 36
Norway, 349
Notwithstanding clause, 422
Nuclear Nonproliferation Treaty, 85
Nunavut, 174, 393
Nunziata, John, 276
Nyerere, Julius, 155, 259

Oakeshott, Michael, 129
October Revolution, 252
Official Opposition, 275
Oil crises, 86, 89
Oil and Gas Conservation Board, 196
Ojibway, 42
Oligarchy, 213
Olson, Mancur, 328, 335
Ombudsman, 411
One-party-dominant system, 346
One-party state, 248–49
One-party system, 346–47
Ontario, 269, 276, 301, 302, 356
OPEC (Organization of Petroleum Exporting
    Countries), 89, 180
Operation Dismantle, 77
Opposition, 273, 274–75, 277, 384
Orders-in-council, 70
Organization, 117
Organization of African Unity, 81
Owen, Robert, 146, 189
Ownership, 143, 159–60
Ozone layer, 90, 91, 196

Paid media, 356–57
Pakistan, 241
Palestine Liberation Organization, 48
Panitch, Leo, 235
Parliament Act (1911), 67, 77, 268
Parliament Act (1949), 268
Parliamentary executive, 395–400
Paliamentary sovereignty, 39–40
Parliamentary systems
    assessment of, 279–81
    in Britain, 267–68, 273, 275, 276,
        277–78

in Canada, 268–78
in France, 278–79
and fusion of powers, 272–77
in Germany, 278
history of, 266–67
in Israel, 279
vs. presidential systems, 290–92
Westminster model of, 267–72
Parochial culture, 321
Participatory culture, 321
Parti Québécois, 42, 54, 71, 298,
    308, 357, 392
Party discipline, 267, 276
Party members, 390–91
Peace-building, 97
Peacekeeping operations, 96
Pearl Harbor, 86
Pearson, Lester, 123, 135
People's Republic of China, 27, 94–95,
    158–59, 160, 175, 241, 245, 246,
    247, 248, 249, 252, 253
Peron, Juan, 345
Perot, Ross, 285, 342, 347
Personal freedom, 109, 110–11. *See also*
    Freedom
Personal parties, 345
Persons case, 187, 419
Peru, 259–60, 362
Peterson, David, 269
Philippines, 176, 179, 241
Philosopher–king, 213
Pinochet, Augusto, 254, 257, 258, 259
Plamenatz, John, 365
Planning, 143, 155–59
Plato, 16, 103, 144, 211–13, 245
Plebiscites, 224
Pluralism, 233–34
Plurality, 222
Poland, 53, 85, 158, 160, 241, 249, 253
Policy community, 317–18
Polis, 16, 144, 166
Political alienation, 379
Political consultants, 330–31
Political culture, 320–24
Political executive. *See* Executive
Political participation, 223–27
Political parties
    assessment of, 349–51
    defined, 338
    described, 338–40
    ideological, 342–43, 343–44